GRAHAM WATSON

ACKNOWLEDGMENTS

Twenty years is a long time, a time in which many friendships were made and nurtured, and all of them are still remembered and appreciated. Through the images in this book, I've been able to pay respect to my colleagues of the road, the cyclists, but I also wish to recognize closer acquaintances and friends. To John Wilcockson go my thanks for having navigated and encouraged me through a minefield of perils in my earlier career, and for the numerous adventures we've enjoyed to this very day. And to Robin Magowan, who invited me to co-author *Kings of The Road* with him in 1986, go my heartfelt thanks for indoctrinating me into the world of book publishing and for pairing me with such a perfectionist as Frances Royle, who edited four of my titles.

Aside from these professional people, and many others too numerous to thank here and now, I've been spoiled by the depth and quality of friendships made over the years in the course of my work. To people like Louis Viggio, Rupert Guinness, Angel Tona, Paul Sherwen and Phil Liggett—and to fellow photographers Roberto Bettini, Hennes Roth, Frédéric Mons, Aldo Tonnoir and Cor Vos—go my sincerest thanks for some great times shared. The many motorcycle drivers who have piloted me in the sport's greatest races deserve thanks, too—especially Ismael Borges, Patrice Diallo, Luke Evans, Jacky Koch and Rafa Landa. Finally, special note must go to Ann McQuaid, who allowed me to appreciate the true value of my work and who influenced me the most with her uniquely demanding attitude to work. And to her brother, Darach, for creating the hugely successful exhibition in Dublin in 1998: "Eyes on the Tour de France."

If I continue to photograph cycling for another twenty years, I hope that many of the same friends mentioned here will still be close by, mixing in with people and friends yet to be embraced.... It's been fun!

GRAHAM WATSON
Middlesex, England

GRAHAM WATSON: 20 YEARS OF CYCLING PHOTOGRAPHY
COPYRIGHT © 2000 GRAHAM WATSON
PAPERBACK EDITION 2002

ALL RIGHTS RESERVED. NO PART OF THIS BOOK MAY BE REPRODUCED, STORED IN A RETRIEVAL SYSTEM, OR TRANSMITTED, IN ANY FORM OR BY ANY MEANS, ELECTRONIC OR PHOTOCOPY OR OTHERWISE, WITHOUT THE PRIOR WRITTEN PERMISSION OF THE PUBLISHER.

PRINTED IN CHINA.
10 9 8 7 6 5 4 3 2 1

DISTRIBUTED IN THE UNITED STATES AND CANADA BY PUBLISHERS GROUP WEST.

INTERNATIONAL STANDARD BOOK NUMBER: 1-931382-14-X

LIBRARY OF CONGRESS CATALOGING-IN-PUBLICATION DATA APPLIED FOR.

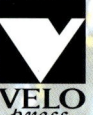

VELOPRESS®
1830 NORTH 55TH STREET
BOULDER, COLORADO 80301-2700 USA
303/440-0601
FAX: 303/444-6788
EMAIL: VELOPRESS@7DOGS.COM

BOOK DESIGN: ANN W. DOUDEN, BOULDER, COLORADO

TO PURCHASE ADDITIONAL COPIES OF THIS BOOK OR OTHER VELOPRESS BOOKS, CALL 800/234-8356 OR VISIT US ON THE WEB AT WWW.VELOGEAR.COM.

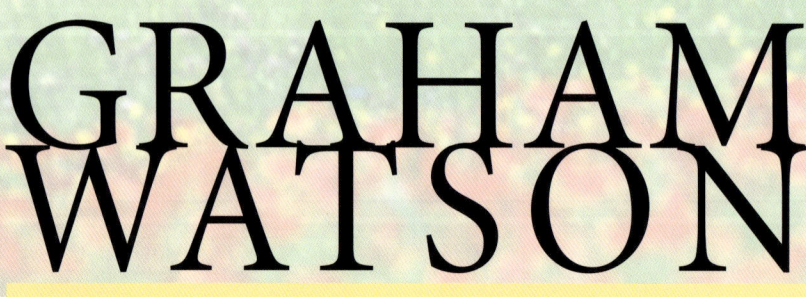

GRAHAM WATSON
20 YEARS OF CYCLING PHOTOGRAPHY

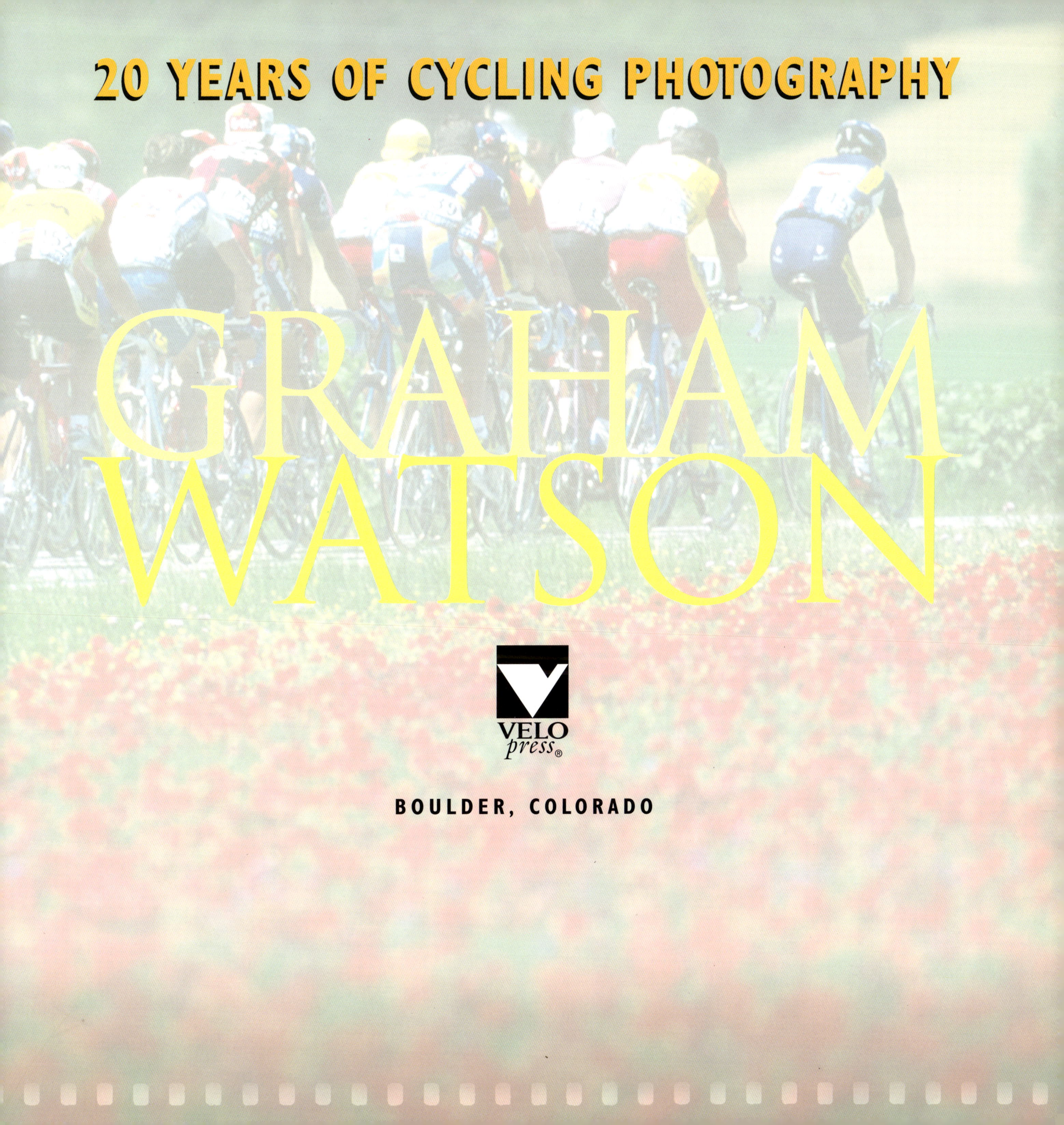

20 YEARS OF CYCLING PHOTOGRAPHY

GRAHAM WATSON

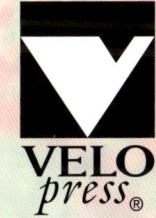

BOULDER, COLORADO

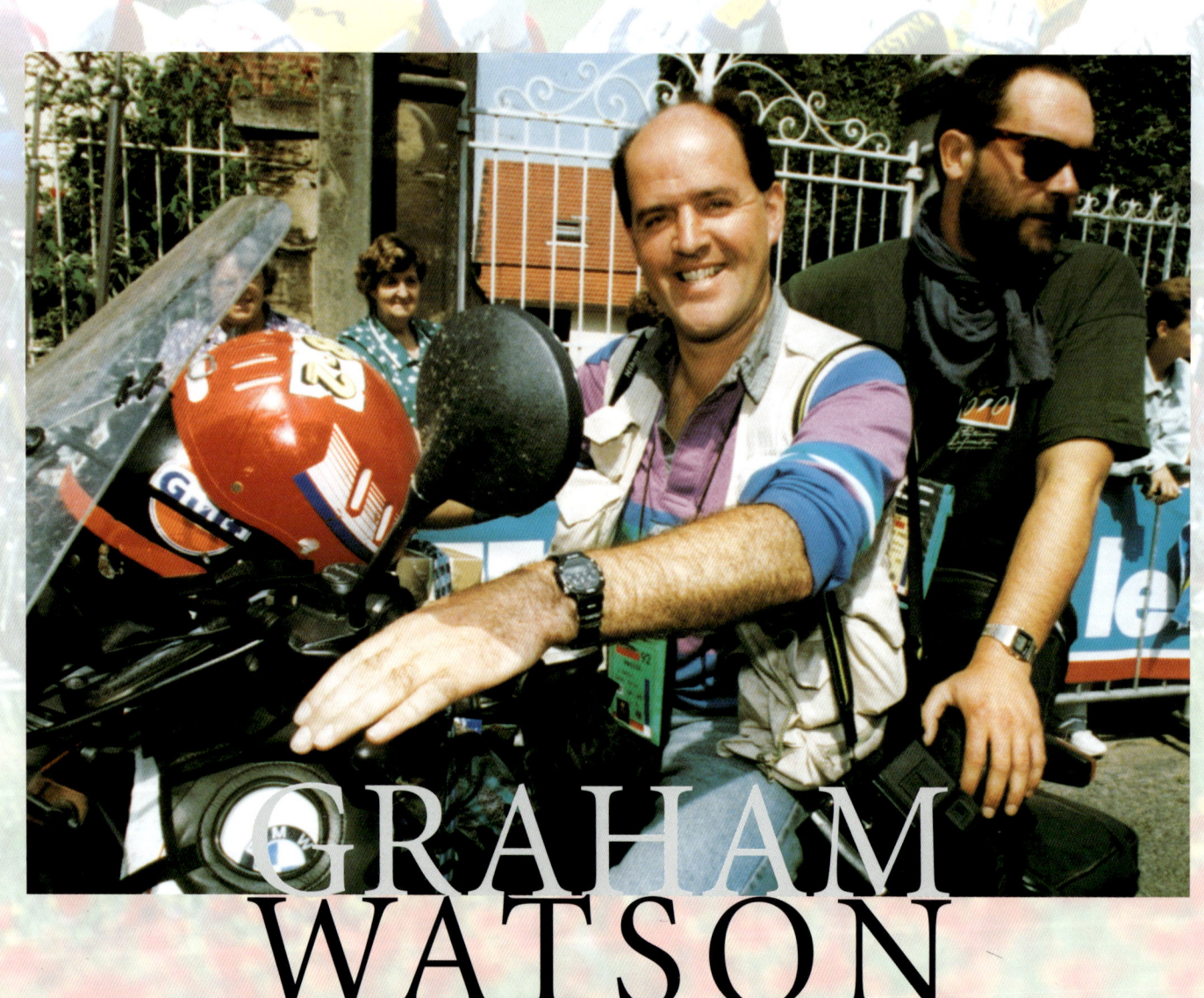

GRAHAM WATSON

20 YEARS OF CYCLING PHOTOGRAPHY

CONTENTS

FOREWORD: Phil Liggett . . . . *vii*

INTRODUCTION: John Wilcockson *1*

CHAPTER ONE   1977–1980 . . . . *7*

CHAPTER TWO   1981–1985 . . . . *19*

CHAPTER THREE   1986–1990 . . . . *61*

CHAPTER FOUR   1991–1994 . . . . *101*

CHAPTER FIVE   1995–1997 . . . . *135*

CHAPTER SIX   1998–2000 . . . . *171*

CHAPTER SEVEN   Beyond 2000 . . . . *207*

INDEX OF PHOTOGRAPHS *225*

ABOUT THE AUTHOR *230*

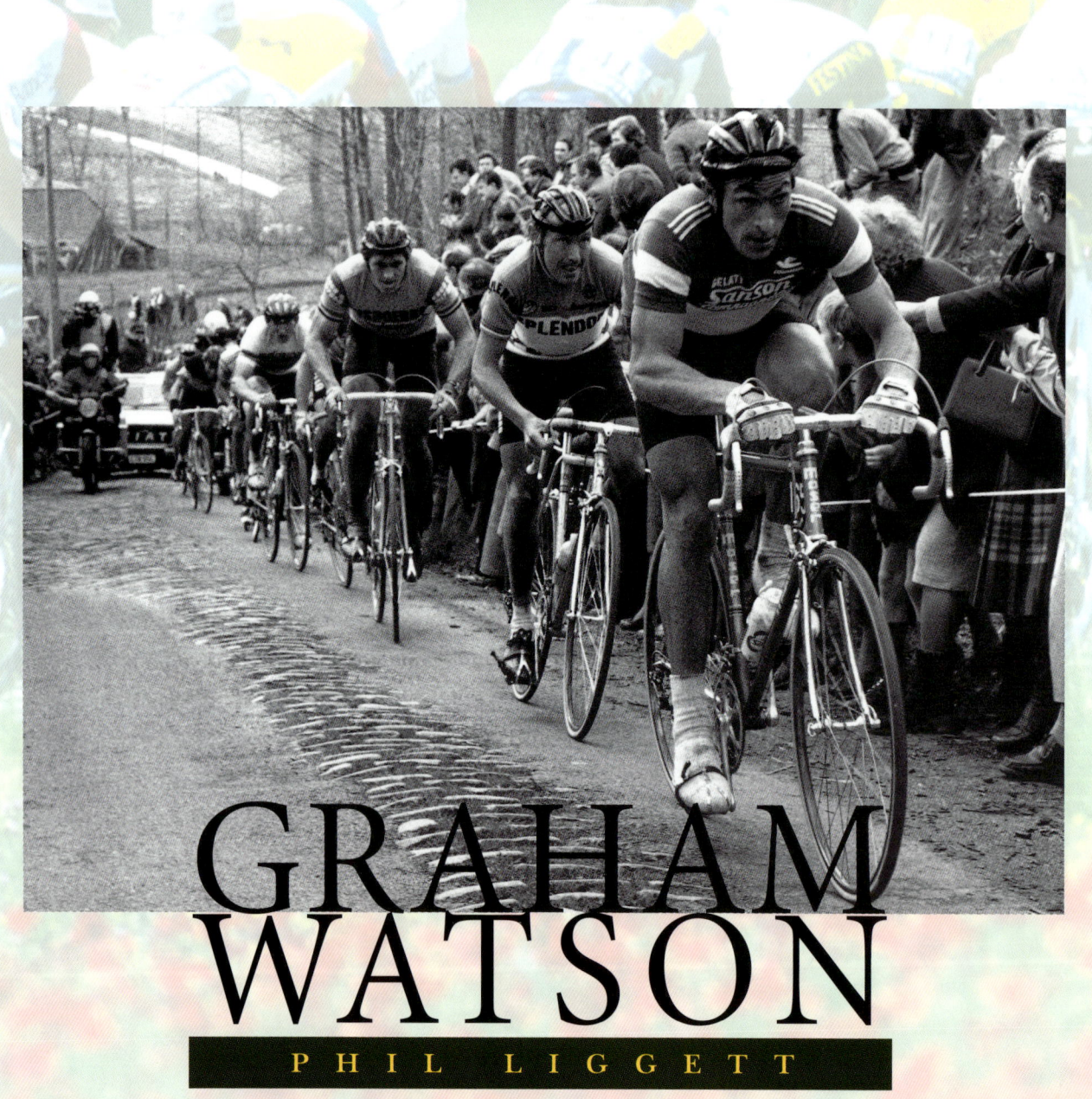

GRAHAM WATSON

PHIL LIGGETT

FOREWORD

GRAHAM WATSON

There are those who can do it, and those who cannot. And those who can will probably never be able to tell you why, because their talent is natural and the result is one of instinct. I remember Graham's first visit to Australia's new race, the Tour Down Under in Adelaide in 1999, where he was working as the official race-photographer and supplying images to magazines and newspapers all over the world.

Like all good men at their job, you rarely see them doing it, yet Graham's images captured the unique atmosphere of a big international stage race being run on strange roads and before an unknowledgeable crowd for the first time. He made everyone looking at those pictures feel as if they had actually been there . . . and one picture stands out the most—a shot of the peloton coursing between the vineyards of the Barossa Valley, with a helicopter and a tiny puff of white cloud being the only blemishes on an otherwise clear blue sky.

I first met Graham in Prague in 1981 at the world championships. It was the year when Freddy Maertens made a shocking, if brief, return to the top, winning the professional road race. Graham remembers our meeting, and I don't, but since then he has become unchallenged in his profession, capturing the greatest moments because of his uncanny instinct to know where to be and when. It is something that talent allows of you, like when Stephen Roche won the Tour de France in 1987, the time the Irishman knew he was going to do it, and when. I know this must be one of Graham's finest memories in a career absolutely smothered by such recollections, the most recent of which is the astonishing return to the top by America's Lance Armstrong in the 1999 Tour de France. Like myself, Graham has followed Lance's career with a mixture of admiration and awe, and it is only natural that many of Graham's best images these past few years have been of Lance Armstrong, as he seeks to emulate America's other cycling great, Greg LeMond.

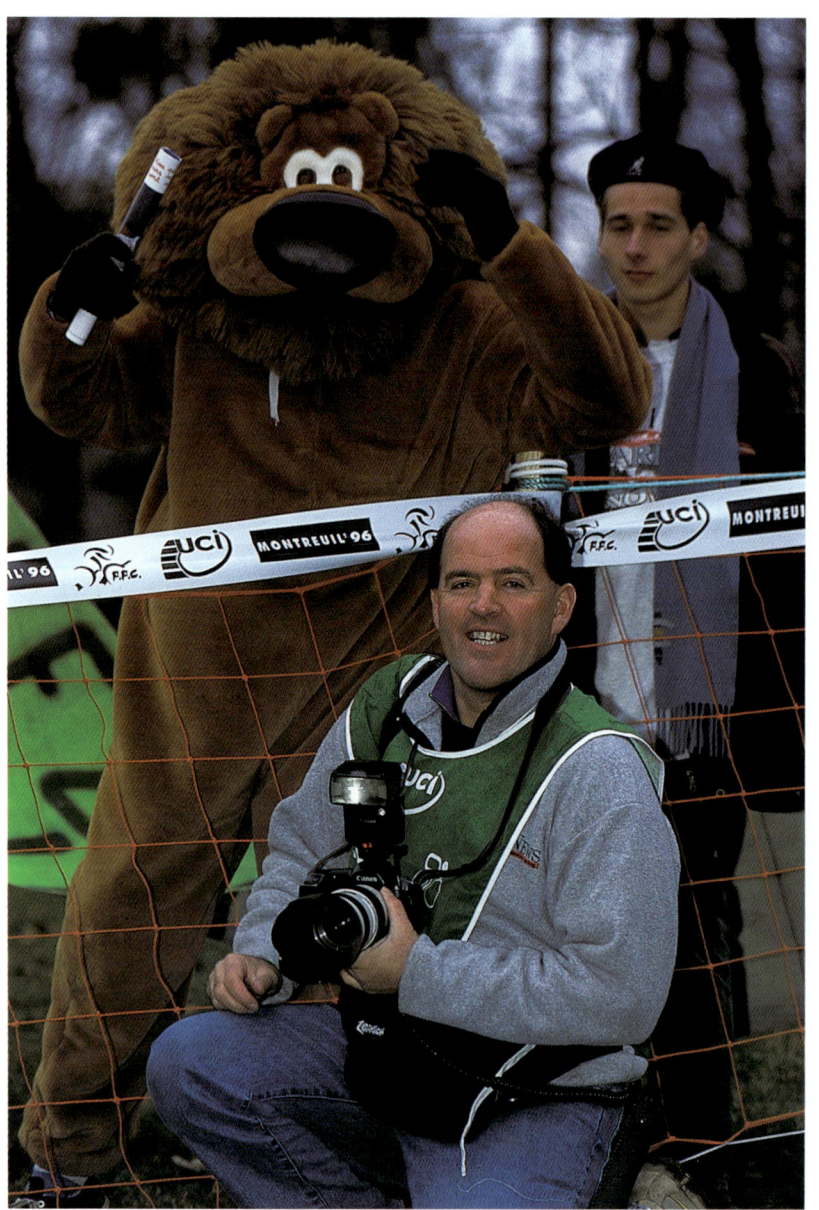

1996: WORLD CYCLO-CROSS CHAMPIONSHIPS: MONTREUIL, FRANCE

Graham is the one with the camera.

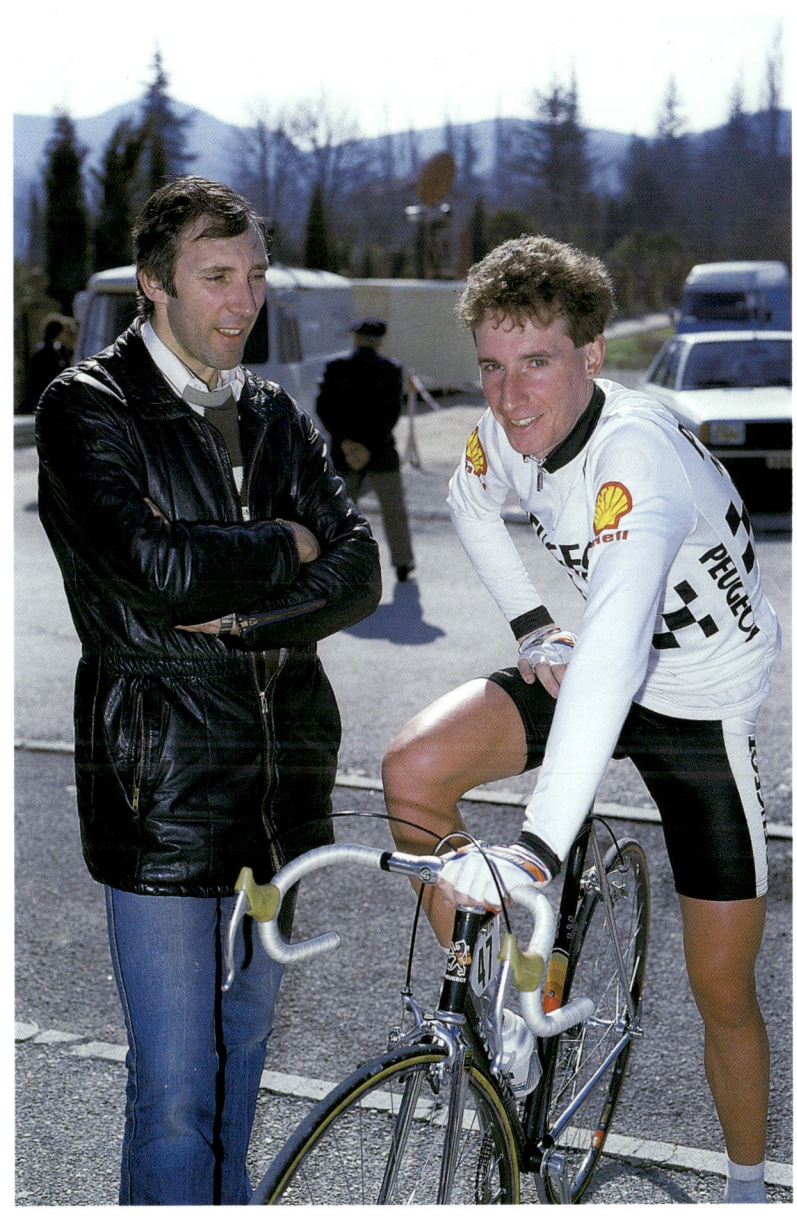

1983: PARIS-NICE: FRANCE

Both Phil Liggett (left) and Robert Millar have played a big part in the author's photographic career.

I've never known Graham to brag about his images, or become involved in any photographers' scuffles after race finishes. Instead, he just quietly gets on with his work, ever striving to maintain his role as one of cycling's greatest photographers. And, as such, he has a unique rapport with race organizers, officials and the cyclists themselves. It's not a job to everyone's liking, though—you wouldn't catch me sitting on the back of a motorcycle in freezing, rainy conditions, or hurtling down mountain descents at crazy speeds, just to have a half-baked chance of getting a decent image now and again. But that is what Graham does, day-in, day-out, for months on end, with little let up between the months of February and October, often rushing into a press room freezing cold and dripping snow on the floor, to then develop and send pictures around the world. I hope and assume that the results in newspapers, magazines and on the Internet make his job worthwhile.

I cannot believe Graham has been living this life for 20 years now; and I certainly can't believe that I am embarking on my 28th year, when my memories are in my commentaries and cannot so readily be recalled for all to see. For Graham, his pictures are to enjoy, and with more than 250 images in this book, I know you will do just that.

PHIL LIGGETT

Hertfordshire, England

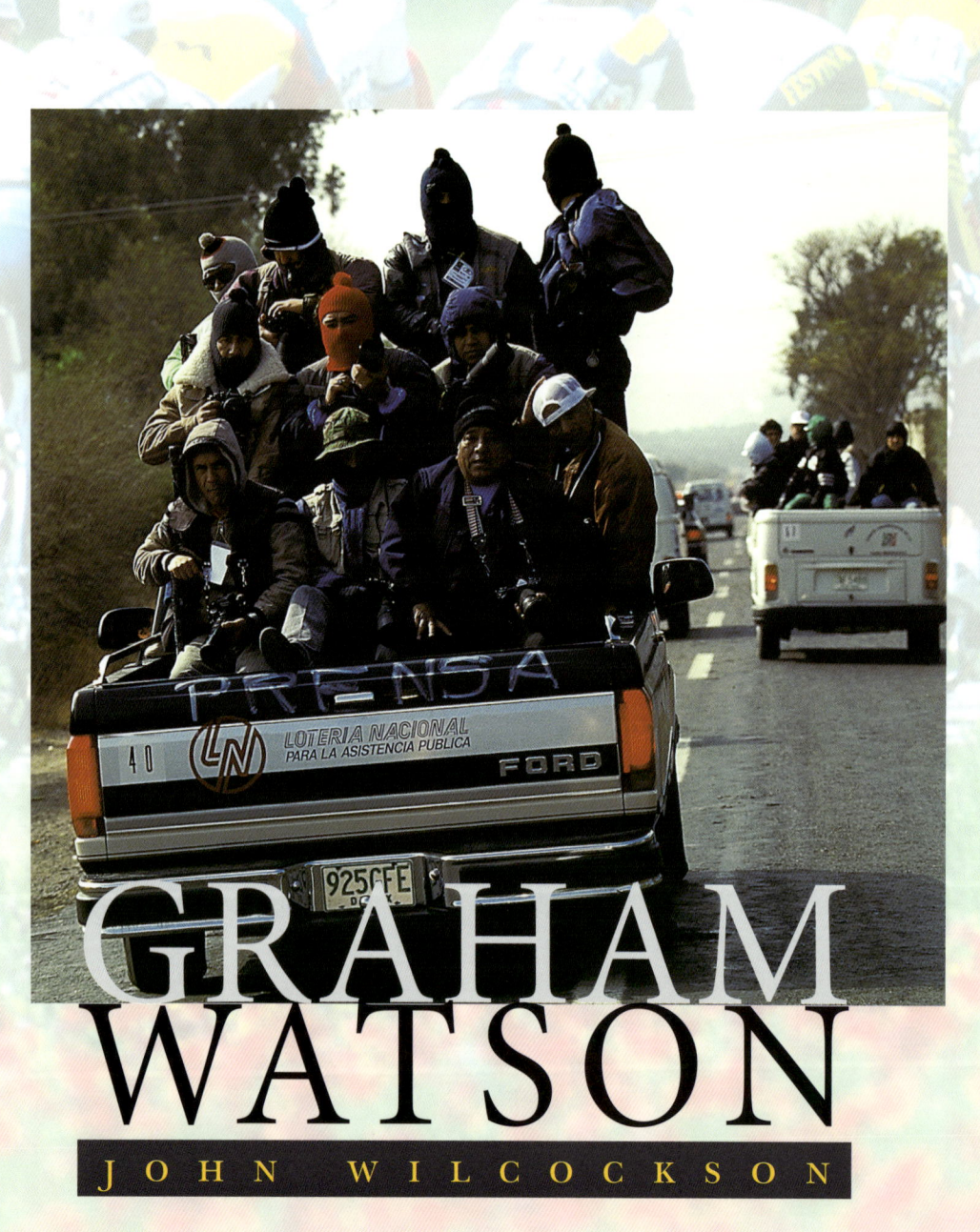

GRAHAM WATSON

JOHN WILCOCKSON

INTRODUCTION

GRAHAM WATSON

Sports photography, at its best, is a beautiful blend of art and actuality. And when it records an emotional and dramatic sport like bike racing, the combination can be exhilarating. Whether reproduced in a glossy four-color magazine or grainy black-and-white newspaper, a single image can capture the very essence of an event. A 1000-word story or a 30-minute telecast may give you the details and background that make a race compelling, but it's the great still photograph that will stay in your mind.

Take Lance Armstrong's comeback to the elite level of his sport, after recovering from cancer. There's one photo of the Texan that encapsulates his re-entry more than any other. It shows Armstrong, slender and hollow-cheeked, his face mud-spattered, his haunting eyes staring ahead through a dull drizzle, as he attacks the steepest part of the Cauberg climb at Valkenburg, in October 1998's world road championship. To shoot such a photo from the roadside is a technically exacting task: In the wet, gloomy conditions, the lens has to be wide open, and the shot's depth of field is miniscule. To successfully make that shot and to frame it precisely, while capturing all of the moment's energy and emotion, is the mark of a true artist.

That photo is but one of hundreds of thousands that Graham Watson has taken over the past 20 years. It

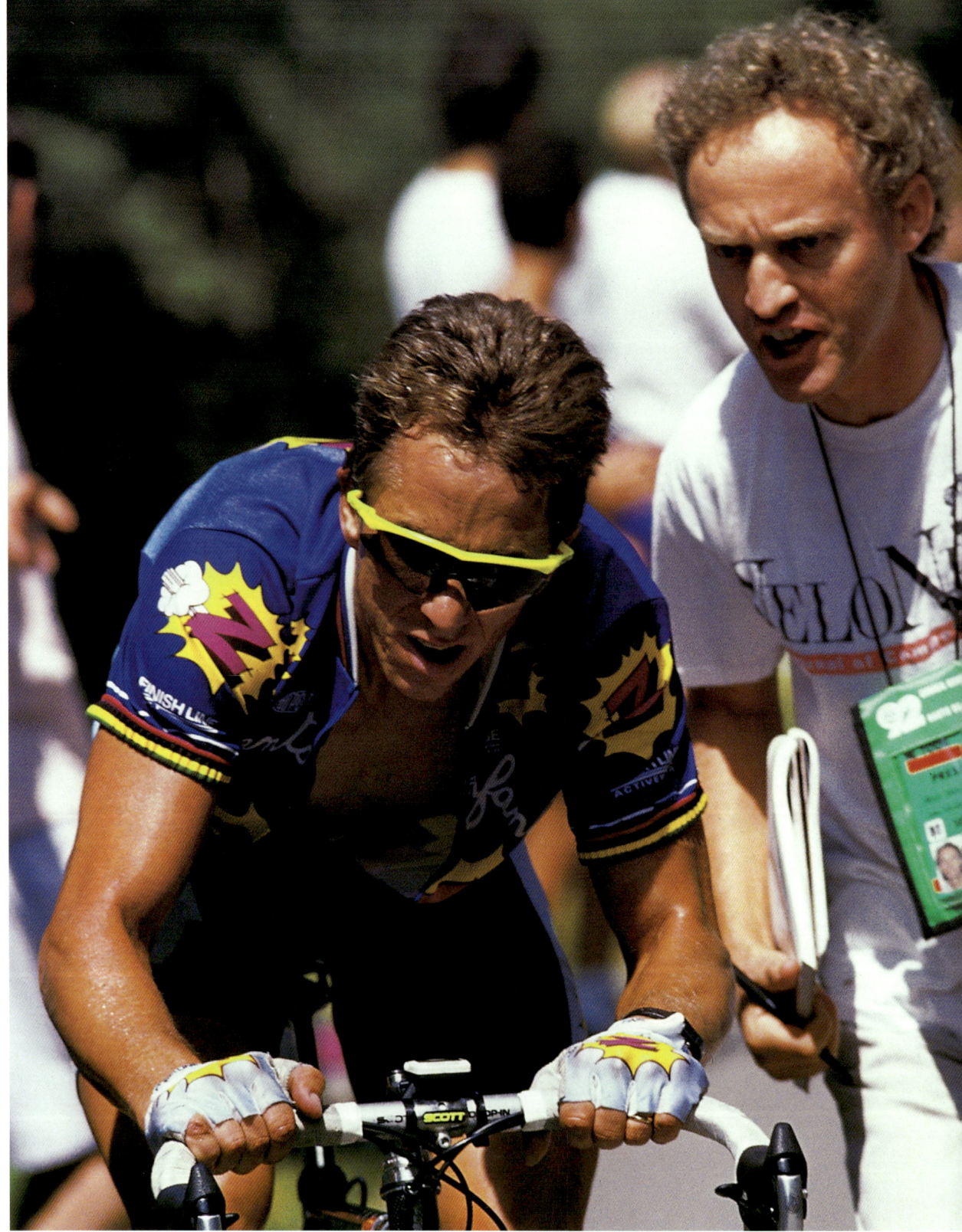

1992: TOUR DE FRANCE: MONT SALÈVE

Graham made a surprise photo at the 1992 Tour of a struggling Greg LeMond being given a word of encouragement by VeloNews editor John Wilcockson.

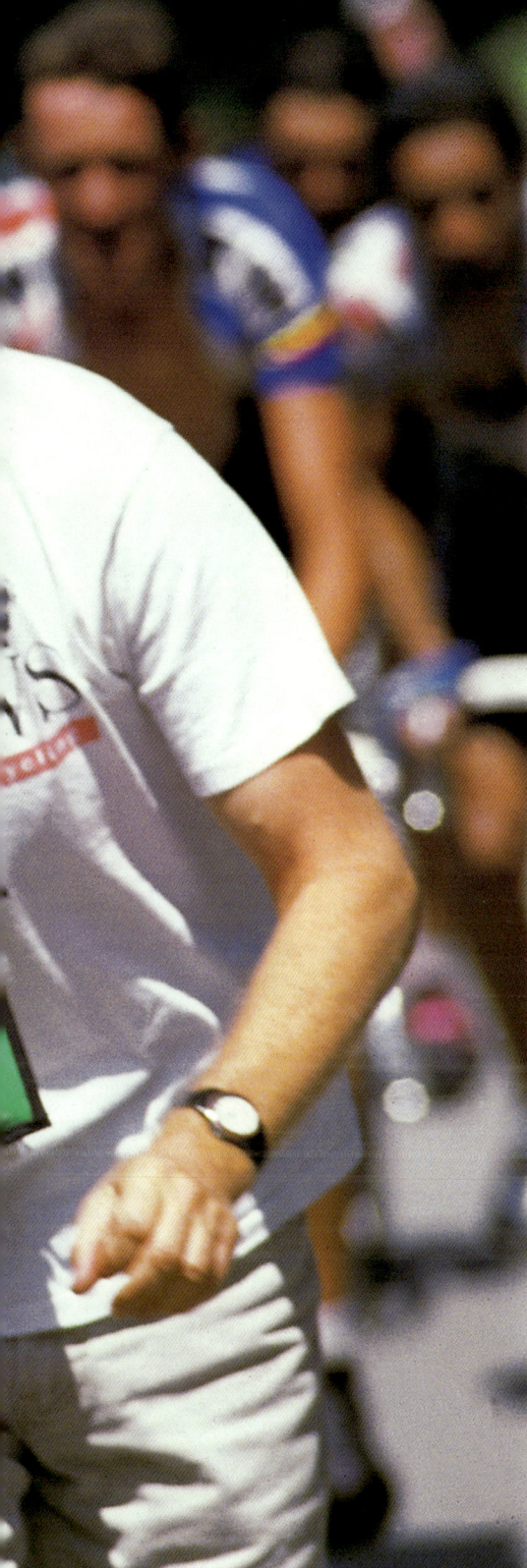

appeared on the cover of the November 26, 1998 issue of *VeloNews*, and it radiates the determination, power and leanness of the "new" Armstrong, who just nine months later shocked the world by winning the Tour de France.

Not every photo can be as stunning as that one, but the 250+ shots we have chosen for this book all reflect the talent that has made Graham the definitive chronicler of cycling today. The book is both a celebration of his work and a tribute to the cyclists who have helped make this English photographer's career such a memorable one.

It has been my good fortune to have worked with Graham throughout the past 20 years. When we first met, I was editing a magazine called *Cyclist Monthly* (the predecessor of today's *Cycle Sport*), and taking many of the photos myself. So "discovering" a near-neighbor who had served an apprenticeship as a portrait photographer and had a passion for cycling, I felt twice blessed.

Through the early 1980s, as Graham traveled more extensively, his images got better and better. And even though it would be a few years before he would start shooting Europe's great professional races from the back of a motorcycle, that never stopped him from seeking the definitive photo at every event he attended.

Graham and I made many of those early trips together. Typical was an early '80s edition of Paris-Nice. We followed the seven-day race across France in Graham's red BMW, leapfrogging past the peloton several times a day—Graham driving, me navigating—using any short-cut that gave us a chance to outpace the pack. One of those "short-cuts" turned into a rocky, dirt road that took us over a high ridge, then down some steep switchbacks into a valley … and we skittered out onto the race course about two-hundred meters ahead of the race. Mission accomplished.

Cycling is not a rote, stadium-confined sport. And giving races a sense of place has been one of the accomplishments of Graham's photography. Back in 1984, when we were both on assignment in Barcelona for the world track championships, we discussed what would make a compelling shot for an opening two-page spread for our coverage in *Winning* magazine. This resulted in Graham clambering up a rocky, 500-foot-high hill at the back of the velodrome, to shoot a wide-angle photo of the well-lit outdoor velodrome at night, with the lights of the city beyond. It was a superb opener.

Cycling is also a sport in which weather and geography play a major part. I'll always remember one of the first one-day classics Graham covered on a motorcycle: Belgium's Tour of Flanders. It was a foul April day of fierce winds and almost continuous, cold rain. With about 90 minutes of the 271km race to go, Graham pulled up alongside our press car. He said that one of his cameras and its flash had stopped working, drowned by the rain, even though he had been using it covered with a big plastic bag. He then asked for something dry to rub down his other camera, which was still barely working. Yet despite being drenched, and laboring in those terrible conditions for nearly seven hours, he still came through with enough good shots to illustrate the day's story.

Graham was an amateur bike racer for a few seasons, before his photography took over his life. But if you had told him back in 1980 that one day he would be riding the classics, the grand tours, the world's, the Olympics, and all the other events that make up this magnificent sport, he wouldn't have believed you.... Well, his bike today may be motorized, but that doesn't prevent him bringing a cyclist's passion to every image he shoots.

We had a lot of fun going through the hundreds of photos that Graham submitted for this book. It was tough leaving any out. The aim was to choose shots that best illustrate the diversity of

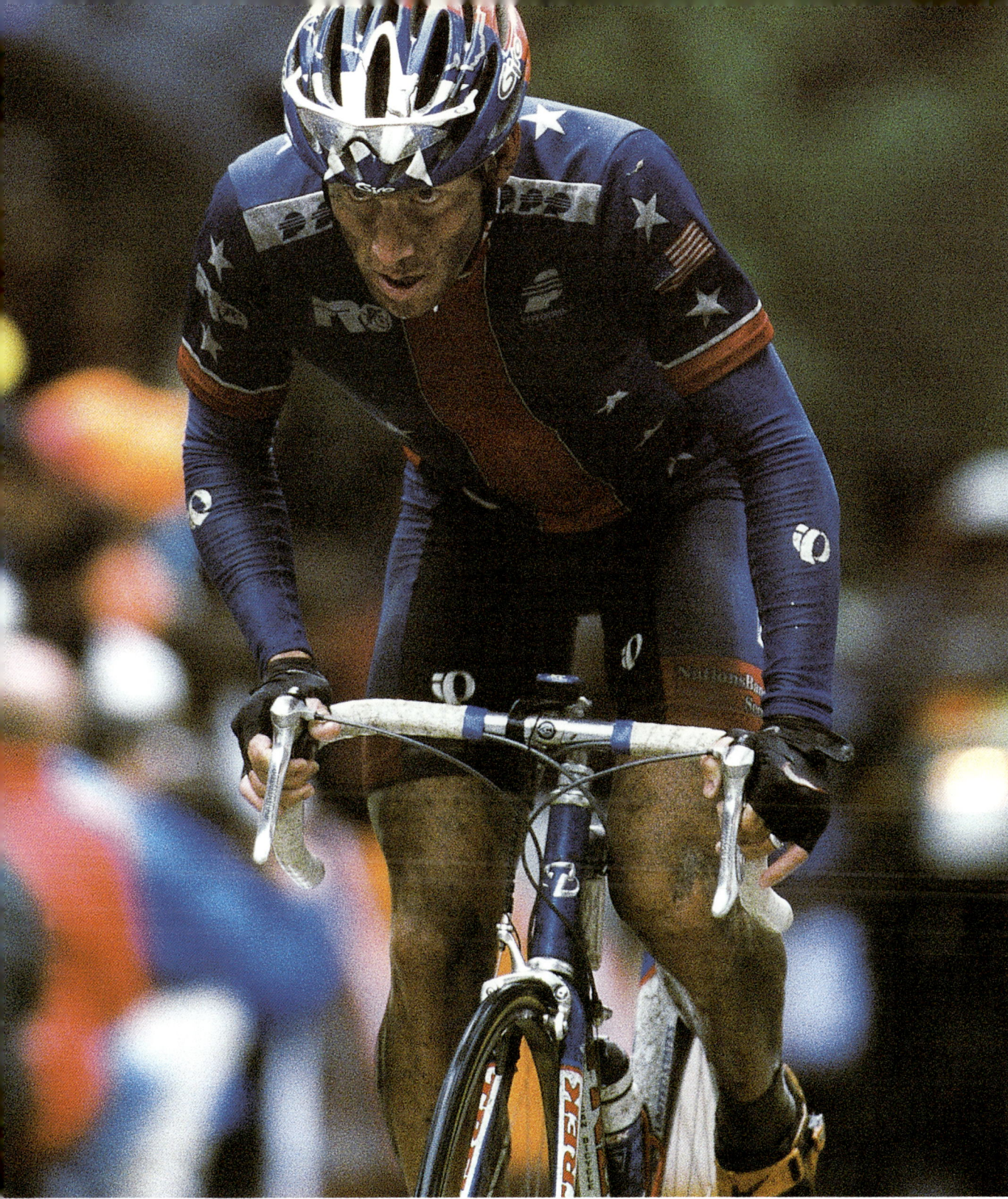

1998: WORLD ROAD CHAMPIONSHIPS: VALKENBURG, THE NETHERLANDS

The photo that captures the spirit of Lance Armstrong's return from cancer to the top level of cycle racing.

his work, while highlighting ones that have not been widely published before. We hope that you like the result.

In 20 years, camera technology has changed dramatically. But throughout these decades Graham's skills and standards have remained consistently high. So, on behalf of all of us who are deeply involved in the sport—and for all the fans of professional bike racing—thanks, Graham, for being our eyes within the peloton. Without your images, this noble sport would be nowhere near as delectable.

20 YEARS OF CYCLING PHOTOGRAPHY

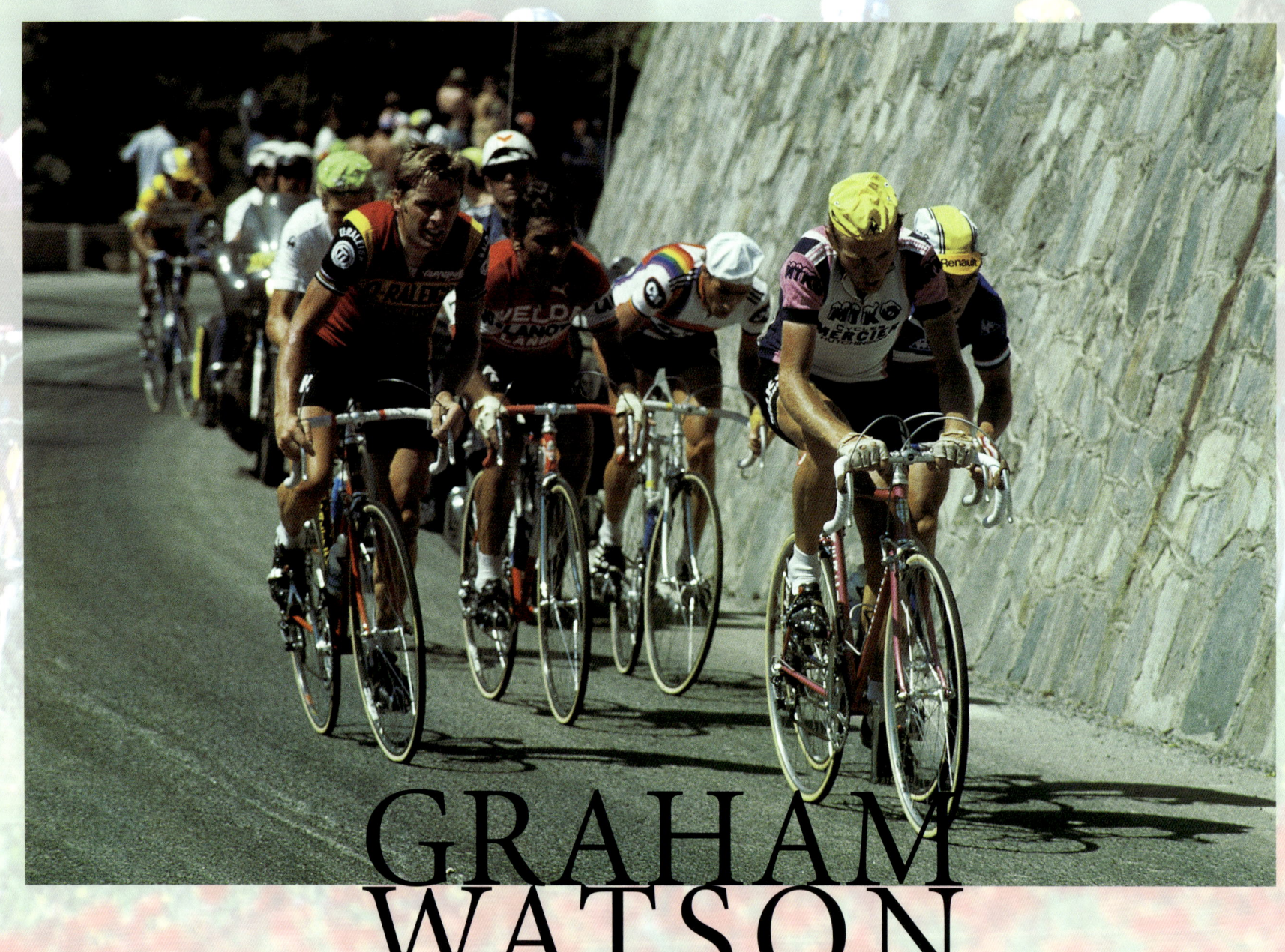

GRAHAM WATSON
1977 TO 1980

GRAHAM WATSON

One of my only regrets in 20 years of cycling photography is missing the great moments of the career of Eddy Merckx. Like any cycling enthusiast, be it pro cyclist, journalist, race-official, photographer or fan, I had come to realize the enormity of Merckx's achievement in crafting a huge niche for himself in cycling's history. Fortunately, I did catch one of Merckx's moments—on the Champs Elysées, at the end of the 1977 Tour de France—and it served me extremely well.

I had traveled to Paris with a group of cycling fans, eager for a sight of Merckx and his rivals at the end of an epic Tour. It was my first glimpse of the Tour, and a hastily taken shot of the Cannibal in the pouring rain won me a tiny award in a photo competition run by *Cycling Weekly*. So I credit Merckx—and the publication of his photograph—for having sent me on my way as a freelance cycling photographer, for each year after that I headed back to France in the hope of achieving more recognition.

As a follow-up to my two days of Tour viewing in 1977, I saw a whole two weeks the following year, and witnessed the arrival onto the scene of Frenchman Bernard Hinault. I was traveling along part of the route by bicycle, and experiencing legendary climbs like the Alpe d'Huez and Col de Porte. It was at Alpe d'Huez that I saw Michel Pollentier make his dramatic attempt to win the Tour against Hinault.

The balding Belgian made a big impression on me, as he flew by where I was standing. But it wasn't until the next day, while scanning a copy of *L'Equipe*, that I realized the true impact his efforts had made: His dramatic exclusion from the Tour ensured that Hinault would not be beaten.

Completely and utterly smitten by now, I expanded my race-watching-and-photographing horizons by catching the 1979 Tour of Flanders, won by Walter Godefroot, and spending another two weeks cycling along the route of that year's Tour, where Hinault was again the dominator. But I knew two weeks was never going to be enough, so 1980 saw me following the entire Tour by car, on a route that started in Frankfurt, Germany, and then went across Belgium, before starting an anti-clockwise trek around France.

Earlier that same spring, I'd paid a visit to the 1980 Paris-Roubaix, and in a rather unconventional way: With a sturdy handlebar bag holding my precious Pentax camera, I cycled from the seaport of Calais to the cobbles near Hem, and back—a round-trip of more than 230km. I'd arrived

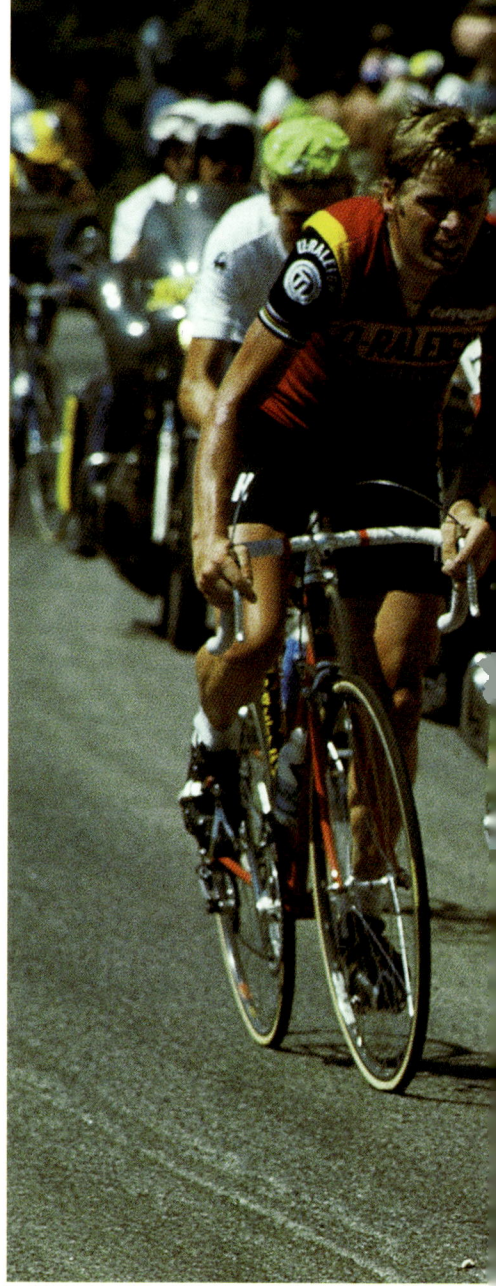

8 1977 TO 1980

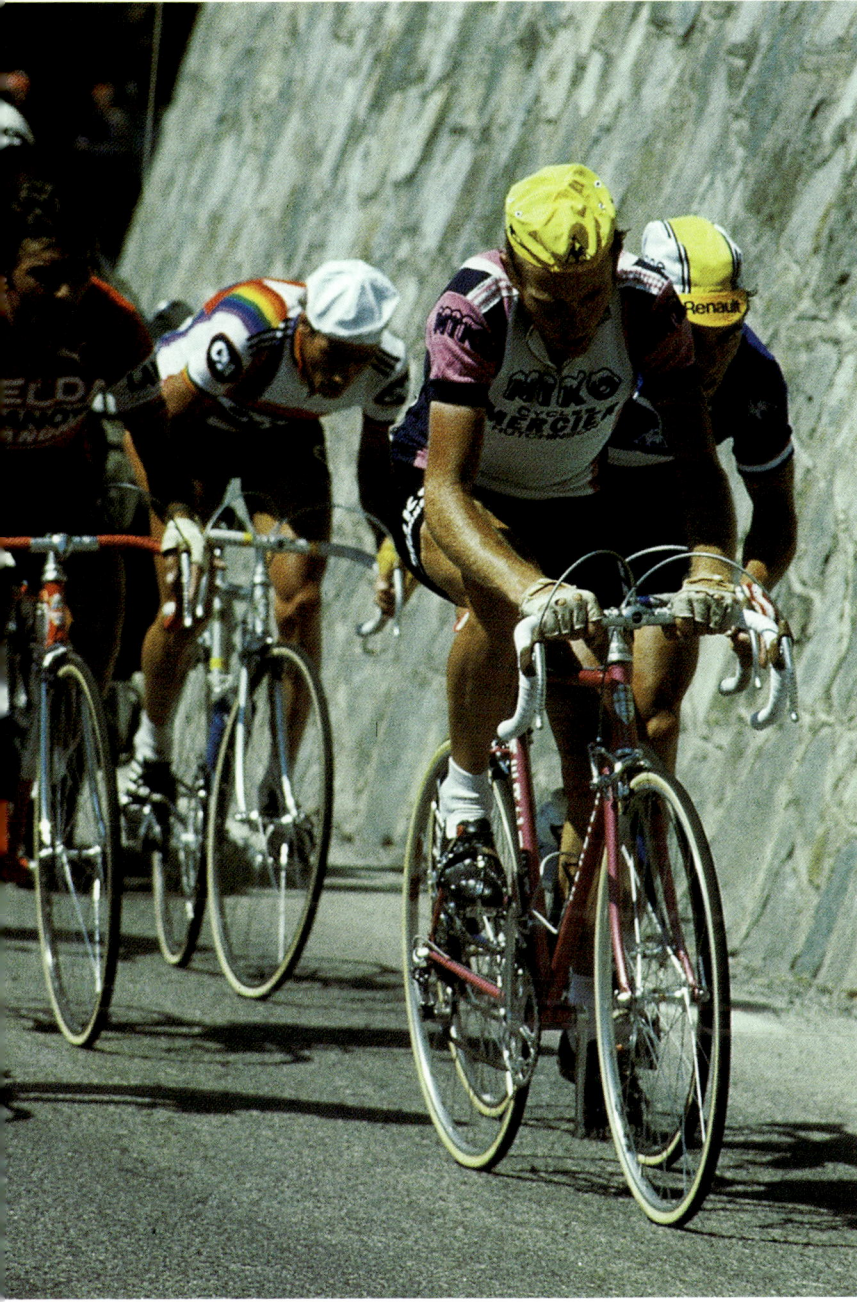

on the dusty cobbles about one hour before the race was due, and had chosen my sacred position very carefully, determined to get a great shot of whichever cyclist was leading at that point, just 10 kilometers from the end.

Thus, my first glimpse of Paris-Roubaix was of the Italian champion, Francesco Moser, nose down almost onto his handlebars, blasting flat-out along the side of the cobbled track—but a French motorcycle photographer obscured my view at the critical moment, his unwieldy BMW cutting half of Moser from my lens.

I could have cried. Still, that dismal experience awakened me to the need to one day follow races by motorcycle. It was to take me another seven years before I finally made it onto an in-race Paris-Roubaix motorcycle . . . and now it is probably me who destroys the aspirations of would-be photographers along the cobblestones of northern France.

In 1980, I saw Dutchman Joop Zoetemelk win the Tour, after years of placing second or third, and that's when the commercial side of my photographic career began—for Zoetemelk was riding a British-built Raleigh bicycle, and the orders for images came through thick and fast from the company's public relations firm, based in Nottingham.

That same Tour woke me to the fact that maybe one day, in the not-too-distant future, there just might be a way to eke out a living from photographing cycling. Stage 19 saw Sean

1978: TOUR DE FRANCE: L'ALPE D'HUEZ

Joop Zoetemelk leads a chase after Michel Pollentier on L'Alpe d'Huez from (left to right) Hennie Kuiper, Joaquim Agostinho, Lucien Van Impe and Bernard Hinault. After taking the stage and the yellow jersey, Pollentier was disqualified for trying to give a false urine sample at the anti-doping control. Zoetemelk took over the race lead that he relinquished to Hinault in the final time trial.

Kelly burst onto the scene at St. Etienne, where he outsprinted his breakaway partner, Ismael Lejarreta. Though unnoticed by me at the time, the Irishman's emergence into the big time was to aid my own progress immensely, for it coincided with the burgeoning careers of other English-speaking stars, like Greg LeMond, Stephen Roche, Phil Anderson, Robert Millar and Paul Sherwen. And what Kelly did for me in the Tour, Millar did even more so in the world championships in Sallanches that August. The Scotsman rode a superb race, always at the side of Hinault in a day-long escape, eventually finishing in a fine 11th place.

After 1980 then, my path was set; it was only a question of seeing where it led. For the old traditions—of a sport once dominated by the French, Dutch, Italians and Belgians—were crumbling fast, and the opportunities for an Englishman like me were rapidly expanding.

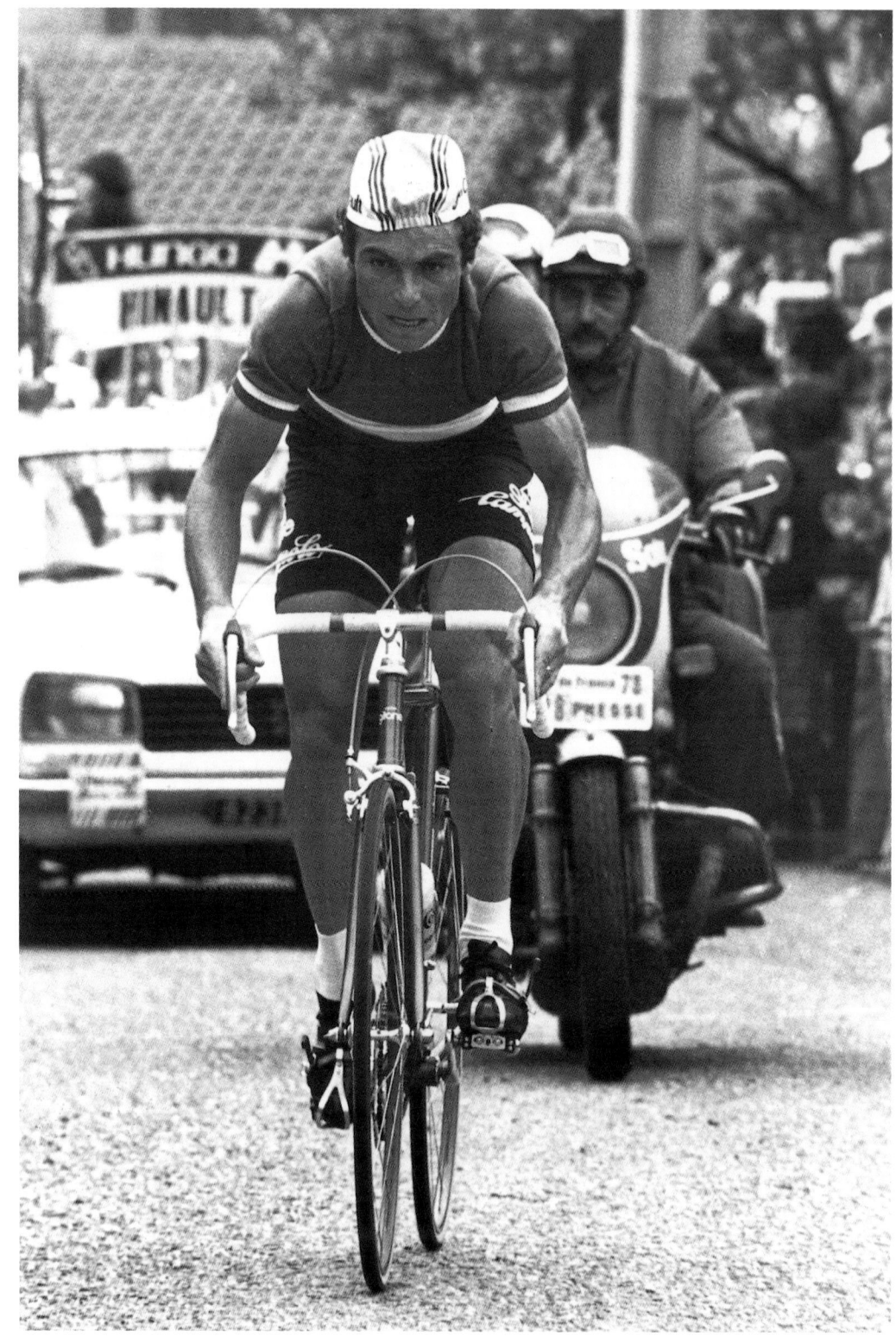

1978: TOUR DE FRANCE: METZ-NANCY

Wearing the French champion's tricolor jersey, Bernard Hinault races alone through the Moselle wine country in stage 20, a 72-kilometer individual time trial between Metz and Nancy. Hinault started the time trial in second place overall, less than half-a-minute behind race leader Joop Zoetemelk. By winning the stage and defeating Zoetemelk (who finished ninth on the stage, more than four minutes slower), Hinault clinched his first victory in the Tour de France.

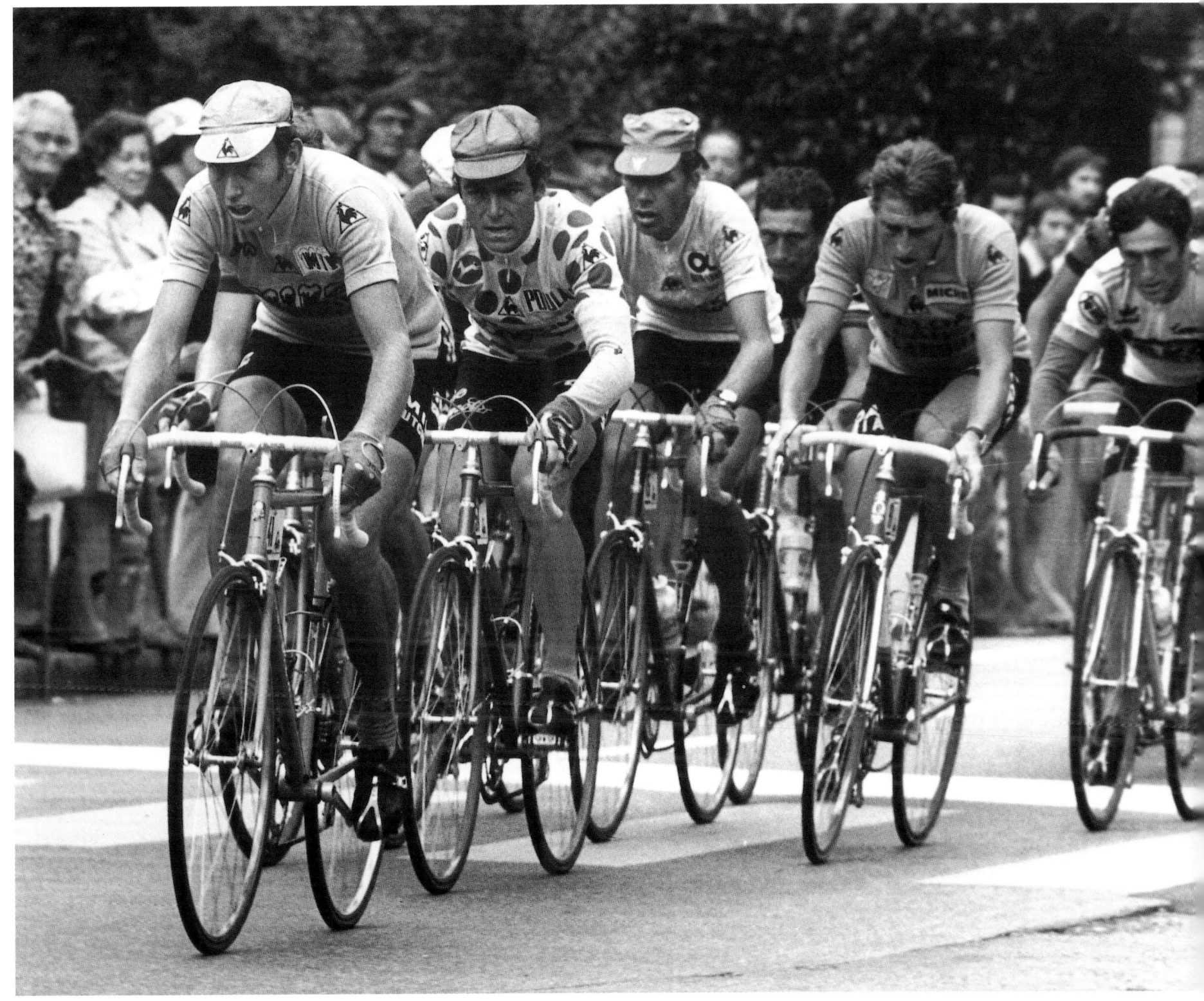

1978: TOUR DE FRANCE: LAUSANNE, SWITZERLAND

No helmets here! Before the era of light, comfortable helmets, the only headwear donned by Tour de France riders were cotton racing caps. Here, coming to the finish of the 16th stage in Lausanne, Switzerland, race leader Joop Zoetemelk leads Bernard Hinault, Johan Van der Velde and Freddy Maertens.

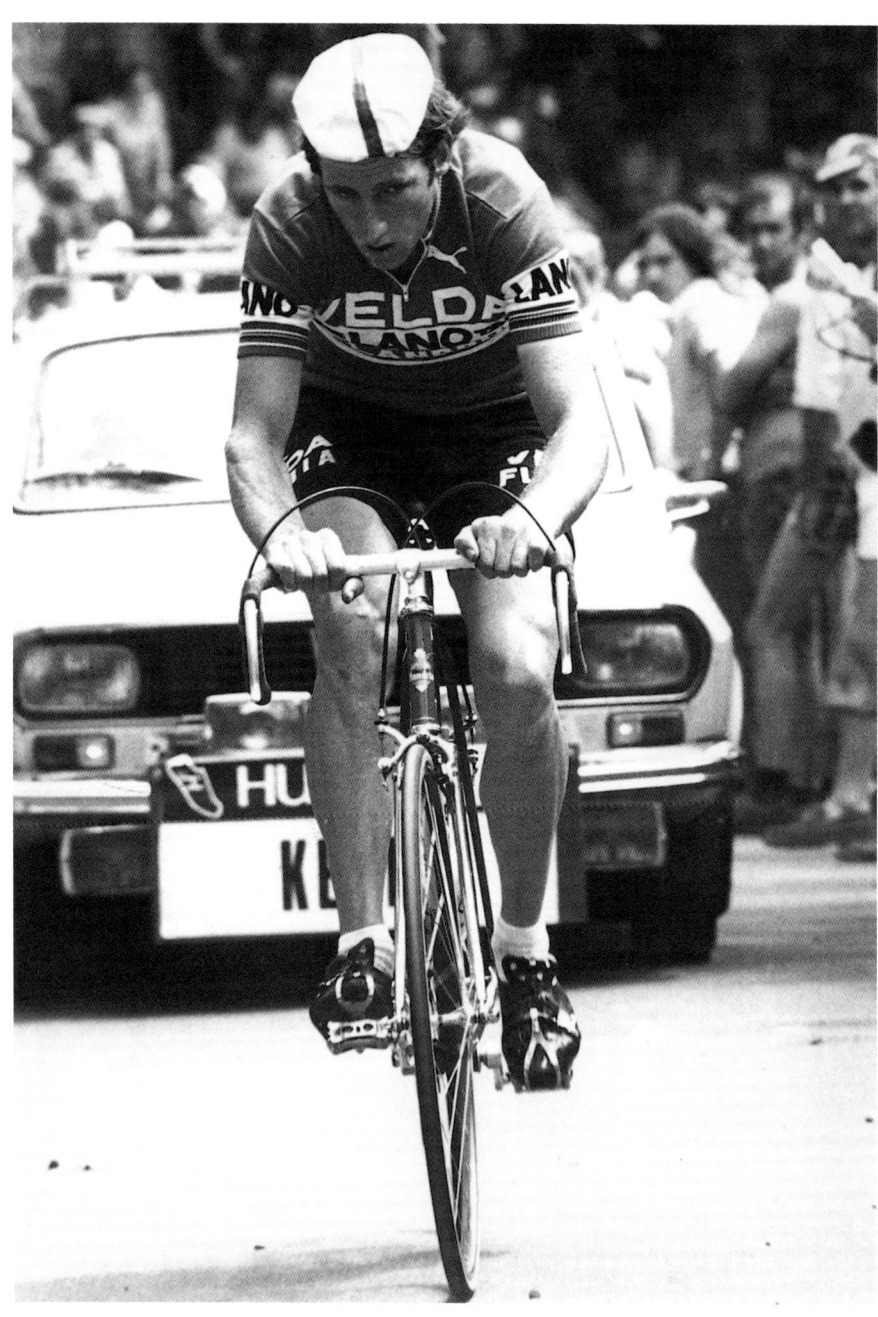

1978: TOUR DE FRANCE: METZ–NANCY

In his first Tour de France, a 22-year-old Sean Kelly rides the final time trial on his way to 34th place overall. Kelly took one stage win in his Tour debut.

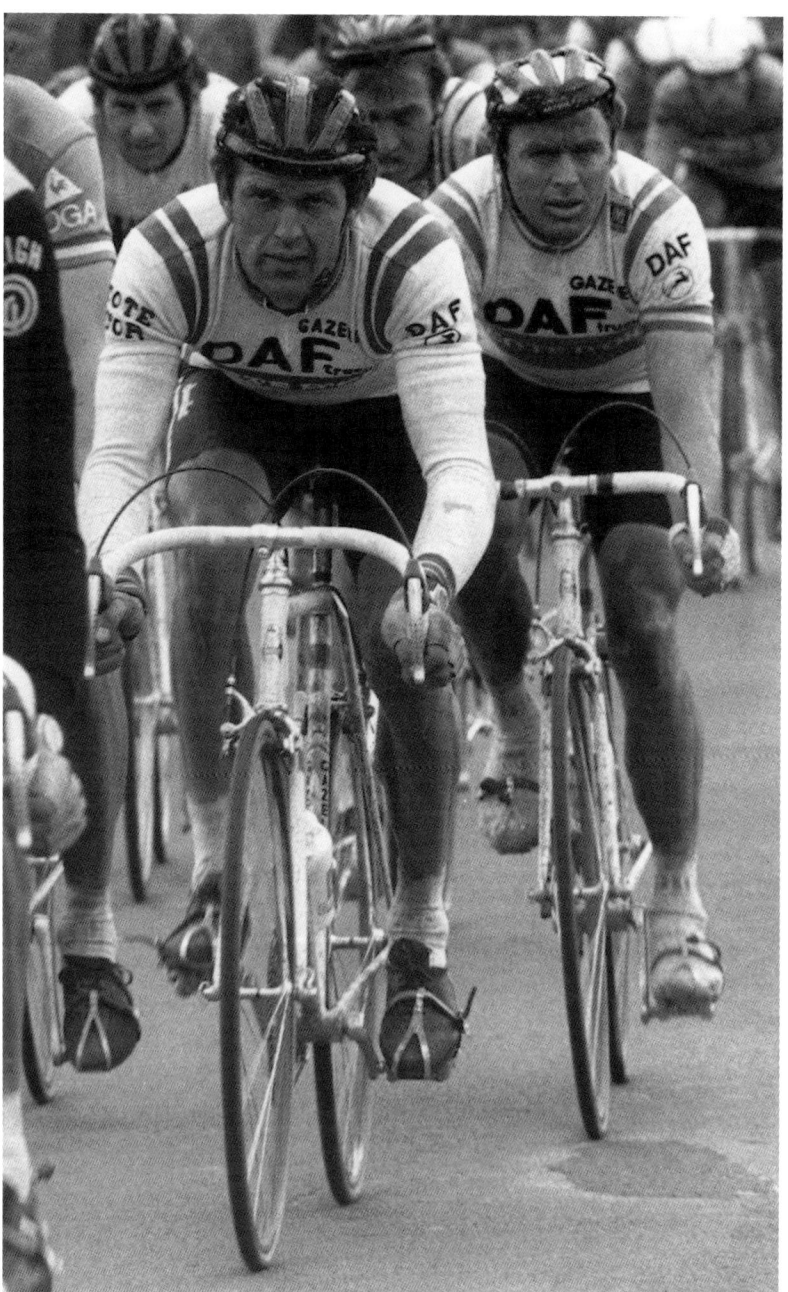

1980: TOUR OF FLANDERS: BELGIUM

Two of the sport's greatest classics riders, Roger De Vlaeminck and Hennie Kuiper, are seen here in the early going of the 1980 Tour of Flanders. De Vlaeminck won this Belgian classic in 1977; Kuiper became the champion in 1981.

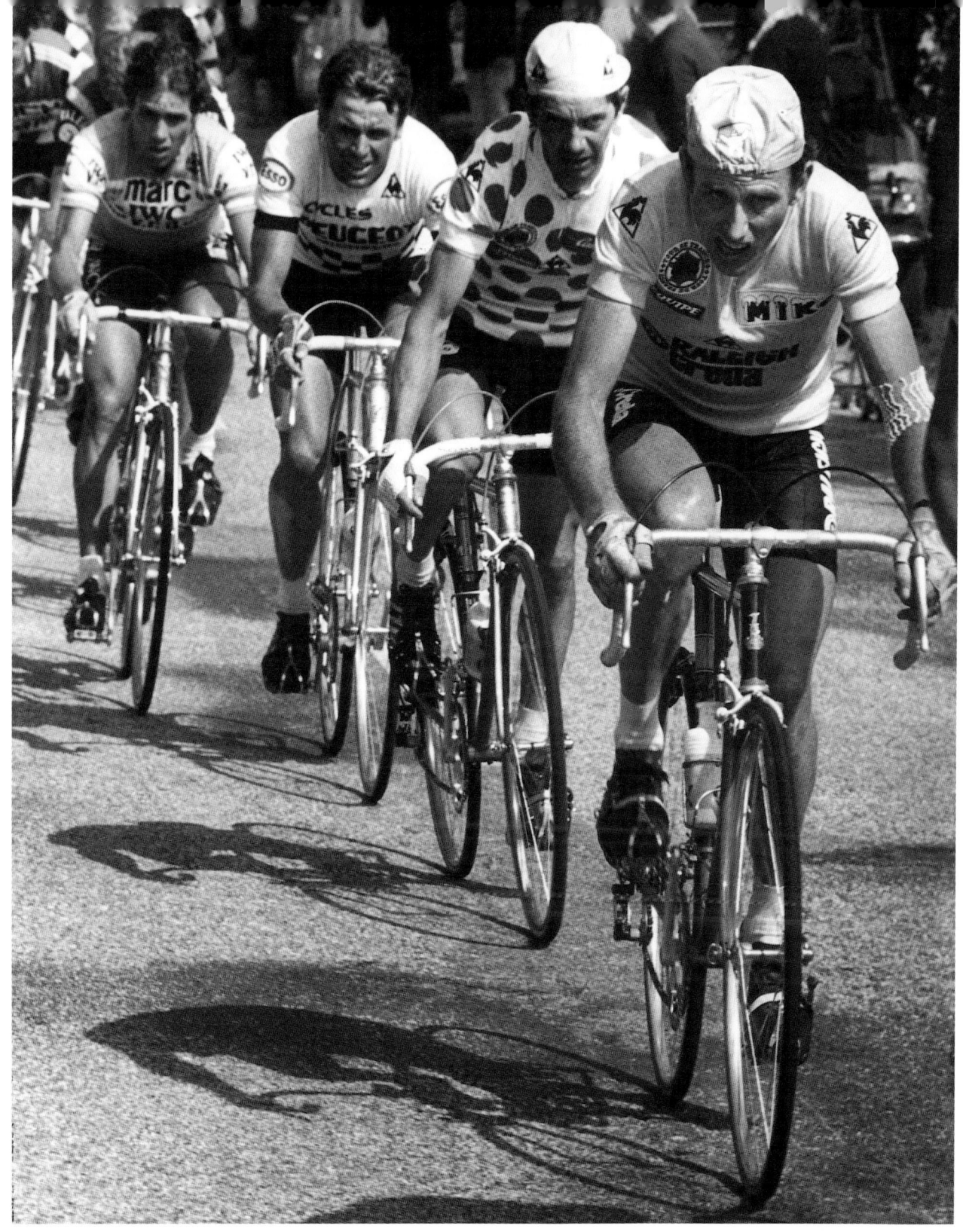

1980: TOUR DE FRANCE: THE FRENCH ALPS

After finishing the Tour de France in second place five times, Joop Zoetemelk finally won the Tour in 1980. He was riding a British-made Raleigh bicycle, which earned the author several commercial sales of his photographs. Here, Zoetemelk leads eventual third- and second-place finishers, Raymond Martin and Hennie Kuiper, with former King of the Mountains Lucien Van Impe following.

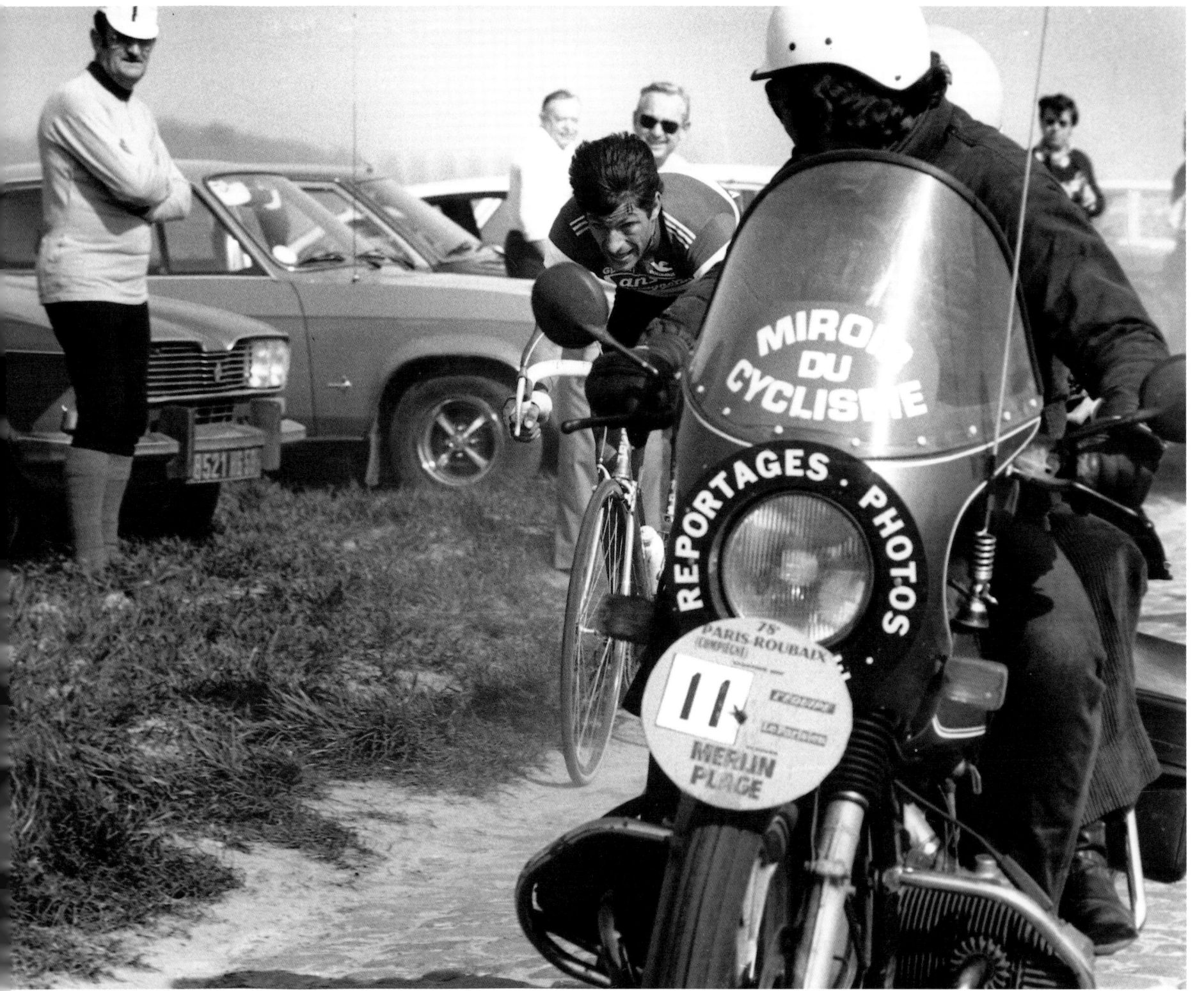

1980: PARIS-ROUBAIX: FRANCE

After riding his bike from England across northern France, the author had one chance of photographing Francesco Moser as he powered to a solo victory in Paris-Roubaix. This was the shot: A motorcycle from French magazine Miroir du Cyclisme *blocked the shot … and gave the author the incentive to one day earn a seat on an official press motorcycle.*

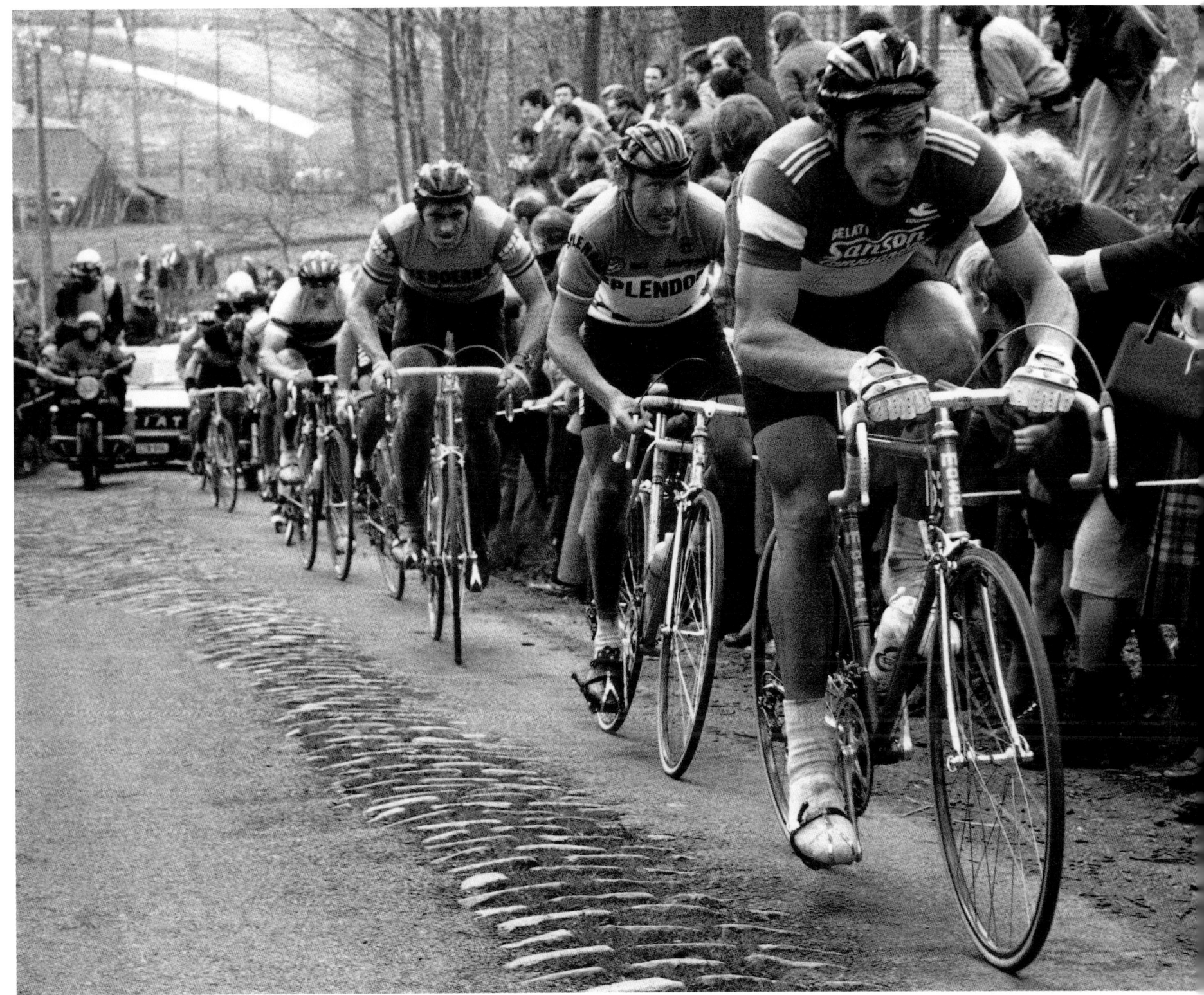

1980: TOUR OF FLANDERS: BELGIUM

The author had better luck at spring 1980's Tour of Flanders. Here, on one of the Belgian classic's many cobblestone climbs, Moser leads eventual winner Michel Pollentier, followed by Marc De Meyer and Jan Raas.

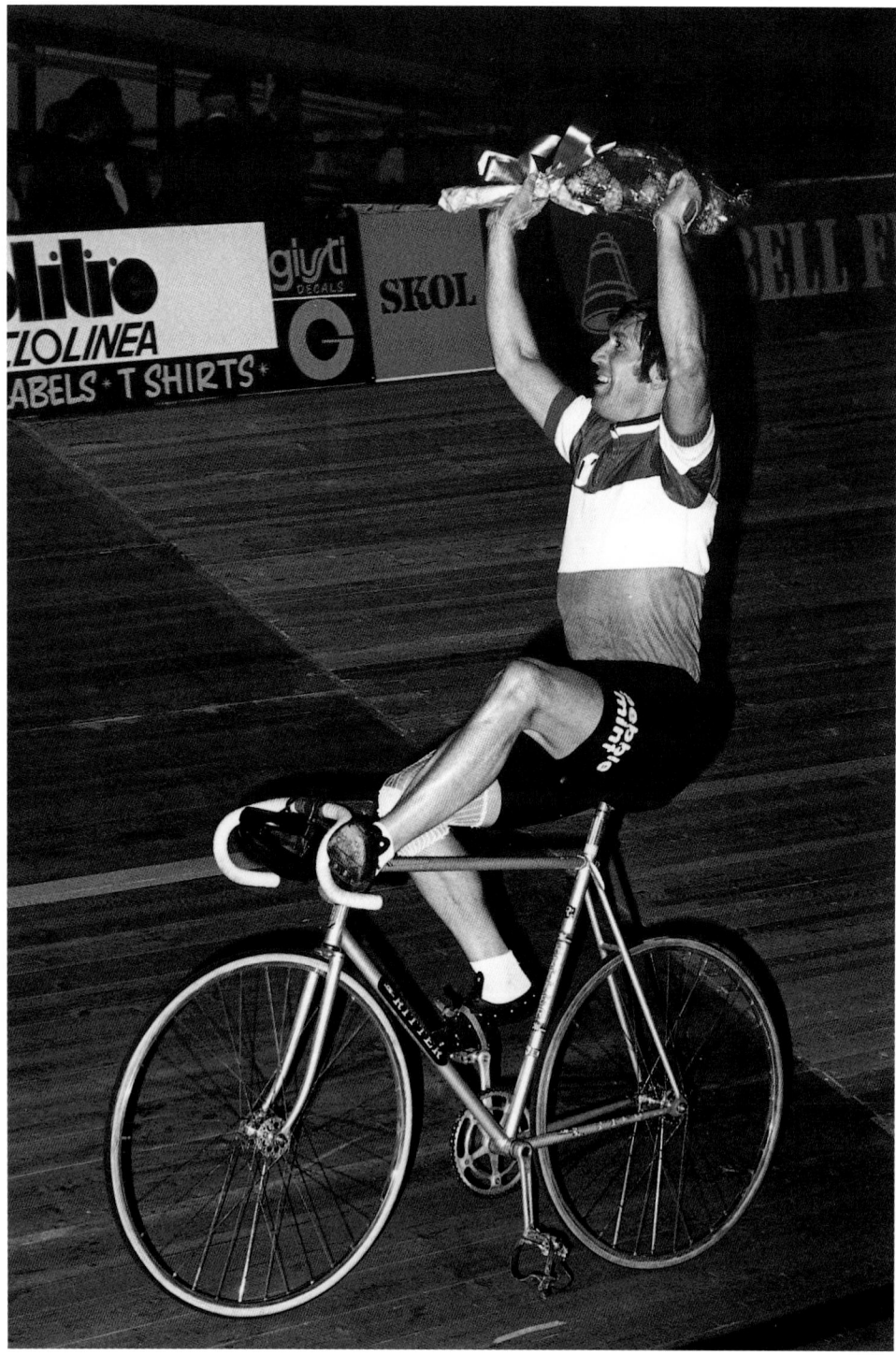

1980: SKOL SIX: LONDON

Besides being the "clown prince" of six-day racing, Belgian track racer Willy De Bosscher was a fast, skillful sprinter. Here, he does a one-legged lap of honor after winning a sprint series during the six-day race sponsored by Skol lager at the arena in Wembley, London.

1980: TOUR DE FRANCE: THE FRENCH ALPS

Between them, Dutchman Hennie Kuiper (leading here) and Belgian Lucien Van Impe rode 27 Tours de France in the 1970s and '80s. Besides taking a record six King of the Mountains titles, Van Impe finished top-five eight times, including his one victory in 1976. Kuiper's best was second place in 1977 (48 seconds behind Bernard Thévenet) and second in 1980 (6:55 behind Joop Zoetemelk).

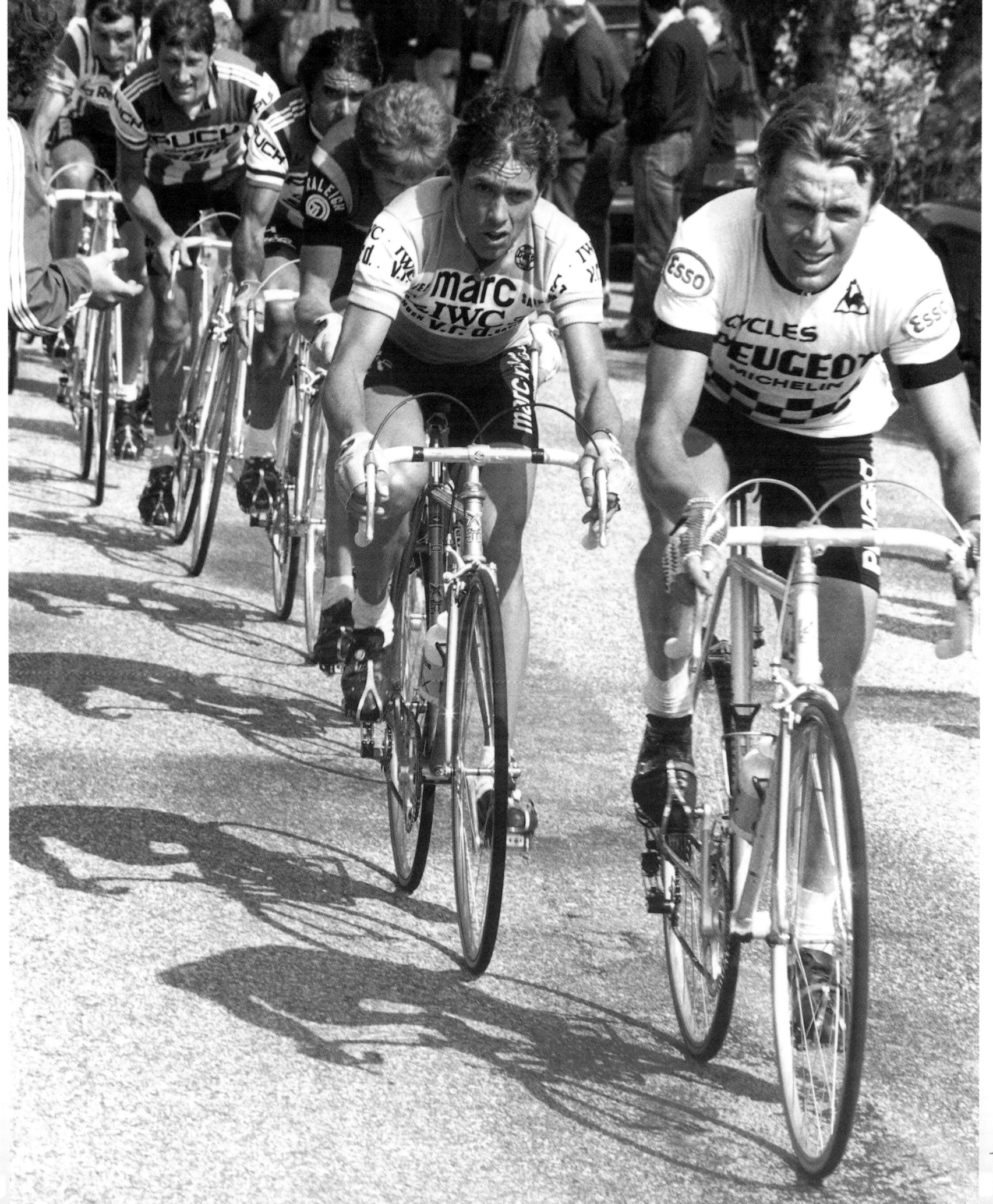

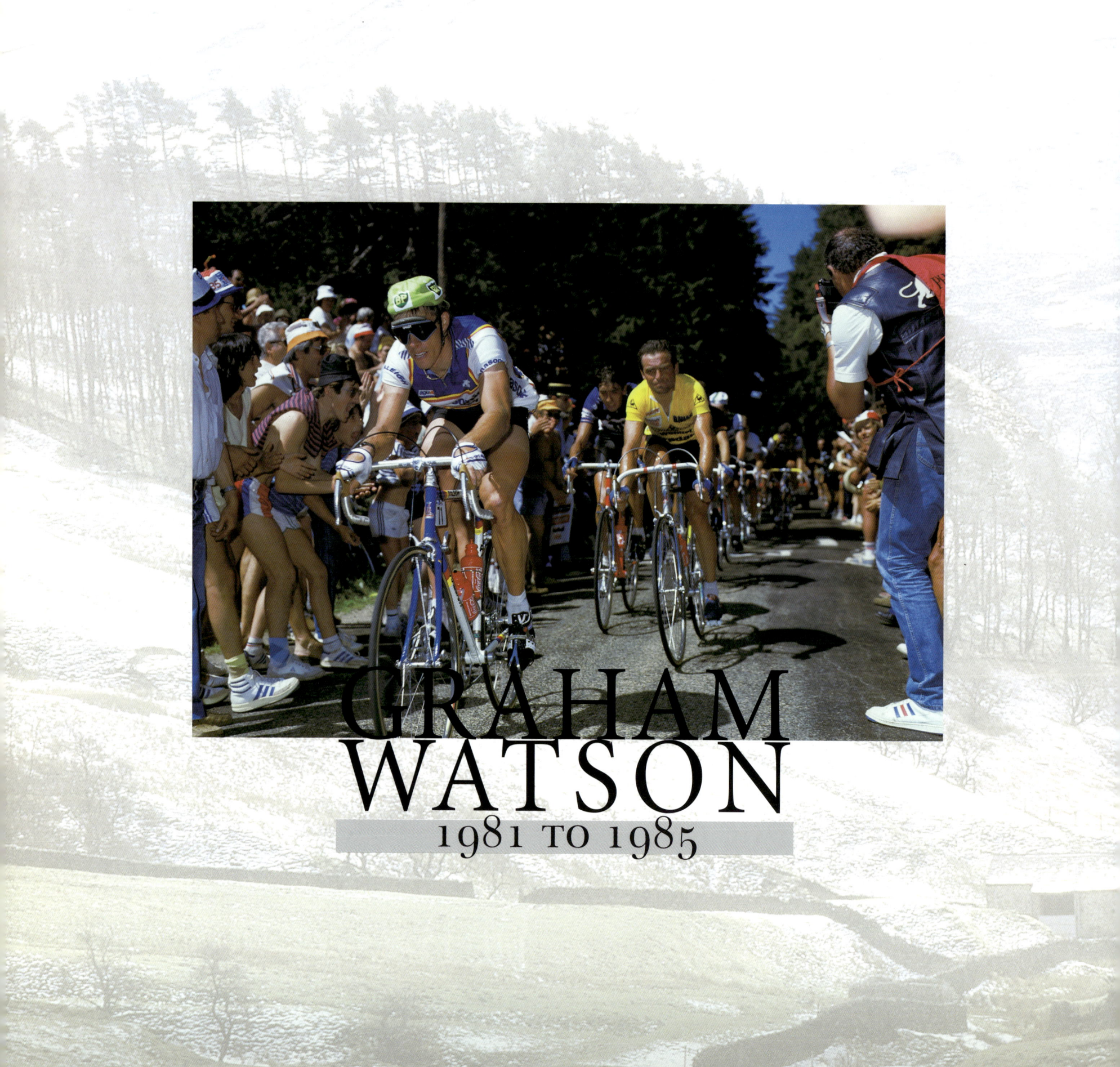

GRAHAM WATSON
1981 TO 1985

GRAHAM WATSON

By the time 1981 dawned, my ambitions had been truly set alight. Frustrated to have missed Stephen Roche's great win in Paris-Nice that March, I began my campaign on the first weekend of April—following a pleading letter to the organizer of the Tour of Flanders that led to my following that race on a motorcycle. The benefits were immediate, as I produced dozens of images of all the great stars—De Vlaeminck, Raas, Kuiper and Thurau. The only one missing was Merckx himself, who by this time had been retired for three years, though his spirit remained very present. I also got to experience a spectacular crash, when my driver lost control on the sinewy descent toward the Koppenberg.

The buzz and excitement of that first Tour of Flanders is still with me today, and though I continue to regret missing Merckx's best days in "De Ronde," there have been so many exciting moments that even this great champion gets pushed to the back of my mind during the race.

Flanders is definitely the hardest race to photograph, being both beautiful and frustrating in equal amounts, with probably the biggest roadside audience of any one-day classic—especially if the great race falls on an Easter Sunday, when hundreds of thousands of dressed-up churchgoers line the roadsides.

Paris-Roubaix is always scheduled one week later, and in 1981, I chose to follow it in my car, rather than by bicycle. With my ascendancy to the big-time at Flanders still a vivid memory, and utterly envious of my new colleagues whenever they drove by me on the cobbles, I yearned for equal access to the French classic. Bernard Hinault won the 1981 "Hell of the North," and I had to settle for a couple of grabbed shots of him in the later stages of the race.

In the Tour that year, Australia's Phil Anderson made a dramatic entrée into professional cycling by grabbing the yellow jersey at Pla d'Adet, in the Pyrénées, after sticking with race-favorite Hinault on the steep climb to the finish in audacious fashion. Though Hinault took revenge the next day, in the short time trial between Nay and Pau, the shot I took of Anderson clad in his yellow skinsuit remains one of my finest Tour memories, though technically it is nothing special. Again, my car did the work this time, with my bike in the back to get me access to the closed mountain roads. And, for the first time, I'd managed to get myself official media credentials . . . things were looking up.

Anderson was again the star in the 1982 Tour de France, this time holding the race lead for a magnificent 10 days . . . before Hinault, once again, trounced him in the time trial in Valence d'Agen. I met with Anderson that July, sitting in on an interview being conducted by John

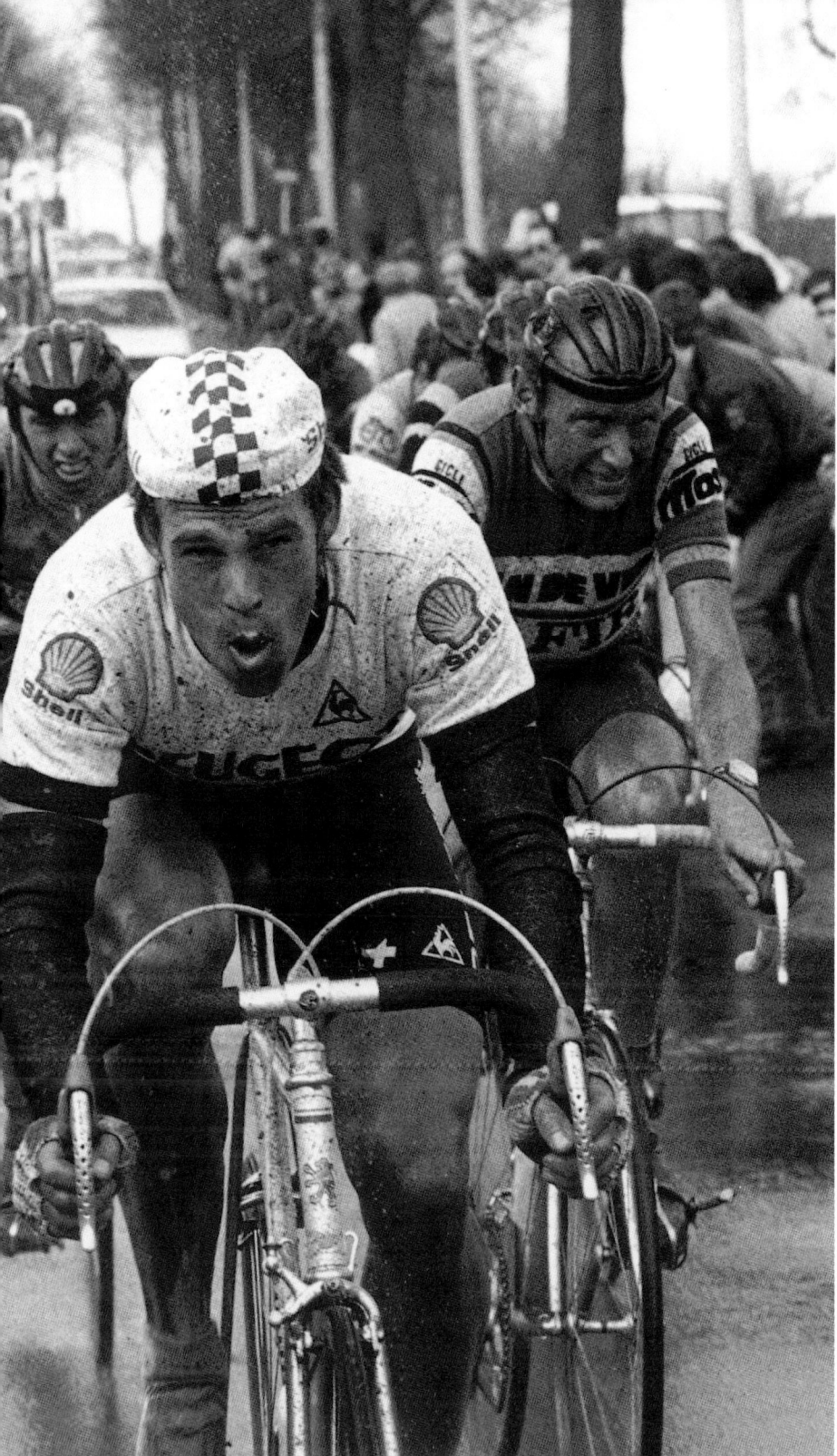

1983: TOUR OF FLANDERS: BELGIUM

Now on a motorcycle, the author was able to start collecting gritty action shots like this one of Aussie Phil Anderson leading a chase with Belgian Michel Pollentier (right) in Belgium's Tour of Flanders classic.

Wilcockson, the English cycling guru, with whom I shared, and still share, some excellent adventures.

I'd met John the previous summer in Brno, Czechoslovakia, on the occasion of the 1981 world championships; and having discovered that we two Brits lived only three miles away from each other in London, our working relationship became the catalyst of my early career, with John editing magazines such as *Cyclist Monthly, Winning, Inside Cycling*, and finally *VeloNews*. As I discovered during his intimate 30 minutes with Anderson, John's love and knowledge of cycling is what sets him apart from his sometimes envious colleagues, most of whom lack that extra percent of sensitivity and understanding of their subject.

With the likes of Australian Phil Anderson and Irishman Sean Kelly now riding high in professional cycling, my career as an English photographer really started to take off, and even by 1982, I had a string of magazines paying for my services, which in turn meant I could go shoot even more races than before.

The world's that year were in England—the track racing in Leicester, and the road events down in very English Goodwood—and I was thrilled by the battle between Gordon Singleton and Koichi Nakano for the professional sprint title in Leicester. Two crashes in two rounds made this pair every pho-

1981 TO 1985 21

tographer's favorites of the championships! Just as Singleton was the ultimate aggressor, so Nakano was the epitome of grace and good manners, and in the next few years he became one of the greatest track stars to grace the sport, winning 10 consecutive world sprint titles.

If the track races were superb, then the road races were even more so, with a "home" win for Britain's Mandy Jones, and a stunning last-kilometer burst by Giuseppe Saronni to win the coveted pro road championship—the Italian was chased home all the way by a precociously talented American, Greg LeMond.

Looking back on those world's, indeed all the world championships of the 1980s, they represented possibly the highlight of the whole season for me. Catering to all disciplines of cycle racing, they offered the chance to see, year after year, the progression of amateur cyclists on their upward path to the top level of the sport. And being held in the summery month of August, the championships were a great big festival for athletes, the public and the media alike. It was the annual coming-together of the great family of cycling—an end-of-summer celebration, even as autumn was starting to show its romantic presence.

In the world of cycling, one cannot talk of romance without talking about the Tour of Lombardy, which, for me, is the most wonderful race on the calendar. Inspired by the racing at the 1982 world's, but bitterly disappointed by the results of some of my photo work, I drove all the way down to northern Italy a month later, determined to put a happy ending on that season. My goal was to capture Saronni, now in the rainbow-colored jersey of world champion, in front of his adoring tifosi. Such was the distance—an 800-mile drive each way—that I took the precaution to photograph another race, the Tour of Piedmont, two

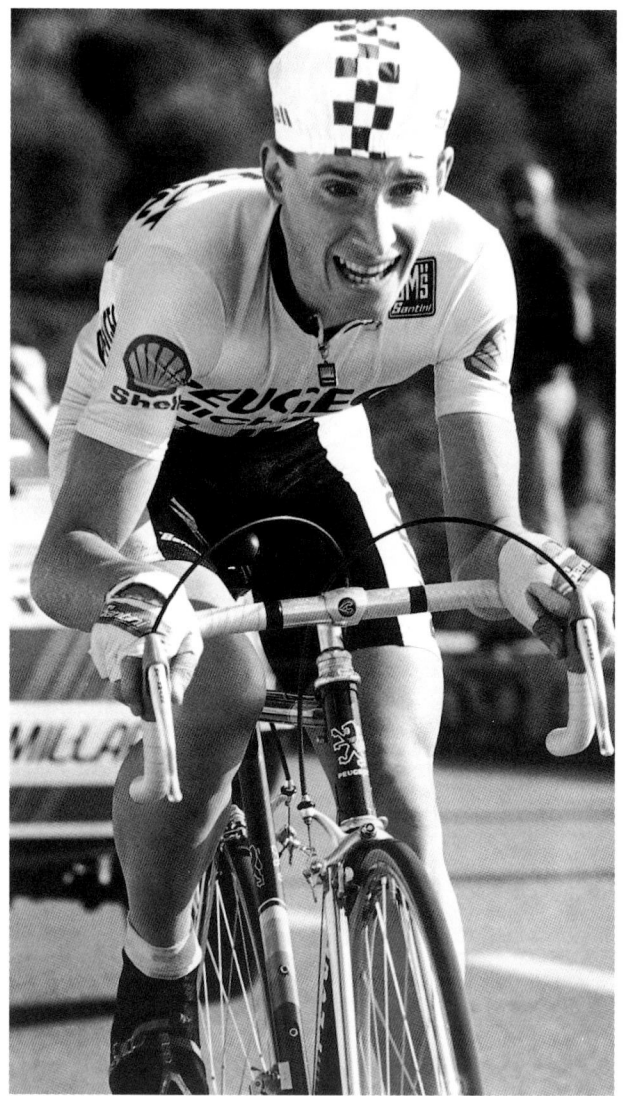

1985: VUELTA A ESPAÑA: SPAIN

Scotsman Robert Millar featured strongly in the author's early portfolio. Here, Millar rides a time trial in the Tour of Spain.

days before the "Lombardia," in case bad weather spoiled my picture-shooting potential at the main event. But in fact, both races were run off under superb sunny conditions, and I was fortunate to see the lakes of northern Italy at their best, and to also see cycling's jewel of a classic, the Tour of Lombardy. There could be no more fitting finale than when Saronni justified my long trip by winning the race, in a sprint, on the lakeshore in Como.

At the Piedmont, I had given a lift to an unusual hitchhiker—English professional Paul Sherwen, who'd waved me down on one of the many climbs, after deciding he'd ridden far enough by that time of the year. We've been friends ever since, and I've now discovered many of Paul's other talents, such as television commentary or safari guiding in his beloved Kenya.

The next year, 1983, was a big one for me. For the first time, I realized that I was turning a passion into a workable existence. Race organizers had started to note my existence, too, and I was now granted motorcycle access to all the one-day races—except Paris-Roubaix. The stubborn French still refused to acknowledge that English-speaking cyclists were winning some of the biggest races, and that there should be an English-speaking photographer in the race.

Yet even though my professional reputation was growing, some mad part of me decided I would follow the entire 1983 Tour on a bicycle. In hindsight, it was as if I knew it would be my last chance to enjoy such an adventure, before my working needs took their natural course over the years to come. So off I rode—though I failed in my attempt to follow every stage, due to a damaged wheel which

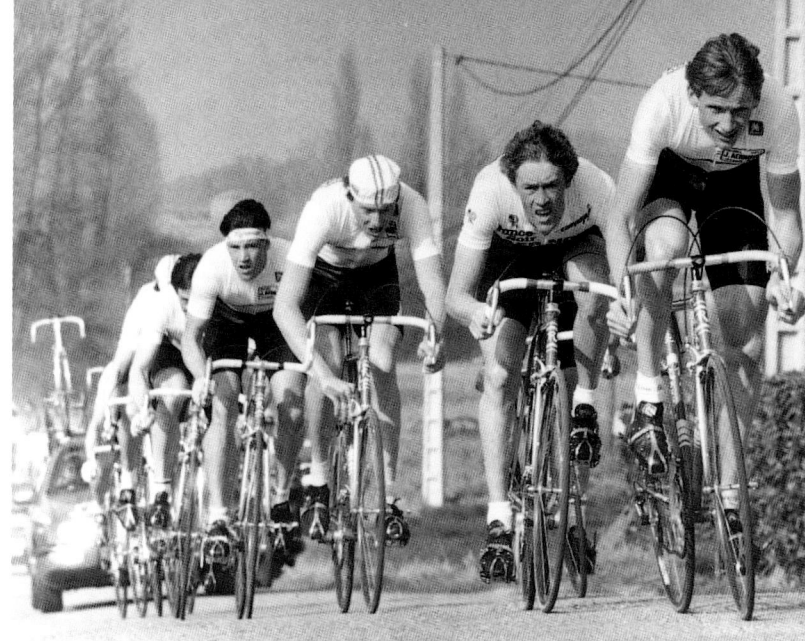

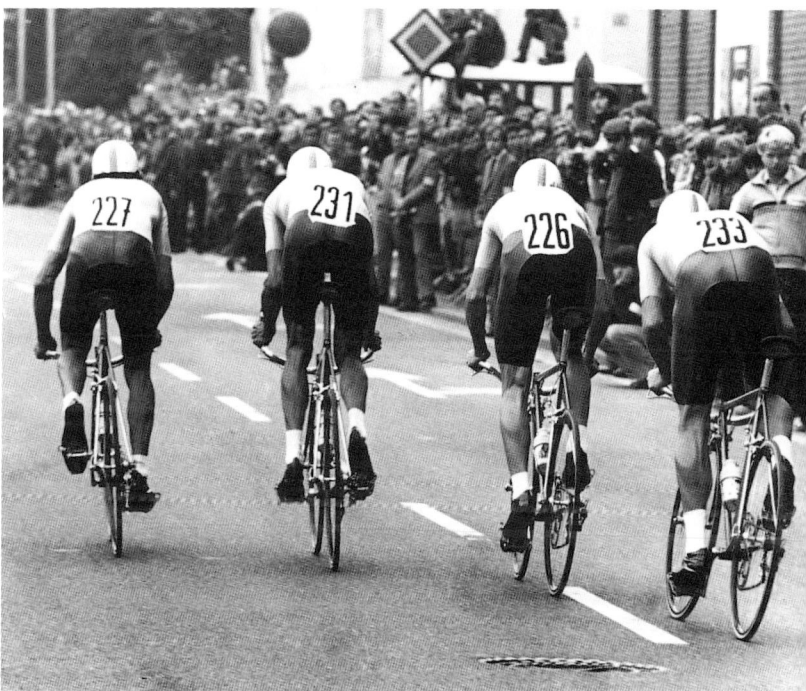

1981 AND 1983: TEAM TIME TRIALS: CZECHOSLOVAKIA AND FRANCE

Team time trialing was one of the major disciplines in the 1980s, shown here by (top) the Aernoudt pro team at the 1983 Paris-Nice and (below) by the amateurs of East Germany at the 1981 world's in Prague.

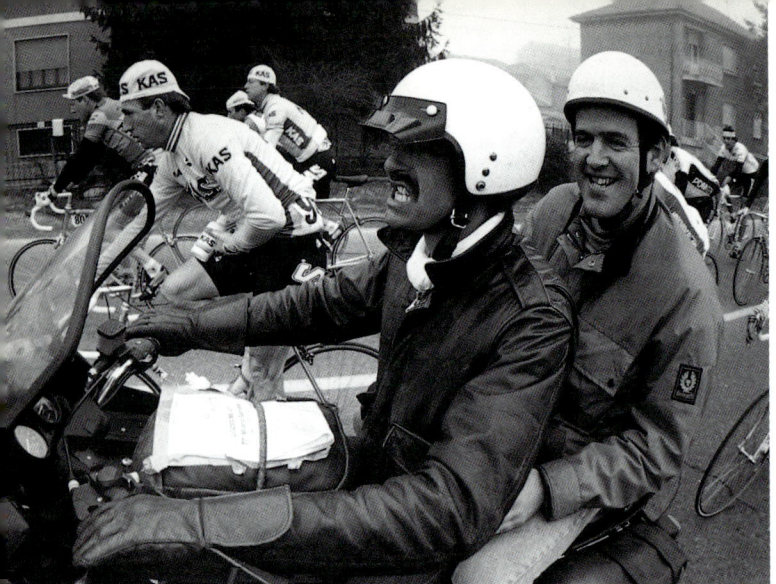
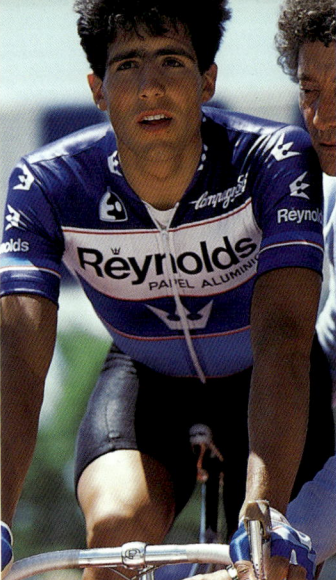

forced me to spend a day in Aurillac, right after I saw Angel Arroyo win the time trial up the fearsome slopes of the Puy-de-Dôme.

The one-day delay waiting for the wheel to be fixed, became a two-day delay after a chance meeting with a very pretty Belgian girl in the campsite where I was stranded. I had to make use of a train to Grenoble to catch up with the race at the Alpe d'Huez.

A year later, the car was my *moyenne de transport*, and I enjoyed seeing Laurent Fignon take his second Tour win. I also enjoyed seeing Greg LeMond make his entry into the Tour, winning the "best young rider" competition, and rapidly increasing my picture sales.

By now, *Winning* magazine had begun to make its presence felt as the premier English-language cycling publication, and, with my photography of the 1984 Tour handsomely displayed within, I moved onto a higher playing field—one that saw me photograph every major race in 1984 and '85, and extend my adventures into Spain with the 1985 Vuelta a España.

The first two images I took in Spain, one sunny April afternoon, were of Federico Echave winning the stage into Oviedo, and then a shot of the new wearer of the race-leader's jersey—a noble-looking youngster named Miguel Induráin.

1985: MILAN-SAN REMO: ITALY

By the mid-1980s, the author (right) became a familiar figure at the European classics.

1985: VUELTA A ESPAÑA: SPAIN

A youthful Miguel Induráin, 20, was first shot by the author at the 1985 Vuelta.

1983: TOUR OF FLANDERS: BELGIUM

No, this is not Paris-Roubaix, but a cobbled farm track in Belgium's Tour of Flanders: the infamous Paddestraat. Here, Gregor Braun of Germany leads Ludo Peeters of Belgium, two of the decade's consistently strong riders.

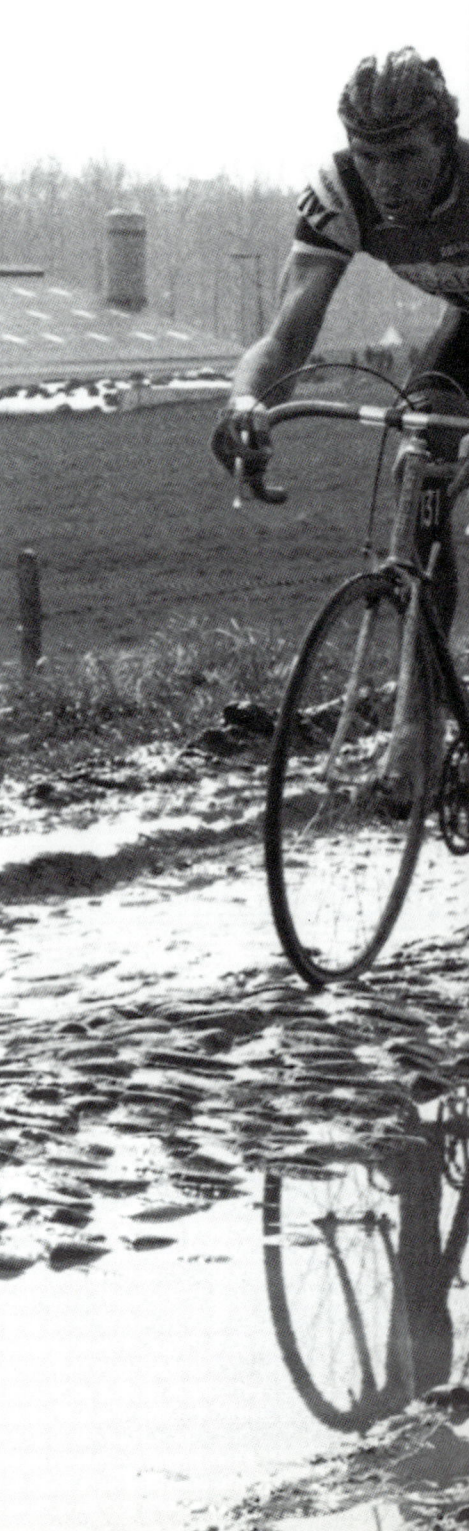

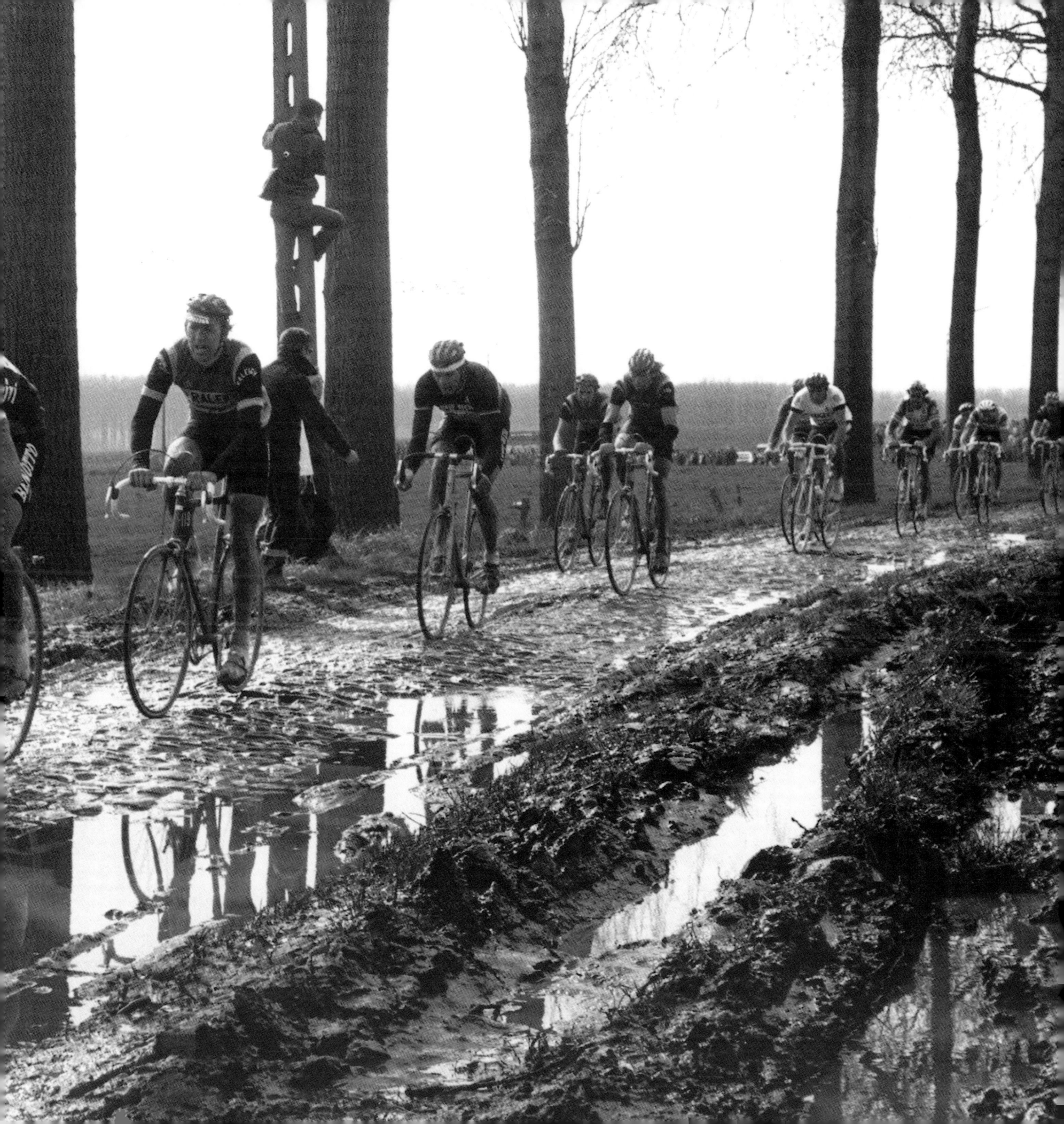

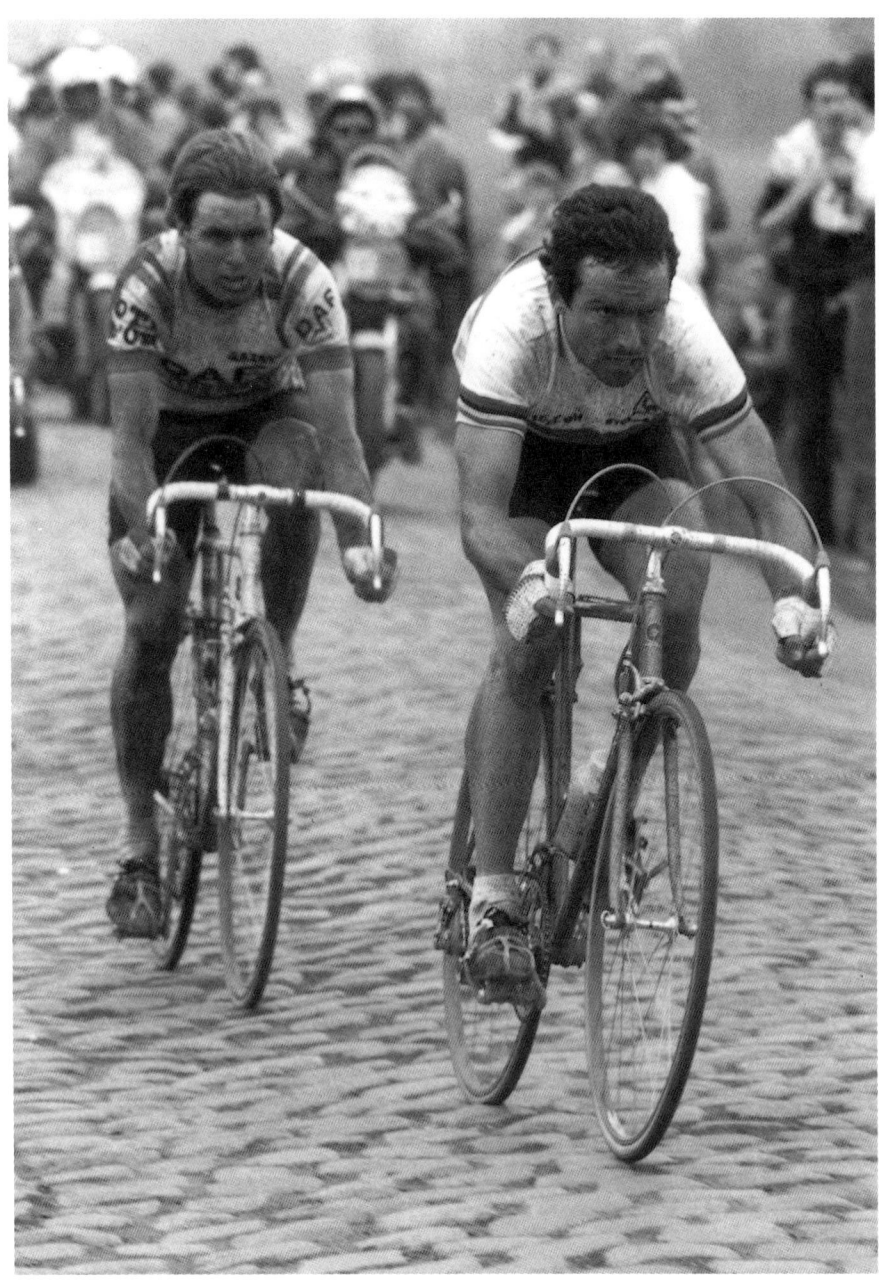

1981: PARIS-ROUBAIX: FRANCE

Five-time Tour de France winner Bernard Hinault (here leading Hennie Kuiper) hated racing in Paris-Roubaix, yet in the 1981 edition he rode tenaciously to win the cobblestone classic in a sprint finish over former winners Roger De Vlaeminck and Francesco Moser.

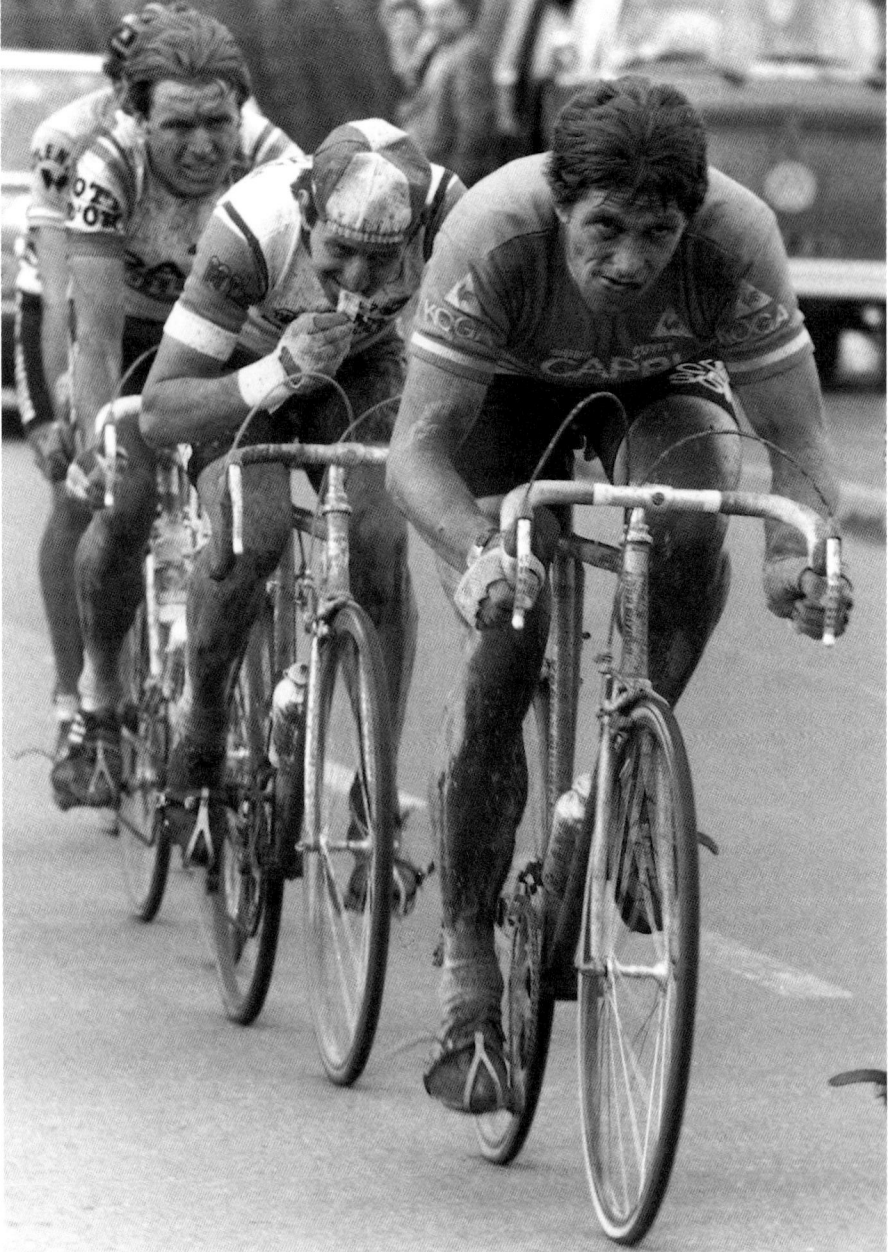

1981: PARIS-ROUBAIX: FRANCE

Marc De Meyer was the ironman of the European peloton in the late 1970s and early '80s. The Belgian was a domestique who rode his heart out for team leaders like Freddy Maertens and yet still managed some major victories, like Paris-Roubaix in 1976.

1982: WORLD TRACK CHAMPIONSHIPS: LEICESTER, ENGLAND

Some spectacular crashes marked the track world's in 1982. Above, Canadian amateur sprinter Pierre Lacouline collides with Dutch champion Rainer Valkenburg. And right, Canada's pro sprinter Gordon Singleton fell in the final after a controversial maneuver by Japan's Koichi Nakano—who went on to win the seventh of his 10 consecutive world titles.

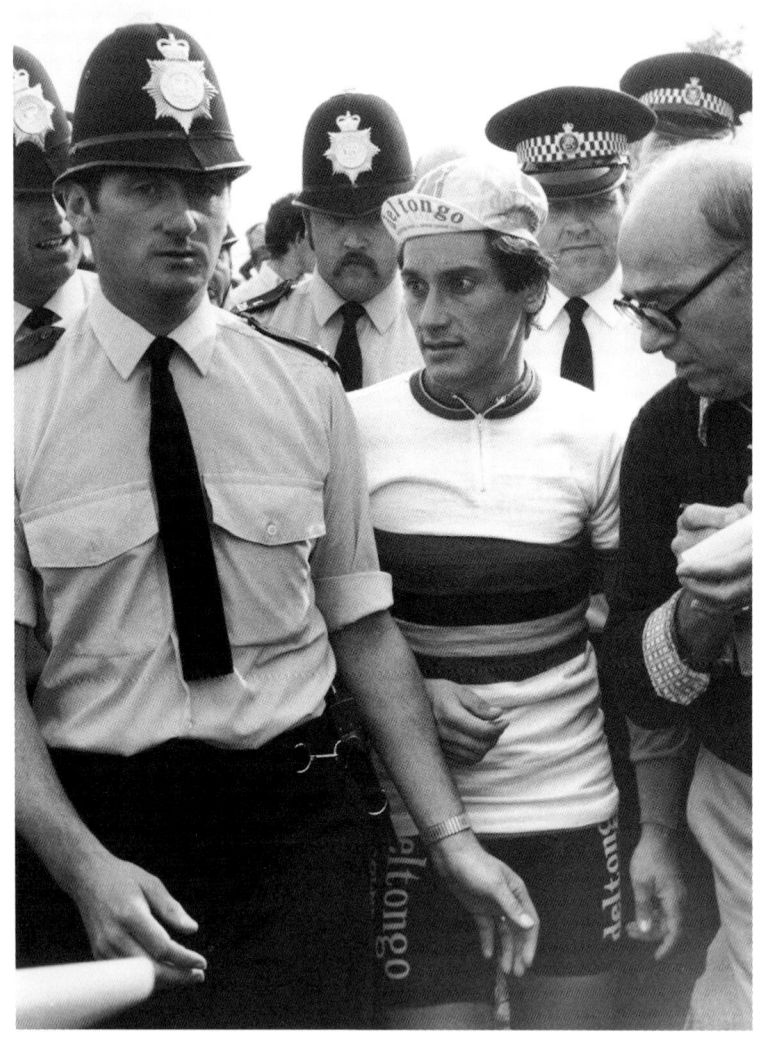

1982: WORLD ROAD CHAMPIONSHIPS: GOODWOOD, ENGLAND

Giuseppe Saronni won the 1982 world road championship with a searing uphill sprint, to earn the rainbow-striped jersey and the respect of some English bobbies.

1983: WORLD ROAD CHAMPIONSHIPS: ALTENRHEIN, SWITZERLAND

A year after his Goodwood triumph, Saronni (No. 101) and his Italian teammates Moreno Argentin (90) and Palmiro Masciarelli (98) again seemed to be in charge at the world professional road race championship. This time, however, Argentin was dropped from the winning break on a climb and American Greg LeMond went on to win.

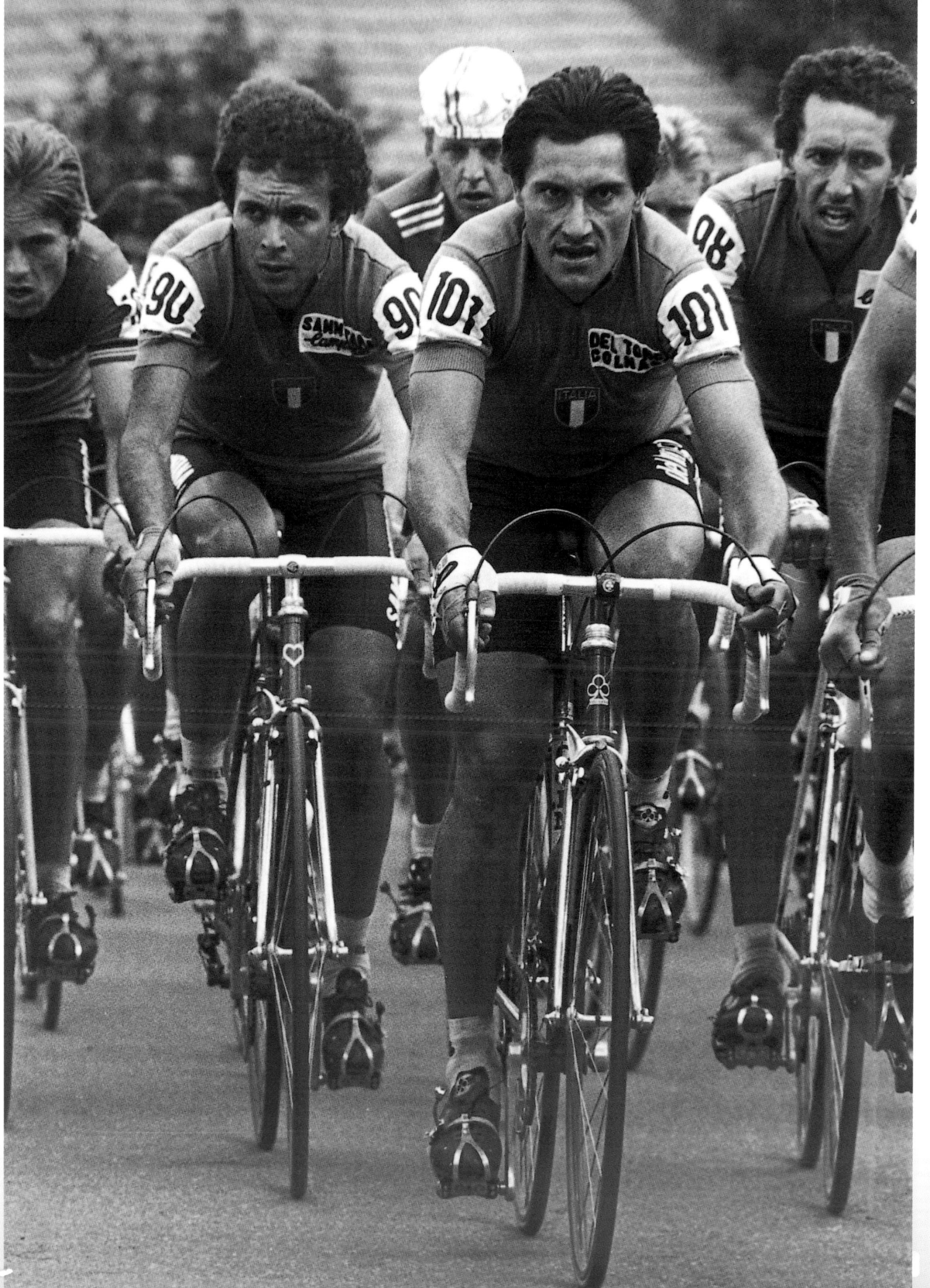

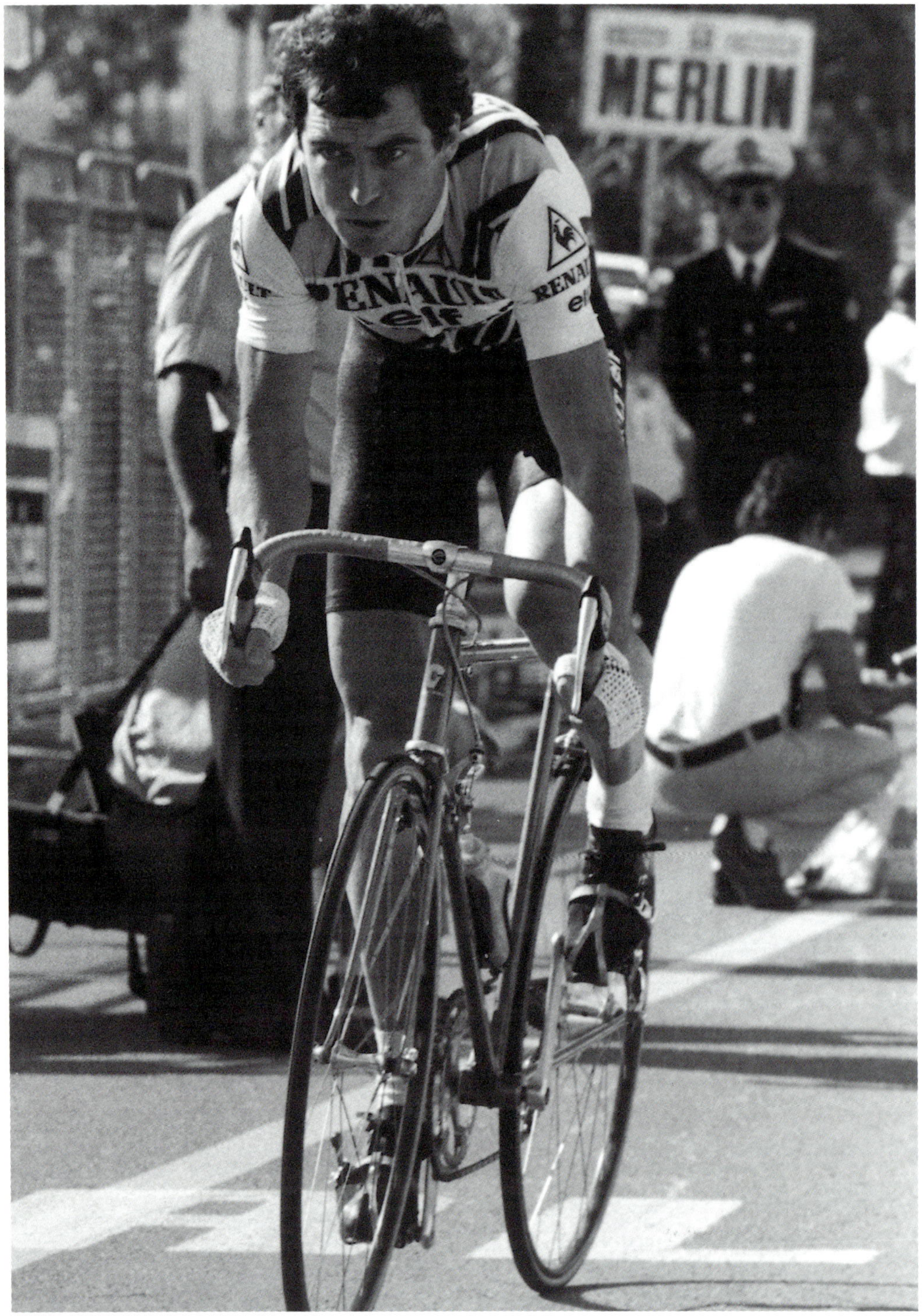

1982: GRAND PRIX DES NATIONS: CANNES, FRANCE

Through the 1980s, the Grand Prix des Nations time trial was one of the top one-day classics. Bernard Hinault was a brilliant winner in 1982, setting a course record on the hilly 90-kilometer course at Cannes on the French Riviera.

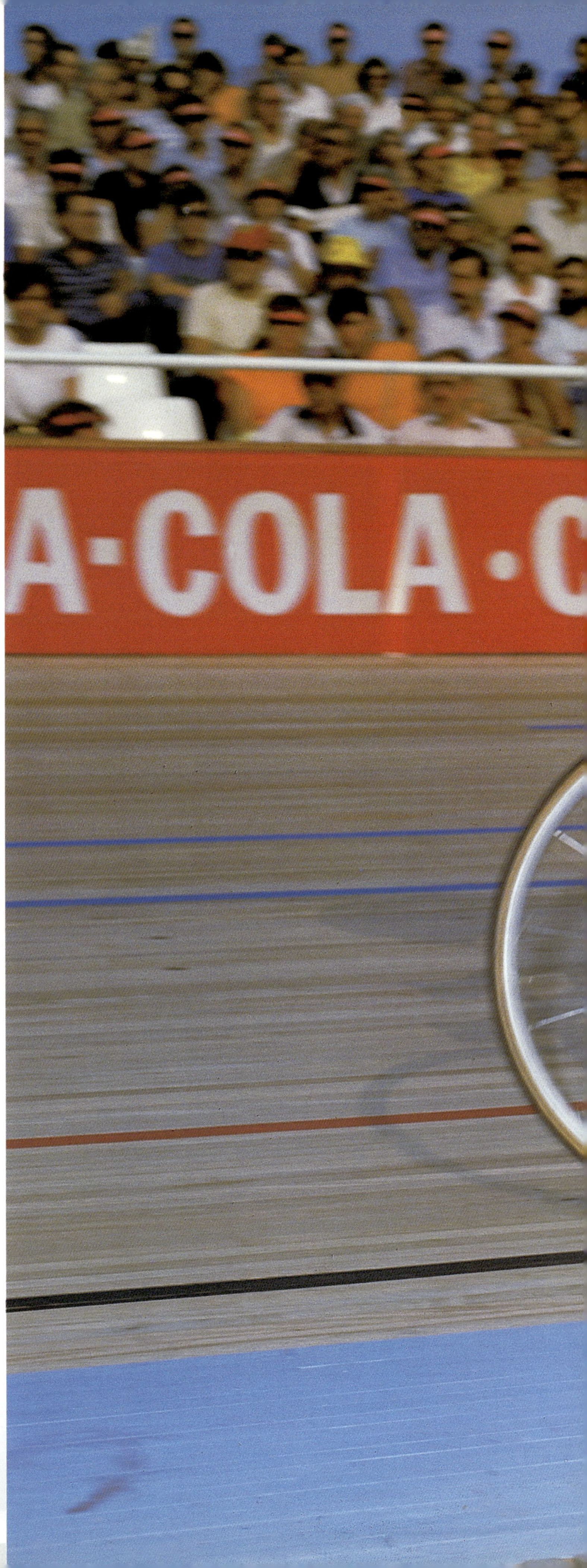

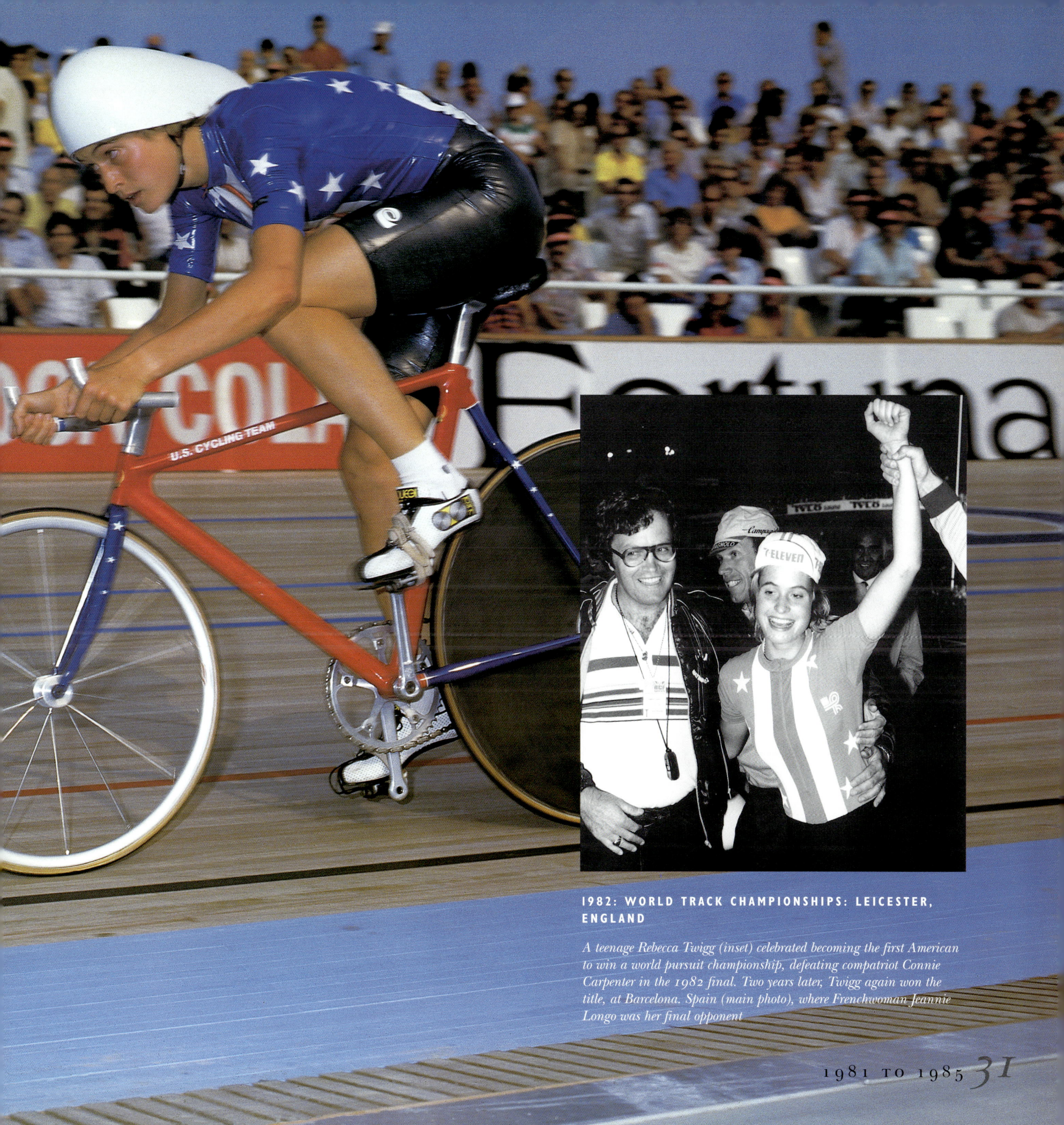

1982: WORLD TRACK CHAMPIONSHIPS: LEICESTER, ENGLAND

A teenage Rebecca Twigg (inset) celebrated becoming the first American to win a world pursuit championship, defeating compatriot Connie Carpenter in the 1982 final. Two years later, Twigg again won the title, at Barcelona, Spain (main photo), where Frenchwoman Jeannie Longo was her final opponent

1981 TO 1985

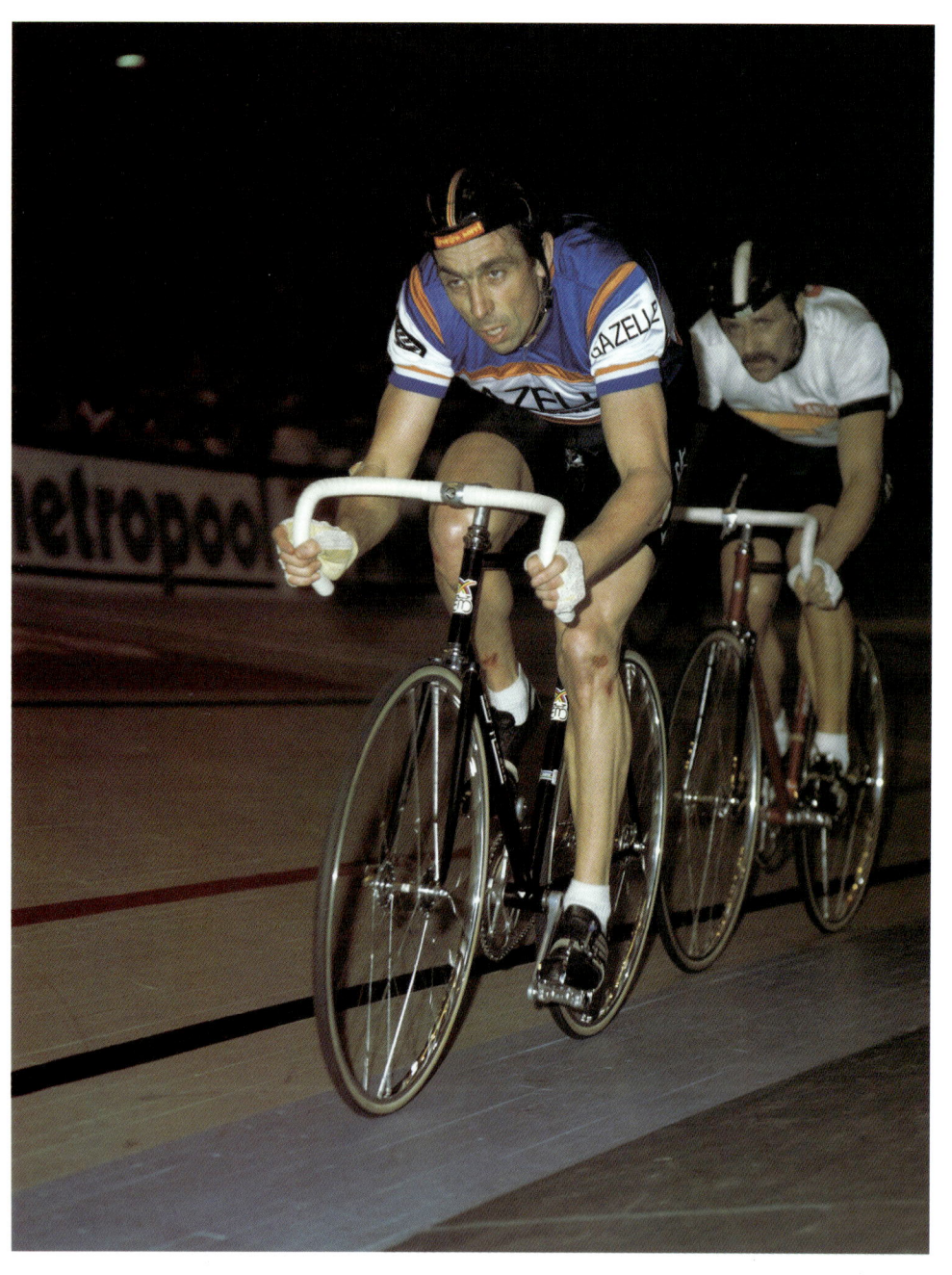

1983: ROTTERDAM SIX DAY: THE NETHERLANDS

Two of the greatest six-day riders of all-time, Patrick Sercu of Belgium and Danny Clark of Australia, do battle at the Ahoy stadium in Rotterdam.

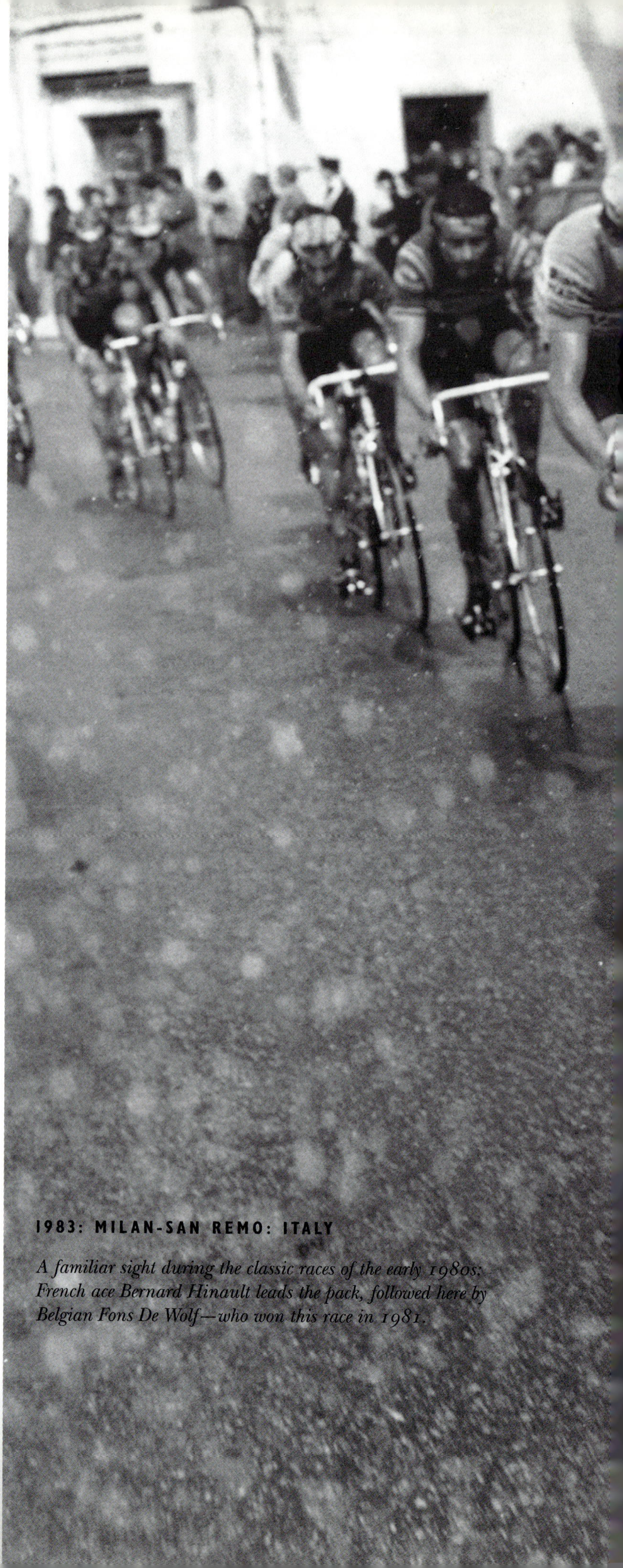

1983: MILAN-SAN REMO: ITALY

A familiar sight during the classic races of the early 1980s: French ace Bernard Hinault leads the pack, followed here by Belgian Fons De Wolf—who won this race in 1981.

32 1981 TO 1985

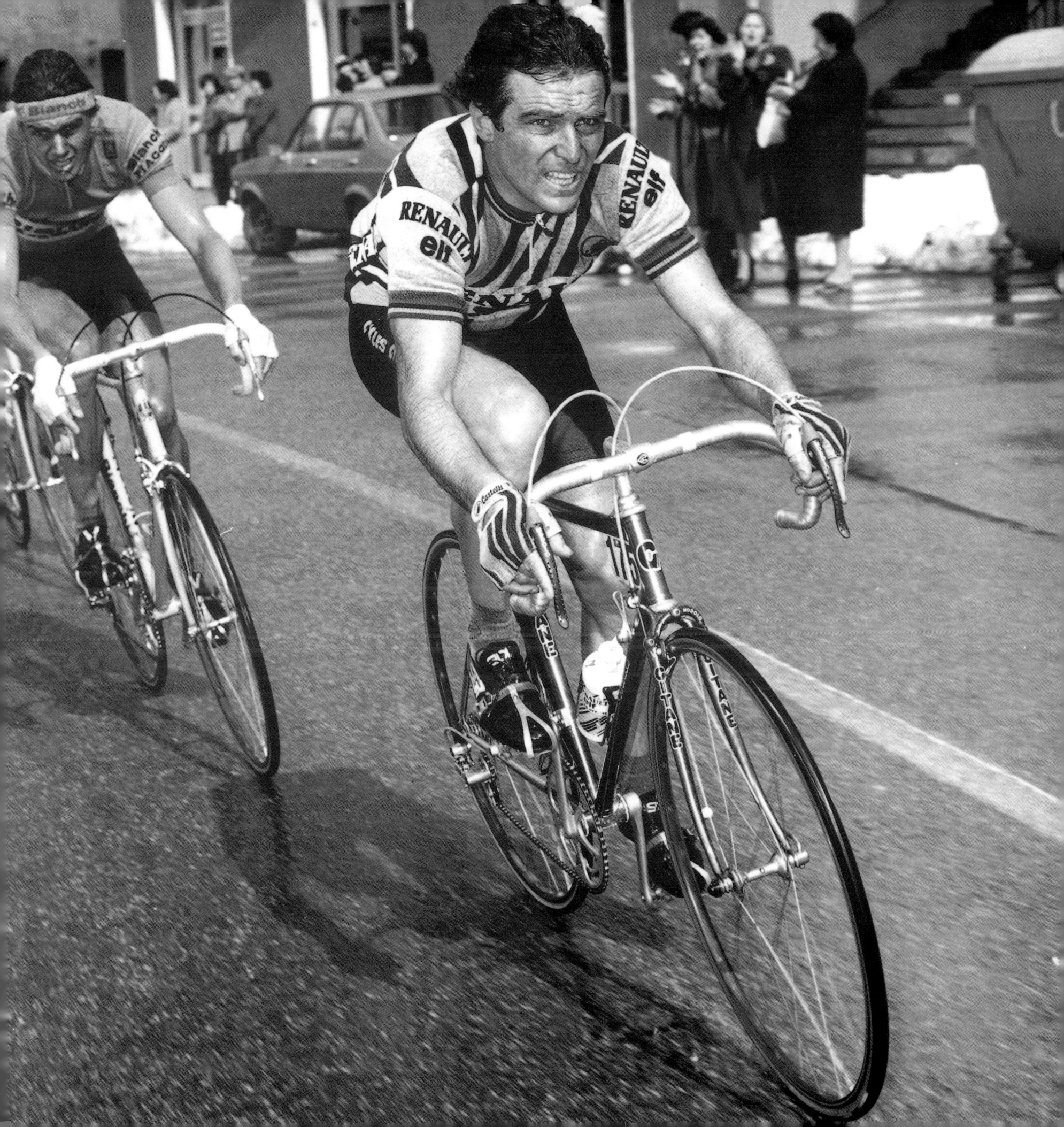

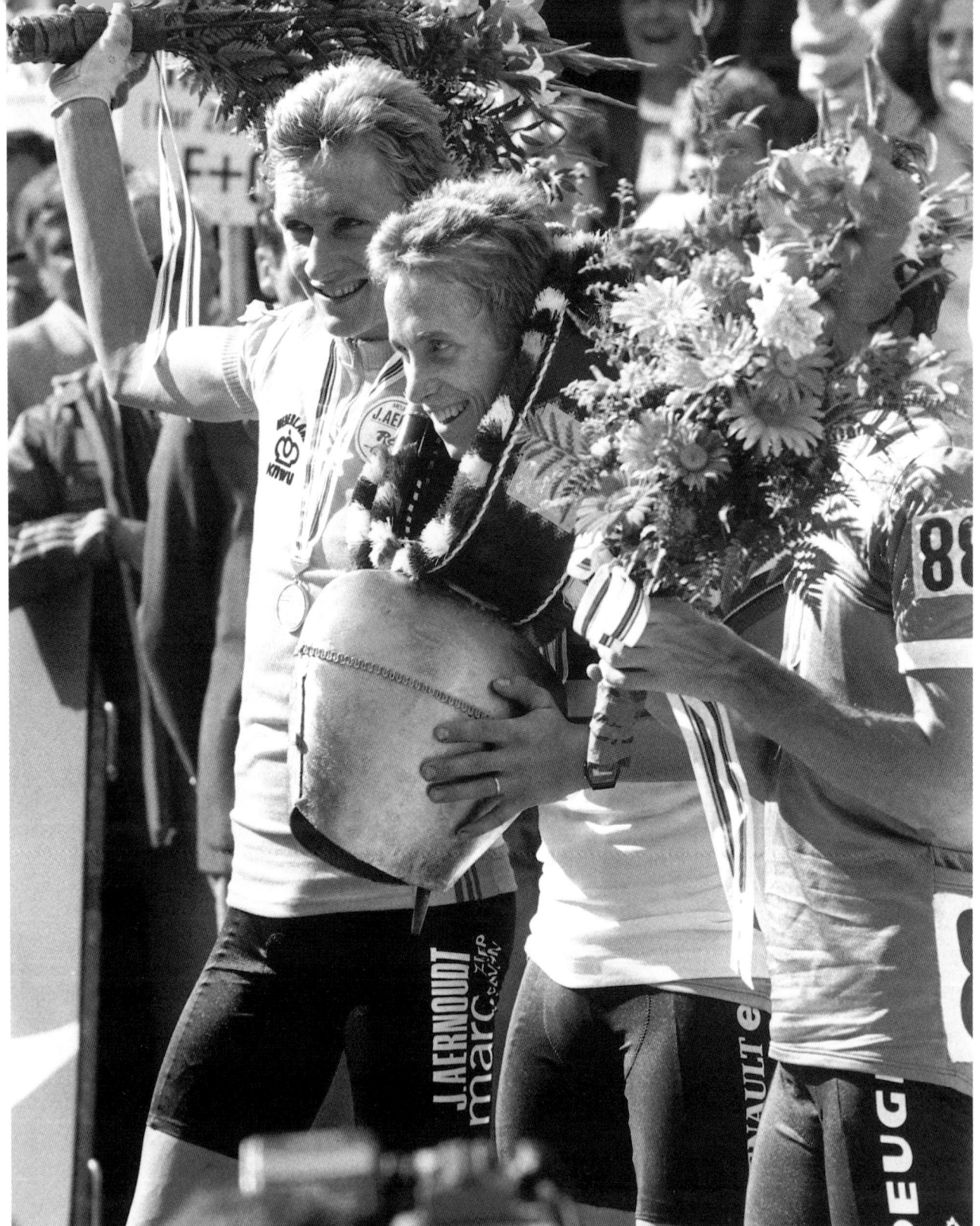

1983: WORLD ROAD CHAMPIONSHIPS: ALTENRHEIN, SWITZERLAND

On a sunny day in northeast Switzerland, Greg LeMond makes a big step in his career by winning the 1983 world road title in a solo break. He shared the podium with (left) Adri Van der Poel of the Netherlands, who went on to become a world champion in cyclo-cross, and (hidden behind the flowers) Irishman Stephen Roche, whose time would come in the late '80s.

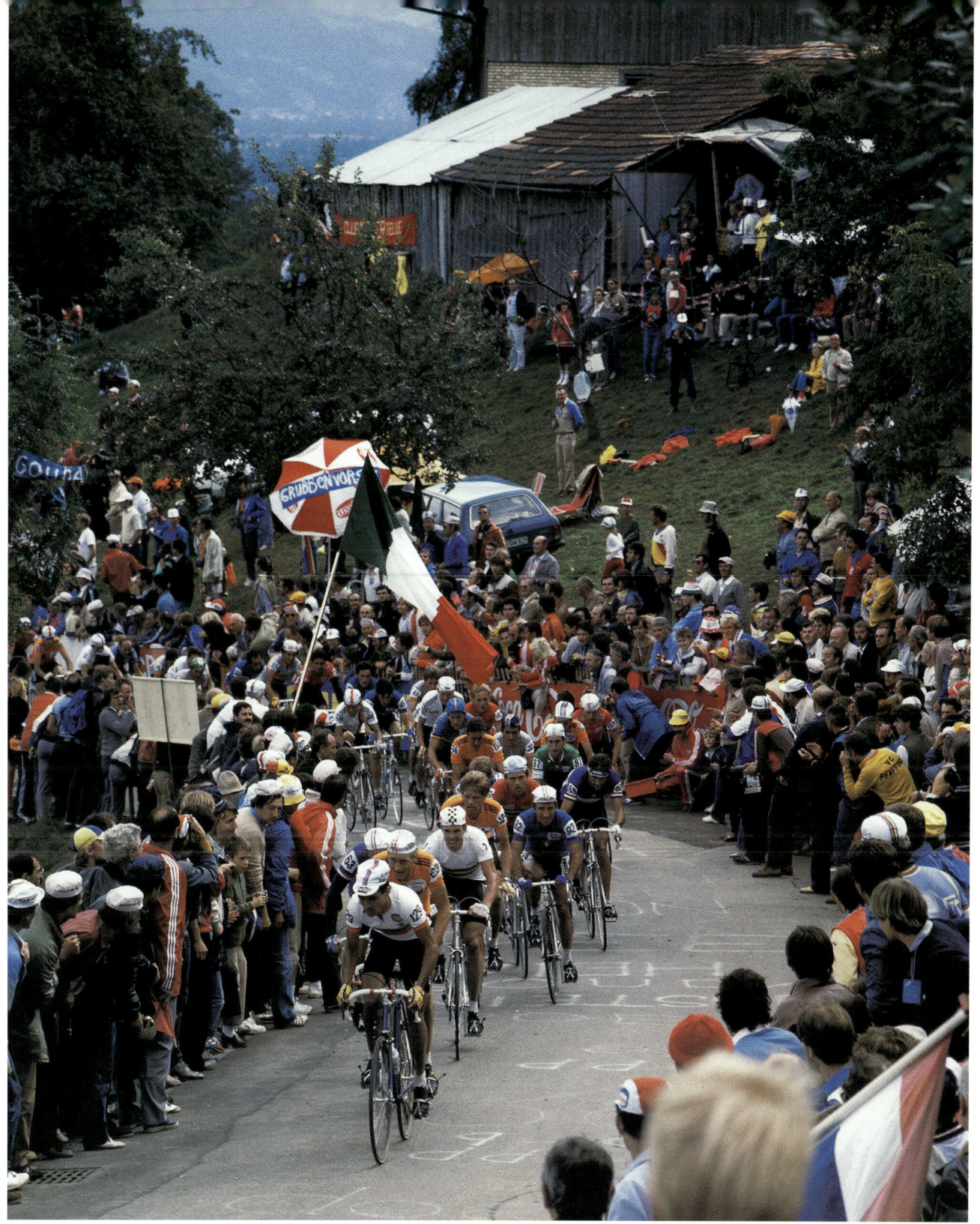

1983: WORLD ROAD CHAMPIONSHIPS: ALTENRHEIN, SWITZERLAND

The world championship is different from the great one-day classics in that it takes place on a circuit. The one in 1983 was 15 kilometers around, covered 18 times, for a distance of 270km. Here, huge crowds gather on the course's main climb, where LeMond made his winning attack.

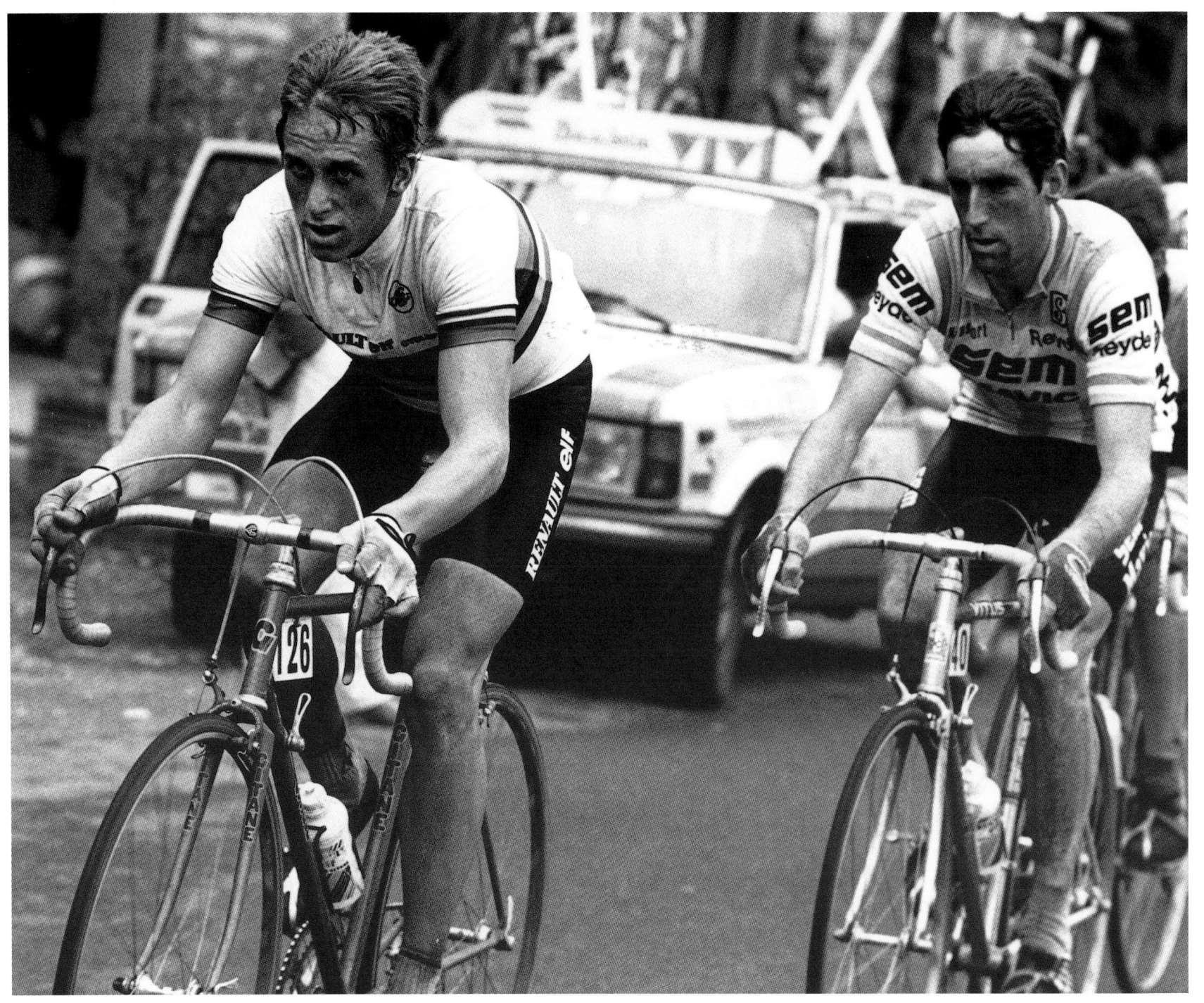

1983: TOUR OF LOMBARDY: ITALY

This was the start of a great rivalry: a highly talented American versus one very determined Irishman. Greg LeMond versus Sean Kelly. The race is the beautiful Tour of Lombardy around the Italian lakes. LeMond (left) wears the rainbow jersey as world champion, but at the finish he will lose the race by a tire's width to Kelly.

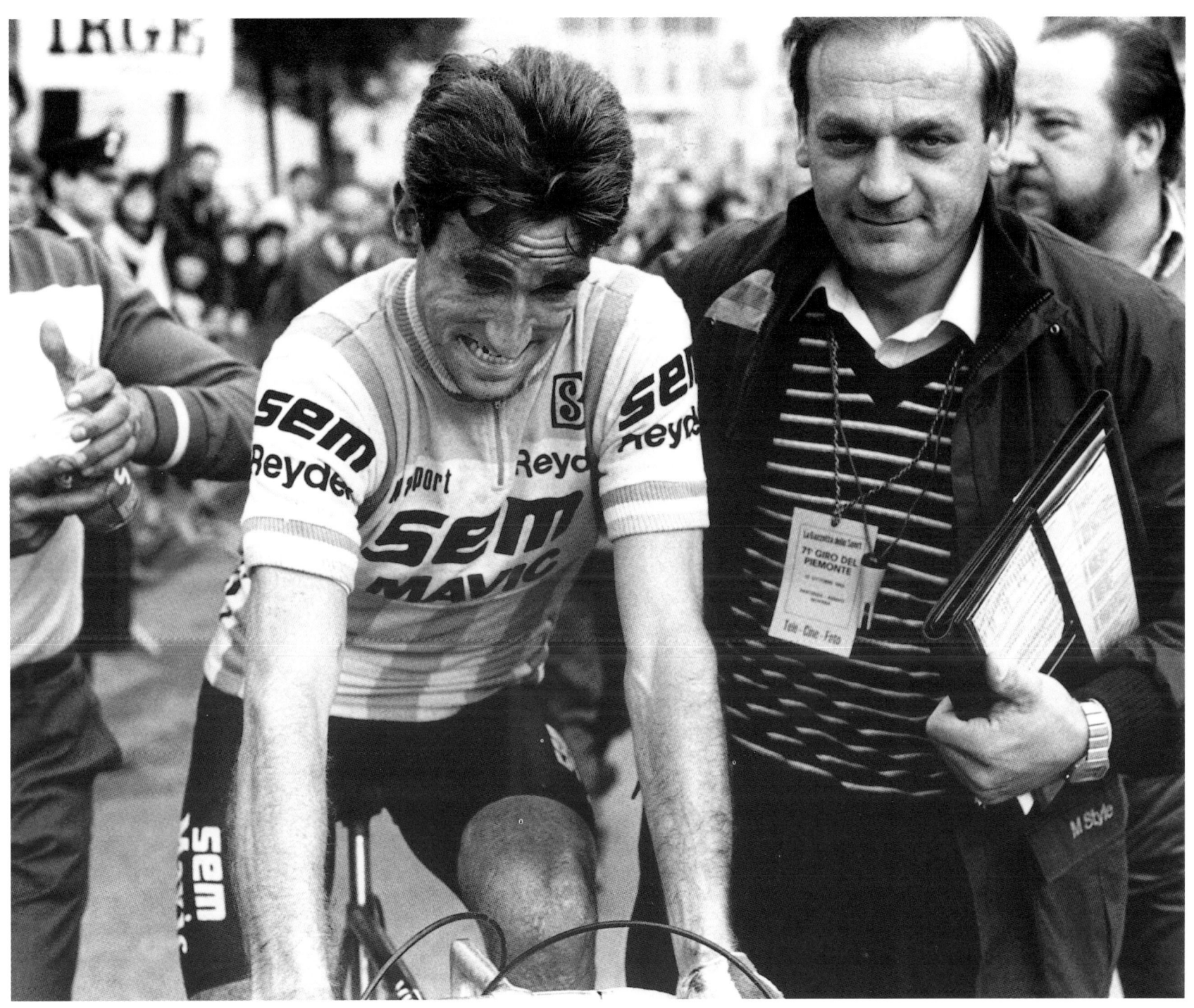

1983: TOUR OF LOMBARDY: ITALY

For an emotional Kelly, the 1983 Lombardia is his first victory in a major classic. He will go on to win most of the sport's major one-day races in the following 10 years, unlike the beaten LeMond who will never add a classic to his palmarès.

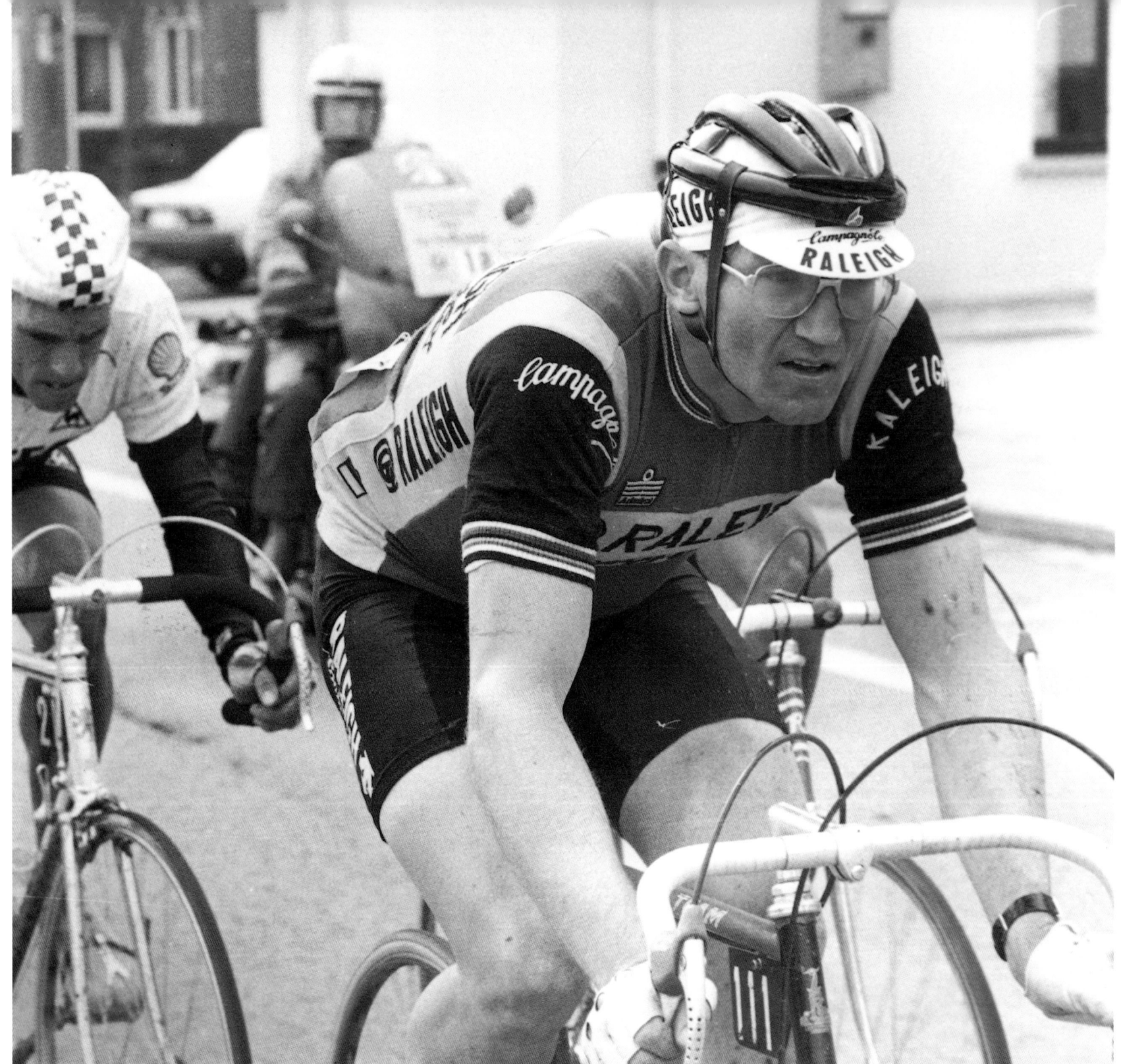

1983: TOUR OF FLANDERS: BELGIUM

Dutchman Jan Raas (here leading Phil Anderson at the Tour of Flanders) was one of the greatest classics riders of the late 1970s and early 1980s, picking up wins in Milan-San Remo, the Tour of Flanders, Paris-Roubaix, the Amstel Gold Race and Paris-Tours.

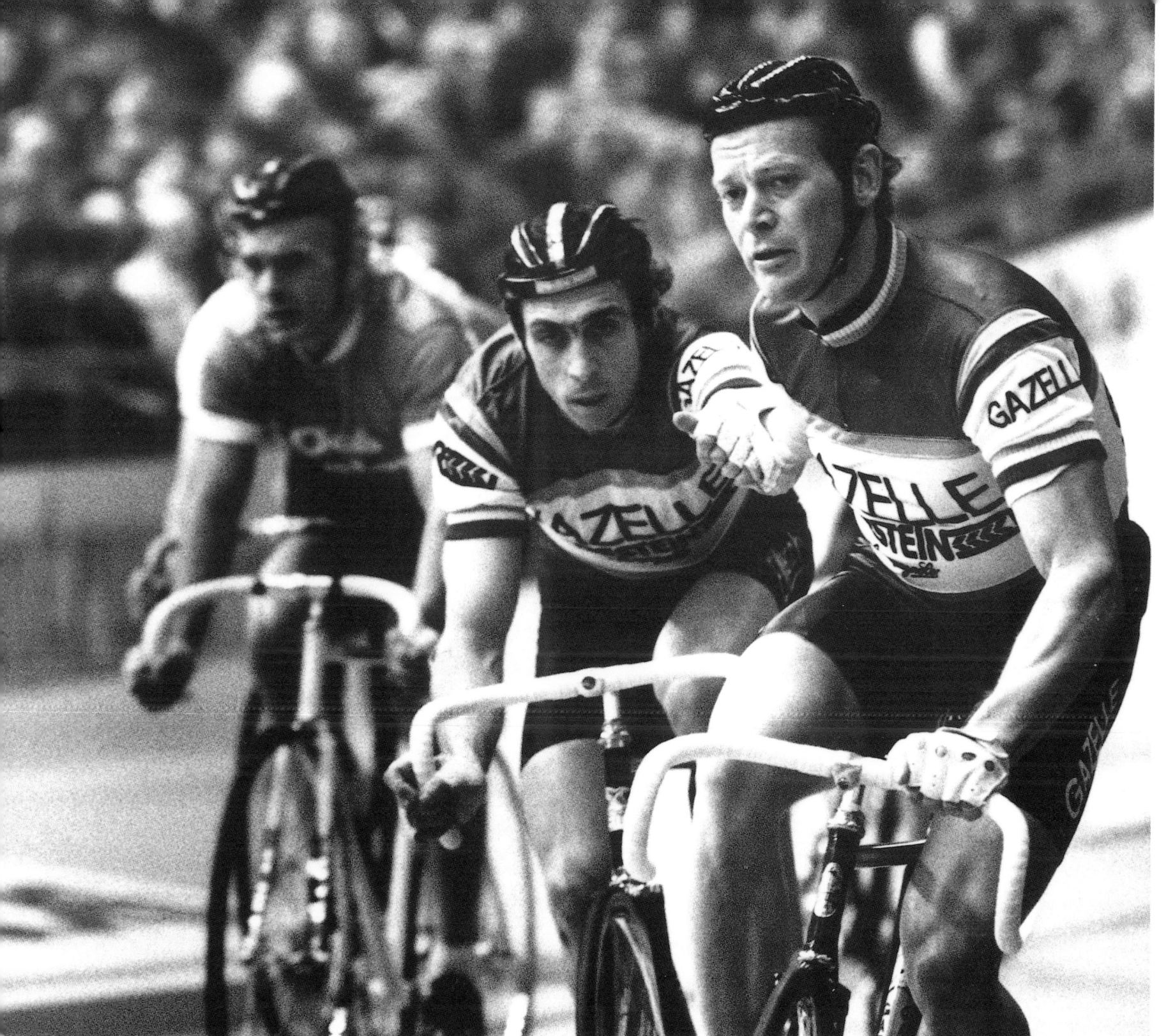

1983: ROTTERDAM SIX DAY: THE NETHERLANDS

Two of the winningest six-day riders ever—they collected a total of 160 wins between them—Patrick Sercu of Belgium (left) and Dutchman René Pijnen teamed up to win the Rotterdam six-day race in 1983.

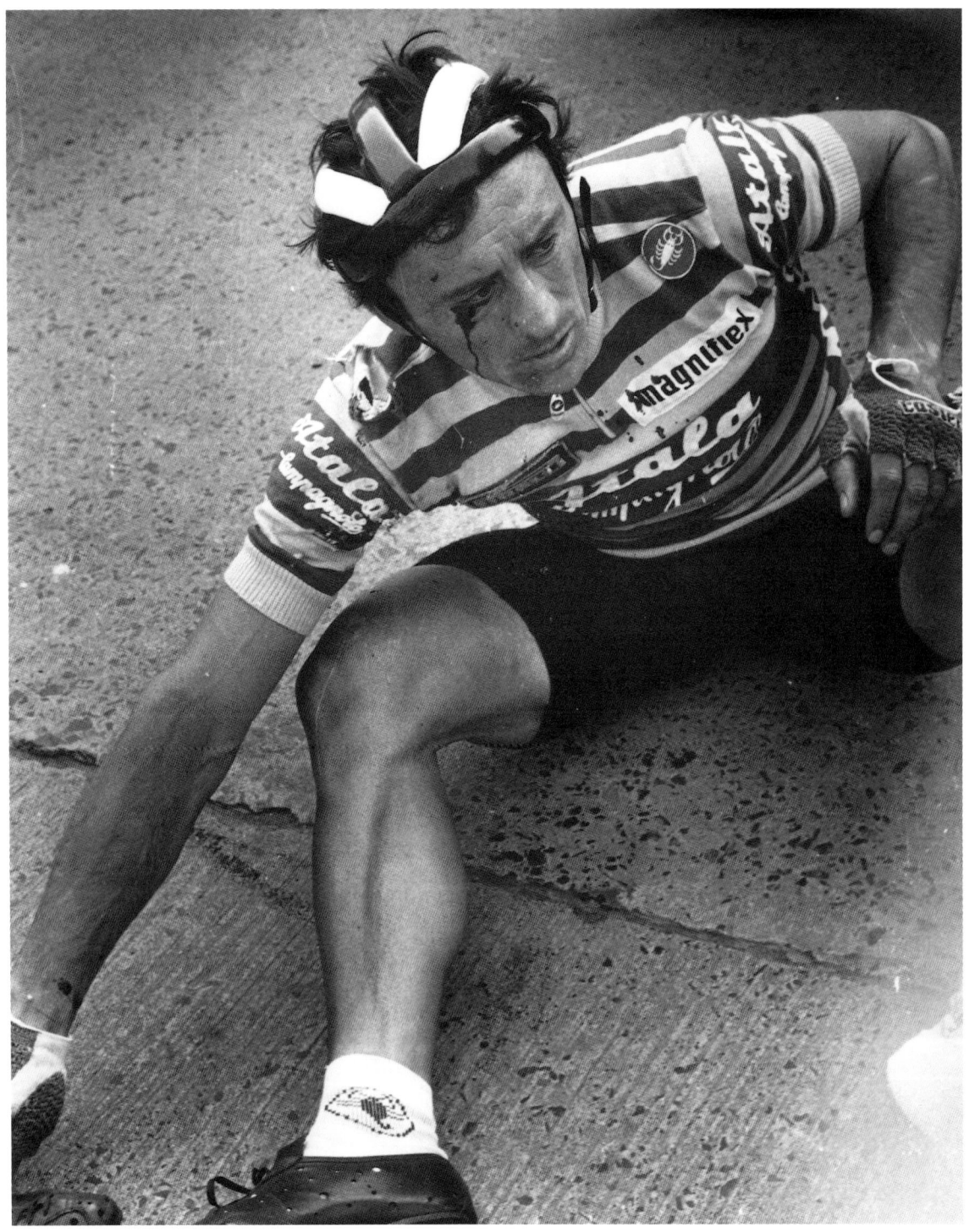

1983: TOUR OF LOMBARDY: BELGIUM

A hard fall on a concrete road for Italian Pierino Gavazzi, who was a great sprinter and won Milan-San Remo in 1980.

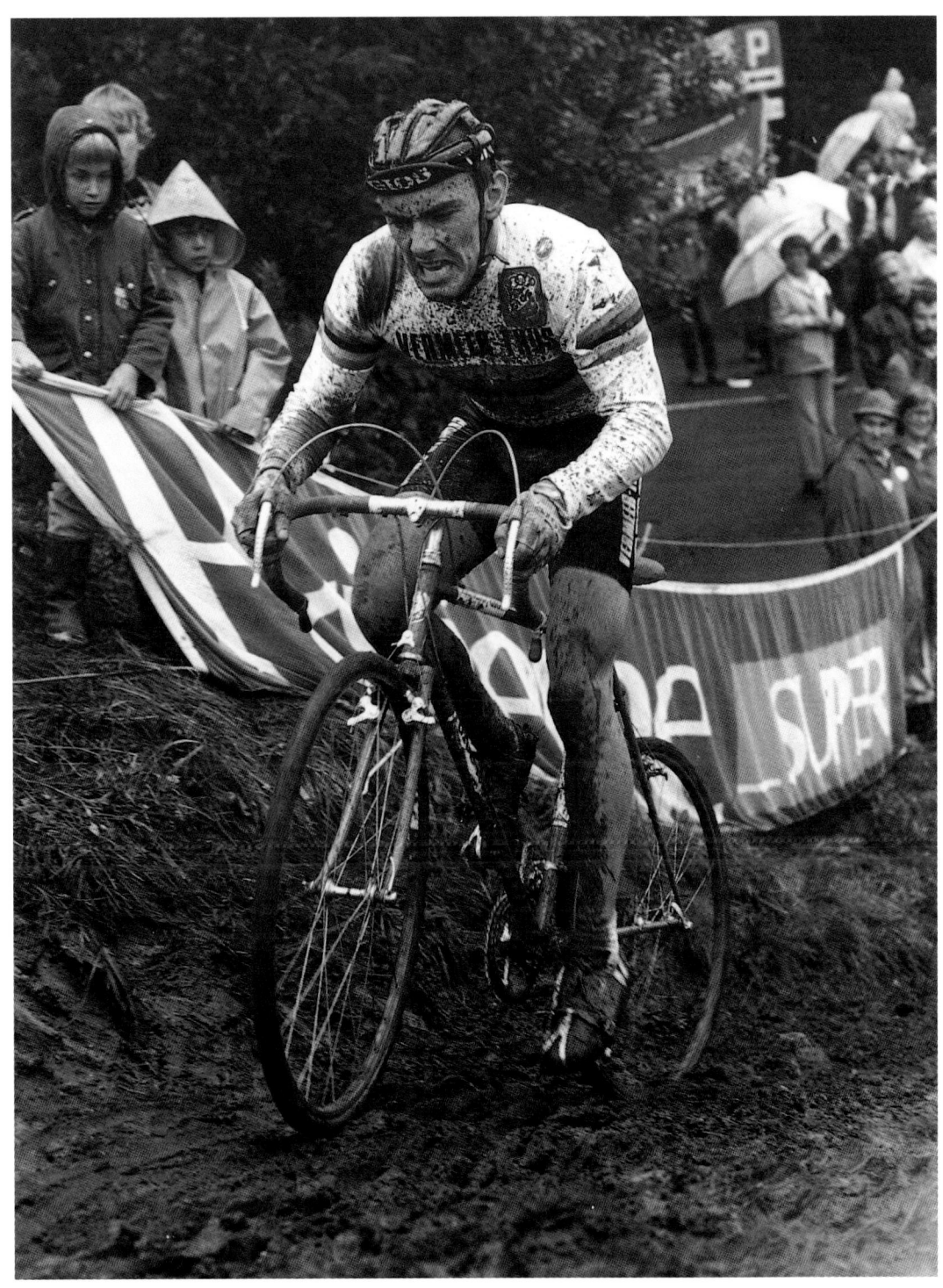

1983: SUPERPRESTIGE CYCLO-CROSS: STEINMAUR, SWITZERLAND

Belgian Roland Liboton won the world professional cyclo-cross championship four times in the early-1980s. Here, he powers up a muddy climb in a pre-world's event.

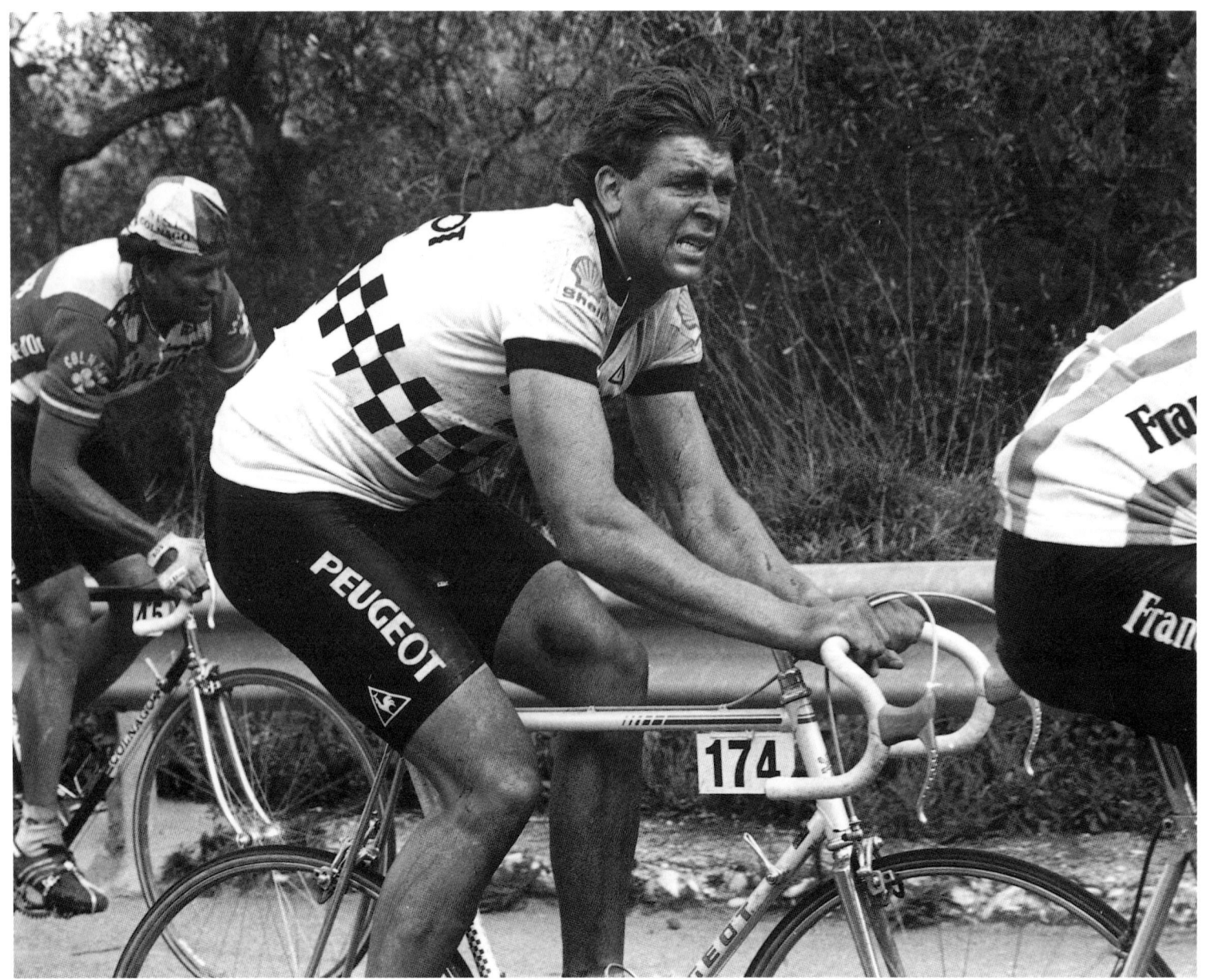

1983: MILAN-SAN REMO: ITALY

A youthful Sean Yates, before he lost weight, struggles up the Capo Berta climb in the 1983 Milan-San Remo. The tall Englishman went on to become an outstanding team rider for the U.S. squads, 7-Eleven and Motorola.

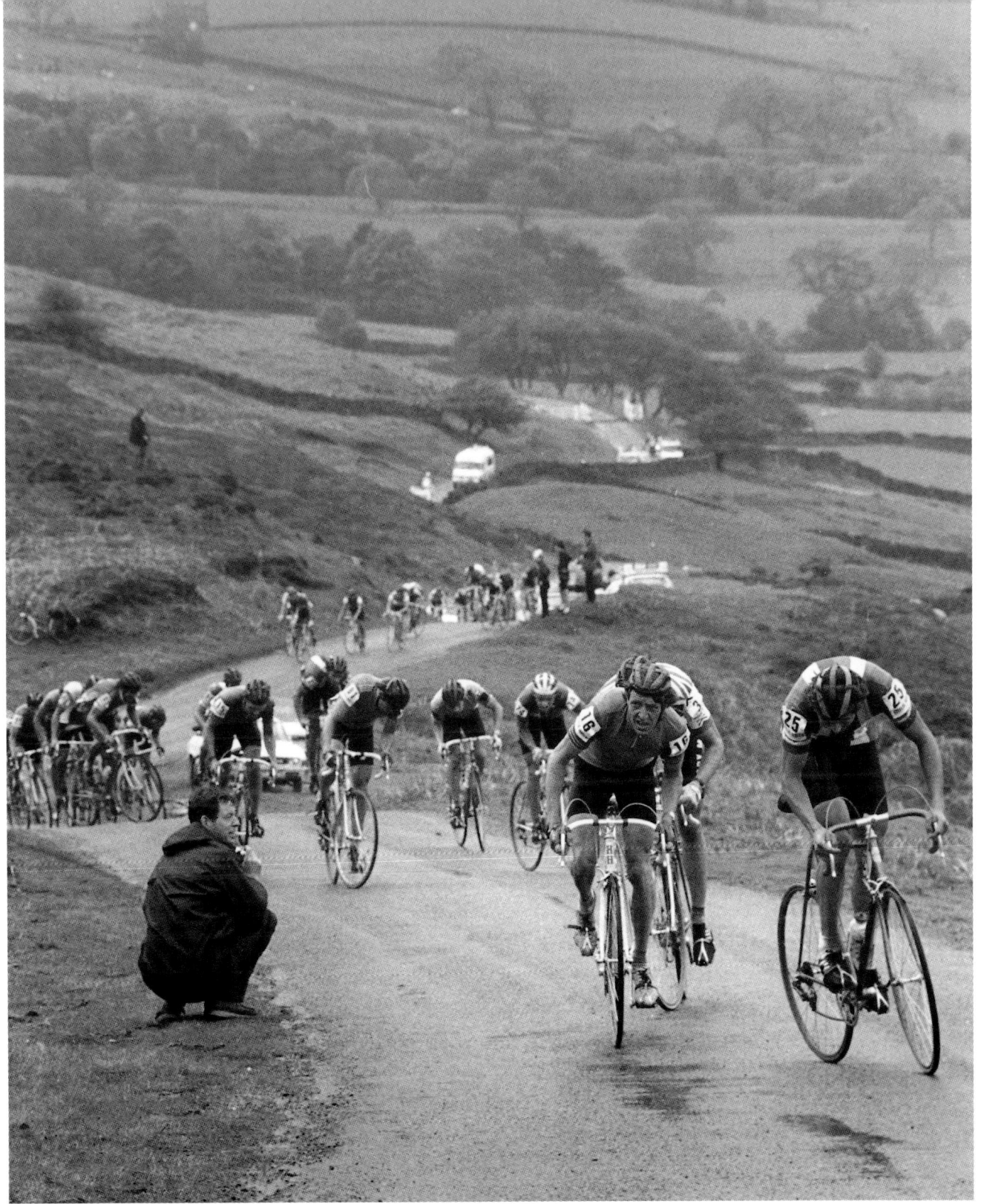

1983: MILK RACE: GREAT BRITAIN

The author's own national race, the Tour of Britain Milk Race, gave him great opportunities to hone his photo skills. Here, England's Jeff Williams leads the race up one of the back-bending climbs in the North York Moors.

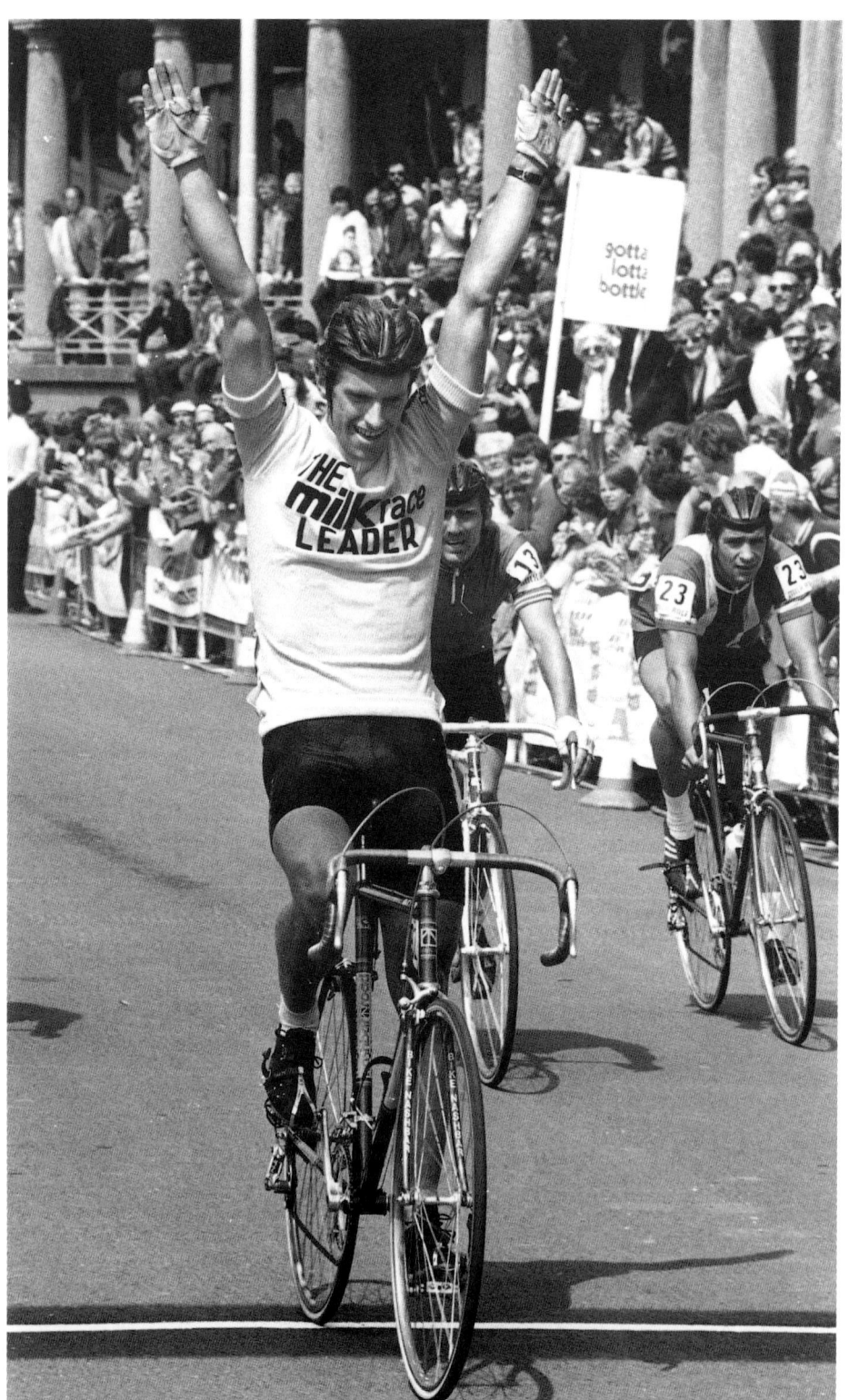

1983: MILK RACE: GREAT BRITAIN

The only American to win the Milk Race was Pennsylvania's Matt Eaton. He was jubilant in crossing the finish line of the final stage in Blackpool.

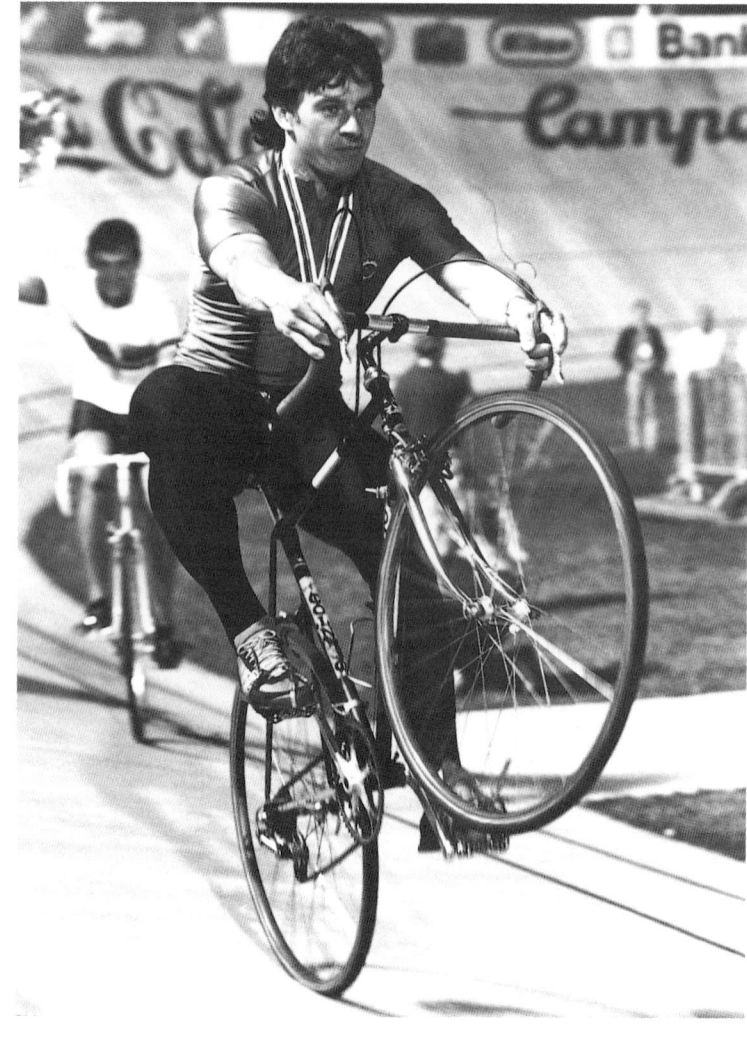

1983: WORLD TRACK CHAMPIONSHIPS: ZÜRICH

After twice winning the world amateur sprint title, acrobatic Soviet sprinter Sergei Kopylov lost to East German rival Lutz Hesslich in 1983. Kopylov pleased the Swiss crowd with his lap-of-honor wheelie on a road bike.

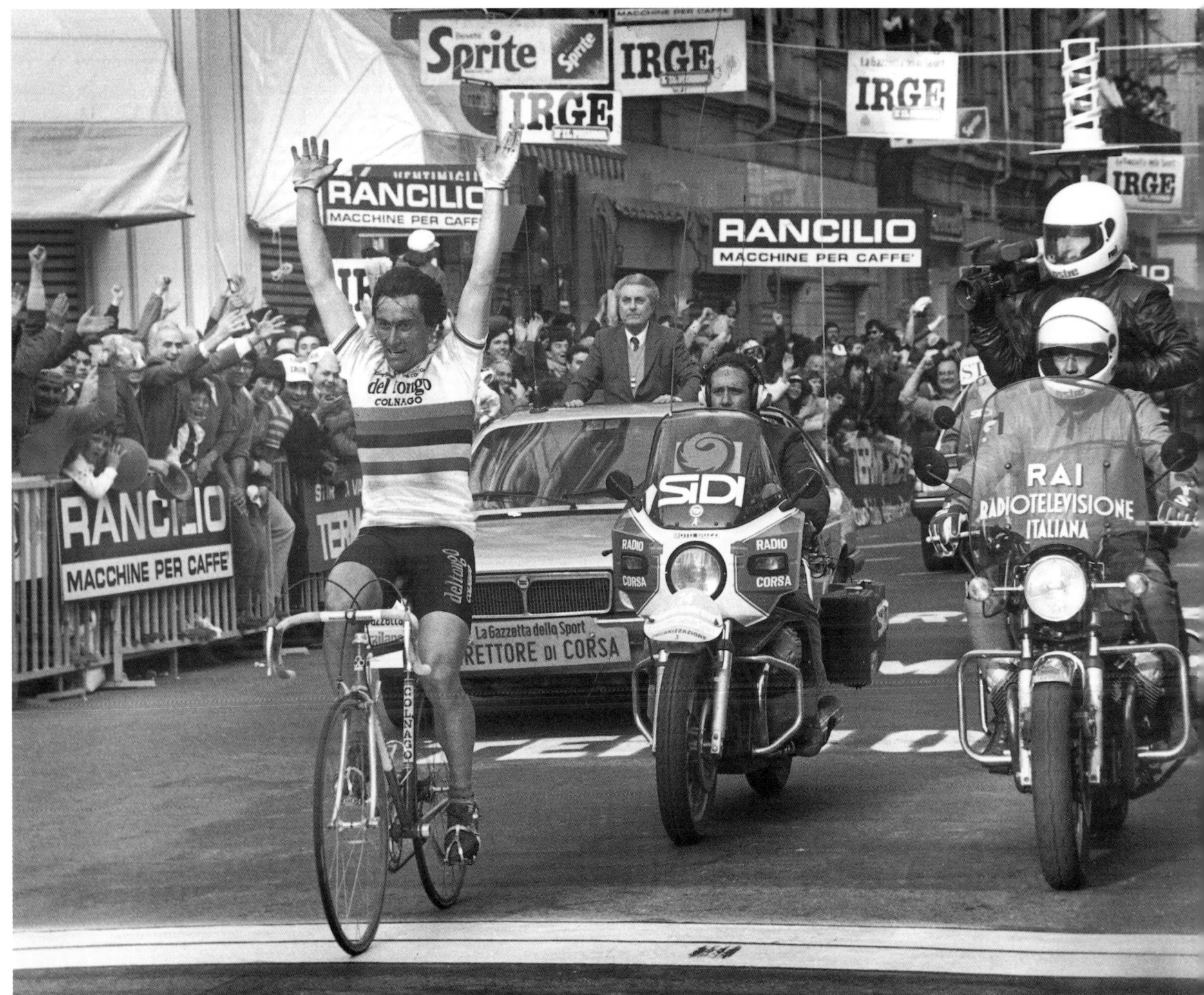

1983: MILAN–SAN REMO: ITALY

Giuseppe Saronni showed he was more than a sprinter by making a late solo effort to win his country's big spring classic, Milan–San Remo. He's wearing the rainbow jersey he earned by taking the world title in England the previous summer.

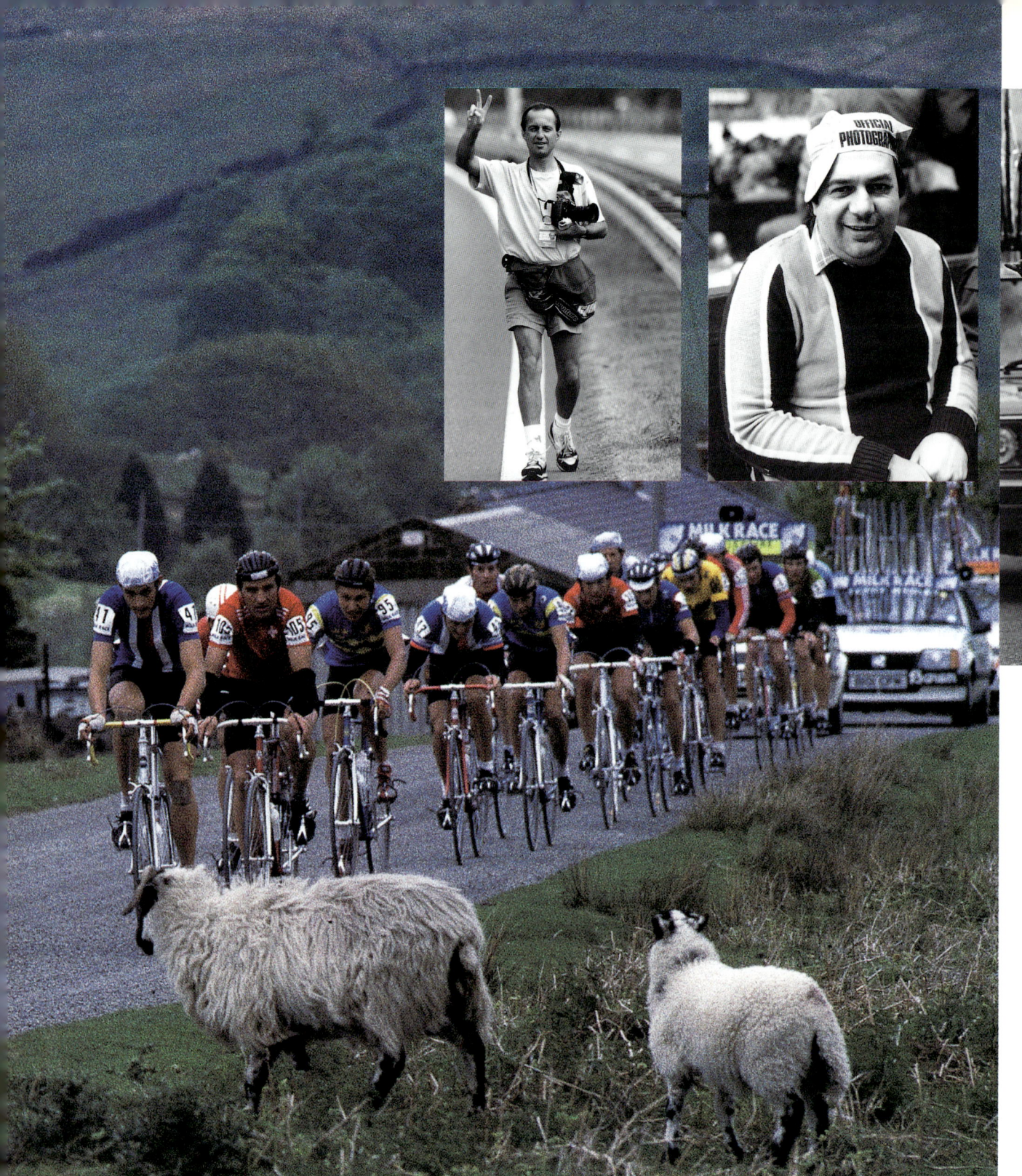

1983: MILK RACE: GREAT BRITAIN

They say there's more sheep than people in the hill country of northern England.

TWO FRIENDS AND A CHAMPION

(At top) Photographer friends Aldo Tonnoir of Belgium (left) and Cor Vos from the Netherlands helped the author's early career, while British rider Mandy Jones (right) gave Watson's portfolio a boost by winning the 1982 world road title at Goodwood, England.

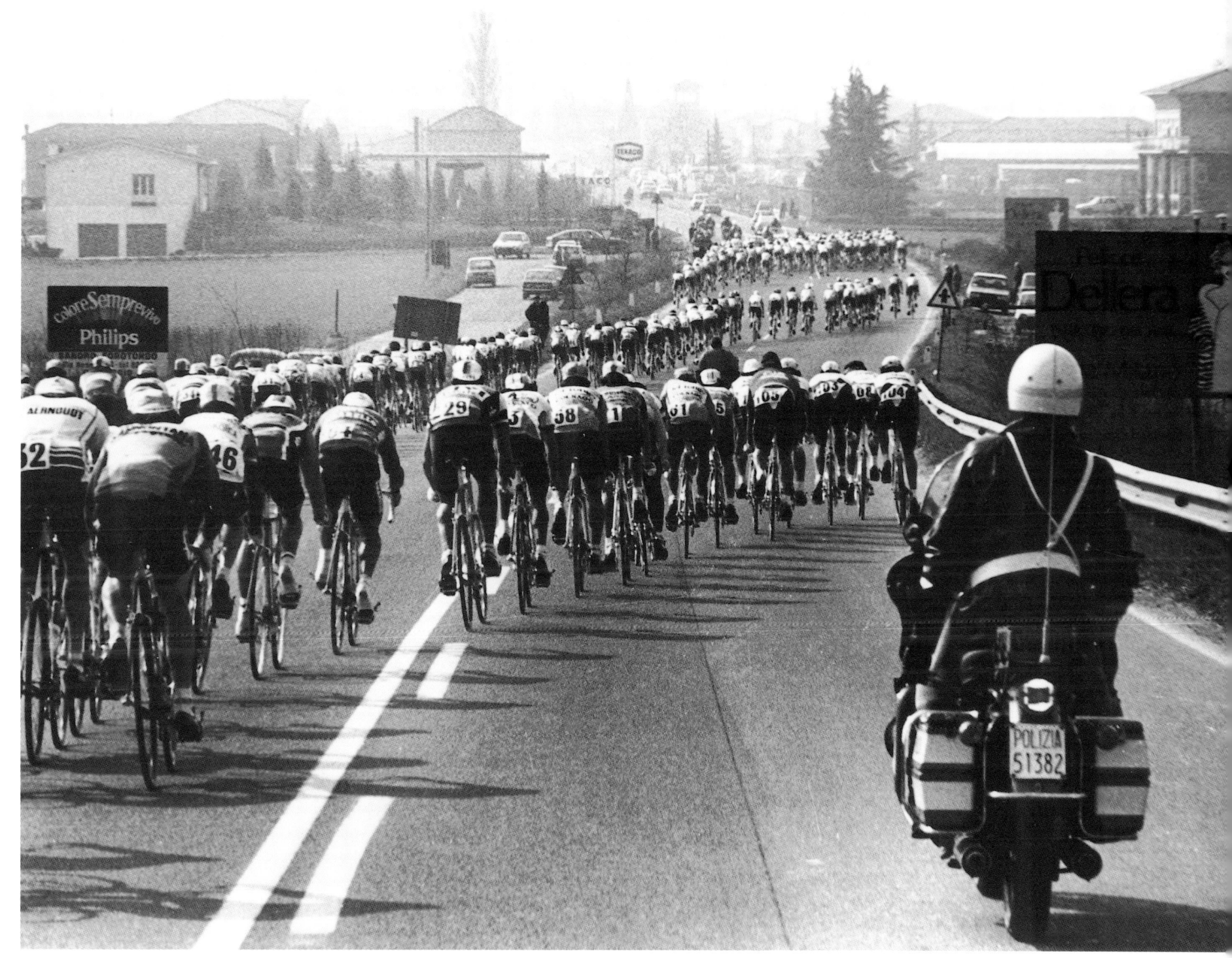

1983: MILAN-SAN REMO: ITALY

Fast going splits the field of nearly 300 into echelons on the early part of Milan-San Remo's near-300-kilometer-long course through northern Italy.

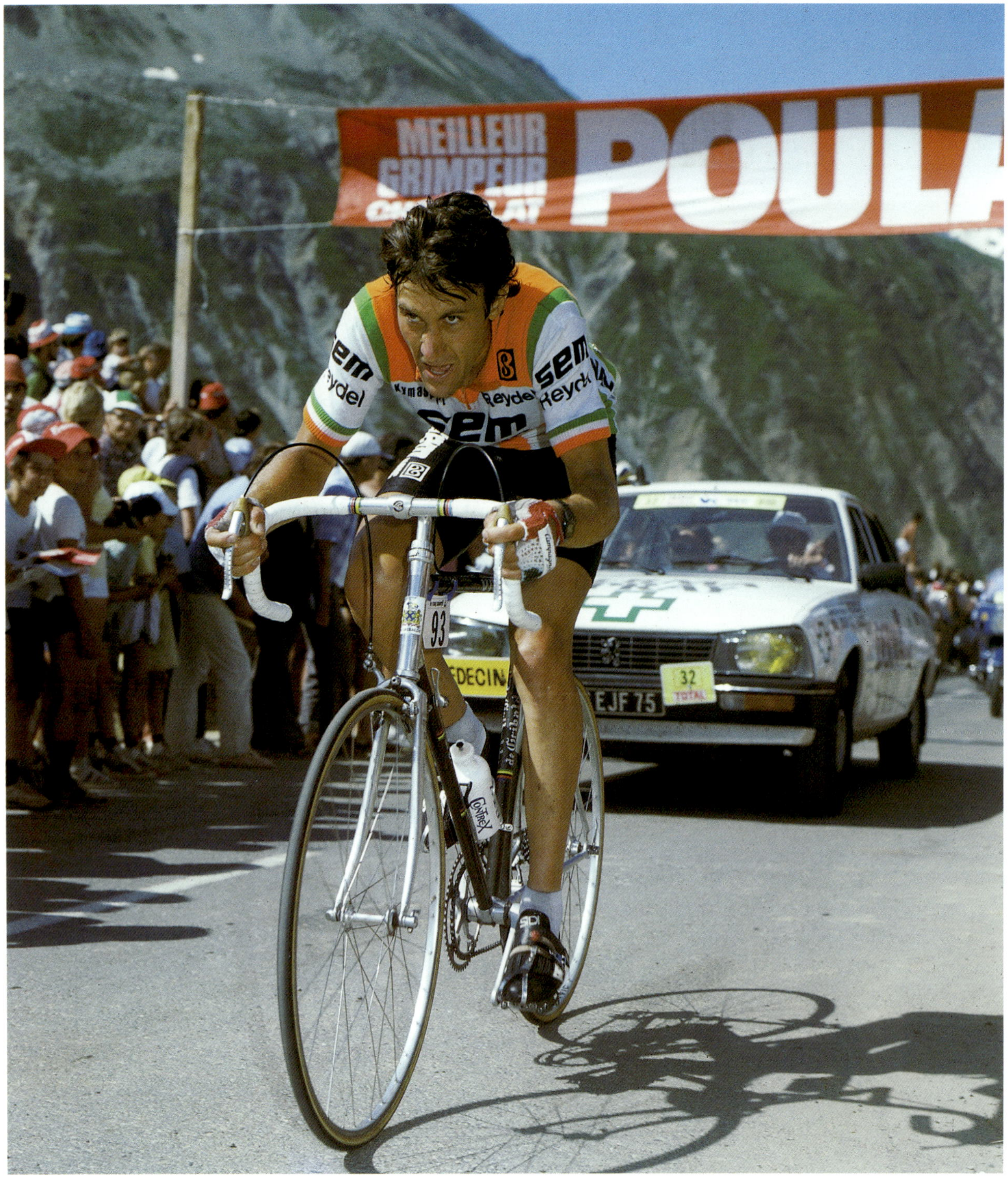

1982: TOUR DE FRANCE: COL DU GLANDON

Californian Jonathan Boyer was the first American to compete in the Tour de France. His best performance was finishing 12th overall in 1983.

1985: PARIS-ROUBAIX: FRANCE

(Opposite page) Despite being splattered by mud from the cobbled roads of Paris-Roubaix, Greg LeMond said he loved this race.

MUD AND WATER

(At top) Swiss "rider" Albert Zweifel (left) won the world professional cyclo-cross championship five times between 1976 and 1986. (Right) A water splash in Westerdale challenged the riders of Britain's Milk Race.

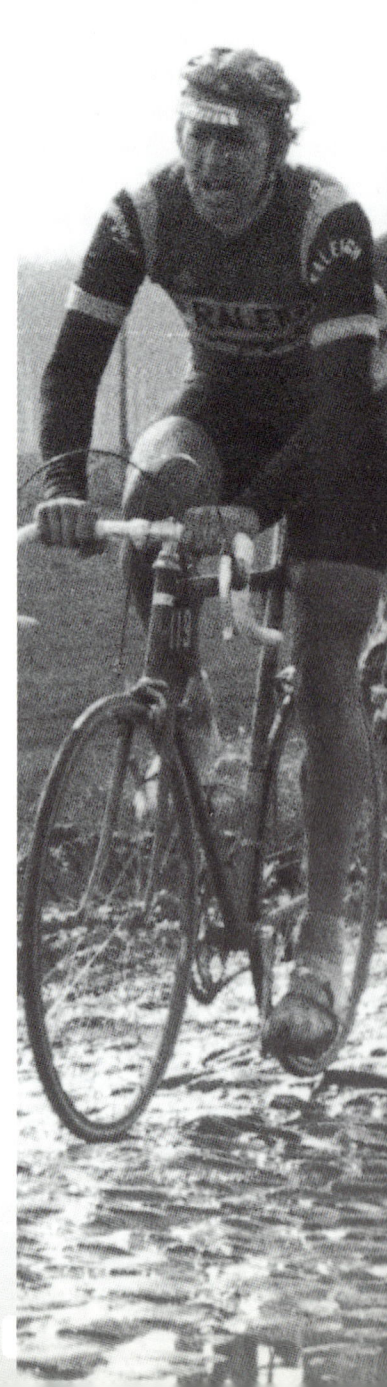

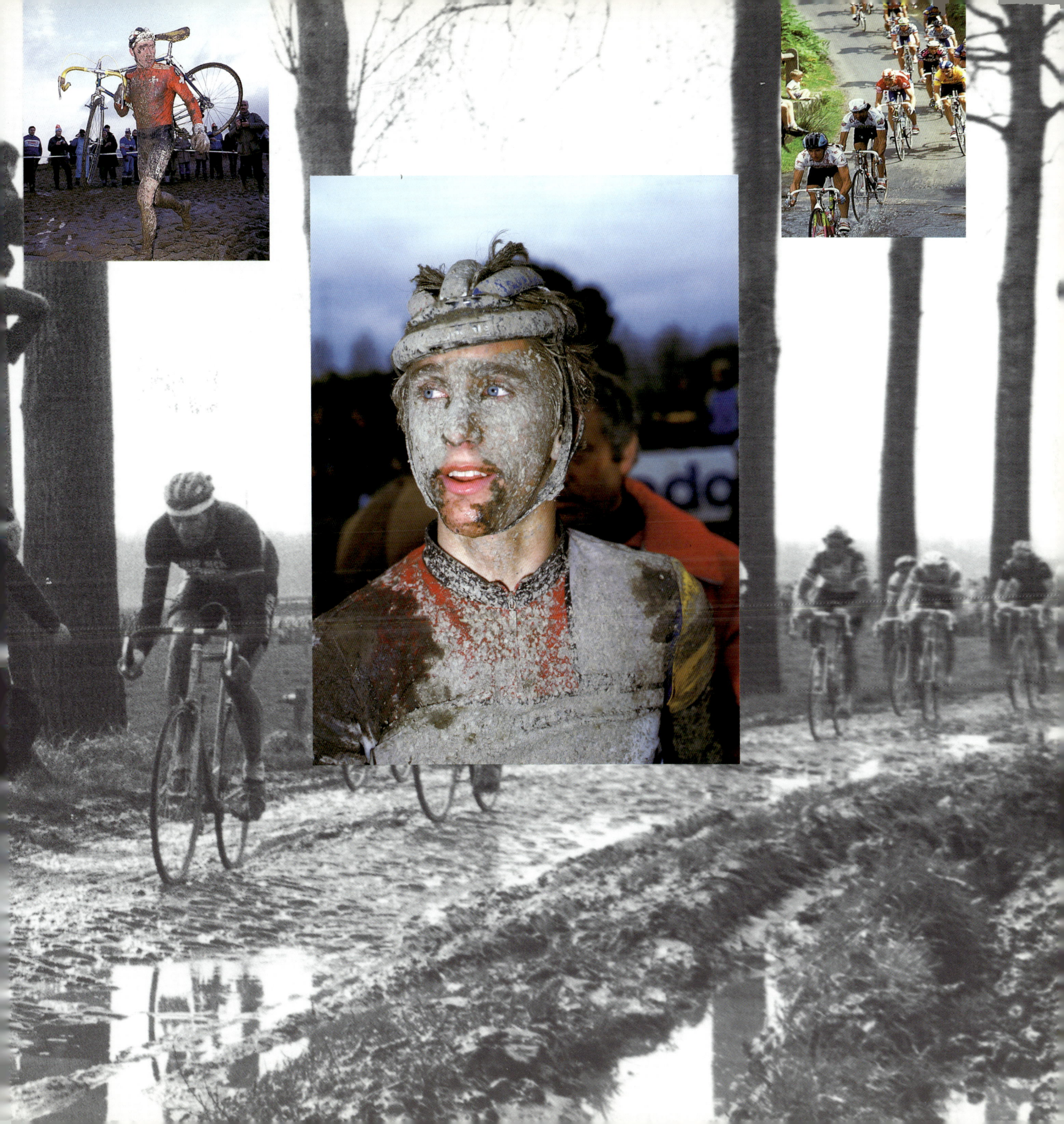

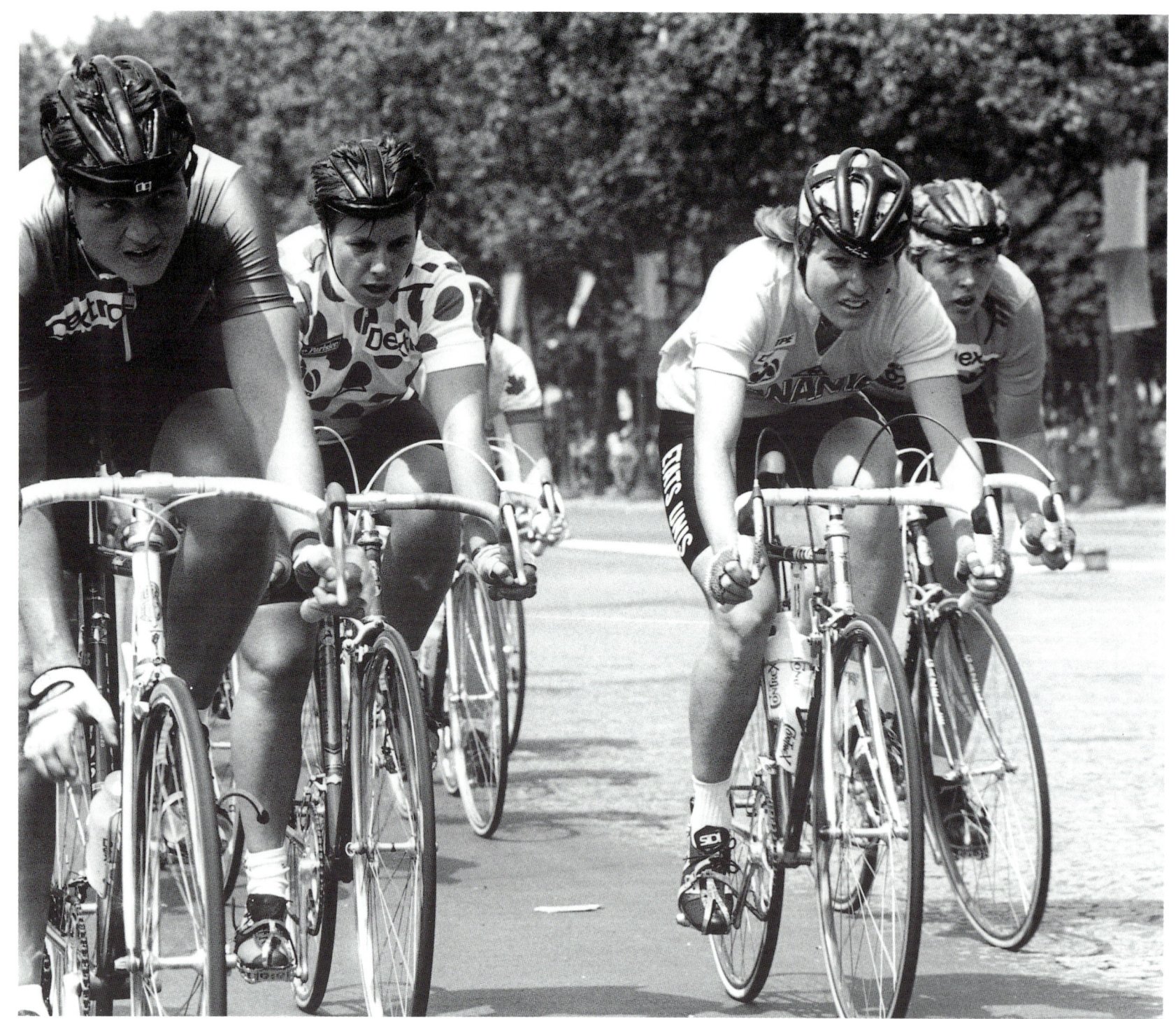

1984: TOUR DE FRANCE FÉMININ: PARIS

At the end of the first Tour de France for women in 1984, American Marianne Martin (right) wore the winner's yellow jersey down the Champs-Élysées. She won the 18-stage race by 3:17 over Dutch racer Helen Hage (in polka-dot jersey); Mieke Havik (left) of the Netherlands won the green jersey points competition.

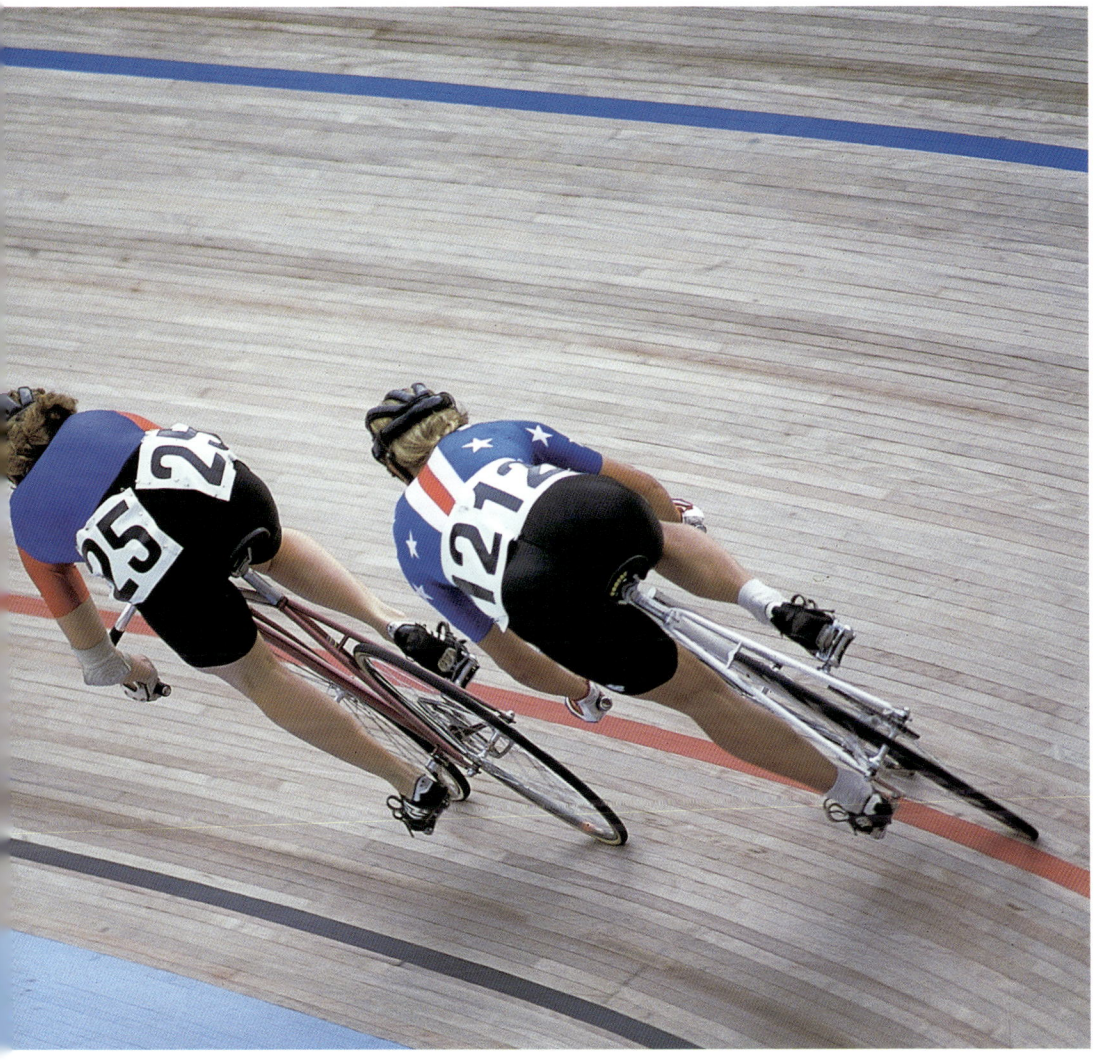

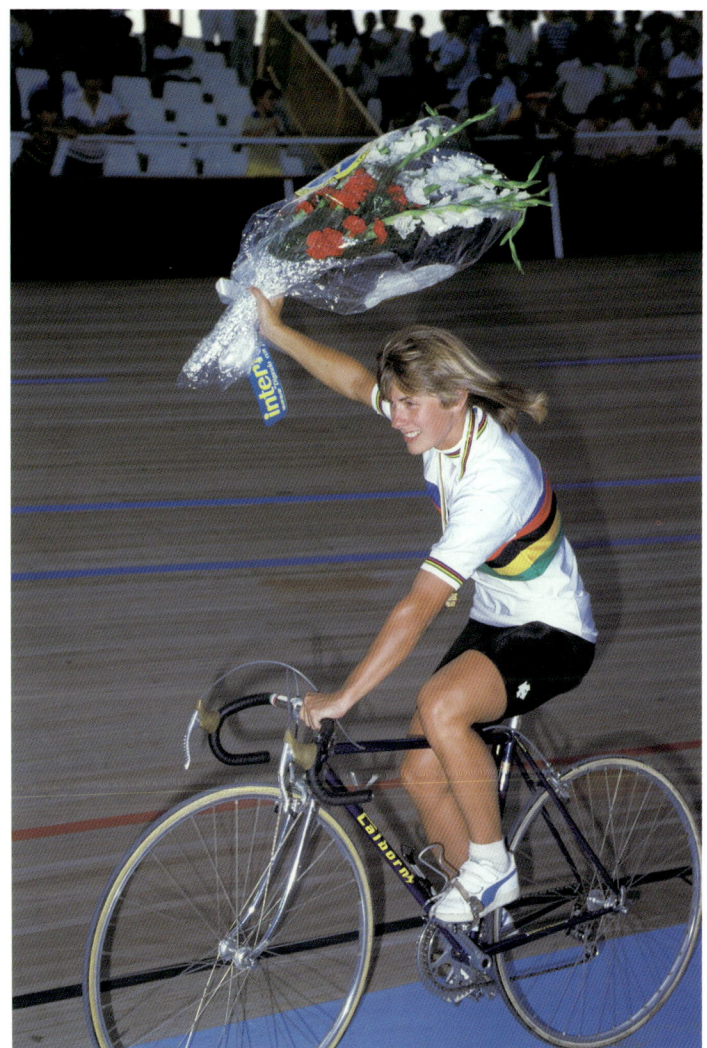

1982: WORLD TRACK CHAMPIONSHIPS: LEICESTER, ENGLAND

America's Connie Paraskevin (at back) emerged as the fastest women's sprinter in the world in 1982.

1984: WORLD TRACK CHAMPIONSHIPS: BARCELONA, SPAIN

In 1984, Paraskevin collected her third consecutive rainbow jersey, at the Barcelona world's.

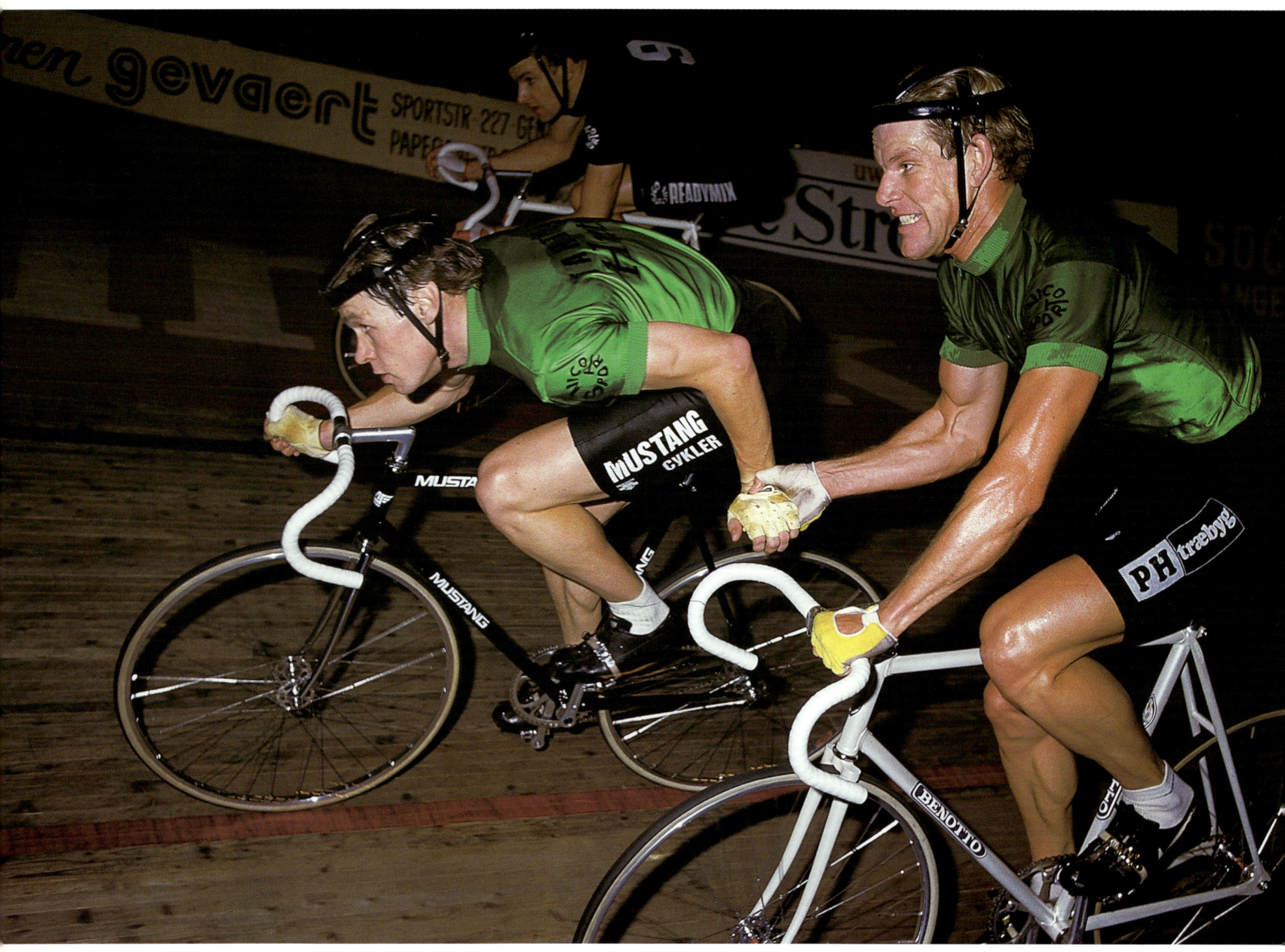

1984: GHENT SIX DAY: DENMARK

The key to the six-day race is the relay, or interchange, between partners at the height of 35-mile-per-hour Madison races. Here, Danish teammates Gert Frank (left) and Hans-Henrik Oersted show how it's done.

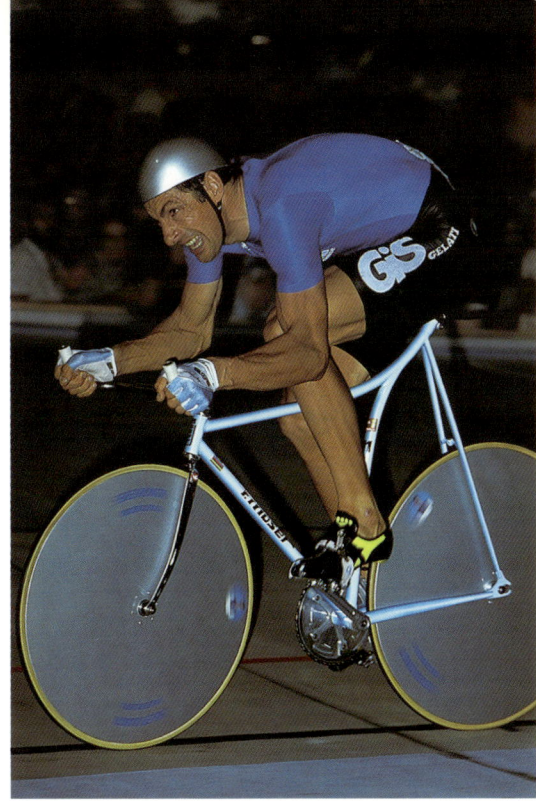

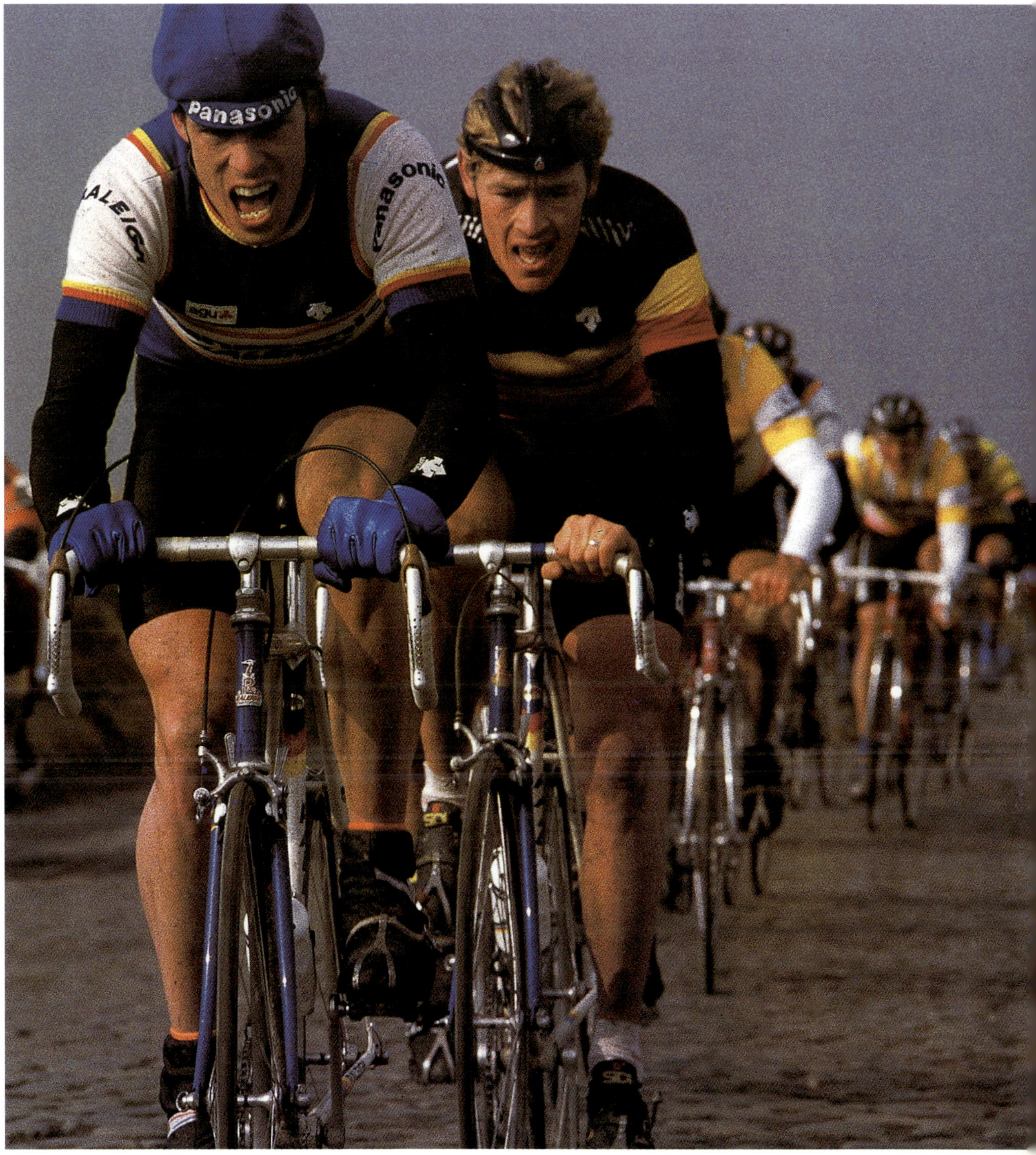

1985: WORLD TRACK CHAMPIONSHIPS: BASSANO DELL GRAPPA, ITALY

Between 1984 and 1988, Italian Francesco Moser held the world hour records at altitude (in Mexico City), at sea level (at Milan) and indoors (at Moscow and Stuttgart). Here, he competes in the 5000-meter pursuit at the 1985 track world's.

1985: HET VOLK: BELGIUM

Australian Phil Anderson leads Belgian teammate Eric Vanderaerden through the early-March sunshine on a cobbled stretch of the Belgian classic, Het Volk.

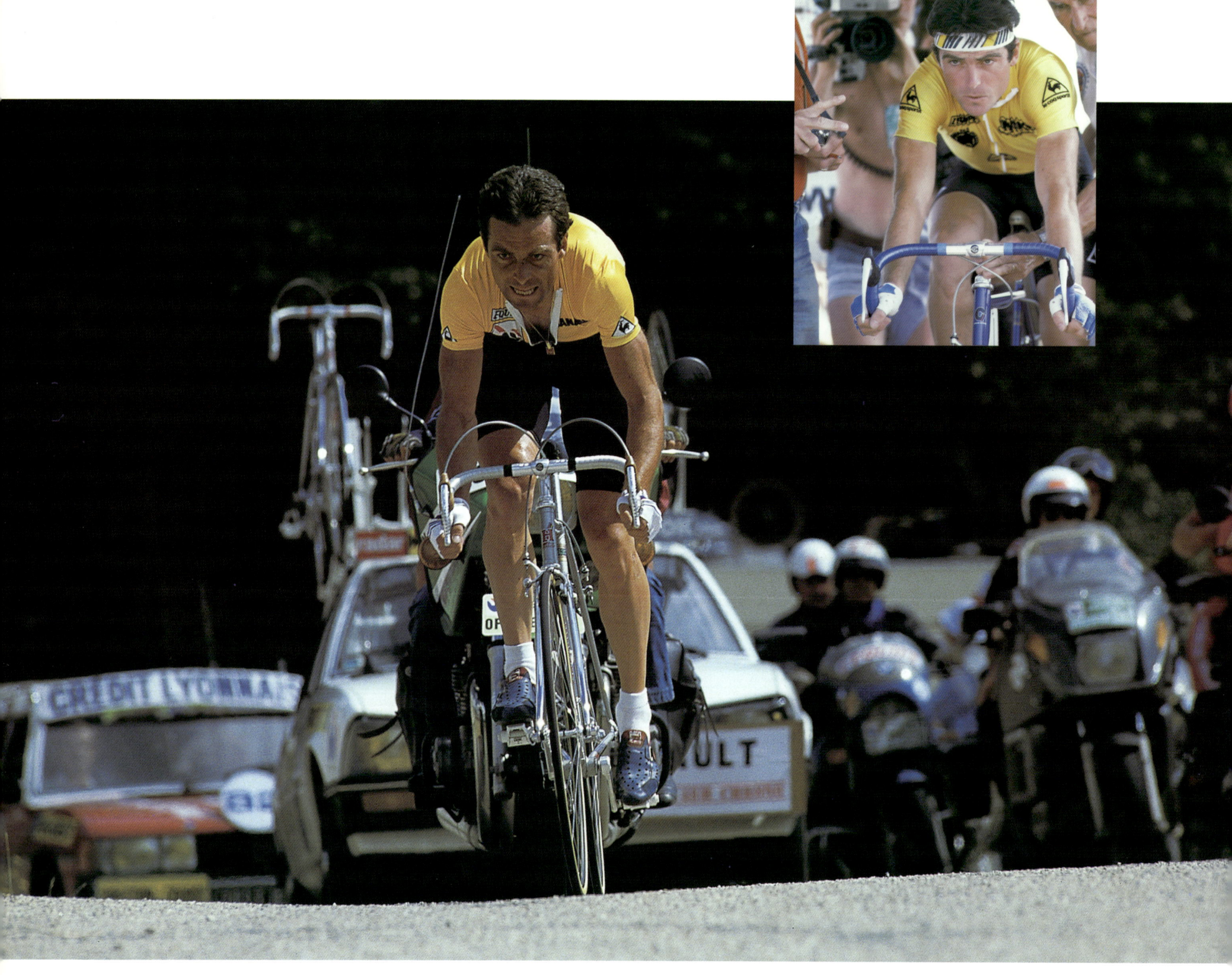

1985: TOUR DE FRANCE: LAC DE VASIVIÈRE

Bernard Hinault won the Tour de France five times between 1978 and 1985. Here, he rides the final time trial of the 1985 Tour, which clinched his overall victory over his La Vie Claire teammate Greg LeMond. (Inset) Hinault at the start of the 1981 Tour.

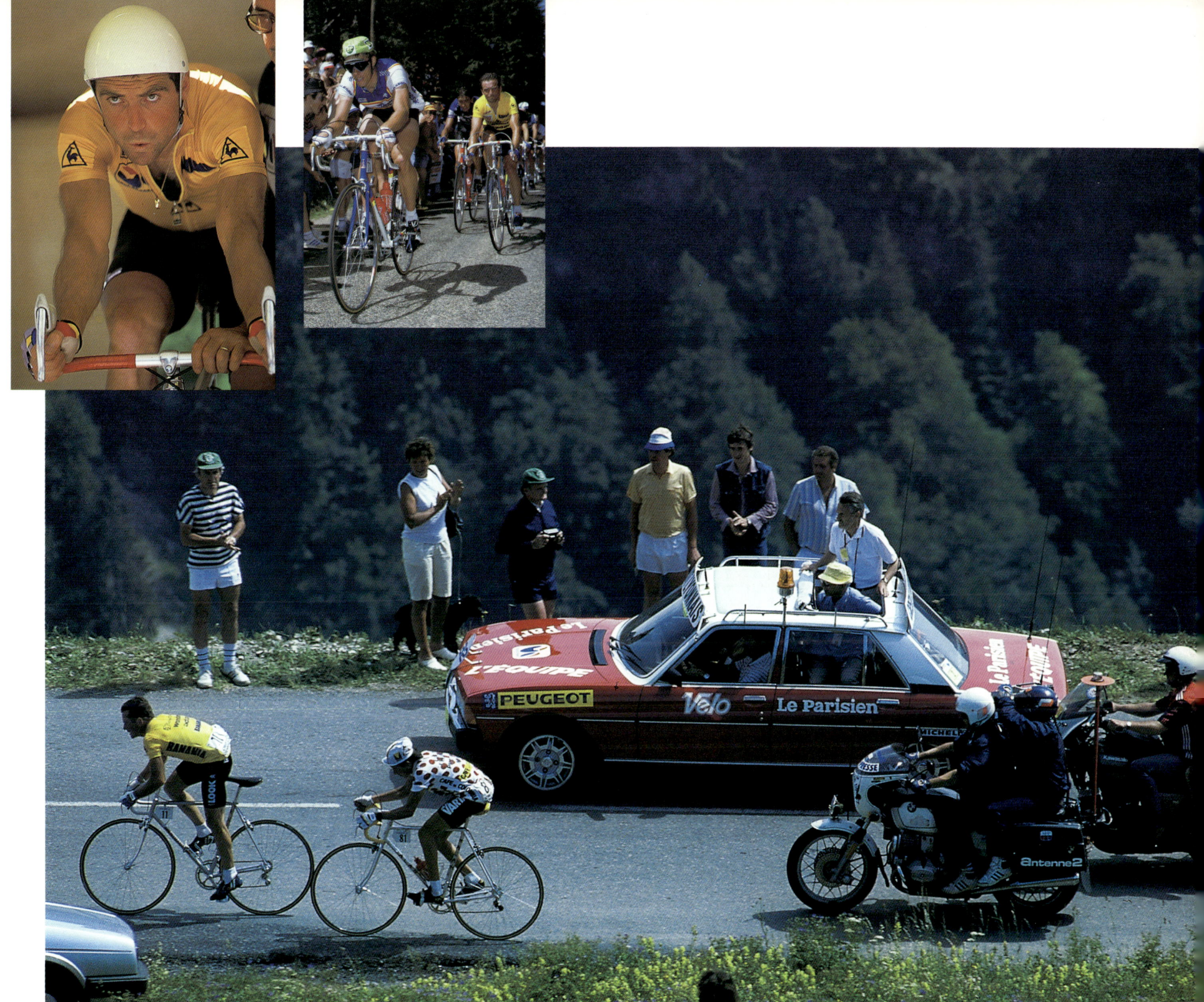

1985: TOUR DE FRANCE: AVORIAZ

Hinault established a big lead in the 1985 Tour when he made a two-man break on the first stage in the Alps with Colombian climbing sensation Lucho Herrera. (Inset) Hinault at a time trial start, and following Australian rival Phil Anderson in the mountains.

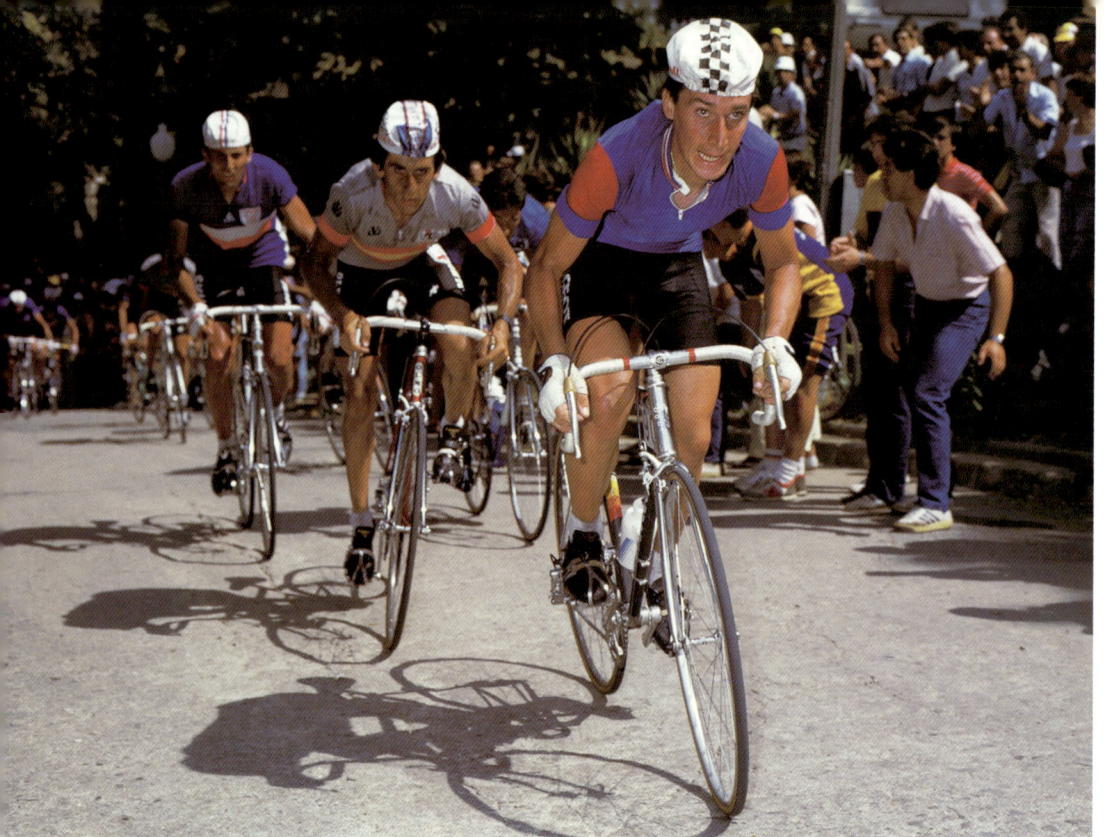

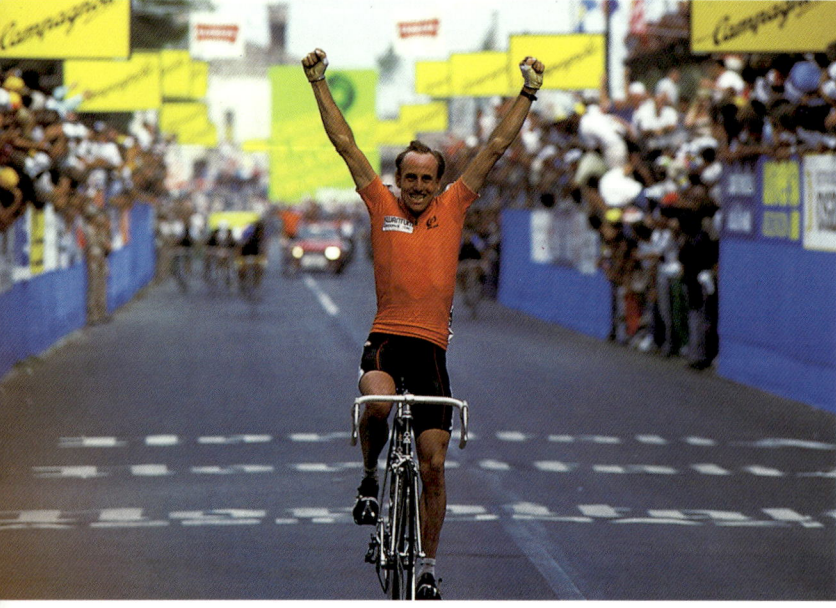

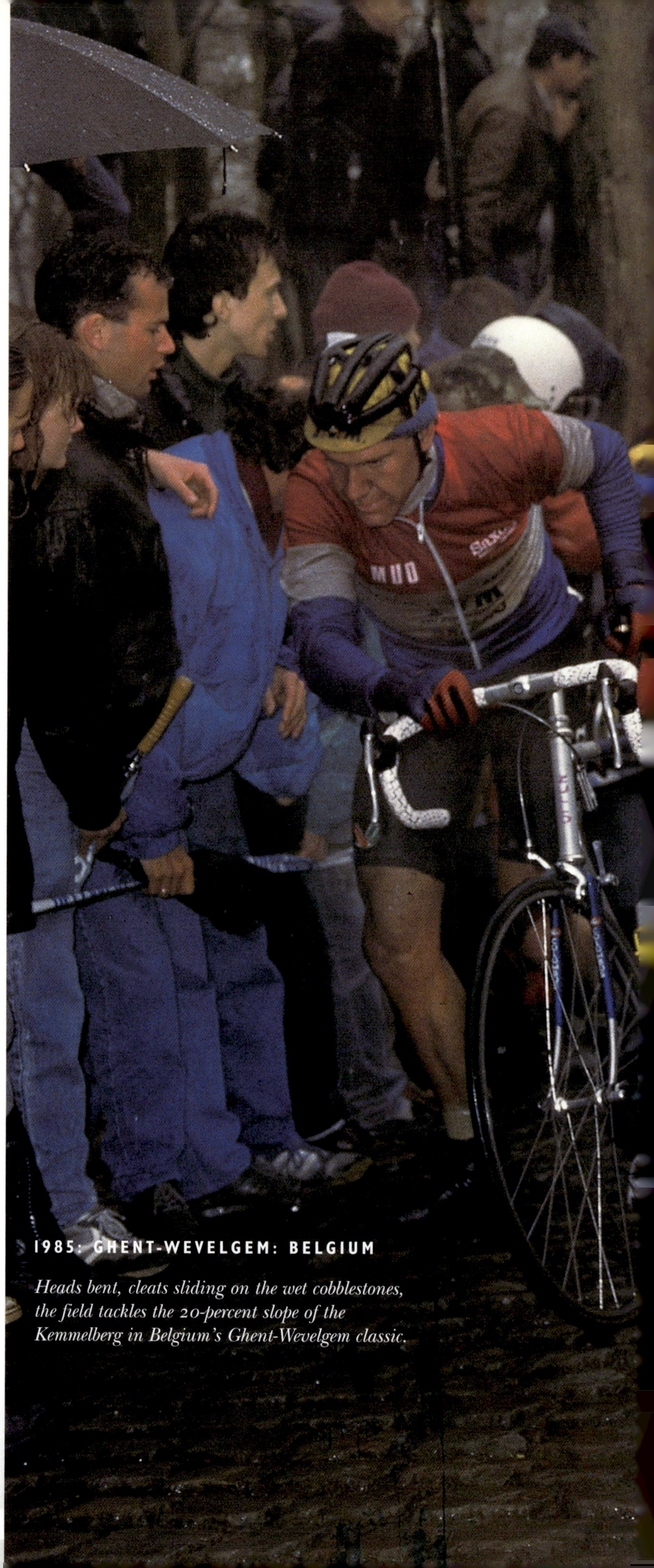

1984: WORLD ROAD CHAMPIONSHIPS: BARCELONA

Robert Millar always rode aggressively at the world championships, as he did on the Montjuich hill at the Barcelona world's.

1985: WORLD ROAD CHAMPIONSHIPS: MONTELLO, ITALY

Considered a climber rather than a sprinter, Dutchman Joop Zoetemelk scored an upset win with a last-kilometer attack at the 1985 world's in Italy. No wonder he was happy!

1985: GHENT-WEVELGEM: BELGIUM

Heads bent, cleats sliding on the wet cobblestones, the field tackles the 20-percent slope of the Kemmelberg in Belgium's Ghent-Wevelgem classic.

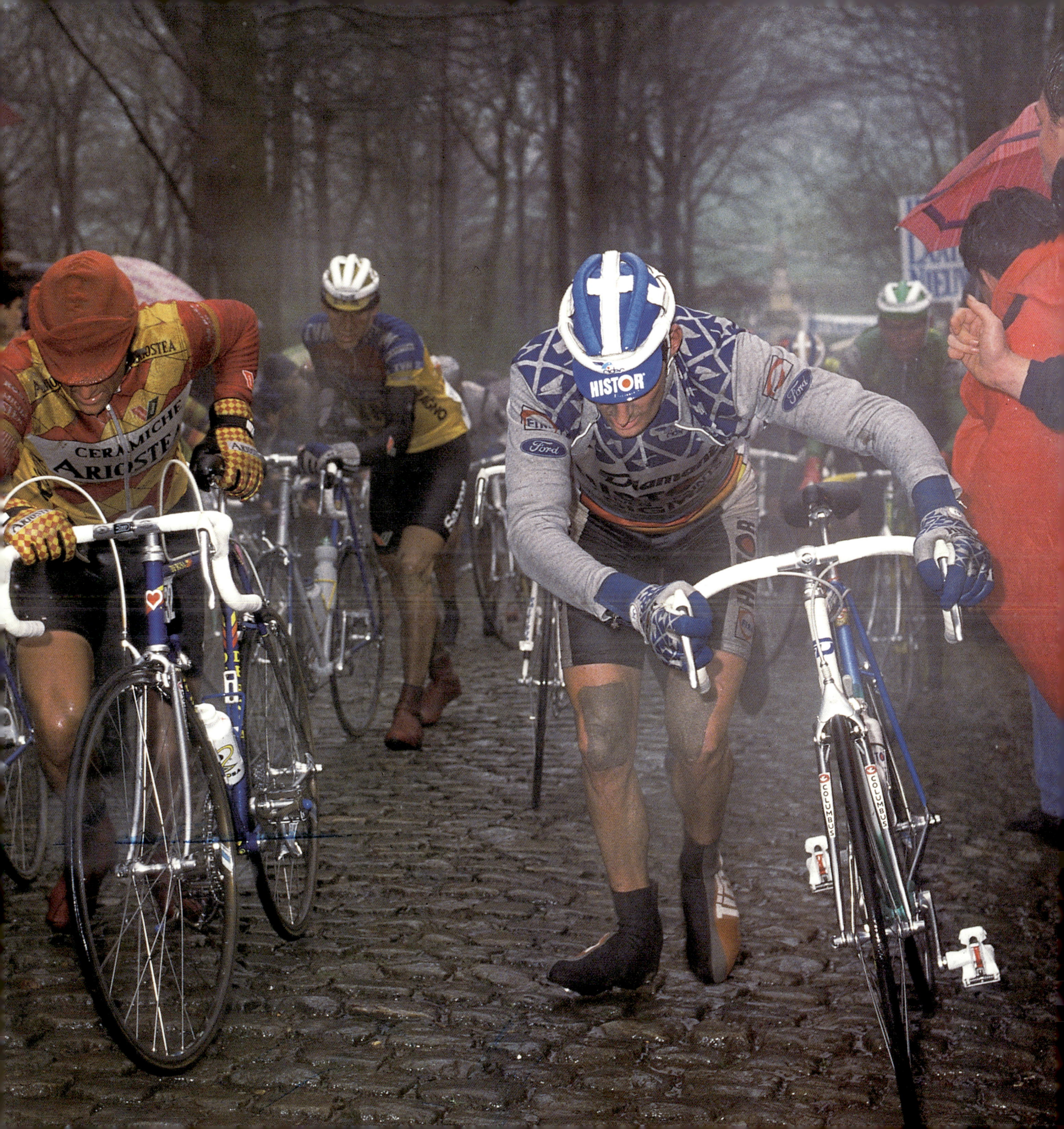

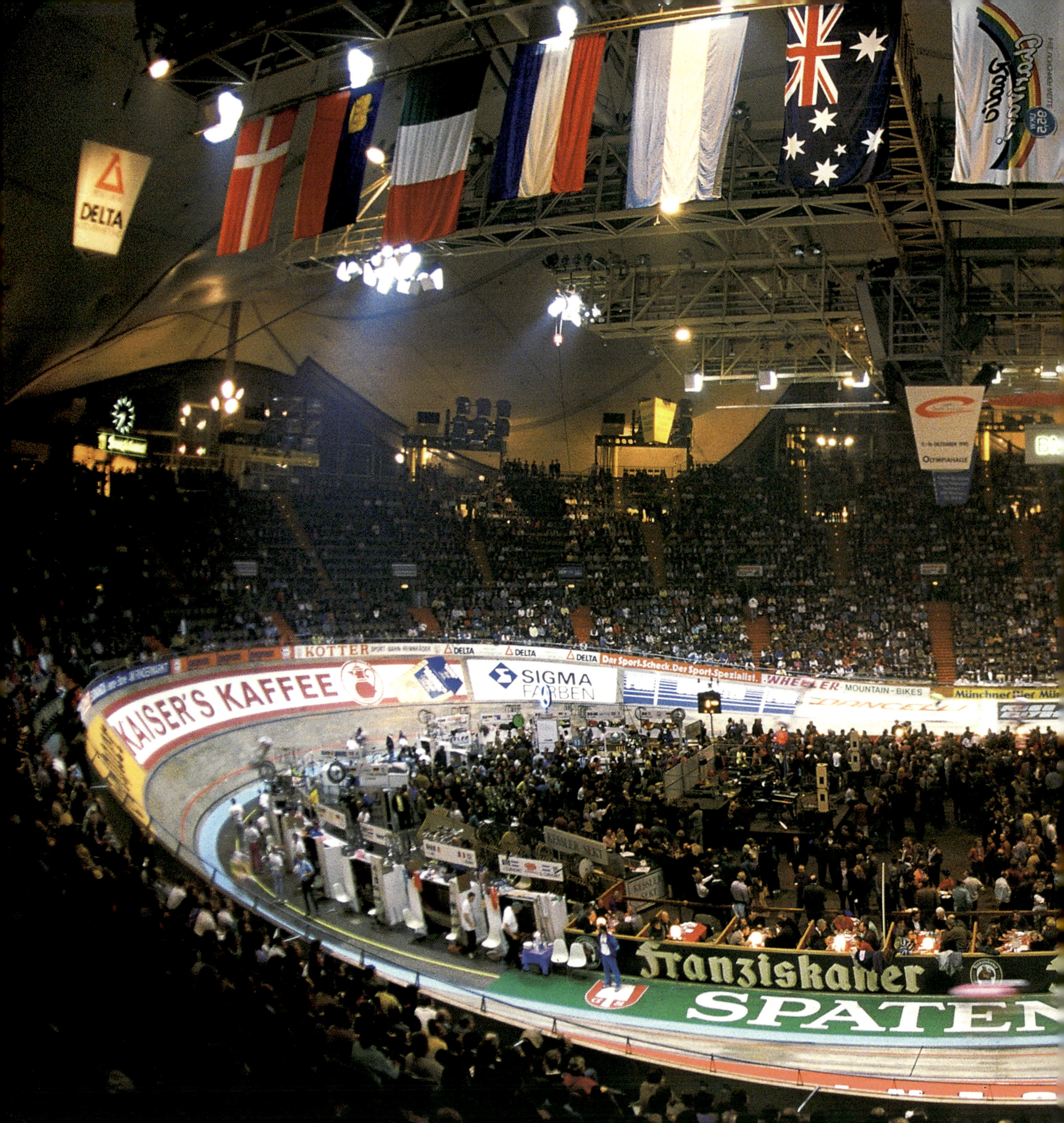

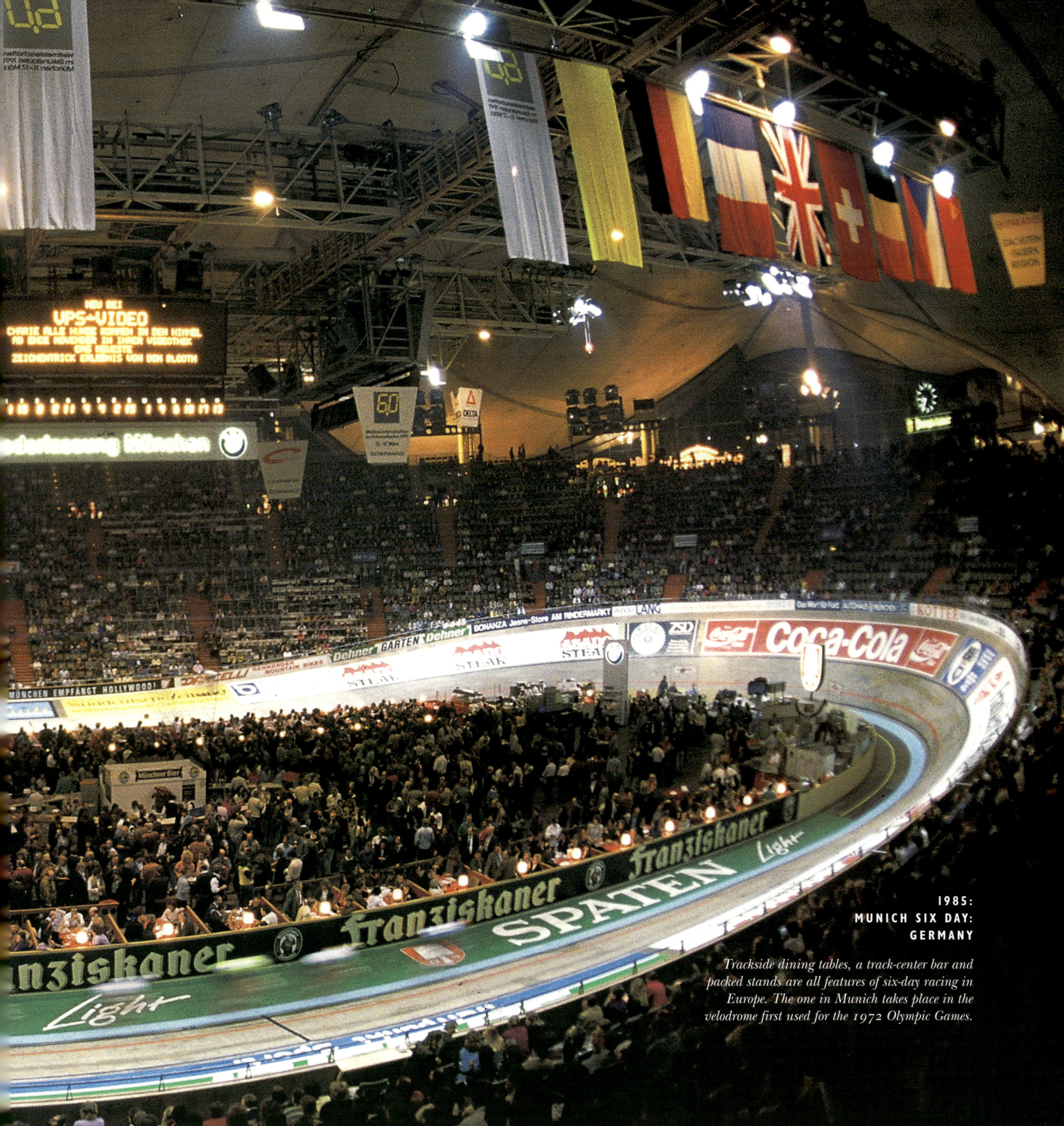

1985: MUNICH SIX DAY: GERMANY

Trackside dining tables, a track-center bar and packed stands are all features of six-day racing in Europe. The one in Munich takes place in the velodrome first used for the 1972 Olympic Games.

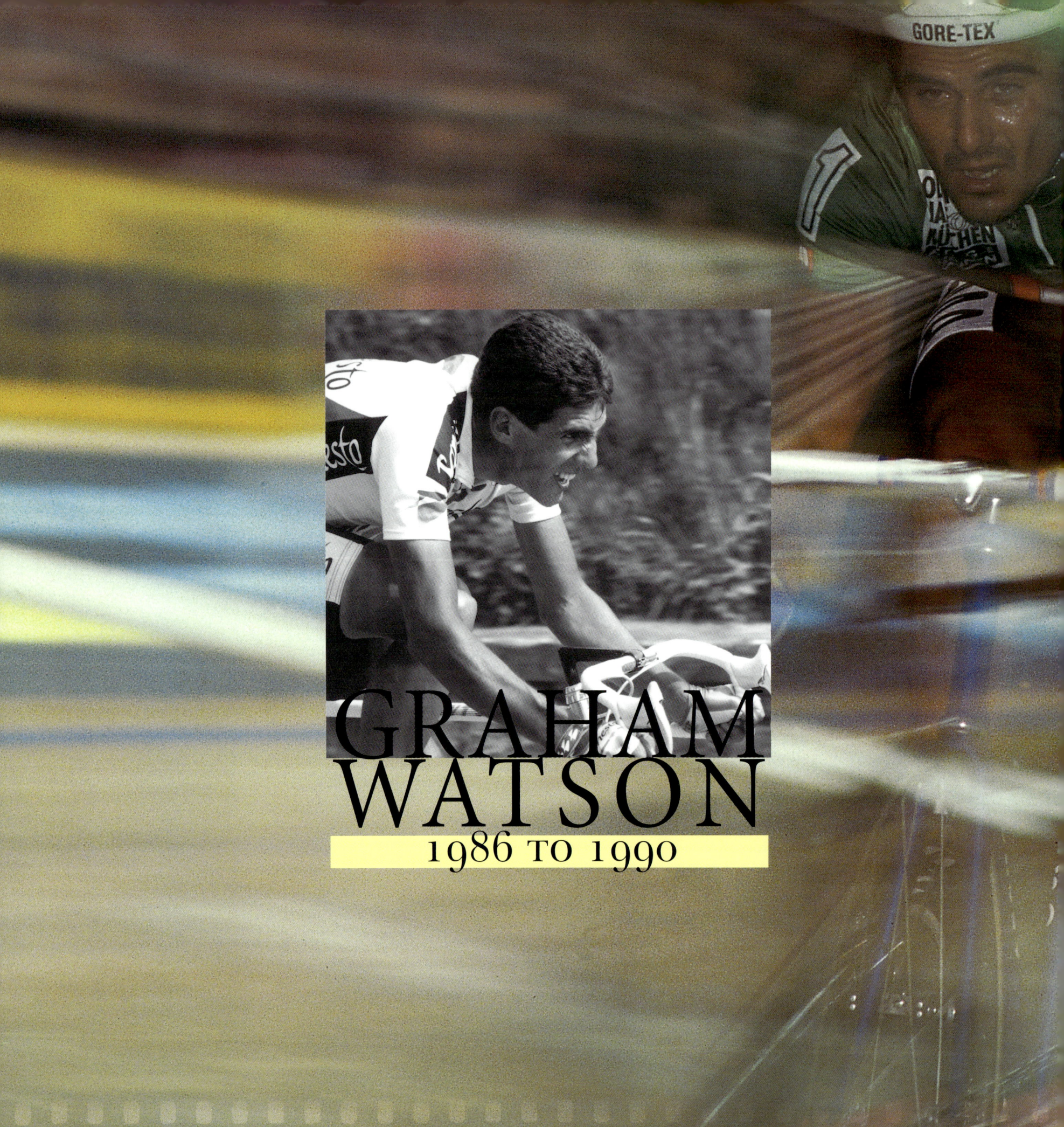

GRAHAM WATSON
1986 TO 1990

GRAHAM WATSON

Miguel Induráin would later come to dominate cycling in the early 1990s, but that brief glimpse of him aside, it was other Spanish cyclists—and Spanish cycling in general—that caught my eye in 1985. I truly believe that the Vuelta put me firmly on the fast track to success, for it opened a new world of opportunity and excitement that I had never even imagined was there. True, riders such as Kelly and Millar were vying for victory in the Vueltas that ran between 1985–89, and my lenses inevitably strayed in their direction. But it was the wealth and depth of Spain's cycling family that woke me to the real cultural appeal of the sport, and I quickly grew to love that country for all its craziness and romance.

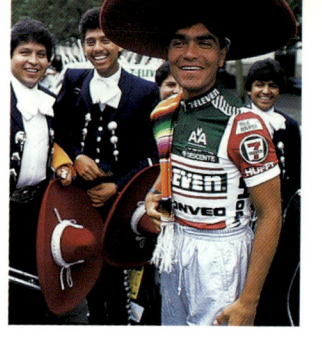
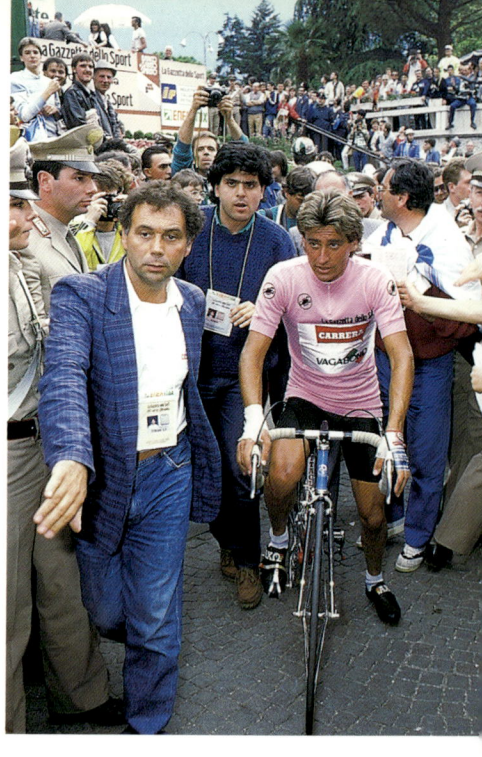

I knew then, as I know now, that I never would have gone to countries like Spain if it had not been for a bike race—a fact I am constantly reminded of as I travel even farther afield. And the joy of discovering Spain, and with it a new flavor of cycling, motivated me to see the Giro d'Italia in 1986. I wanted to see if the Giro could be as good as the Vuelta, to see if Italy could possibly be as majestic and colorful as its Latin sister, and if the people could be anywhere near as friendly.

I was not disappointed. Clearly, the Giro was a step up from the Vuelta in terms of organization, and it unquestionably had a higher-class peloton racing for attention. For while the May–June Giro was used as preparation by riders aiming to do well in the Tour de France, the earlier Vuelta was largely an all-Spanish affair—save for the few star foreigners looking to earn easy money, or earn a victory in what was considered the least competitive of the three grand tours.

I also discovered from the start how different the Giro and the Vuelta are from one another, each as distinct as their country's lifestyles and weather. Yet to this day, I cannot adequately explain what those differences are, and I still cannot decide which of the two races I prefer to work in, for they both give so much pleasure. My abiding memories of that first Giro are of seeing the Dolomites for the first time—the steep rocky spires above the Passo Sella, on a stage to Bassano del Grappa—and of the time-trial battle between Francesco Moser and Dietrich Thurau into Cremona, in which Moser's high-tech Benotto racing bike rattled daringly to victory over the city's ancient cobblestones.

My personal organization that year left a little to be desired, for to really discover the Giro, one has to follow the race with a motorcycle—something I'd not managed to arrange in my haste to get from Spain to Italy, while somehow placating my anxious bank manager along the way. In

1986 AND 1988: GIRO D'ITALIA: ITALY

Italian Roberto Visentini, wearing the leader's pink jersey, was the main attraction of the 1986 Giro, while in '88 Mexican Raúl Alcála brought publicity for the U.S. team, 7-Eleven.

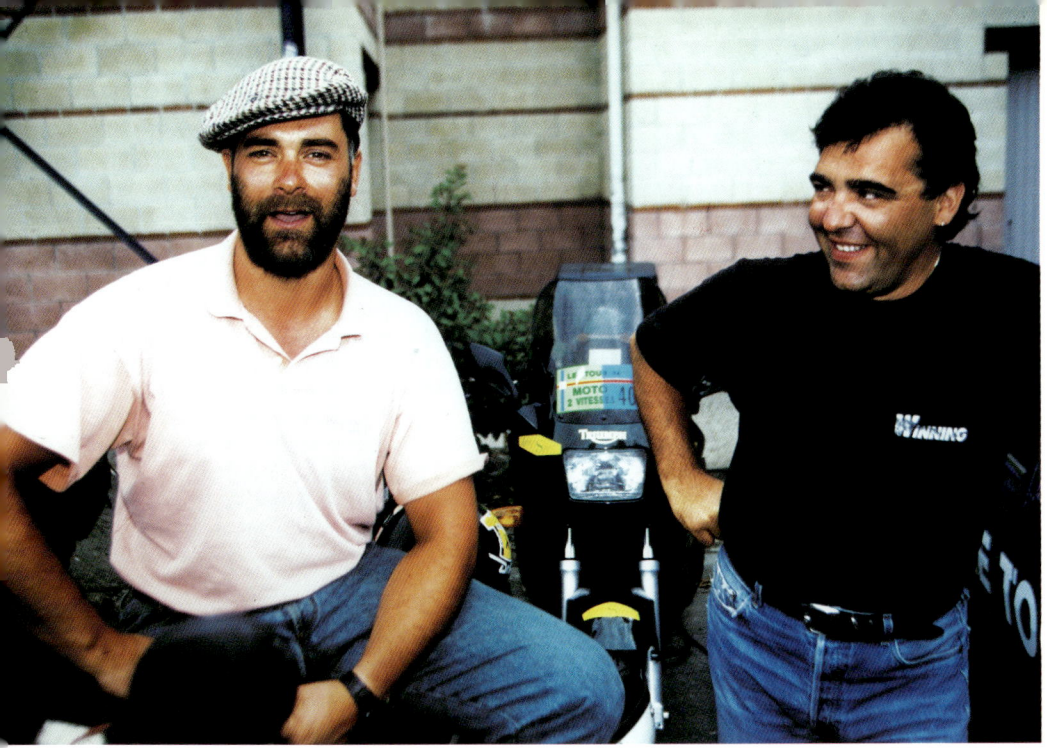

1990: TOUR DE FRANCE: PYRENEES

Basque motorcycle drivers Ismael Borges (right) and Rafa Landa helped the author get to know the Vuelta better than any other major race—and also gave him a longtime relationship with Spain.

Spain, I'd been relatively well-off, established, employed and entertained by the new Spanish cycling magazine, *Ciclismo a Fondo*. But in Italy, I was once again struggling to make ends meet, and to make myself accepted by officials and fellow photographers with whom I knew, even if they didn't, that I was starting a long-term relationship.

As harsh as my experiences were that year, they helped me enormously in 1987, when I stretched my presence on the Giro to a full two weeks, with motorcycle, to witness one of the greatest race battles in my 20 years—Stephen Roche versus Roberto Visentini. As only a foreigner could, I loved every minute of the tussle in Italy between the homegrown Visentini and Dublin's ever-smiling Roche. I became quite close with the Irishman, as he found himself more and more rejected by his Italian teammates and their *tifosi*. Yet little did I know then that I'd witnessed the commencement of a historic achievement in cycling, for Roche was to go on to win the Tour de France and world championships that same summer, something that only the great Eddy Merckx himself had done, many years earlier.

Feeling proud of Roche's triumph over the odds, my return to London after the race brought me my own not-insignificant achievement: Thanks to a deal that had been struck between the American magazine, *Inside Cycling*, for which I then was working, and *Sports Illustrated*, I was slated to follow the Tour de France that year on a motorcycle, exactly 10 years after first seeing the Tour in 1977.

And what a Tour it was! I couldn't have chosen a better debut than this one, which had the yellow jersey changing hands no less than nine times, and contained drama after drama before Roche finally emerged as the winner against Spain's Pedro Delgado.

Now, instead of coming away from the Tour with 20 rolls of undeveloped film in my shorts, I had up to 20 rolls of film a day to dispose of, often couriered by the Tour's helicopter to Paris, where a *Sports Illustrated* agent took possession, before processing the film overnight and placing it on board the Concorde for an early delivery into New York that same day.

Times had changed, and at last I had become one of the elite . . . though there was still plenty of work to be done in the years ahead, if I were to keep my hallowed place in the motorcycle-photographers' ranks.

The only thing missing in that 1987 Tour was its defending champion, Greg LeMond, who had been accidentally shot earlier that spring. And yet, to be fair, the race was so good without him that only two years later did one consider how good it could have been with him.

Just how good became blatantly clear in the 1989 Tour, an event of outstanding drama and excellence, with a stunning last week that saw Greg battling against an impressively competitive Fignon, in a titanic duel that only ended on the very last day in the now-famous time trial. I have never known such excitement as a photographer as when, surprisingly isolated from my colleagues who'd been expecting Fignon to

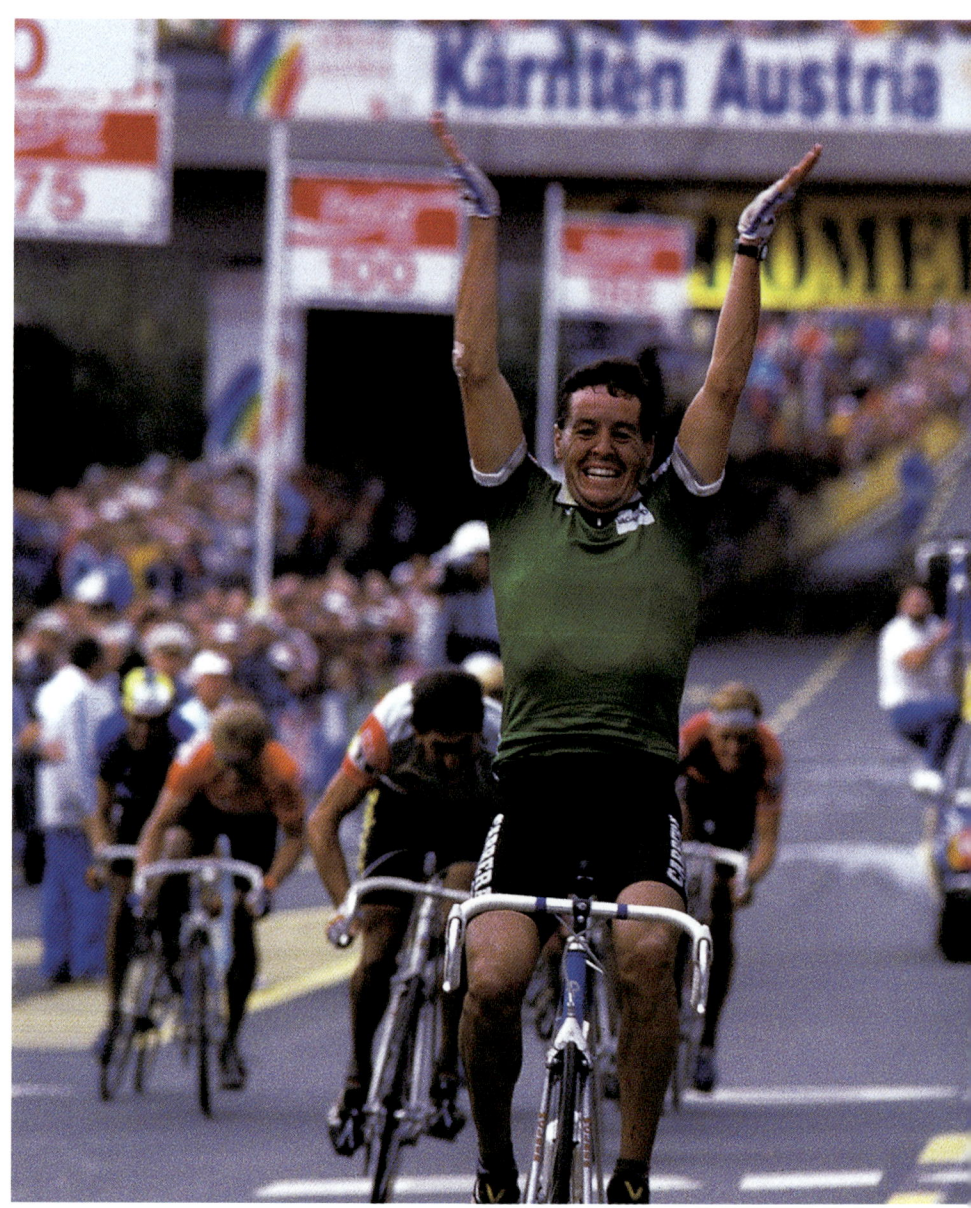

1987: WORLD ROAD CHAMPIONSHIPS: VILLACH, AUSTRIA

Irishman Stephen Roche crowned a season that had already included winning the Giro and Tour, to score a surprise victory in the 1987 world road championship in Austria, by outspeeding Moreno Argentin (right) and other fast-closing riders.

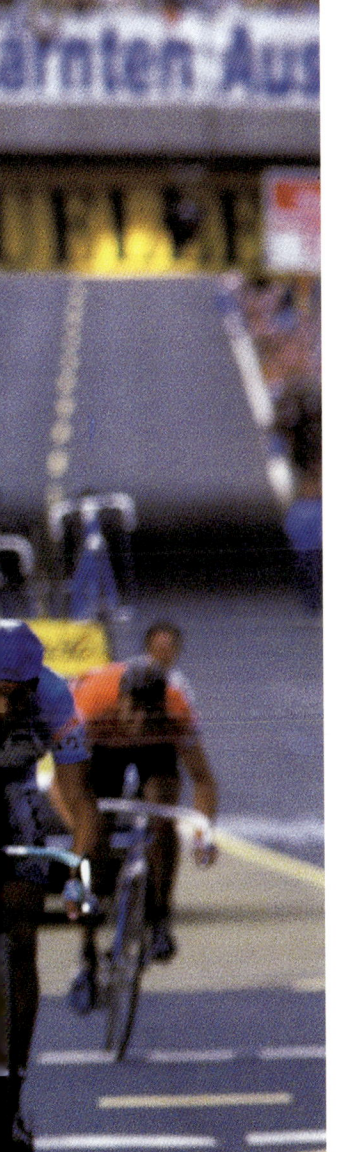

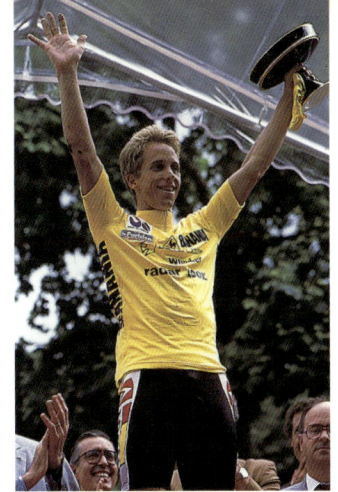

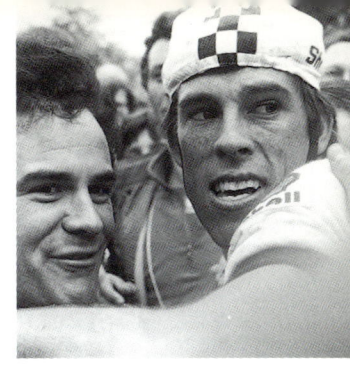

win, I found myself at LeMond's side as he fought with his emotions, not yet believing he'd finally won! On that humid afternoon in Paris, I became the proud owner of a set of images that showed the true drama of the occasion, images I still treasure today, more than 10 years later, for they have yet to be superseded by a similar event.

As the decade drew to a close, with LeMond winning the 1990 Tour from Claudio Chiappucci, and veteran Rudy Dhaenens winning the world road championship in Japan, I was able to reflect on a remarkable change of fortune for myself, for I'd made the transition from a would-be photographer riding a bicycle on the roads of the Tour, to a photographer proudly following all the great races, just inches away from the greatest champions of the era. And even though I had missed Merckx, I had enjoyed the best of Kelly's years—including all seven of his Paris-Nice wins—and gotten to know people like Phil Anderson and Stephen Roche, two icons of our time whose efforts brought a whole new meaning to the word "competition." I'd also marveled at seeing Robert Millar try to out-climb the Spaniards in Spain, and at Andy Hampsten beating the Italians in Italy, in 1988.

So, too, I wondered at the potential of Miguel Induráin in the next decade, for his solo stage win in the Pyrénées at the 1989 Tour had been followed this summer by another upset stage win in the Pyrénées: At Luz-Ardiden, Induráin attacked LeMond to win, and thus relegated his teammate and friend, Pedro Delgado, to a supporting role in the years to come.

1986: TOUR DE FRANCE: PARIS

Two other English-speaking riders to boost the author's career were Greg LeMond, winner of the 1986 Tour, and Aussie Phil Anderson, seen here with French mechanic Patrick Valcke.

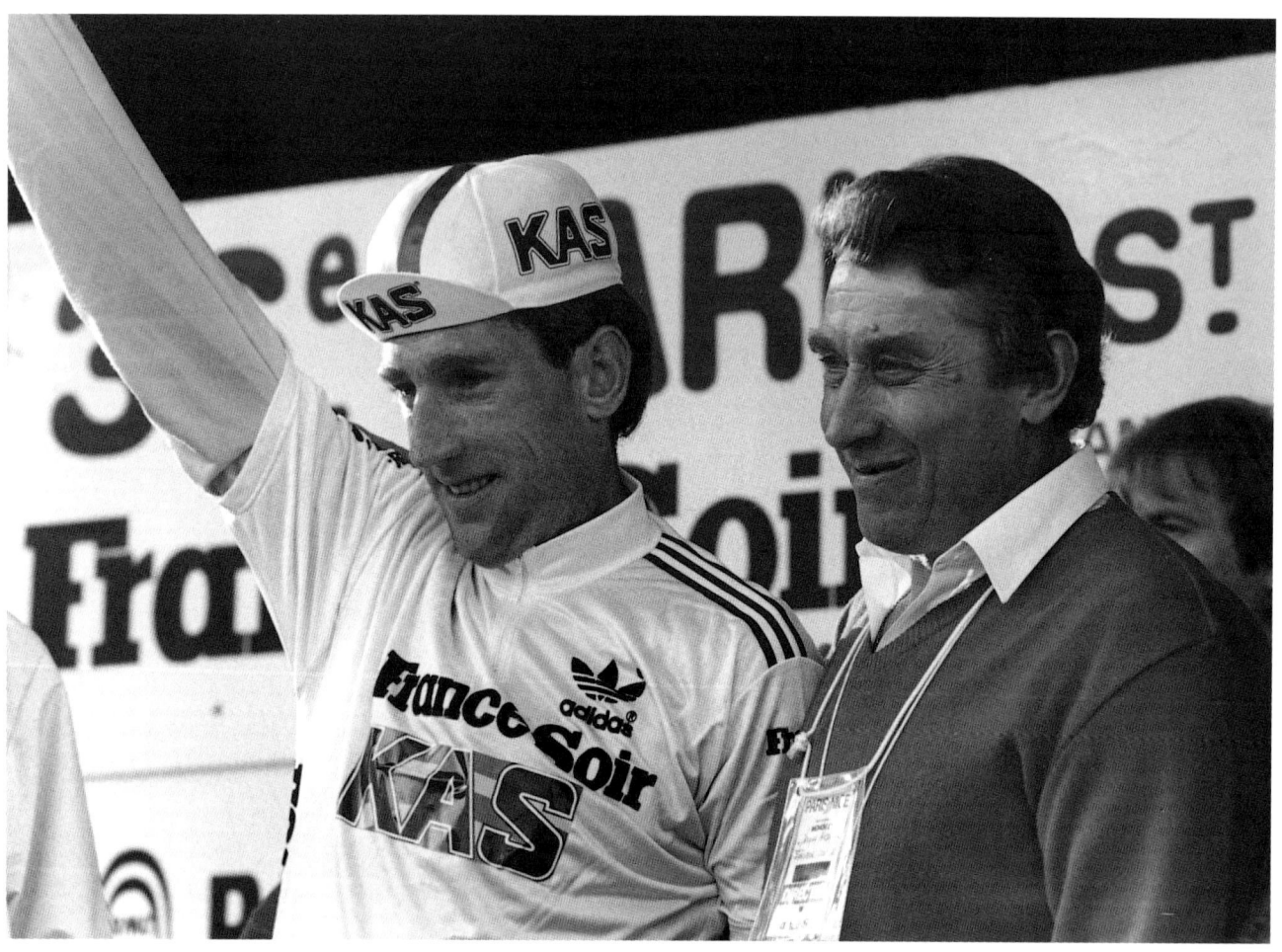

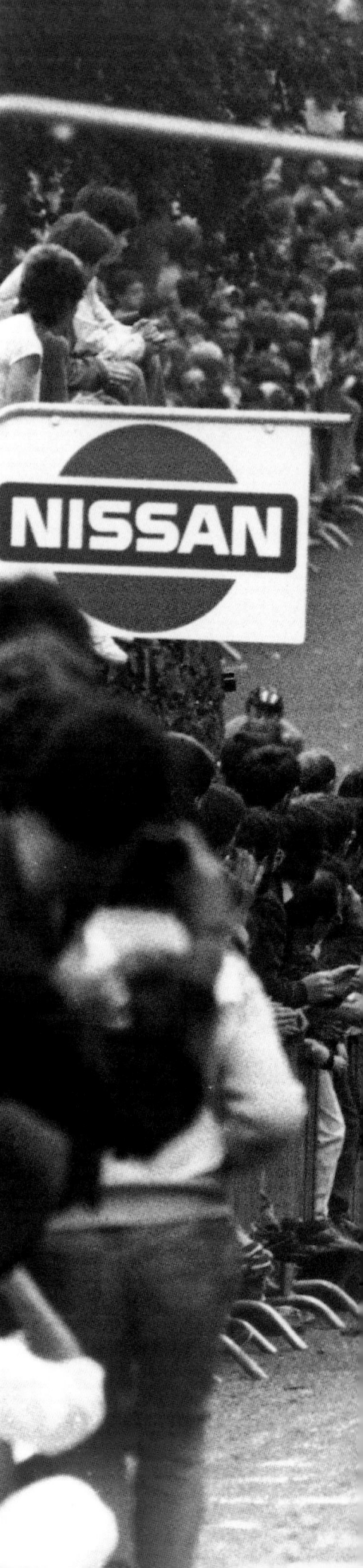

1986: PARIS-NICE: COL D'EZE

In 1986, Sean Kelly won the fifth of his seven consecutive victories in Paris-Nice, to beat the previous record of four wins held by French legend Jacques Anquetil (right), who was then the race director.

1986: NISSAN CLASSIC: CORK, IRELAND

Huge crowds, steep grades and spectacular racing were hallmarks of Ireland's Nissan Classic. Here, at the foot of the ultra-steep St. Patrick's Hill in Cork, Sean Kelly (at front on right) pulls his foot from the pedal before recovering to finish third on the stage.

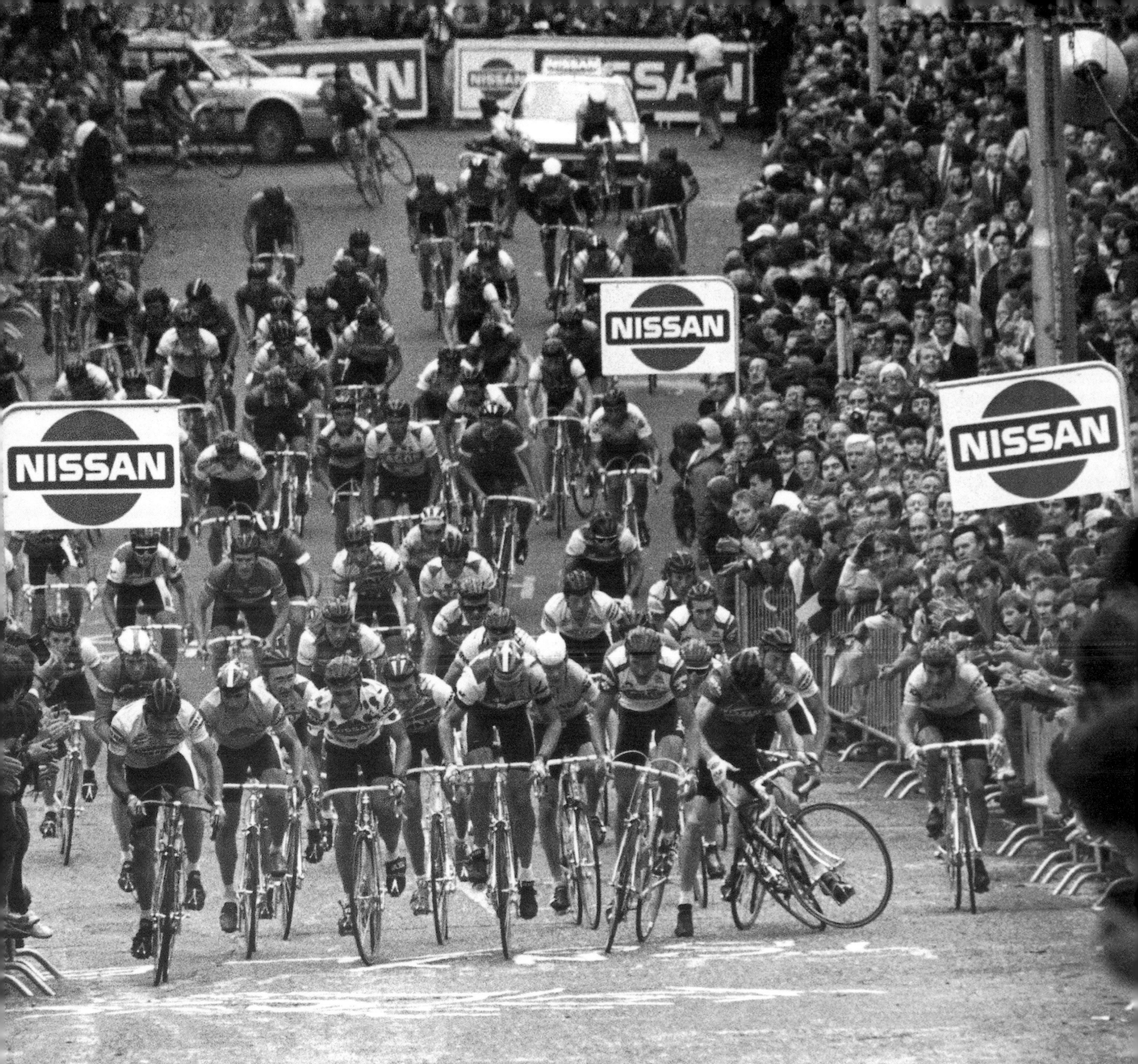

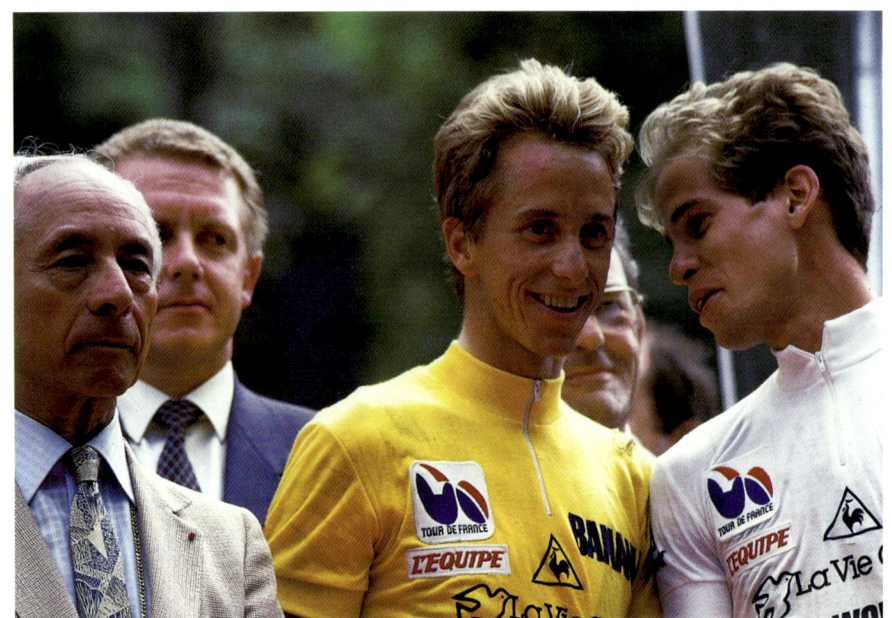

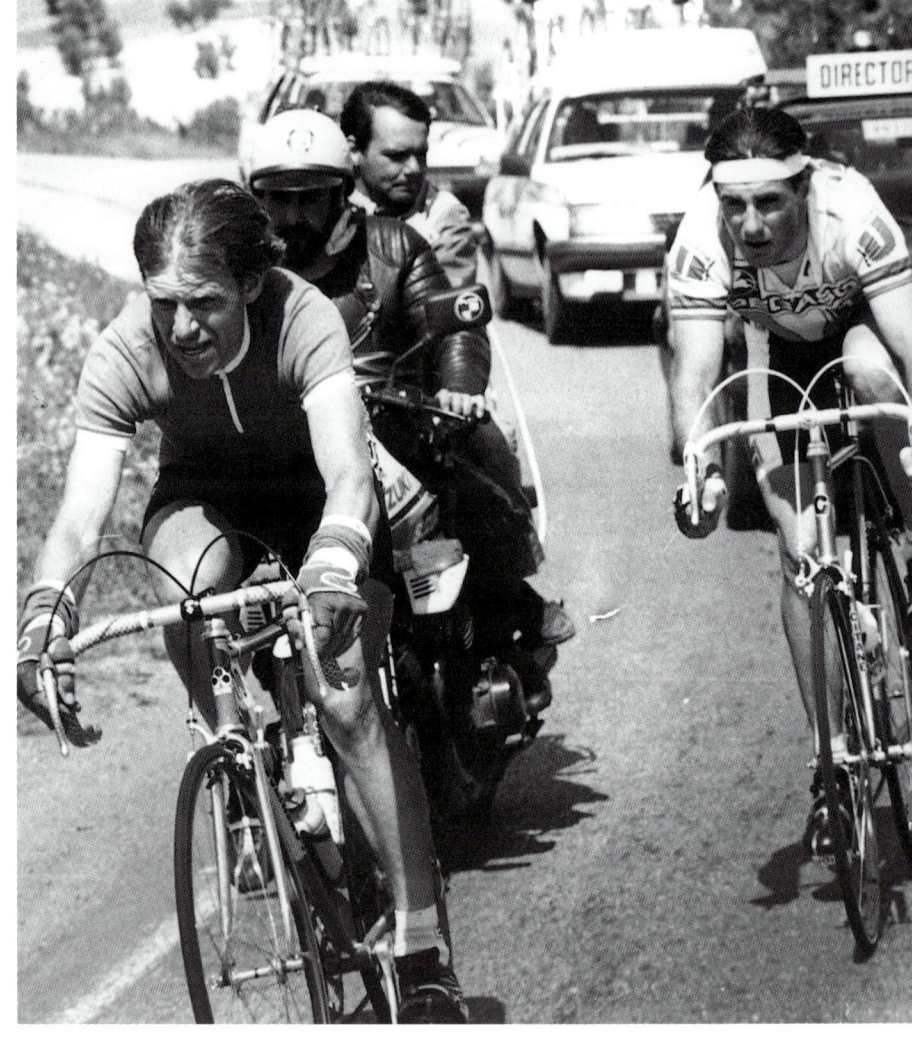

1986: TOUR DE FRANCE: PARIS

Two American teammates on the Tour de France podium in 1986: Winner Greg LeMond shares a joke with best young rider Andy Hampsten, as race director Félix Lévitan (far left) and UCI president Hein Verbruggen look on.

1986: VUELTA A ESPAÑA: SPAIN

Sergei Soukhoroutchenkov (left) was one of the greatest cyclists ever, but his best years preceded the lifting of the Iron Curtain, and the Russian star was restricted to riding in amateur-only races. When he contested the Vuelta with the Soviet team in 1986, he was well past his prime, but still showed his class in this breakaway with Frenchman Alain Bondue.

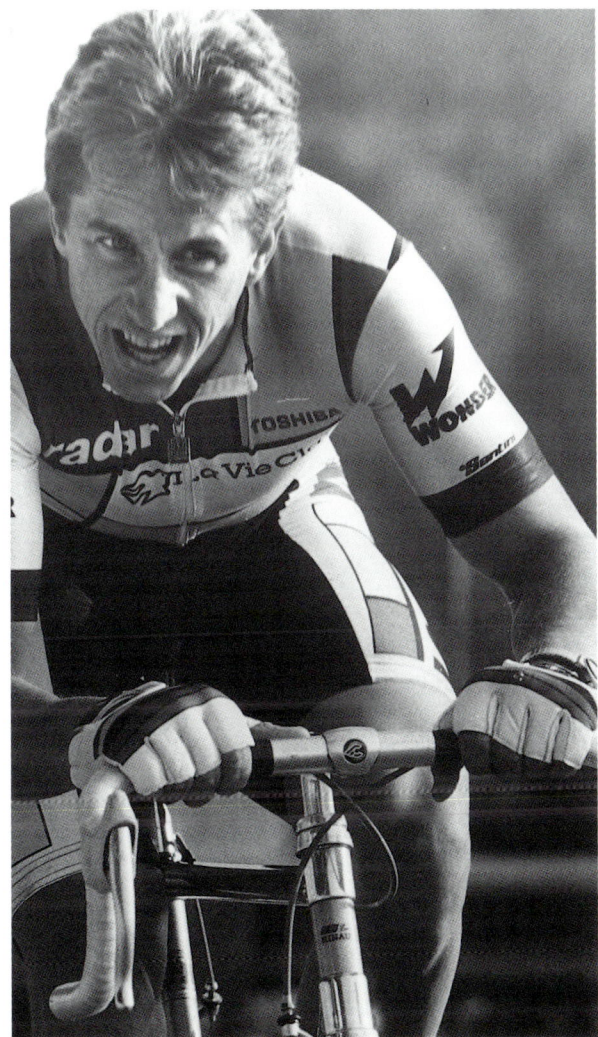
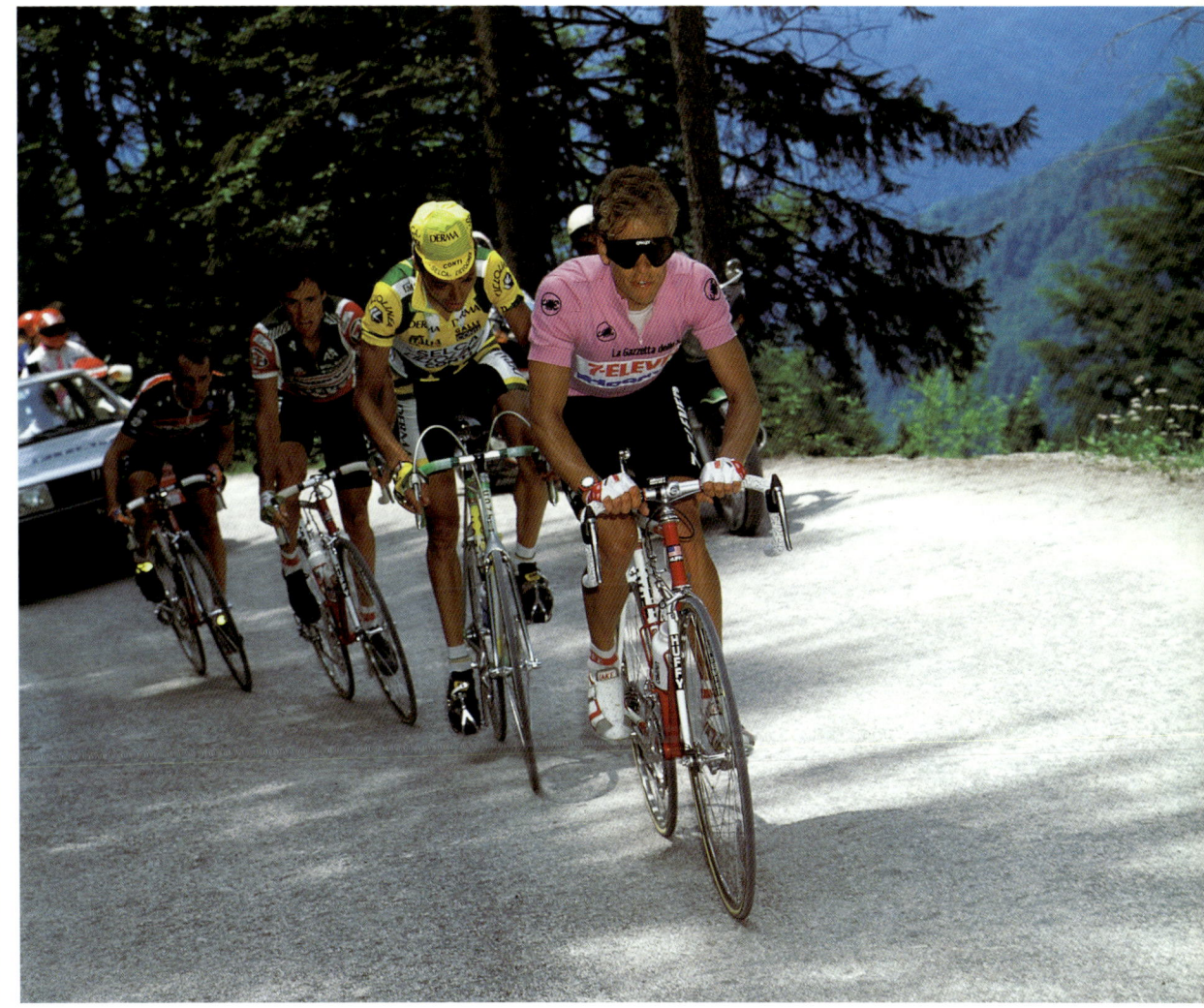

1986: PARIS-NICE: COL D'EZE

Greg LeMond finished third in the 1986 Paris-Nice, an early-season race he generally rode in his build-up toward the bigger events of the summer.

1988: GIRO D'ITALIA: PASSO DURAN

Andy Hampsten led a desperate chase through the Dolomite mountains to defend his Giro d'Italia pink jersey when Swiss rider Urs Zimmermann made a long-distance breakaway, starting on the Passo Duran.

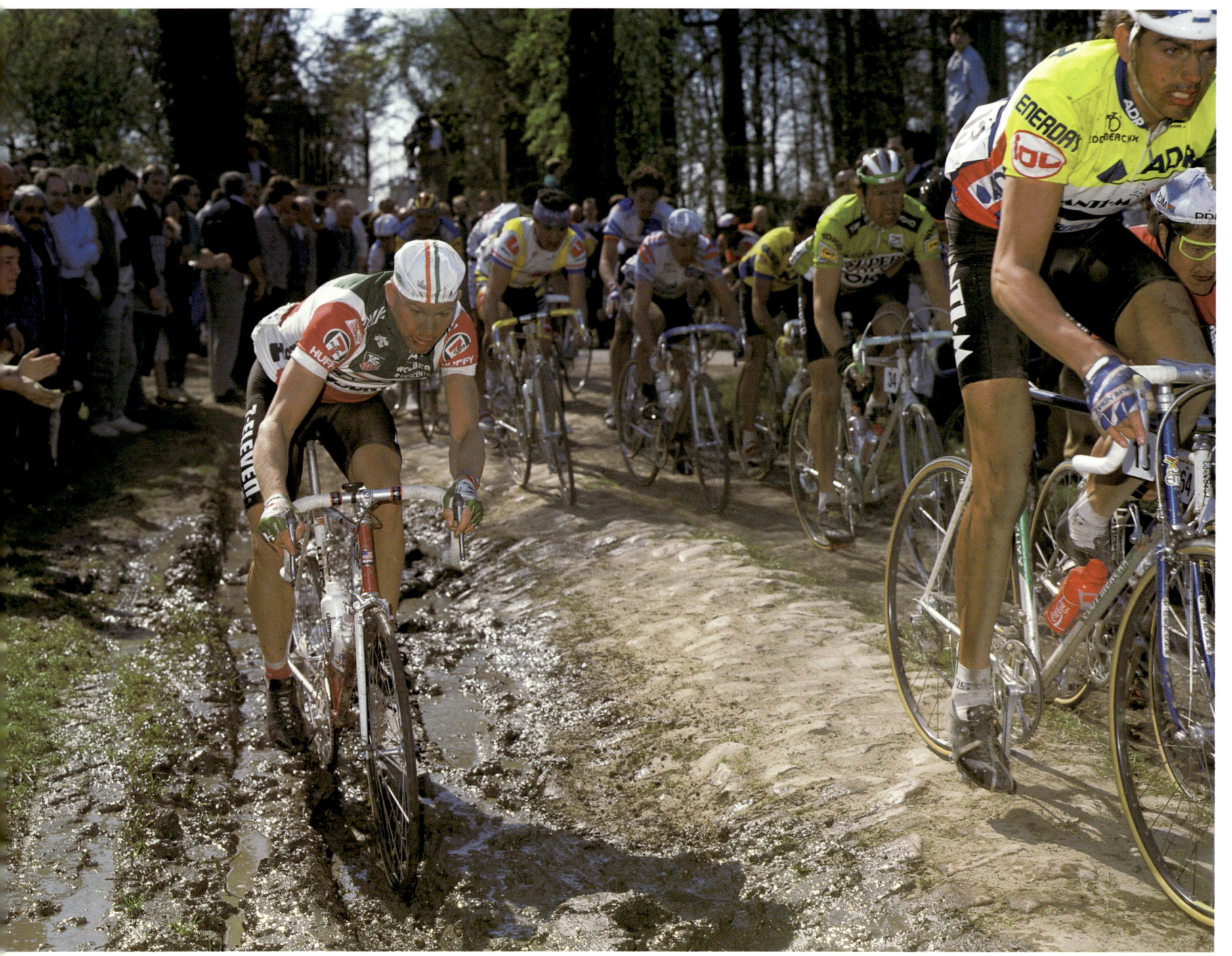

1989: PARIS-ROUBAIX: FRANCE

Bob Roll (left) personified the gritty professional more typical in Europe than America: The Californian finished all five editions of Paris-Roubaix that he started, despite difficulties like this in the 266-kilometer cobblestone classic.

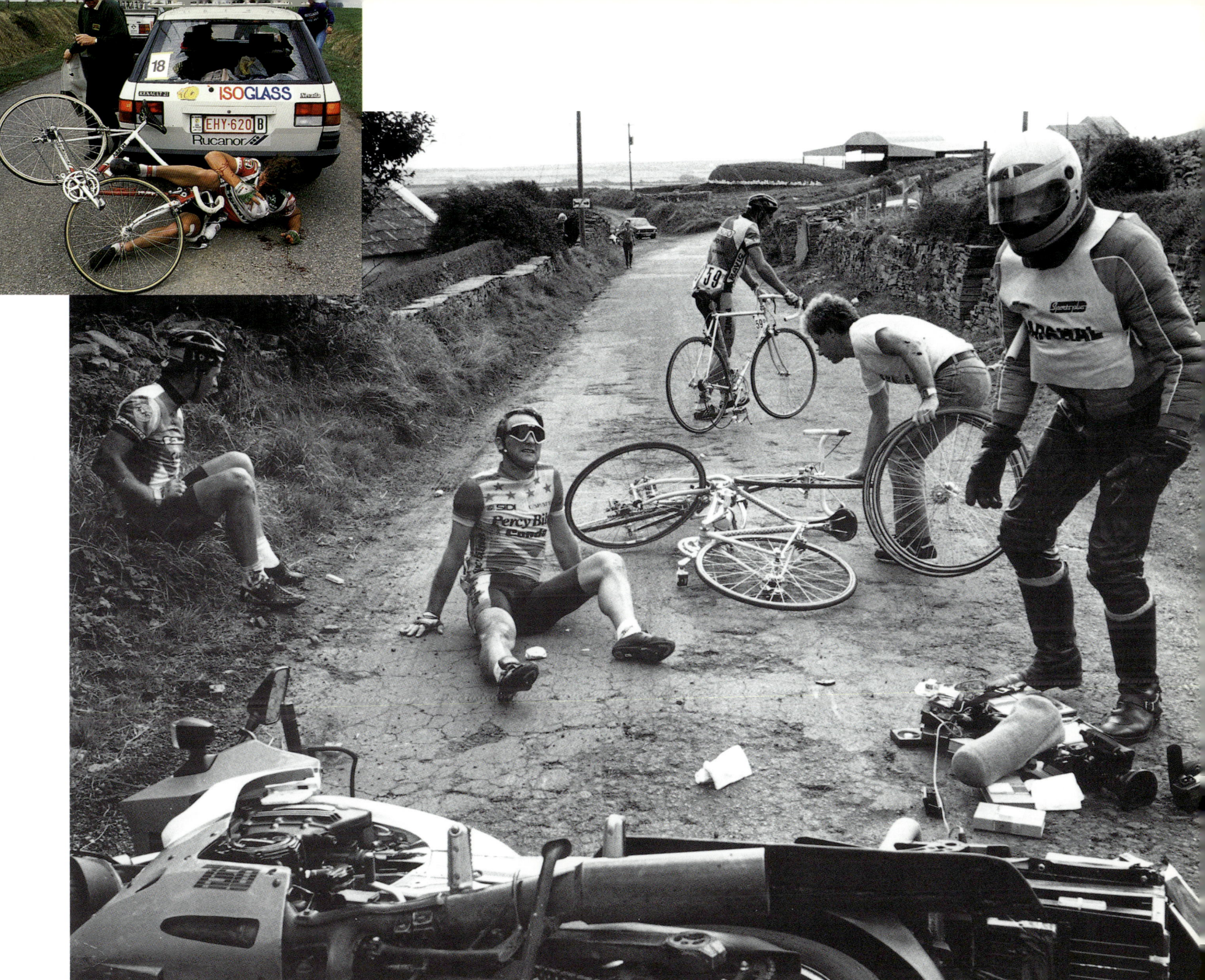

1988: LIÈGE-BASTOGNE-LIÈGE: BELGIUM

American sprinter Davis Phinney "escaped" with multiple facial lacerations after crashing head-first into a team vehicle when chasing back to the peloton after an earlier pileup.

1986: NISSAN CLASSIC: CLIFFS OF MOHR, IRELAND

A motorcycle goes down on a narrow Irish back road, destroying a TV camera and leaving riders like Englishman John Herety (sitting on the road) stunned by the impact.

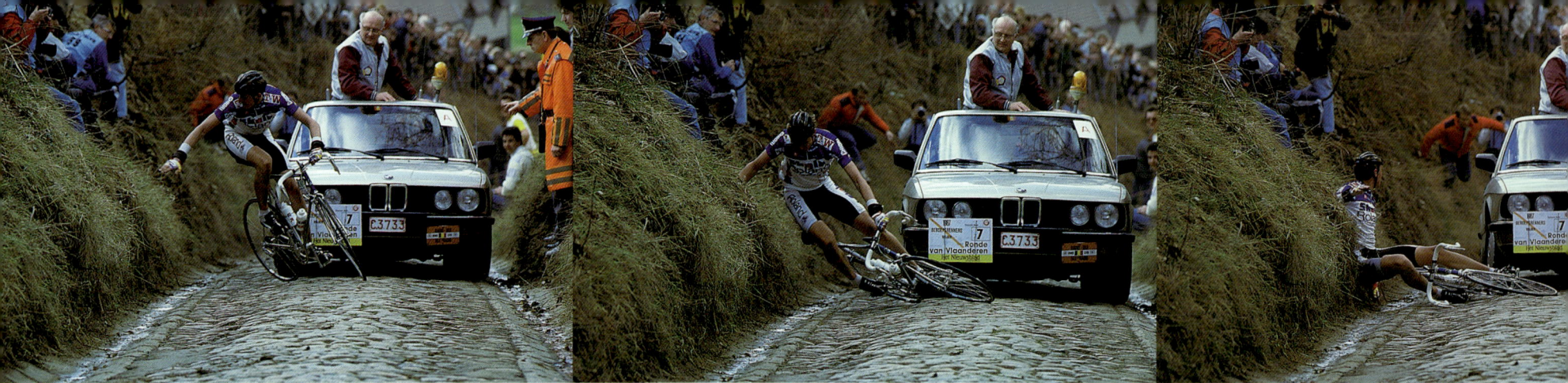

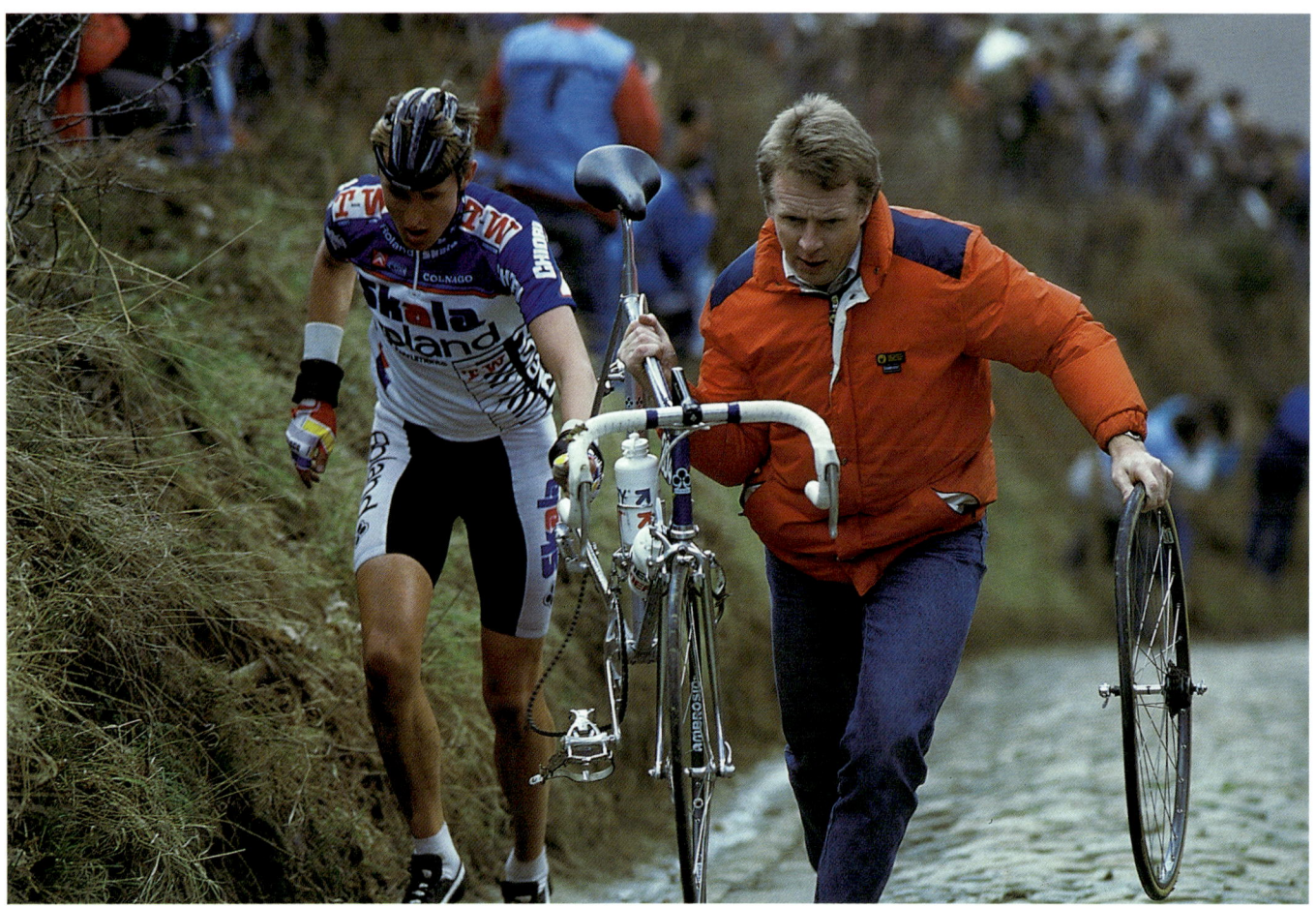

1987: TOUR OF FLANDERS: BELGIUM

Nearing the end of a long solo breakaway in the Tour of Flanders, Dane Jesper Skibby lost his balance on the 25-percent cobbles of the Koppenberg — and watched in horror as the race director's car drove over his bike, and nearly his leg!

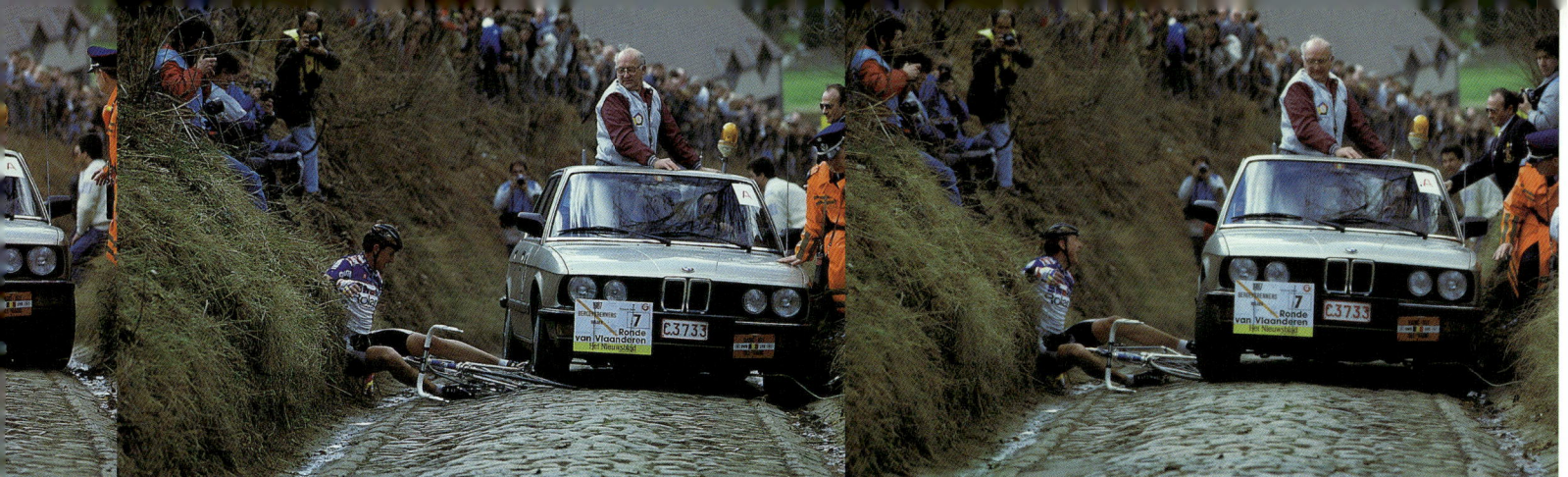

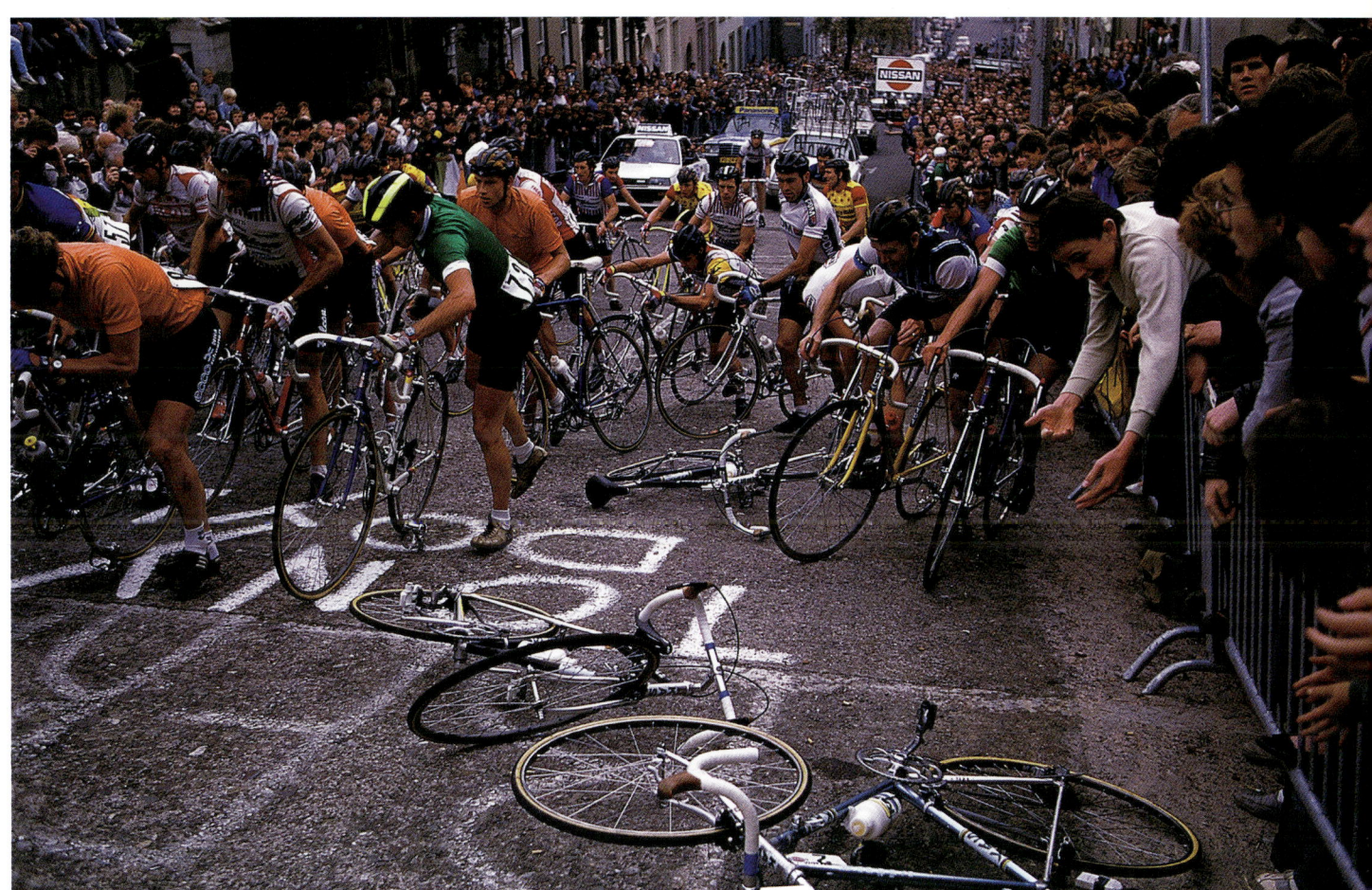

1986: NISSAN CLASSIC: CORK, IRELAND

The wrong end of the pack near the top of St. Patrick's Hill in Cork: no cobbles here, but a grade that is almost 30 percent!

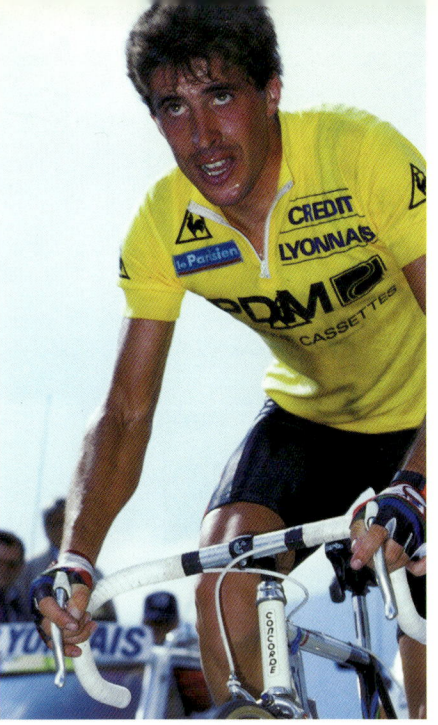
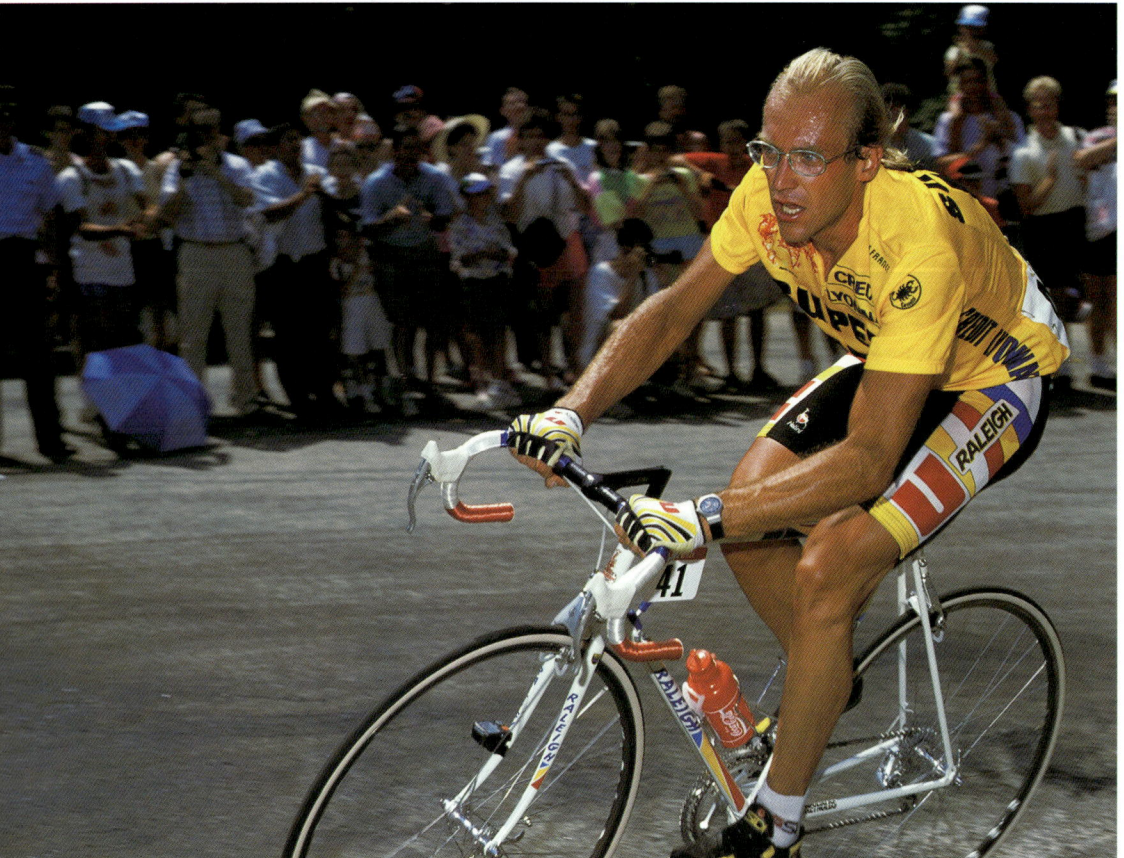
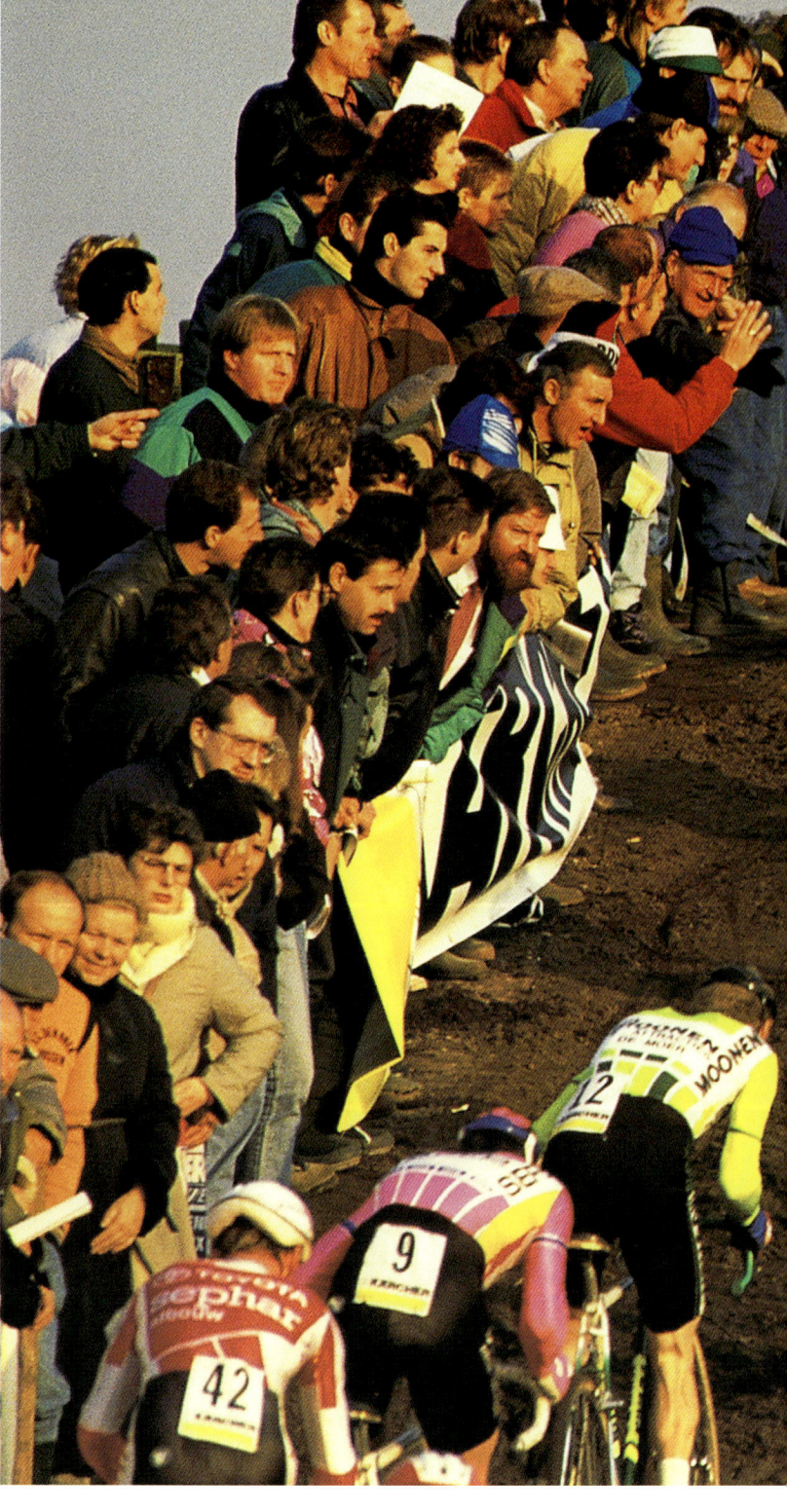

1987: TOUR DE FRANCE: FRENCH ALPS

Spanish climber Pedro Delgado (top) was leading the 1987 Tour when he made a strong attack on the uphill finish to La Plagne, but Stephen Roche fought back to limit his losses and three stages later claimed the yellow jersey in a time trial at Dijon.

1989: TOUR DE FRANCE: FRENCH ALPS

Another rider destined to lose the yellow jersey he wore in the Alps was Frenchman Laurent Fignon. He, too, lost it in a time trial: the famous Versailles-Paris stage that earned Greg LeMond the final victory by eight seconds.

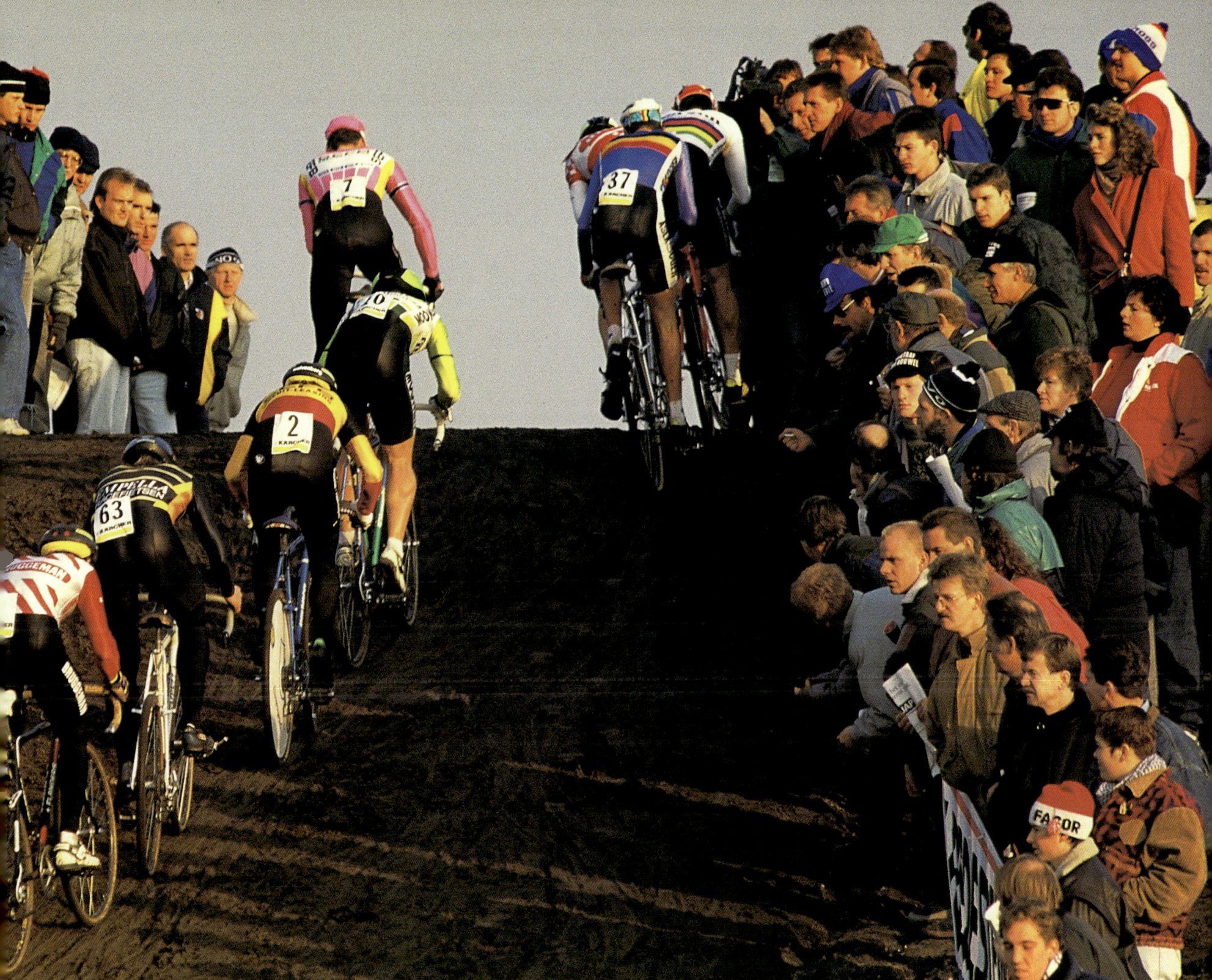

1990: SUPERPRESTIGE CYCLO-CROSS: VALKENSWAARD, THE NETHERLANDS

The author was always happy when the road season ended in October—so he could go off to the Continent again and shoot cyclo-cross.

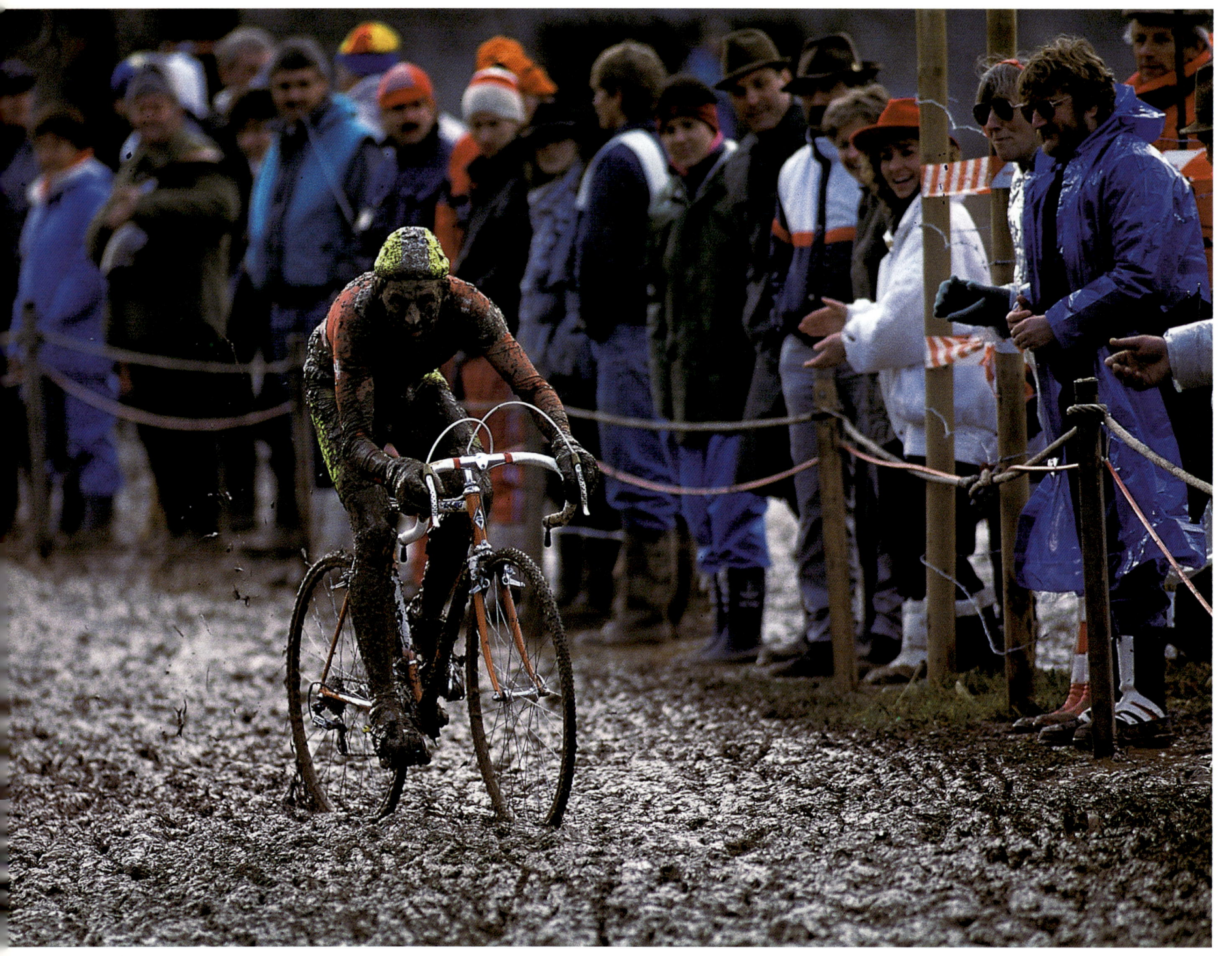

1988: WORLD CYCLO-CROSS CHAMPIONSHIPS: HÄGENDORF, SWITZERLAND

Riders change bikes and have them washed by support staff every lap in a cyclo-cross race, but mud like this soon dirties them again. Swiss rider Beat Breu went on to finish third in this 1988 World Championship.

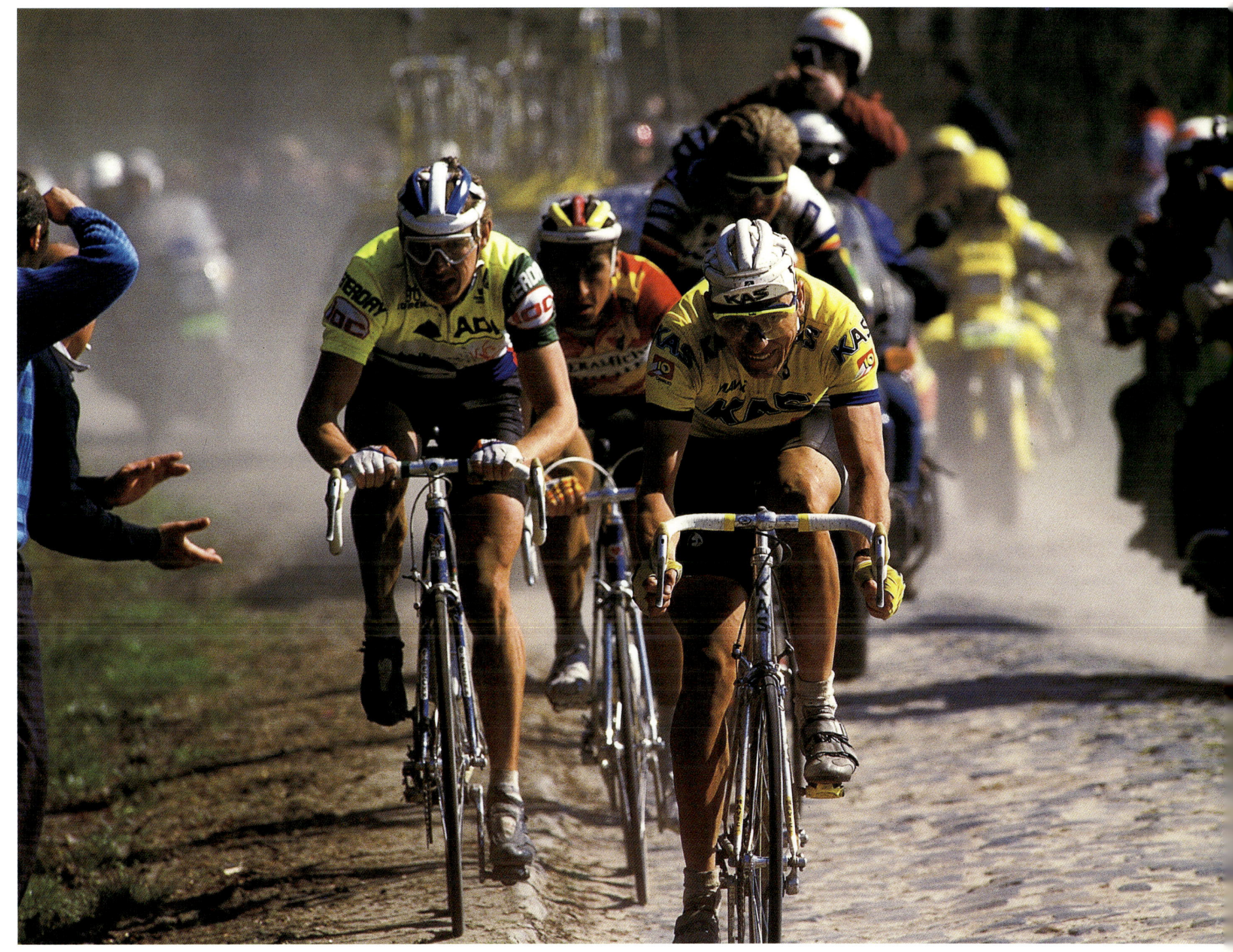

1988: PARIS-ROUBAIX: FRANCE

One of the author's favorite photos: Thomas "The Tank" Wegmüller of Switzerland led a long, long breakaway at the 1988 Paris-Roubaix that resulted in a shocking win for Belgian Dirk Demol (left)—who is now an assistant director of the U.S. Postal Service team.

1986 TO 1990

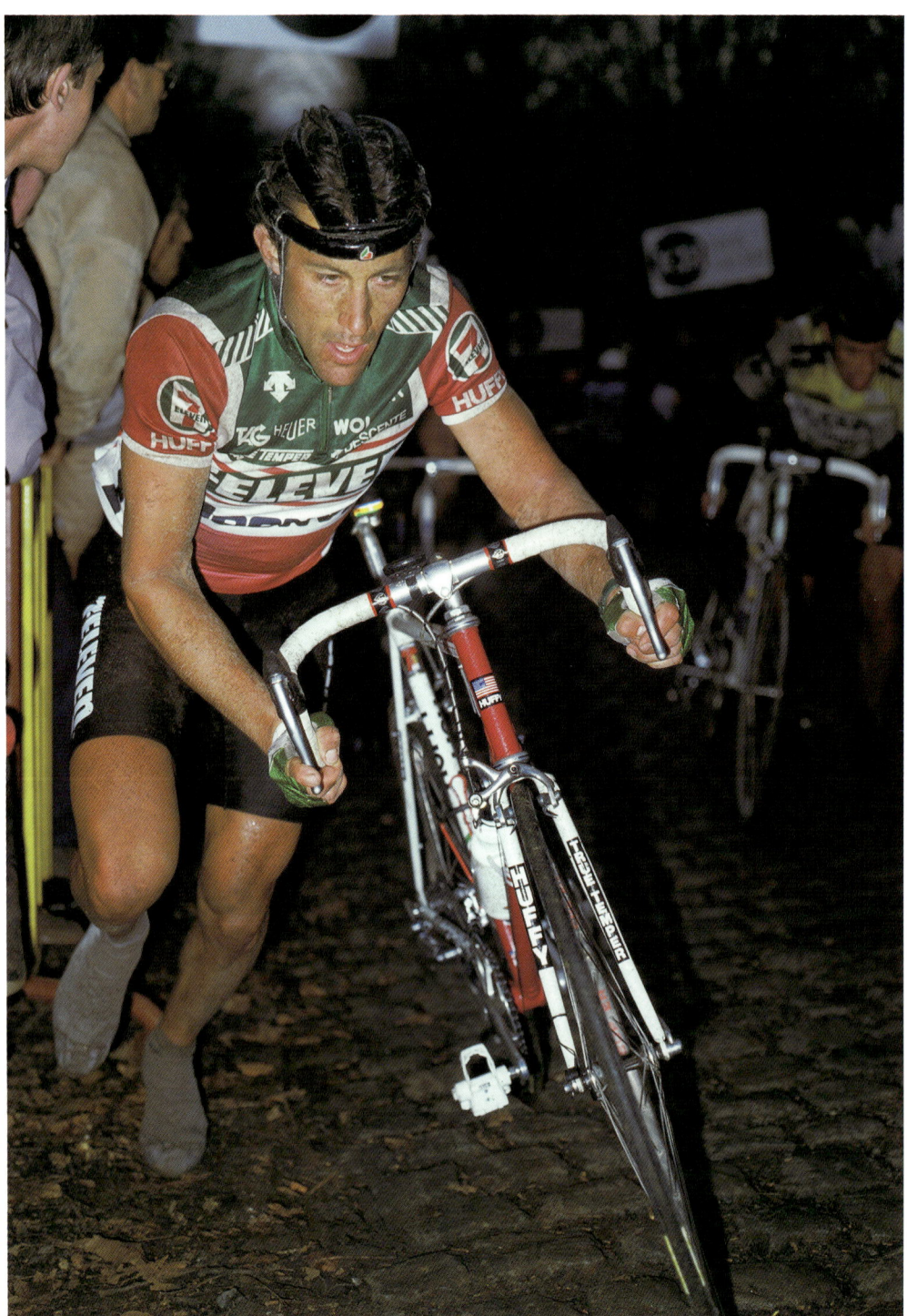

1986: GHENT-WEVELGEM: BELGIUM

No, Jonathan Boyer's not doing cyclo-cross, he has to jog his bike up the wet cobblestones of the Kemmelberg.

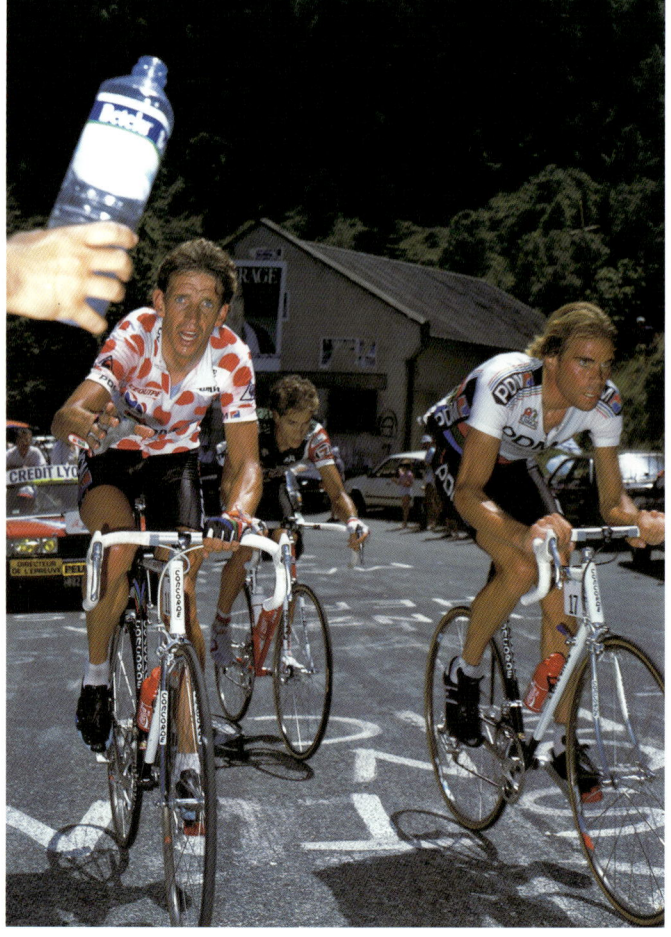

1988: TOUR DE FRANCE: FRENCH ALPS

The Dutch had a great Tour de France in 1988, with Steven Rooks (left) finishing second overall and winning the best climber's polka-dot jersey, while friend and teammate Gert-Jan Theunisse came in fourth overall.

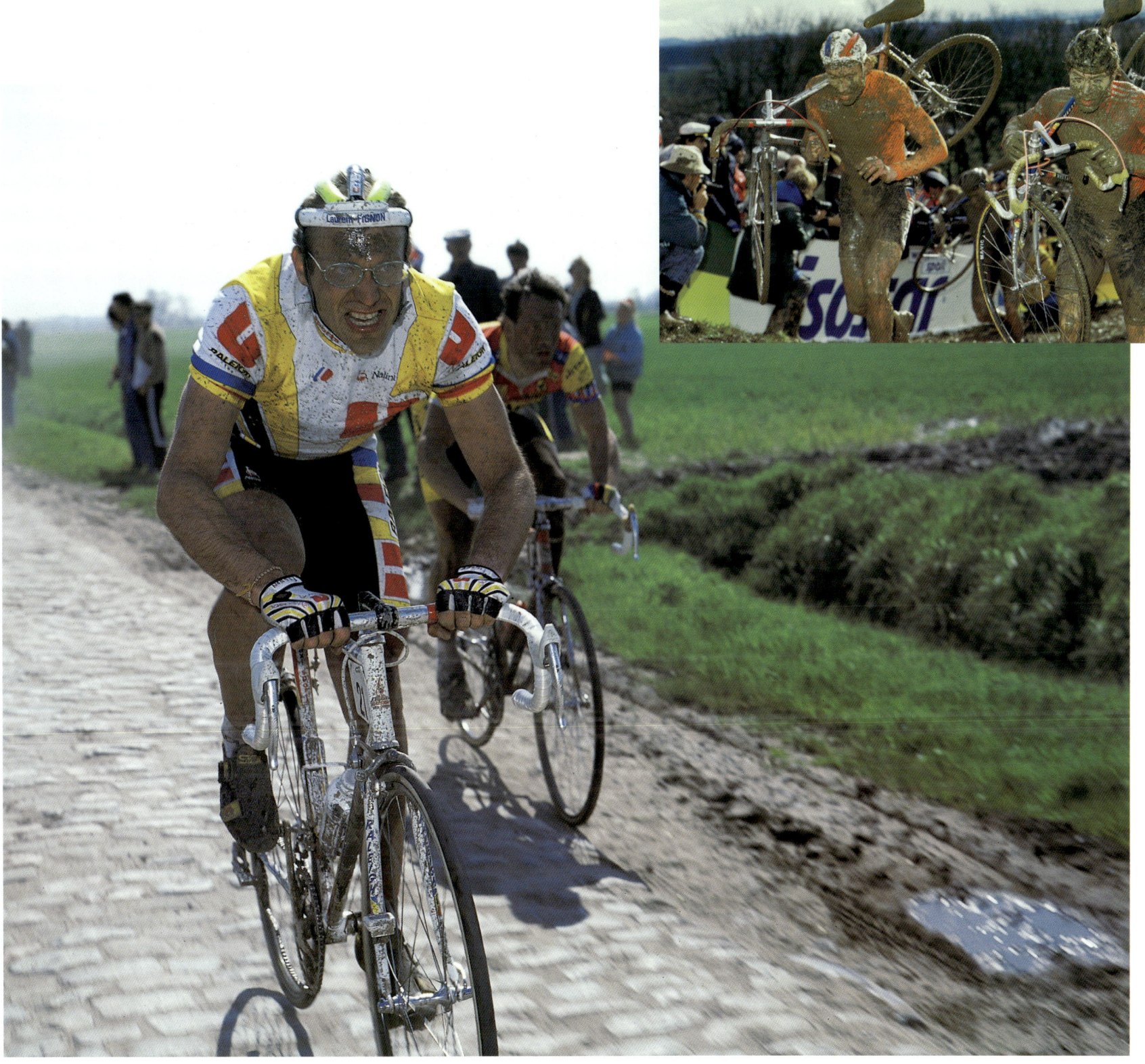

1989: PARIS-ROUBAIX: FRANCE

Beside winning the Tour and the Giro, Laurent Fignon was a great one-day classics rider—as he showed with a gutsy attack at the 1989 Paris-Roubaix.

1988: WORLD CYCLO-CROSS CHAMPIONSHIPS: HÄGENDORF, SWITZERLAND

Although Adri Van der Poel (left) and Pascal Richard both won stages of the Tour de France, they were also world champions in cyclo-cross. Here, Richard (right) is on his way to defeating Van der Poel for the 1988 crown.

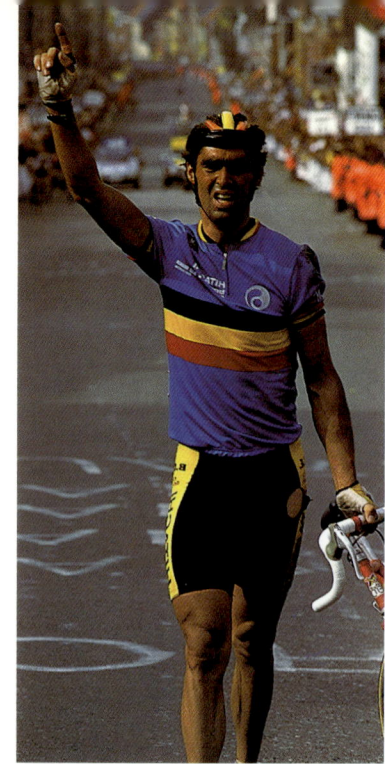

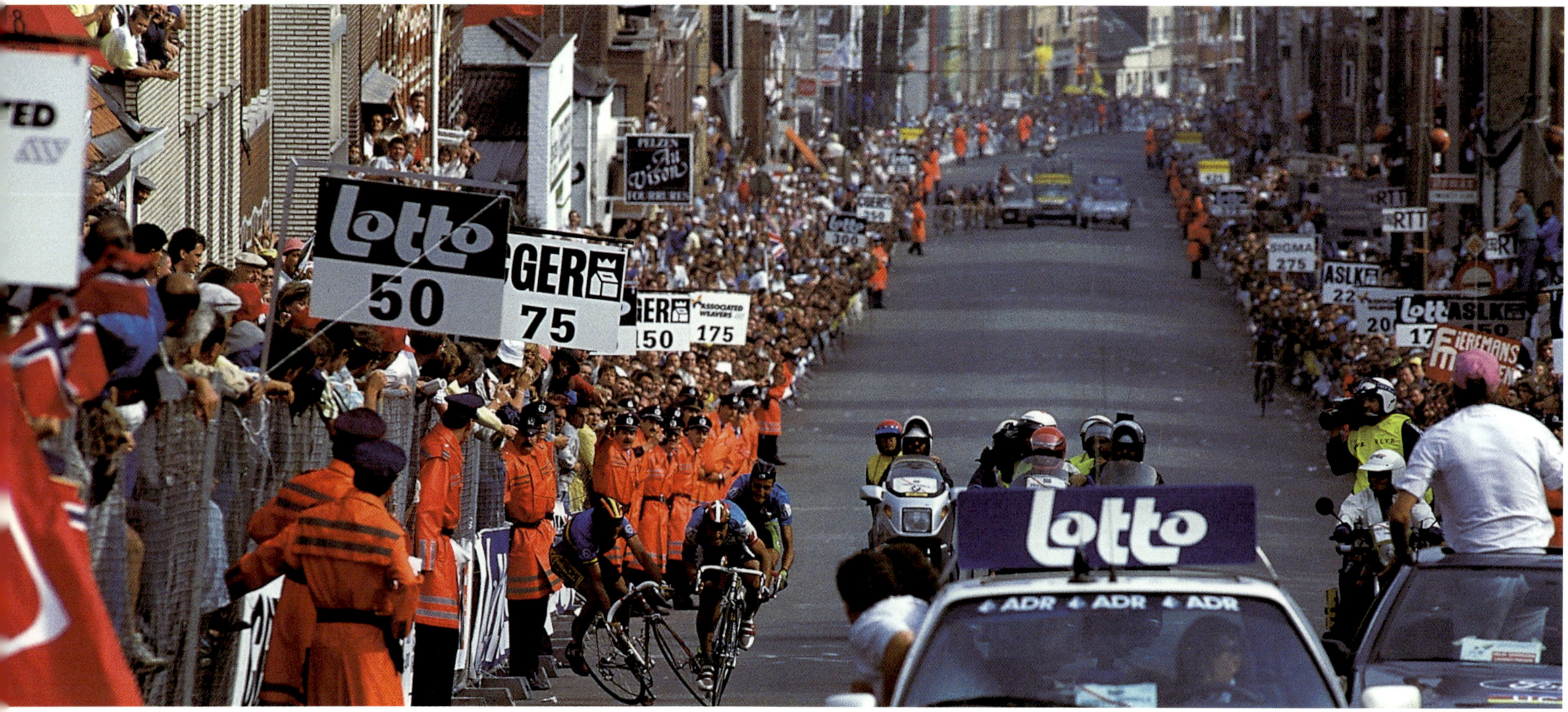

1988: WORLD ROAD CHAMPIONSHIPS: RENAIX, BELGIUM

The controversial sprint at the 1988 world's: Canadian Steve Bauer (right) and Belgian Claude Criquielion were sprinting for the title when their bikes collided, forcing Criquielion to the street, causing Bauer to slow, and allowing Italian Maurizio Fondriest to come past and win. Criquielion (top) protested the result and later sued Bauer for damages (unsuccessfully).

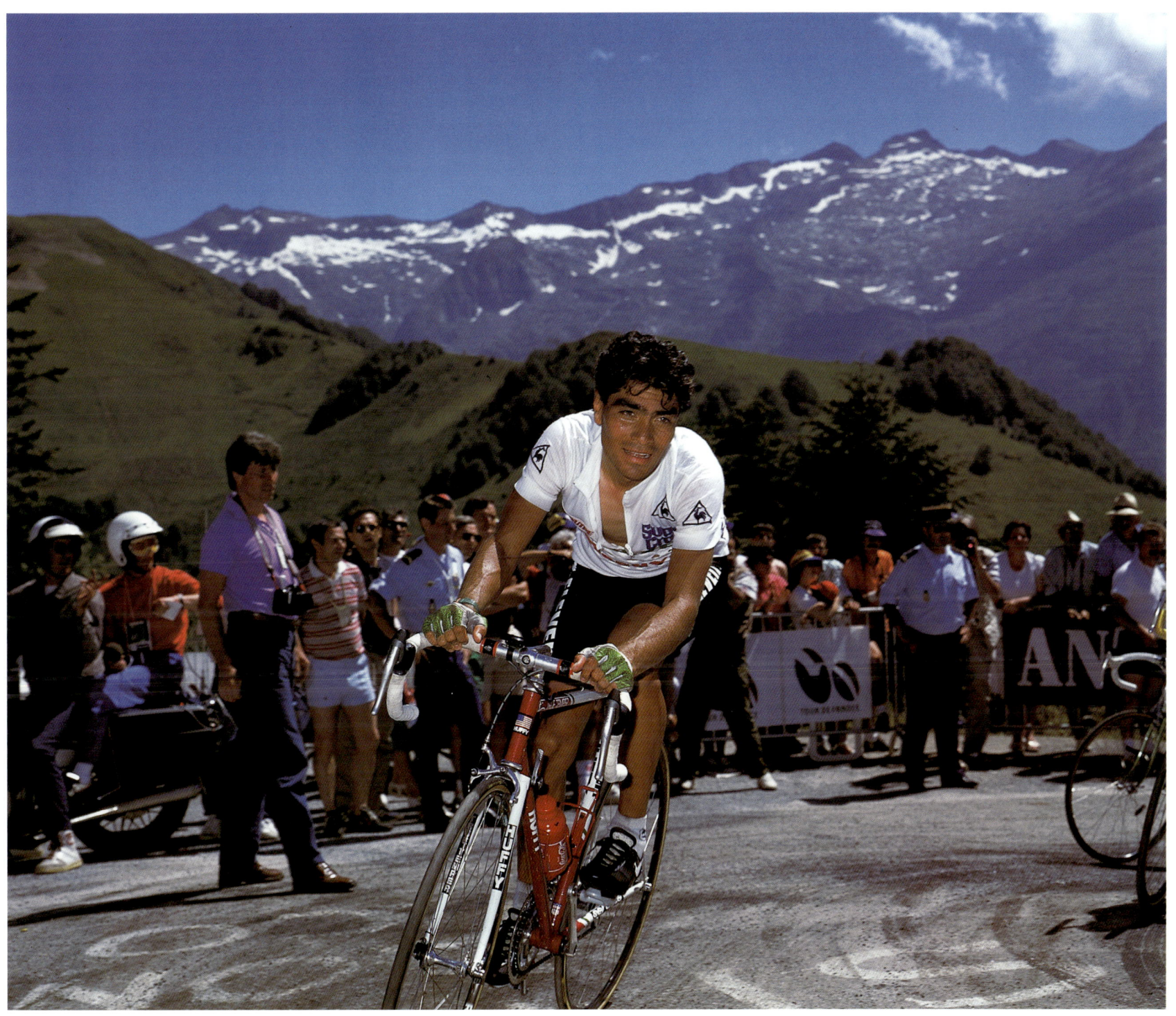

1988: TOUR DE FRANCE: GUZET-NEIGE

Mexican Raúl Alcalá had a fairy-tale ride in the Tour de France, when he won the best young rider's white jersey in 1987. He would go on to win two stages of the Tour, the only Mexican to do so.

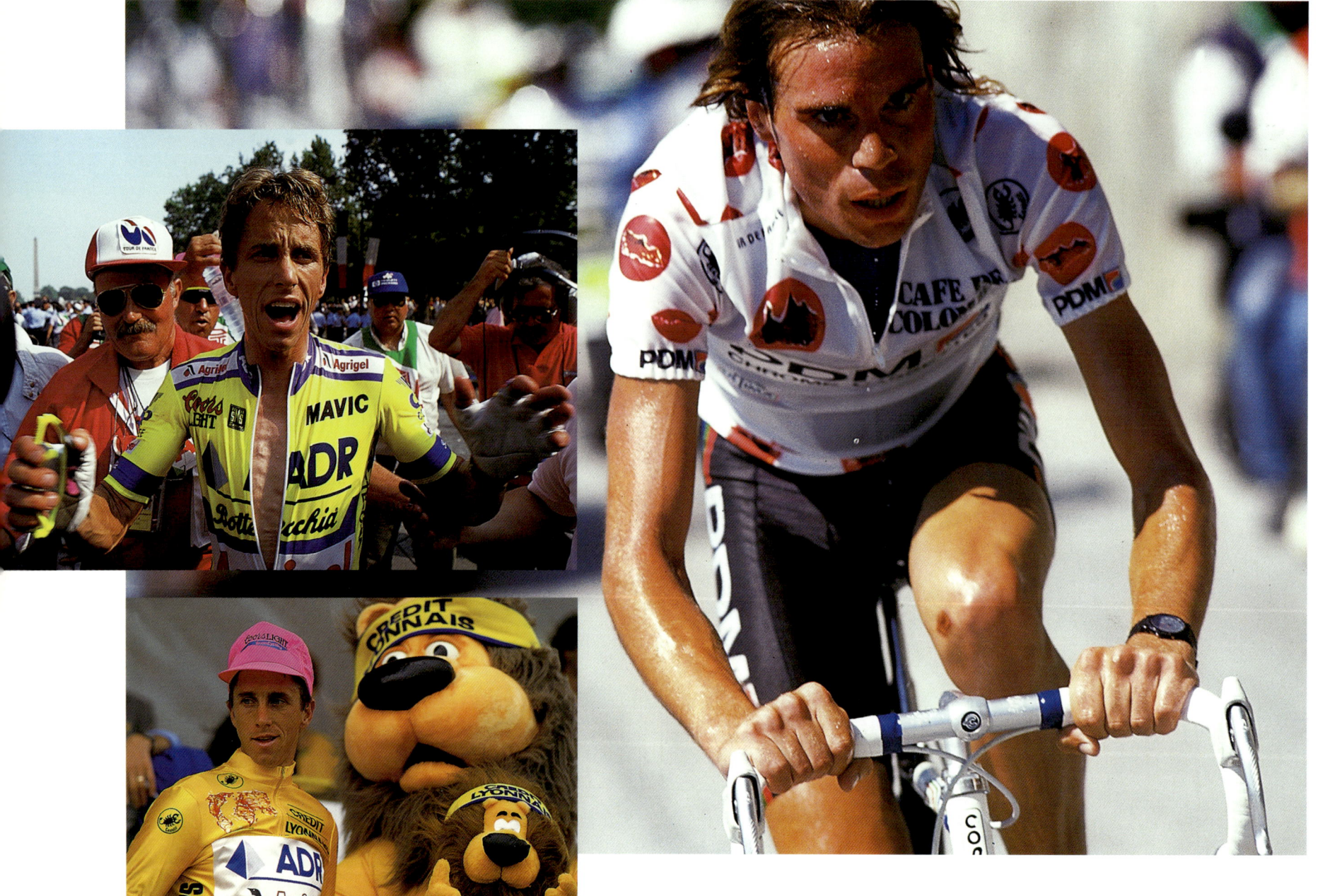

1989: TOUR DE FRANCE: PARIS

The author captured the excitement and disbelief on Greg LeMond's face when he realized he'd won the Tour by eight seconds. Later, with the main sponsor's mascot, the Crédit Lyonnais lion, the American still seems in a state of shock.

1989: TOUR DE FRANCE: L'ALPE D'HUEZ

Gert-Jan Theunisse of the Netherlands had his finest hour when he won the Alpe d'Huez stage of the Tour wearing the polka-dot jersey.

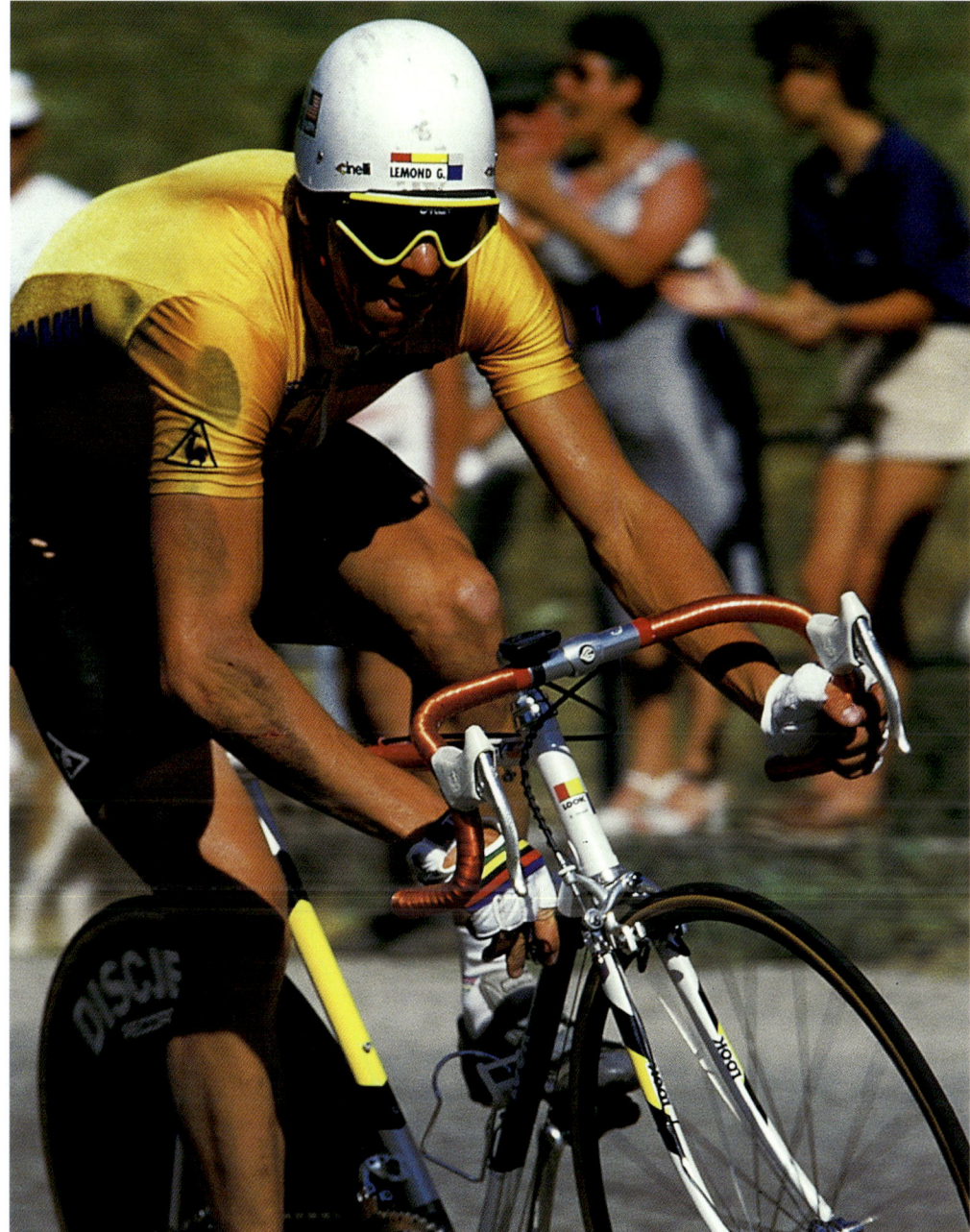

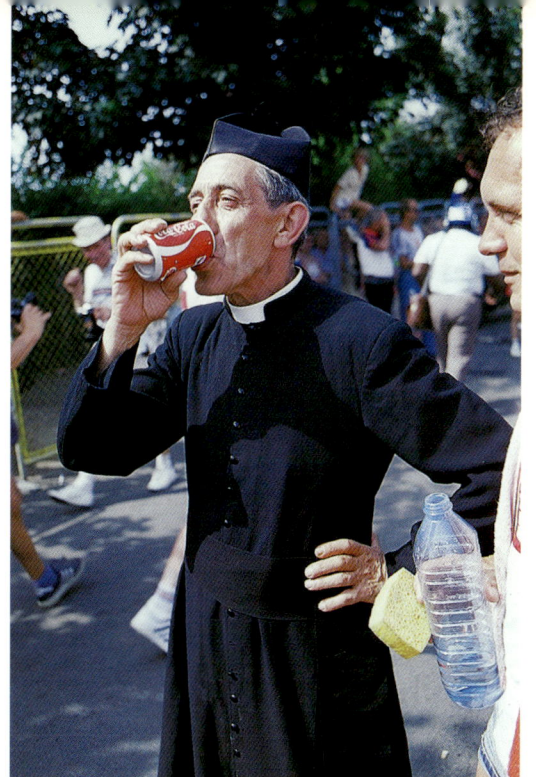

1986: TOUR DE FRANCE: ST. ETIENNE

Despite a fall on a sharp turn, Greg LeMond defended his yellow jersey in the 1986 Tour's final time trial over teammate Bernard Hinault.

1988: TOUR DE FRANCE: ON THE ROAD

One of the Tour sponsor's products gets divine endorsement during a heat wave.

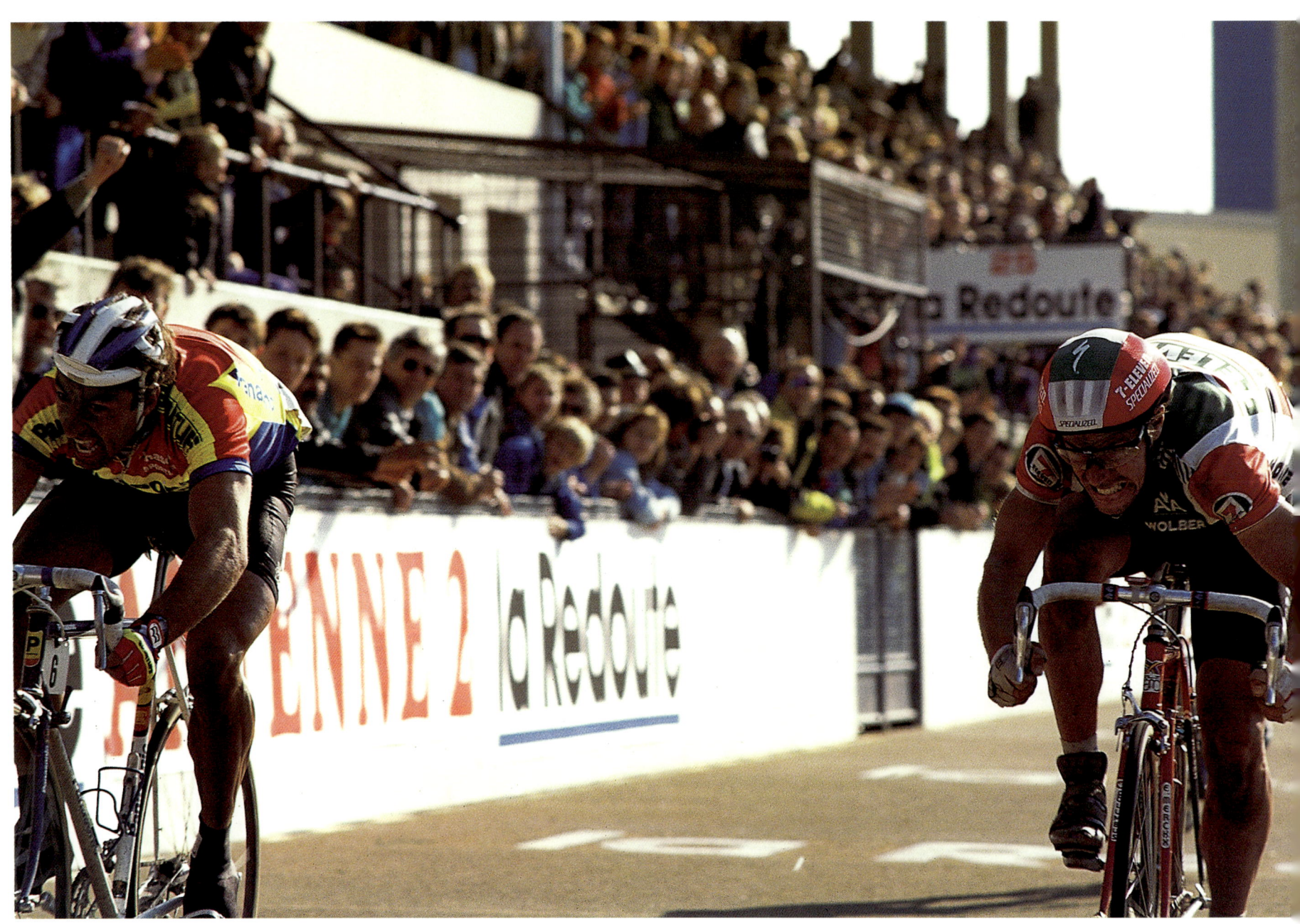

1990: PARIS-ROUBAIX: FRANCE

After racing for more than seven hours over the cobblestones and farm roads of northern France, only a centimeter separated winner Eddy Planckaert of Belgium (left) and Steve Bauer, the unlucky Canadian, in the sprint at the Roubaix Velodrome.

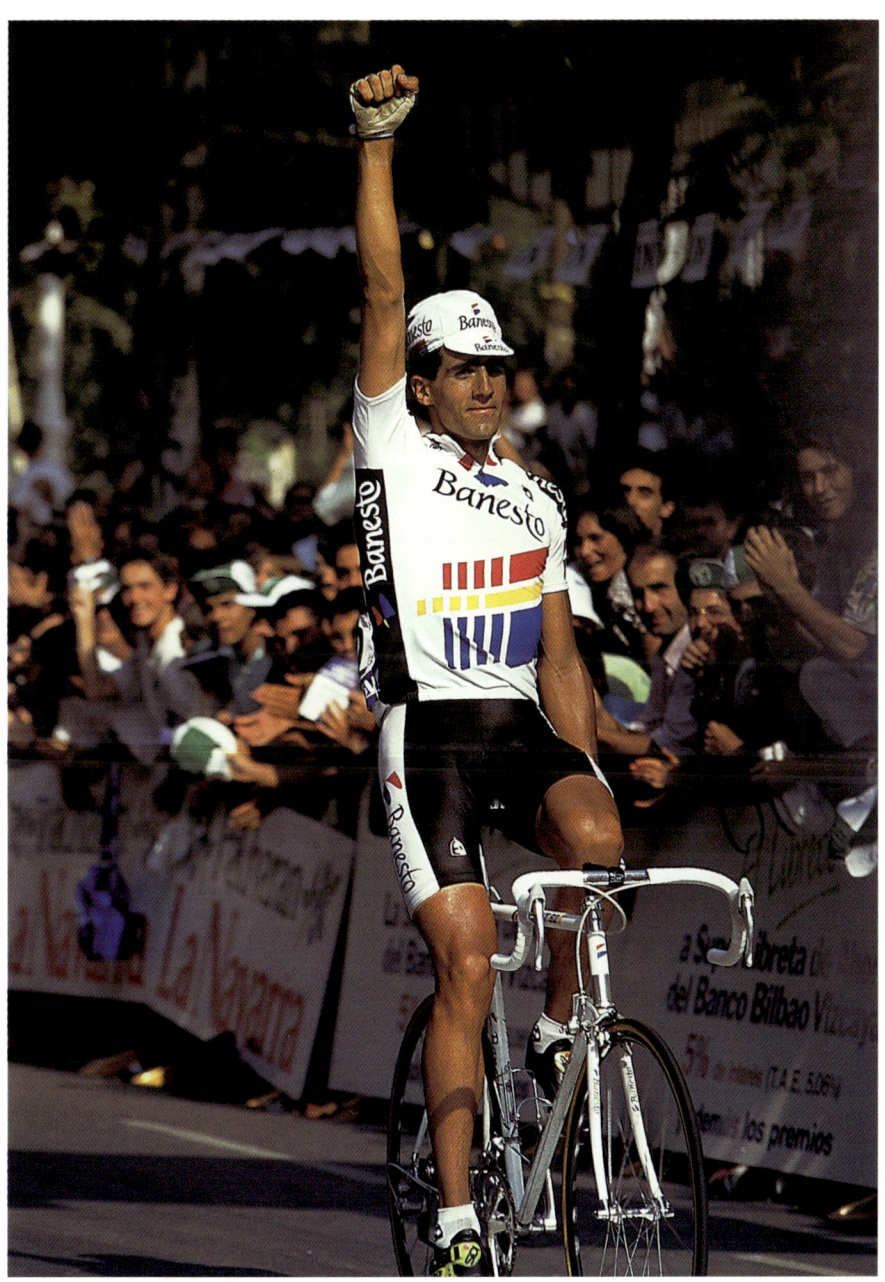

1990: CLASICA SAN SEBASTIAN: SPAIN

Before he took the first of his five consecutive Tour de France wins, Spaniard Miguel Induráin won his national World Cup classic at San Sebastian in a solo break.

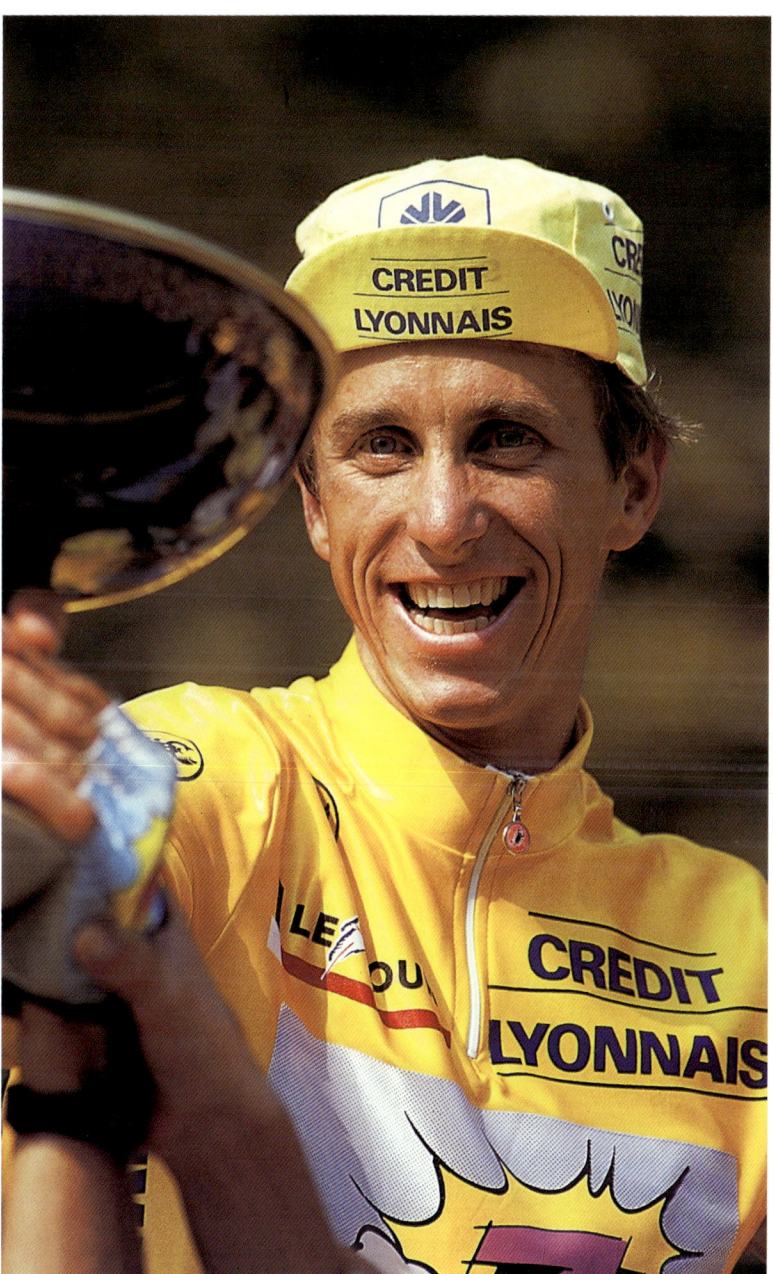

1990: TOUR DE FRANCE: PARIS

Greg LeMond celebrated his third victory at the Tour de France in 1990. Without his shotgun accident in 1987 he would probably have win five successive Tours, like Induráin.

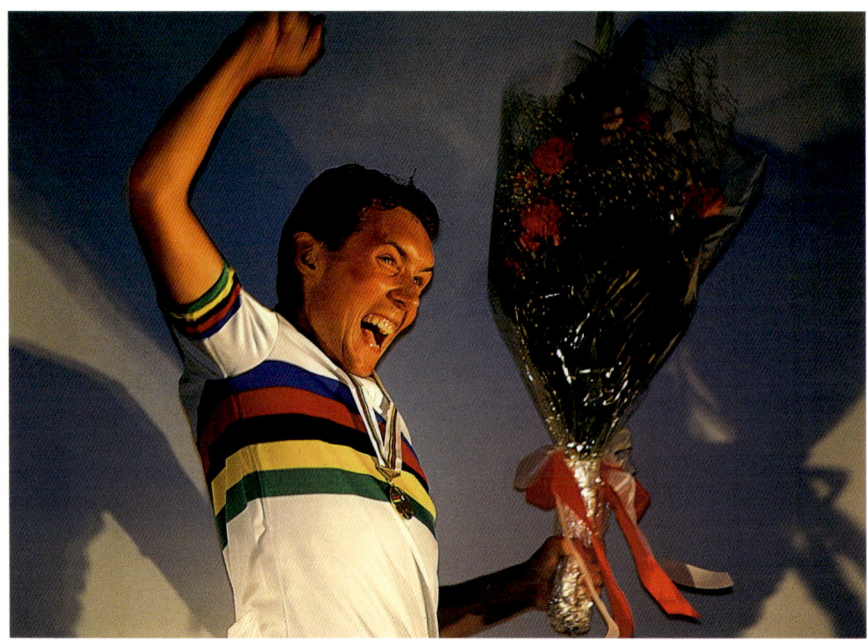

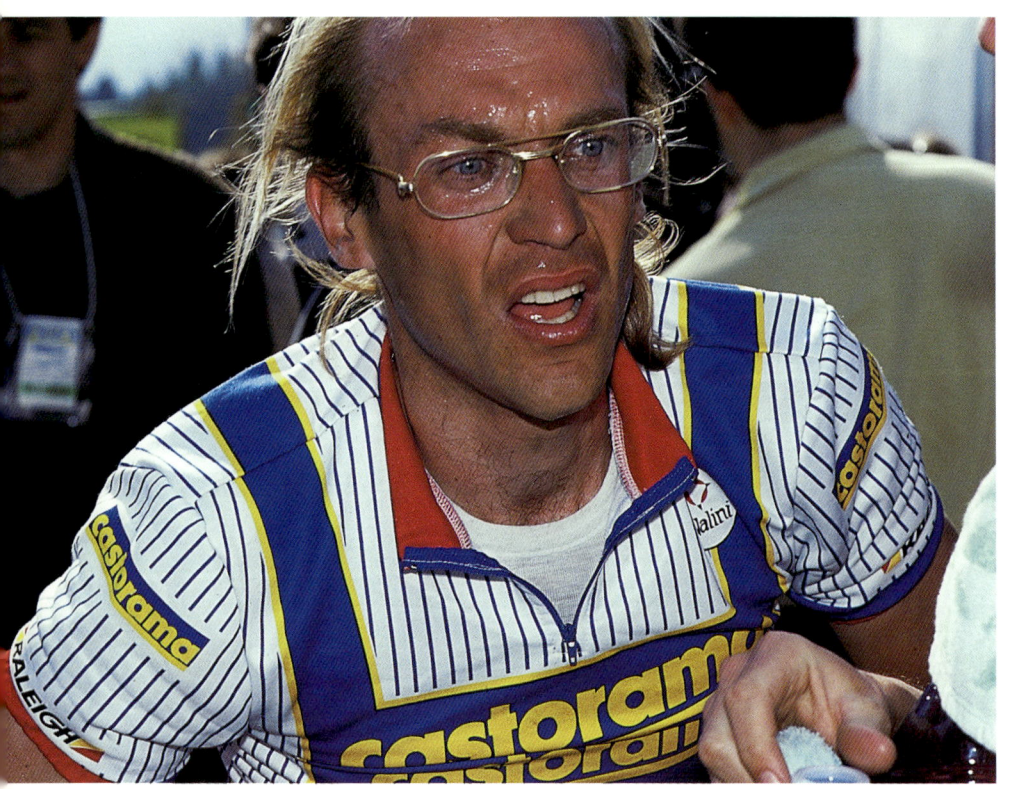

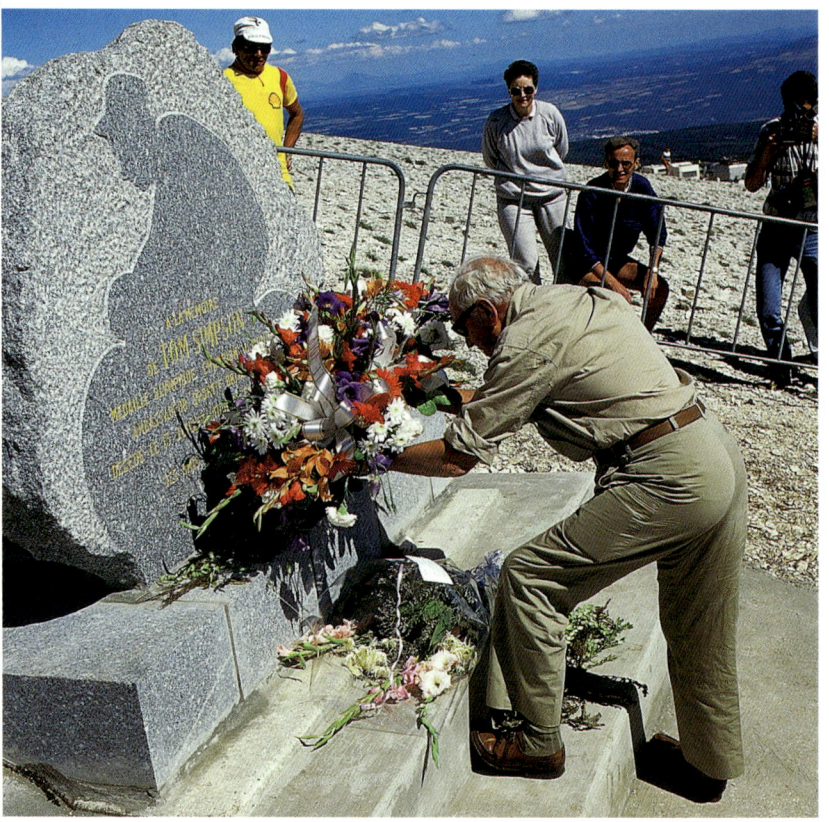

1990: WORLD ROAD CHAMPIONSHIPS: UTSUNOMIYA, JAPAN

Mirko Gualdi (top) celebrated in Japan after winning the 1990 world amateur road title—an event that became restricted to non-professional under-23 riders in 1996.

1990: PARIS-NICE: MONT FARON

Paris-Nice was not a race that agreed with Laurent Fignon. He never won France's early-season stage race.

1987: TOUR DE FRANCE: MONT VENTOUX

Twenty years after English star Tom Simpson collapsed and died on the barren slopes of Mont Ventoux, race director Jacques Goddet laid a wreath on the granite memorial stone just above the spot where Simpson fell.

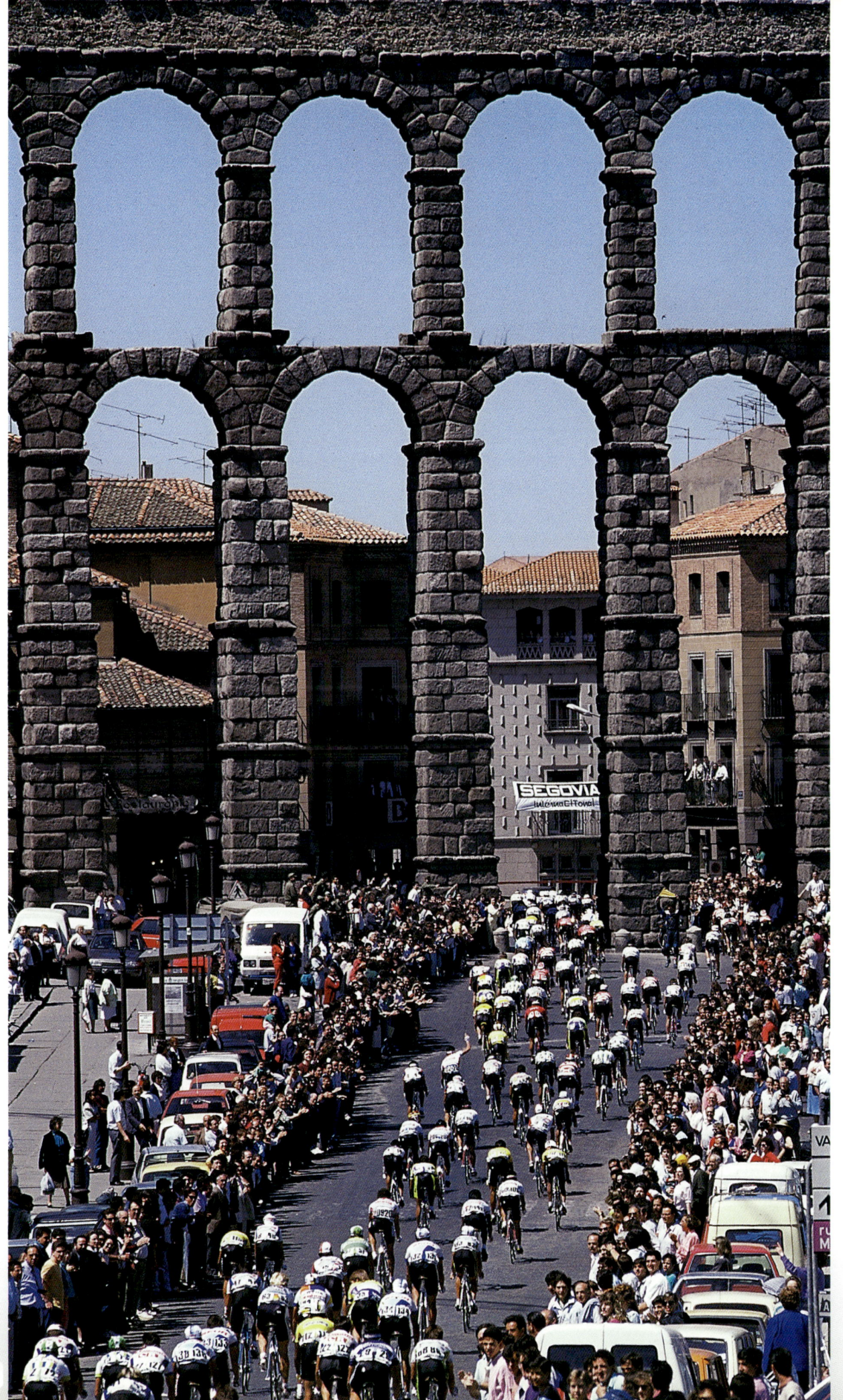

1989: VUELTA A ESPAÑA: SEGOVIA, SPAIN

Stage 21 of the '89 Vuelta passed below the city of Segovia's 2000-year-old Roman aqueduct.

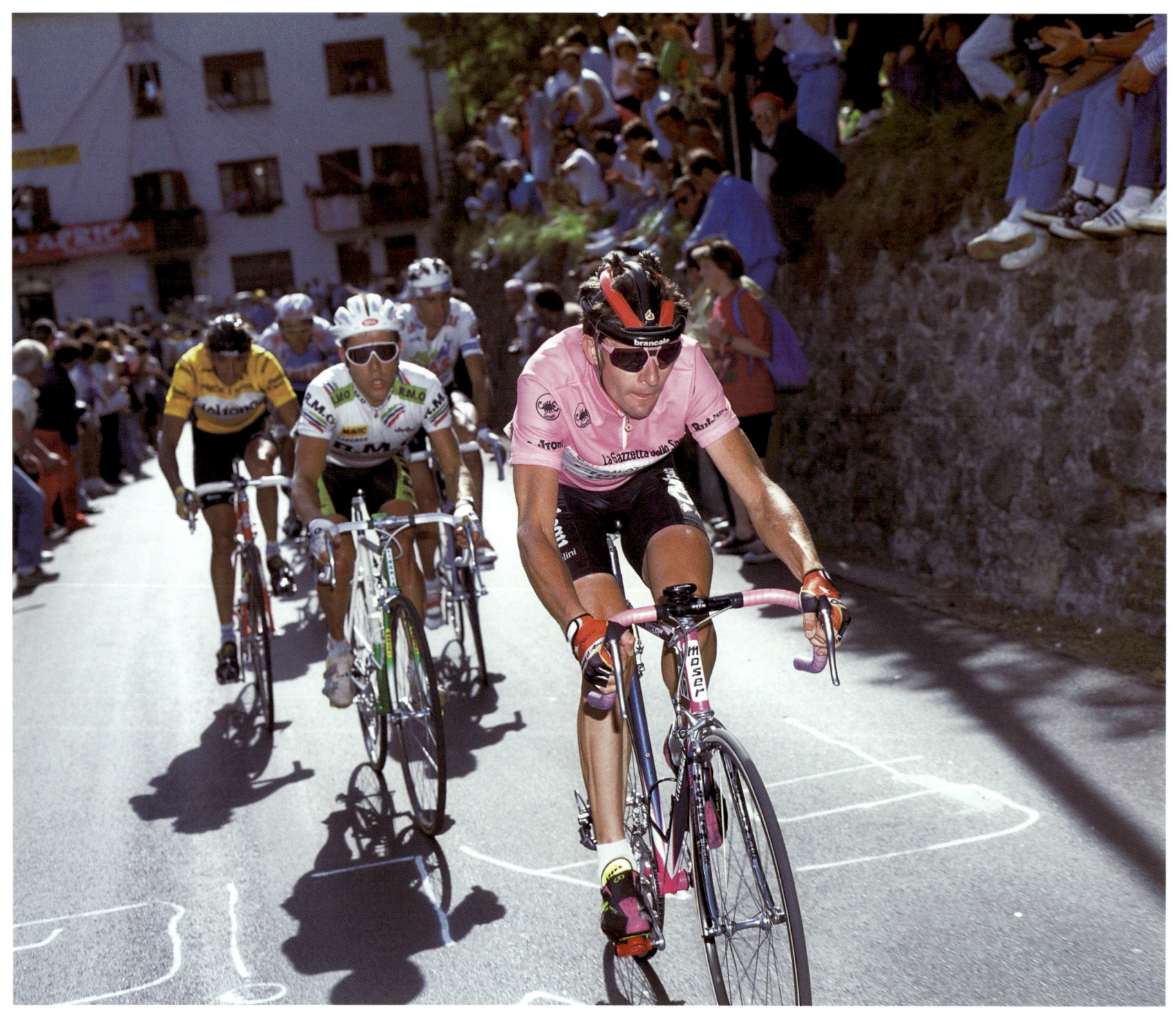

1990 GIRO D'ITALIA: THE ITALIAN ALPS

Gianni Bugno led the 1990 Giro from start to finish of the 20-day race, finishing 6:33 ahead of runner-up Charly Mottet of France—who is riding behind Bugno on the climb to Aprica.

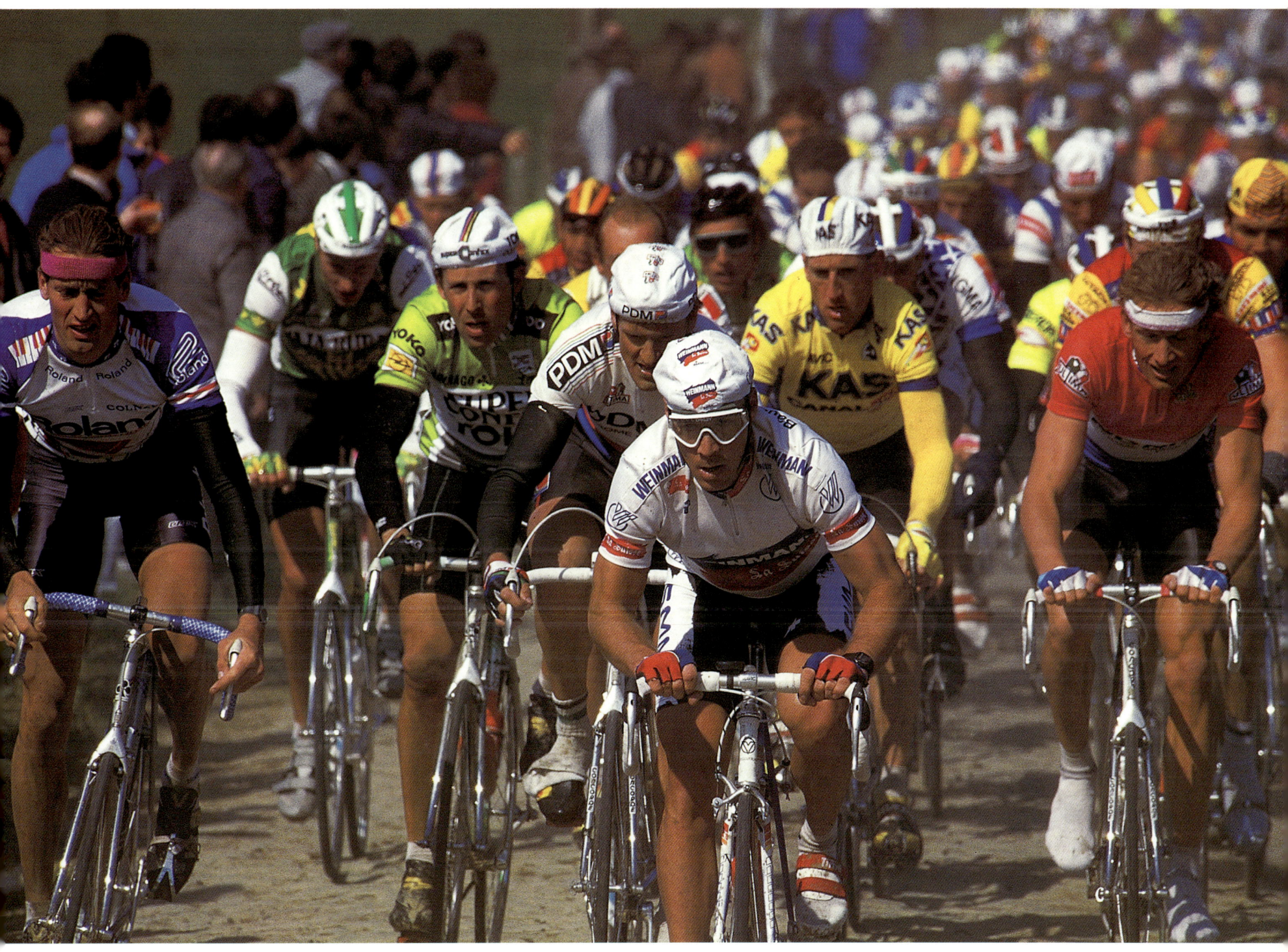

1988: PARIS-ROUBAIX: FRANCE

Three specialists of Paris-Roubaix lead the peloton as it heads toward the cobbles: Steve Bauer (in white) leads Sean Kelly (in yellow) and Adri Van der Poel (in headband, on right). Getting to the front of the pack is more vital in the French classic than any other one-day race.

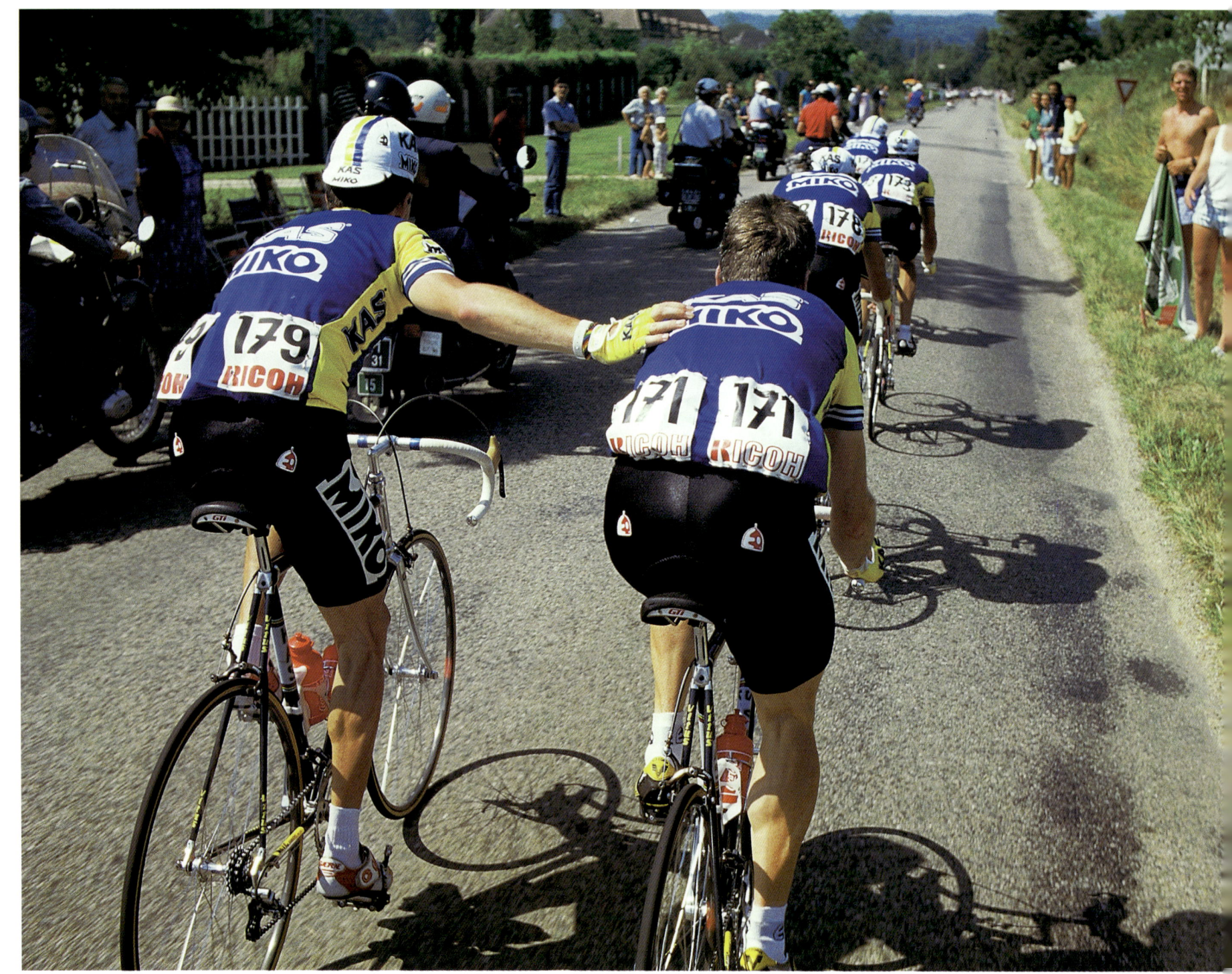

1987: TOUR DE FRANCE: DORDOGNE

After a crash on the Brive-Bordeaux stage of the 1987 Tour de France, Sean Kelly was helped back to the peloton by his Kas teammates. Unfortunately, his injuries forced him to quit the race, and the stage into Bordeaux was won by American Davis Phinney.

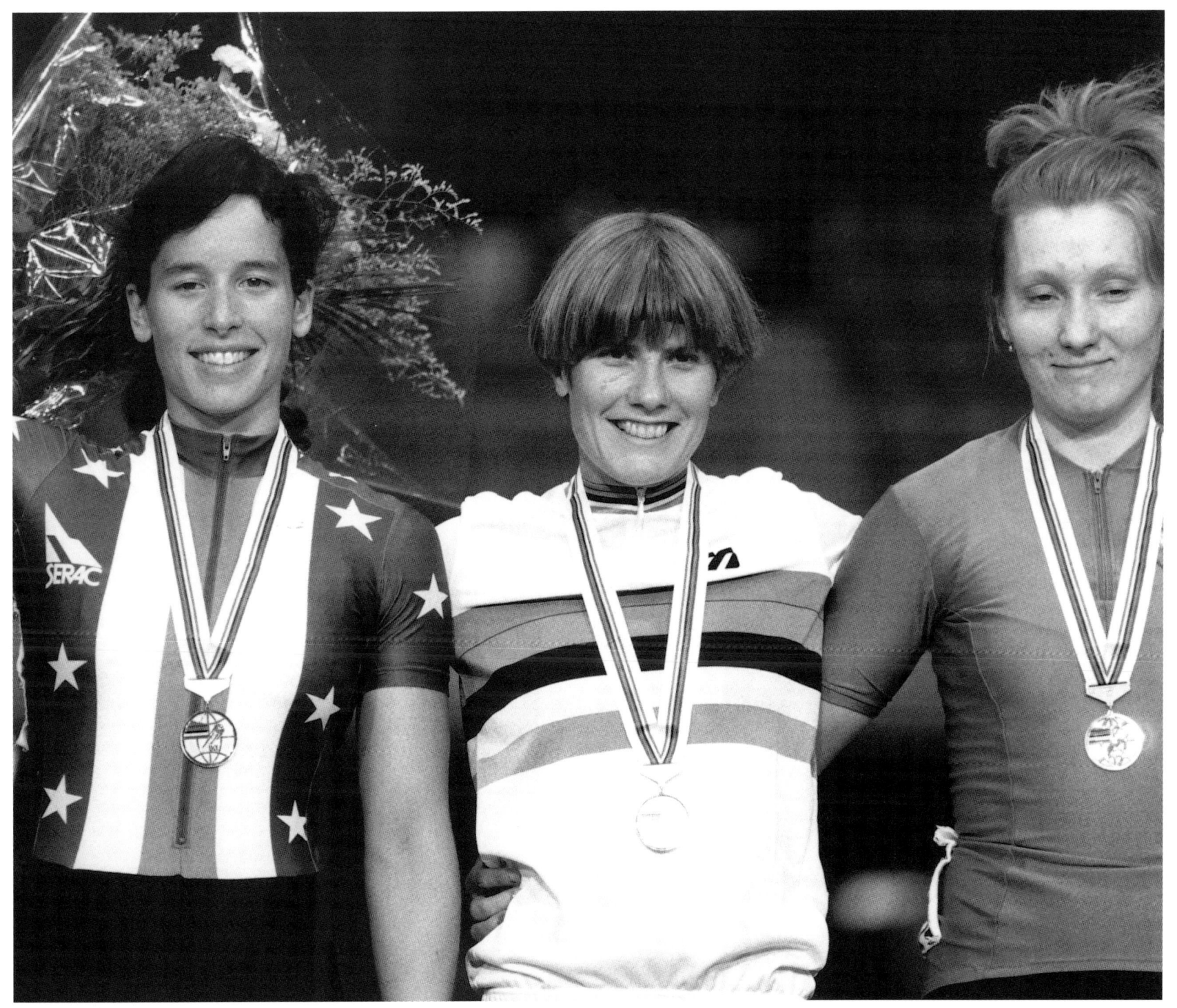

1990: WORLD TRACK CHAMPIONSHIPS: MAEBASHI, JAPAN

Connie Paraskevin won her fourth world sprint title in 1990, sharing the podium with teammate Renée Duprel (left) and Russian Rita Rasmaite.

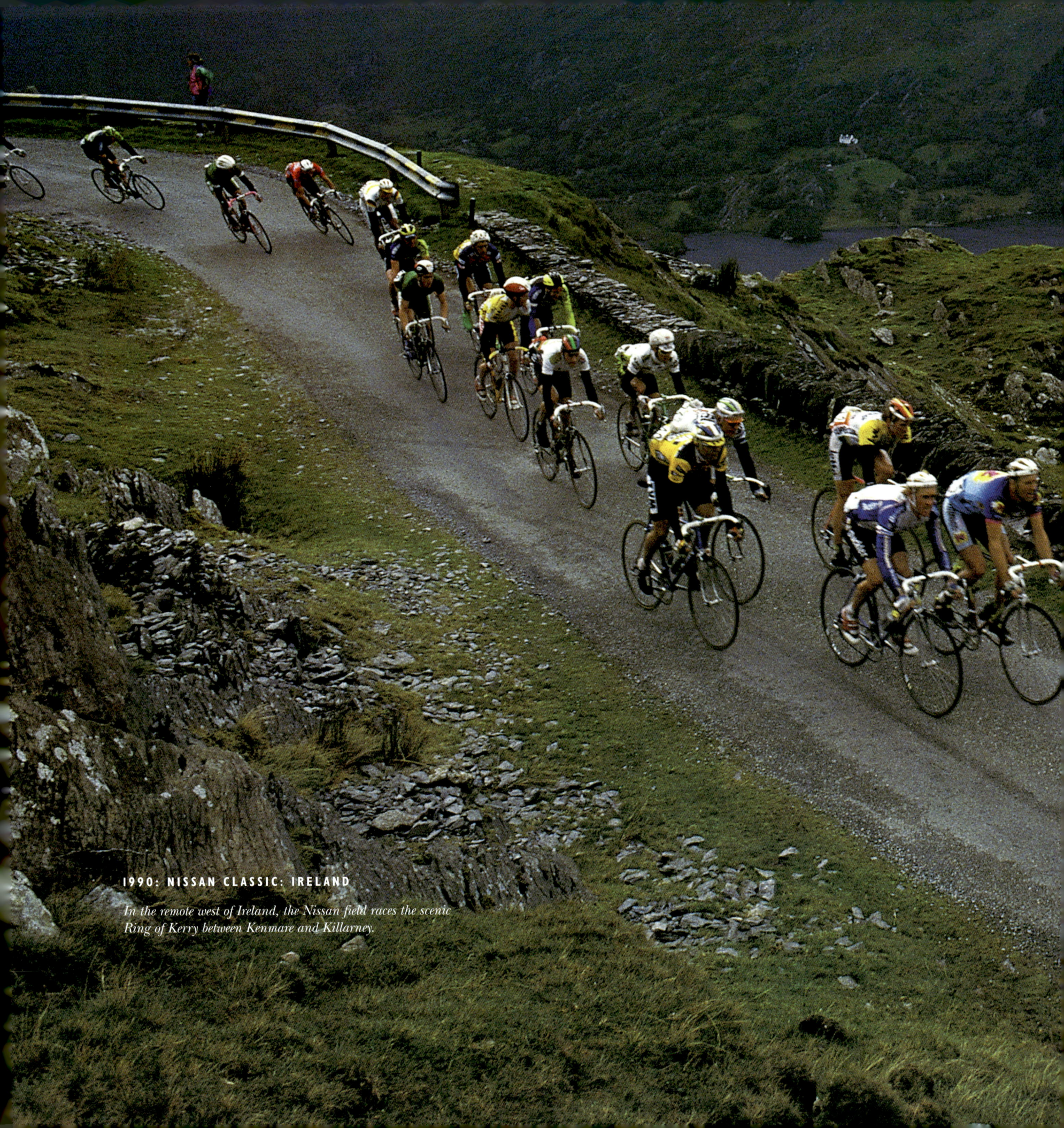

1990: NISSAN CLASSIC: IRELAND

In the remote west of Ireland, the Nissan field races the scenic Ring of Kerry between Kenmare and Killarney.

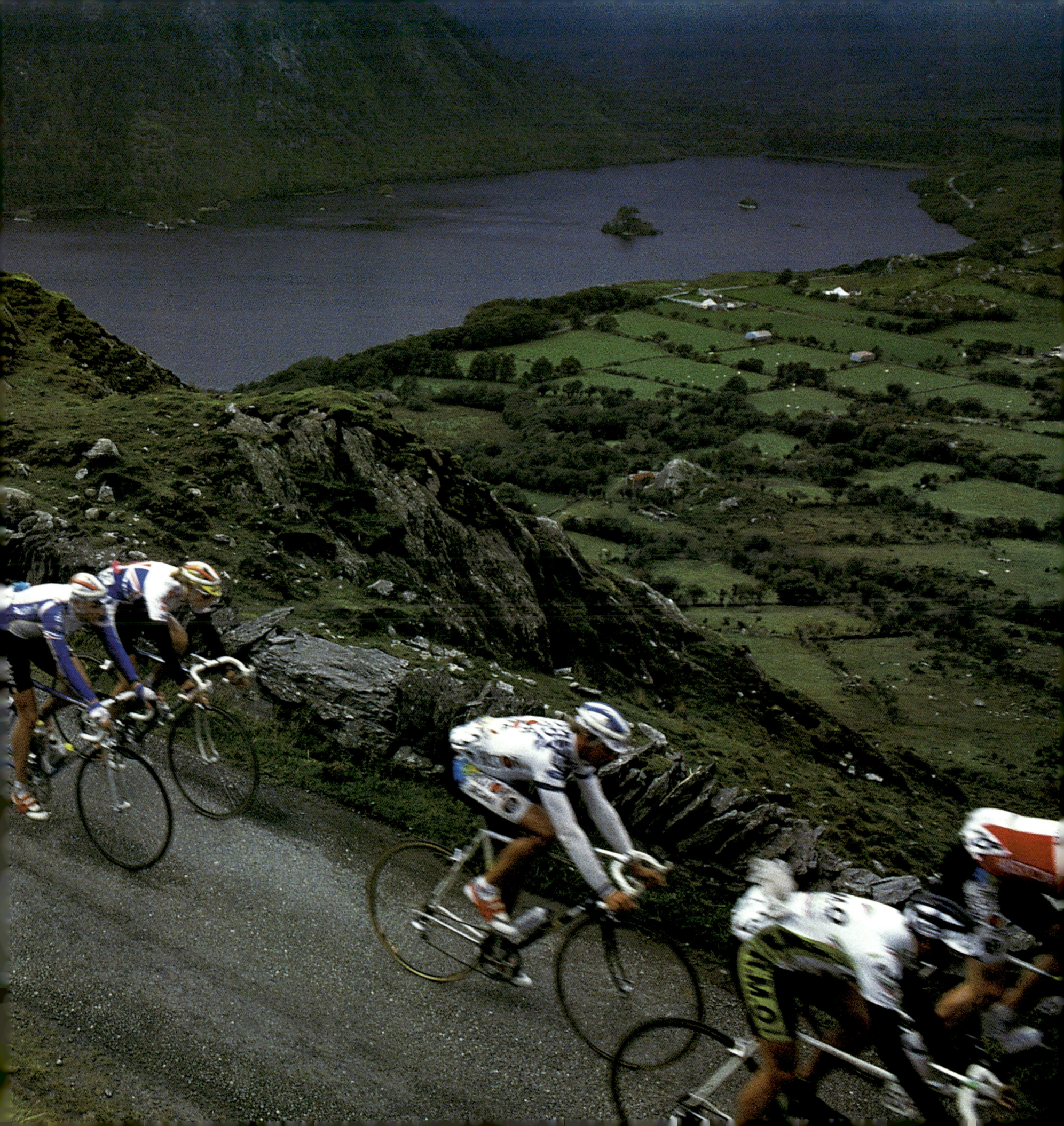

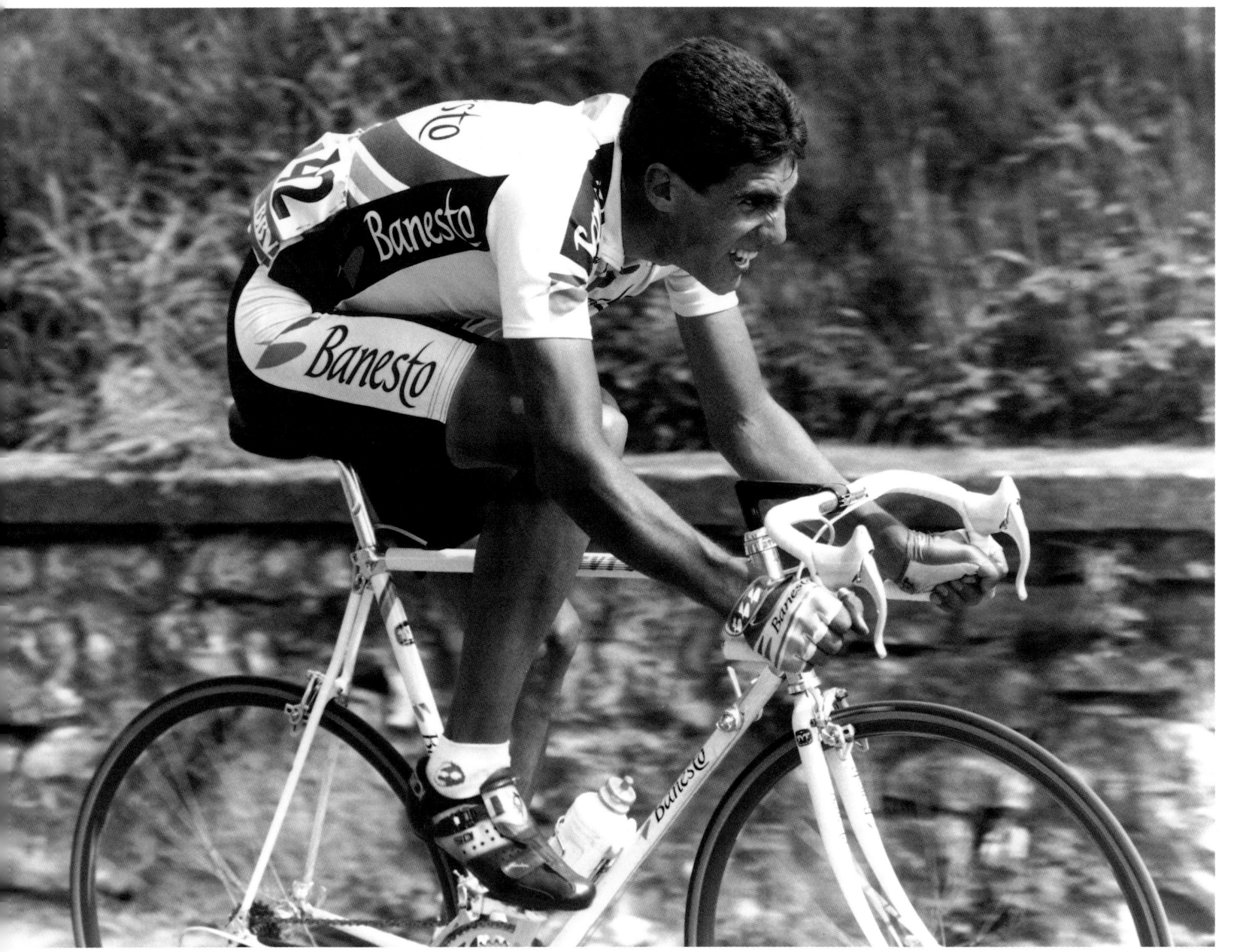

1990: CLASICA SAN SEBASTIAN: SPAIN

Miguel Induráin (above) showed all the style and courage in this solo break at the 1990 San Sebastian classic and earlier that year on the Mount Faron climb in Paris-Nice (right). He would win the Tour de France five times from 1991 to 1995.

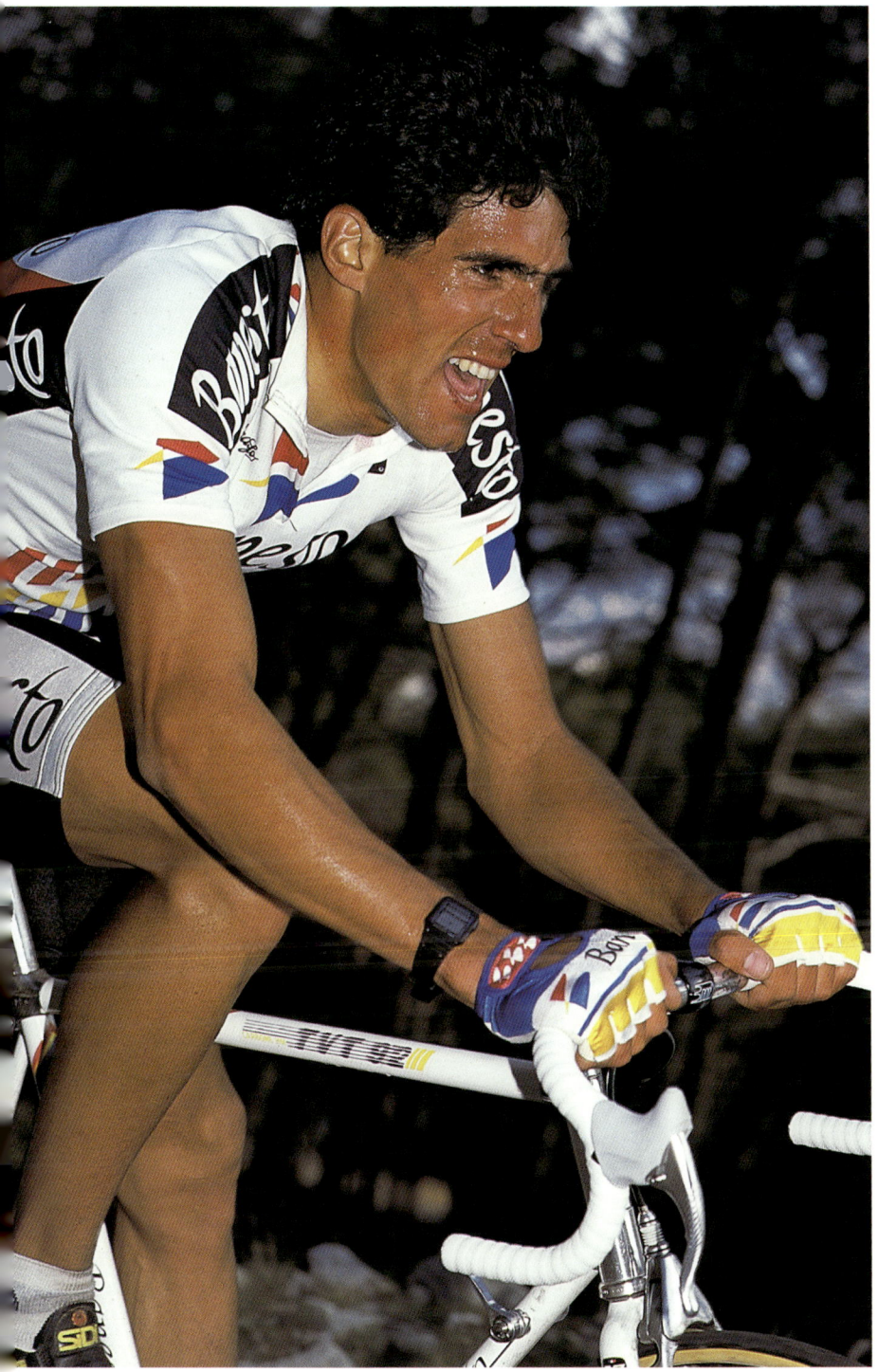
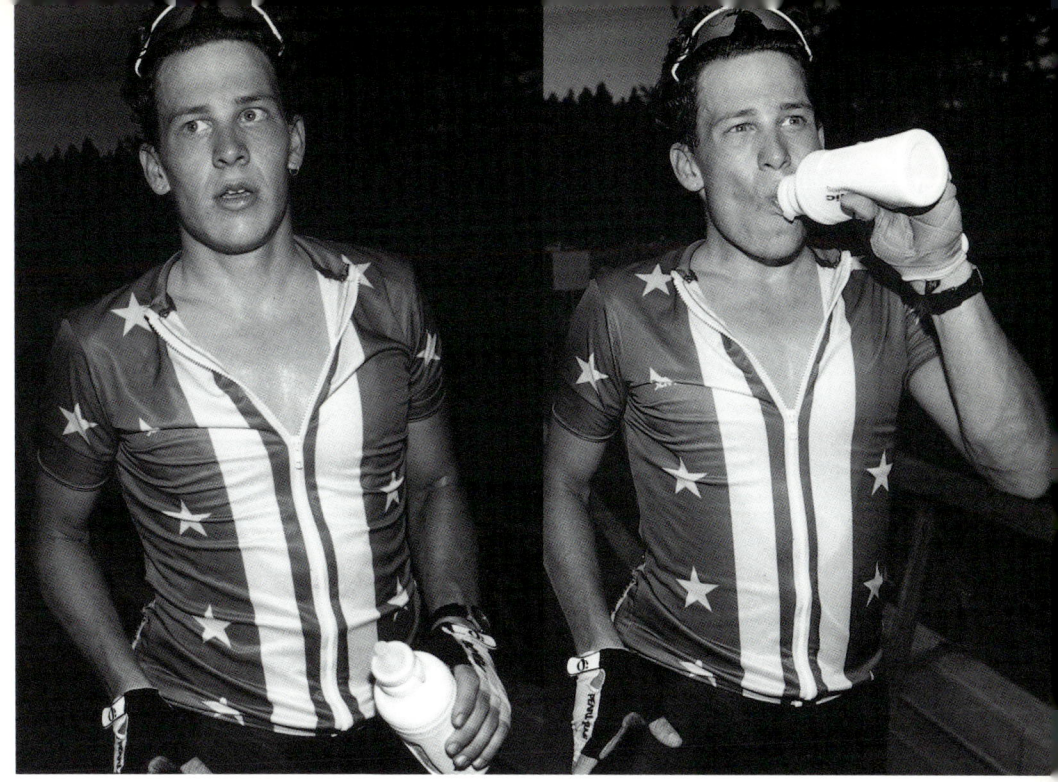

1990: WORLD ROAD CHAMPIONSHIPS: UTSUNOMIYA, JAPAN

Another future Tour winner, Lance Armstrong, only 18, showed he was a fearless rider in the amateur road race at the 1990 world's in Japan.

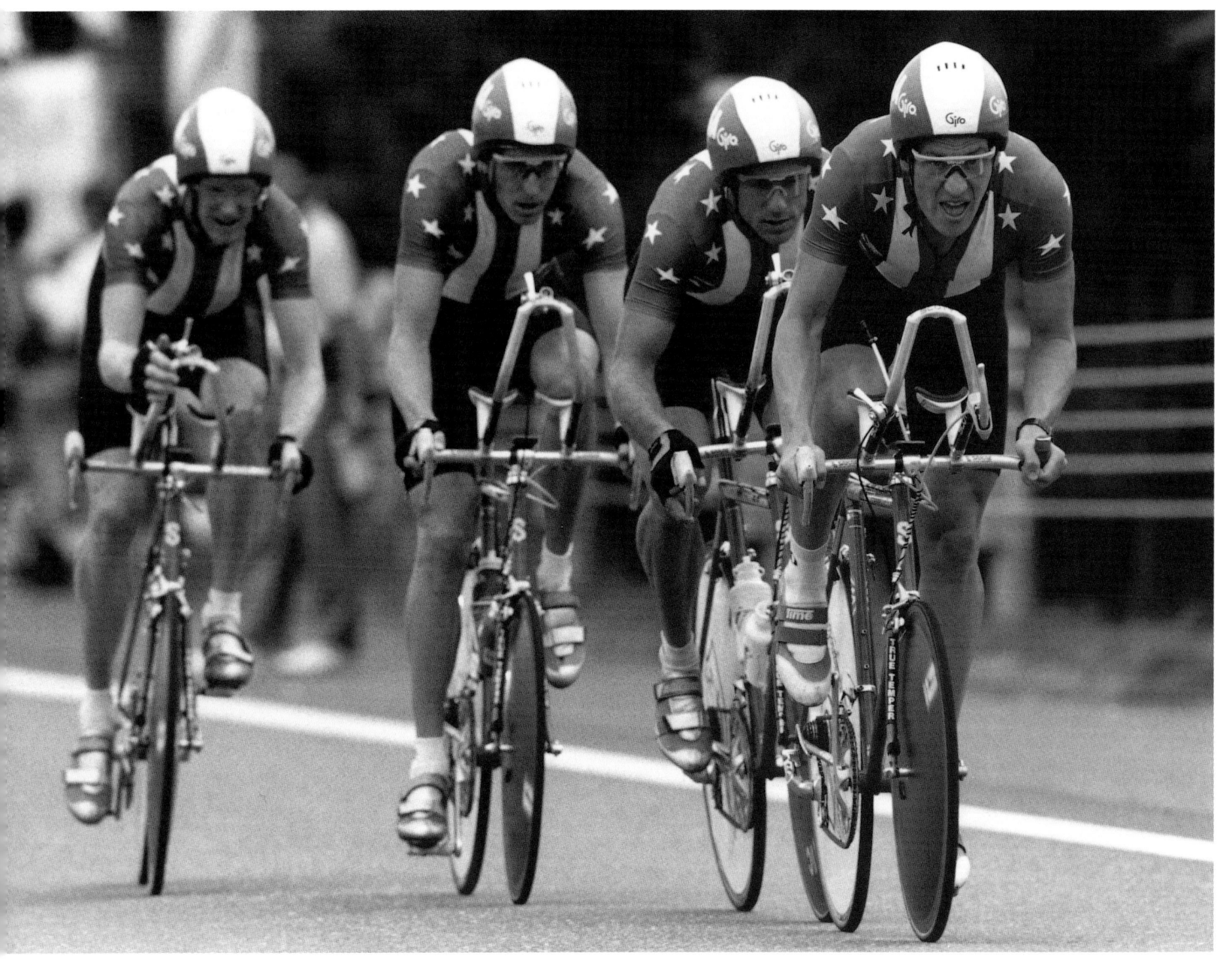

1990: WORLD ROAD CHAMPIONSHIPS: JAPAN

Lance Armstrong, still a teenager, was the driving force of the U.S. foursome's seventh place in the 100km team time trial at the 1990 world's. Armstrong is followed by Jim Copeland, Nate Reiss, and Nathan Sheafor.

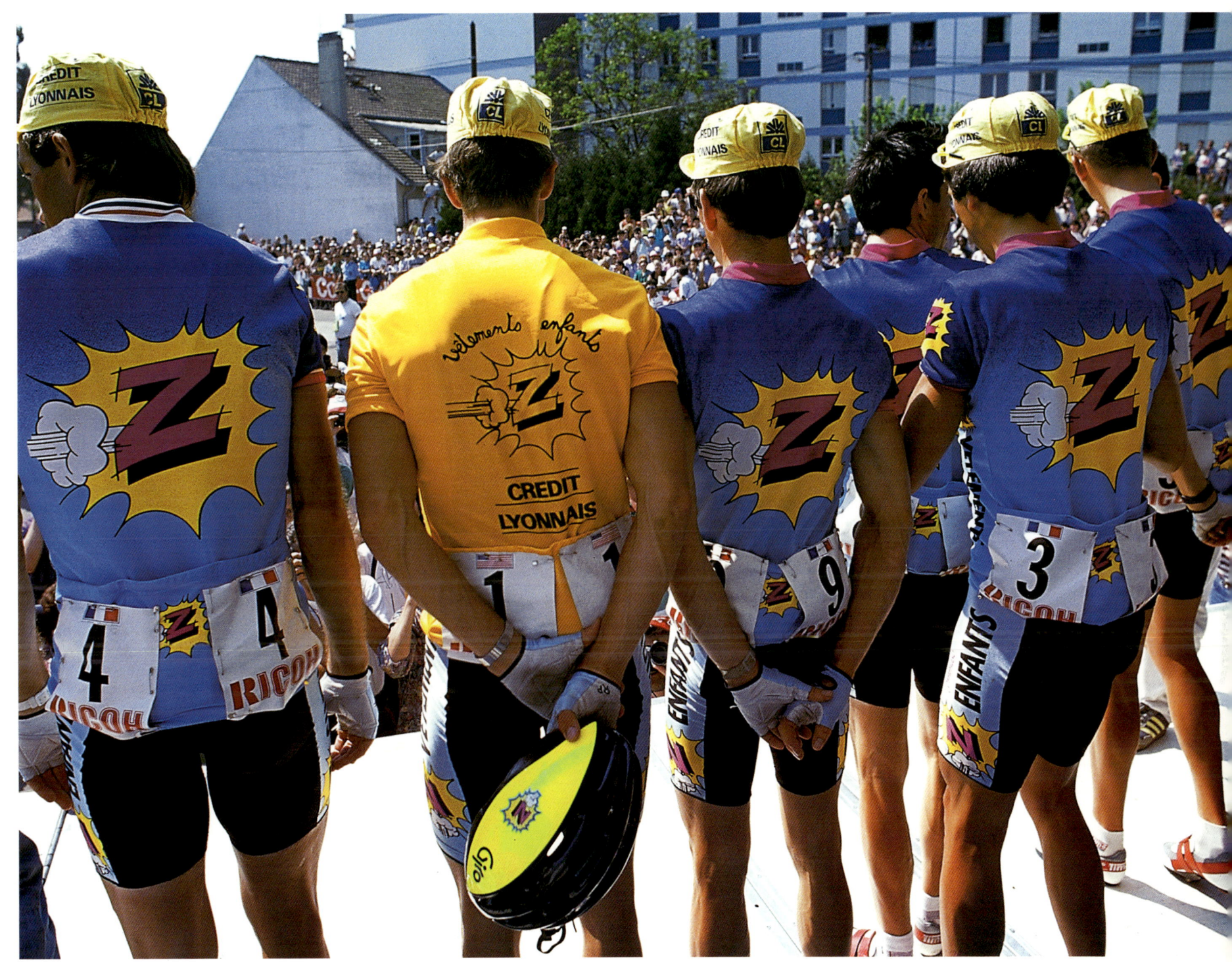

1990: TOUR DE FRANCE: BRÉTIGNY

Greg LeMond was well supported by his French team, Z, on his way to victory at the 1990 Tour. They were introduced to the crowd at the start of the final stage into Paris.

1990: WORLD TRACK CHAMPIONSHIPS: MAEBASHI, JAPAN

The sleek, almost sinister, silver-and-gray outline of East German track racer Antonella Bellutti flashes through a spotlight at the Green Dome velodrome in Maebashi, Japan.

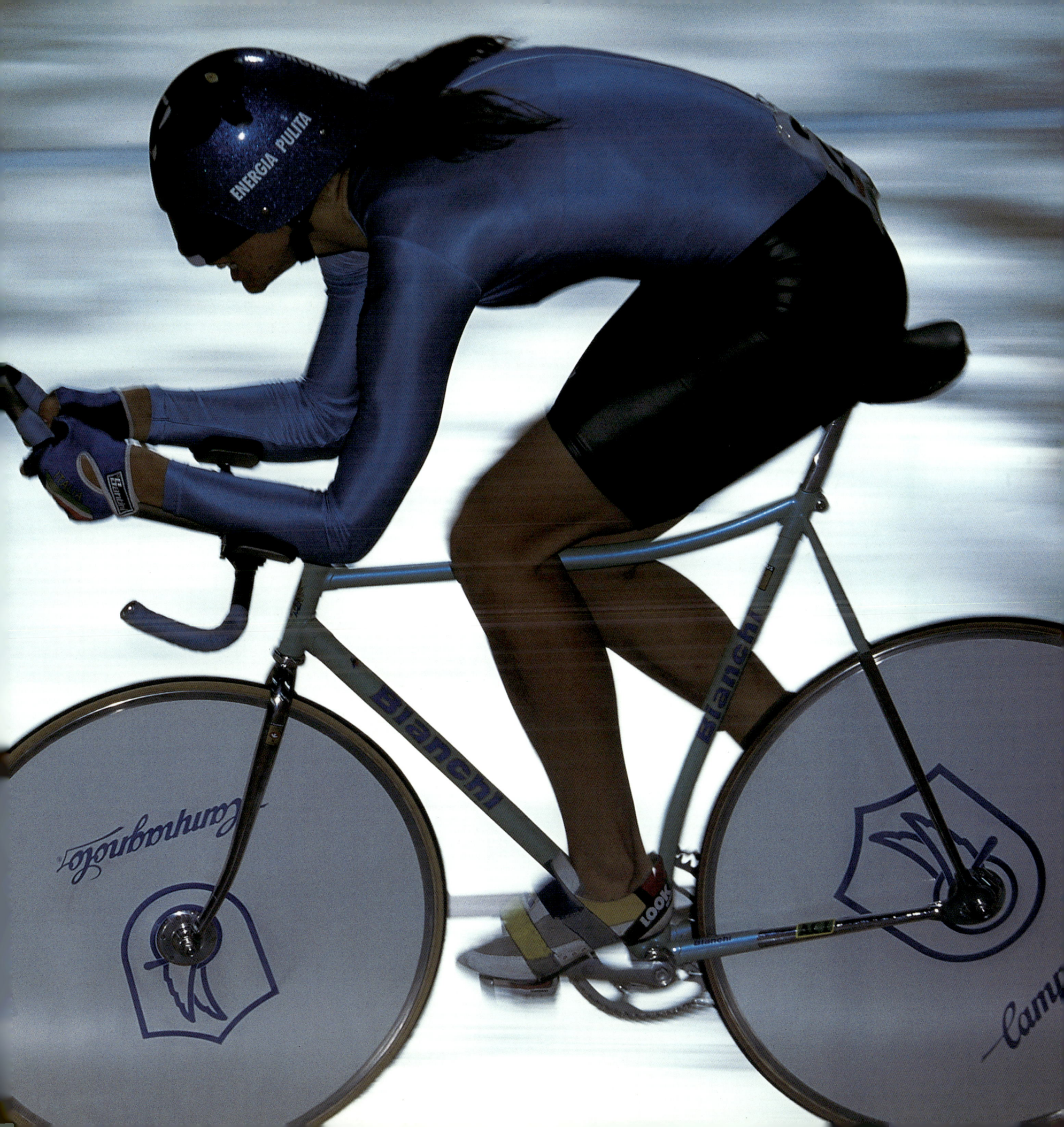

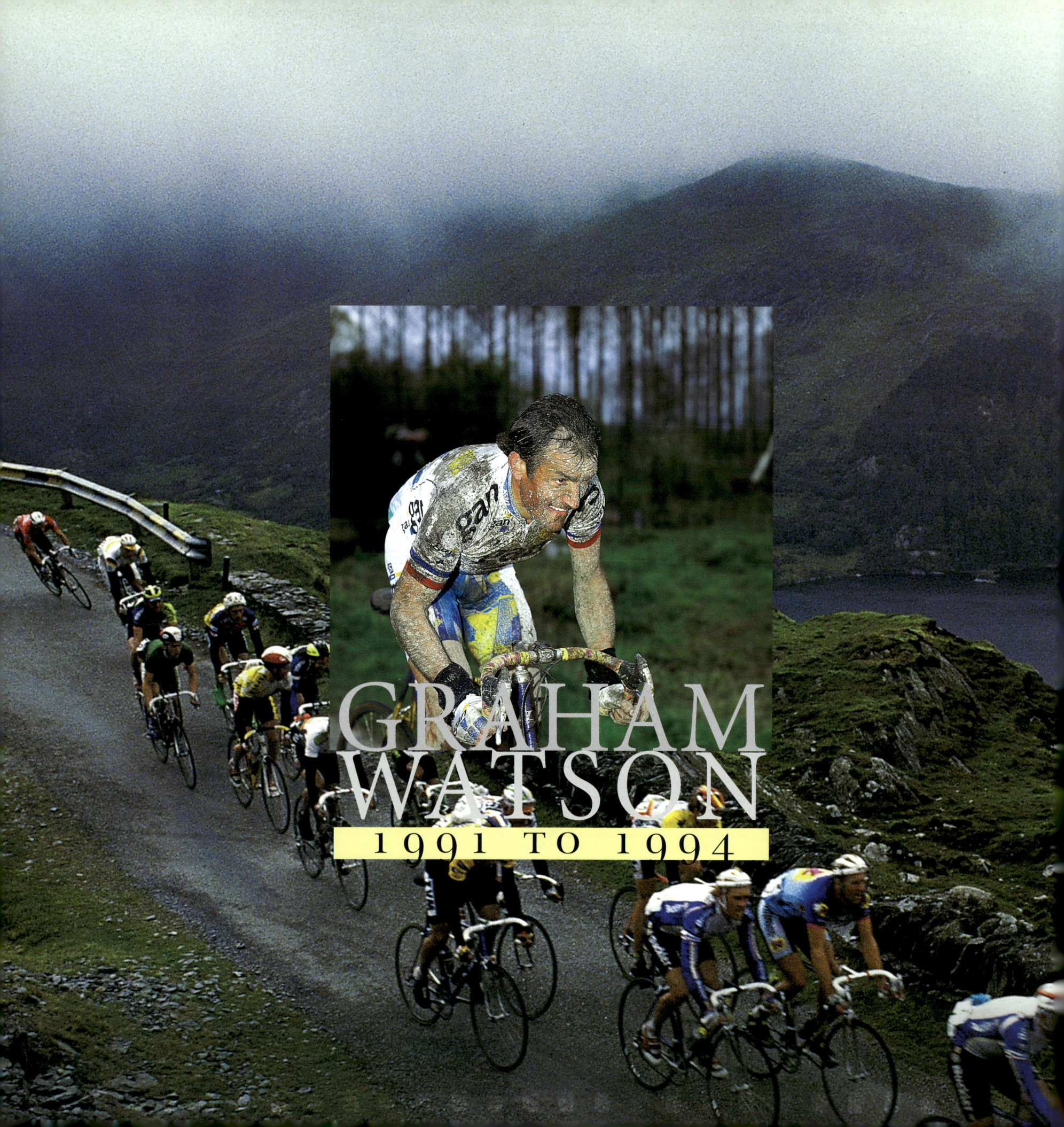

GRAHAM WATSON
1991 TO 1994

GRAHAM WATSON

The new decade started for me in the freezing cold environment of the northern Netherlands. I was covering the world cyclo-cross championships in Gieten, where the Czech star Radomir Simunek won his third championship ahead of Adri Van der Poel, the "eternal second" of professional cyclo-cross. Away from the glamor of races like Paris-Roubaix and the Tour de France, cycling's calendar is reinforced by smaller races—hundreds of them—and other branches of the sport, like cyclo-cross and six-day racing. These are two extremely exhausting disciplines, in which sweat and tears are the blood that is spilled—hence the attraction for someone like me.

Even now, spoiled by choices between the big races, it is the world of cyclo-cross in particular that I love; and barely has the road season ended with the Tour of Lombardy, than I am looking for the dates of the first big 'cross race, and of the 'cross world's that always kick-starts the next road-racing season, four months hence. Six-day racing also has its attractions, though my enjoyment of races like the London "Skol-6" and those in Rotterdam and Ghent has been severely diminished since the early 1980s, now that we no longer have a clown like Willy Debosscher to entertain us.

My two distinct memories of the 1991 season are of Greg LeMond's Tour defeat at the hands of Miguel Induráin and the "comeback from death" by Britain's six-day star Tony Doyle. Doyle's six-day career began at the Skol-6, a few months after he won his first world pursuit title in 1980. A decade later, the Englishman was almost killed in a crash at the 1990 Munich Six, but after months spent in hospital, he recovered, returned to Munich in '91, and won the six-day with his long-time partner Danny Clark.

Years earlier, in 1982, Doyle had won the European points championship in Herning, Denmark, and I'd driven to that race with the late Dennis Donovan, of *Cycling Weekly*. After the long drive across credit-card-free Germany, we arrived almost stripped of our cash reserves; and it was Doyle who lent us the money to take the ferry home from Denmark to England, after the event. Dennis's report of the race was undoubtedly the most pro-Doyle story he ever wrote!

The year 1991 marked a noticeable turnaround in the hierarchy of the European peloton. Induráin won his first Tour, ahead of the two Italians, Gianni Bugno and Claudio Chiappucci. That same year saw the "death throes" of LeMond, who would never finish another Tour before retiring in 1994. Another star on the decline was Pedro Delgado, who,

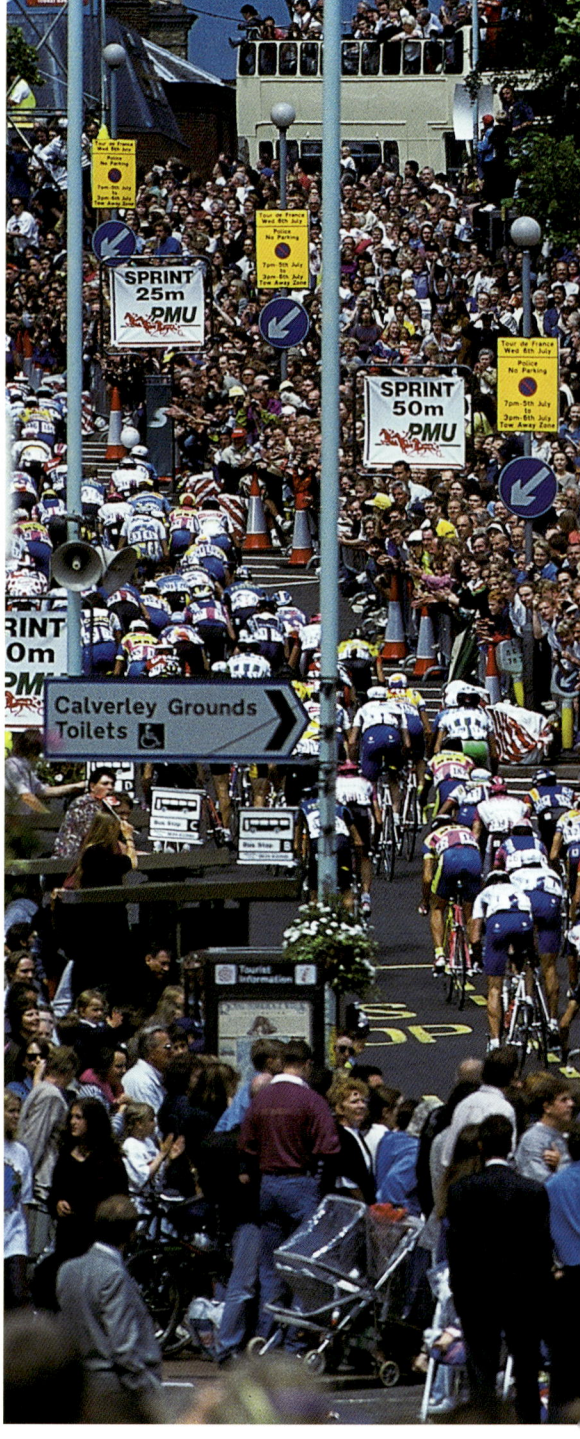

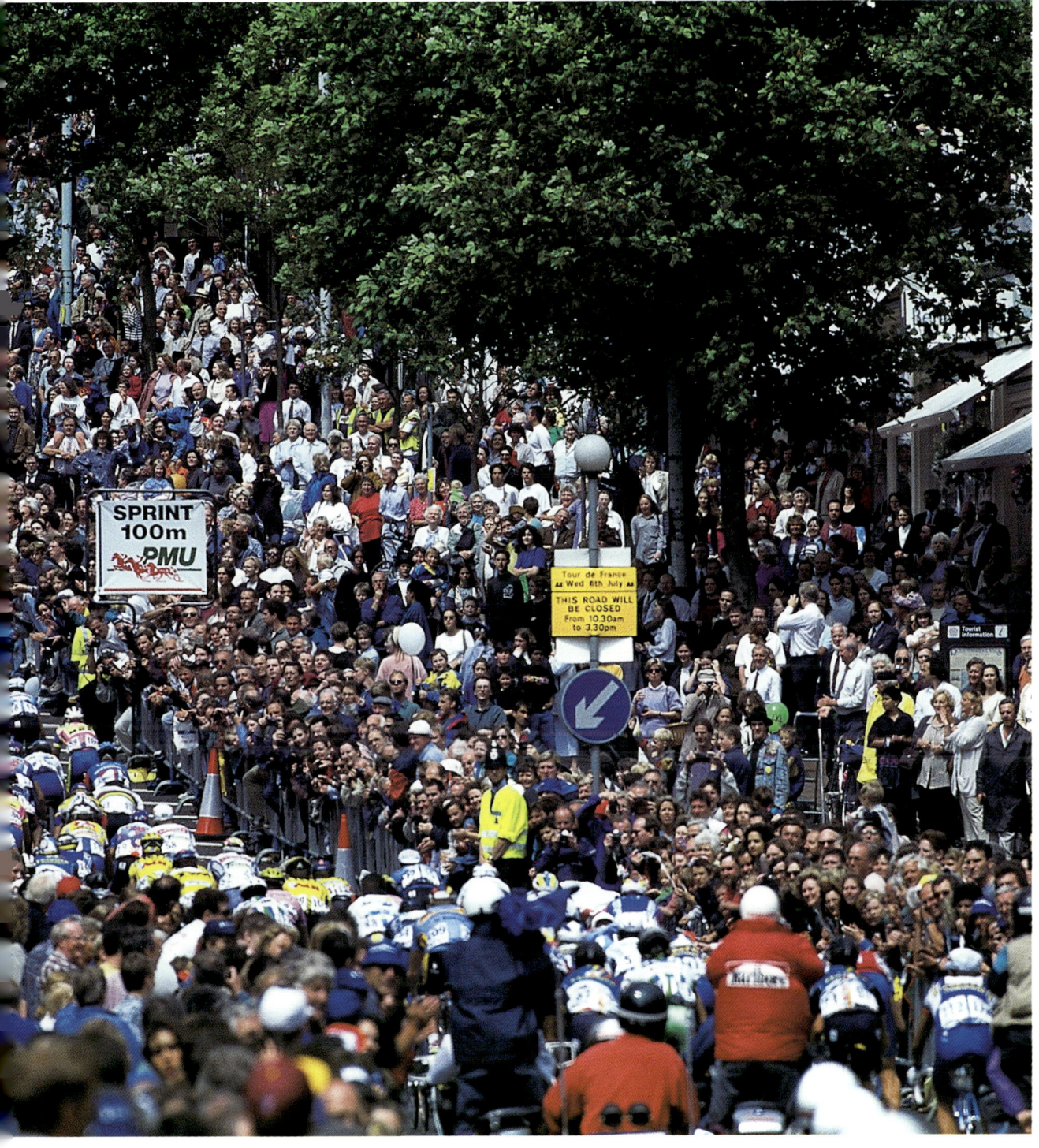

1994: TOUR DE FRANCE: ENGLAND

When the Tour came to Britain for the second time in its history, the two stages drew huge crowds, like this one in Royal Tunbridge Wells.

after winning the Tour in 1988, was now reduced to the role of super-domestique in Induráin's favor. I could also sense the end coming to the great career of Sean Kelly, who had broken his collarbone in the '91 Paris-Nice, at the age of 34, and had then been forced out of that year's Tour with a serious virus.

It was Kelly's retirement that concerned me the most, for he had been the colossus whose career had seemingly underpinned my own at that time. His departure, I feared, would be a severe blow to my morale. So it was especially nice to see Kelly win a third Tour of Lombardy in October '91, and he won it in true Kelly style—the hard way—by forging a commanding breakaway with 30km left, and then outsprinting his fellow escapee, Martial Gayant of France.

1991 TO 1994

Maybe Kelly sensed his fans' anxiety, for he started the 1992 season as he'd finished the last, in winning form. This time it was the Milan-San Remo classic that fell to him after a crazy descent from the Poggio summit. So I could postpone my worries for a while longer!

When Kelly finally did retire—effectively at the end of the 1992 season—he took with him into retirement the Nissan Classic, a five-day race that was created around the success of Kelly and fellow Irishman Stephen Roche in the mid-1980s. This annual trek around Ireland had become the year's most sought-after race for the media, and the streets were filled with tens of thousands of fans reveling in its carnival-like atmosphere. Behind this great little race are stories that will never be told, publicly, of the antics of many a famous cyclist in the bars and clubs of Limerick or Dublin, and of the inebriated journalists needing close supervision in the nightly search for their hotels.

Coming late in the year, in October, when Ireland is perhaps seen at its best, race photographers spoke lovingly of the autumnal light ... the glow of a Galway sunset ... the mist hanging low over the Kerry mountains . . . the enthralling drama of seeing the peloton hit the slopes of St Patrick's Hill in Cork. Yes, there never was anything quite like "the Nissan."

As Kelly was going, so Induráin was arriving, and in 1992 and '93 the Spaniard won both the Giro and the Tour, something not achieved since Bernard Hinault achieved the Giro-Tour double in 1982 and '85. Induráin's participation in the Giro drew me closer to that race, and in 1994, I covered the event in its entirety for the first time—and was stunned at Induráin's defeat

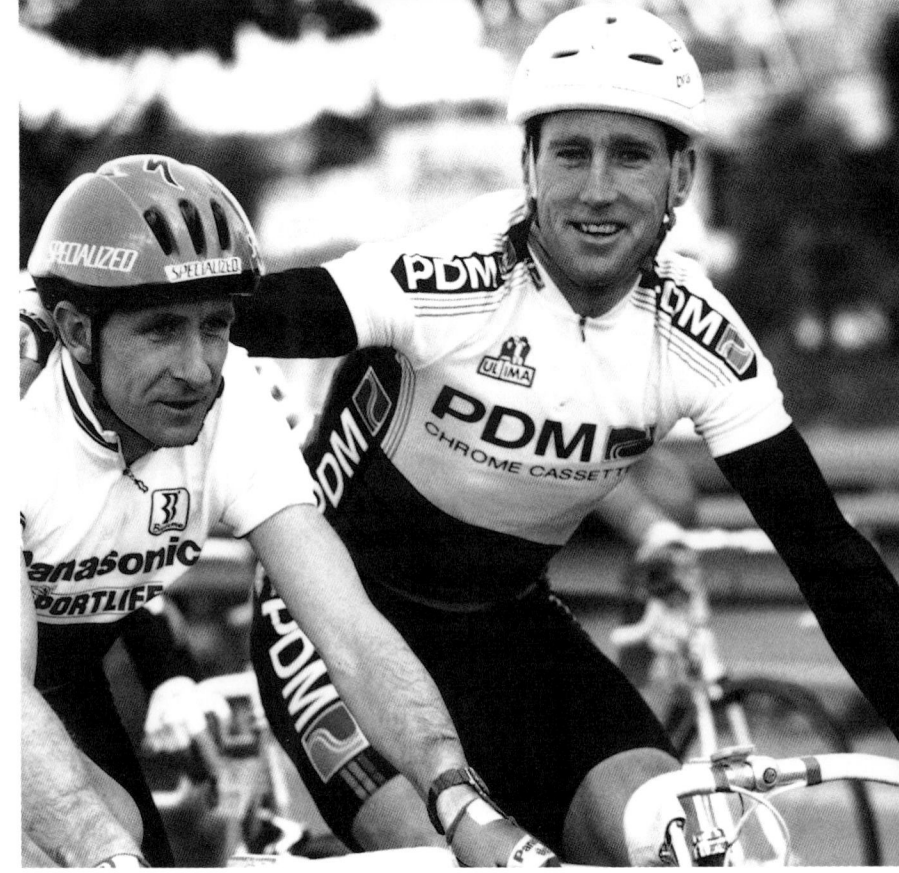

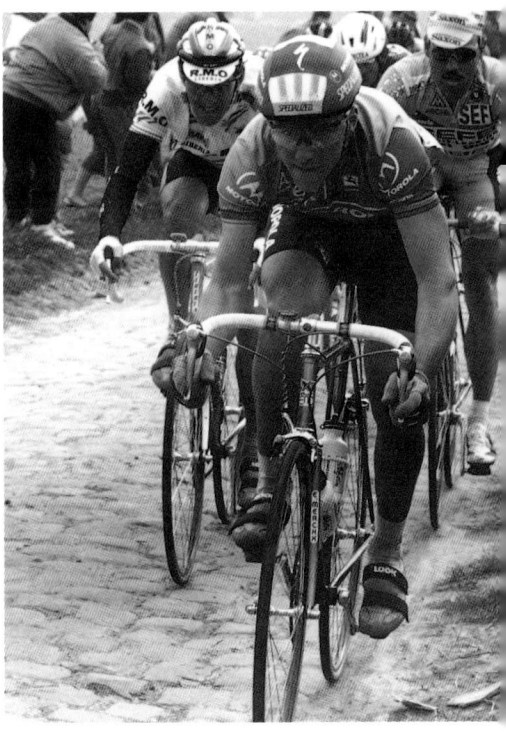

1991: TOUR OF FLANDERS: BELGIUM

The helmets were not too pretty in the early '90s! Sean Kelly (right) greets his Belgian friend Rudy Dhaenens, winner of the world title the previous October, at the start of the 1991 season. [Dhaenens retired from racing in 1993 and died in an auto accident in April 1999.]

1991: PARIS-ROUBAIX: FRANCE

The guy in the Motorola jersey looks comfortable riding on the dirt at Paris-Roubaix; and so he should. Later that season, John Tomac won the world mountain bike cross-country championship.

by the young Russian, Evgeni Berzin.

Following a whole Giro has to be one of the most delightful ways of making a living, for Italy is the one European country where the food is always good, the wine beyond praise, and the companionship never to be forgotten. The weather is almost always good as well, and the racing never fails to live up to expectations, with an intoxicating blend of lethargy, tremendous, dramatic efforts, and outright emotion. It seemed strange to consider that by 1994, I had already followed nine complete Vueltas yet was only just completing my first full Giro. This was another small regret in my career, for in discovering the true Giro d'Italia, I realized how much I'd missed by not having done so earlier.

The 1994 Giro introduced the world of cycling to a balding youth named Marco Pantani, who, at the outset of the alpine stages, unleashed a series of seemingly crazy attacks which threatened to dislodge such leading contenders as Berzin and Induráin. Pantani saved his biggest effort, however, for a stage that would climb the mighty Stelvio Pass, swoop down to Bormio, then climb up to Aprica twice—the first time via the feared Mortirolo climb, then over the nasty little climb of Santa Christina. That Pantani won the stage went partially unnoticed, for in accelerating on the Santa Christina, he put paid to Induráin's attack on Berzin, who was struggling to restrict his losses further down the climb. The big Navarran was not happy, and he did his utmost in the remaining week's racing to spoil Pantani's Giro fiesta. But by then, we all knew we were witnessing the arrival of a very special cyclist, possibly the best to come out of Italy since the days of Felice Gimondi.

The Tour de France came to England in July of that year, and massive crowds

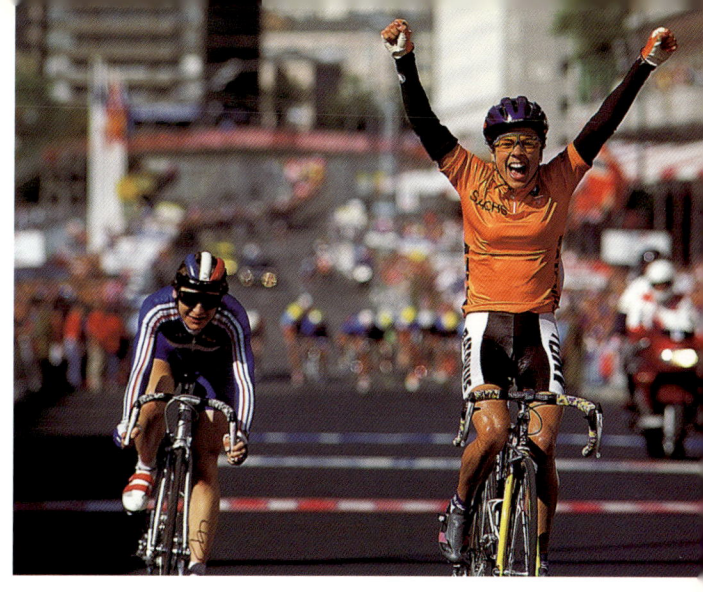

1993: WORLD ROAD CHAMPIONSHIPS: NORWAY

Dutch diva Leontien Van Moorsel outkicks French ace Jeannie Longo to take the women's road race title in Oslo.

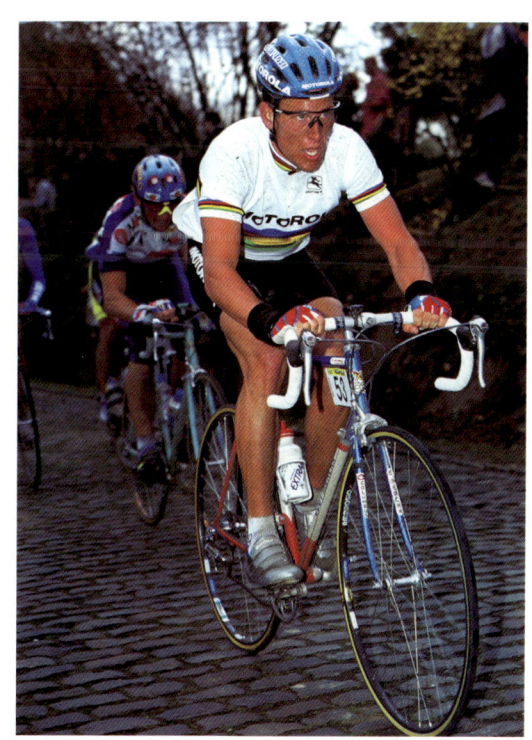

1994: TOUR OF FLANDERS: BELGIUM

Lance Armstrong paraded his world champion's rainbow jersey at the spring classics, leading up to a second place in Liège-Bastogne-Liège.

turned out to salute the Tour's cyclists, a group that included Englishmen Chris Boardman and Sean Yates. The French organizers and media were stunned that England could produce such a big turnout: From the garden county of Kent through deepest Sussex and into Hampshire, the roads were lined with tens of thousands of cheering fans. The only ingredient missing was that Boardman had lost his yellow jersey to Johan Museeuw the day before the race arrived in Dover; and the final irony was that Yates won the yellow jersey after the first stage back in France, in Rennes. I was personally chuffed to see Sean clad in yellow—if ever a man deserved this recognition, it was Sean. As he waved his bouquet, and shyly accepted the podium girls' kisses, my mind drifted back to 1983 and the world championships in Switzerland, where Sean had just finished the road race. I was penniless after the drive down from England and the week's stay in Europe's most expensive country; and it had been Sean who'd lent me £200 (roughly $400 at the time) to get home.

The years 1994–95 will be remembered as the Tony Rominger years. True, it was Induráin, now recovered from his '94 Giro defeat, who won the next two Tours de France. But it was Rominger, a three-time winner of the Vuelta in consecutive years, who tore the record books apart by twice beating the world hour record in Bordeaux during late 1994. And he then went on to win the 1995 Giro at a canter.

My experience at photographing six-day races allowed me to really enjoy Rominger's incredible double feat in the Bordeaux velodrome. His first attempt was almost a private affair, with just a few cunning journalists managing to sneak inside to watch, and only myself and a French photographer from *L'Équipe* allowed in the velodrome to take pictures. A Spanish colleague had gone home in disgust a few days

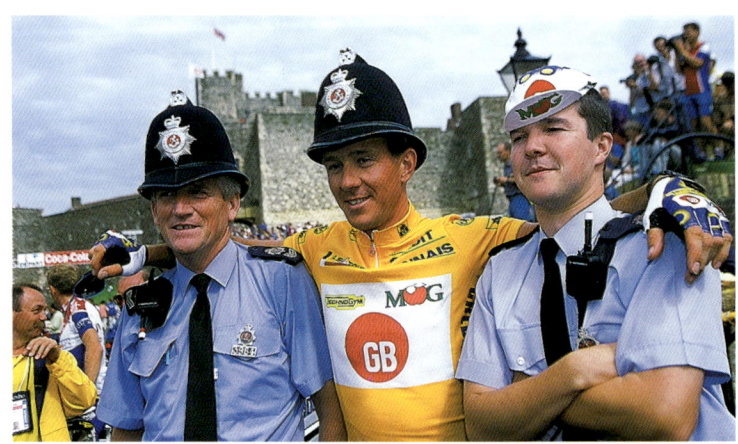

1994: TOUR DE FRANCE: ENGLAND

Arresting new headwear for Tour yellow jersey Johan Museeuw at Dover Castle, as Le Tour arrives en Angleterre.

earlier, after having been forced to photograph Rominger's training rides through a half-closed window on the outside of the building!

Rominger's second record attempt was far more serious, and he rose to the occasion superbly, in front of a full-house of spectators and a full complement of the world's press. That was his high point and one of my high points for the year.

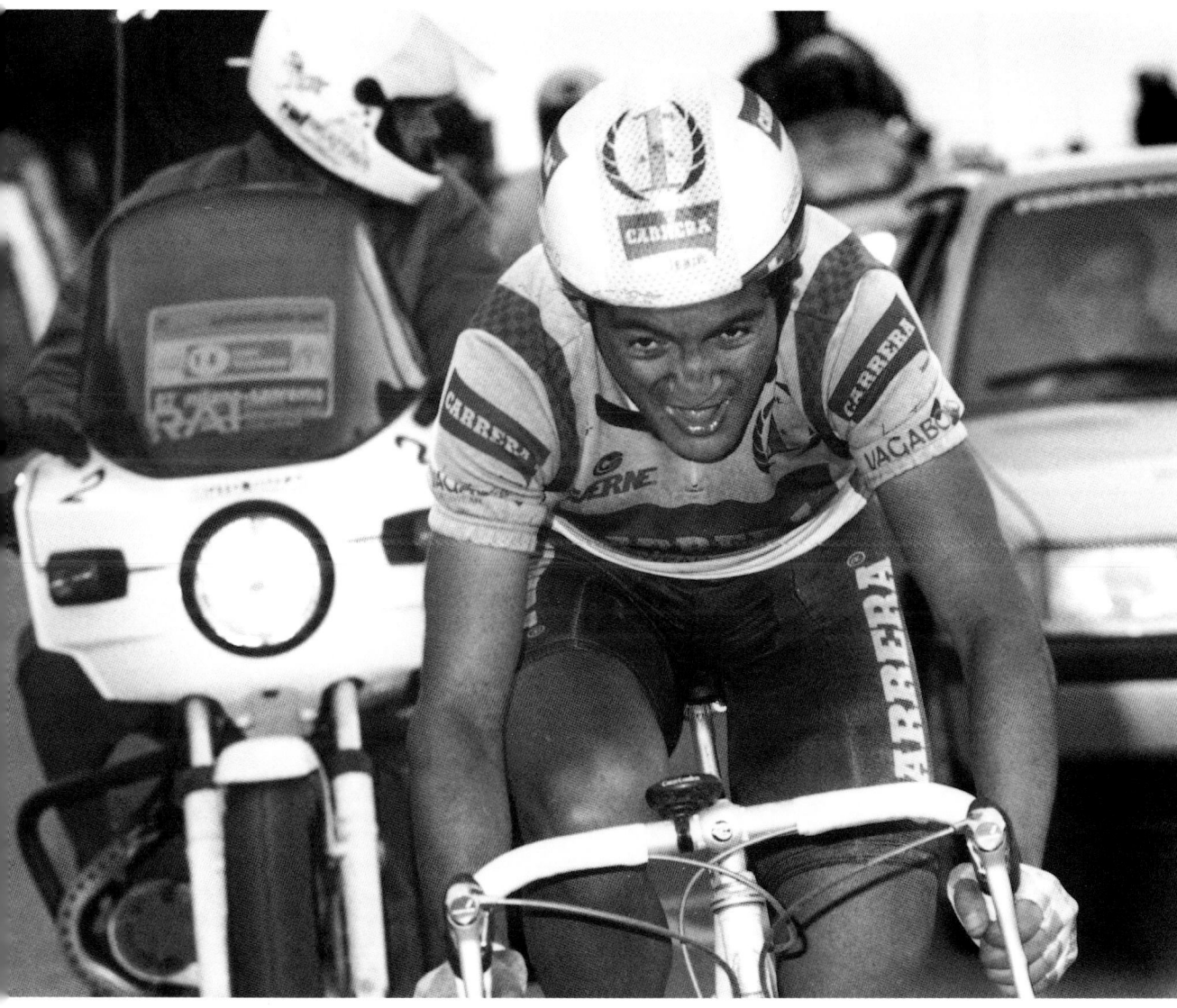

1991: MILAN-SAN REMO: ITALY

Avanti! Claudio Chiappucci heads over the Poggio hill into San Remo for a solo win in Italy's springtime classic.

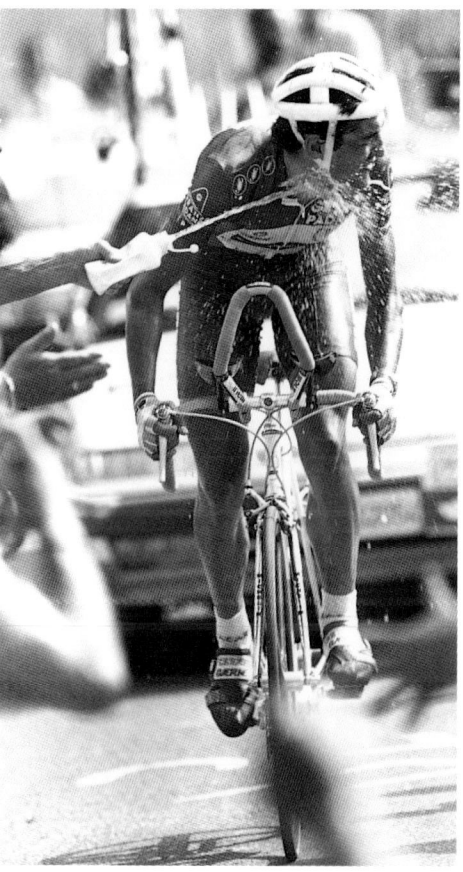

1991: GIRO D'ITALIA: CASTEGGIO

Three months later, Chiappucci races to second place at the Giro, after taking third in this final time trial.

1991 TO 1994

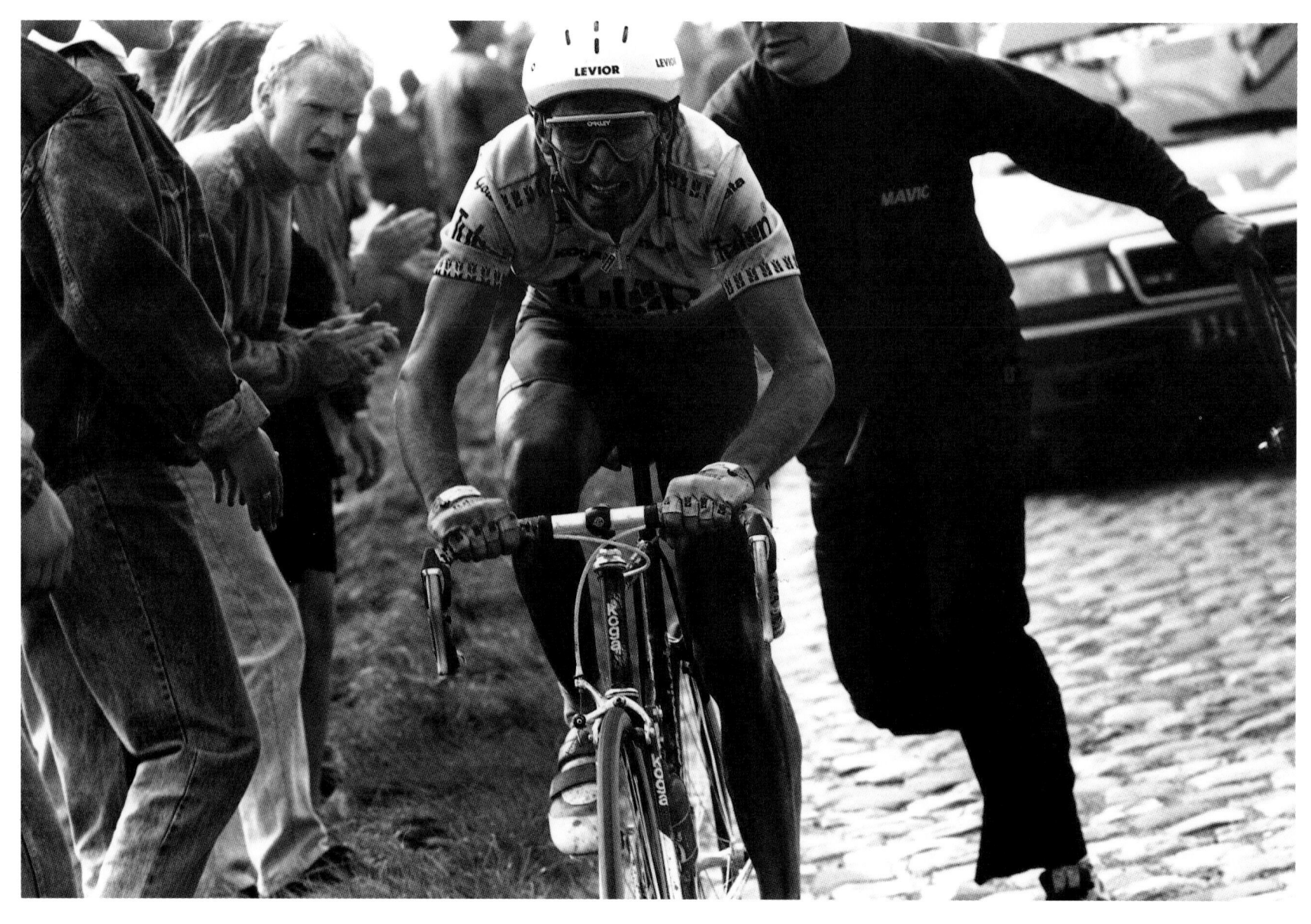

1991: PARIS-ROUBAIX: FRANCE

A new wheel and a big push for Australia's Allan Peiper in one of his favorite races.

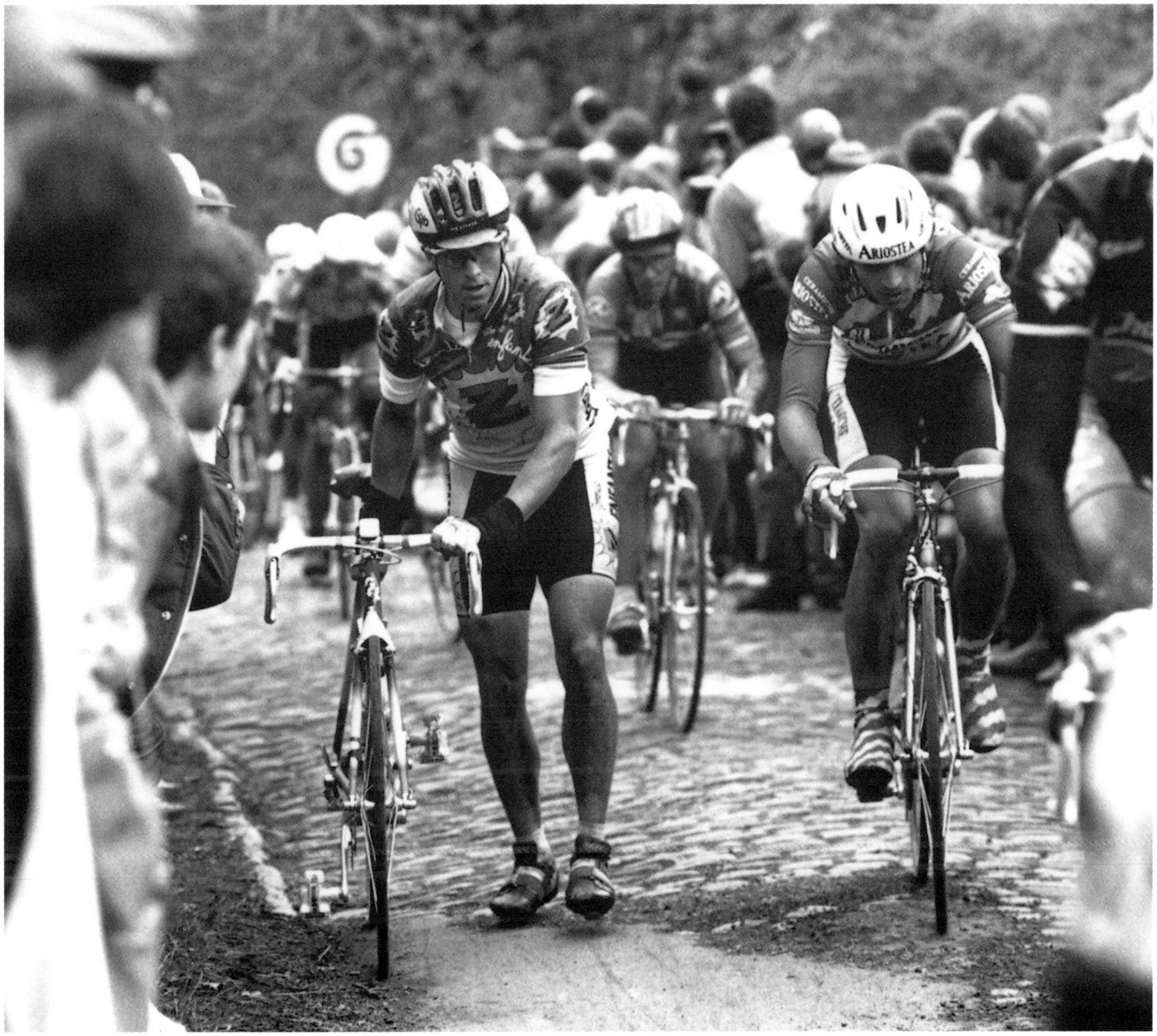

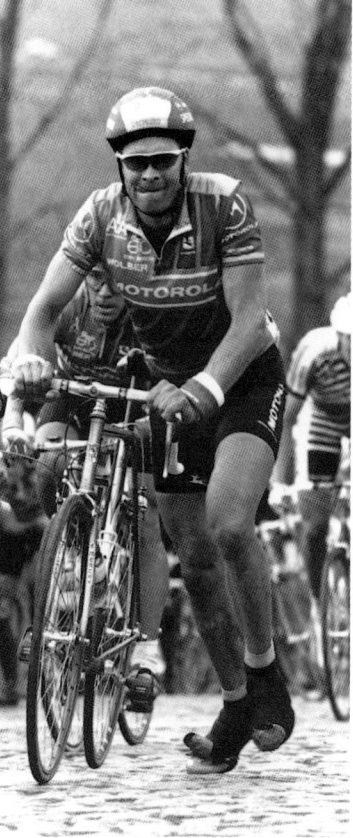

1991: TOUR OF FLANDERS: BELGIUM

Those cobblestone climbs in Flanders are steep! Greg LeMond (left) and Sean Yates (top right) both had to hoof it in the '91 Ronde.

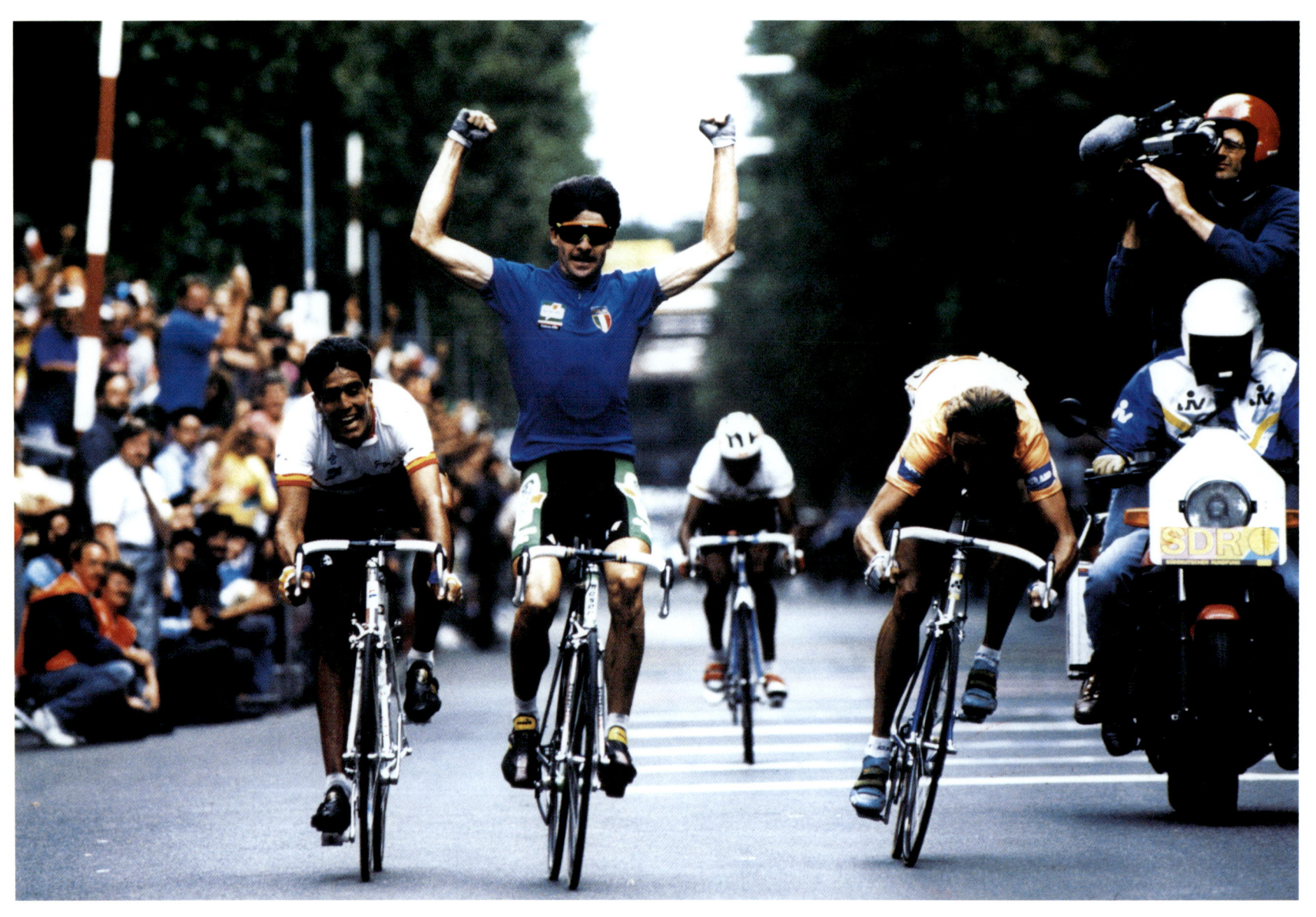

1991: WORLD ROAD CHAMPIONSHIPS: GERMANY

A narrow victory for Gianni Bugno over Steven Rooks (right) and Miguel Induráin (left) at the world pro road championship in Stuttgart.

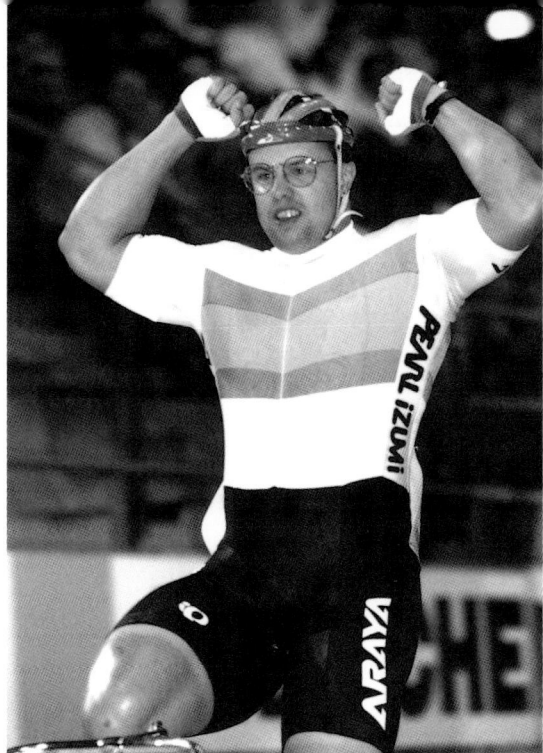

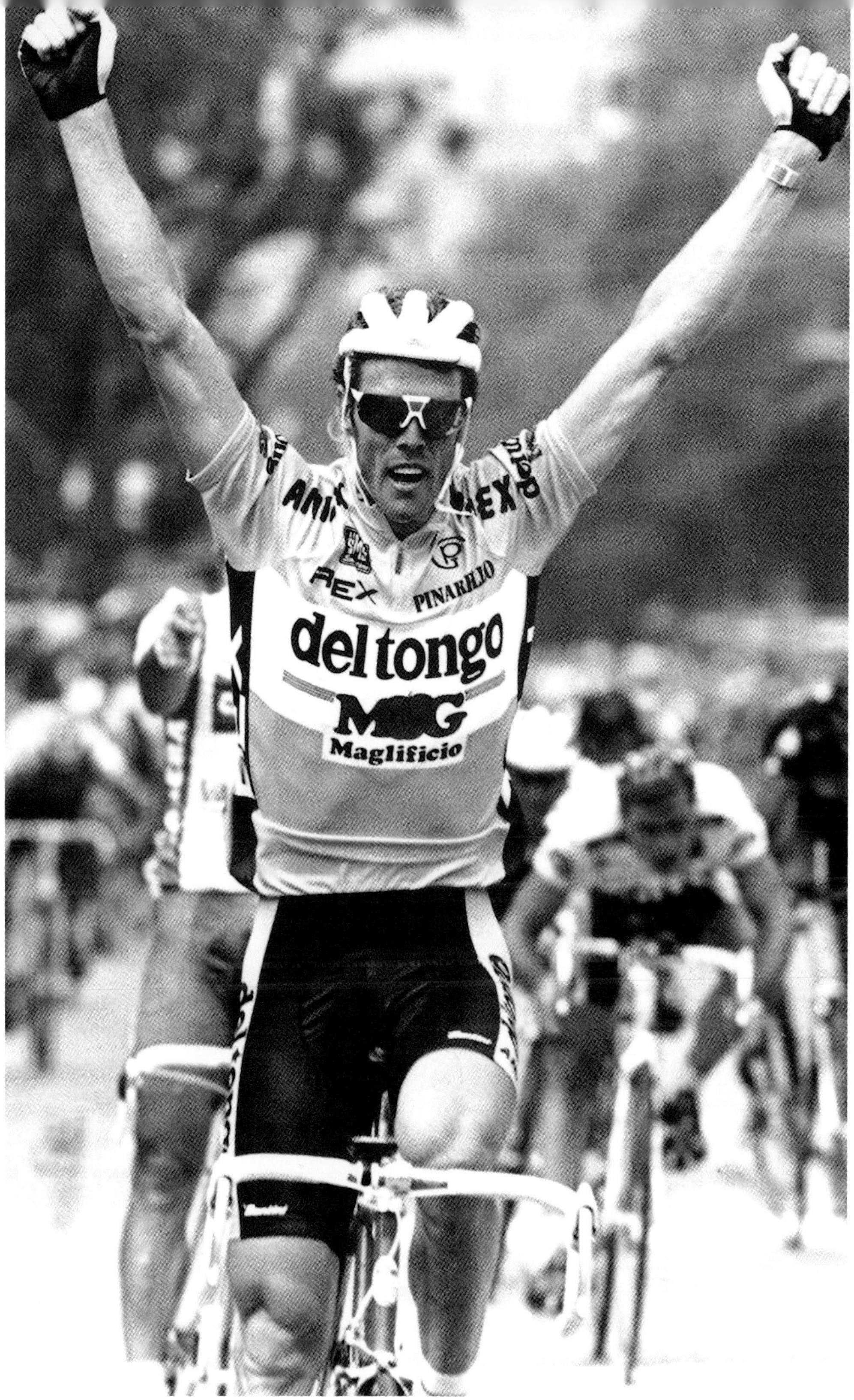

1991: WORLD TRACK CHAMPIONSHIPS: GERMANY

A hollow victory for Aussie sprinter Carey Hall, who lost the world title at the doping control: positive for steroids.

1991: GIRO D'ITALIA: MILAN

An easy victory for Mario Cipollini, his third stage win at the '91 Giro.

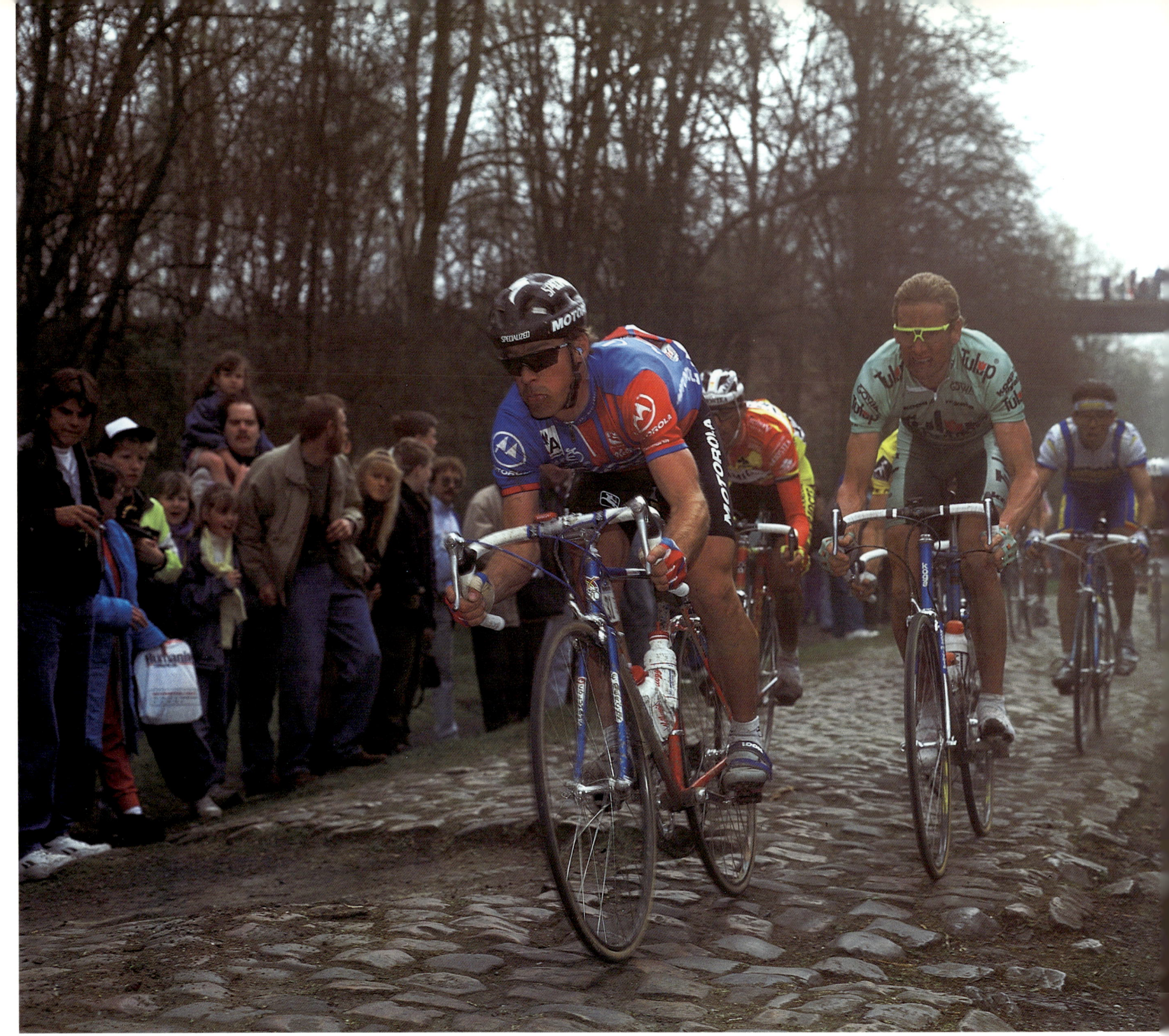

1992: PARIS-ROUBAIX: FRANCE

Anxious faces ... high speed ... an imminent crash? Steve Bauer (left) leads Adri Van der Poel and the rest of the pack onto the broken cobblestone "alleyway" of the Wallers-Arenberg Forest: the most notorious section of pavé in Paris-Roubaix.

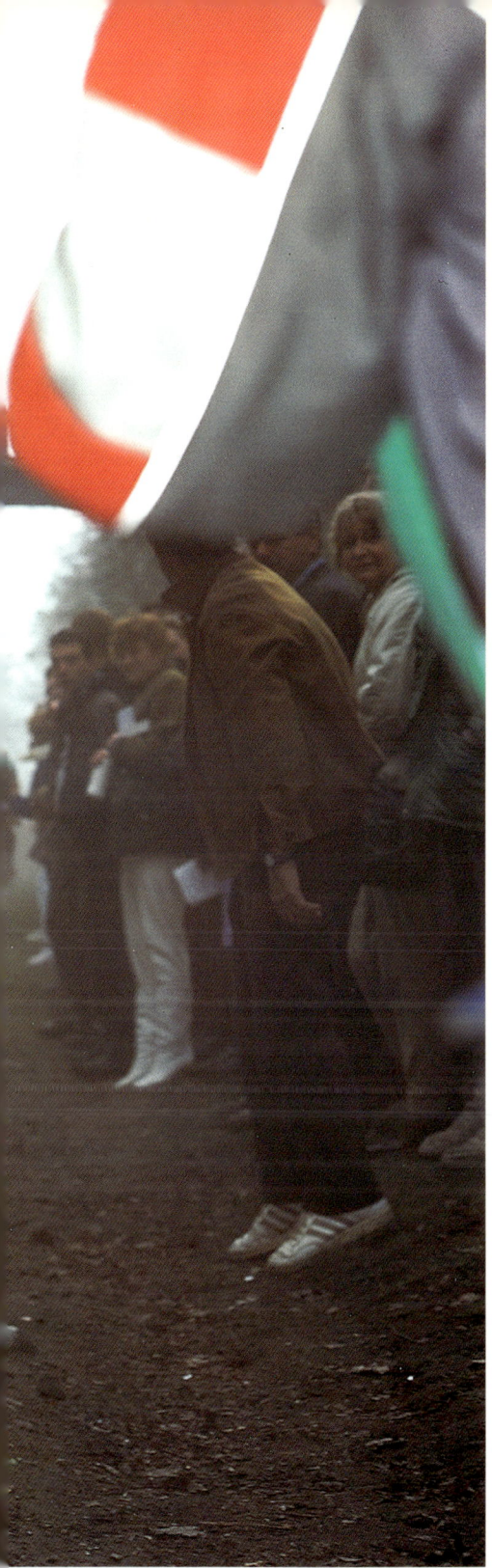
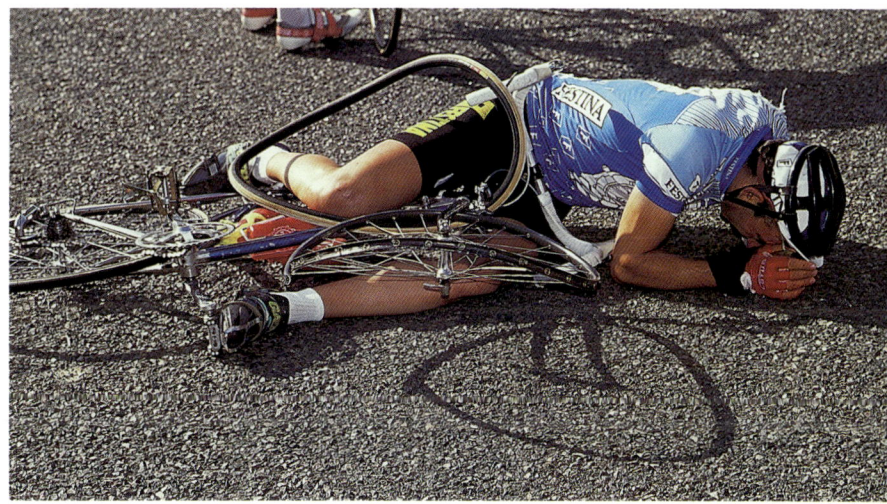

1992: PARIS-TOURS: FRANCE

A rolled tire, a heavy spill is the fate of Festina team rider Jean-Jacques Henry at France's other World Cup classic, Paris-Tours.

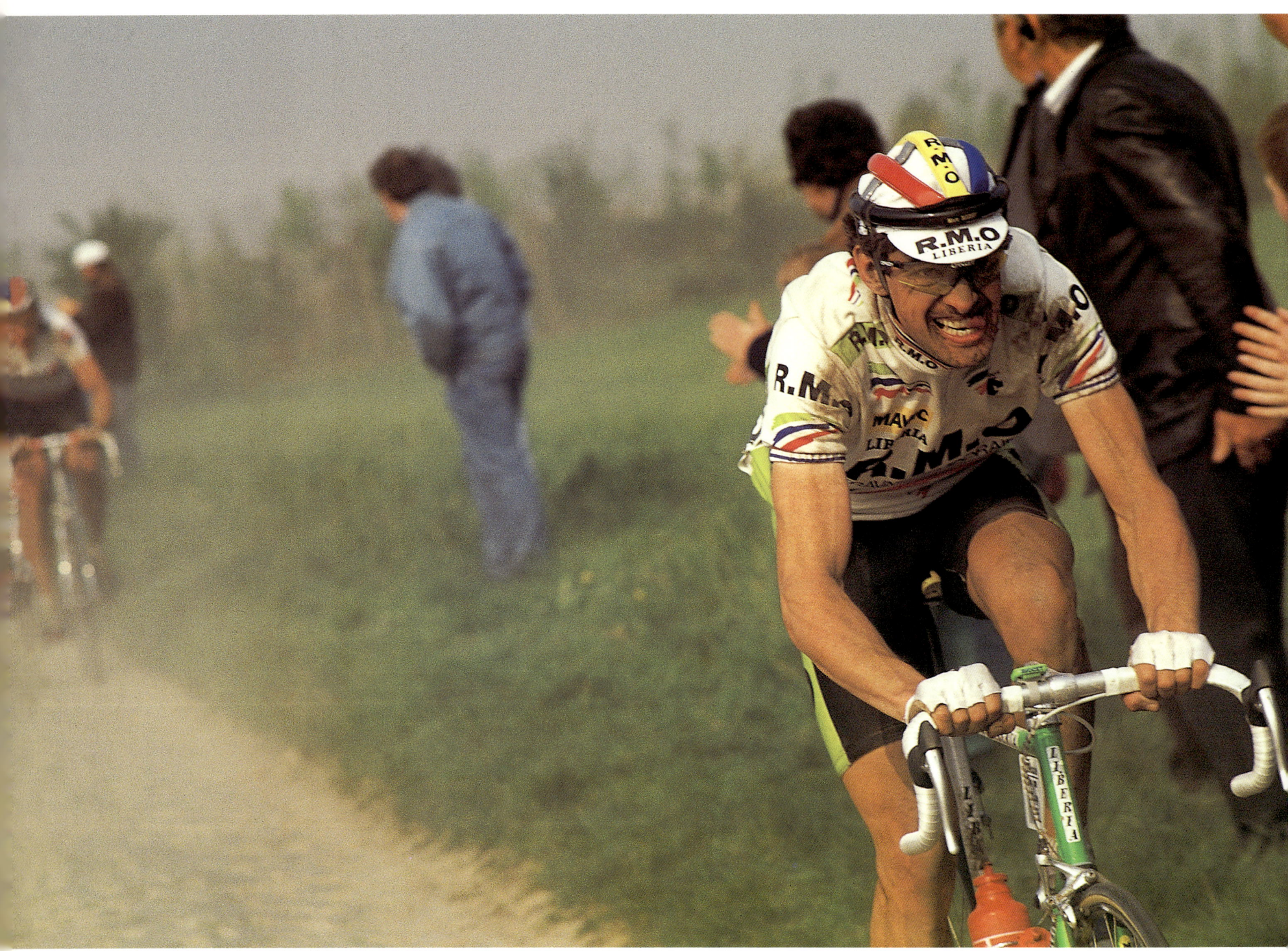

1991: PARIS-ROUBAIX: FRANCE

On the cobbled rise toward the Carrefour de l'Arbre—often the critical section of pavé at Paris-Roubaix—Marc Madiot of France makes the decisive attack that will take him to the finish as the solo winner.

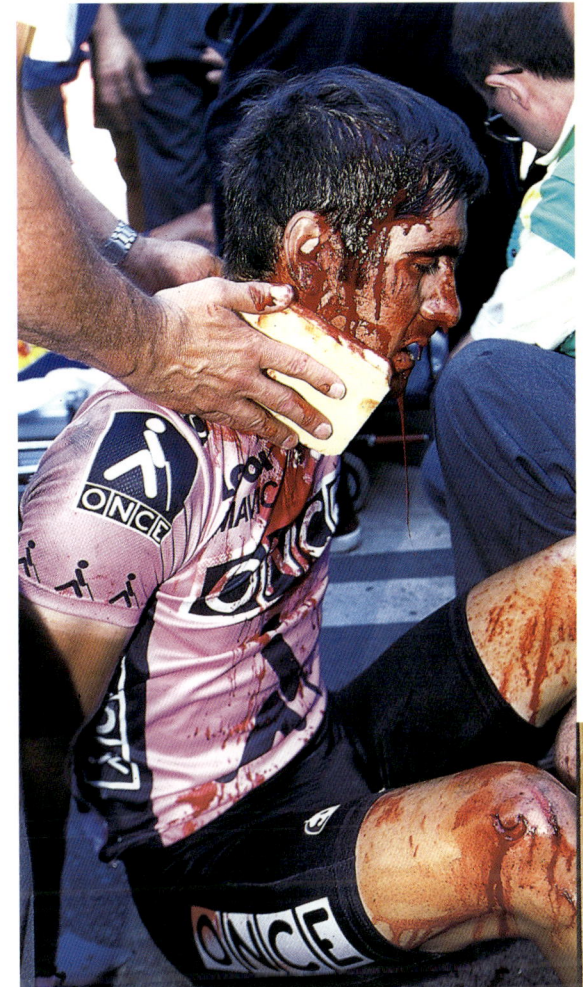
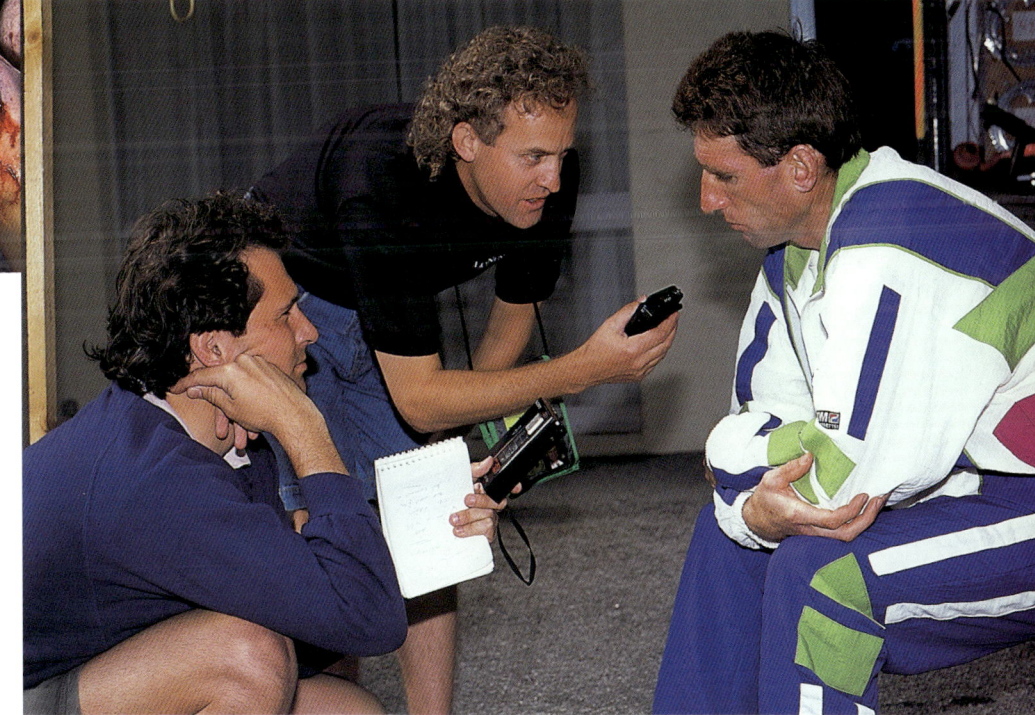

1994: TOUR DE FRANCE: ARMENTIÈRES

After colliding with a gendarme at the height of the finish sprint into Armentières, Laurent Jalabert gets help from his soigneur. That dramatic crash landed him in the hospital for extensive dental surgery, and marked the end of the sprinting phase of the Frenchman's career.

1991: TOUR DE FRANCE: QUIMPER

During the ninth and 10th stages of the 1991 Tour, every member of the PDM team became sick with a high fever. It was later revealed that their team doctor injected each rider with an unrefrigerated batch of medication. All of them left the race, including Sean Kelly (right), who was interviewed on his departure by journalists Rupert Guinness (left) and John Wilcockson.

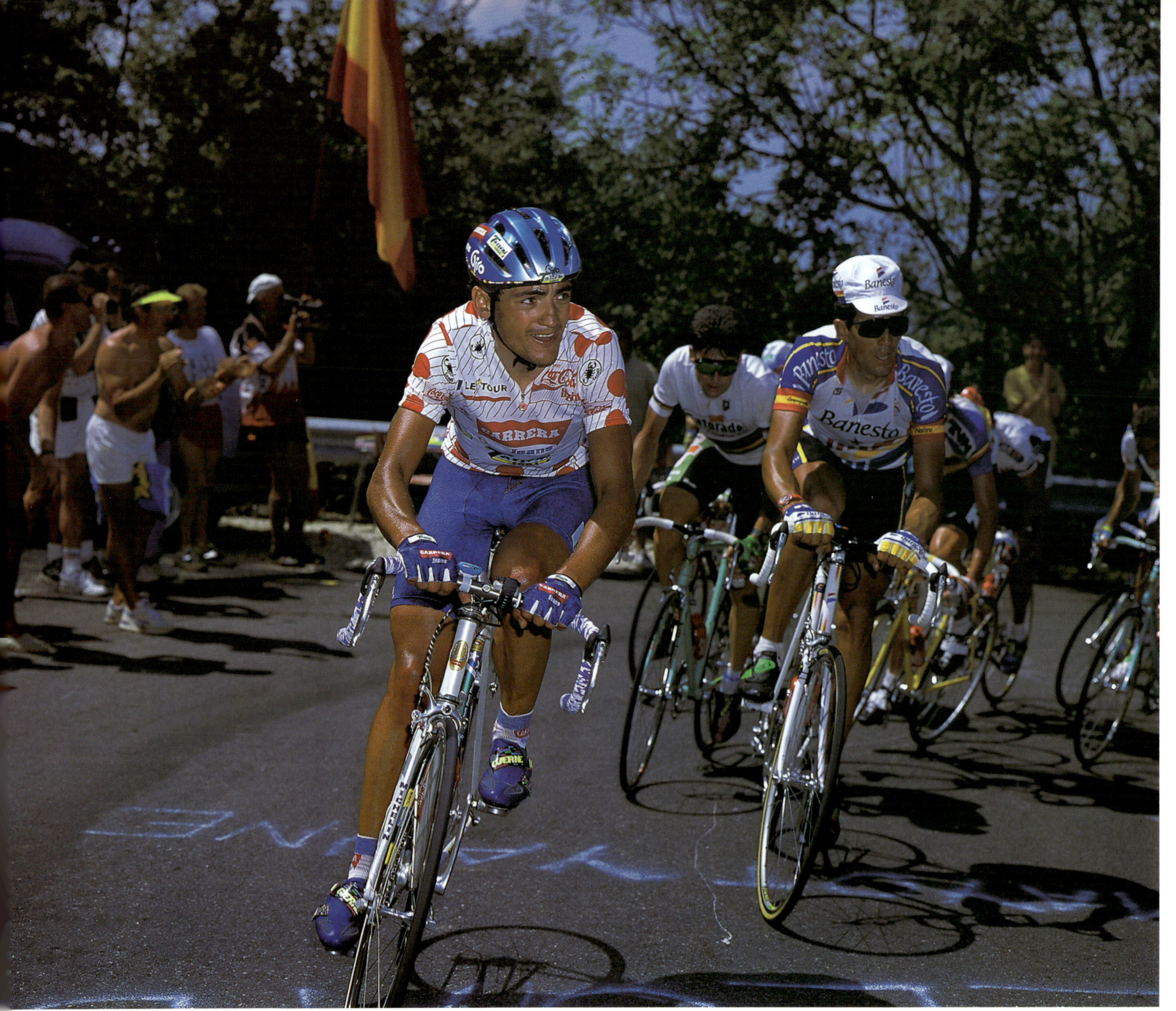

1992: TOUR DE FRANCE: MONT SALÈVE

Claudio Chiappucci—the day before his epic break to Sestriere—leads Miguel Induráin (right) and Gianni Bugno (in rainbow jersey) up the steep slopes of Mont Salève, near Geneva.

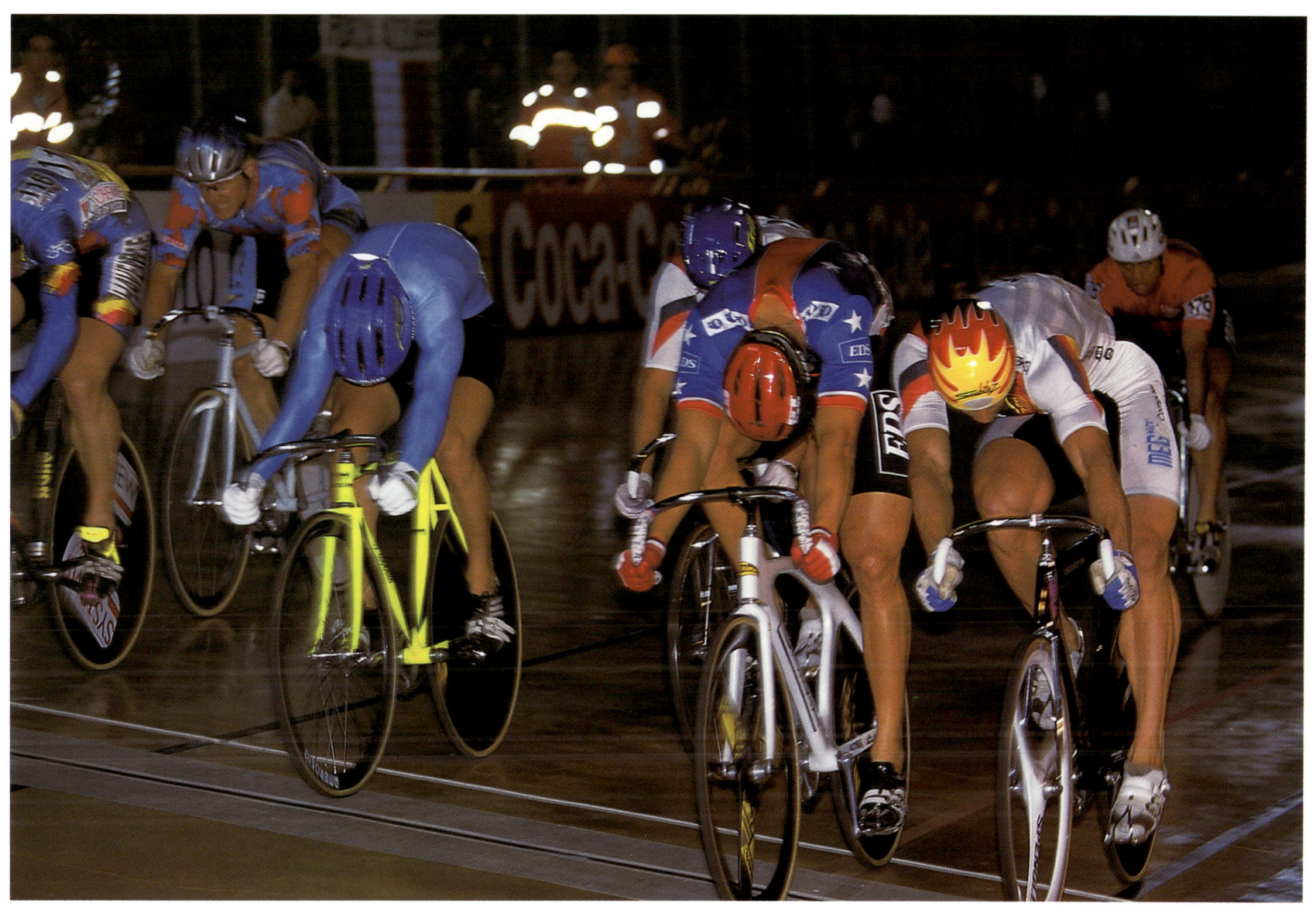

1994: WORLD TRACK CHAMPIONSHIPS: PALERMO, ITALY

The keirin is often one of the most exciting—and often crash-marred—events at the track world's. Here, at an outdoor velodrome on the island of Sicily, American Marty Nothstein holds off German Michael Hübner for the gold medal.

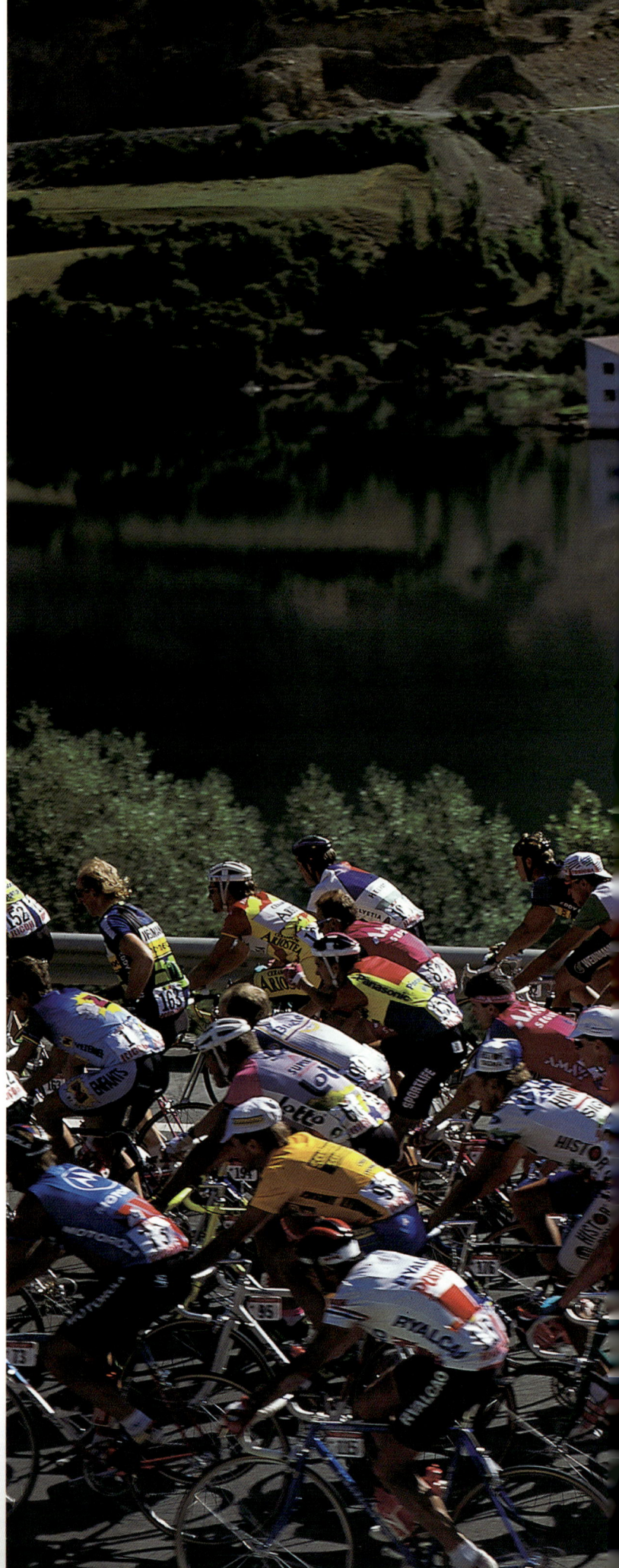

1991: TOUR DE FRANCE: PYRENEES

On the Spanish side of the Pyrenees mountains, a back road carries the Tour peloton past the lakeside hamlet of Lanuza on its way to the Col du Pourtalet. The man in the yellow jersey is French climber Luc Leblanc; Miguel Induráin would take over the race lead by the end of the day for the first time in his career.

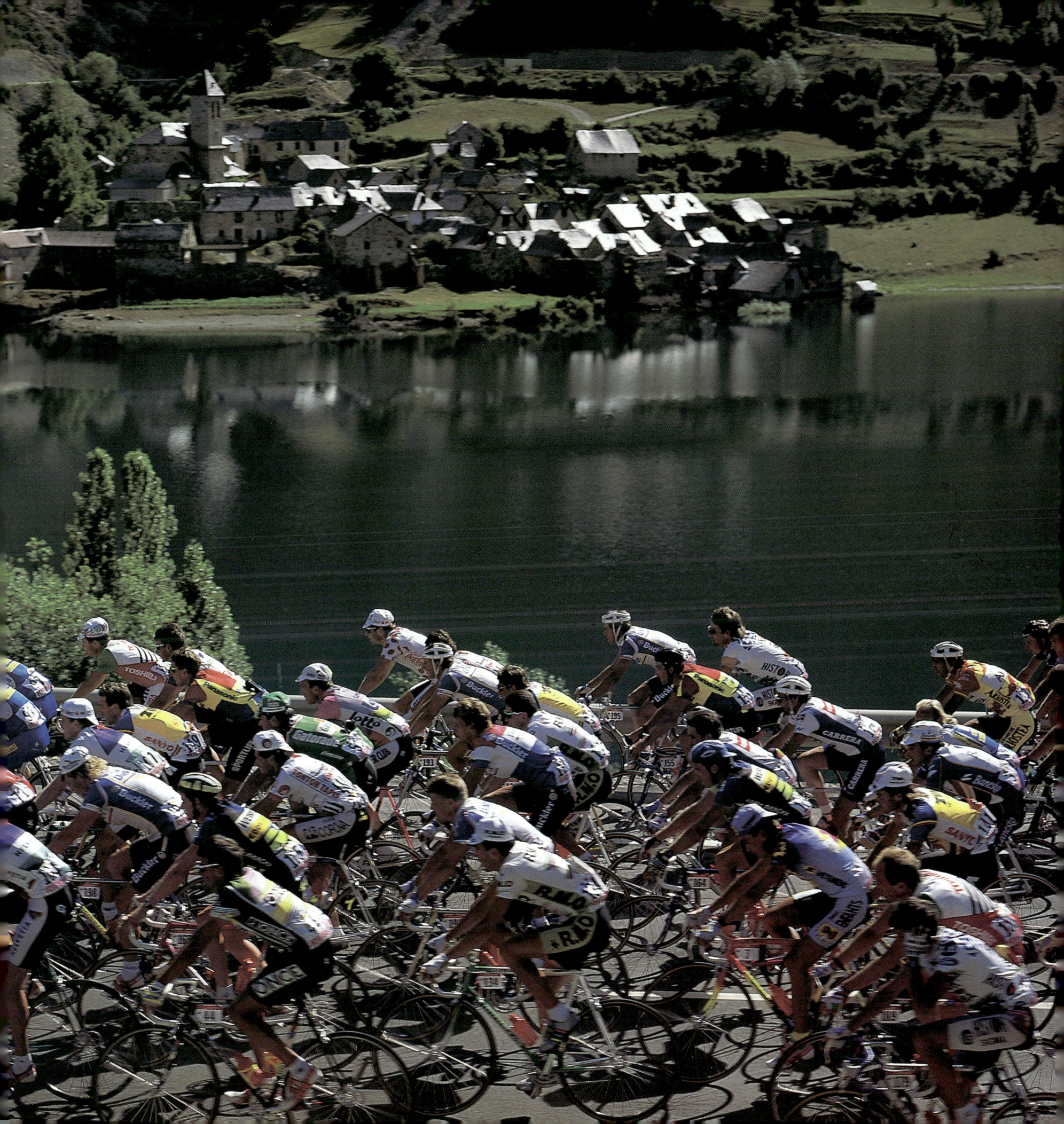

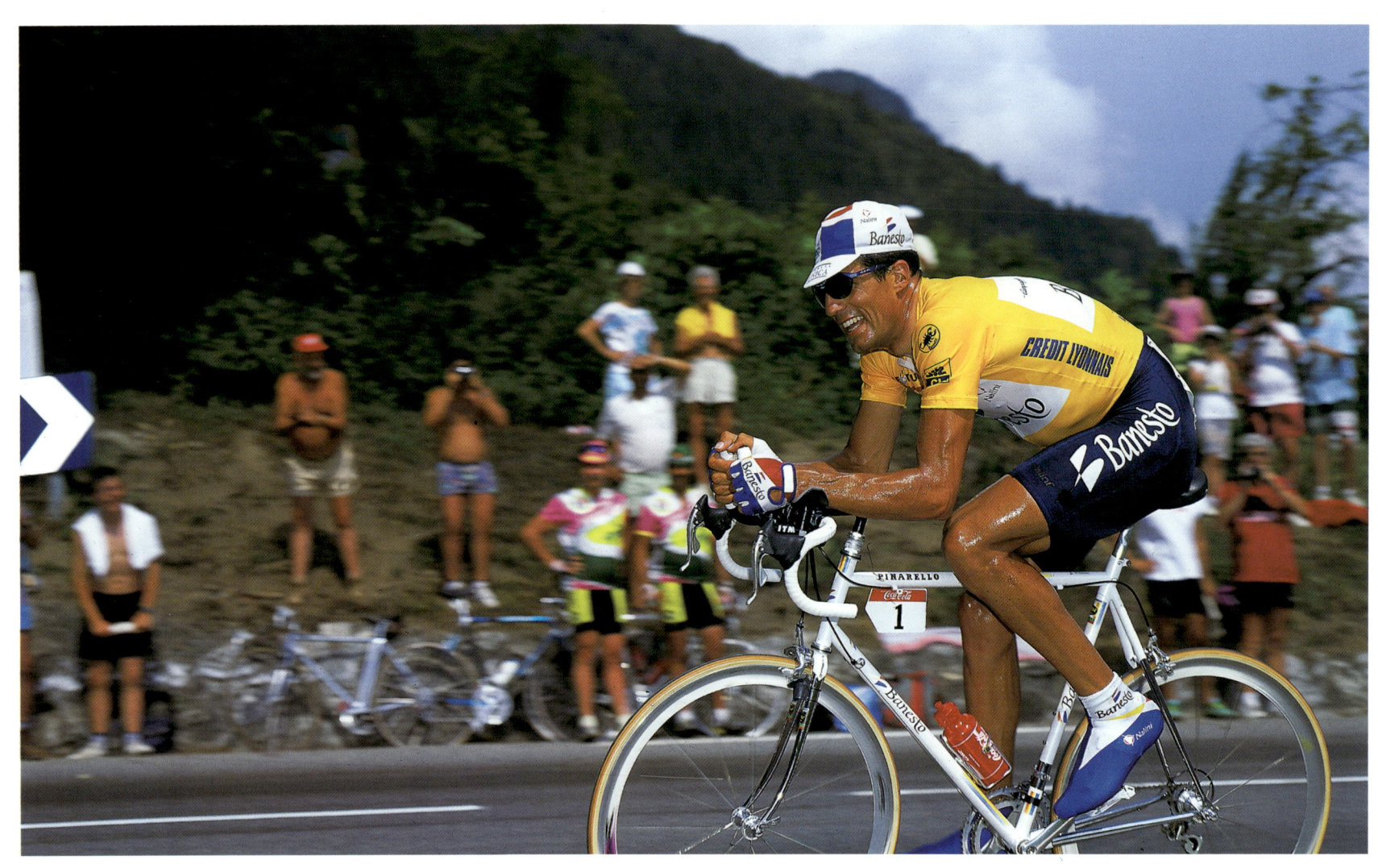

1994: TOUR DE FRANCE: FRENCH ALPS

In the fourth year of his Tour de France reign, Miguel Induráin rides the mountain time trial between Cluses and Avoriaz.

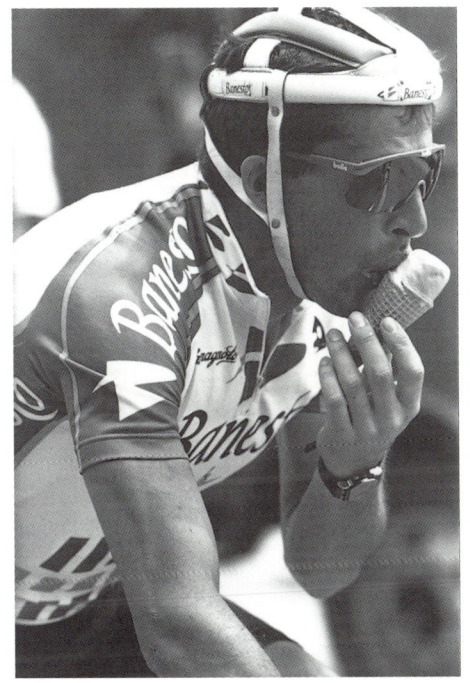

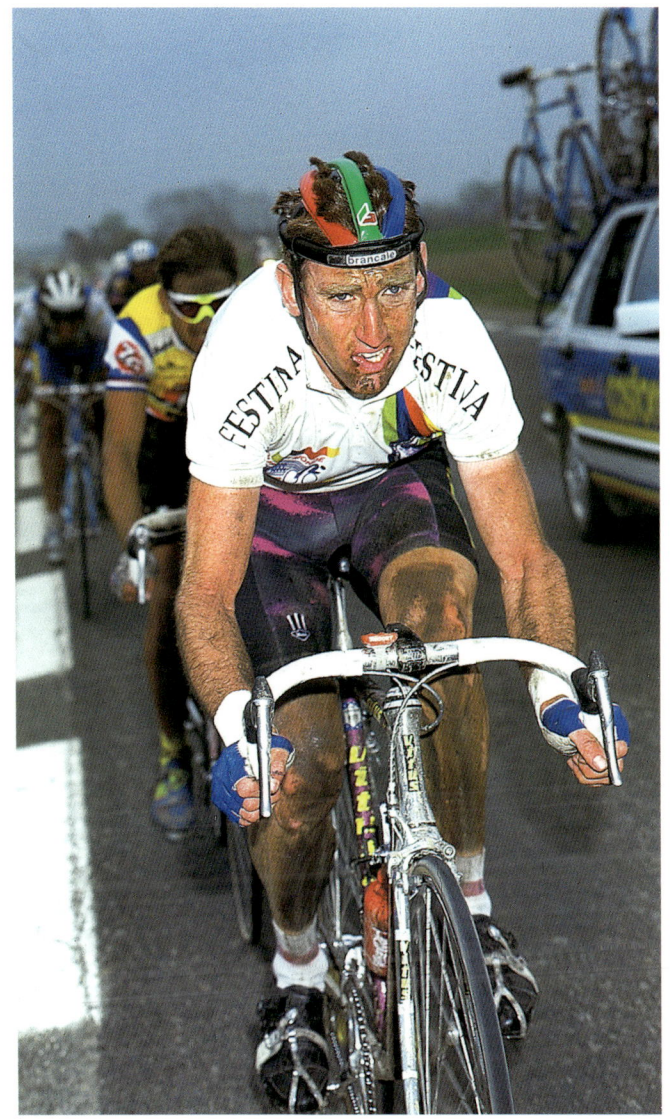

1991: GIRO D'ITALIA: ITALY

Gelato has its attractions, even for a Tour de France winner like Pedro Delgado.

1992: TOUR OF FLANDERS: BELGIUM

Wearing the leader's jersey of the World Cup, two weeks after winning Milan-San Remo for the second time, Sean "King" Kelly rides through the rain in his adopted Flanders.

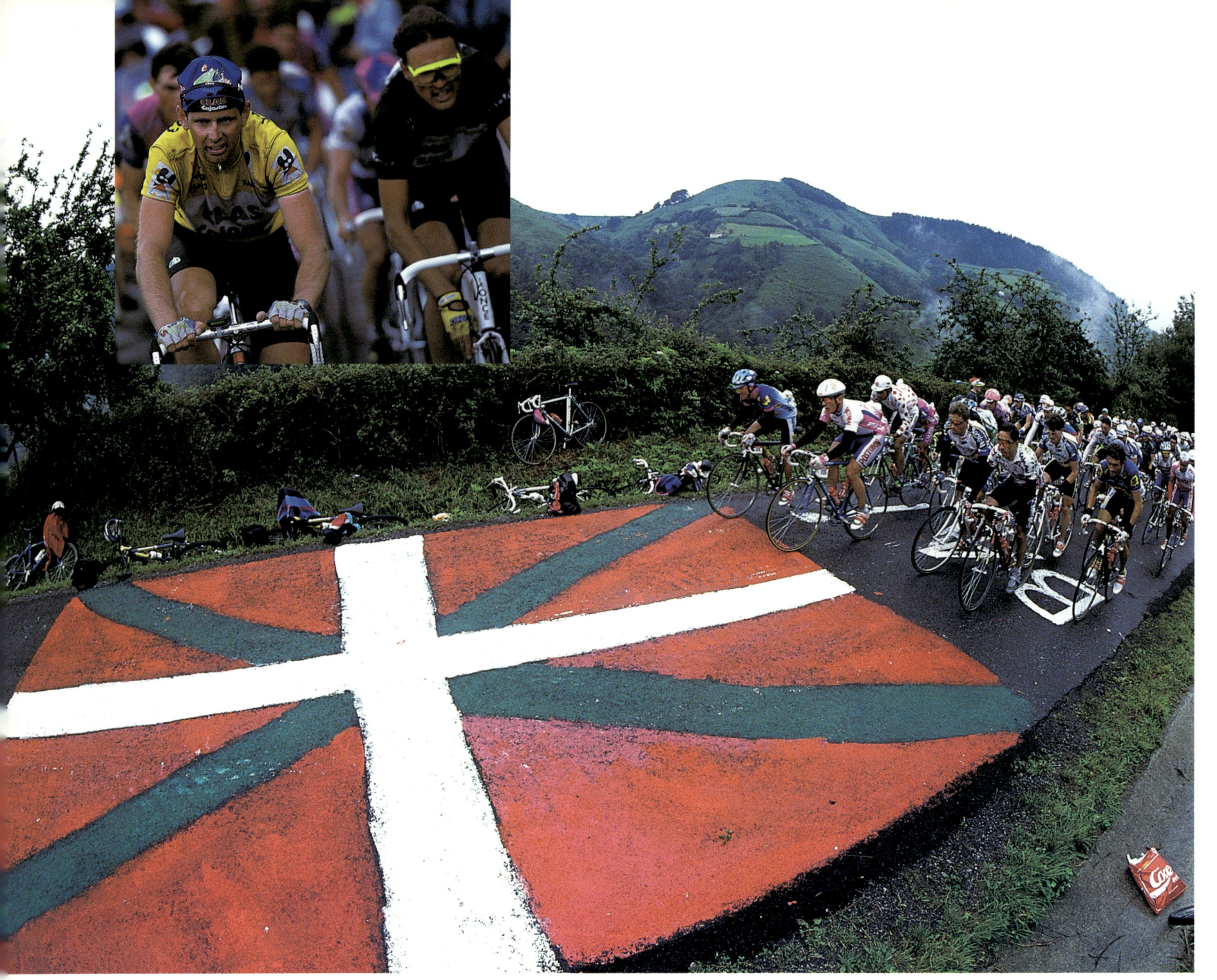

1993: VUELTA A ESPAÑA: SPAIN

Two Swiss riders dominated the Vuelta in 1993. Here, race leader Tony Rominger (in yellow) races with eventual runner-up Alex Zülle on the mountain stage between Gijon and Oviedo.

1992: TOUR DE FRANCE: SPAIN

The Basque fans of northern Spain proudly painted their distinctive flag on the Tour route between San Sebastian and Pau in 1992.

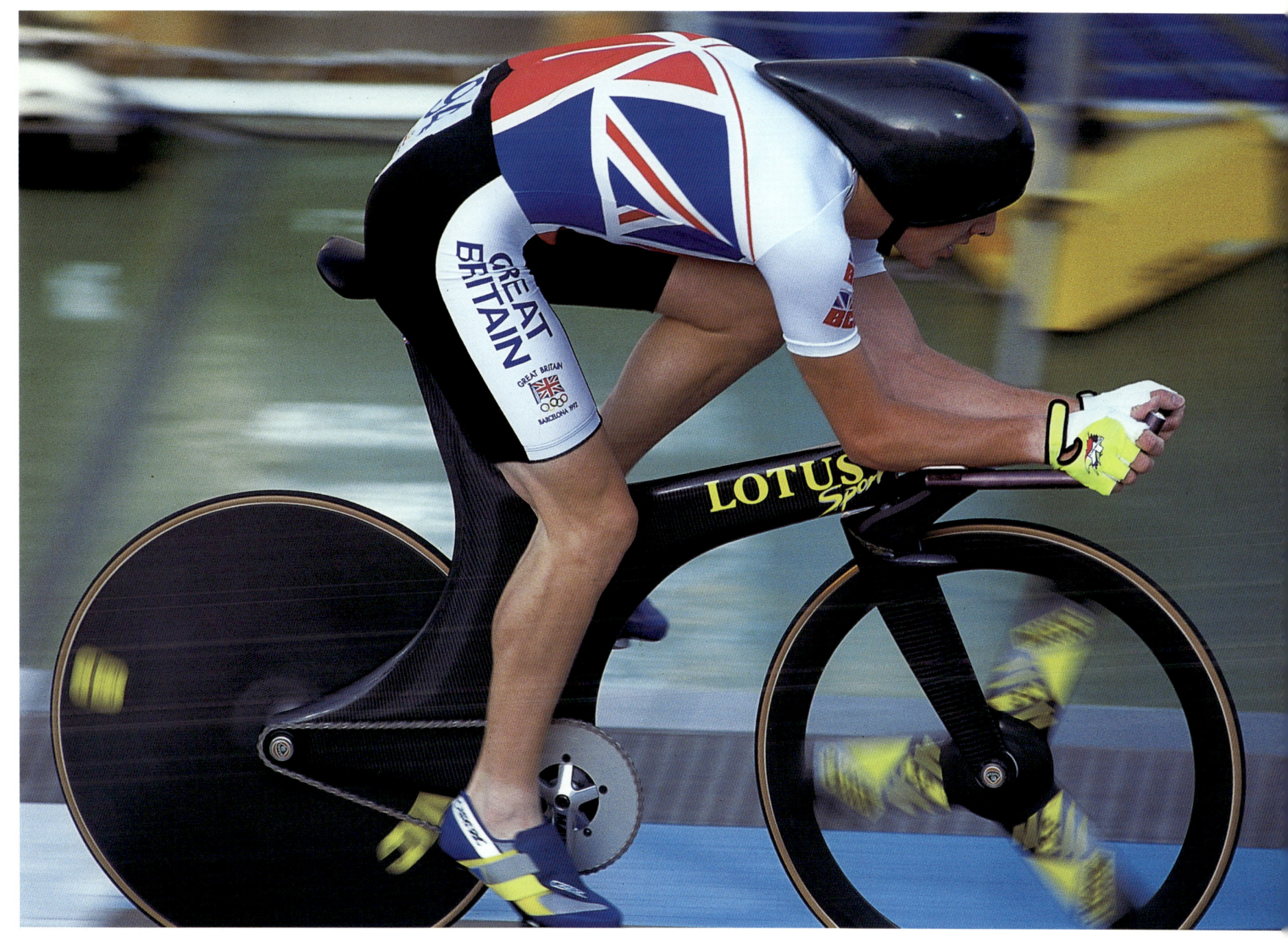

1992: OLYMPIC GAMES: BARCELONA

Aboard a revolutionary monoblade, monocoque carbon-fiber frame, Britain's Chris Boardman races to a world 4000 meters record on his way to an Olympic gold medal in the individual pursuit at Barcelona.

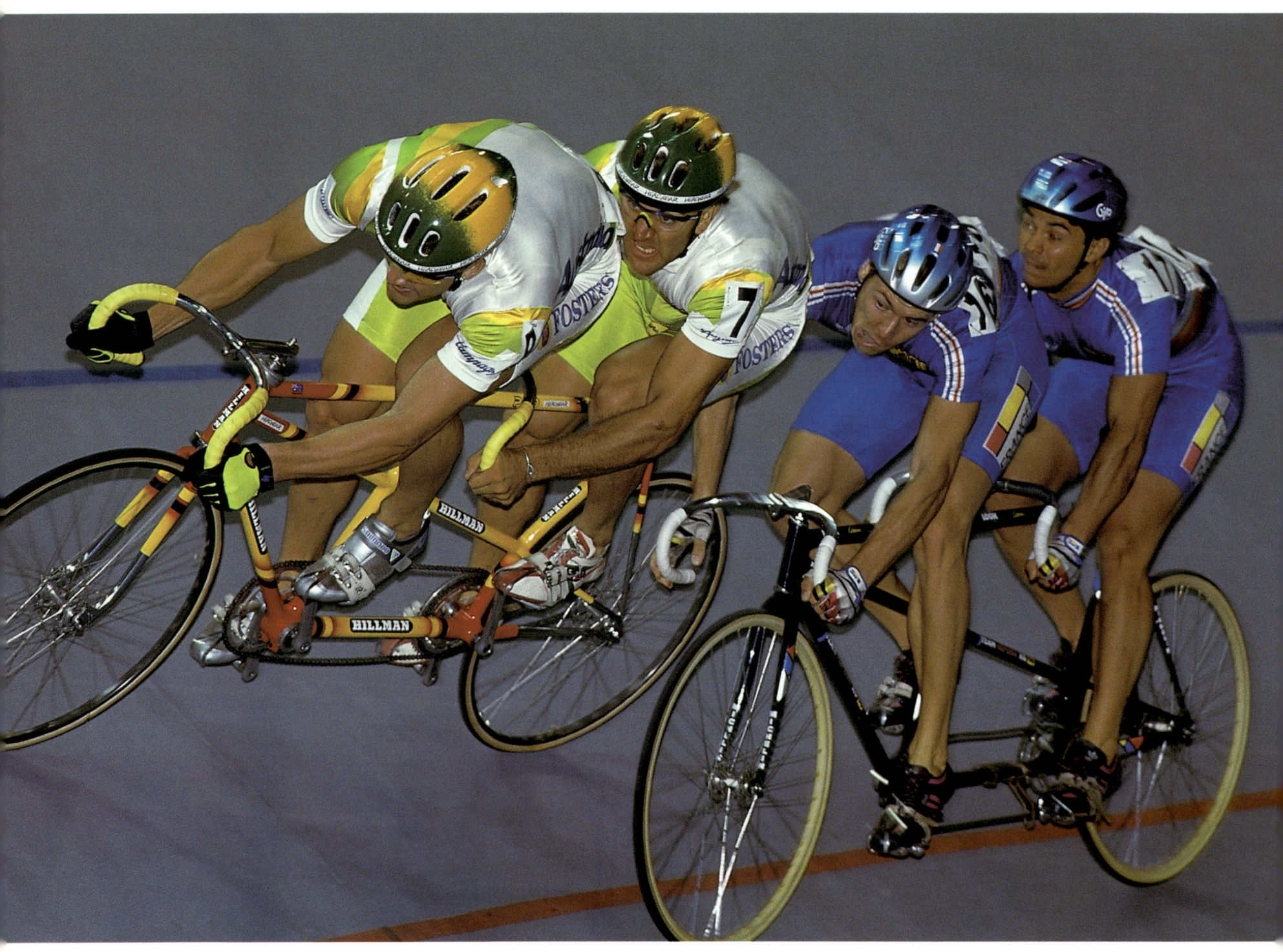

1992: WORLD TRACK CHAMPIONSHIPS: VALENCIA, SPAIN

Whoops! French tandem pilot Frédéric Lancien and teammate Denis Lemyre suddenly realize they have no way past their quarter-final opponents Tony Peden and Dave Dew of Australia at the '92 track world's.

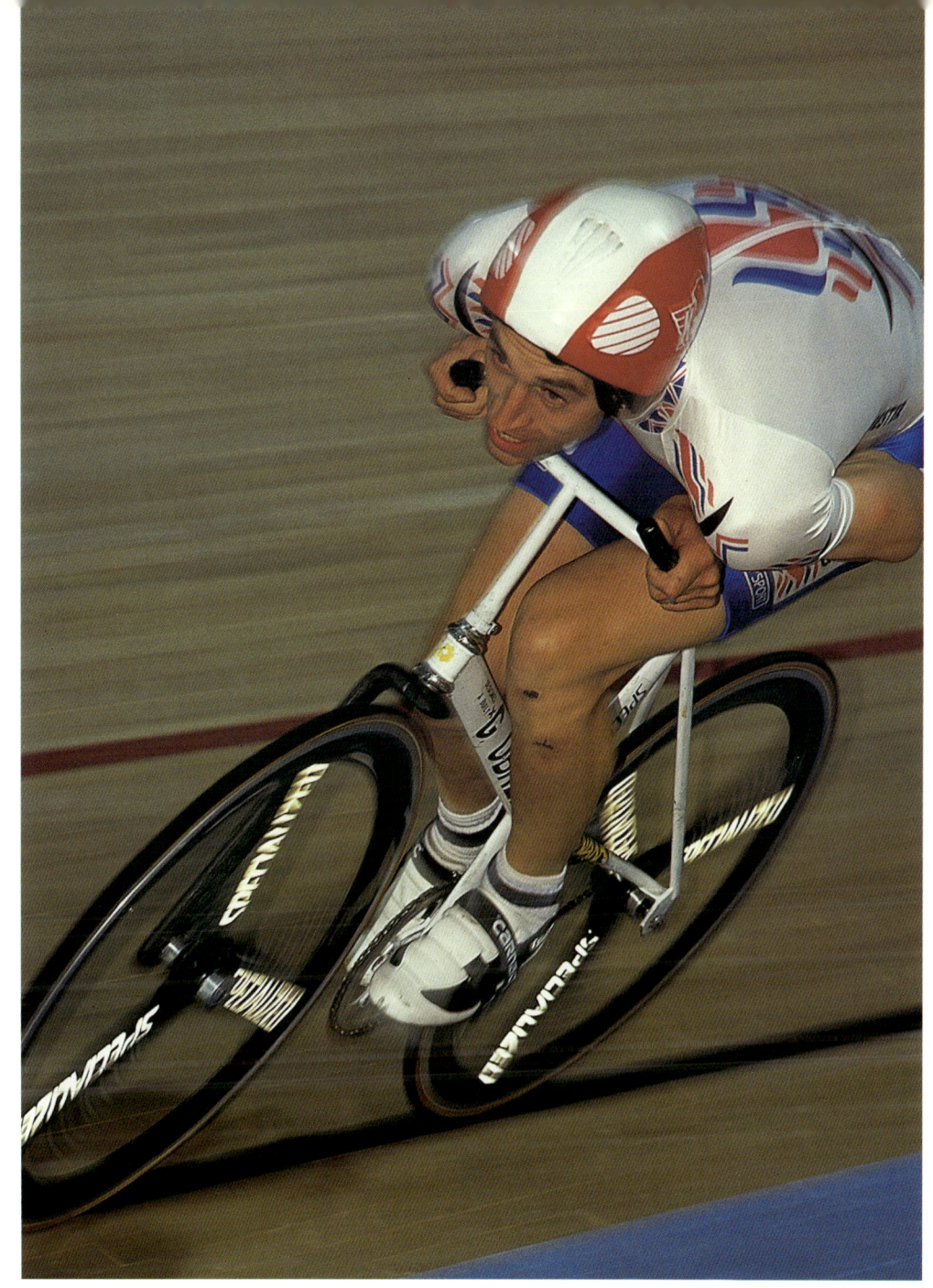

1993: WORLD TRACK CHAMPIONSHIPS: HAMAR, NORWAY

On his home-built bike and in his patented "egg" position—which was later banned by the UCI—Scotsman Graeme Obree wins the world pursuit championship in Norway, a month after breaking Francesco Moser's long-standing world hour record.

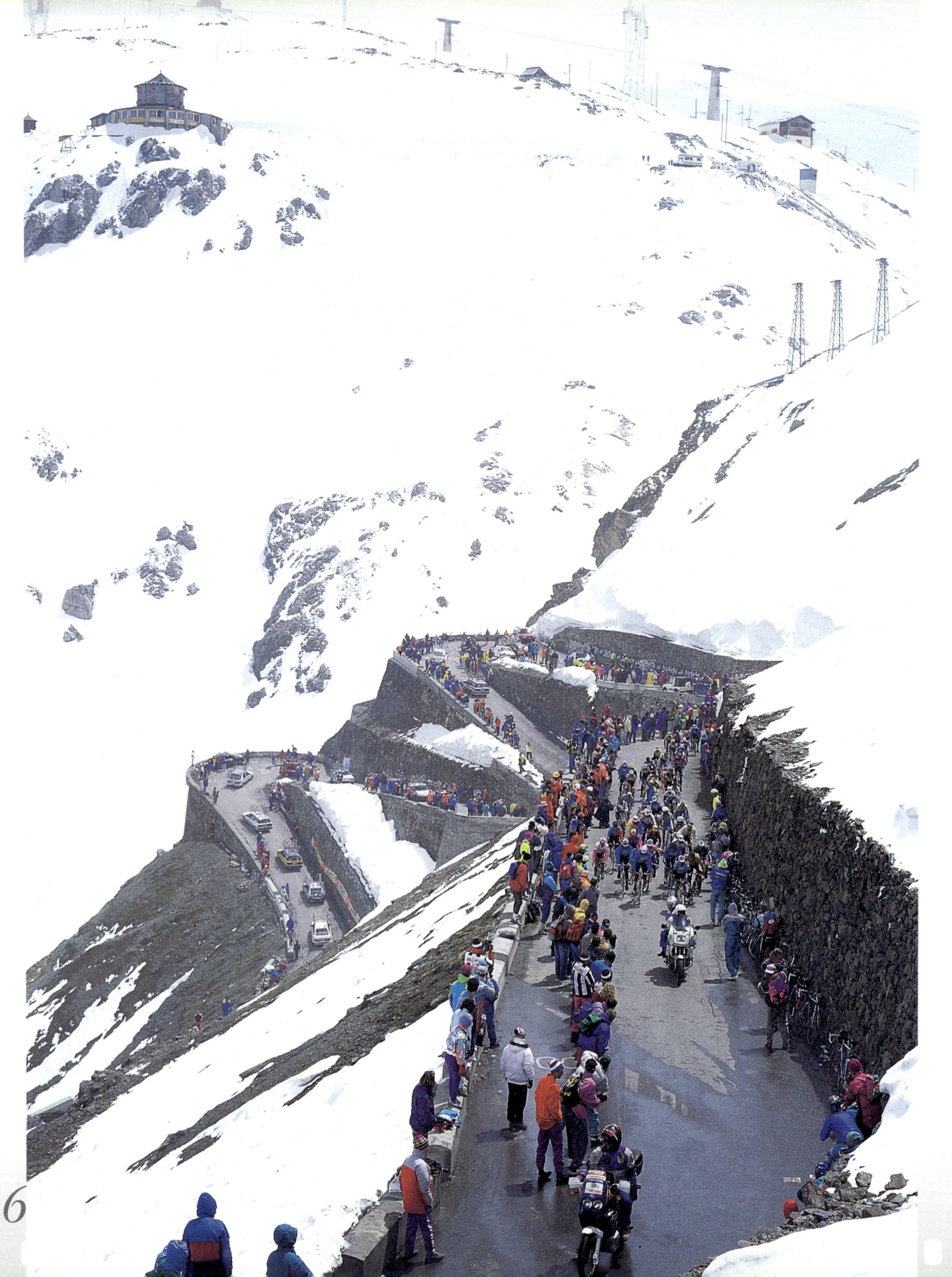

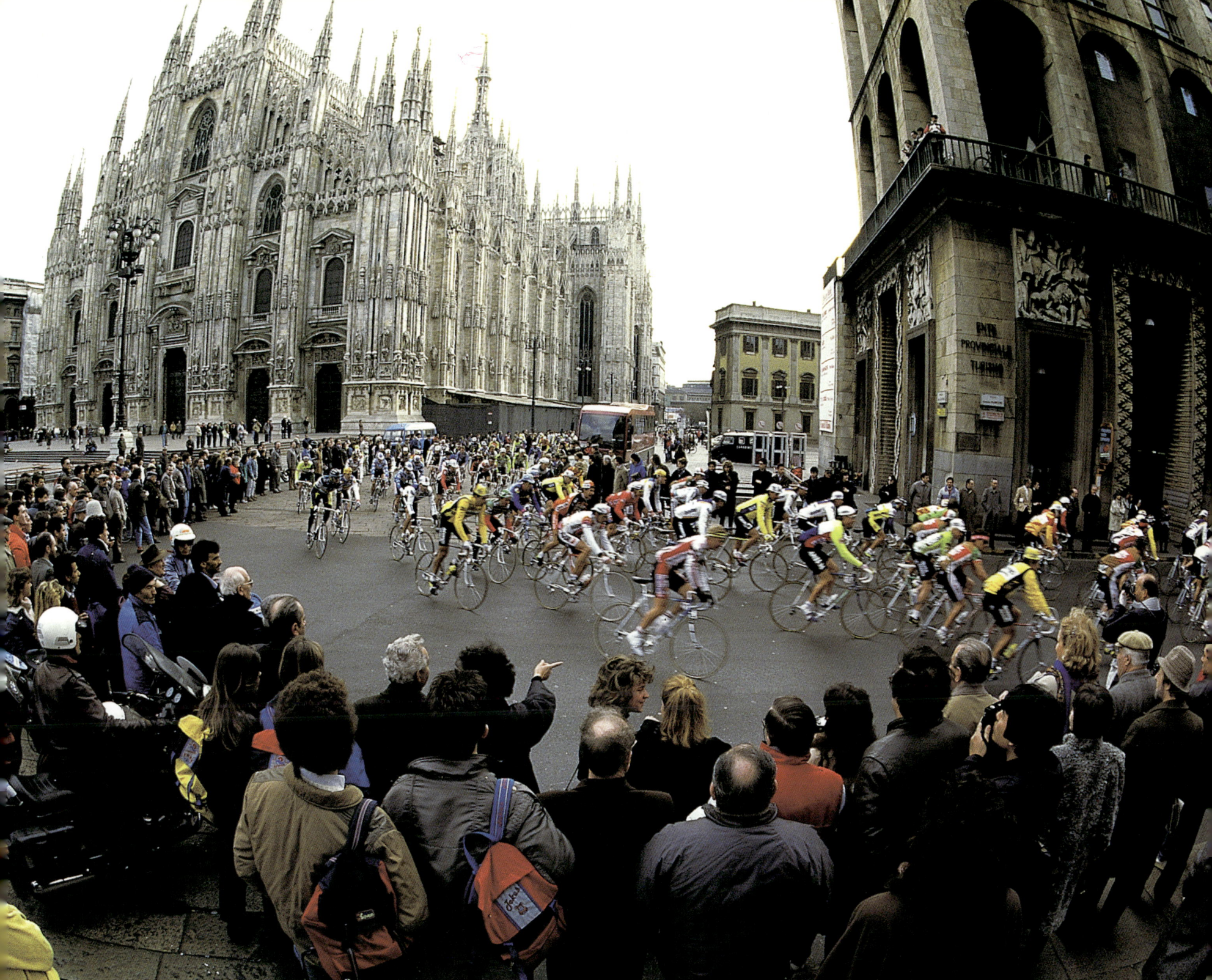

1994 GIRO D'ITALIA: ITALIAN ALPS

At 2758 meters (9048 feet), the Stelvio is the highest and most famous mountain pass in the Italian Alps. Snow banks still lined the switchback ascent on June 5, 1994, when the Giro peloton scaled the giant climb on the stage between Merano and Aprica.

1991: MILAN-SAN REMO: ITALY

Milan's grandiose Gothic cathedral is the traditional starting point for Italy's marvelous spring classic, Milan-San Remo.

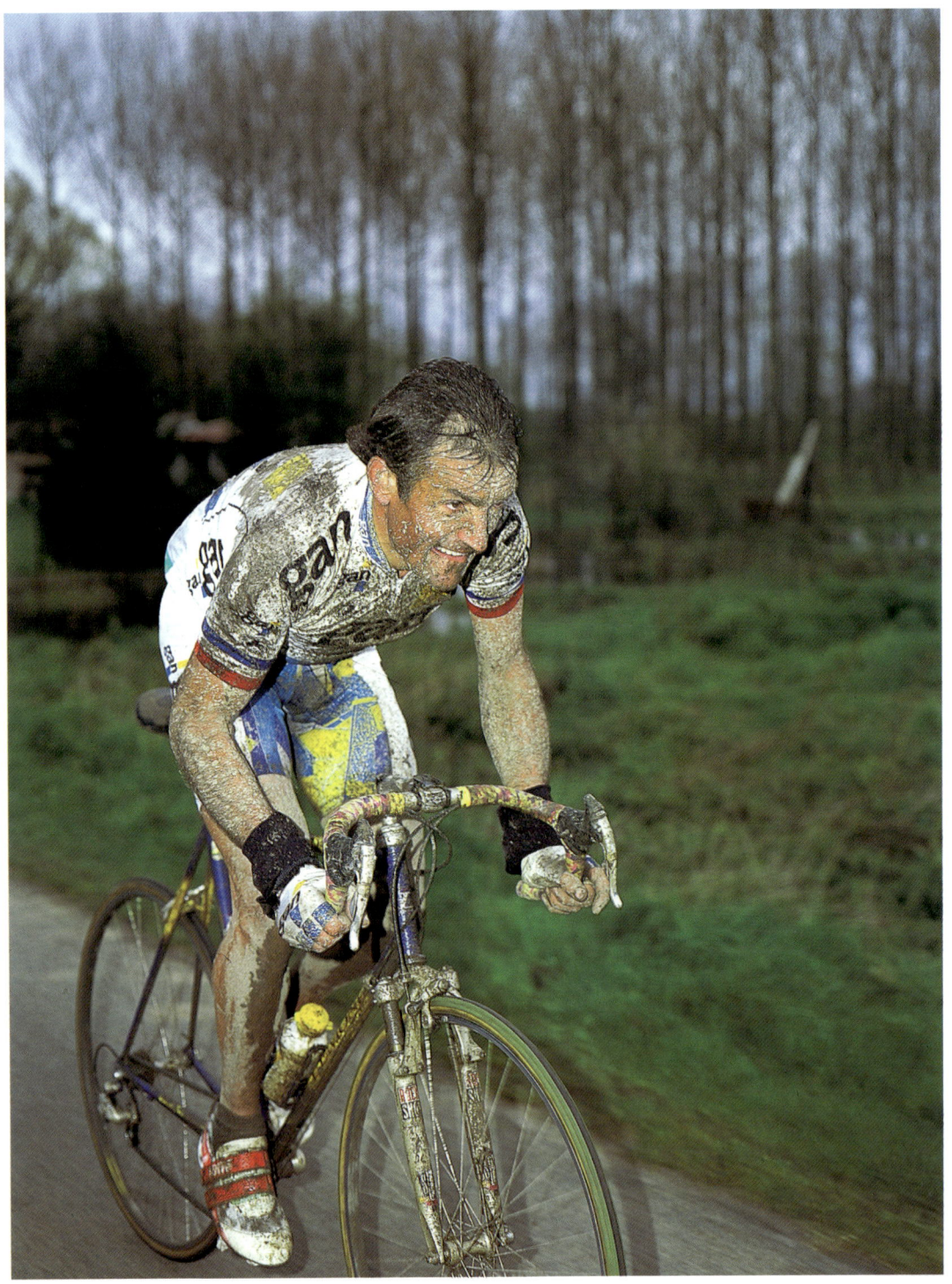

1994: PARIS-ROUBAIX: FRANCE

At age 39, two-time Paris-Roubaix champion Gilbert Duclos-Lassalle of France battles back from a crash and two flats to finish seventh at the '94 edition.

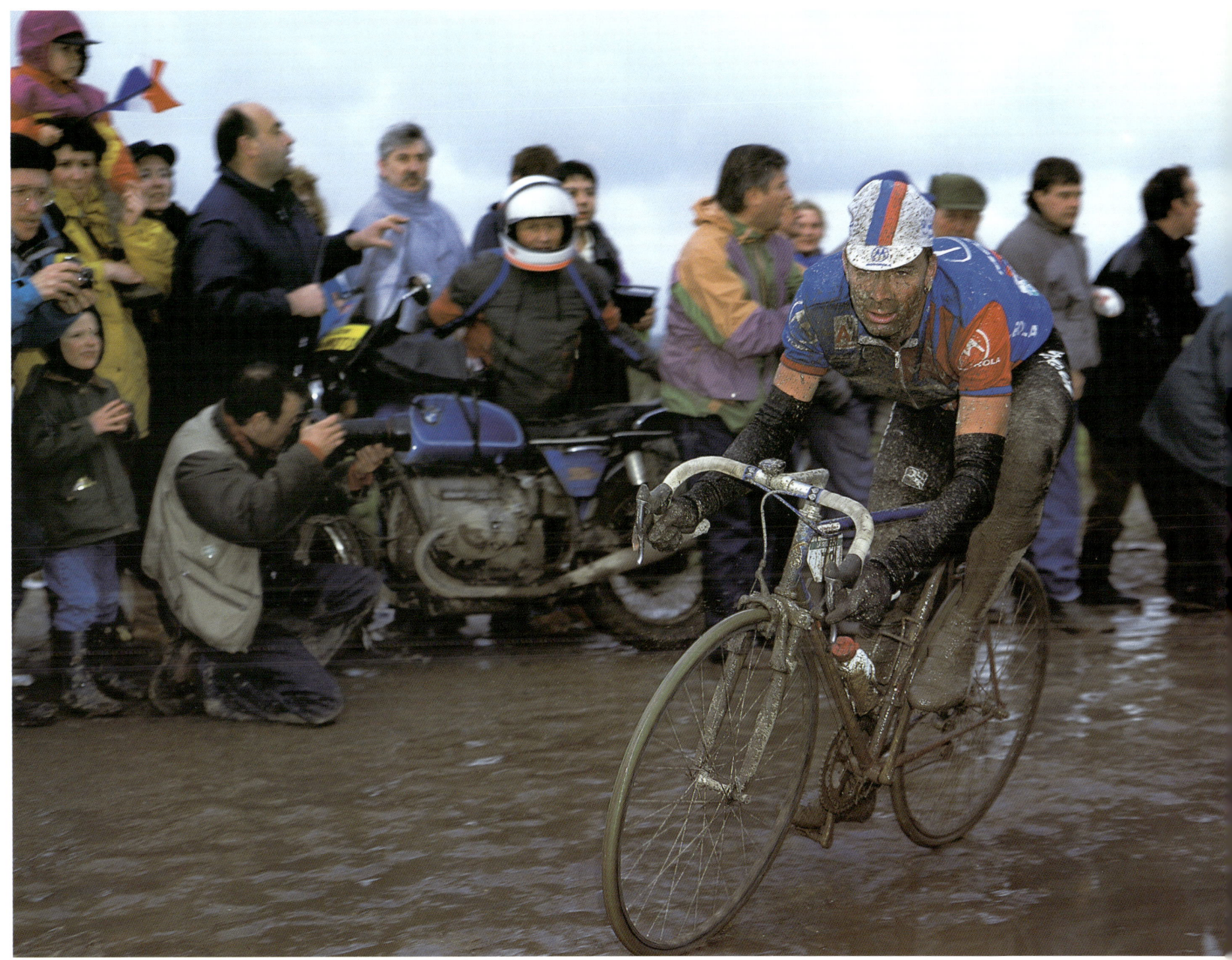

1994: PARIS-ROUBAIX: FRANCE

Englishman Sean Yates always raced strongly through the cobbled hell of Paris-Roubaix. In the rain-battered '94 edition, the Motorola man ended up in fifth place.

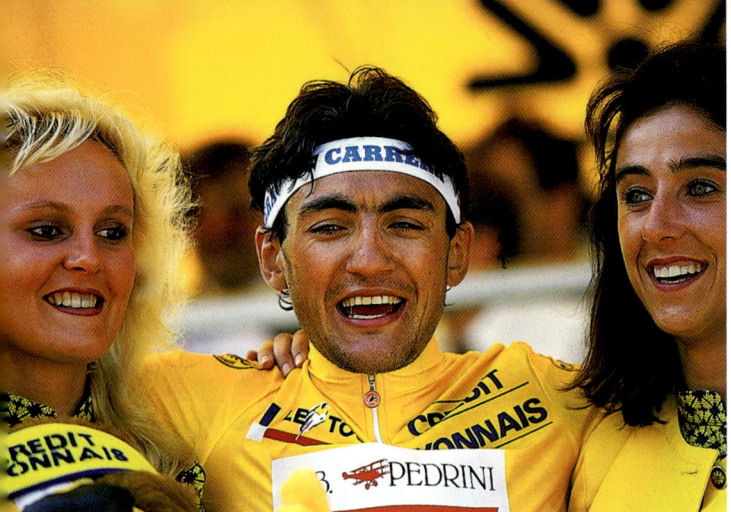
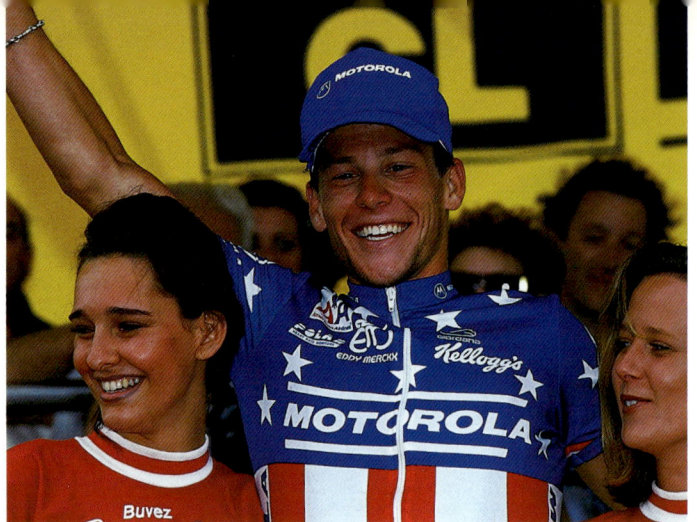
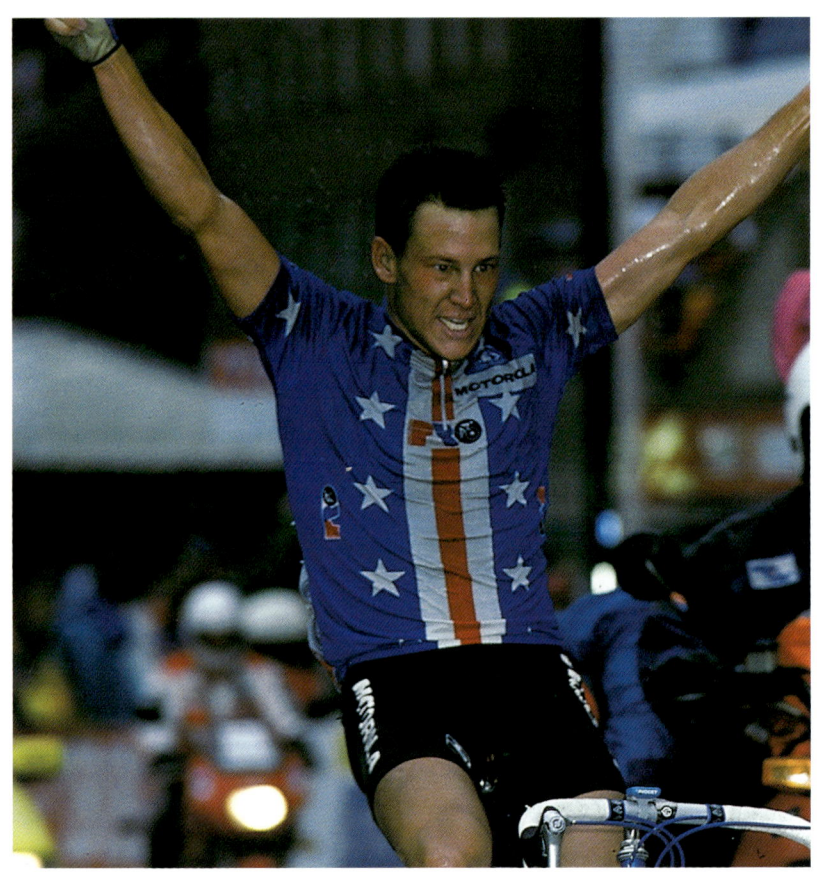

1990: TOUR DE FRANCE: VILLARD-DE-LANS

Long way, baby! Claudio Chiappucci metamorphosed from a team worker into a champion at the 1990 Tour de France—where he eventually finished second to Greg LeMond.

1993: TOUR DE FRANCE: VERDUN

Lance Armstrong's first Tour de France resulted in a brilliant stage win at Verdun, where he outsprinted Mexican Raúl Alcalá and the rest of a six-man breakaway group.

1993: WORLD ROAD CHAMPIONSHIPS: OSLO, NORWAY

At age 21, just a year after turning professional, Lance Armstrong became the world champion after racing away from a pack that included Tour de France maestro Miguel Induráin.

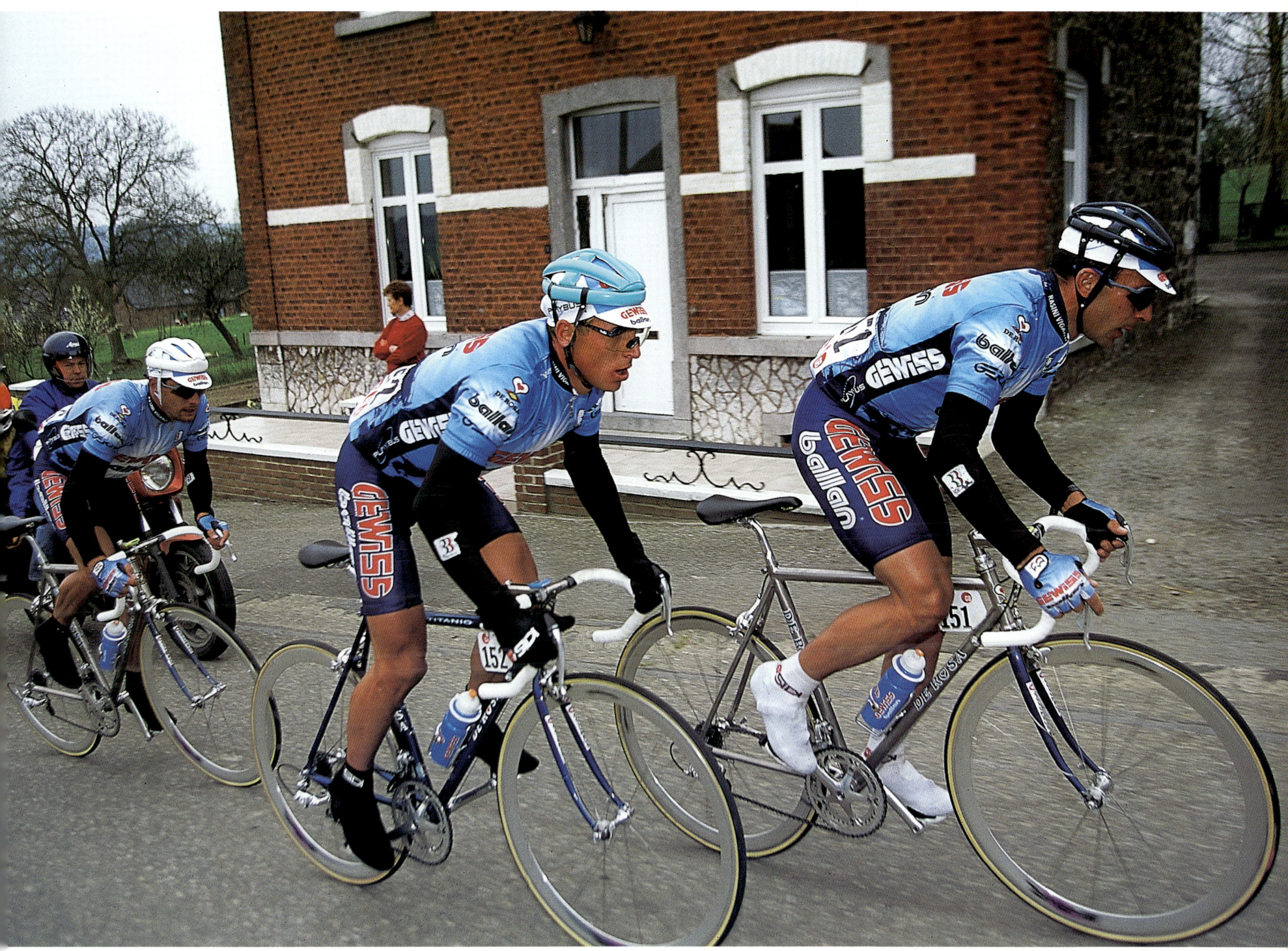

1994: FLÈCHE WALLONNE: BELGIUM

Three men. Three Gewiss-Ballan riders. Moreno Argentin (at the front), Evgeni Berzin and Giorgio Furlan conducted a 70km-long breakaway, to finish 1-2-3 at the Flèche Wallonne classic in '94. There was talk of their dominance not being entirely natural....

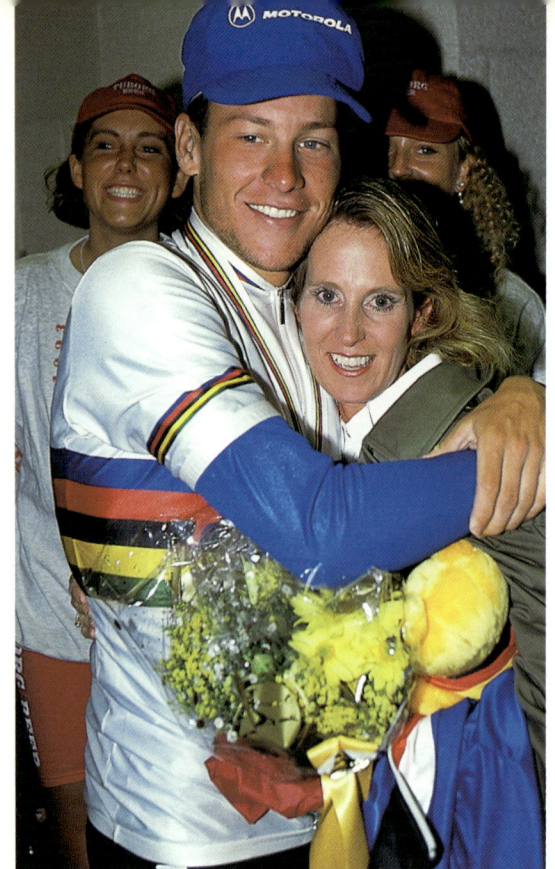

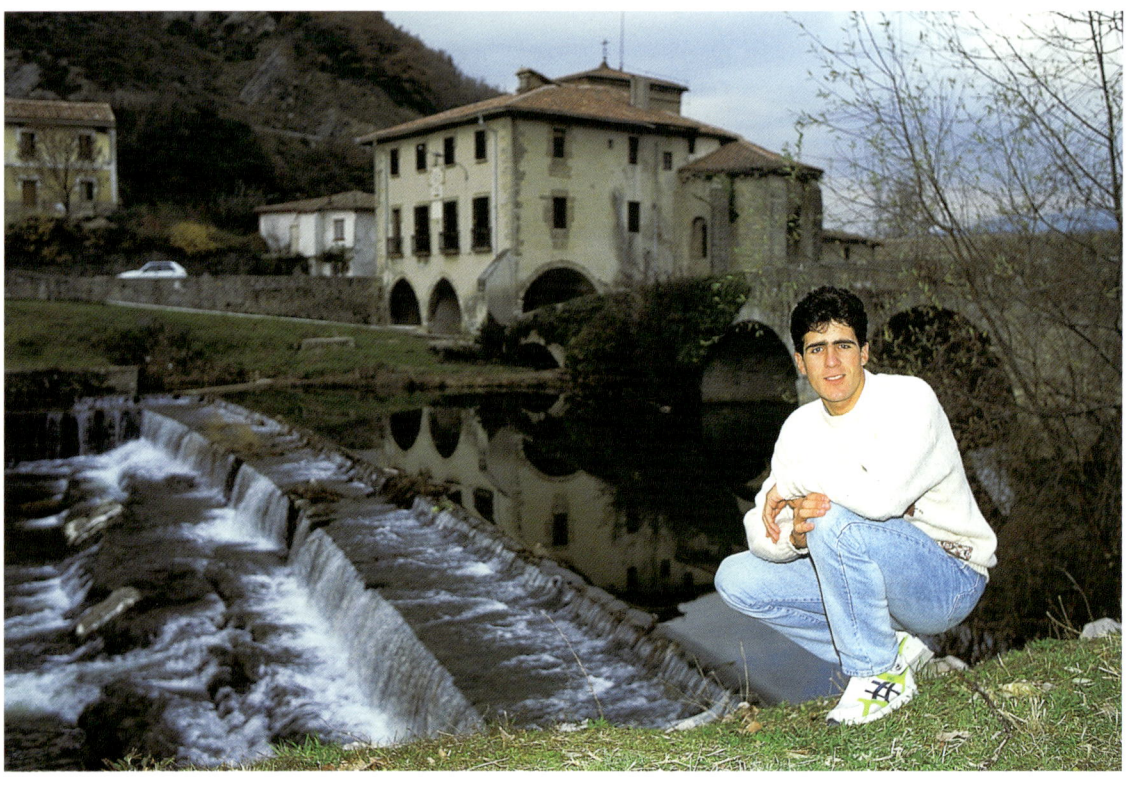

1993: WORLD ROAD CHAMPIONSHIPS: NORWAY

Son and mother: Lance Armstrong celebrates with Linda Walling after his victorious world's.

1993: INDURÁIN'S HOME: VILLAVA, SPAIN

Home alone: Miguel Induráin relaxes by a bridge on the pilgrim route to Santiago de Compostela, near his family home in Navarra.

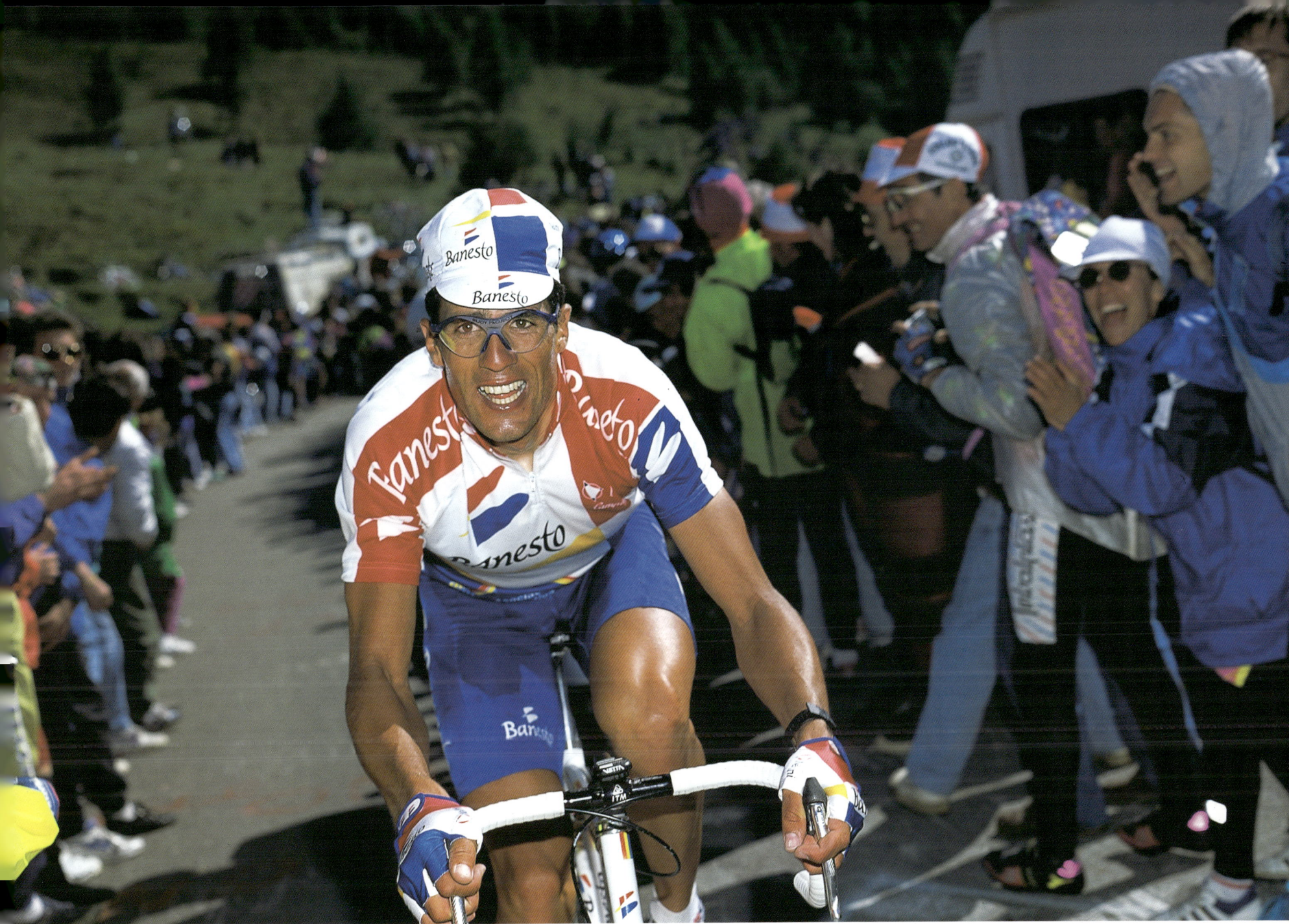

1994: GIRO D'ITALIA: ITALY

Two-time Giro winner Miguel Induráin was just below his best and placed only third in the 1994 edition.

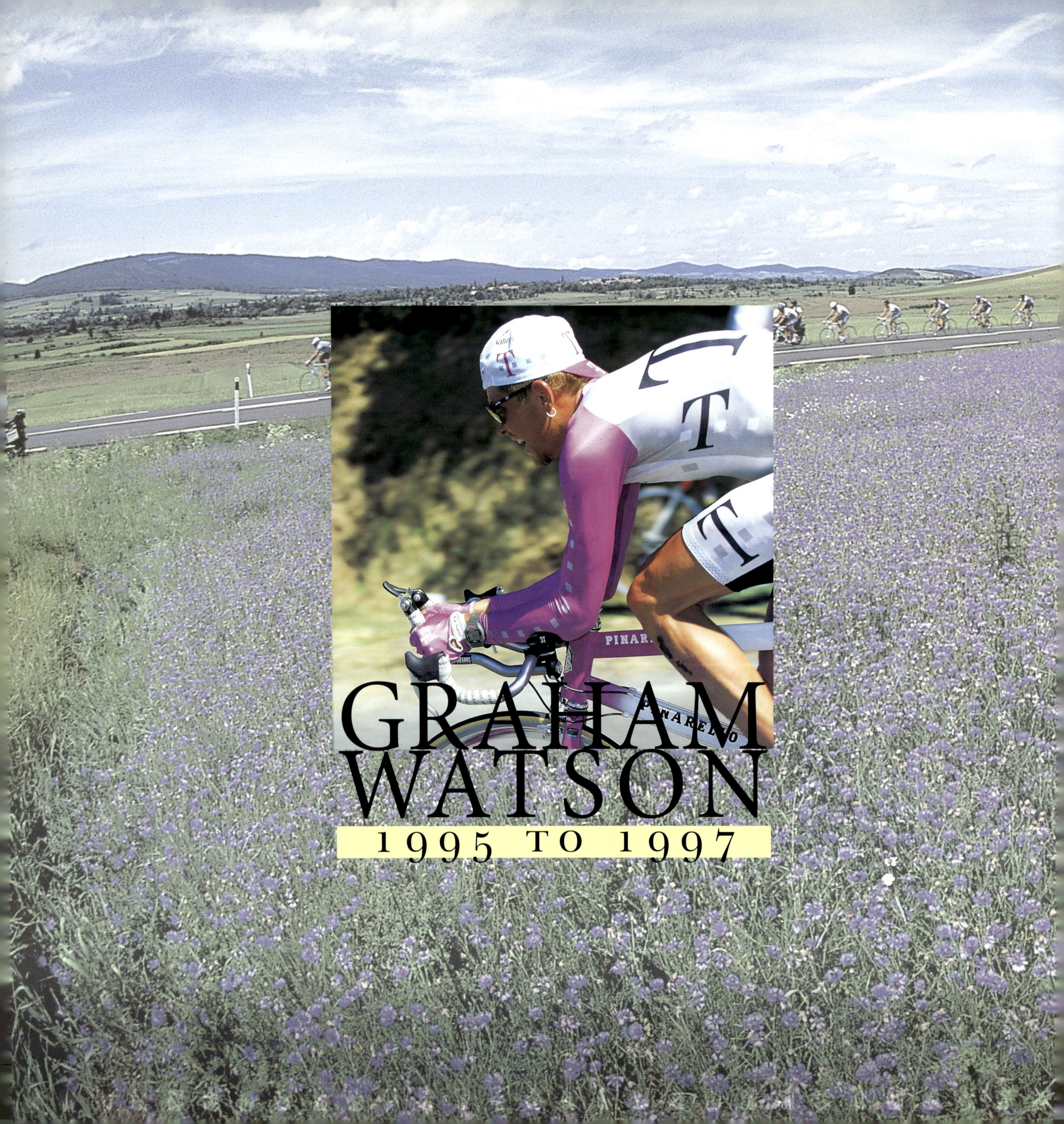

GRAHAM WATSON

Sadly, 1995 will always be remembered for the death of Fabio Casartelli, during stage 15 of the Tour de France. One of the quandaries a cycling photographer faces is whether or not to take pictures when there has been a serious crash, or, as in this instance, when someone's life is clearly in peril. In the case of Casartelli, I was thankful that I wasn't there and didn't have to make that decision. Some of my colleagues were there, and, though hardened by war assignments and road accidents—the less glamorous side of being a professional photographer—many arrived in the press-center that evening in a state of shock.

The following day was deeply moving, for the whole peloton rode as one in tribute to the young Italian from the Motorola team. It was a stage that stretched to more than eight hours and took its toll on the riders, who climbed passes like the 20-kilometer-long Col du Soudet in searing temperatures. And at the end of the day, with the entire Motorola team having ridden on the front for the last 50km into Pau, the rest of the peloton sat up within sight of the line, allowing Casartelli's distressed teammates to make a dignified and very poignant tribute to him by crossing the finish line together. It was a very touching end to a highly emotional day, and I felt privileged to have witnessed the riders' magnificent tribute.

More sadness came with the news that broke in October 1996: One of Casartelli's teammates, the brilliant American cyclist, Lance Armstrong, had been diagnosed with testicular cancer. Unlike Casartelli, whom I had only photographed at a Motorola training camp in 1995, and therefore hardly knew, I had always enjoyed a friendship of sorts with Armstrong. I'd first met him some years earlier at a California training camp, and in March 1996 he helped celebrate my 40th birthday, the day after he finished second overall in Paris-Nice.

That birthday aside, 1996 hadn't been a great year for me on a sporting front, for I'd seen the downfall of Induráin in that summer's Tour de France, and at the hands of someone far less deserving, or so it seemed at the time. Bjarne Riis was never going to be regarded with the same affection that Induráin enjoyed throughout his career—even if Riis had gone on to win five Tours de France. But that didn't stop him from tearing into Induráin's defenses like a man possessed,

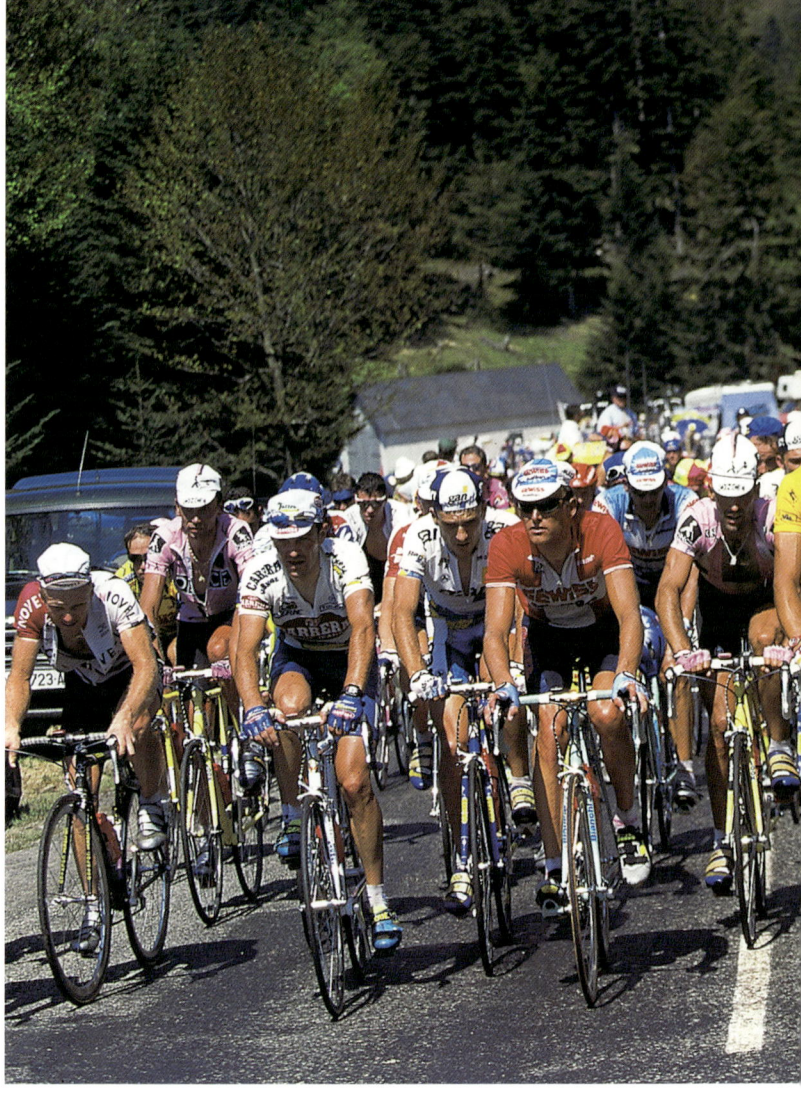

1995: TOUR DE FRANCE: PYRENEES

In homage to Fabio Casartelli, who died in a tragic crash the day before, the Tour de France peloton rode the 16th stage as a tribute to the fallen Italian rider. The 117 survivors rode as one over six mountain passes and 237km from Tarbes to Pau. Everyone agreed, it was the toughest day of the Tour.

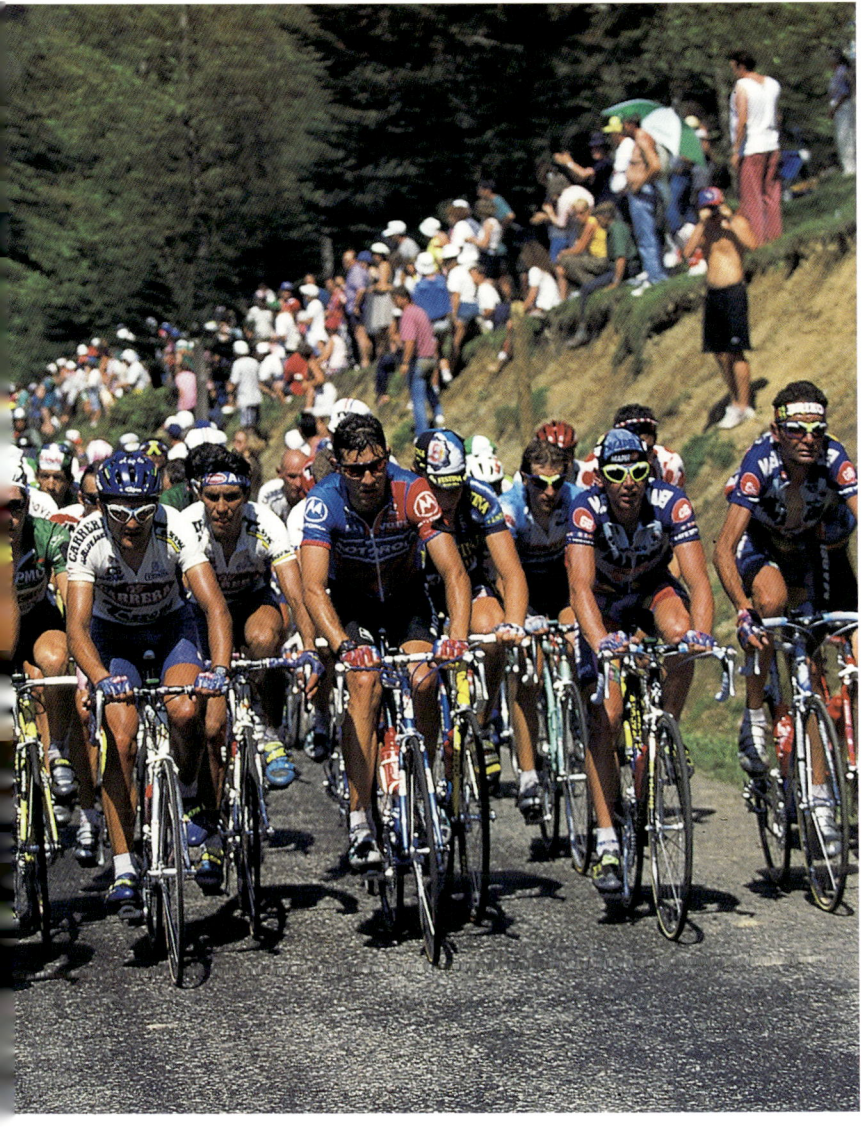almost belittling the great Spaniard's stature on the very approach to Induráin's hometown of Villava. Of course, Induráin would have expected no less, for that is the nature of the sport. Yet even hardened race-watchers winced at seeing Riis pile on the agony on that marathon stage to Pamplona, when perhaps a greater man would have eased off the gas a little and allowed Induráin some dignity in his own backyard.

To make my Tour worse, I'd collected a penalty on stage 8, the uphill time trial to Val d'Isère, by driving against the race route in order to find a better position. And this happened just a few days after we'd been tangled up with Induráin himself during a "hot" moment, as his team car arrived unannounced to change his front wheel. Because of these two incidents, I was thrown out of the race for a day. Fortunately, it was a day whose stage was severely shortened, due to snow and dangerous winds on the Iseran and Galibier passes.

The only bright side to this Tour, as far as I was concerned, was the emergence of Jan Ullrich. The carrot-haired German rode his first Tour as if it were his fifth, with a display of strength and determination that belied his 22 years. There is still a suspicion that he was ordered to slow down by his directeur sportif in the St. Emilion time trial, one day from the end, to avoid embarrassing his team leader, Riis! Ullrich eventually beat his senior teammate by 2:18 in the time trial—just 1:41 short of taking the yellow jersey. And Induráin showed his true courage by finishing second that day to Ullrich, setting himself up as the favorite for the Olympic Games time trial a few weeks later.

Atlanta '96 was a big disappointment to just about everyone but the medal winners. Coming as it did after the vibrant Games of Barcelona in 1992, the Georgia city just wasn't in the same league, with *tapas* bars and *cervezarias* nowhere to be seen among the fast-food outlets of Coca-Colaville. And whereas Barcelona had the warmth of its Catalonian inhabitants to welcome the visitors, the Atlanta Games seemed to be run by thousands of untrained volunteers, brought into the city from all over the States to try and make things run smoothly. Nonetheless, the track racing got the cycling competitions off to a good start, on a superb track built to be destroyed immediately after the competitions! On what will probably be the last outdoor velodrome to be used for a major title event, the photographic possibilities were endless; and names like Collinelli, Bellutti, Rousseau and Ballanger found their pictures in all sorts of sporting magazines for the first time in their lives. But the star of the track Olympics was without doubt Jens Fiedler, the German sprinter who successfully defended the Olympic title he won in Barcelona. His exuberance at winning put a lighter note on what was otherwise a fairly solemn track series.

The road races came next, with great expectations for the yet-to-be diagnosed Armstrong. But the easiness of the circuit worked hopelessly against his talents, causing him to watch from afar as his friend and teammate, Frankie Andreu, rode into fourth place behind surprise winner Pascal Richard of Switzerland.

All eyes now turned to the eagerly awaited individual time trial—the first-ever Olympic competition in this discipline—and my hopes were high on Induráin regaining his strength to wrest something from his disastrous season. Since the event was based on four laps of a 13-kilometer circuit, we photographers had never had it so easy, with four clear chances to shoot each passing cyclist. And Induráin did not disappoint when he came in fastest of all to accept the gold medal from fellow Spaniard Juan Antonio Samaranch, president of the International Olympic Committee.

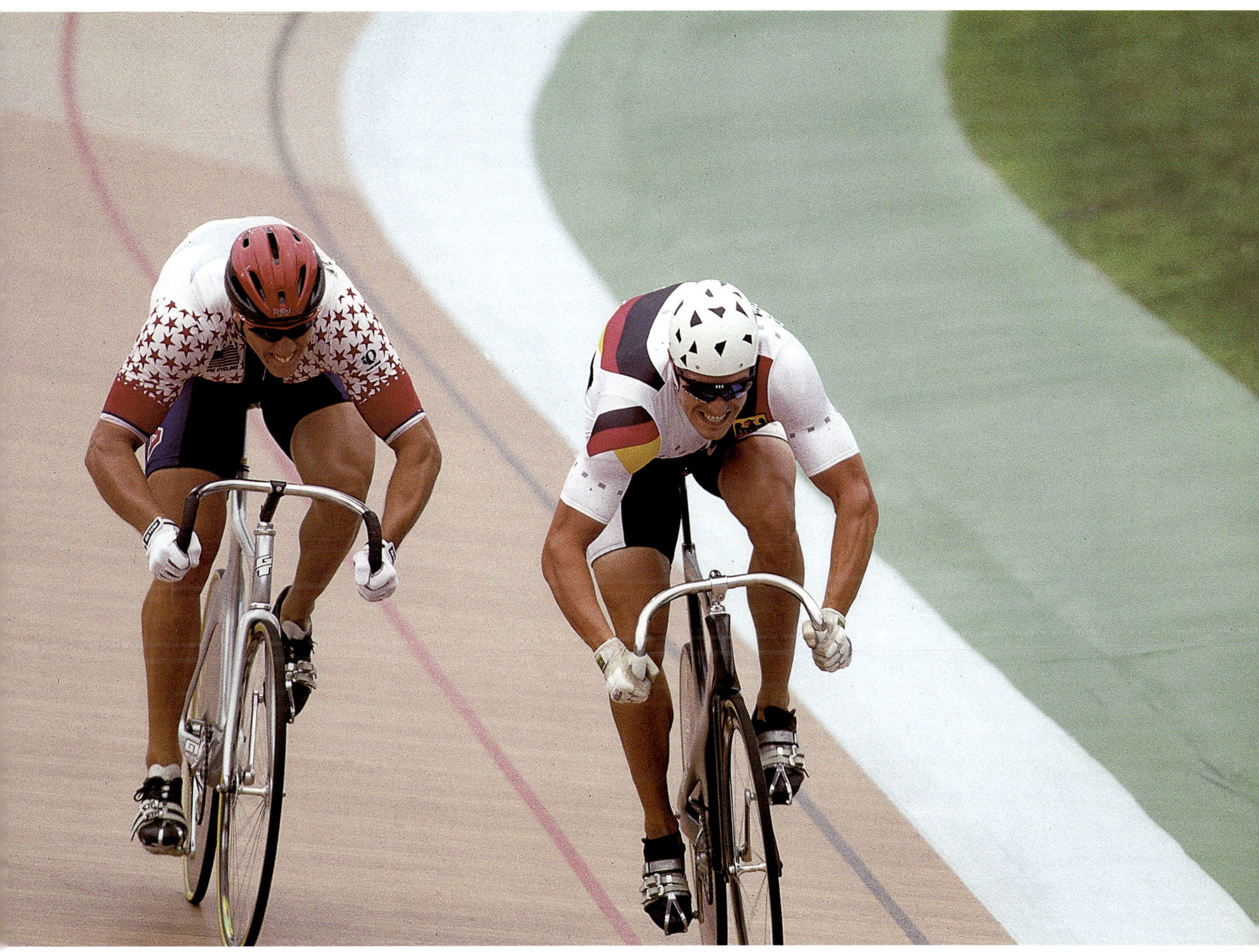

1996: OLYMPIC GAMES: ATLANTA

At Atlanta's Stone Mountain velodrome, the exuberant German rider, Jens Fiedler (right), conquered America's Marty Nothstein to win the Olympic sprint competition for the second time. Fiedler was planning to go for his third gold in Sydney.

Meanwhile, out on the course, where we'd been since 8 A.M. that morning, we'd survived a bomb scare when a security guard mistook a discarded photographer's monopod for something more sinister, and ordered everyone away. Problem was, we had ordered a batch of pizzas by cell phone to be delivered to that same spot where we'd been standing, only to be sent away just as the food was due to arrive. I cracked that afternoon: Sorry Miguel, I confess, I ate a McDonald's hamburger, a double one in fact, and at the very moment you were giving your press conference.

Third-placed in the Atlanta time trial, Chris Boardman provided me with the outstanding sporting highlight of the year, if not the decade, by shattering Rominger's seemingly invincible hour record in Manchester. Boardman had already broken the world pursuit record a few weeks earlier on the same track, during the 1996 track world's, and I was thankful to have delayed my journey to the start of the Vuelta in order to witness this incredible ride. I've never heard 3000 people get so behind their hero as they did in Manchester that day. Boardman's performance was out of this world, and the fans knew it.

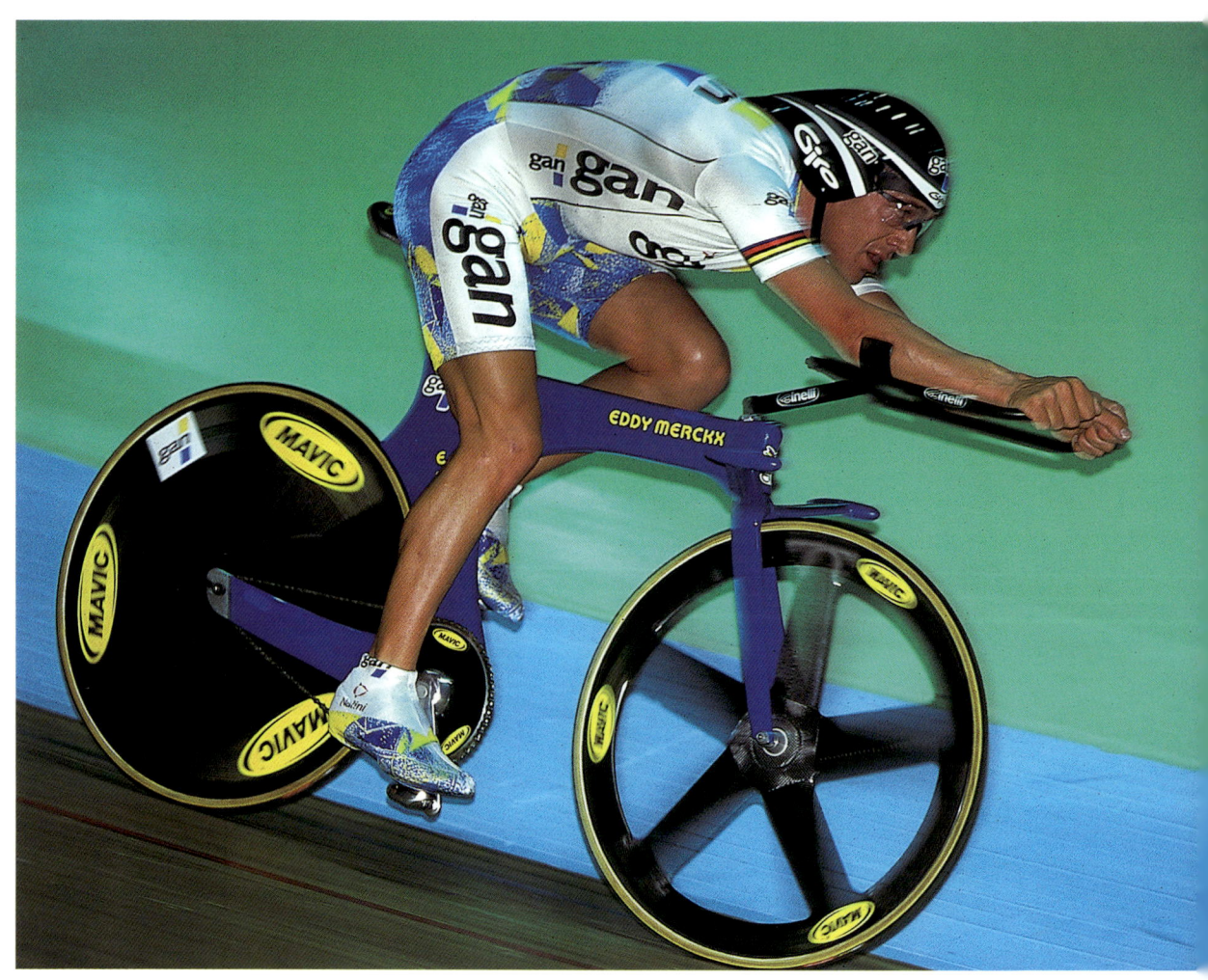

1996: WORLD HOUR RECORD ATTEMPT: MANCHESTER, ENGLAND

In 60 short minutes at Manchester's veldorome, Chris Boardman pedaled his "Superman" machine to an incredible 56.375 kilometers (35 mph!): a new world hour record. The extended-arm position and non-traditional frame have since been banned from international competition.

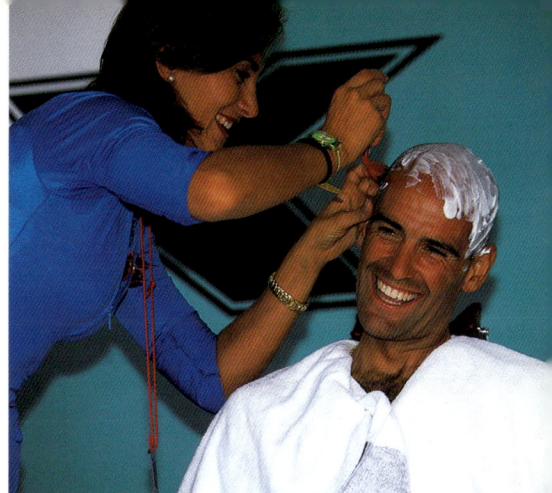

On the next day, the newly scheduled Vuelta began in Valencia, Spain, and Beppe Conti won the first stage. I'd made it to the finish only a few minutes before—after the dash from London to Valencia, and with no sleep—as the film of the historic hour record just had to be developed first. I happened to be staying in Rominger's Valencia hotel that night, and had to force myself not to show him the images I had of Boardman on his "Superman" bike. Even this unusually bubbly Swiss wouldn't have appreciated my teasing him.

Armstrong's shocking news broke at the beginning of the world championships in 1996. A high-tech Internet link-up enabled journalists in Switzerland to talk directly with the Texan in Austin, where he was already recovering from the first of many life-saving operations.

Those world's were so absorbing that I had little time to reflect on Armstrong's illness. It was only later, after dispatching the images of Zülle and Museeuw—respective winners of the time trial and road events—that the facts fully hit me. My archive of Lance was enormous: In just a few short years he'd created for me a memorable wealth of images, the sheer numbers of which were more appropriate for a five-time winner of the Tour than for a young Texan still unsure of which direction his career would take. Each time I sought an image, I had to go through the letter "A" in order to get where I needed to. And each time I found myself distracted and delayed, studying every image of Armstrong, and still unbelieving of the situation in which he now found himself.

By the time the 1997 season began, I had begun to accept the reports that said Armstrong was fighting back, would survive, and would maybe come back to cycling in 1998. With this hope alive, I managed to enjoy the spring races that saw Laurent Jalabert win Paris-Nice, Erik Zabel win his first Milan-San Remo, Rolf Sørensen win the Tour of Flanders, and, surprisingly, Frédéric Guesdon win Paris-Roubaix.

1997: VUELTA A ESPAÑA: CORDOBA, SPAIN

One shampoo and shave coming up! Herminio Diaz-Zabala of the ONCE team before the 10th stage of Spain's national tour.

Lance visited Europe in April, and on the eve of the Paris-Roubaix race, he held a press conference to announce his intention to race again, just as soon as his health was fully restored. I was there photographing him and couldn't believe how well he seemed: the glint in his eyes, the warm smile spreading across his face, the confident "I'll be back" statement ringing in every word he spoke that afternoon in Compiègne's Palais de Congrés.

He was back again in July, on a holiday with his fiancée Kristin. This time he spent a few days following the Tour . . . where Jan Ullrich was wearing the yellow jersey, and where his old Motorola teammate, Bobby Julich, was completing his first-ever Tour ride with an eventual 17th place in Paris.

I wondered if, and when, Lance would return to the Tour....

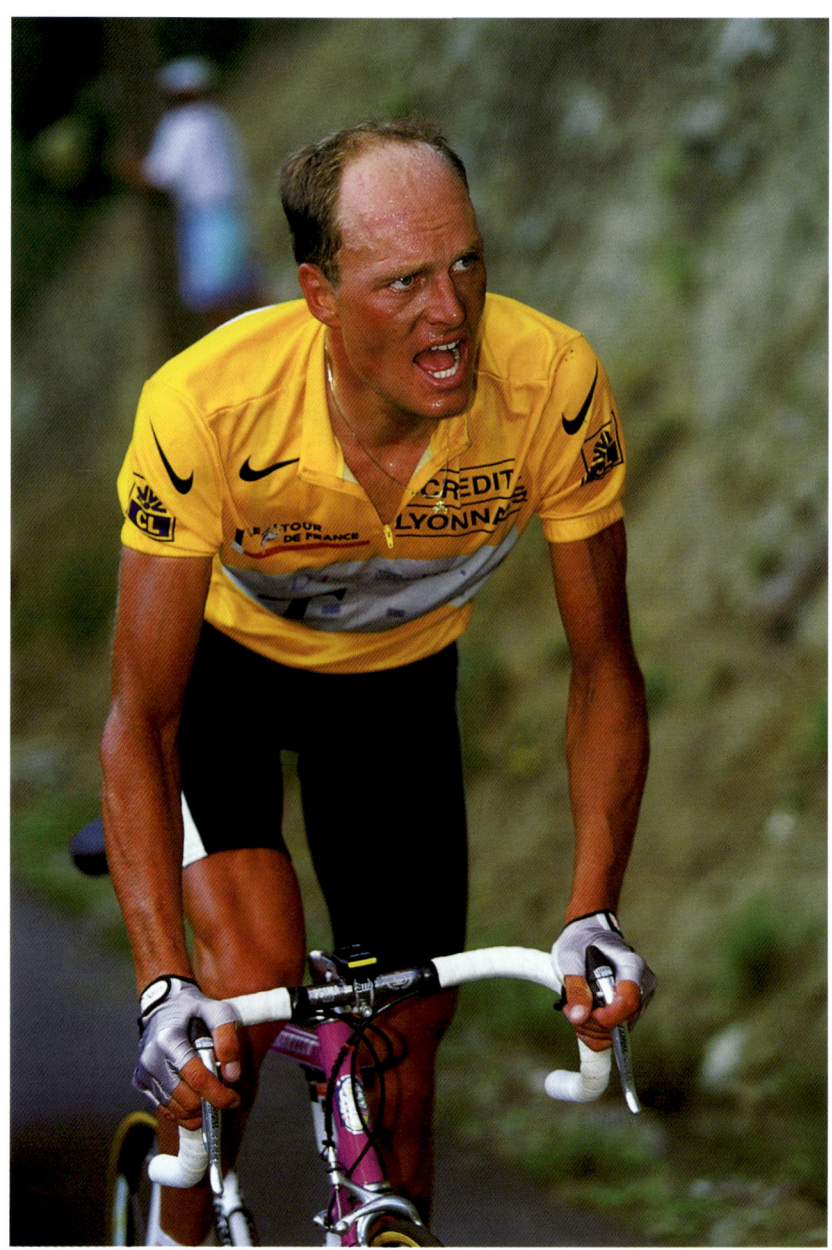

1996: TOUR DE FRANCE: HAUTACAM

After attacking halfway up the final climb, Bjarne Riis won stage 16 at Hautacam, to cement his leadership of the '96 Tour.

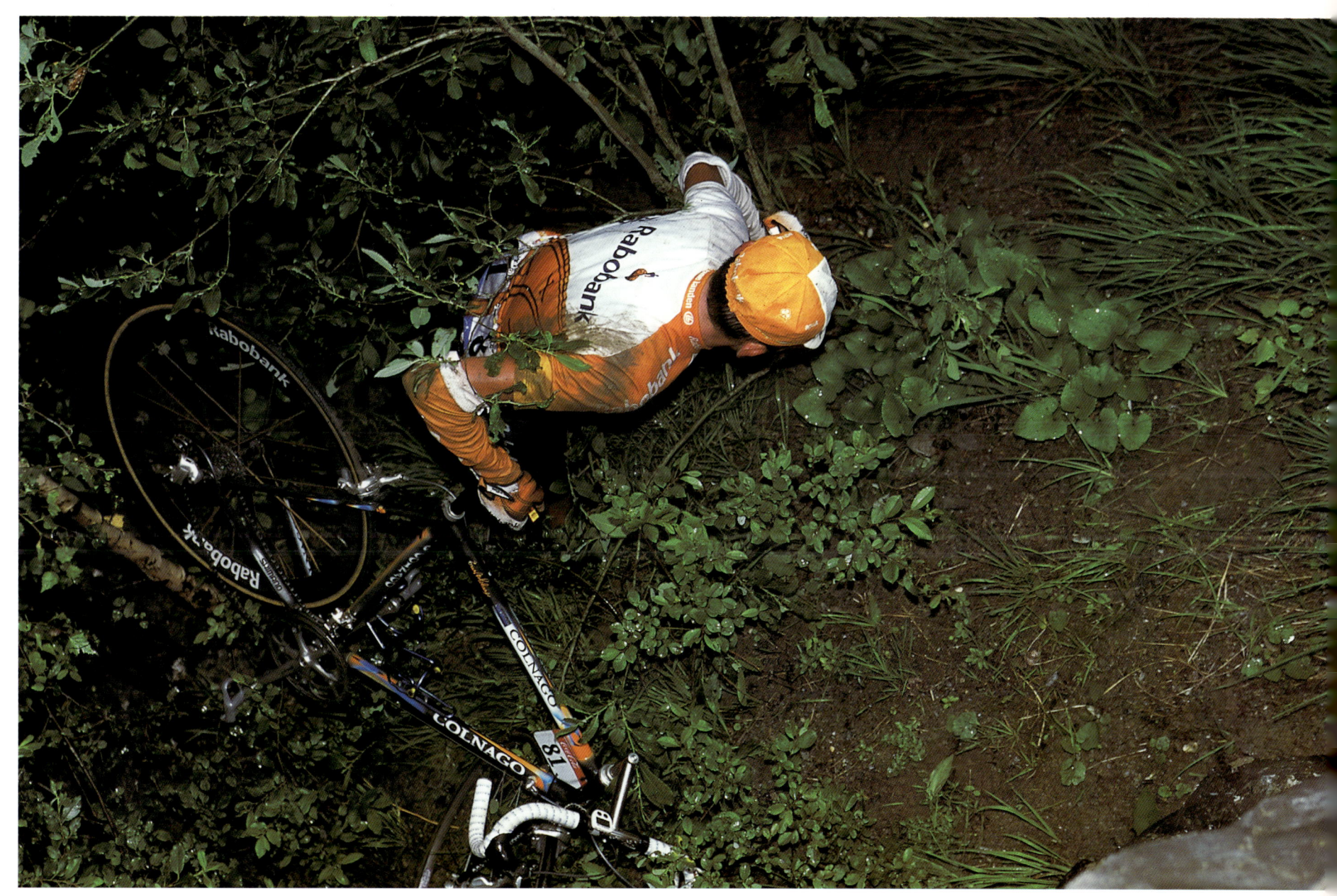

1996: TOUR DE FRANCE: CORMET DE ROSELAND

Oh, lucky man! Descending the Cormet de Roseland mountain in the French Alps, Belgian rider Johan Bruyneel overshot a bend, slotted through a gap in a retaining wall, and landed in the trees. Bruyneel is now the U.S. Postal Service team's directeur sportif.

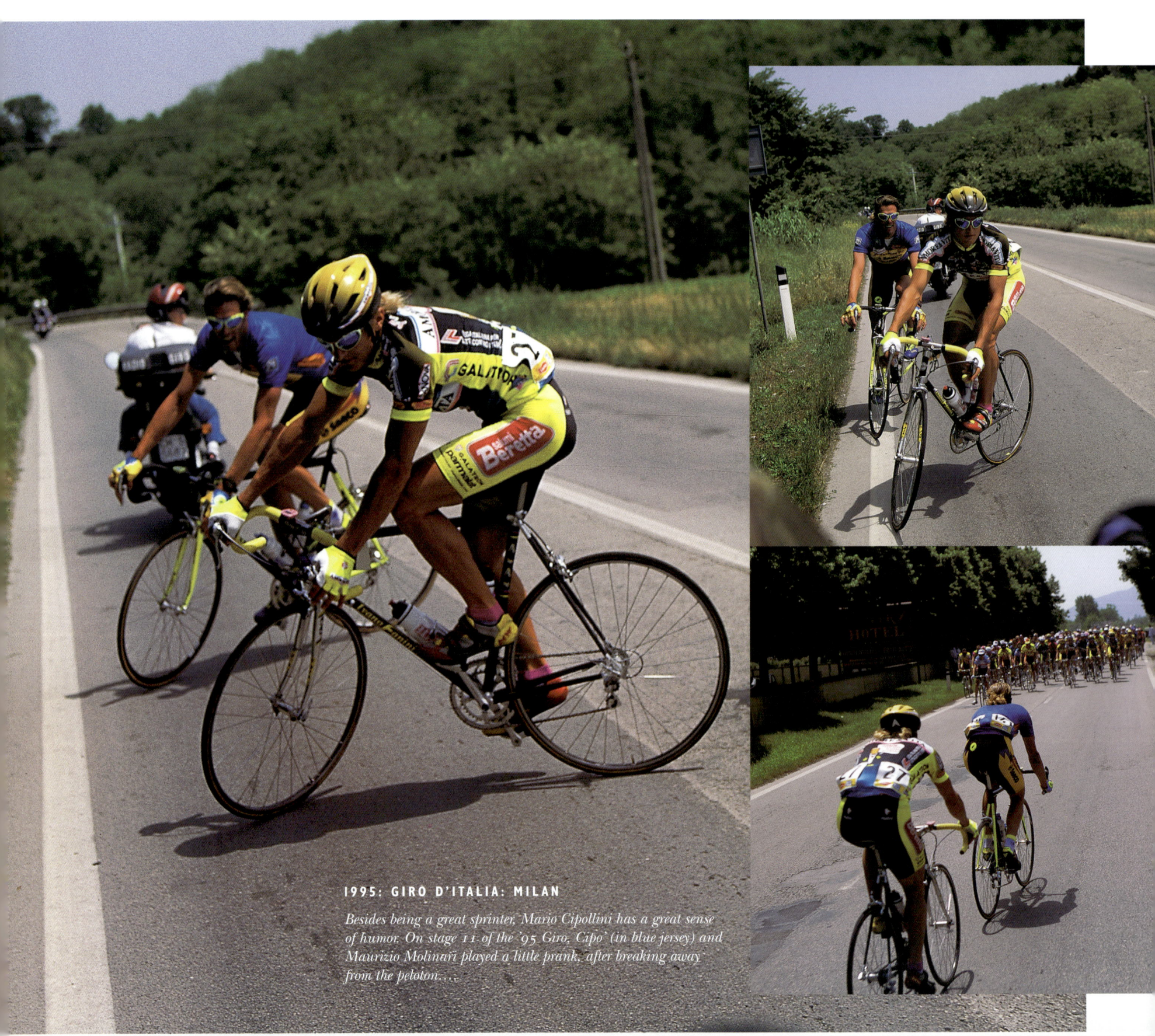

1995: GIRO D'ITALIA: MILAN

Besides being a great sprinter, Mario Cipollini has a great sense of humor. On stage 11 of the '95 Giro, 'Cipo' (in blue jersey) and Maurizio Molinari played a little prank, after breaking away from the peloton....

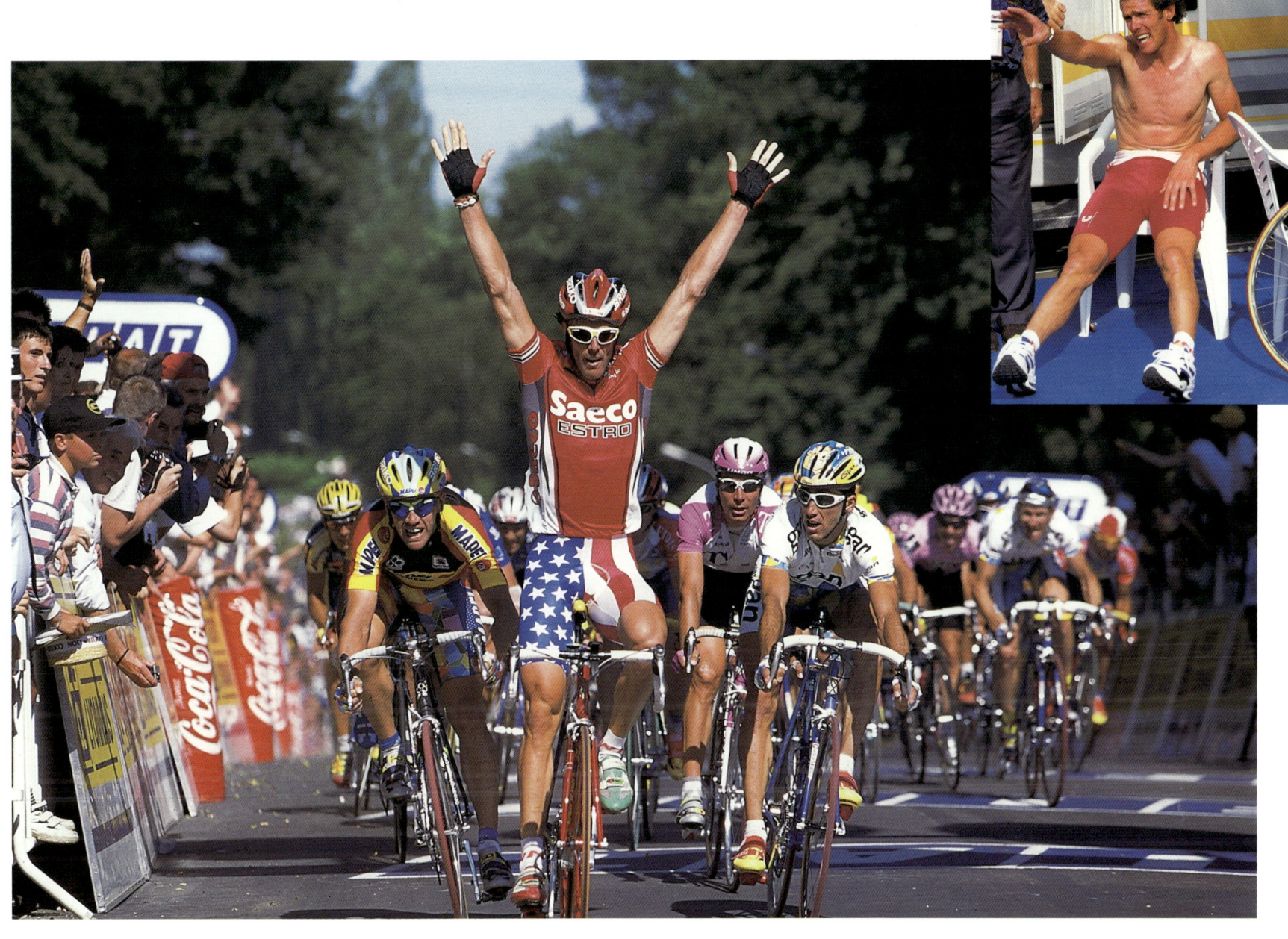

1997: TOUR DE FRANCE: FORGES-LES-EAUX

Dressed to kill! To publicize his Saeco team's new association with the American bike company, Cannondale, Cipollini wore stars-and-stripes shorts to win the opening stage of the 1997 Tour, by outspeeding Tom Steels (left), Frédéric Moncassin (right) and Erik Zabel. The stage winner's time bonus gave the Italian sprinter (seen after a stage at top) the race leadership—and, of course, the yellow jersey, which he complemented the next day with yellow shorts.

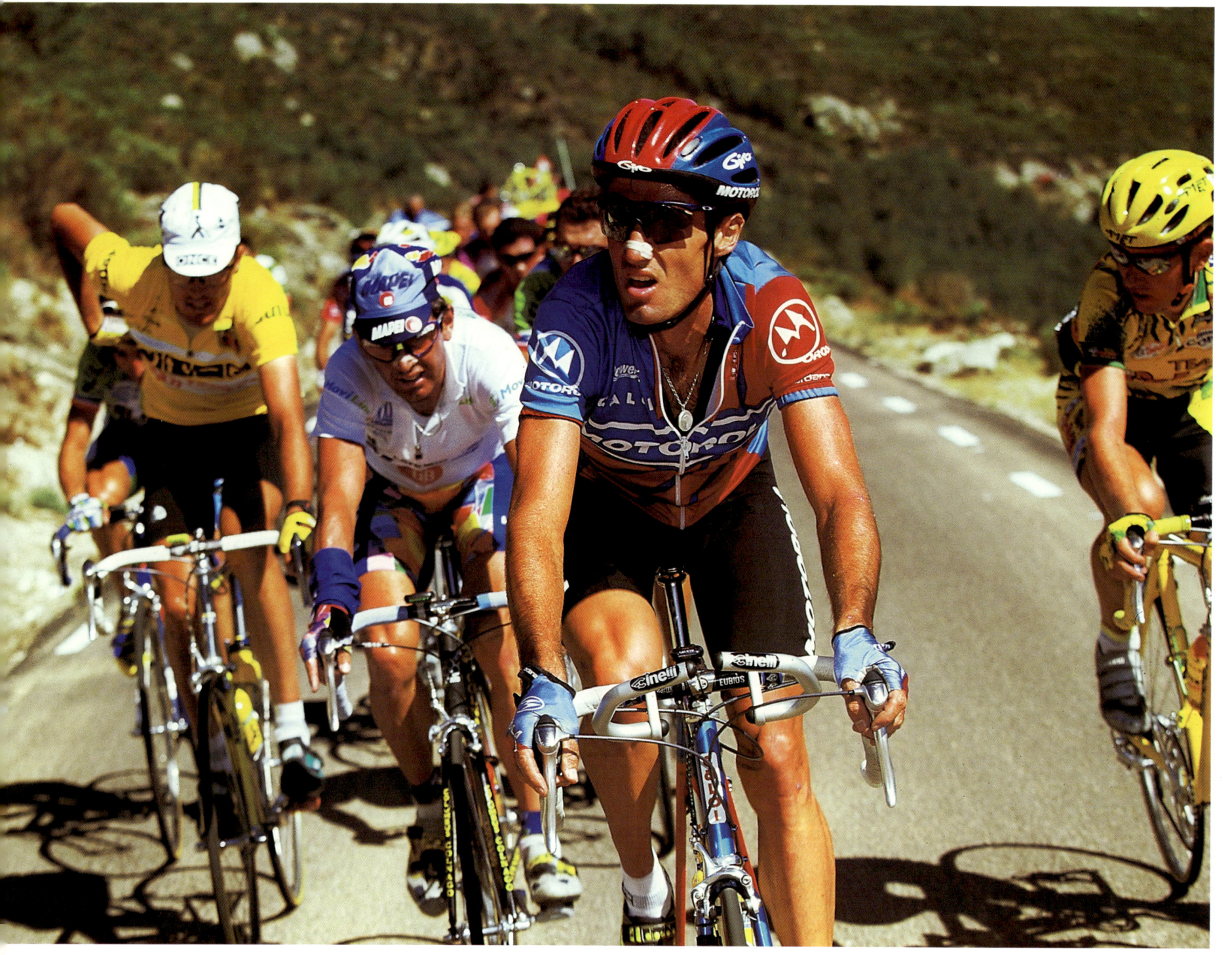

1996: VUELTA A ESPAÑA: PUERTO DE SERRANILLOS

In his breakthrough year at the '96 Veluta, American Bobby Julich leads three-time Vuelta winner Tony Rominger (in white) and race leader Alex Zülle (in yellow, on left) up the Puerto de Serranillos climb on stage 9.

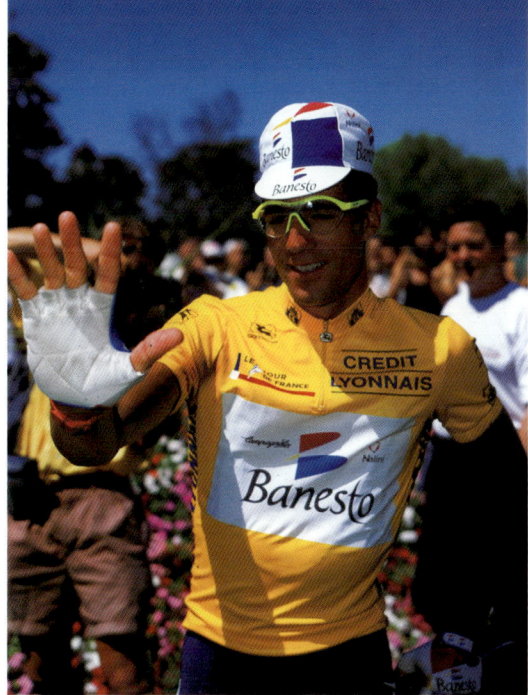

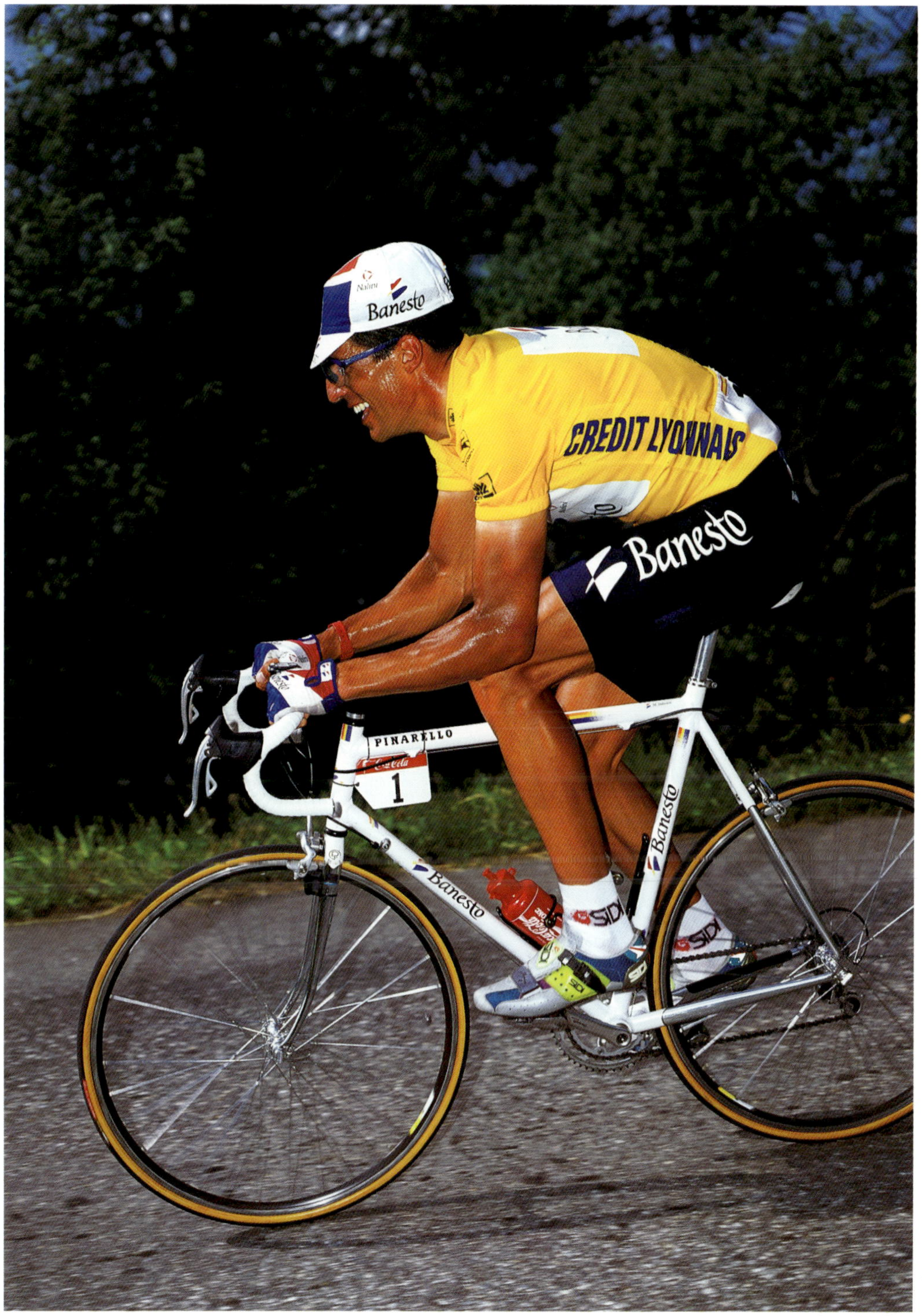

1995: TOUR DE FRANCE: PARIS

His hand says it all: Miguel Induráin has just won his fifth consecutive Tour de France.

1995: TOUR DE FRANCE: FRENCH ALPS

Winning the Tour just once is a huge accomplishment. Doing it five times in a row is a feat that no one had accomplished before Induráin—here seen racing flat out in defense of the yellow jersey.

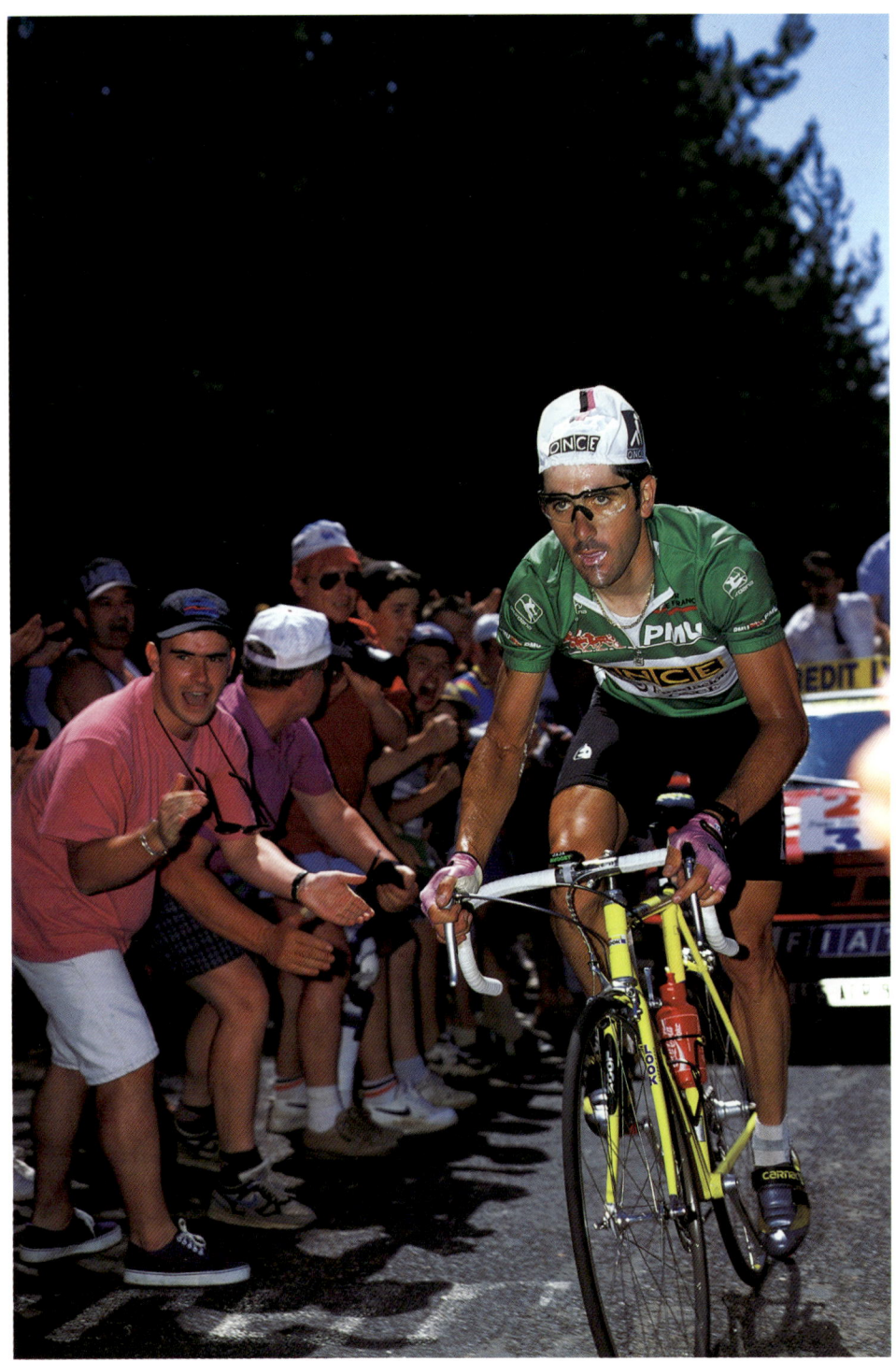

1995: TOUR DE FRANCE: MASSIF CENTRAL

The Tour and Laurent Jalabert has been a love-fate relationship. The French star never did better than in 1995, the year he finished the Tour in fourth place and won the green jersey— paraded here by Jalabert on his famous solo break to win stage 12 at Mende on July 14, the French national holiday.

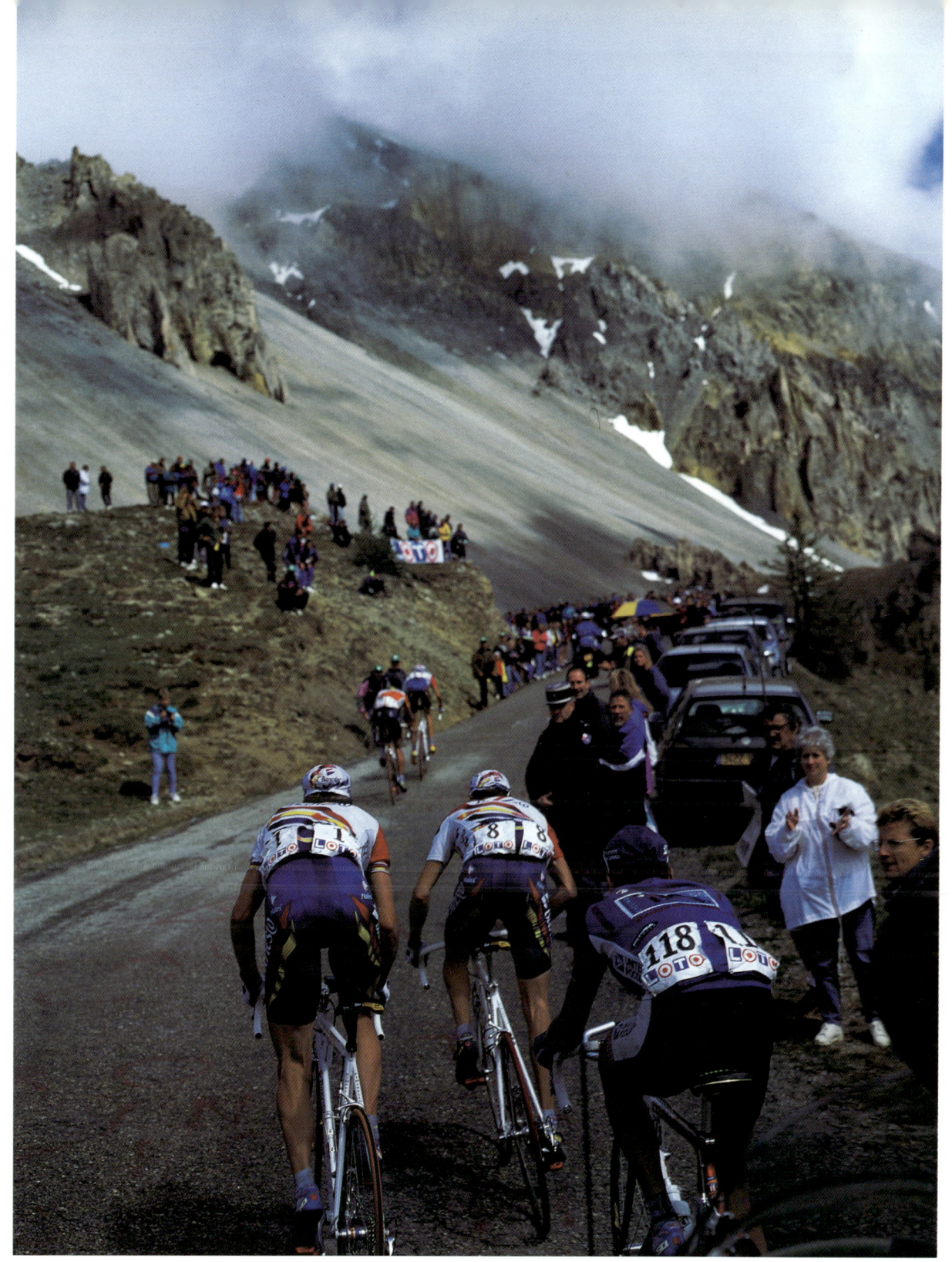

1997: DAUPHINÉ LIBÉRÉ: COL D'IZOARD

Abraham Olano (No. 1)—here following the pace of teammate Miguel Angel Peña and trailed by U.S. Postal's Jean-Cyril Robinóis on his way to the race leadership of the '97 Dauphiné at Briançon. The two riders attacking on the Col d'Izoard are Michael Boogerd and a Rabobank teammate.

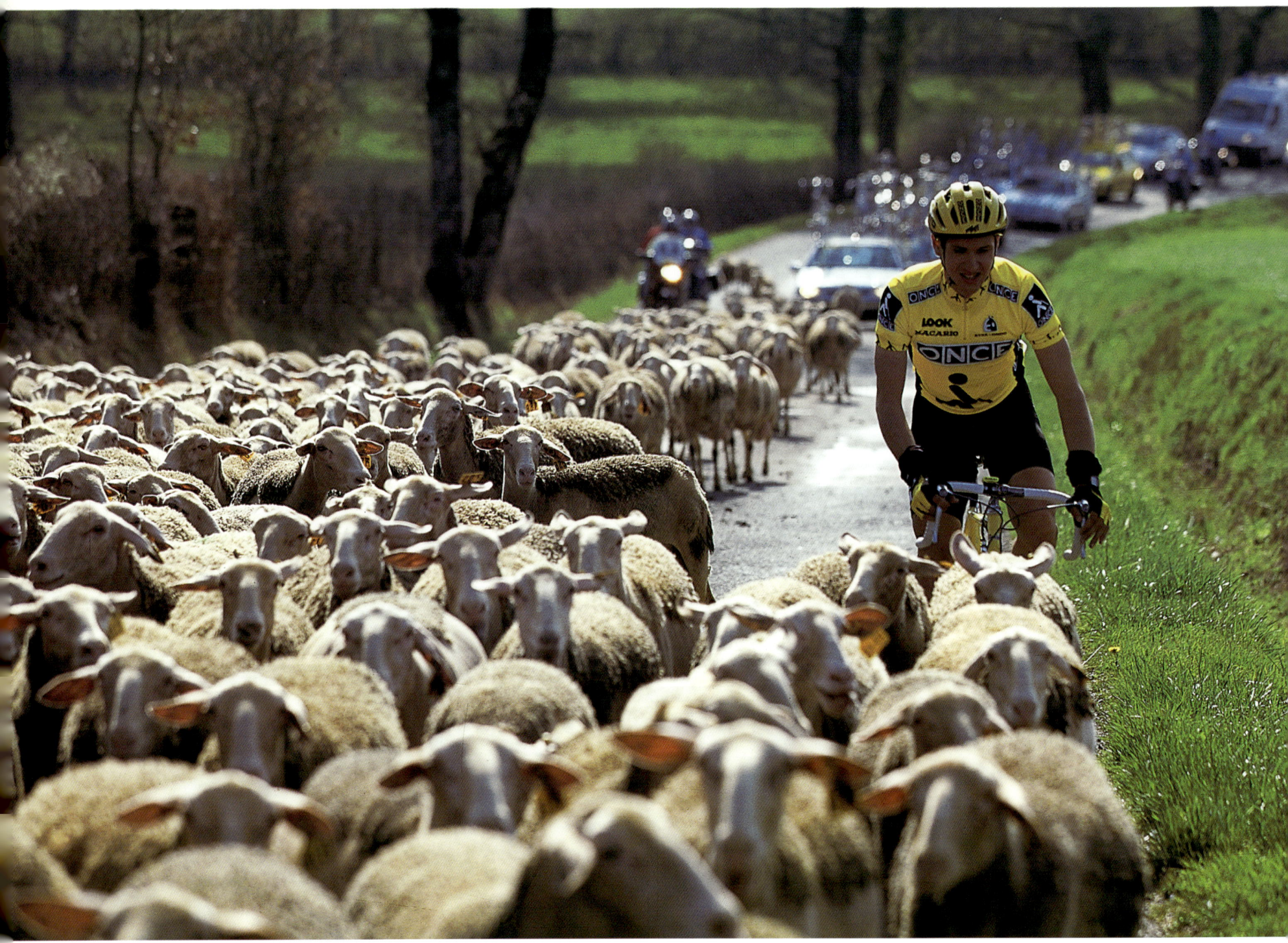

1996: CRITÉRIUM INTERNATIONAL: FRANCE

ONCE's Miguel Morras must have felt like Harry Potter after turning the rest of the peloton into sheep on stage 1 of the 1996 Critérium International in the hill country of the Tarn region.

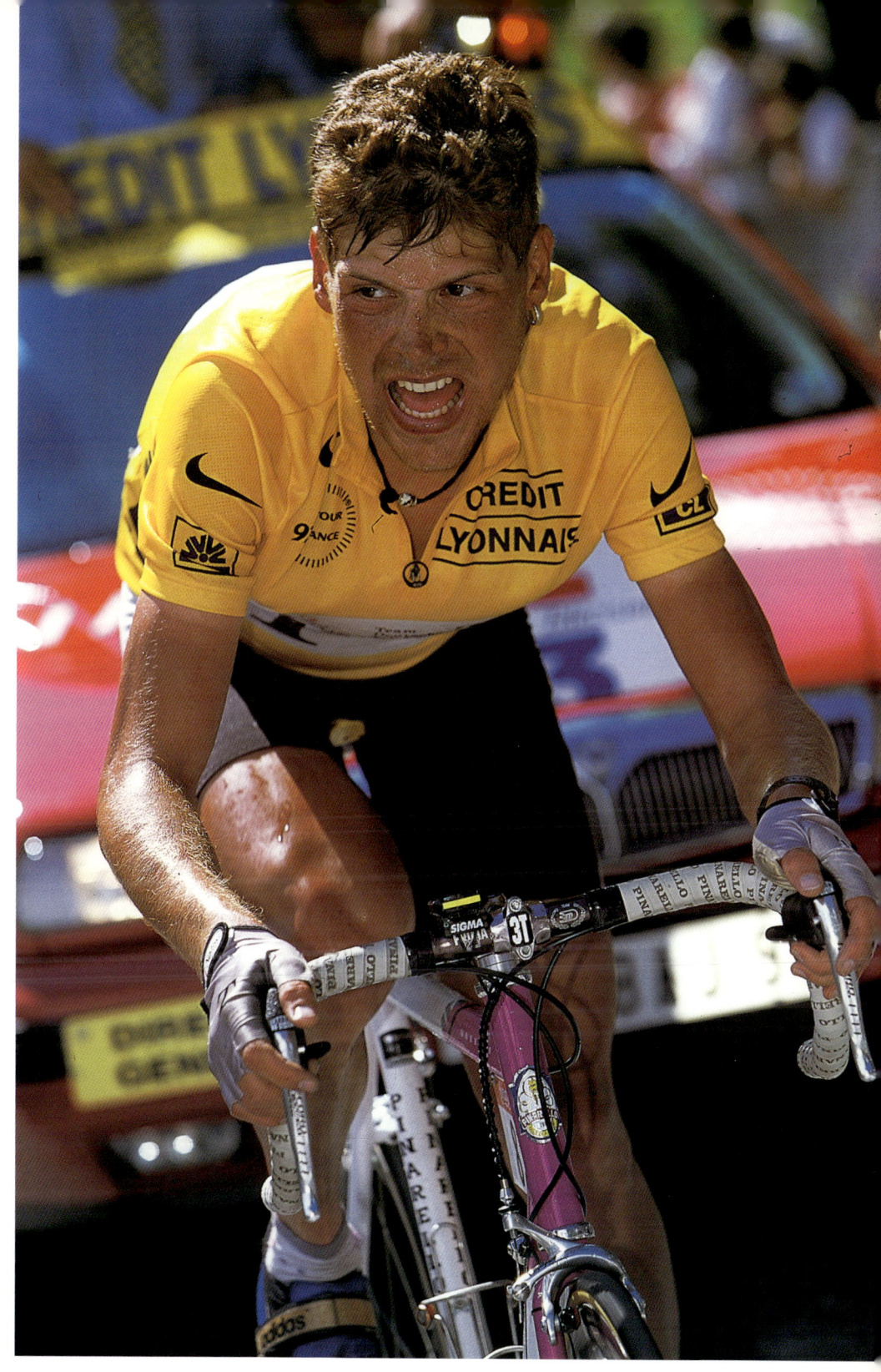

1997: TOUR DE FRANCE: L'ALPE D'HUEZ

In all his glory, German wunderkind Jan Ullrich defends his yellow jersey with style and vigor after an attack by Marco Pantani on the mountaintop finish at L'Alpe d'Huez.

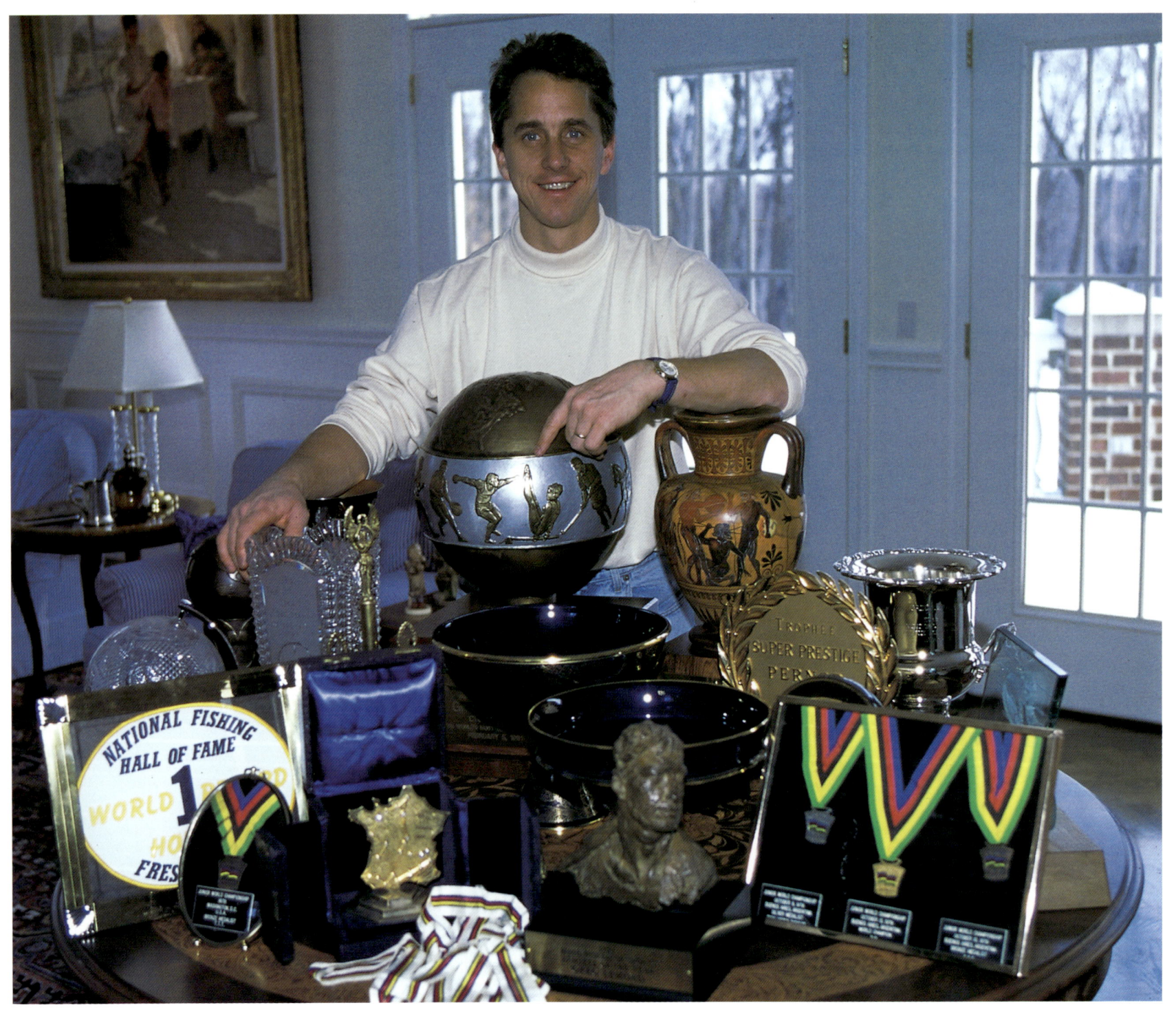

1995: GREG LEMOND'S HOME: MINNESOTA, USA

After announcing his retirement from racing due to a rare muscular disease, Greg LeMond displays some of his career milestones at his Minnesota mansion: (above) Tour de France trophies, world championship medals and Sportsman of the Year trophies; (top right) a selection of Tour yellow jerseys, rainbow jerseys and other significant leader jerseys; (above right) two front page stories from 1989: taking the Tour lead at Rennes, and winning the race in Paris.

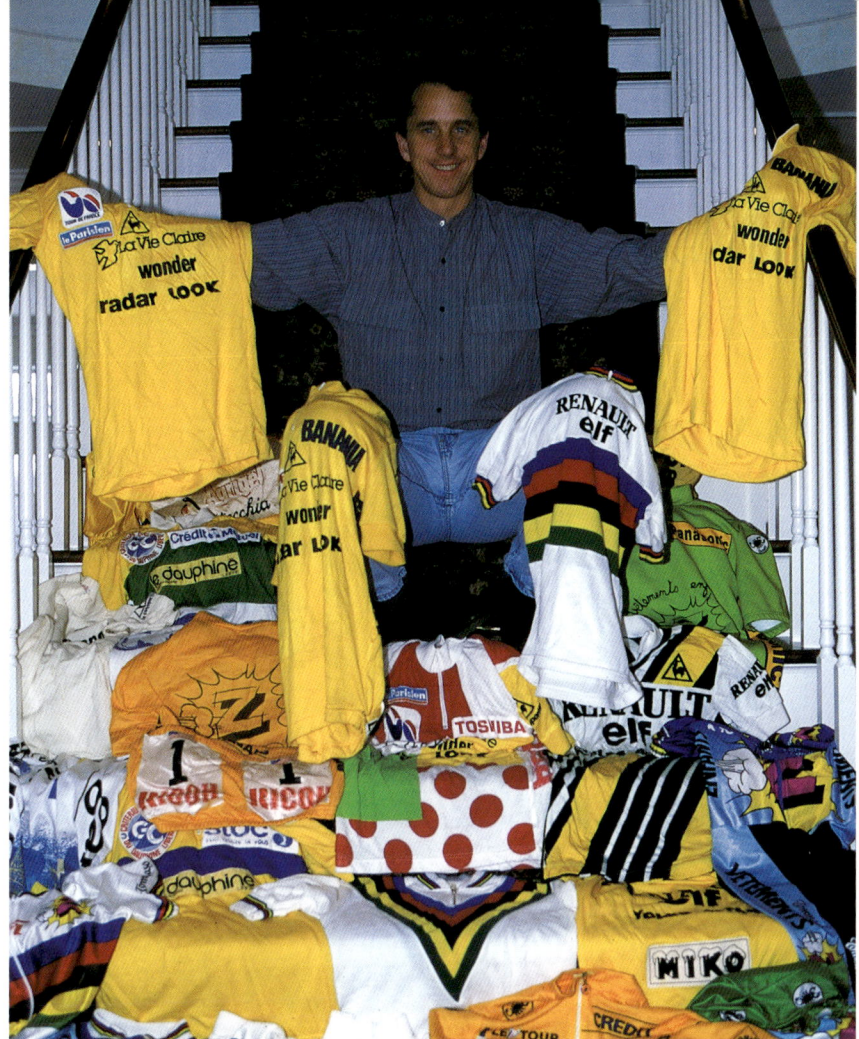

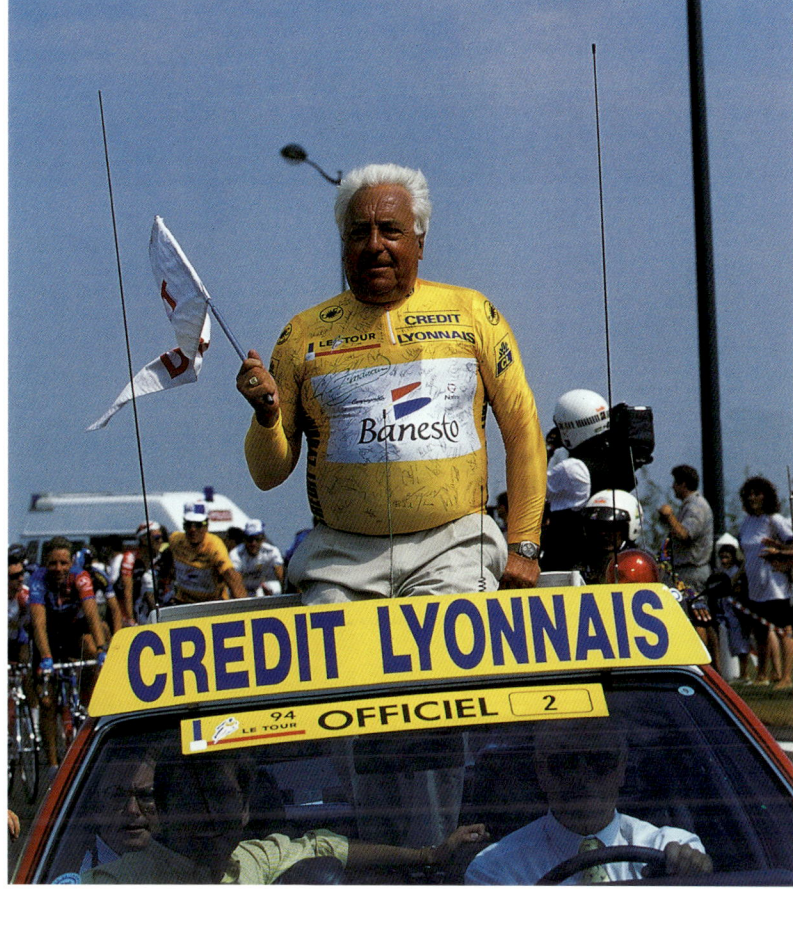

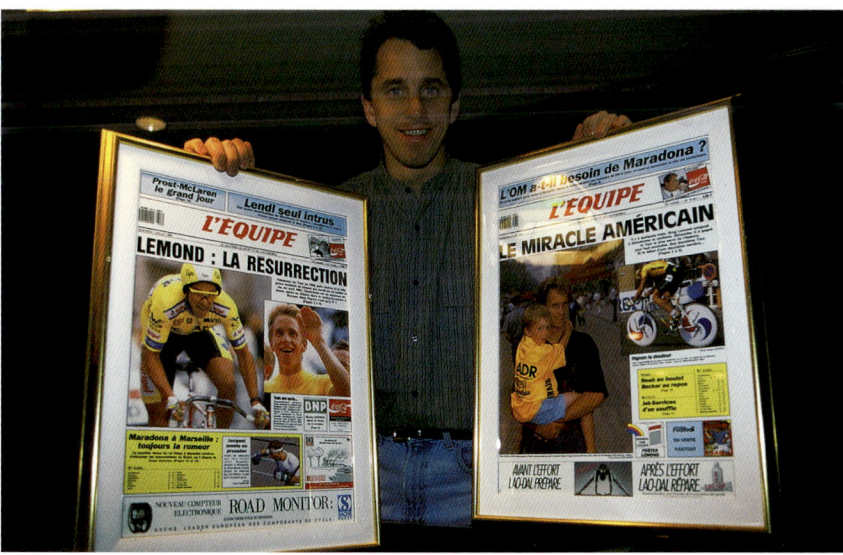

1995: TOUR DE FRANCE: PARIS

Another who announced his retirement (from officiating) was Frenchman Albert Bouvet (top right), who wore a symbolic yellow jersey on his last day as technical director of the Tour de France.

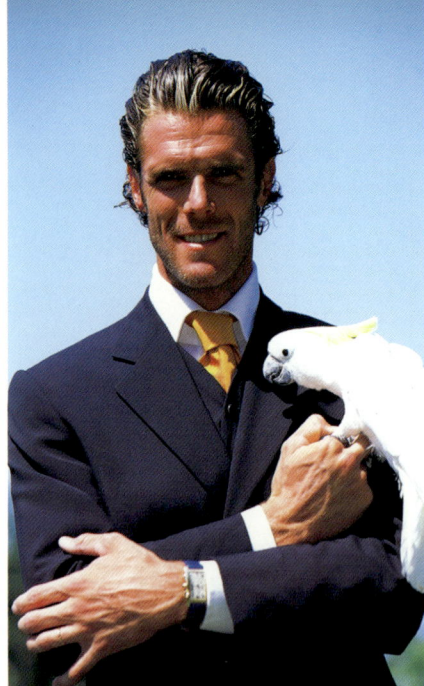

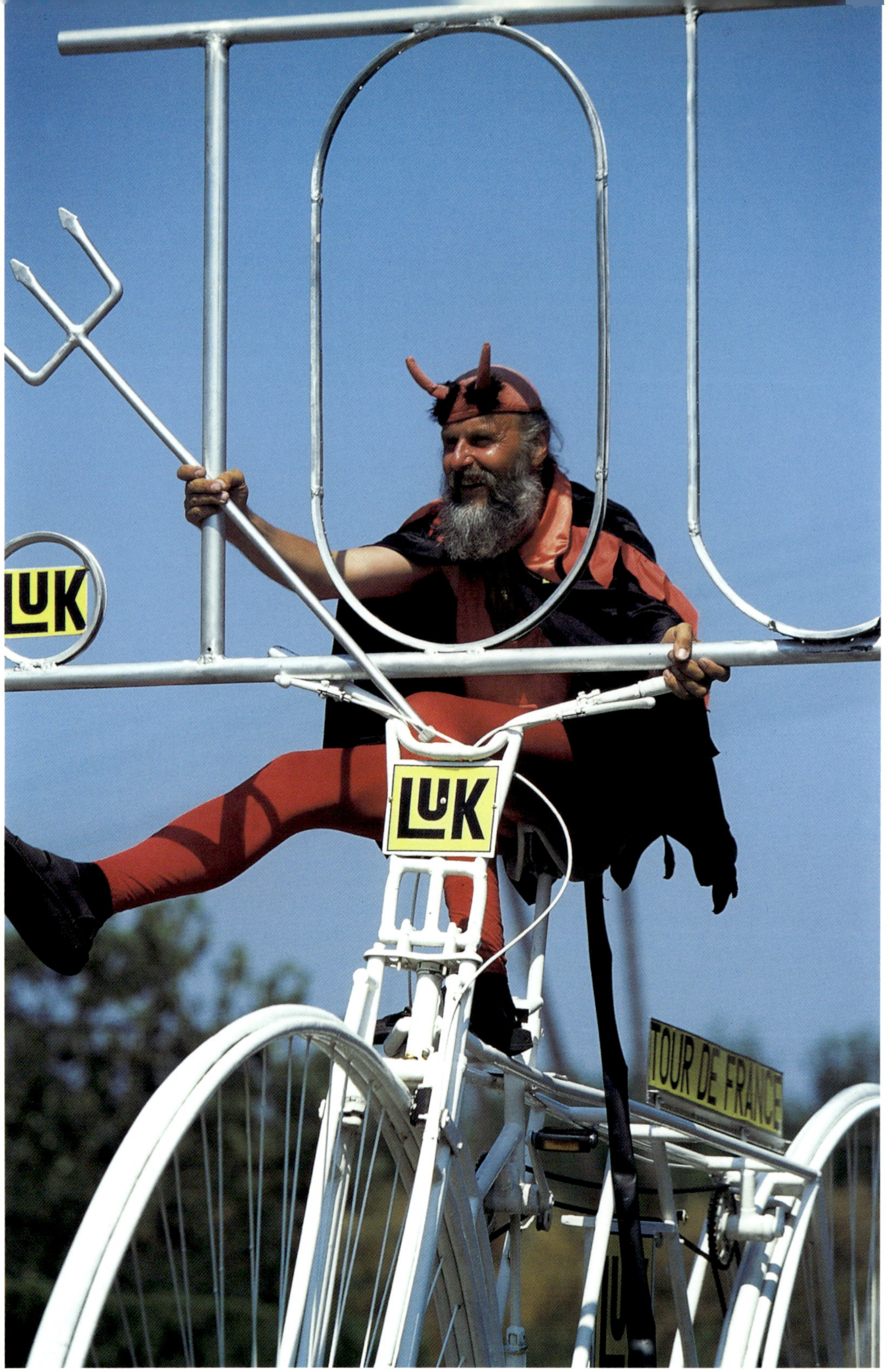

1997: CHEZ CIPOLLINI: TUSCANY, ITALY

Italian superstar Mario Cipollini keeps a menagerie at his Tuscan estate, including this white parrot.

1995: TOUR DE FRANCE: LIMOGES

German race fanatic Didi Senft dresses up as the devil and displays one of his bike sculptures at every stage of the Tour de France and Giro d'Italia, and at the annual world road championships. Here, he mounts his special Tour bike at Limoges in 1995.

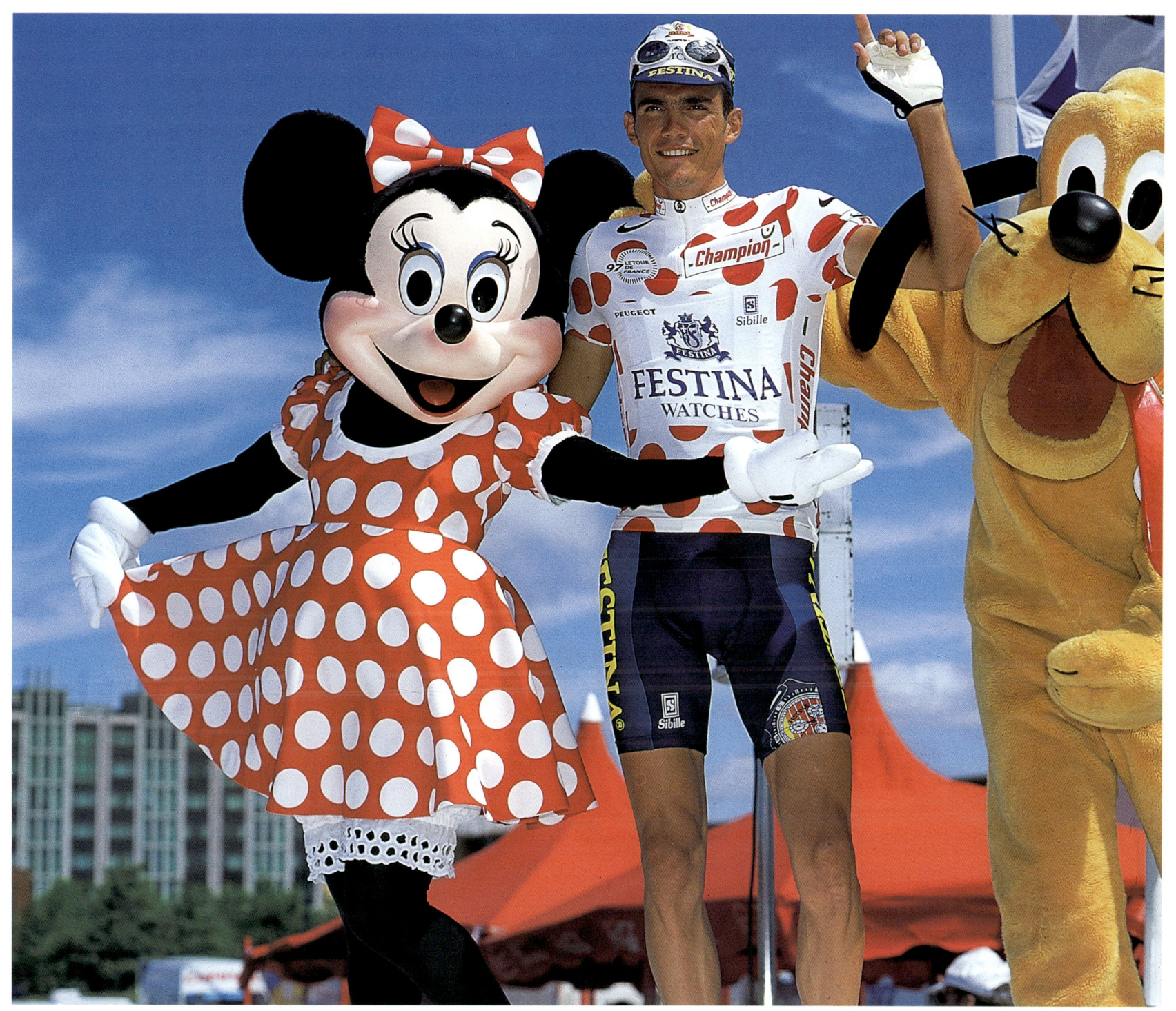

1997: TOUR DE FRANCE: DISNEYLAND PARIS

Who's wearing the prettier polka-dot outfit? Miss Mouse or Mister Virenque?

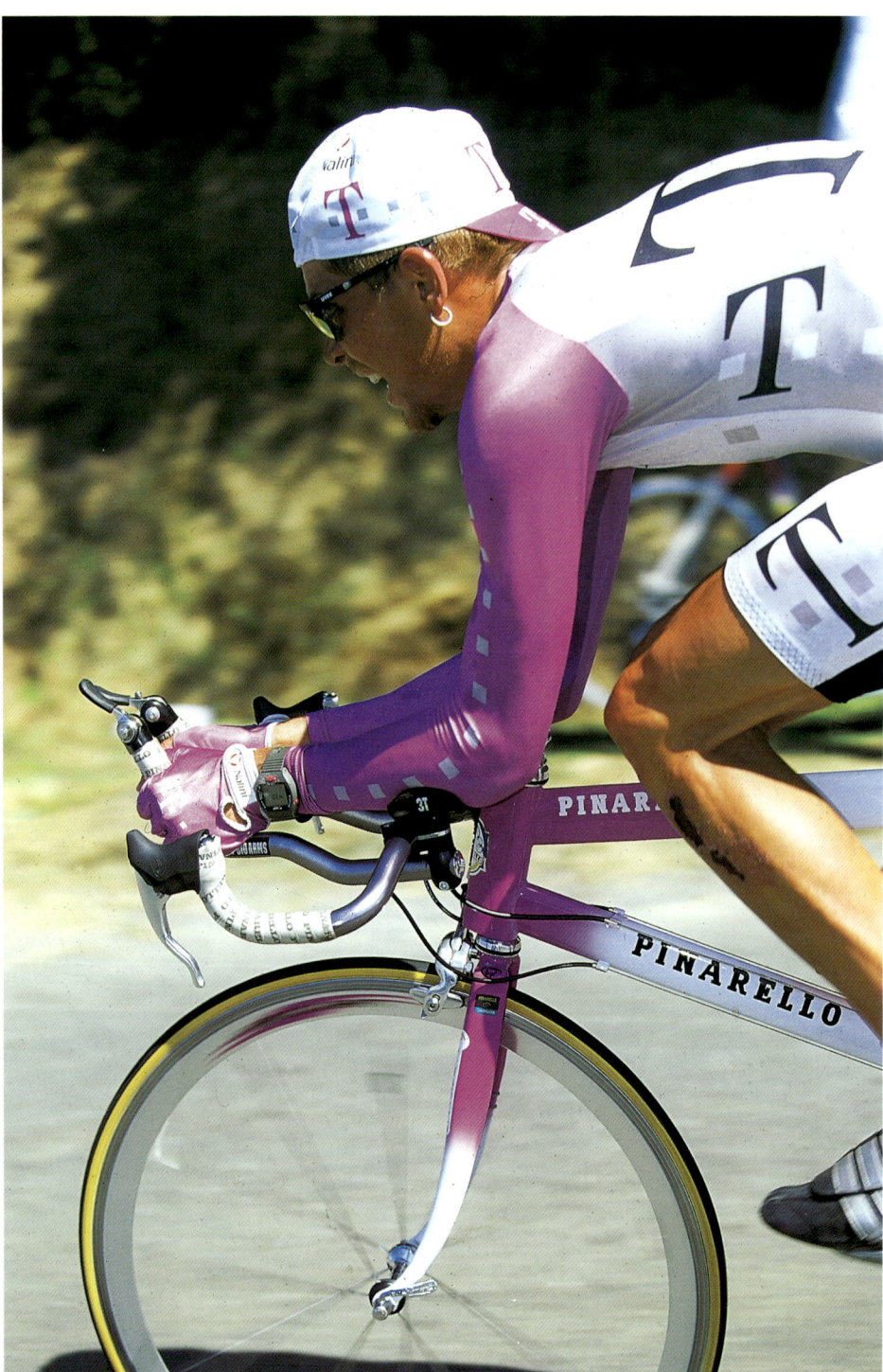

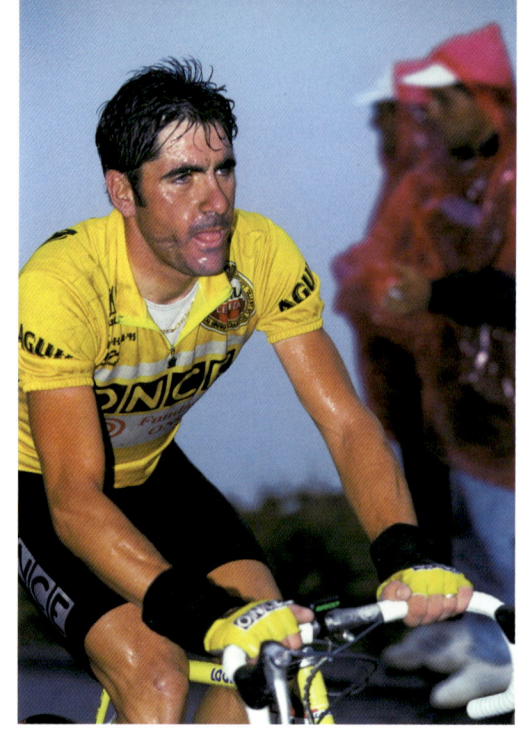

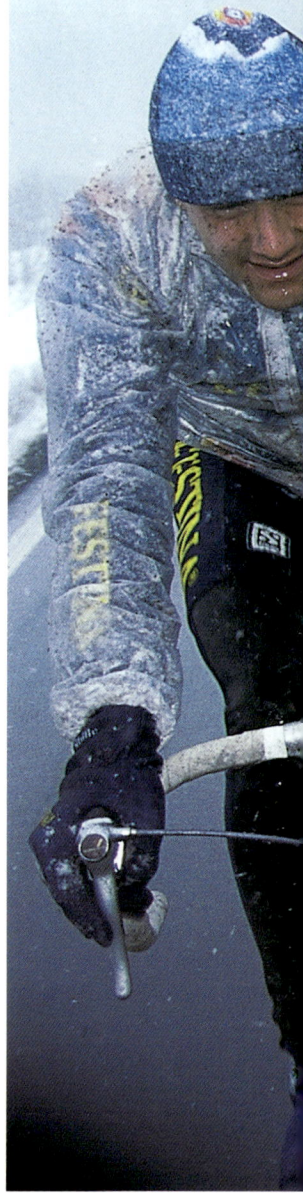

1996: TOUR DE FRANCE: ST. EMILION

Jan Ullrich, aged 22 and in his third season as a professional, clinched second place overall in his debut Tour de France by winning the Bordeaux-St. Emilion stage 20 time trial.

1995: VUELTA A ESPAÑA: PYRENEES

Laurent Jalabert raced brilliantly to win the '95 Vuelta, taking five stages on the way—including this one to the summit of Luz-Ardiden in the French Pyrenees.

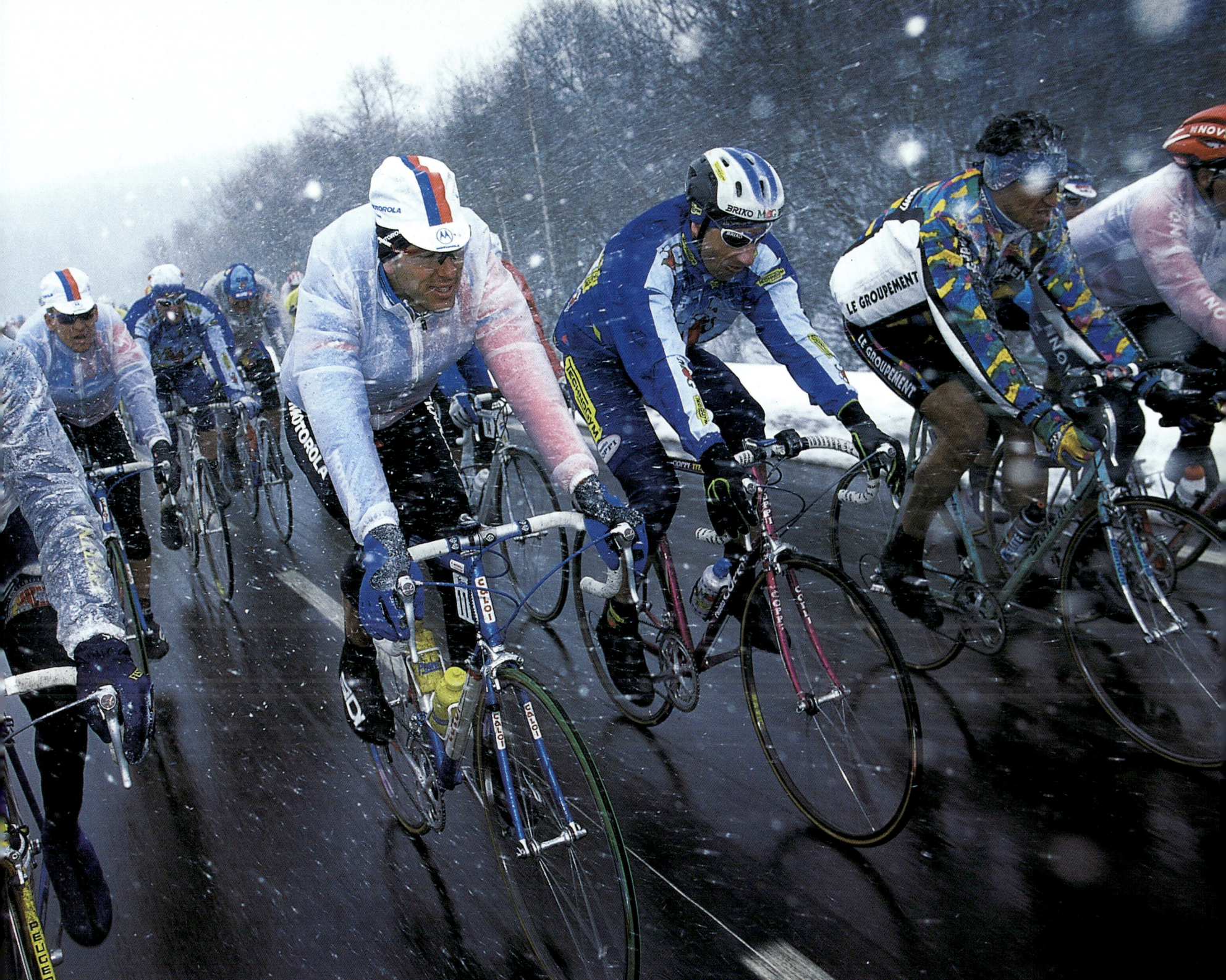

1995: PARIS-NICE: MASSIF CENTRAL

After riding in snow for two hours on stage 4 of Paris-Nice, the peloton came to a halt, with Frenchman Thierry Bourgignon (second from right in photo) leading a rider protest. American Frankie Andreu (in center, wearing Motorola uniform) argued with Bourgignon, and the stage continued for another 20km before finally being abandoned.

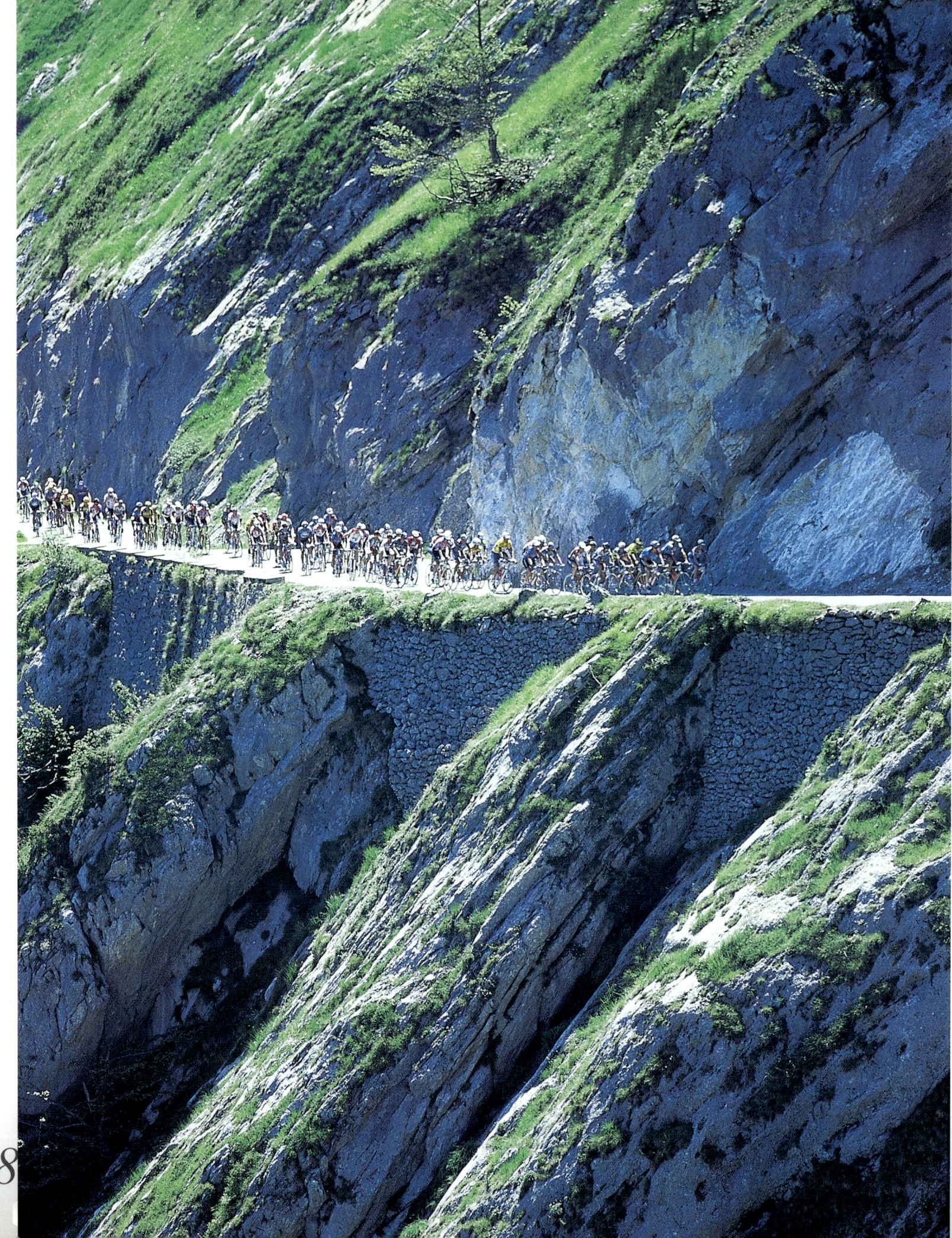

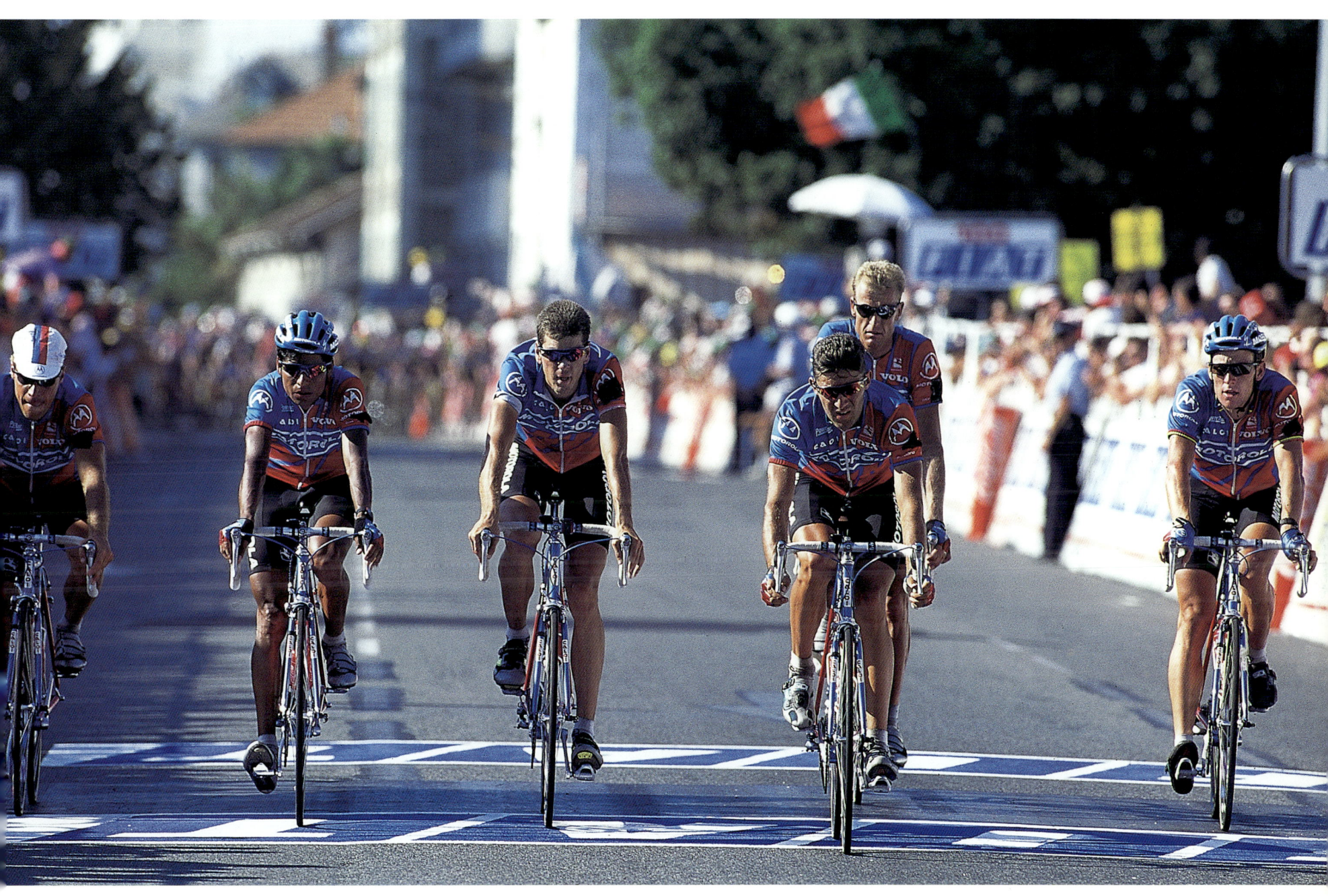

1995: TOUR DE FRANCE: PYRENEES

The death of 1992 Olympic champion Fabio Casartelli during stage 15 of the 1995 Tour de France remains one of cycling's darkest moments. The following day, the riders paid homage to their fallen colleague by riding, not racing, a difficult mountain stage in silent respect. The climb up the Col d'Aubisque (left) came partway through the eight-hour ride, which ended with Casartelli's six Motorola teammates (above) riding into Pau alone: (left to right) Steve Bauer, Alvaro Mejia, Frankie Andreu, Andrea Peron, Stephen Swart and Lance Armstrong.

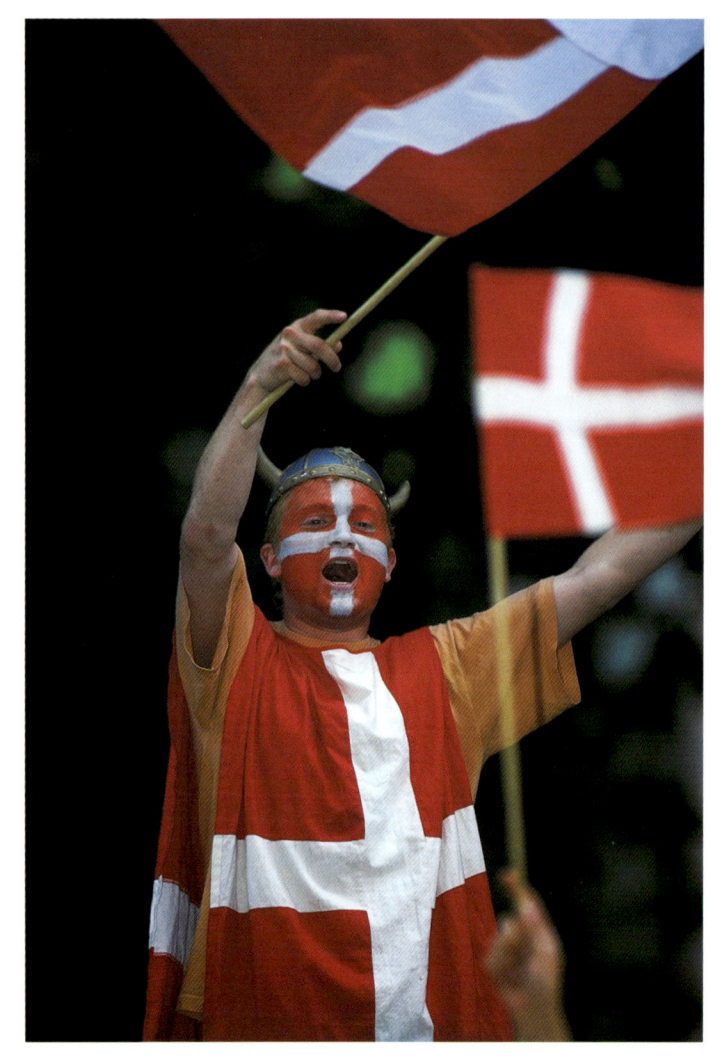

1996: TOUR DE FRANCE: PARIS

When Bjarne Riis became the first Danish cyclist to win the Tour de France, his fans celebrated with colorful patriotism.

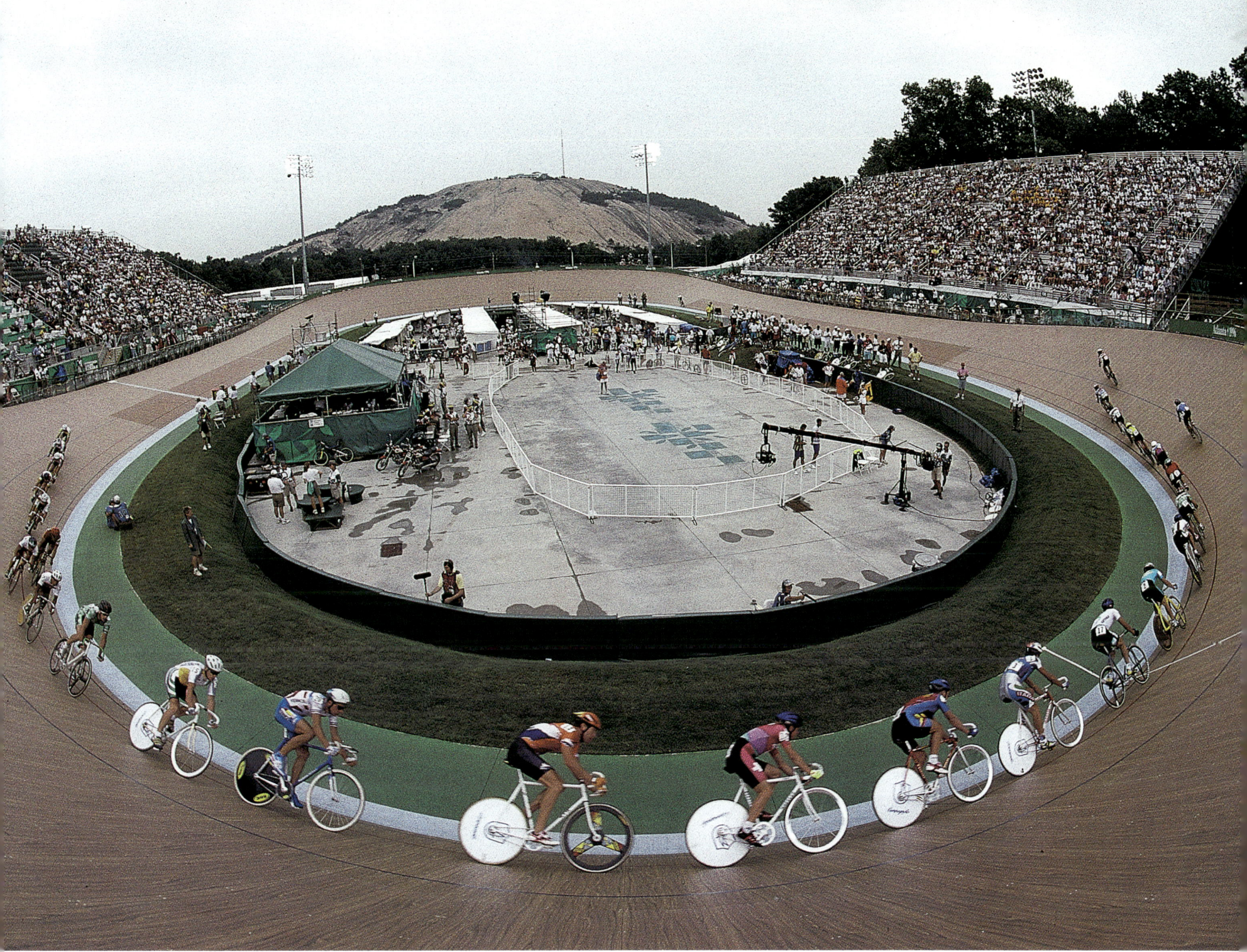

1996: OLYMPIC GAMES: ATLANTA

The Olympic velodrome at Atlanta, next to Stone Mountain, was probably the last outdoor track to be used for an international championships. Cycling's world governing body, the UCI, has since decreed that all Olympics and world championships can only be held at indoor velodromes.

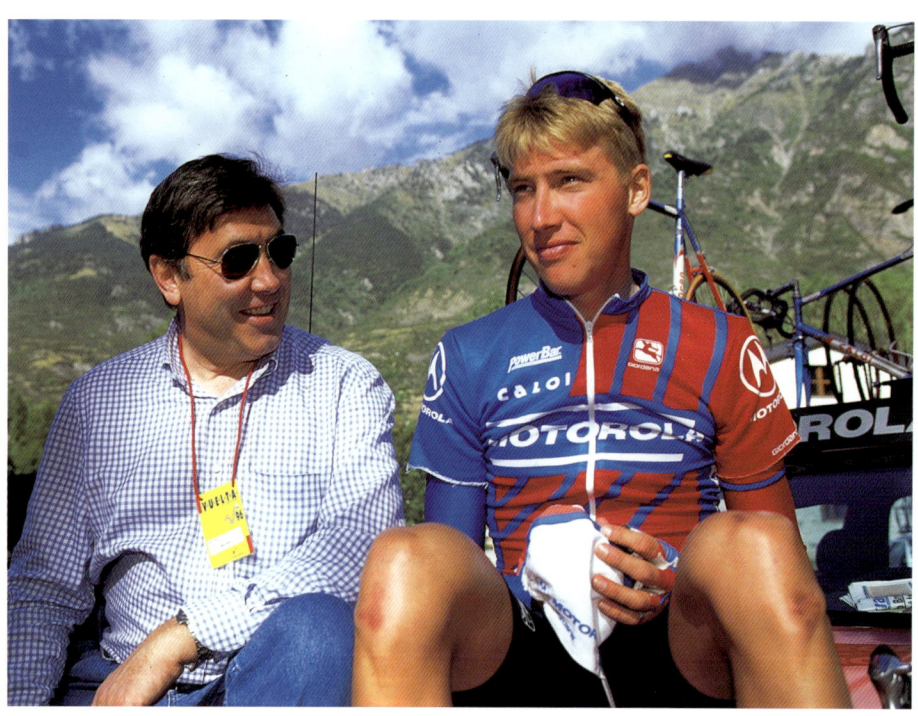

1996: VUELTA A ESPAÑA: BENASQUE

There's never been a prouder cycling parent than Eddy Merckx (left), pictured here with son Axel before stage 18 of the 1996 Vuelta.

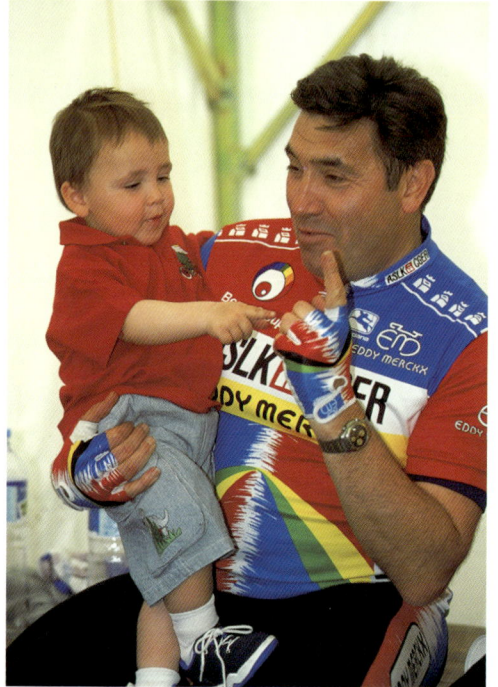

1996: GENTLEMAN'S CHARITY RACE: LIÈGE, BELGIUM

Nice to have a granddad like Eddy Merckx! The cyclist of the century relaxes with his first grandchild after riding a charity event with his son Axel.

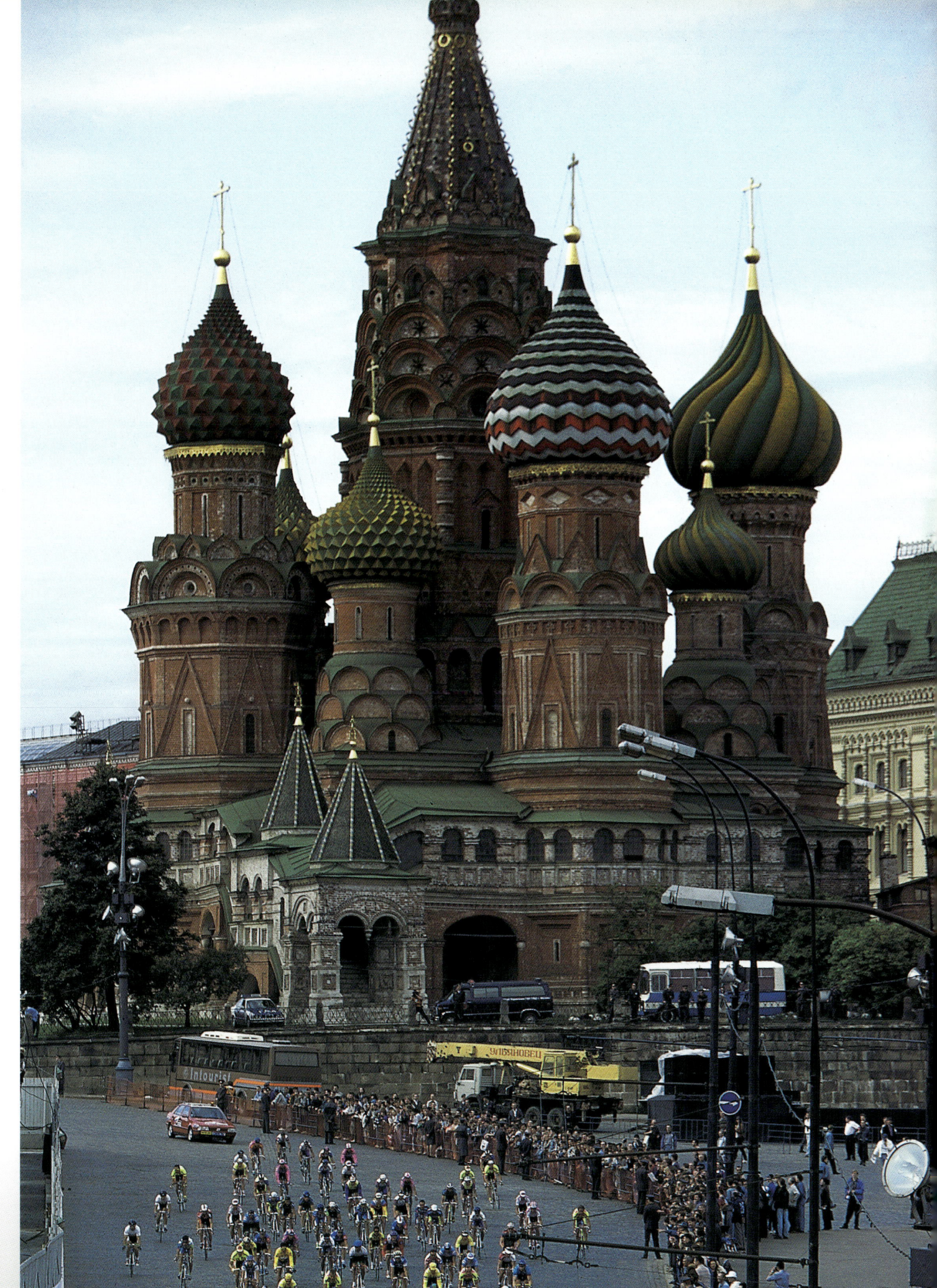

1995: POST-TOUR DE FRANCE CRITERIUM: MOSCOW

The big stars from the 1995 Tour de France were flown to Moscow for a criterium around St. Basil's Cathedral in Red Square.

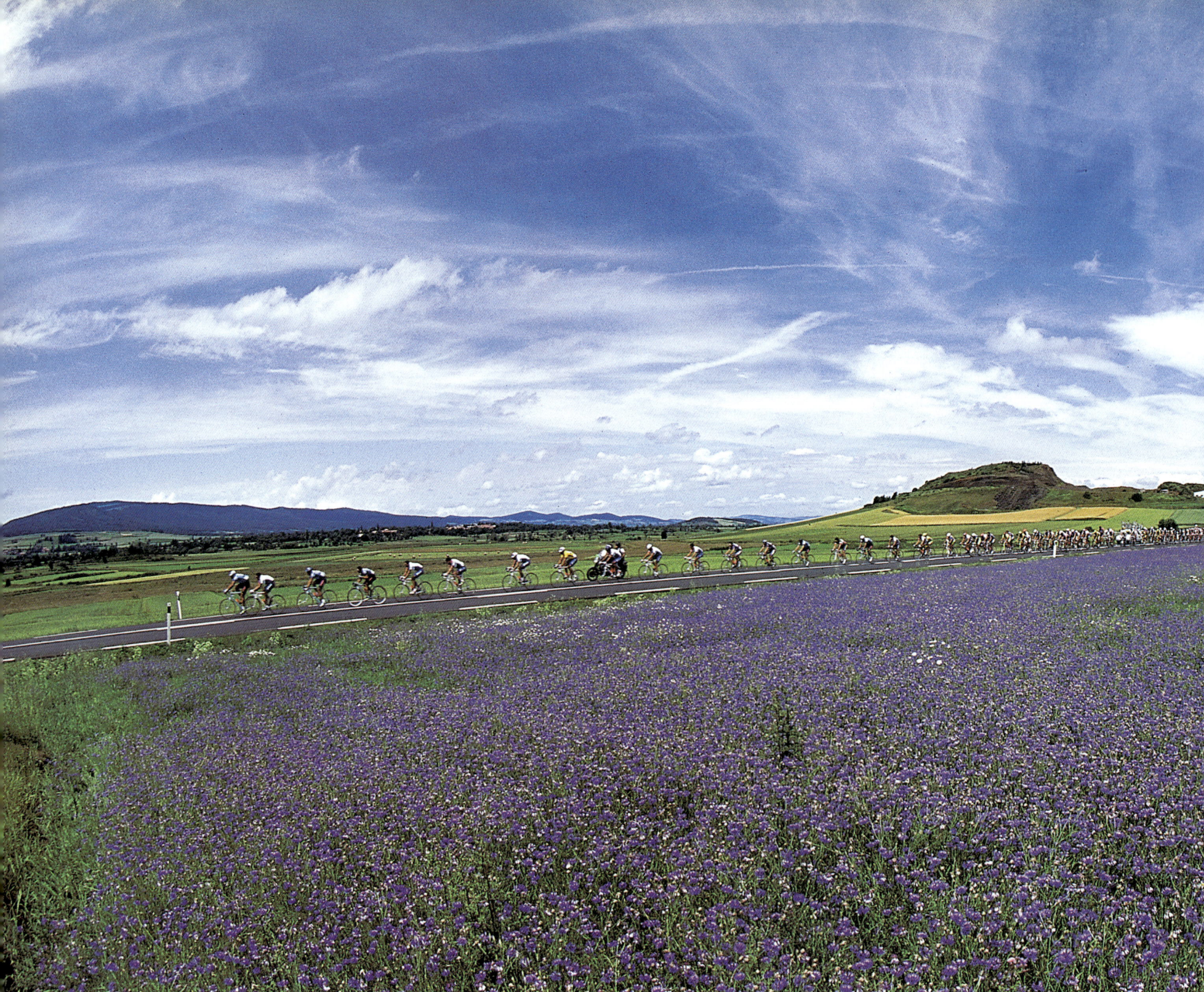

1995: TOUR DE FRANCE: MASSIF CENTRAL

On the St. Etienne to Mende stage of the '95 Tour, Miguel Induráin (in yellow) and his Banesto team chased a breakaway led by French rival Laurent Jalabert that threatened to give Jalabert the race lead.

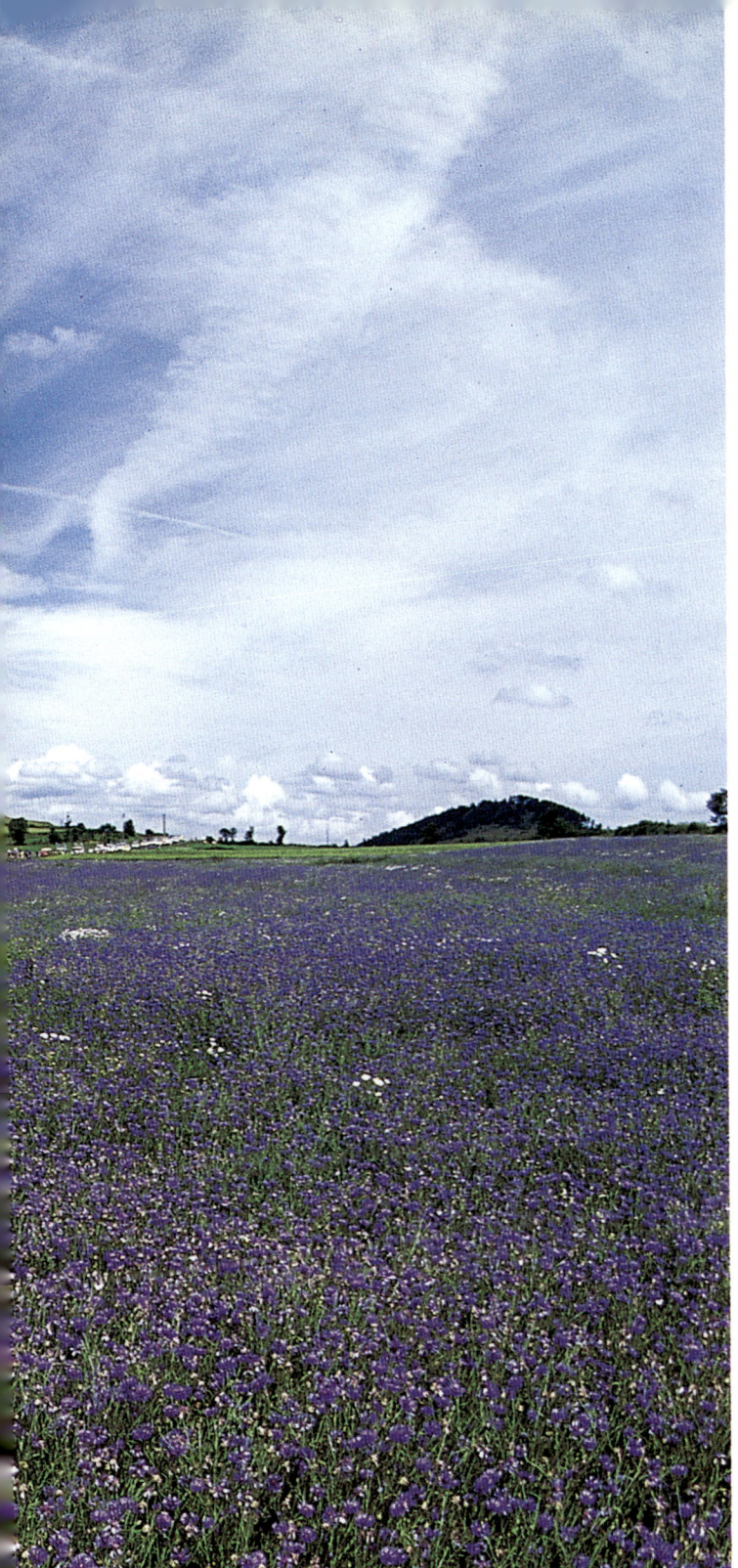
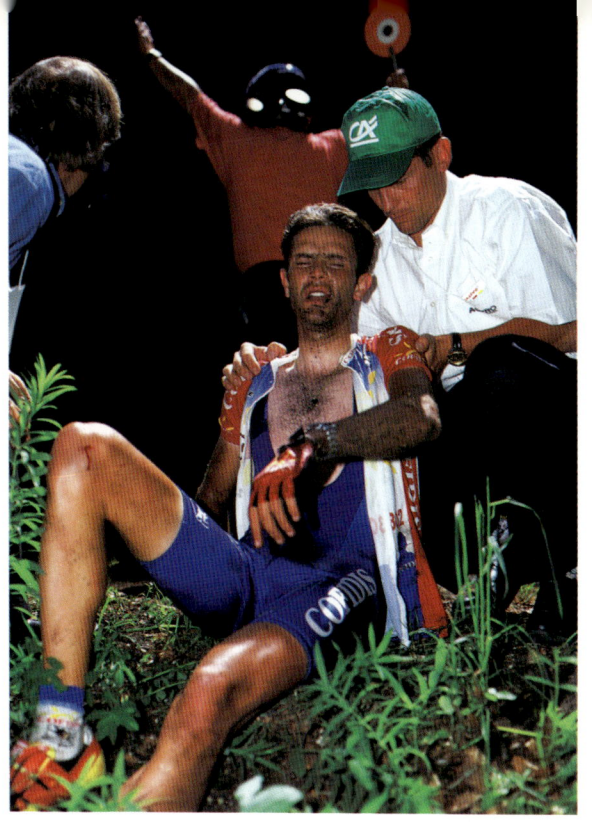

1997: DAUPHINÉ LIBÉRÉ: COL DE PORTE

Five riders crashed on a tricky turn descending the Col de Porte at the '97 Dauphiné, including this rider, Stéphane Goubert, who after colliding with a tree perforated his abdomen.

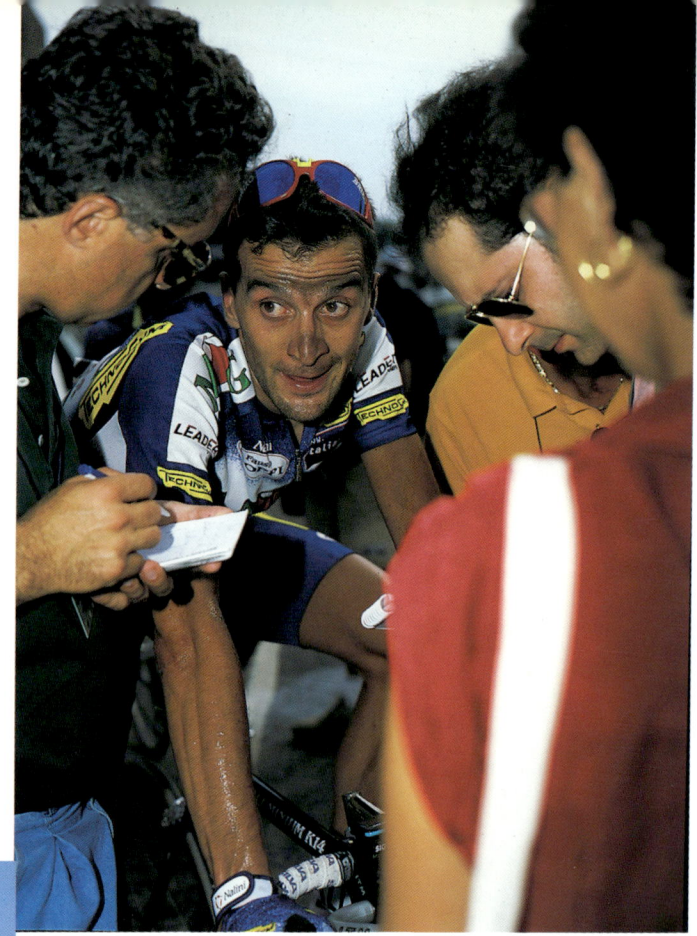

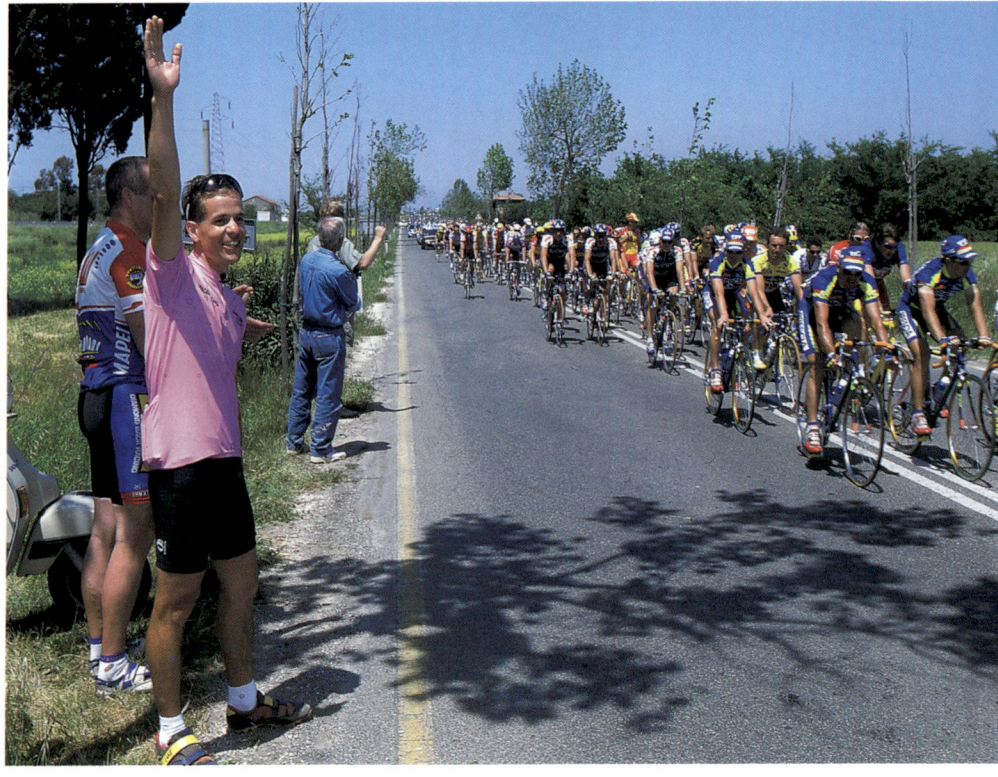

1997: GIRO D'ITALIA: TUSCANY

Andy Hampsten, winner of the 1988 Giro, came out to greet the 1997 peloton when it passed near his adopted home in Tuscany.

1997: ROCHESTER CLASSIC: ENGLAND

Italian ace Michele Bartoli received a lot of attention when he came to race in England's World Cup race at Rochester, Kent, in 1997.

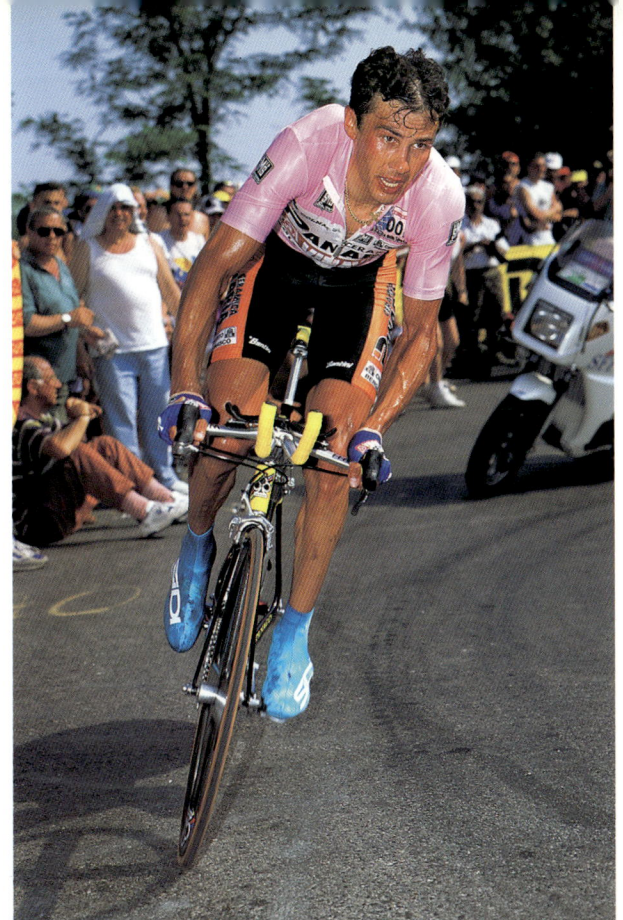
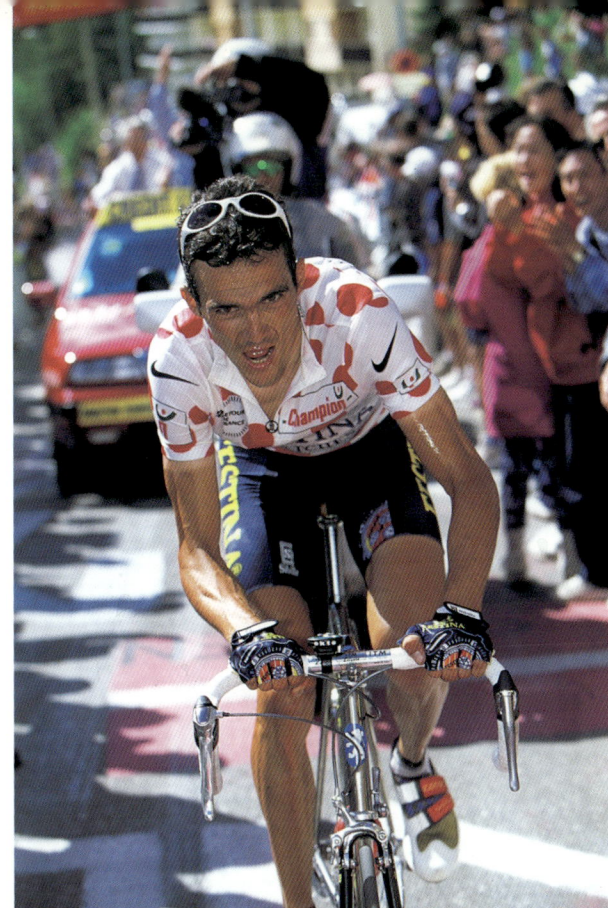
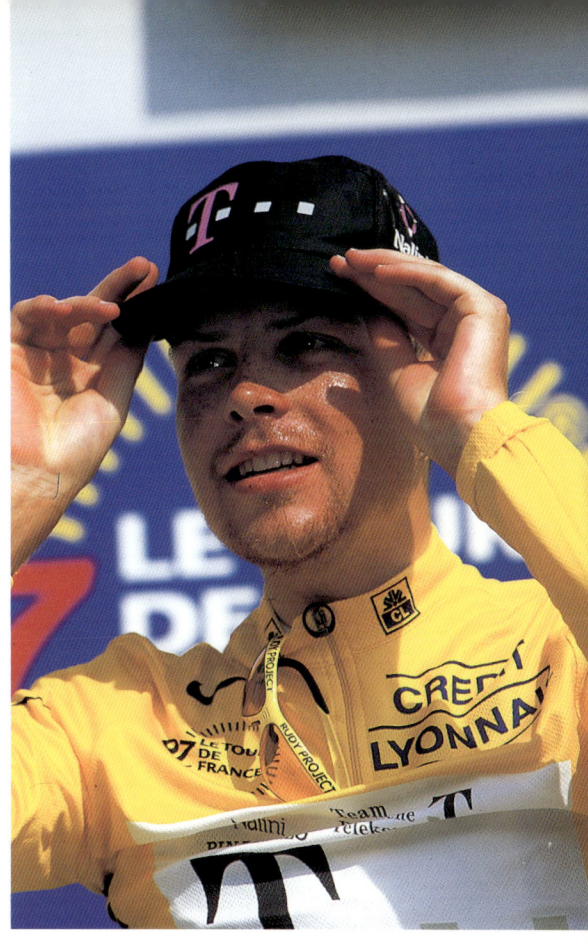

1996: GIRO D'ITALIA: MAROSTICA

In 1996, Pavel Tonkov became the second Russian cyclist to win the Giro, strongly defending his leader's pink jersey with a fourth-place finish in the 62km time trial from Vicenza to Marostica.

1997: TOUR DE FRANCE: FRENCH ALPS

Richard Virenque—here in a solo break on stage 14 over the Col de la Madeleine—finished second overall and took his fourth King of the Mountains title at the Tour in 1997.

1997: TOUR DE FRANCE: PARIS

By winning the Tour at age 23, Jan Ullrich seemed to be headed for a multi-year domination of the world's biggest bike race.

1995 TO 1997   167

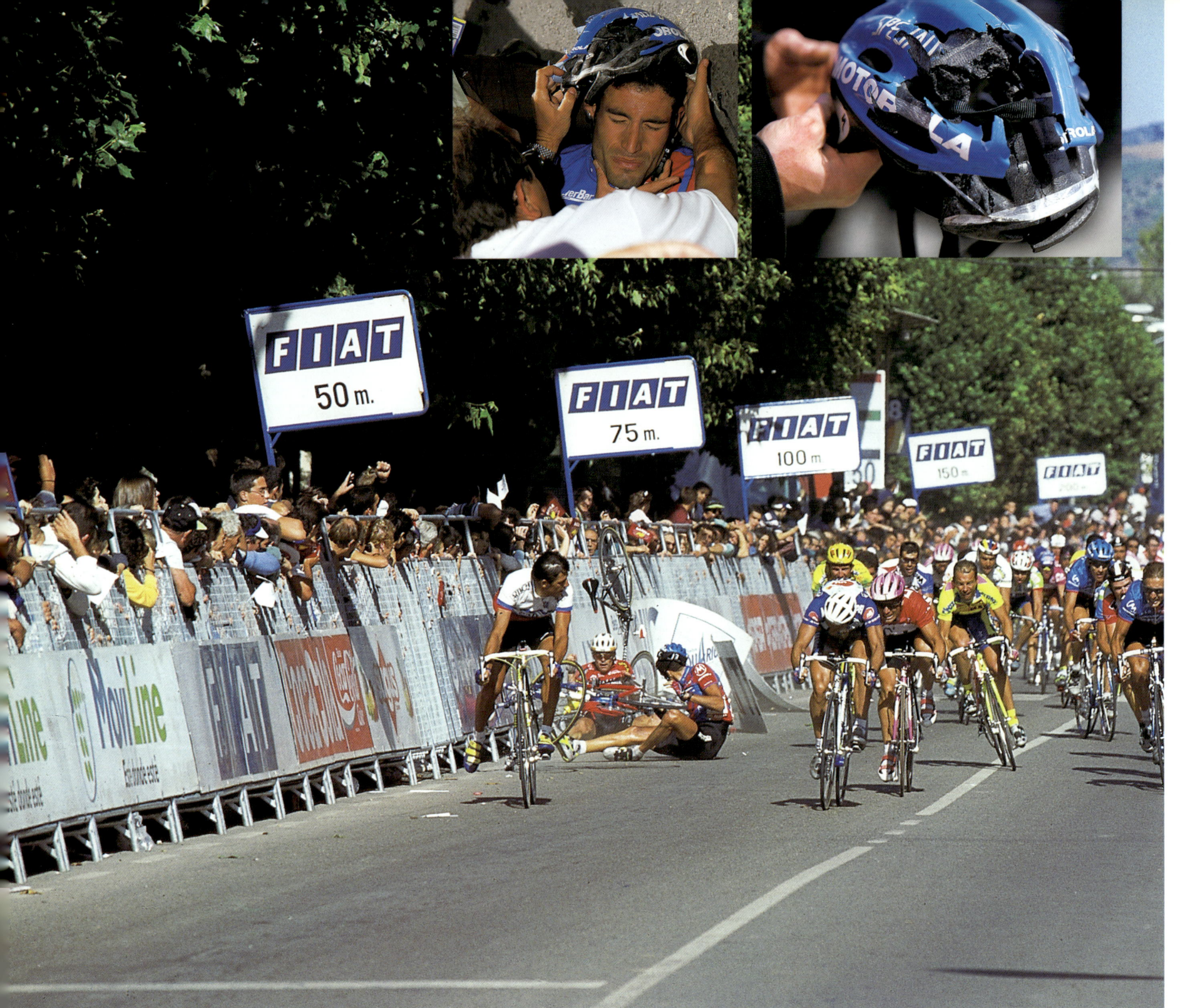

1995: VUELTA A ESPAÑA: CALATAYUD

A clash of wheels, a collision with the barricades, and two sprinters—George Hincapie and Marcel Wüst—hit the tarmac at the stage 19 finish of the '95 Vuelta. His fall broken by his helmet, Hincapie had no more than a bad headache, and he was able to continue in the race the next day. Wüst was penalized for causing the crash when he tried to squeeze between Hincapie and the barriers at the height of the sprint.

1997: GIRO D'ITALIA

The peloton at the '97 Giro races along the Amalfi coast, just south of the Bay of Naples, on stage 8 between Mondragone and Cava dei Tirreni.

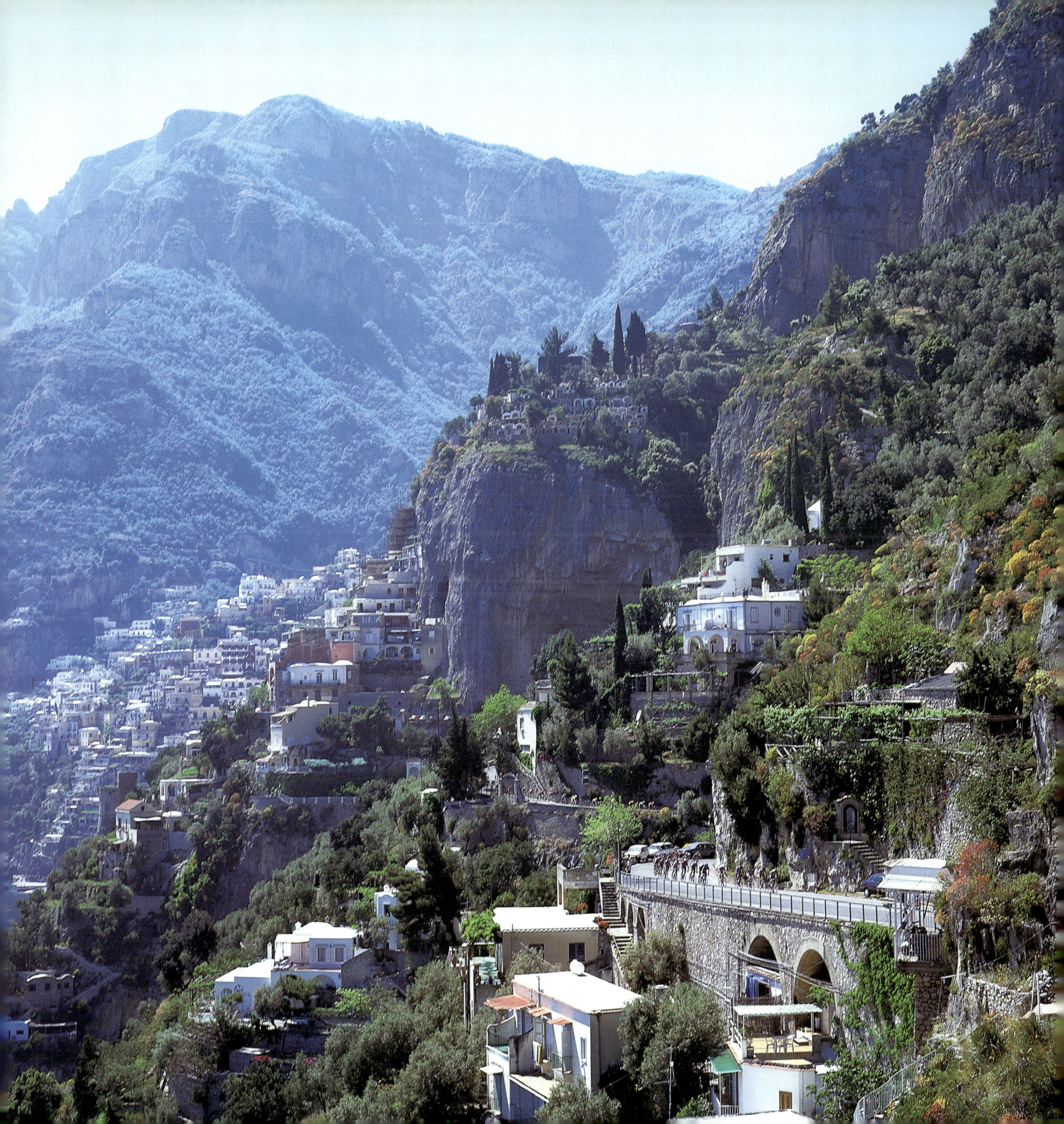

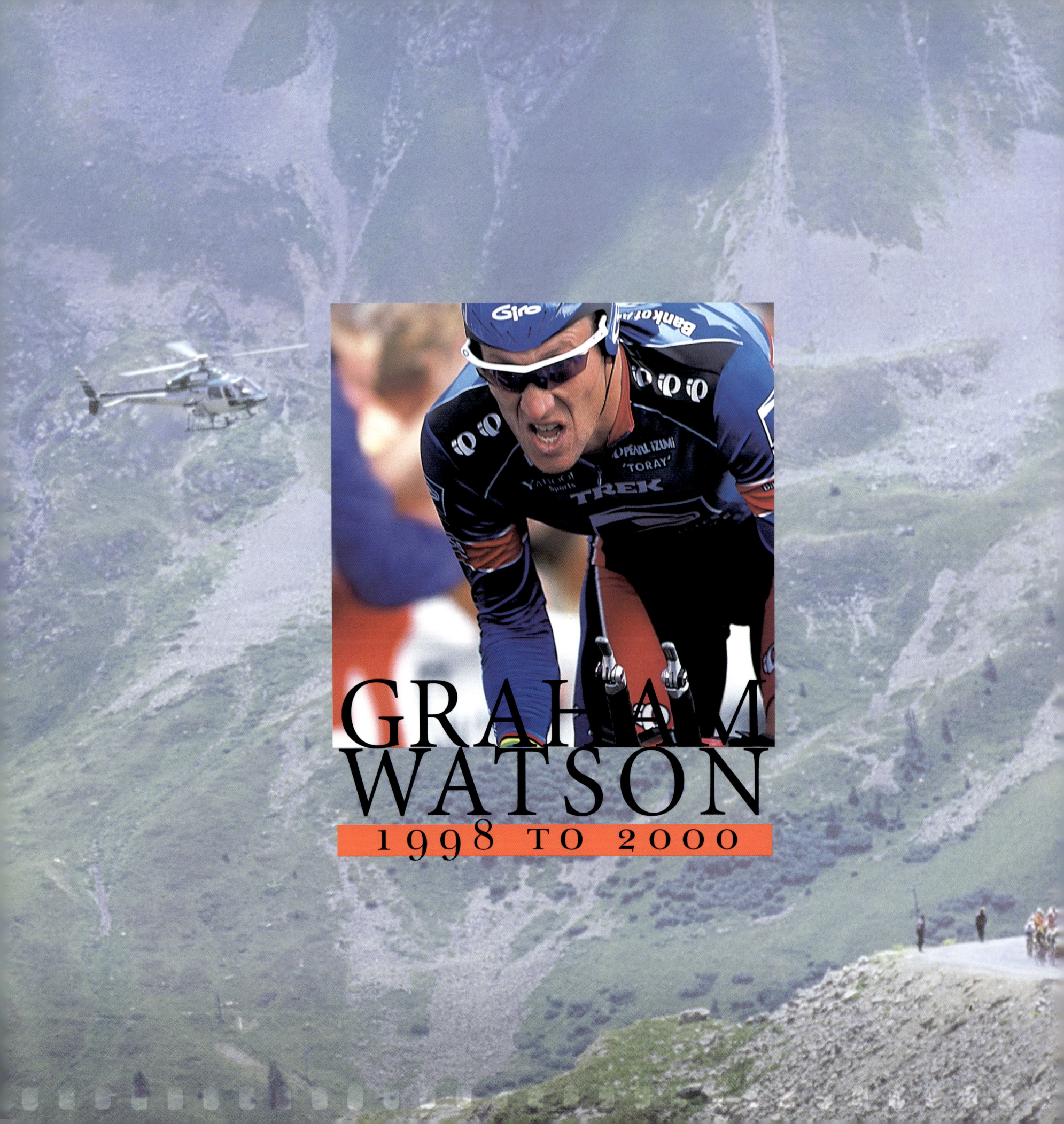
GRAHAM WATSON
1998 TO 2000

GRAHAM
WATSON

It was perhaps inevitable that my first assignment of 1998 was a visit to Lance Armstrong in Santa Barbara, California. He was spending a relaxing few weeks there, prior to attending training camp with his new team, sponsored by the U.S. Postal Service. In doing four-hour training rides and early-morning weight exercises in a local gym, Lance showed himself to be a completely new, revitalized man, totally focused on his hoped-for comeback to the top level of the sport. I noticed, too, how much thinner he was—apparently a natural reaction to the cancer therapy he'd undergone in late-1996.

I'd made the trip to California out of choice, sensing this man's determination to prove to the world that he could be as good as before, if not better. And Lance was totally accommodating of my requests for photographs—be it riding a bike, training at the gym, walking on the beach with Kristin, or drinking wine with some local friends. Everything I asked for was granted, and the resulting pictures were sold in magazines throughout the world, both sporting and otherwise.

Lance's comeback went on hold, however, when he withdrew from Paris-Nice at the end of the first road stage. Some journalists, desperate for some interesting news during a somewhat ordinary Paris-Nice, declared: "Armstrong's career is over." I thought otherwise, benefiting from that trip to California that had allowed me such close-up understanding of Lance's mental state. And I was right: Barely three months passed before he was back in Europe and winning, in the Tour of Luxembourg. After hearing that Lance had won the first stage of this quite difficult four-day race in the Ardennes, I cut short my regular seven-day-long devotion to a particularly boring Dauphiné Libéré to head north 300 miles overnight. So I got to see Lance break the defense of challenger Lauri Aus, and begin the comeback that seemed like a creation of Hollywood, if not of some place higher and holier.

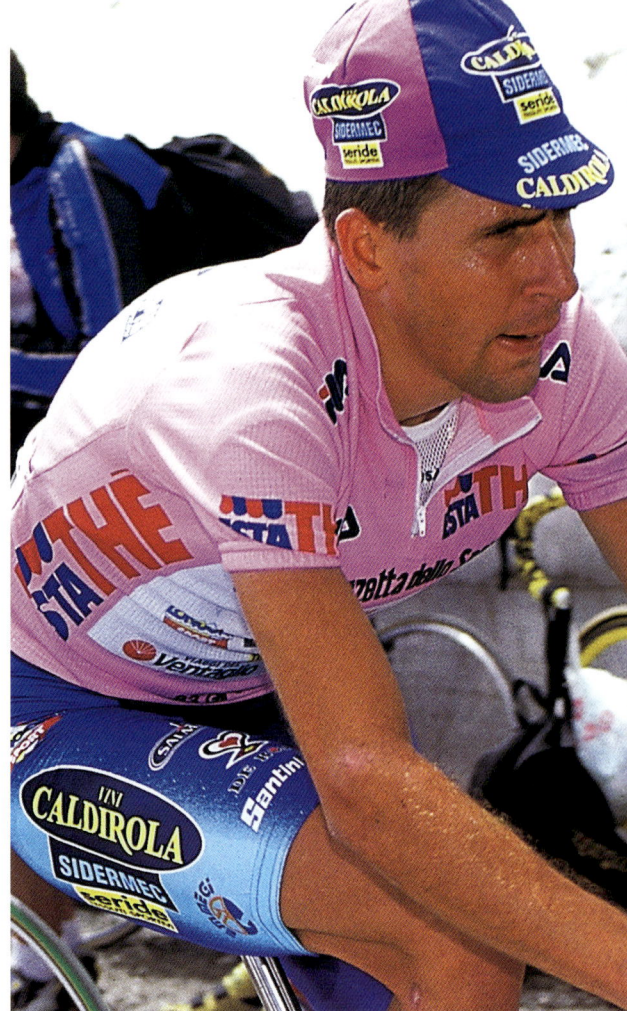

In between the Tour of Luxembourg and the absolute confirmation of Armstrong's comeback—the 1998 Vuelta—the sport of cycling faced one of its darkest moments: the police arrests of the Festina team during the Tour de France, and the ensuing period in which cycling came under the cruel spotlight of media and legal persecution. I was personally hurt by the "revelations" attached to the criminal investigations, having never quite realized that a sport so beautiful and exciting could also be a sport so corrupt and tarnished.

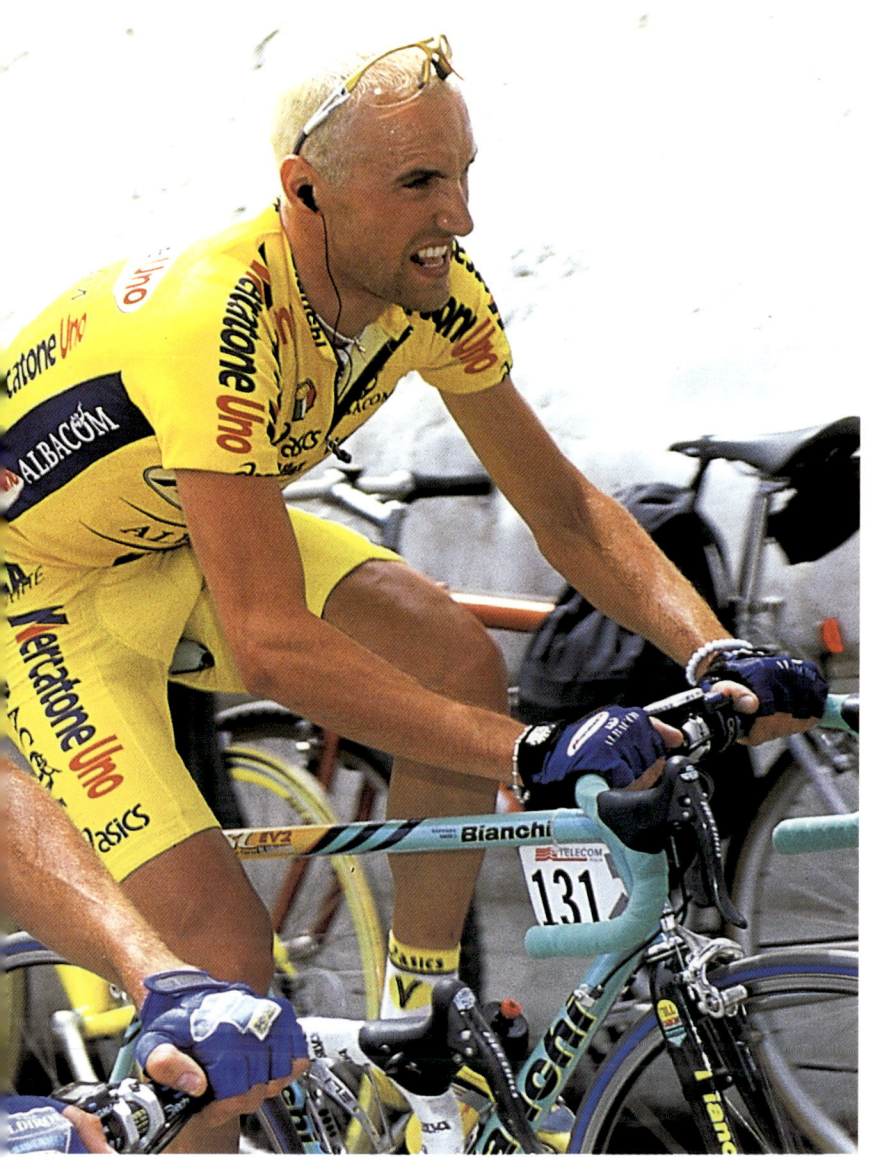

I remember one night during the '98 Tour when we had just encountered the riders' strike of stage 17 to Aix-les-Bains. Confused, depressed, and not knowing if the next day's stage would even begin, we pondered the ritualistic idea of continuing our Tour de France to Paris no matter what, staying in hotels long-since booked, in order to alleviate the harsh reality that perhaps the sport of cycling was about to become extinct. It only partially helped that the stop-start '98 Tour was a stunner, with Marco Pantani delivering a fatal blow to Jan Ullrich's defense of his '97 Tour win, after a searing attack on the Col du Galibier in atrocious conditions. For Pantani's win seemed almost too good to be true: Suddenly, the little climber had become a time trialist as well, taking third-place in the next-to-last day's time-test at Le Creusot, just behind Julich — who continued racing in the best form of his life to secure third-place overall.

Ironically, Julich's success helped motivate Armstrong even more, and the Texan became the savior of the season—if not of cycling itself—by blitzing the end of the year with consecutive fourth places in the Vuelta, the world time trial championship and the world road championship. In contrast to my experience at the Tour de France, I had thoroughly enjoyed the Vuelta—enjoyed seeing Lance better than his old best, faster than his old self, and now climbing with the likes of José Maria Jiménez and Fernando Escartin on Spain's most difficult mountain passes.

But just when it seemed that the sport was getting itself back on its feet in the spring of 1999, two incidents threatened to send our little world crashing down once again. First, a group of cyclists,

2000: GIRO D'ITALIA: COL D'IZOARD, FRANCE

With three days remaining of the 2000 Giro, Francesco Casagrande (left) seemed to be headed for overall victory over fellow Italian Stefano Garzelli (right) as they headed to the stage 18 finish in Briançon; but a muscle spasm wrecked Casagrande's time trial the next day, and Garzelli took the race overall by 1:27.

some professionals, were arrested by French police in connection with drug trafficking, together with two accomplices, a lawyer and a pharmacist. One of the arrested was 23-year-old Frank Vandenbroucke, the star of the future it had seemed, following his storming win in the Liège-Bastogne-Liège race a few weeks earlier, preceded by his win at Paris Nice. The world of cycling held its breath once again, and I was happy to take off on another Lance Armstrong mission: an all-day training ride in the Pyrénées, where Lance was planning on riding every centimeter of the 173km, 15th stage of that year's Tour.

As I sat down to dinner with Lance and his wife Kristin—as well as his mini-team of soigneur, mechanic and directeur sportif—I appreciated this diversion from the sport's latest problems, and I began to realize how serious Lance was about the Tour. I enjoyed listening to the Texan's plans on how he was going to win the event, and by the time we'd reached Piau-Engaly, after nearly seven hours of enduring constant rain and cold, I had no doubts at all—Lance would win. My cameras were nearly ruined by the rain, I was soaked through to the skin, Gore-Tex or no Gore-Tex, and my motorbike driver was shivering down to the bone. But this cold, miserable day had also been a day so inspiring and motivating that I'd barely felt the cold at all. And when I cheerfully left Lance and his team in a deserted parking lot amid this ski station's cluster of concrete buildings, I knew that the images I'd captured of him climbing and descending seven cols, would complement the images of him later that July, on these very same roads. My only regret was not being able to do a repeat the next day, on Lance's second sortie over the Col du Tourmalet and Col d'Aubisque climbs. But the Tour de Romandie beckoned me to Switzerland, followed by the Giro d'Italia that started on the island of Sicily—a much warmer prospect!

Sadly, that Giro ended in even worse circumstances than the previous year's Tour, following the exclusion of race leader Marco Pantani two days before the end. By this point, Pantani had the

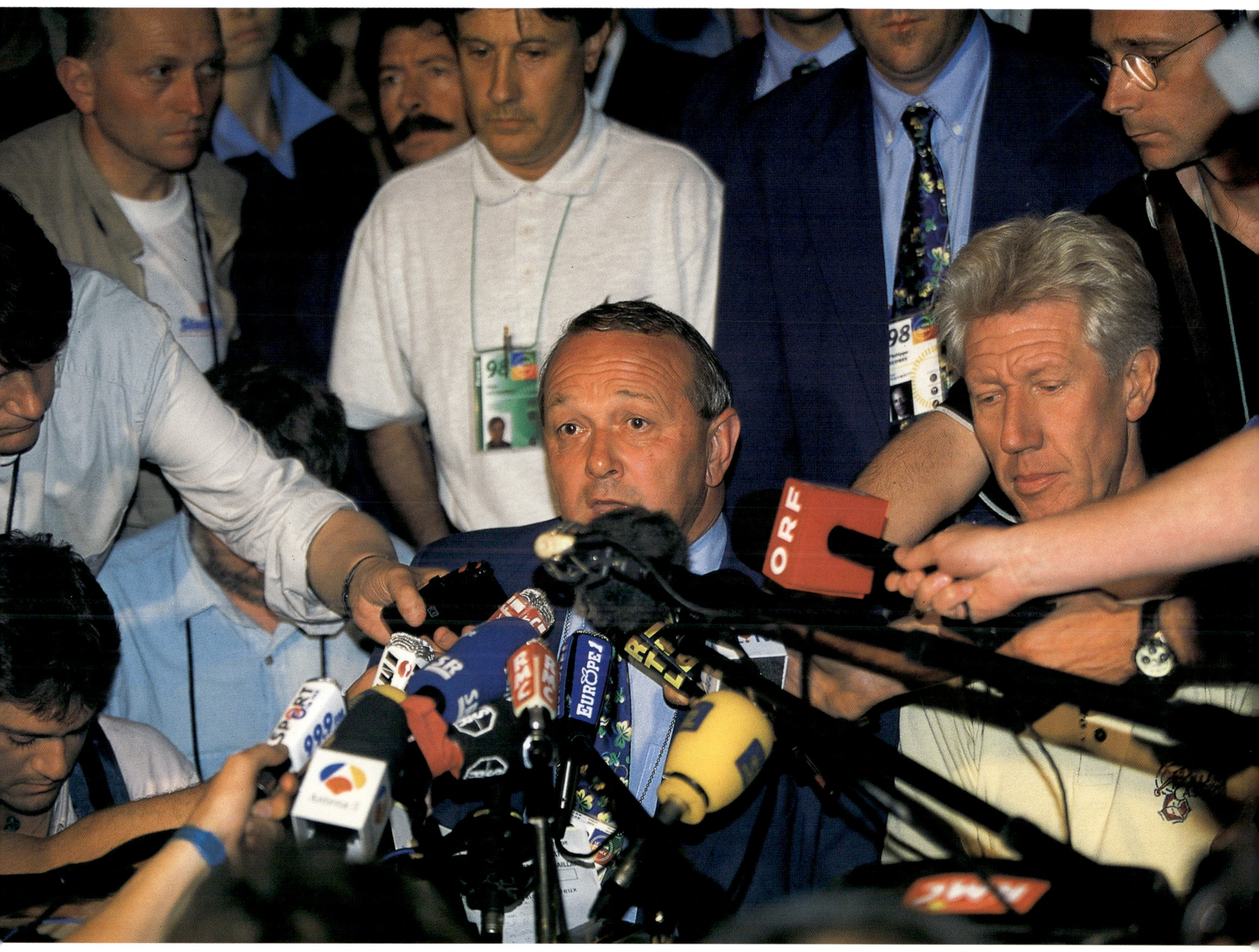

1998: TOUR DE FRANCE: BRIVE-LA-GAILLARDE

At 11 p.m., after hours of discussions and deliberations, Tour de France director-general Jean-Marie Leblanc announces after stage 6 that the entire Festina team is being excluded from the 1998 Tour. The technical reason given for the French team's exclusion was contravention of Rule No. 29—after its directeur sportif Bruno Roussel admitted to the police that Festina used a systematic doping plan, involving the banned drugs, EPO and human growth hormone.

Giro won, had taken the four hardest stages of the race, and would most certainly have saved his best for the last—an epic stage over the passes of the Tonale, Gavia, Mortirolo and Santa Christina. Instead, after testing above the 50-percent hematocrit limit that morning, Pantani locked himself into his team's hotel in Madonna di Campiglio, while the rest of the peloton raced this awesome stage in an atmosphere of complete and utter anticlimax. It would be months—if ever—before the truth would be revealed, but I knew then, as did most of my colleagues, that if Pantani had cheated at the 1999 Giro, then his race-saving victory in the '98 Tour was also in question.

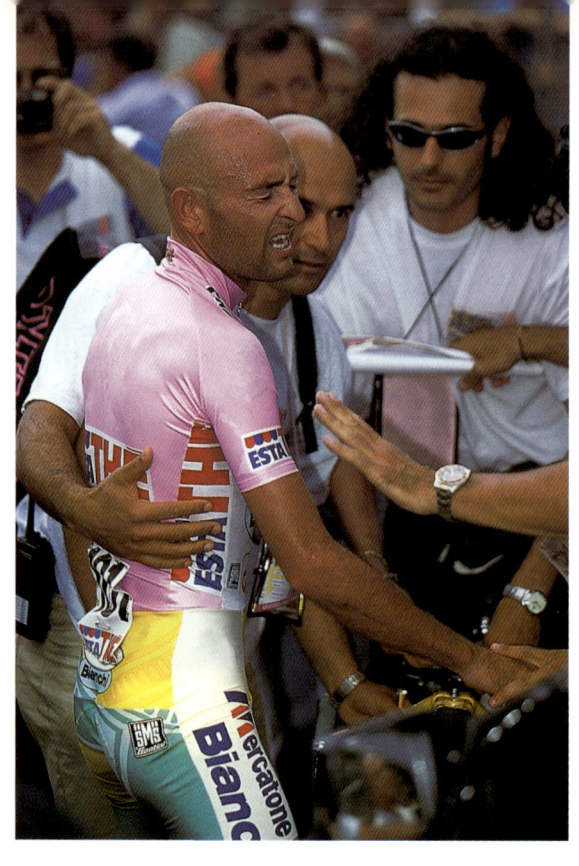

I was happy yet again to leave the mourning to others, and left the next day for the Dauphiné Libéré. Here, Armstrong was building up to the Tour by racing in the service of his teammate Jonathan Vaughters, who had won the Mont Ventoux time trial and was hoping to win the race overall, just a few weeks before the Tour began.

The 1999 Tour delivered everything I could possibly have asked for: great weather, inspired racing, a degree of drama, and the triumph of Mr. Lance Armstrong, who won his Tour as planned. From the moment he won the prologue in Le Puy du Fou, I felt he had the race within his grasp. And knew for sure a week later, after he'd trounced his rivals in the time trial around Metz. The Alps came and went—all too quickly as far as I was concerned—and then came the Pyrénées and that same stage Armstrong had ridden a few months earlier, to Piau-Engaly. Only now, it was sunny and hot.

We'd begun our Tour, a group of roughly a dozen journalists, photographers and drivers, with the agreement that whenever a Brit, American or Australian won a stage or took the yellow jersey, a bottle of champagne had to be opened to honor them. Fortunately, this tradition was aban-

1998: GIRO D'ITALIA: LUGANO, SWITZERLAND

After finishing third in the stage 21 time trial from Mendrisio to Lugano, Marco Pantani wrapped up his triumph at the 1998 Giro—which he followed a month later by winning the Tour de France.

doned after just the prologue and the Metz test; for Lance's success meant double workloads for everyone, and would have created enormous hangovers for the last 10 days, not to mention empty bank accounts. Nonetheless, it was a Tour I will never forget, for I felt as if I were watching a friend win, and that doesn't happen too often in one's lifetime. His repeat victory in 2000 was just as exciting and even more impressive.

I have enjoyed the last 20 years enormously. I enjoyed watching the likes of Armstrong race, and I enjoyed witnessing the successes and fortunes of so many other cyclists, too numerous to name. Each winter, when the season finally winds down to a halt, I spend many long hours re-filing that year's collection of color slides—possibly up to 25,000 of them—carefully throwing away unneeded images, while storing only the best ones for future use. By now, my Armstrong file has grown considerably, and I draw similarities between that and my archive of Sean Kelly, 20 years earlier, and my more recent archive of Miguel Induráin—for the images of these men form the bulk of my collection to date.

As I look back through my archives, I also look ahead, and wonder who will be the Kellys, Induráins and Armstrongs of future years and whether they'll be English speakers or from the more "traditional" lands of cycling.

I like to think I have the best job in the world, working with some of the best people in the world, and I know for sure that I'll be doing my work for as long as possible in the years to come. I wouldn't want it any other way.

1999: TOUR DE FRANCE: BOURG D'OISANS

With the Alps behind him and his yellow jersey secure, Lance Armstrong was viewed with a sense of awe by the media at the '99 Tour.

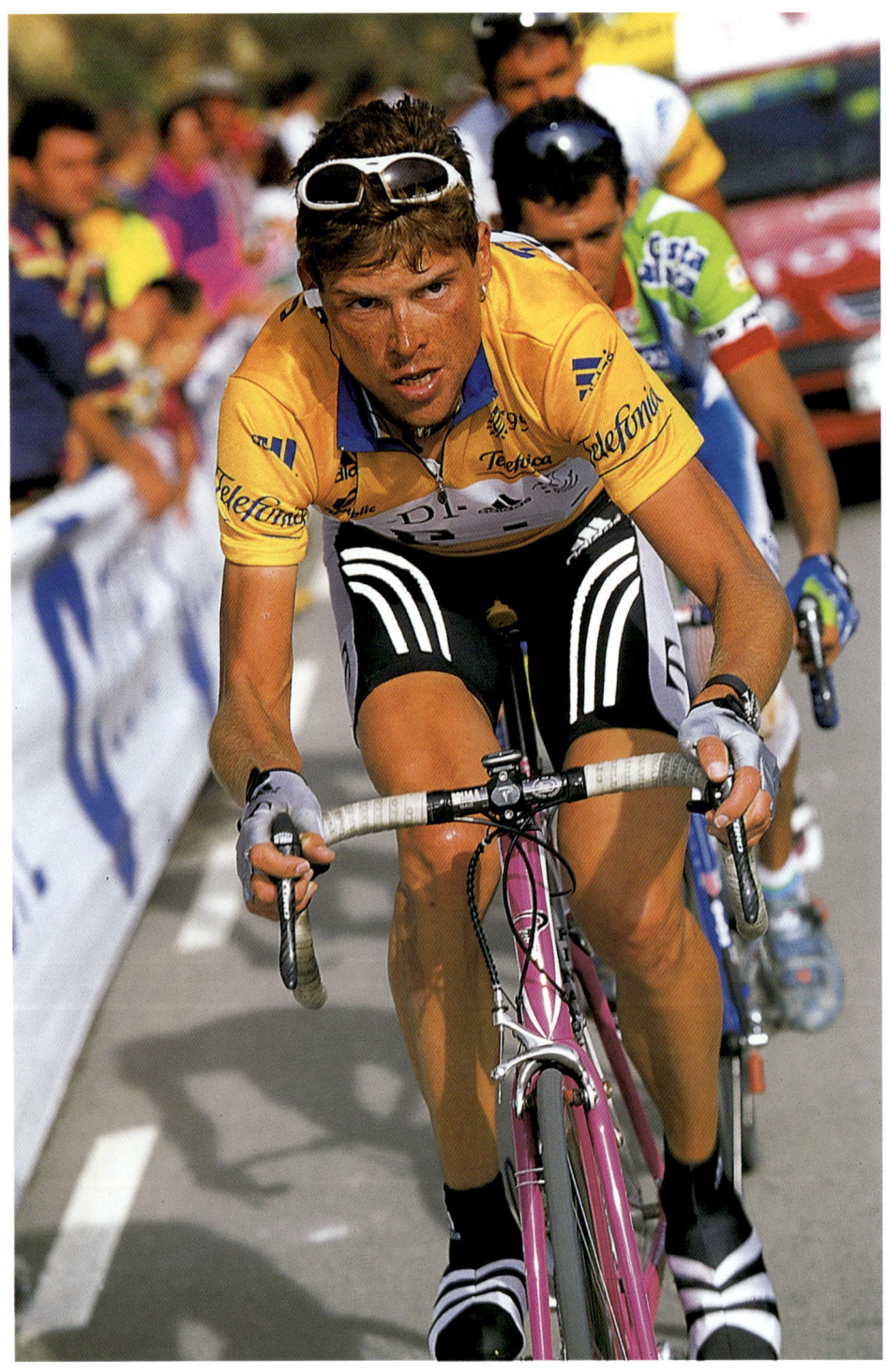

1999: VUELTA A ESPAÑA: CASTELLAR DEL RIU, SPAIN

Defending his yellow jersey, Jan Ullrich leads Roberto Heras up the finishing climb to Castellar del Riu on stage 13 of the '99 Vuelta.

1999: LIÈGE-BASTOGNE-LIÈGE: BELGIUM

The crowds come out in force every April in the Belgian hill town of Houffalize, to watch the Liège-Bastogne-Liège field tackle its first serious climb of the day, the Côte St. Roch.

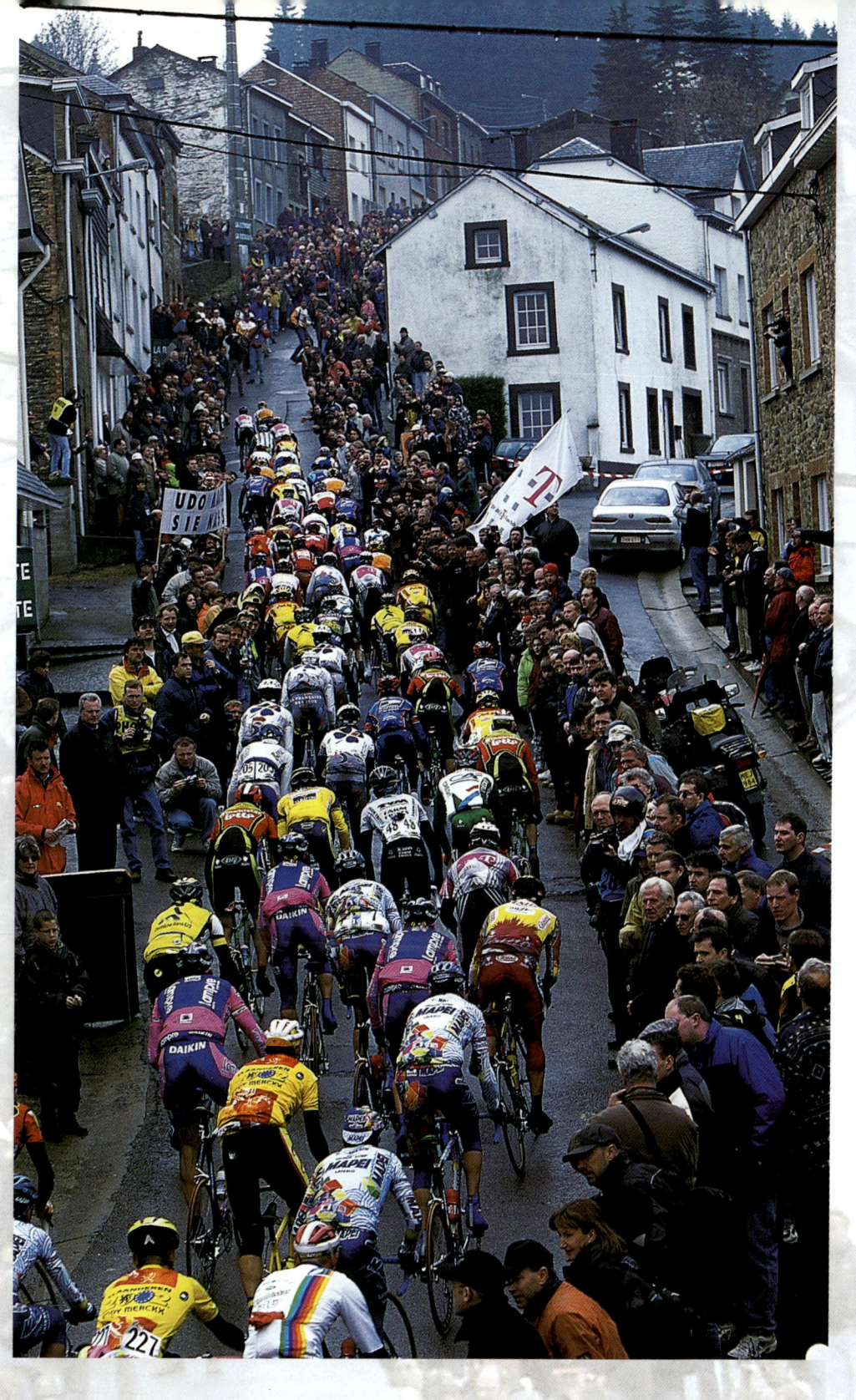

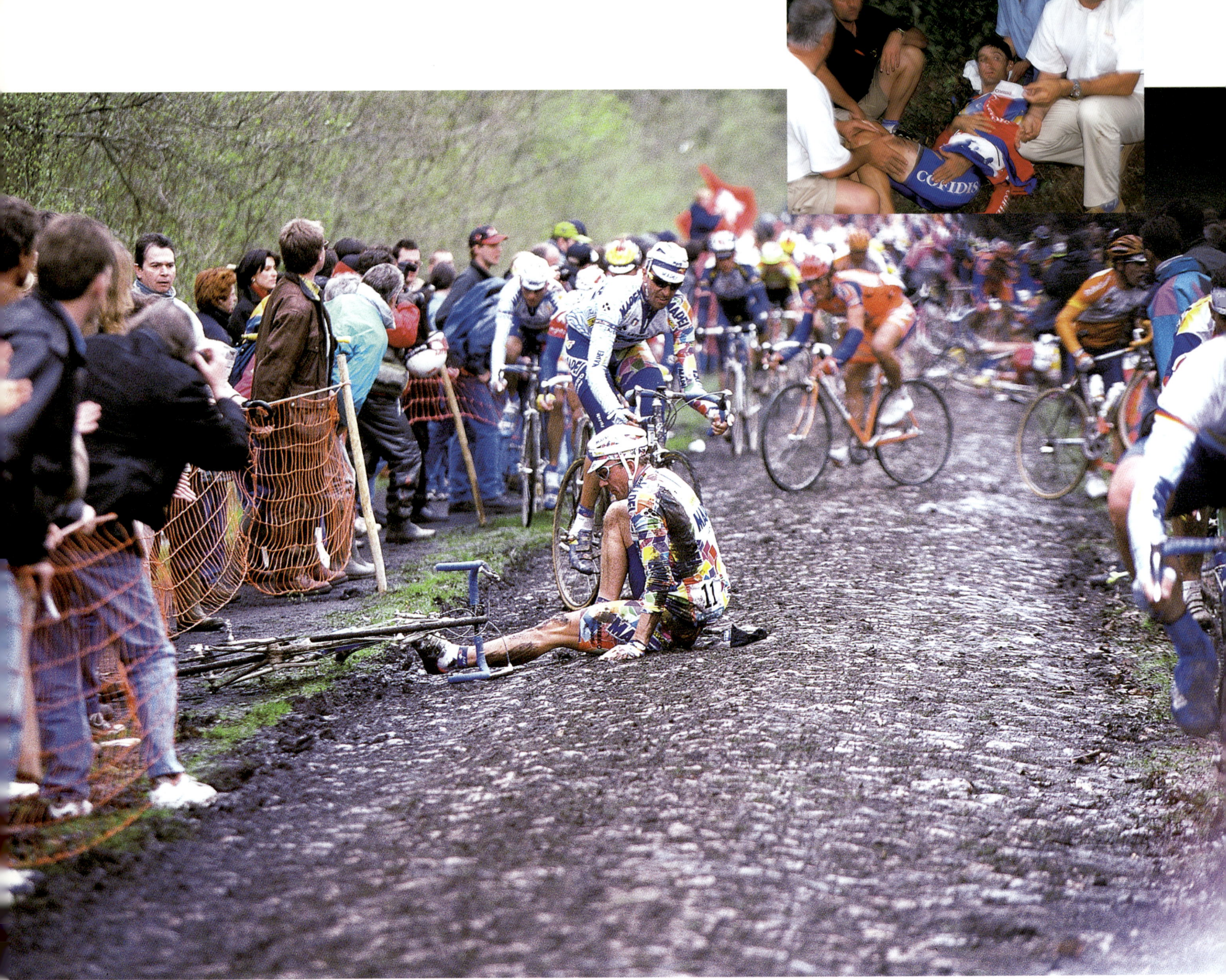

1998: PARIS-ROUBAIX: WALLERS, FRANCE

The crash that nearly ended a career: Johan Museeuw (No. 11) has just fallen on the mud-slick cobblestones of the Wallers-Arenberg Forest in Paris-Roubaix. Dirt on a knee wound was not properly treated and the Belgian star narrowly averted having a leg amputated because of a gangrenous infection.

1999: TOUR DE FRANCE: METZ

An ambulance was needed to evacuate Bobby Julich after a high-speed crash in the stage 8 Metz time trial at the '99 Tour.

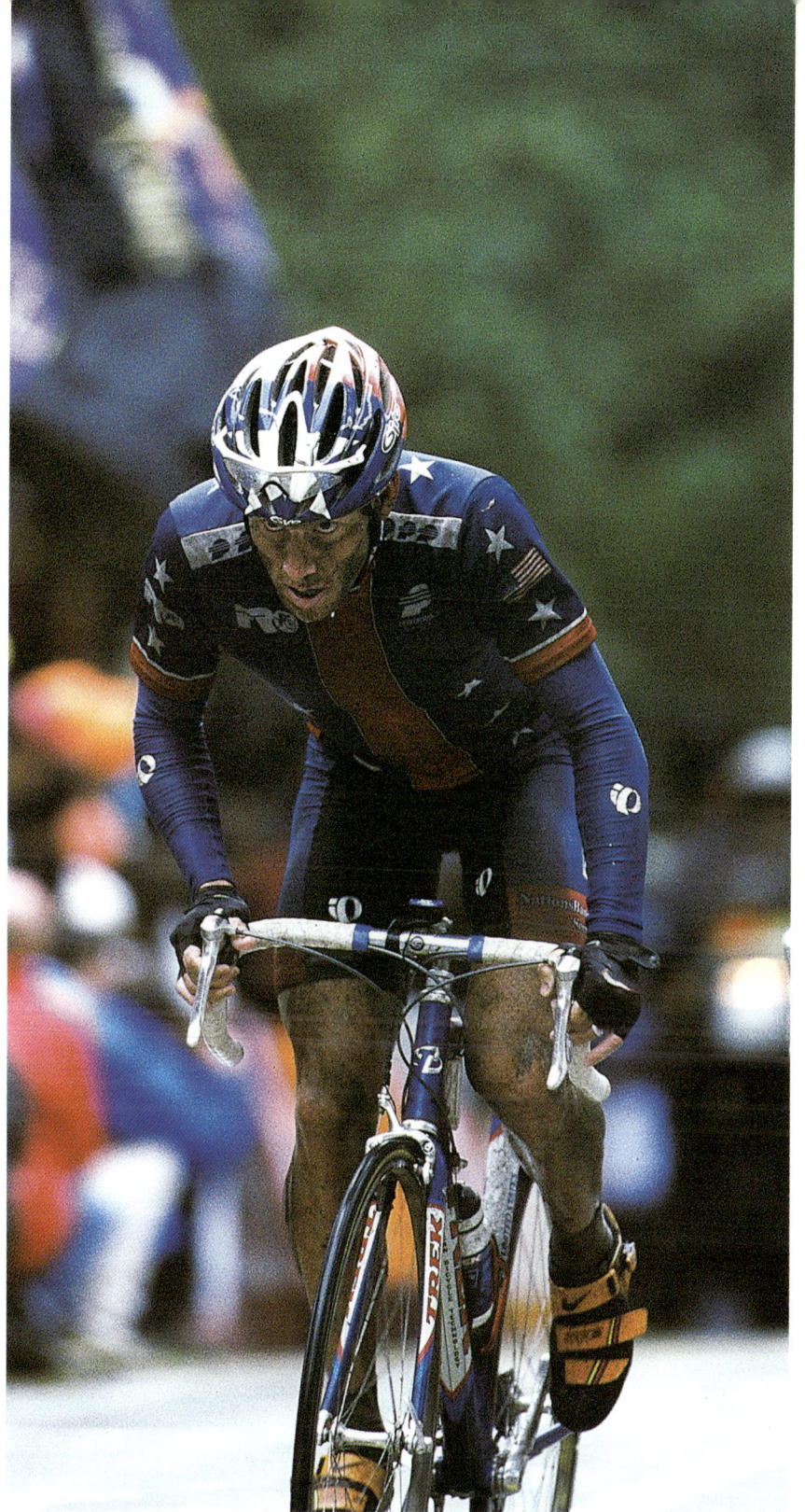

1998: WORLD ROAD CHAMPIONSHIPS: VALKENBURG, NETHERLANDS

Determination was etched on the face of Lance Armstrong as he climbed the Cauberg on his way to fourth place at the 1998 world road championship in the Netherlands.

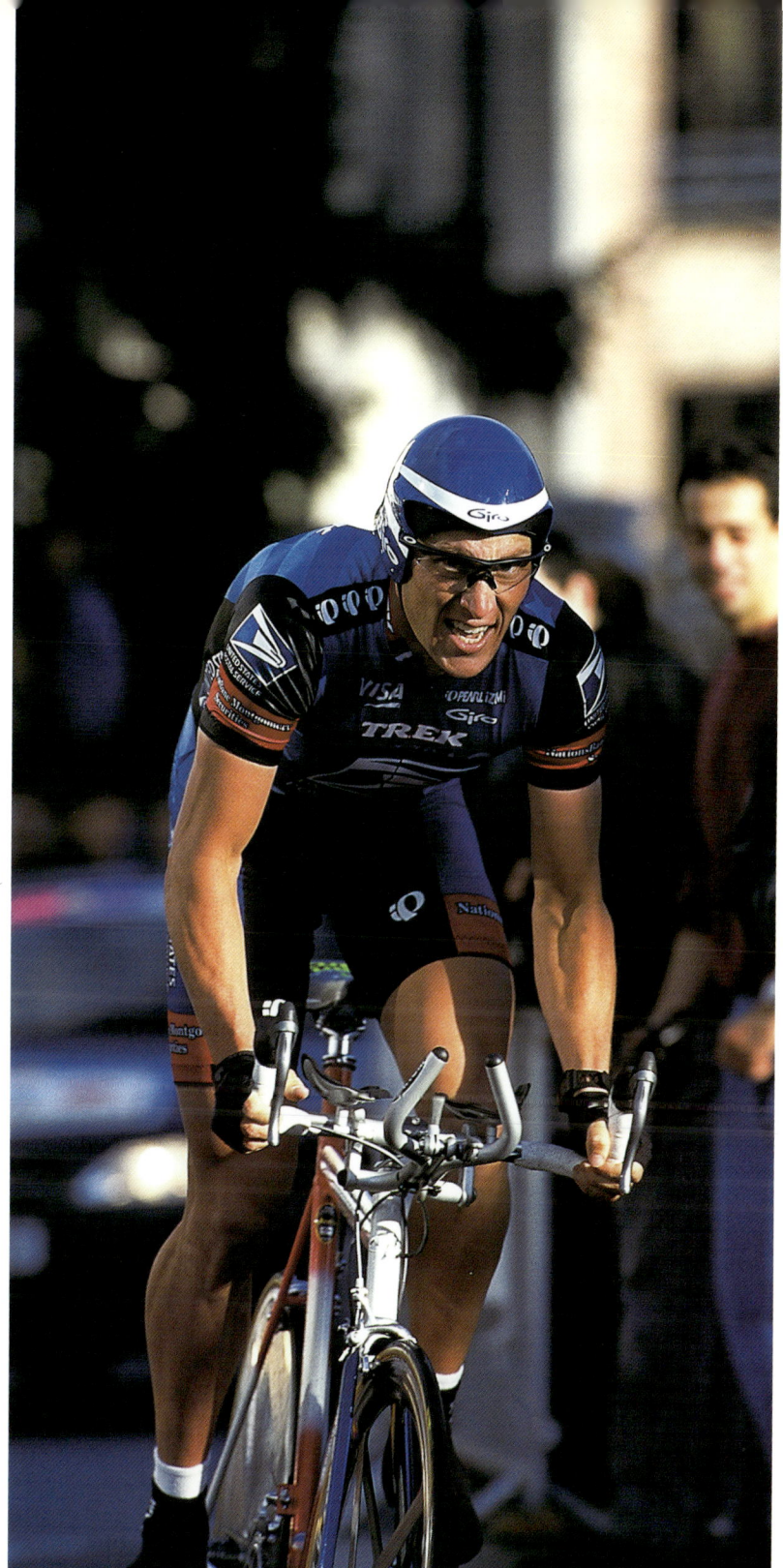

1998: PARIS-NICE: PARIS

Some journalists said this would be the last race of Lance Armstrong's career: He rides the stage 1 time trial from Suresnes to Paris at the '98 Paris-Nice. This initial comeback from cancer ended the next day, when the American quit near the end of the first road stage at Sens. But he returned to racing within two months....

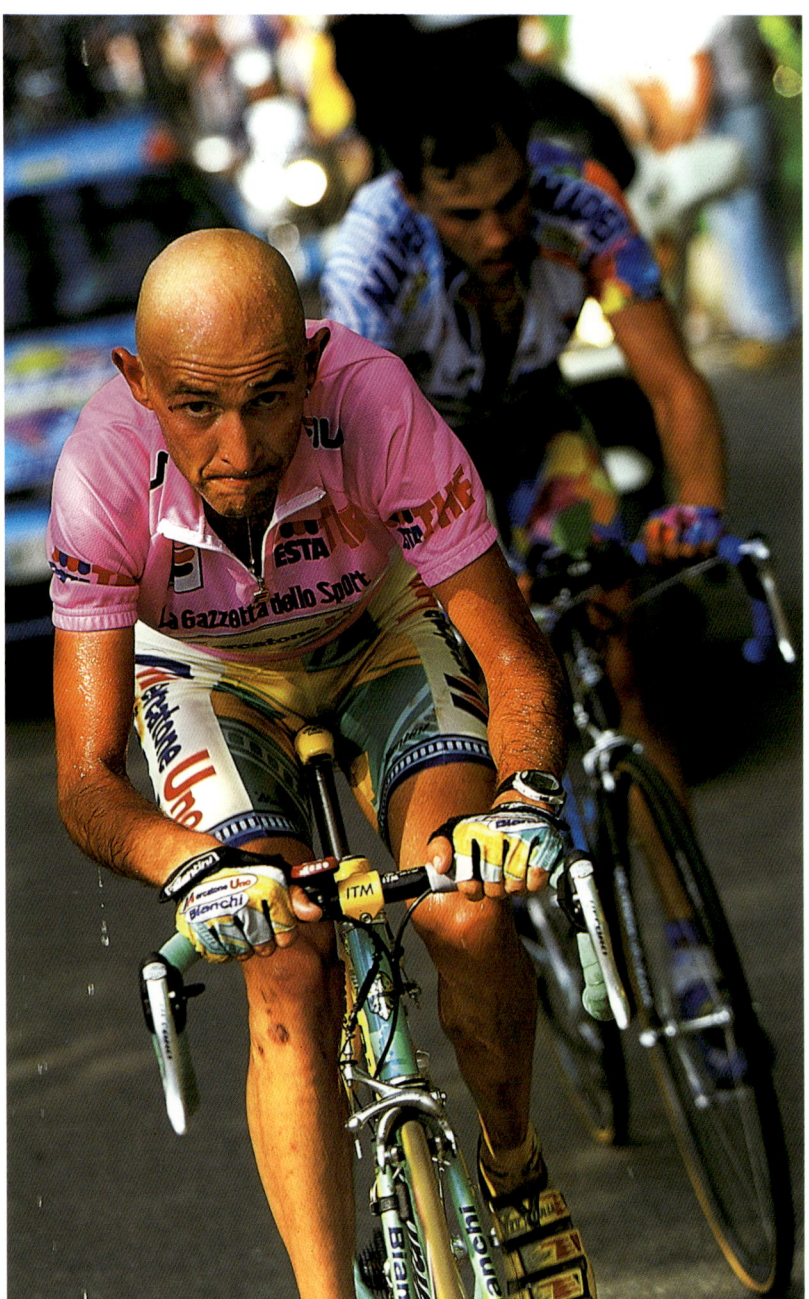

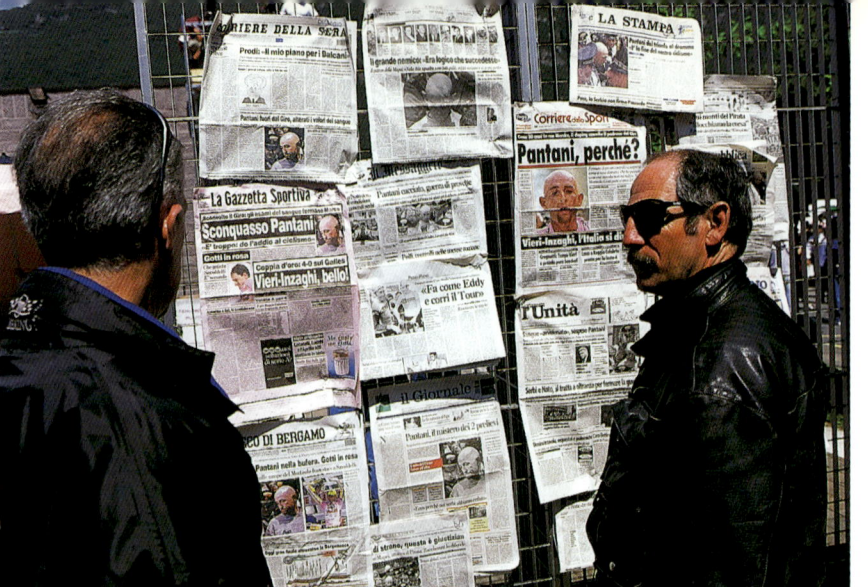

1998: GIRO D'ITALIA: MONTECAMPIONE

On the final big climb of the '98 Giro, the Montecampione, Marco Pantani knows he has to get rid of Russian rival Pavel Tonkov if he wants to win the race. Just after this shot, Pantani indeed dropped Tonkov and arrived at the summit with a one-minute advantage.

1999: GIRO D'ITALIA: BOARIO TERME

Fast forward one year, Pantani is on his way to a second consecutive Giro victory when he tests over the 50-percent hematocrit limit in an early-morning blood test. The next morning, before the stage start in Boario Terme, all the Italian newspapers have the Pantani story on the front page.

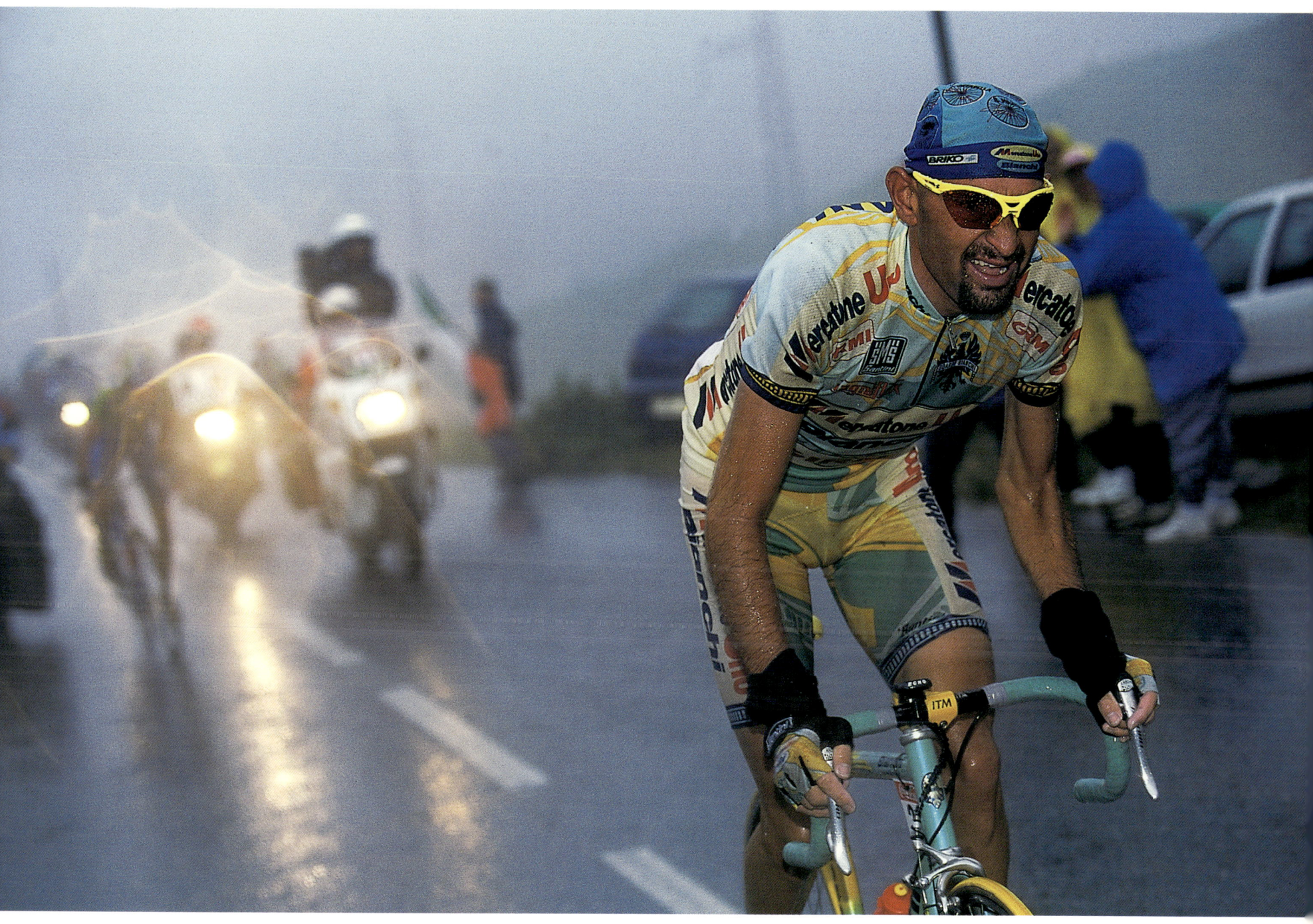

1998: TOUR DE FRANCE: COL DU GALIBIER

If the blood-test fiasco was the low point of Pantani's career, the high point was surely his attack (above) on the Col du Galibier that saw him go on to win the 15th stage, at Les Deux-Alpes, and take the 1998 Tour de France yellow jersey from Jan Ullrich.

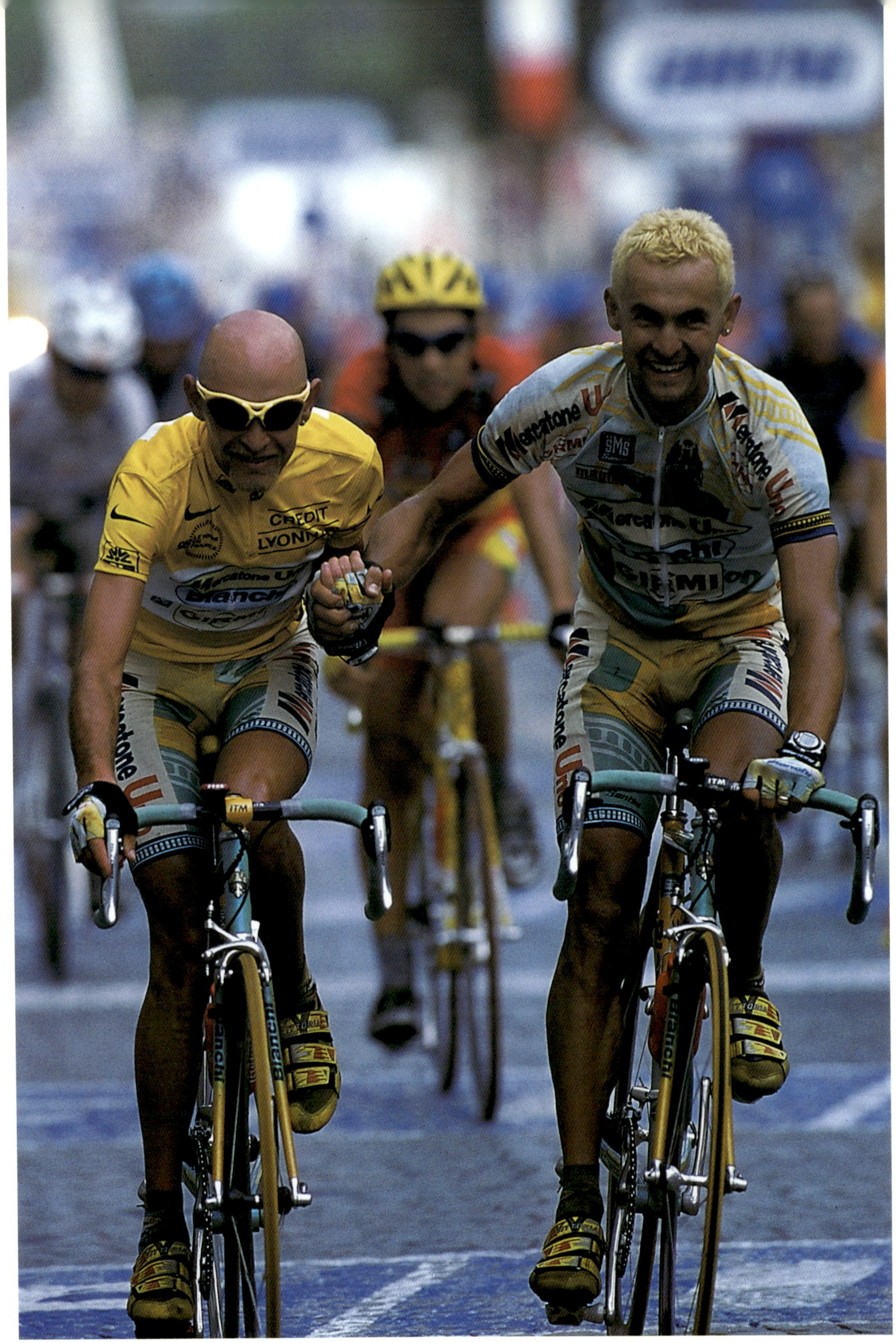

1998: TOUR DE FRANCE: PARIS

To celebrate Marco Pantani's victory in the '98 Tour, all his Mercatone Uno teammates dyed their hair yellow for the final stage in Paris. Here, Fabio Fontanelli shakes his team leader's hand as they cross the final finish line.

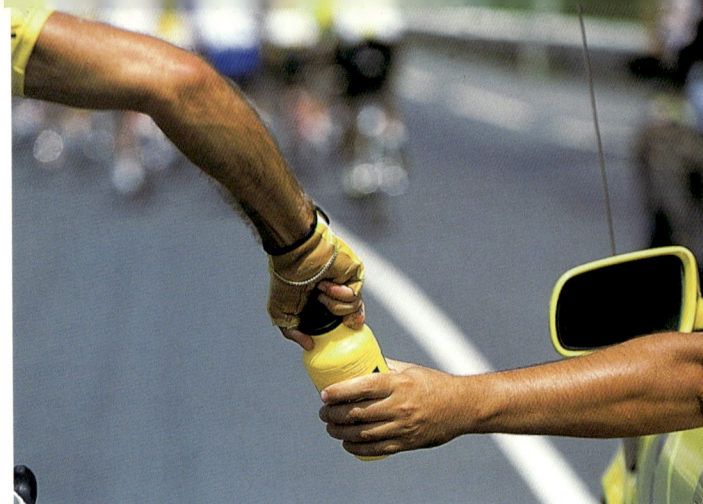

1998: VUELTA A ESPAÑA: SPAIN

A helping hand: An ONCE team rider takes a water bottle (and a friendly push) from his team mechanic.

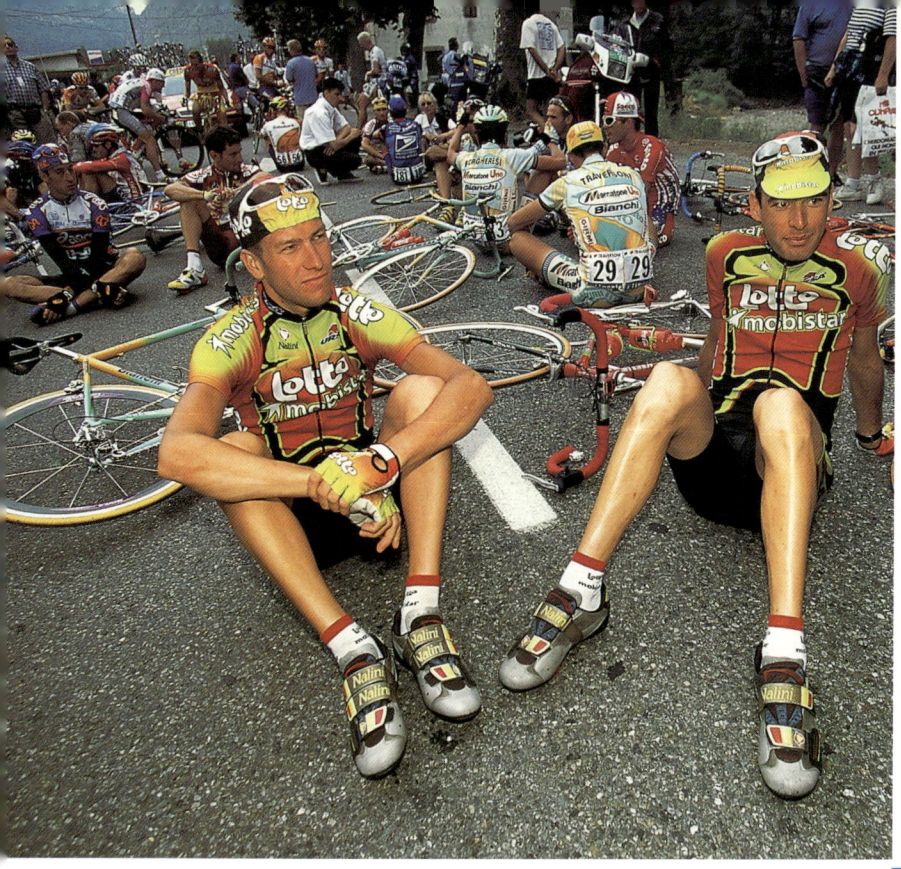

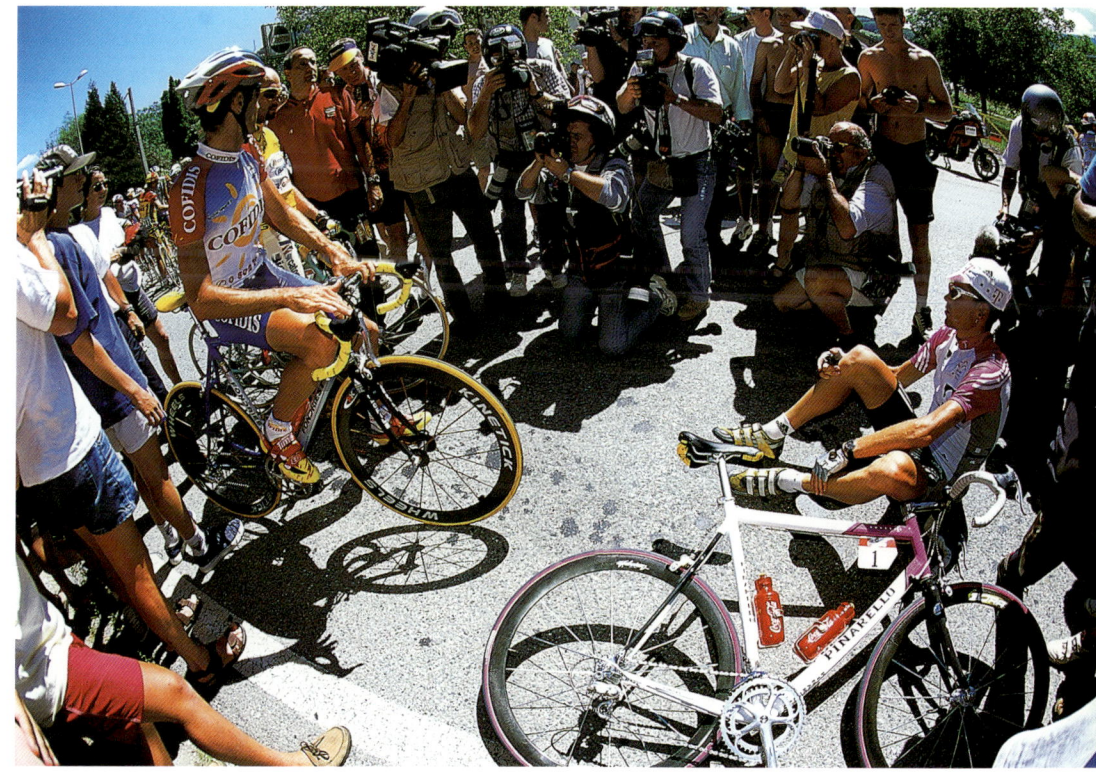

1998: TOUR DE FRANCE: TARASCON-SUR-ARIÈGE

Tour threatened, part I: With the news coming through that morning of the Festina riders' harsh overnight imprisonment by the police in Lyon, the Tour riders refused to start stage 12 of the '98 Tour. A compromise was finally negotiated between officials and riders, and the stage proved the fastest of the Tour at 48.764 kph.

1998: TOUR DE FRANCE: ANNECY LAKE

Tour threatened, part II: A week later, in the early kilometers of stage 17 between Albertville and Aix-les-Bains, word spread through the peloton of another case of repugnant police action, this time against riders from TVM. Here, the cameras are trained on the Tour top three: Bobby Julich (left), Jan Ullrich (right) and yellow jersey Marco Pantani. Again, the race survived, but only after six teams quit in protest.

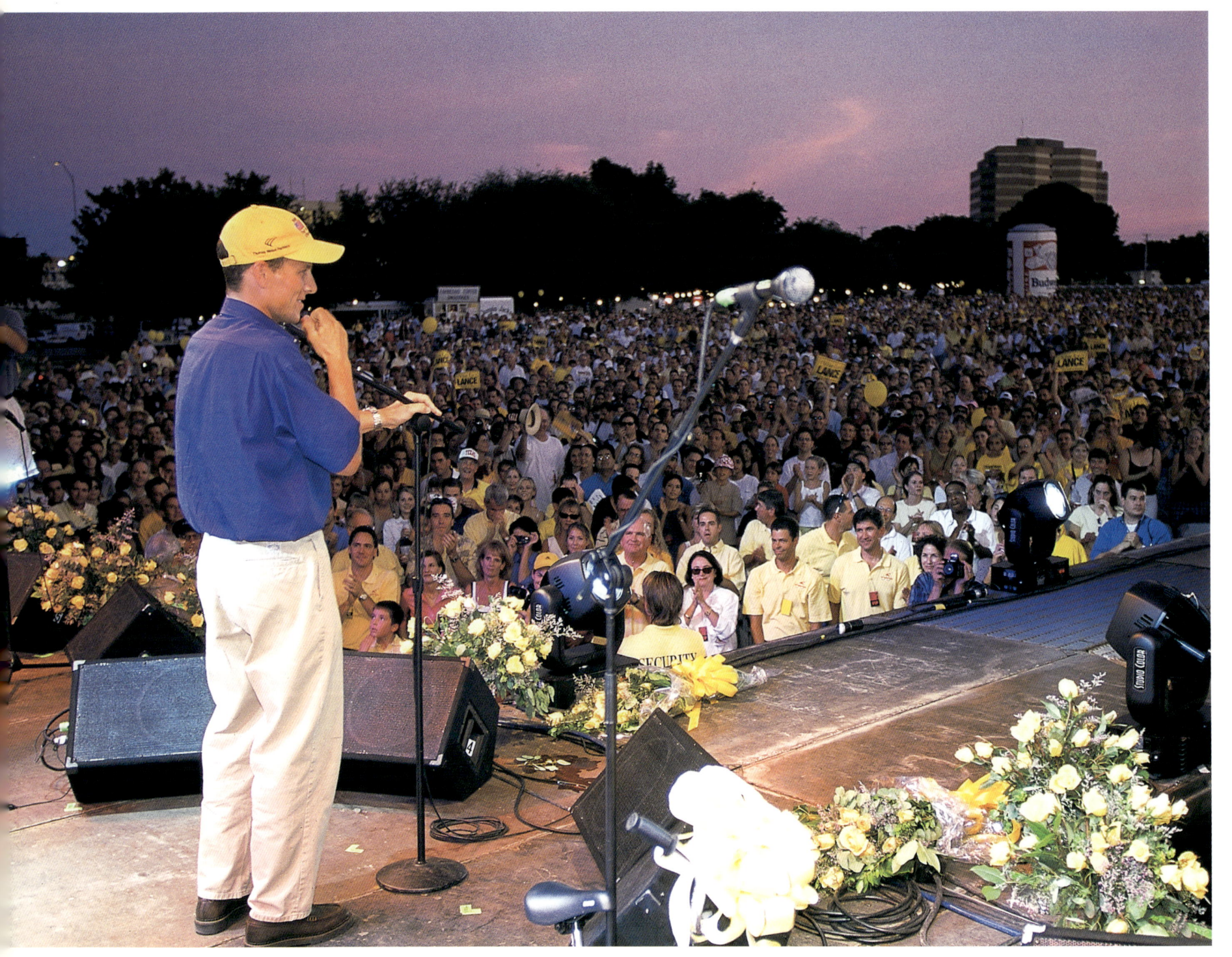

1999: ARMSTRONG HOMECOMING: AUSTIN, TEXAS

A man who battled back from cancer. A man who then won the toughest sports event in the world. Lance Armstrong was welcomed back to Austin by thousands of his fellow citizens in August 1999.

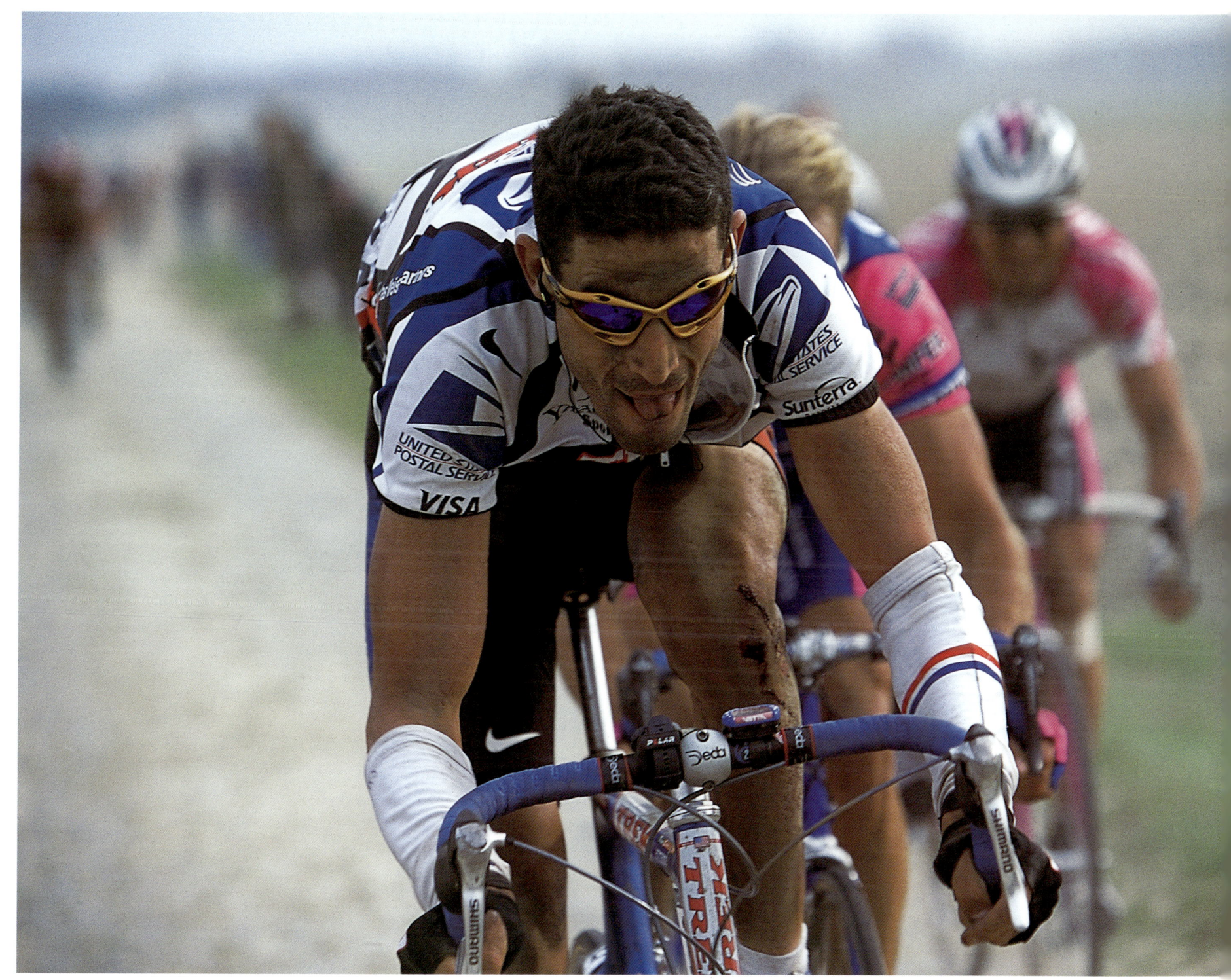

2000: PARIS-ROUBAIX: FRANCE

After finishing fourth at the 1999 Paris-Roubaix, George Hincapie was a pre-race favorite in 2000. He rode to a strong sixth-place, for his seventh consecutive finish in the toughest spring classic.

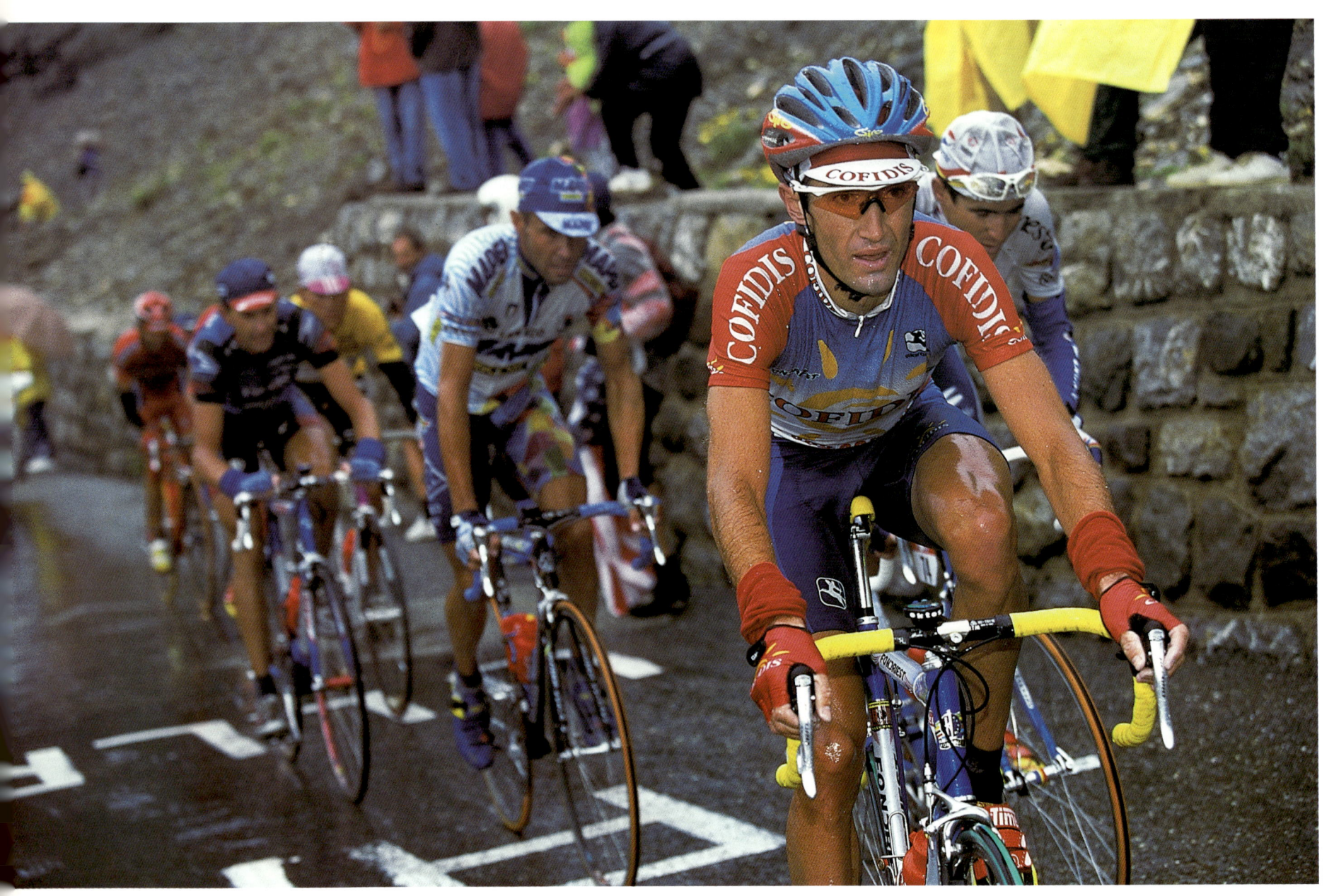

1998: TOUR DE FRANCE: COL DU GALIBIER

Marco Pantani has already disappeared into the mist in search of winning the '98 Tour; race leader Jan Ullrich (in yellow) is struggling on the race's highest climb; so Bobby Julich (in helmet) takes up the chase on the Galibier.

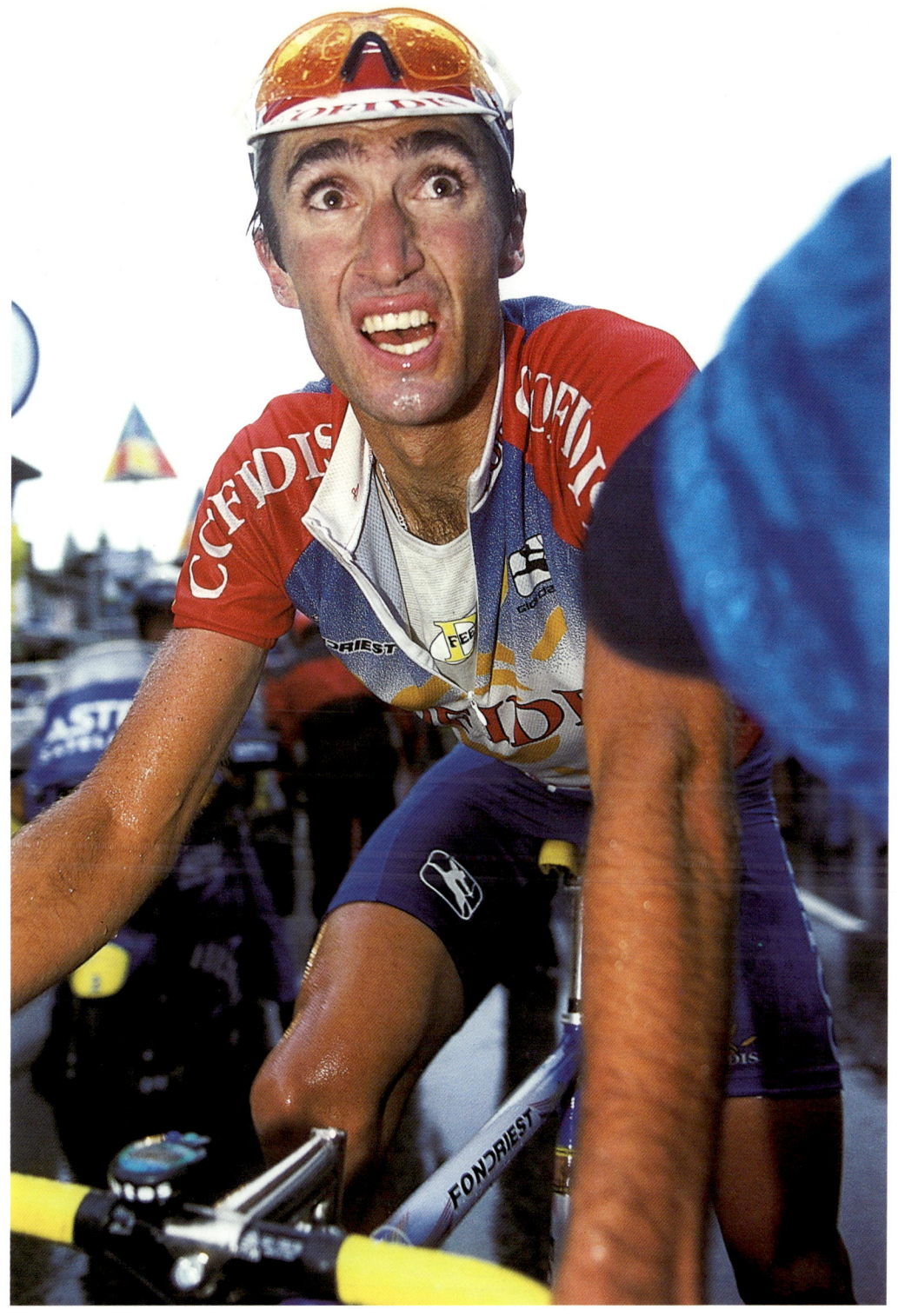

1998: TOUR DE FRANCE: LES DEUX-ALPES

Just over an hour later, on reaching the stage finish at Les Deux-Alpes 5:43 after Pantani (and 3:14 ahead of Ullrich), Julich is exhausted by his chase and astonished by the margin of Pantani's victory.

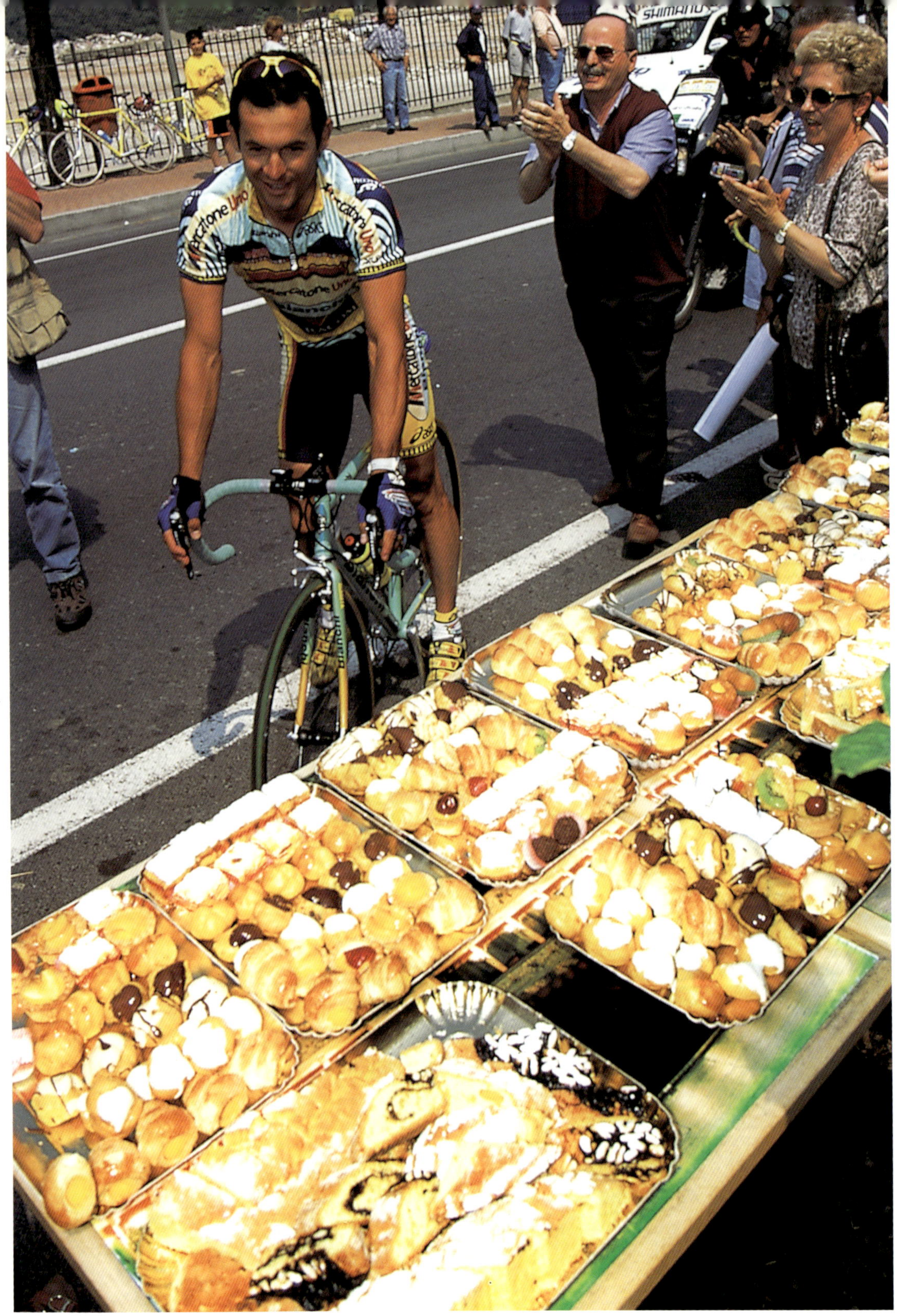

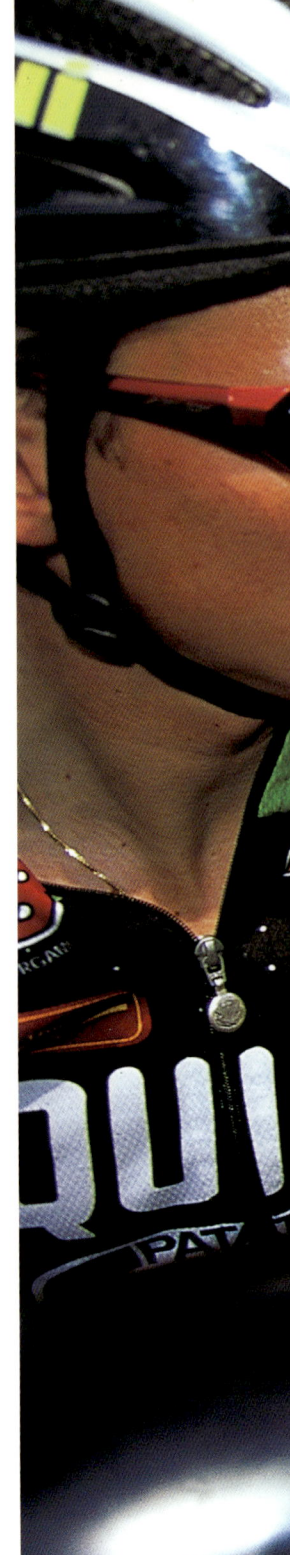

1999: GIRO D'ITALIA: ROMAGNA, ITALY

Mercatone Uno's Fabiano Fontanelli was the first rider of the '99 Giro peloton to spot a roadside display of delicious pastries on stage 12 between Cesanatico and Sassuolo....

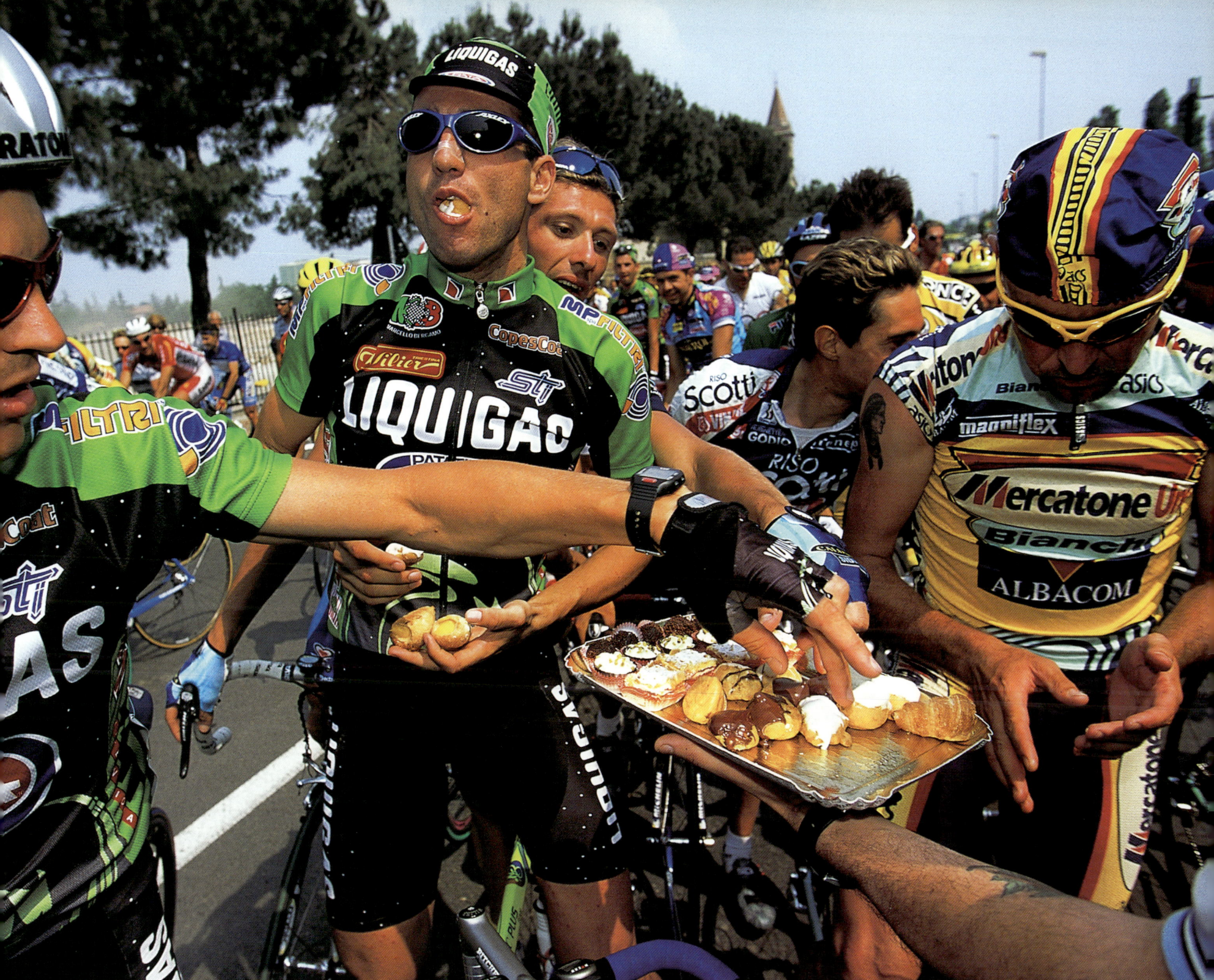

1999: GIRO D'ITALIA: ROMAGNA, ITALY

... Soon, most of the riders had joined him at the impromptu feeding station.

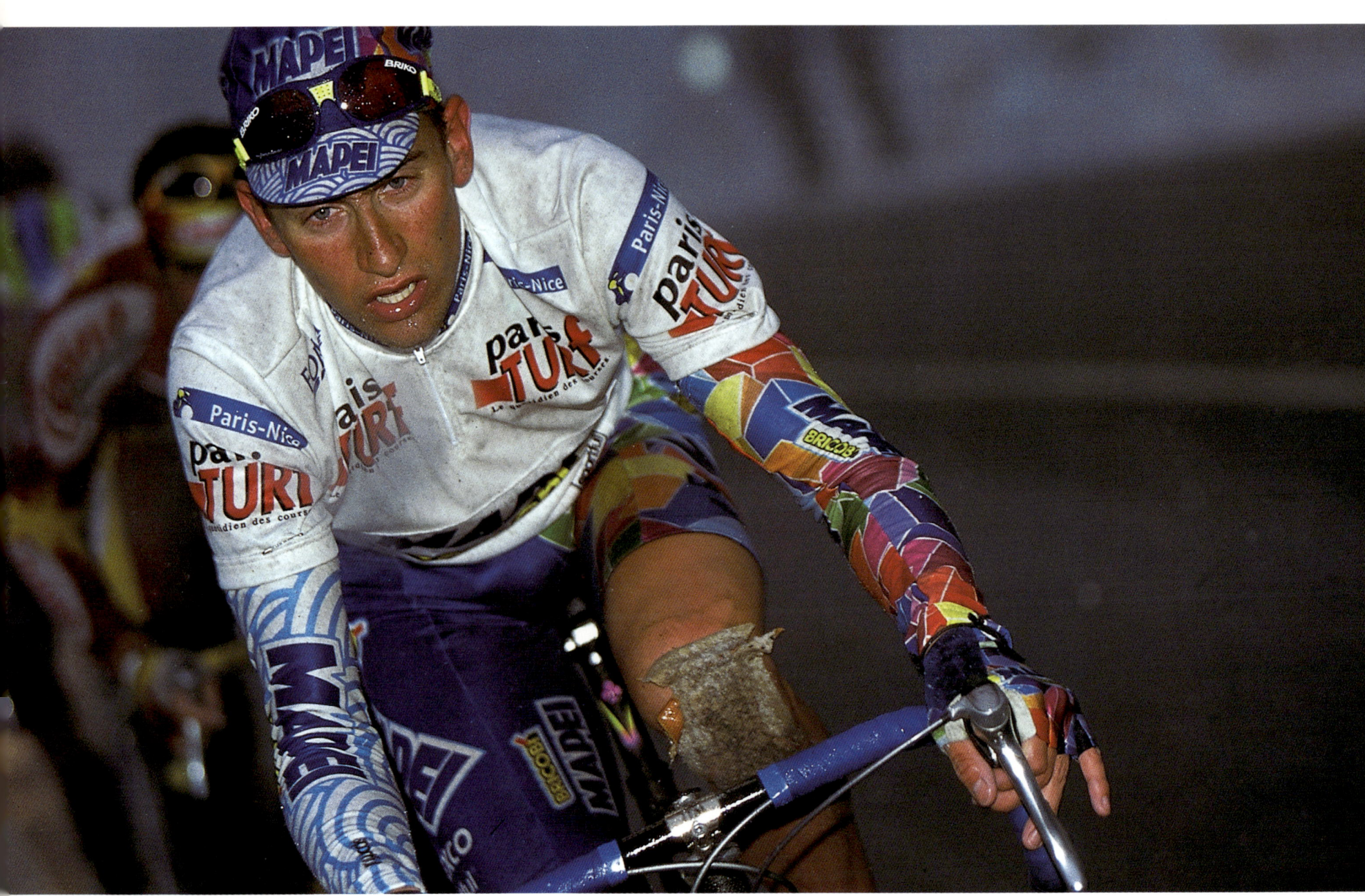

1998: PARIS-NICE: COL DE LA RÉPUBLIQUE

When Frank Vandenbroucke dominated the 1998 Paris-Nice—including his imminent stage win (above) at St. Etienne—the 23-year-old was hailed as Belgium's next contender at the Tour de France. Things have yet to work out....

1999: DAUPHINÉ LIBÉRÉ: MONT VENTOUX

American Jonathan Vaughters exploded onto the world stage when he set a new record of 56:51 for the 21km Mont Ventoux climb in the time-trial stage of the '99 Dauphiné.

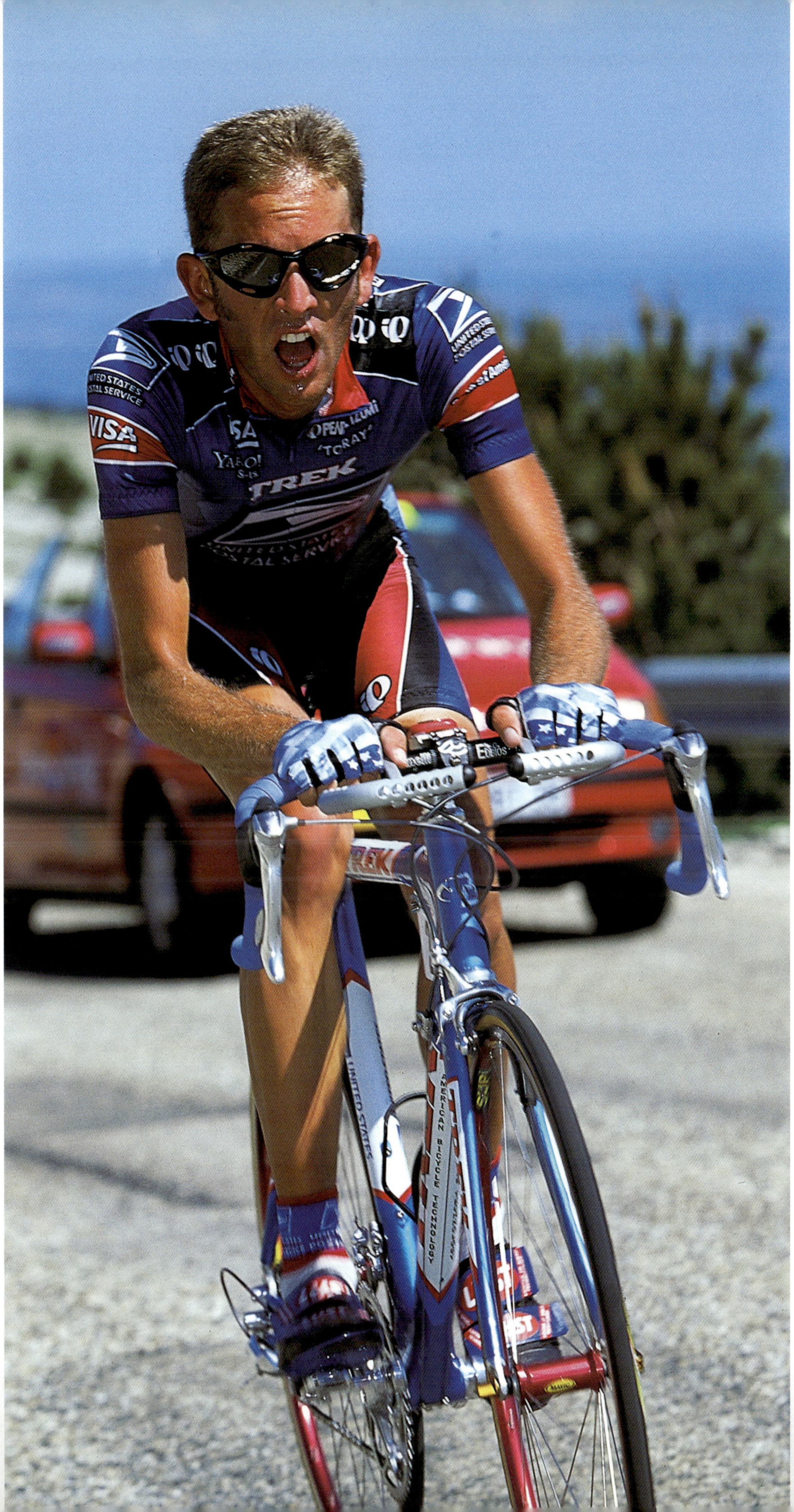

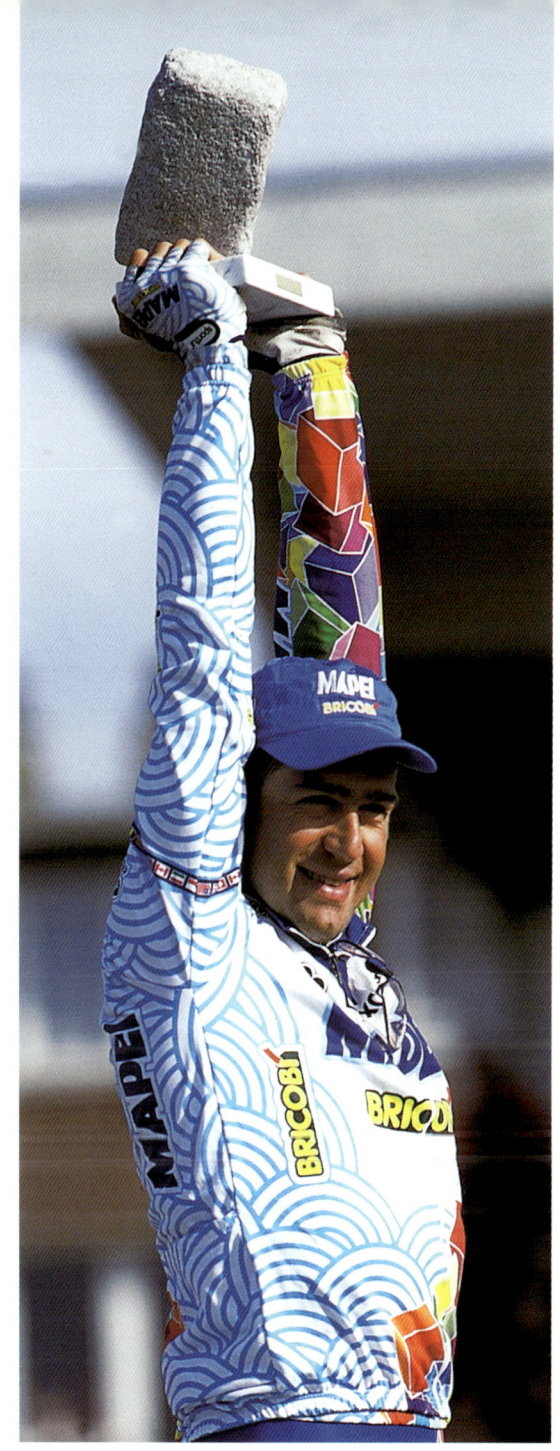

1998: PARIS-ROUBAIX: FRANCE

Every winner of Paris-Roubaix is awarded a cobblestone trophy. In 1998, Italian Franco Ballerini received his second award in four years.

1998 TO 2000

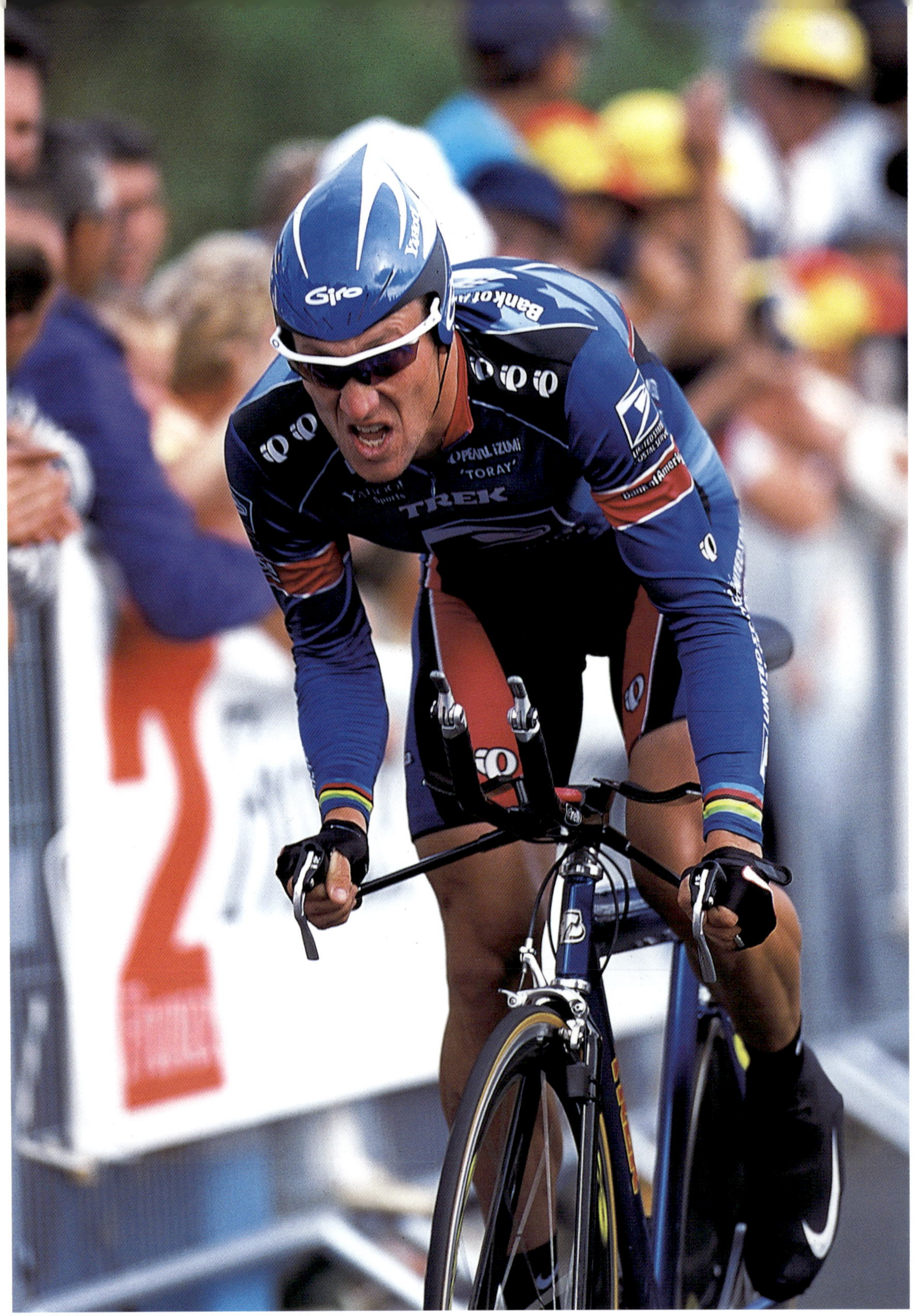

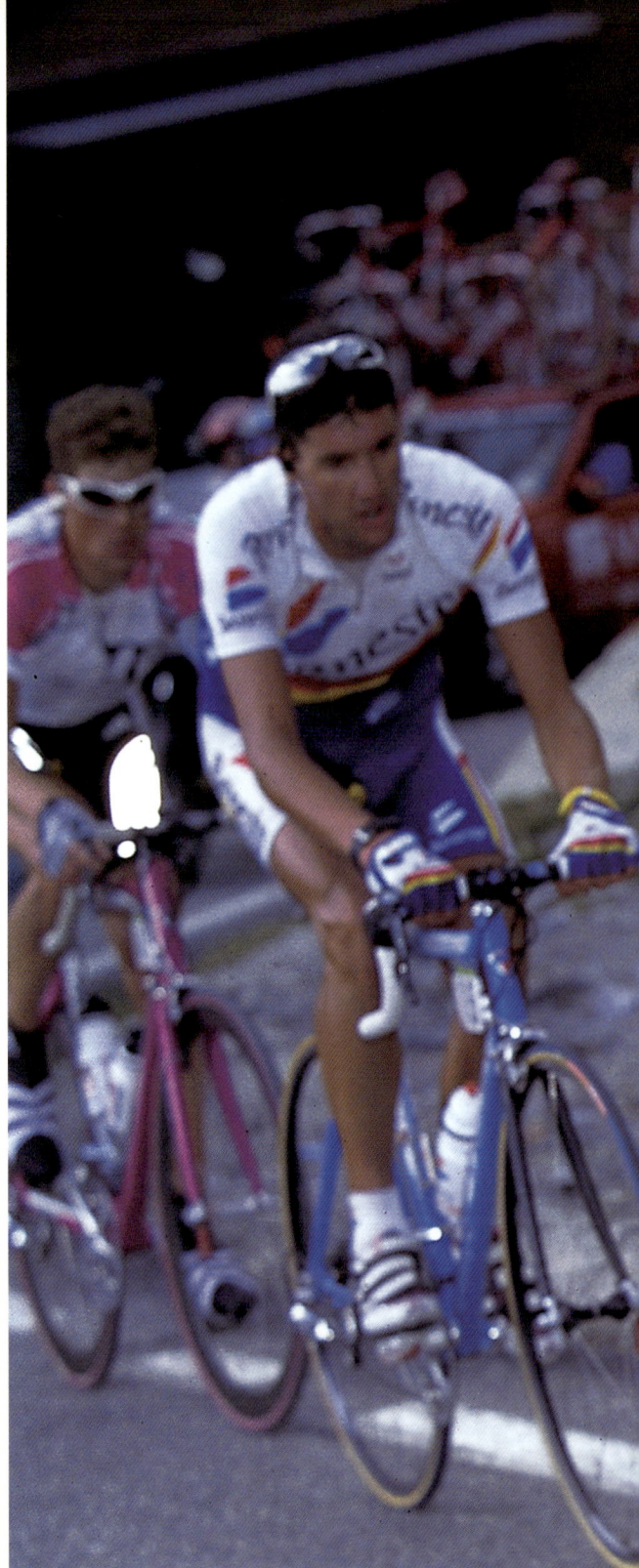

1999: TOUR DE FRANCE: PUY-DU-FOU

After all the build-up to the 1999 Tour and the high expectations in Lance Armstrong, the Texan came through in the 6.8km prologue time trial with a resounding victory. Armstrong thus became the first American since Greg LeMond in 1991 to wear the yellow jersey.

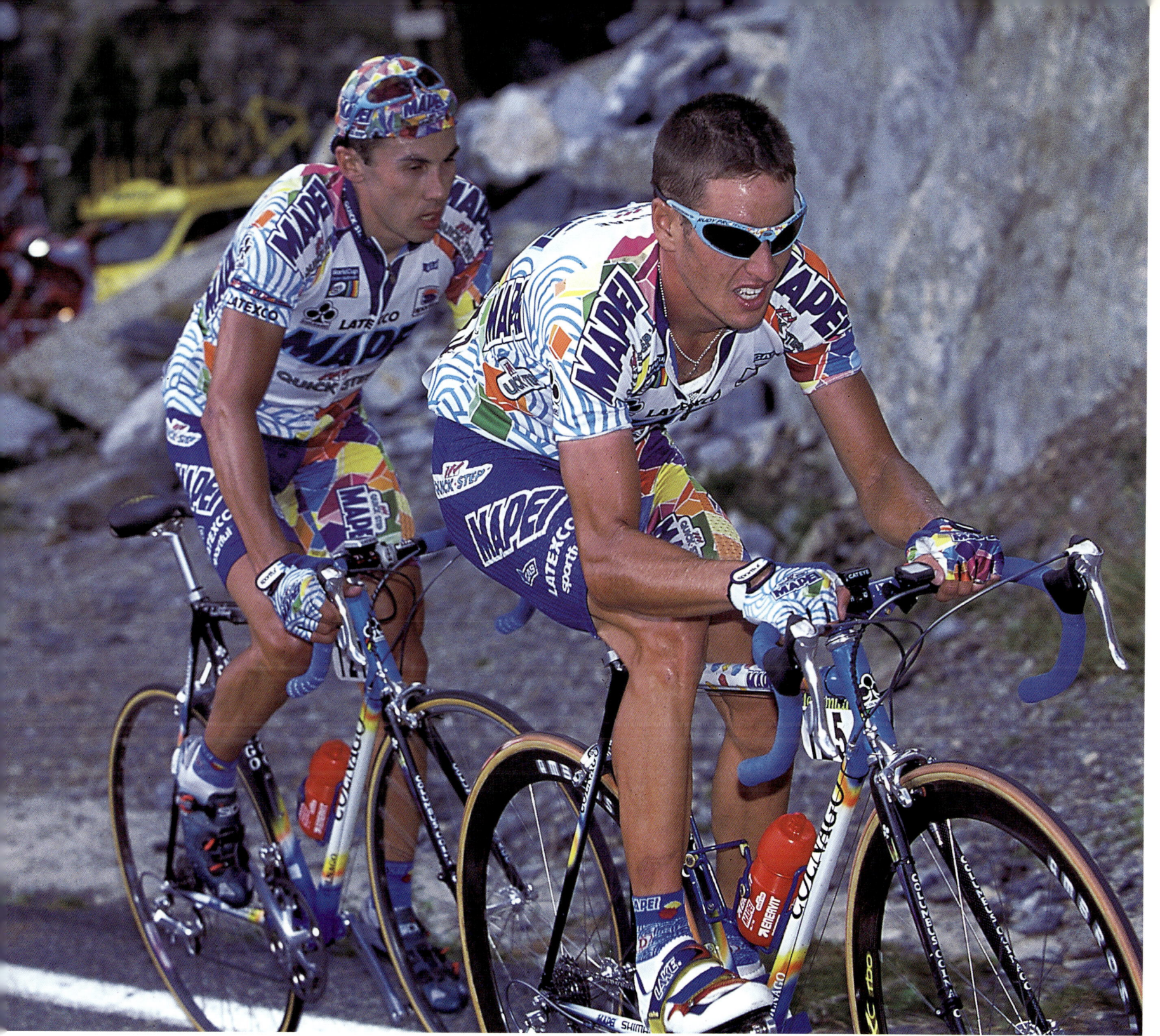

1999: VUELTA A ESPAÑA: ANDORRA

Riding in service of Pavel Tonkov, his Mapei team leader, American Chann McRae leads Tonkov, Spanish climber José Maria Jiménez and soon-to-be race leader Jan Ullrich on the Collet de Montaup climb, prior to the mountaintop stage 12 finish at Arcalis.

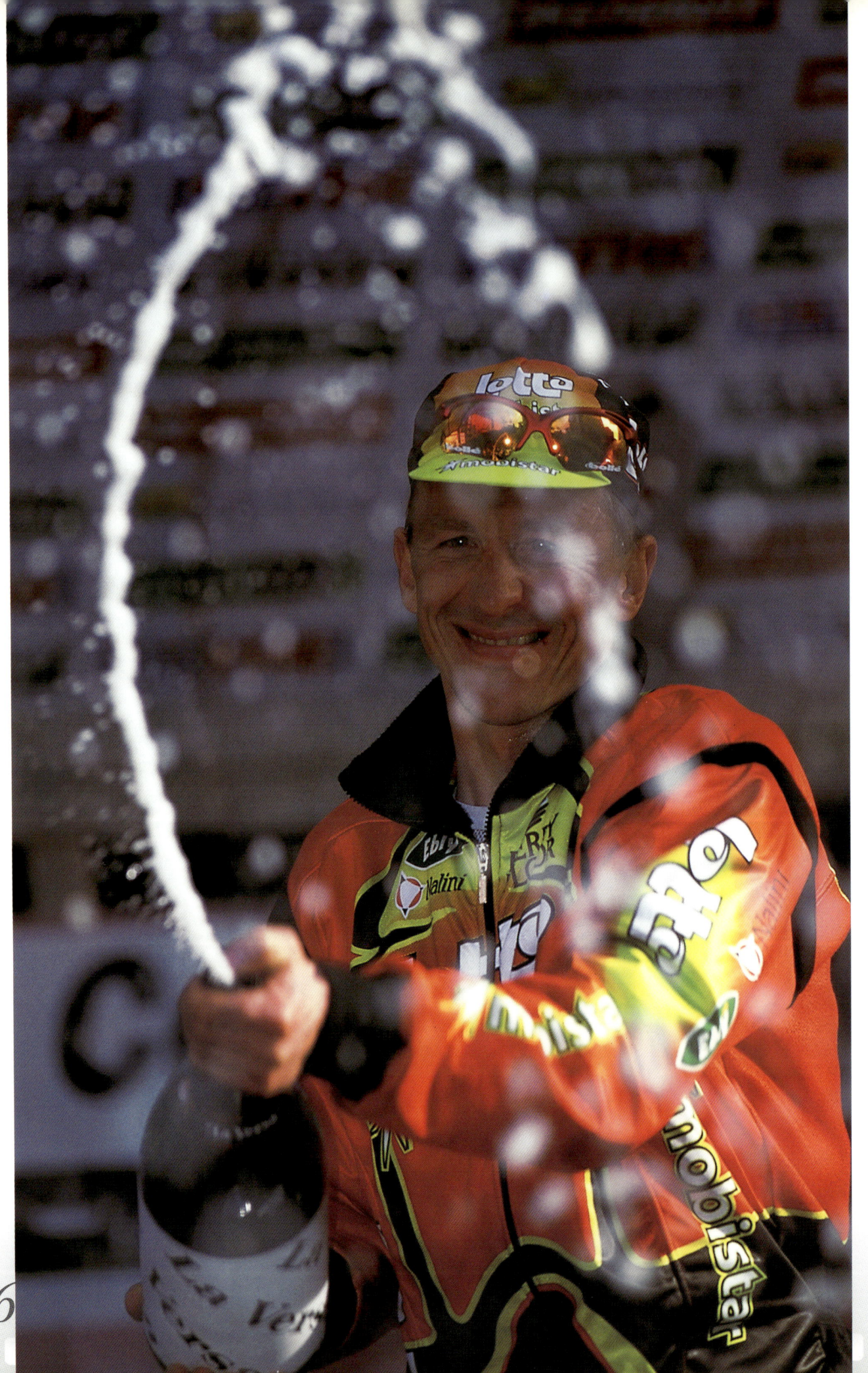

1999: MILAN–SAN REMO: ITALY

Andreï Tchmil celebrates after a dramatic, last-minute victory at Milan–San Remo—a win that set him on the road to winning the 1999 season's 10-race World Cup.

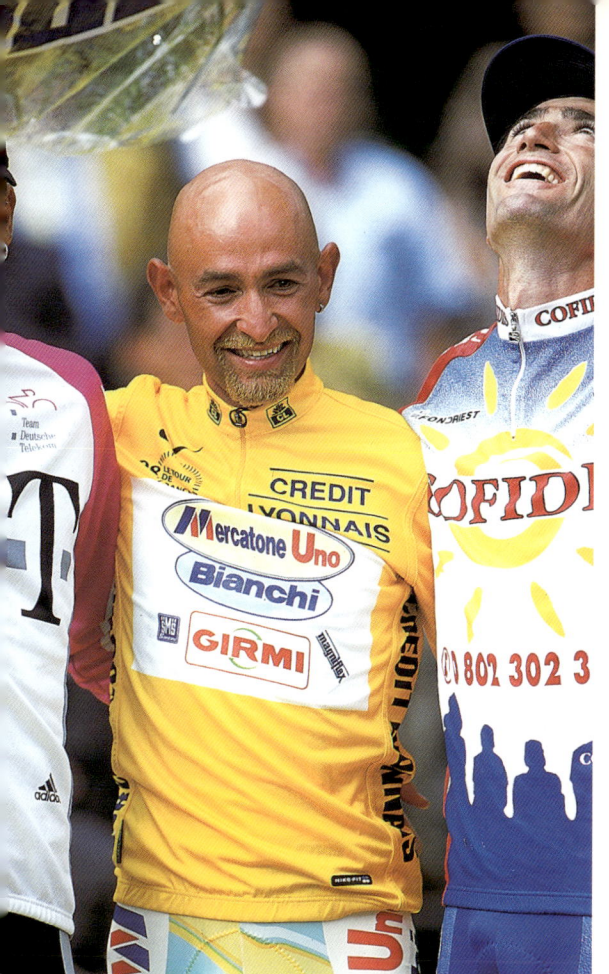
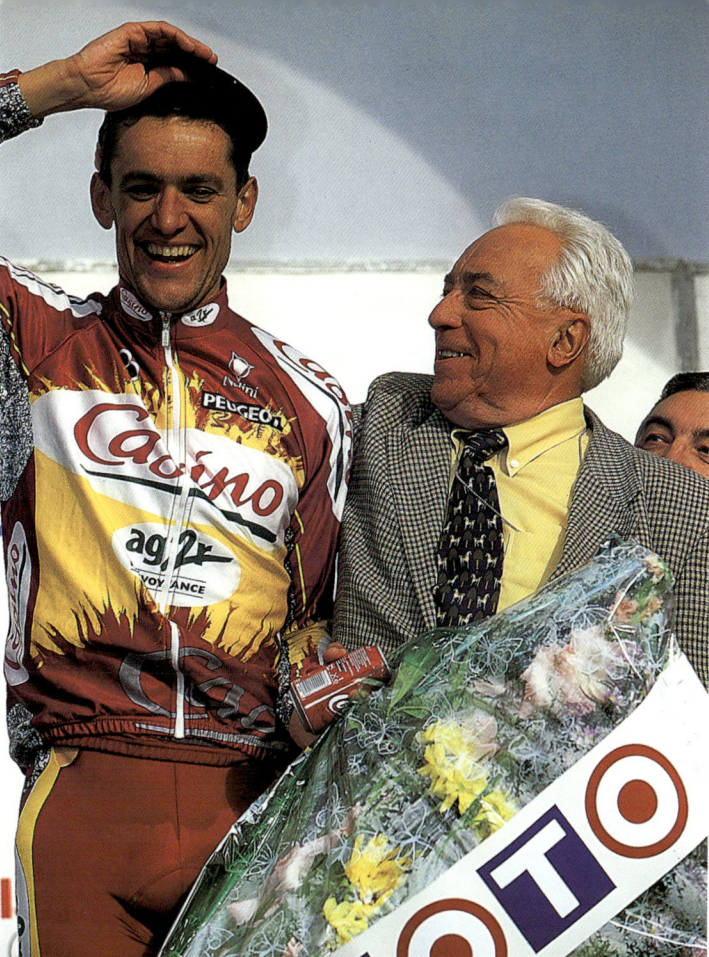
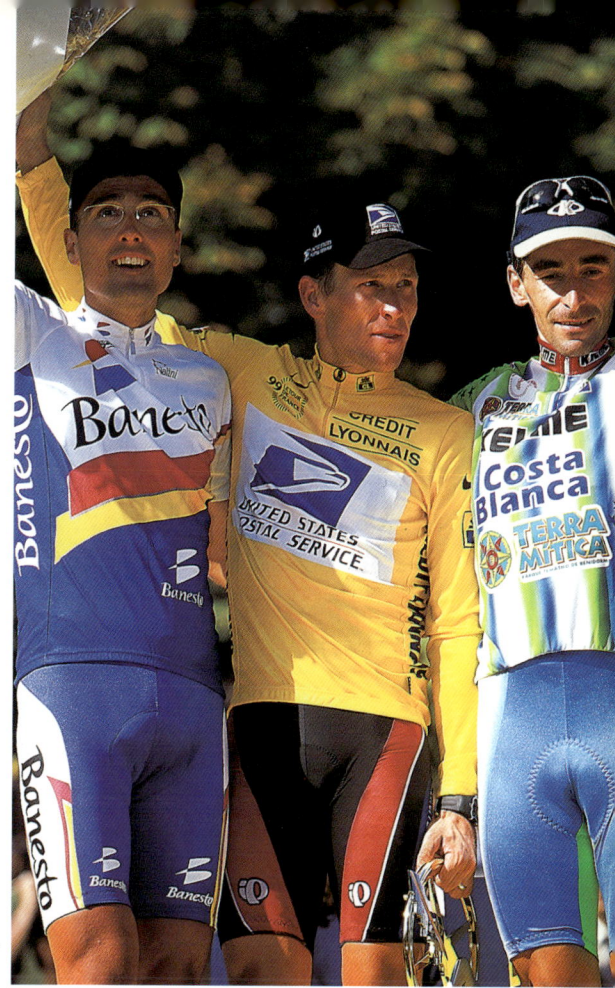

1998: TOUR DE FRANCE: PARIS

Podium of a troubled Tour: Ullrich, Pantani, Julich.

1998: PARIS-TOURS: FRANCE

History made: Jacky Durand celebrates victory at the Paris-Tours classic, 42 years after the last French winner, Albert Bouvet (right).

1999: TOUR DE FRANCE: PARIS

Podium for a new start: Zülle, Armstrong, Escartin.

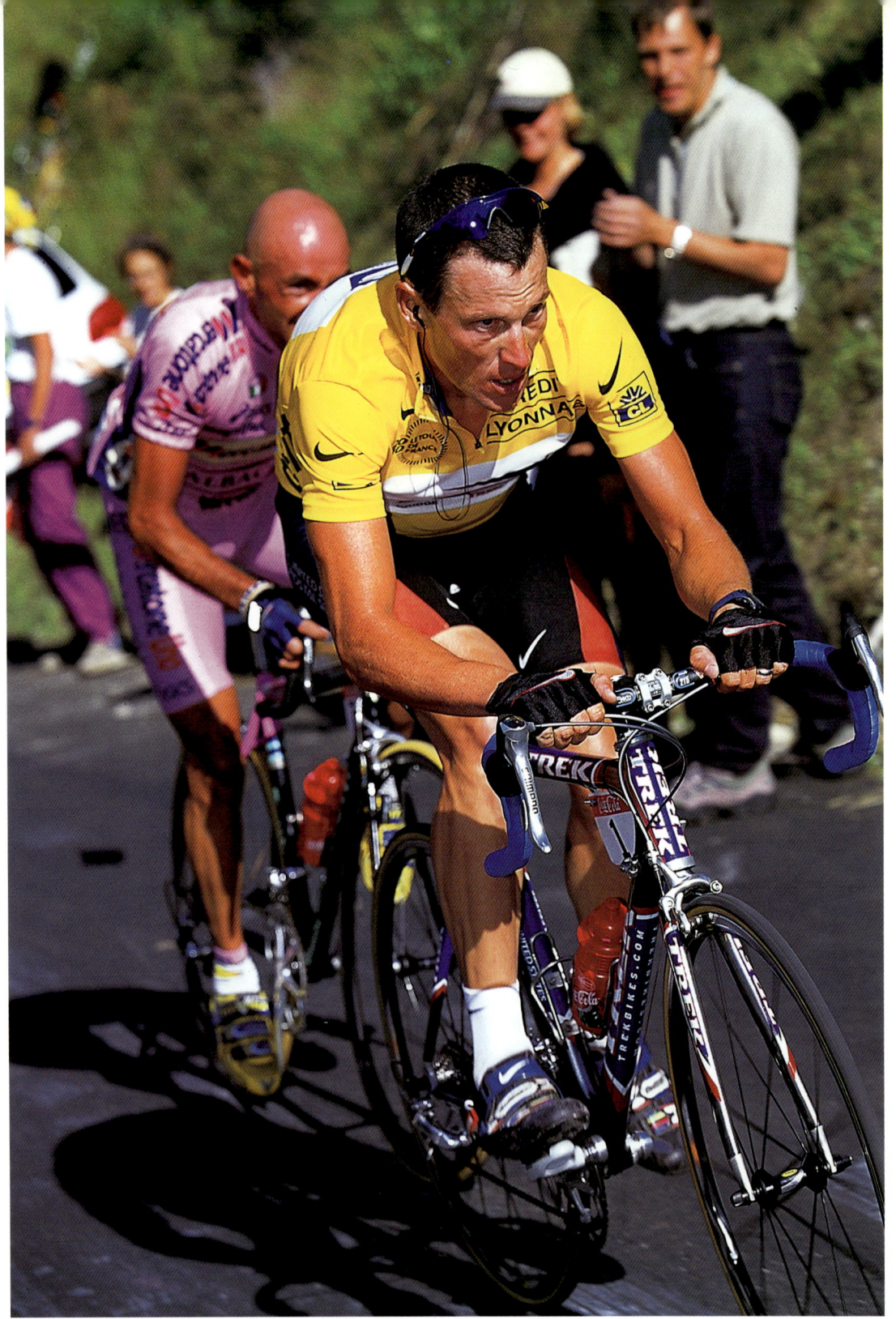

2000: TOUR DE FRANCE: FRENCH ALPS

Lance Armstrong astounded the Europeans—including Marco Pantani (left)—with his climbing strength at the 2000 Tour. Here, the American lead the Italian on the legendary Col d'Izoard.

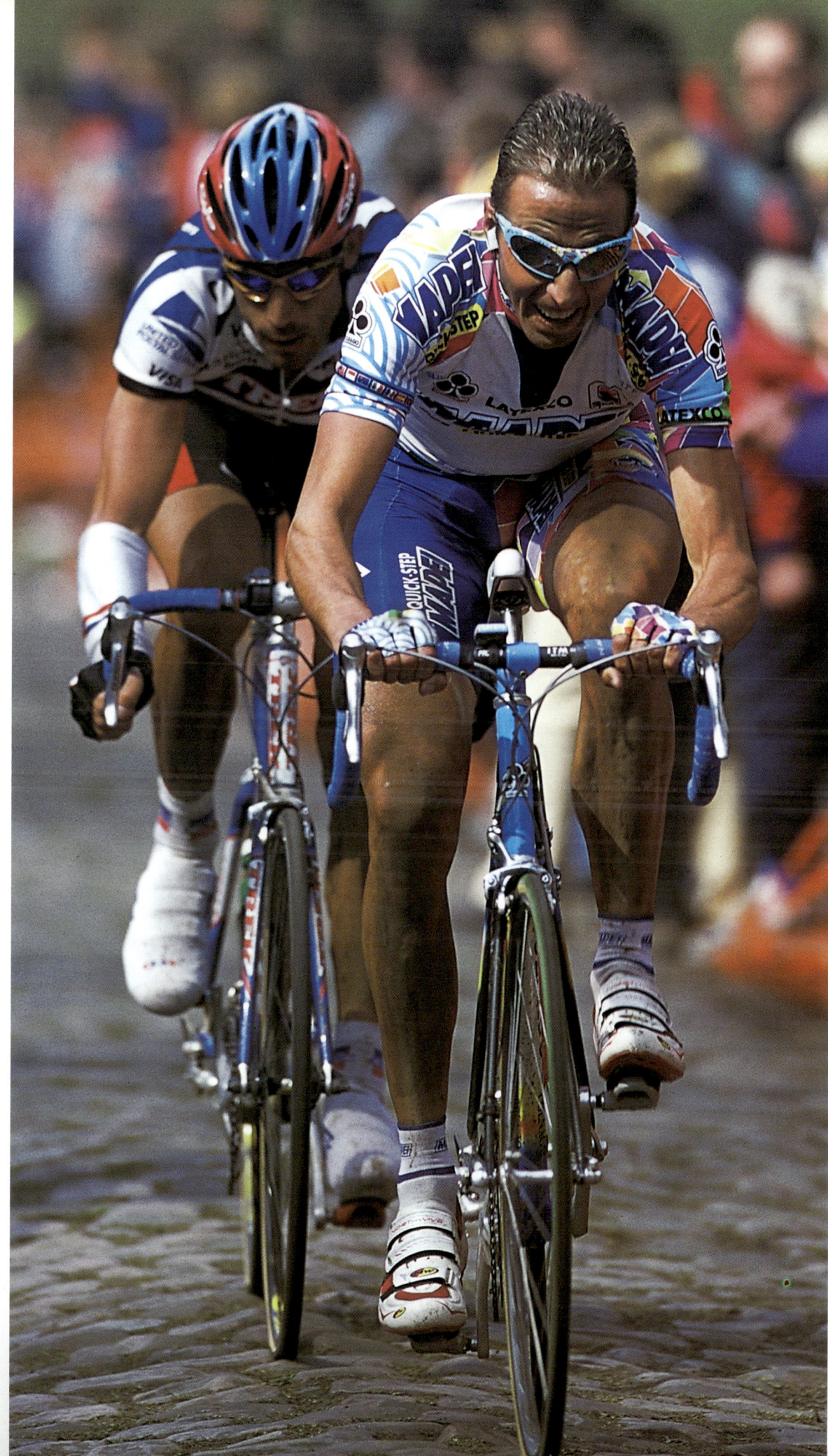

2000: PARIS-ROUBAIX: FRANCE

Two powerful performers in the Hell of the North: Former winner Andrea Tafi (front) and still-knocking-at-the-door George Hincapie show different techniques of tackling the pavé at Paris-Roubaix.

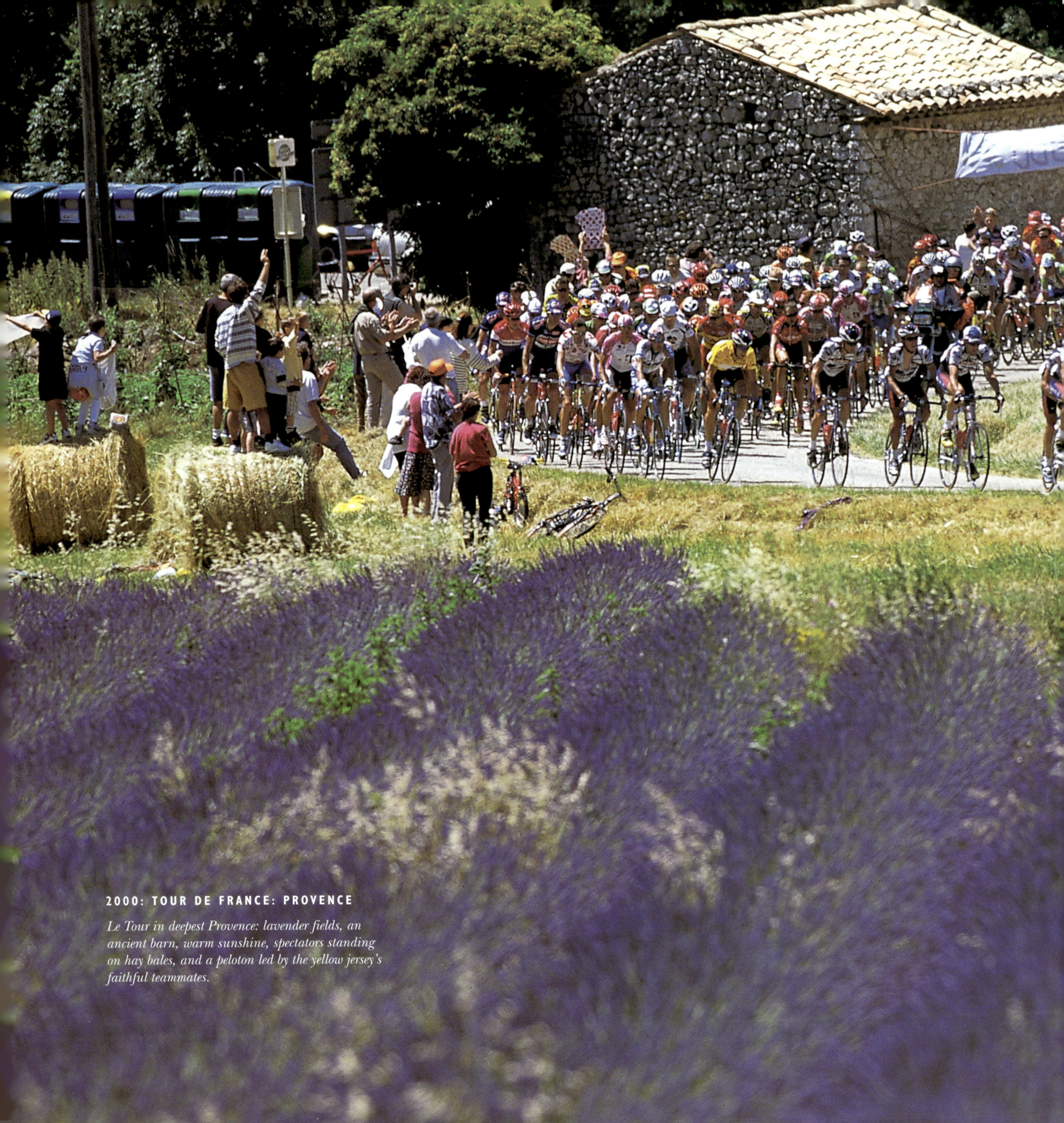

2000: TOUR DE FRANCE: PROVENCE

Le Tour in deepest Provence: lavender fields, an ancient barn, warm sunshine, spectators standing on hay bales, and a peloton led by the yellow jersey's faithful teammates.

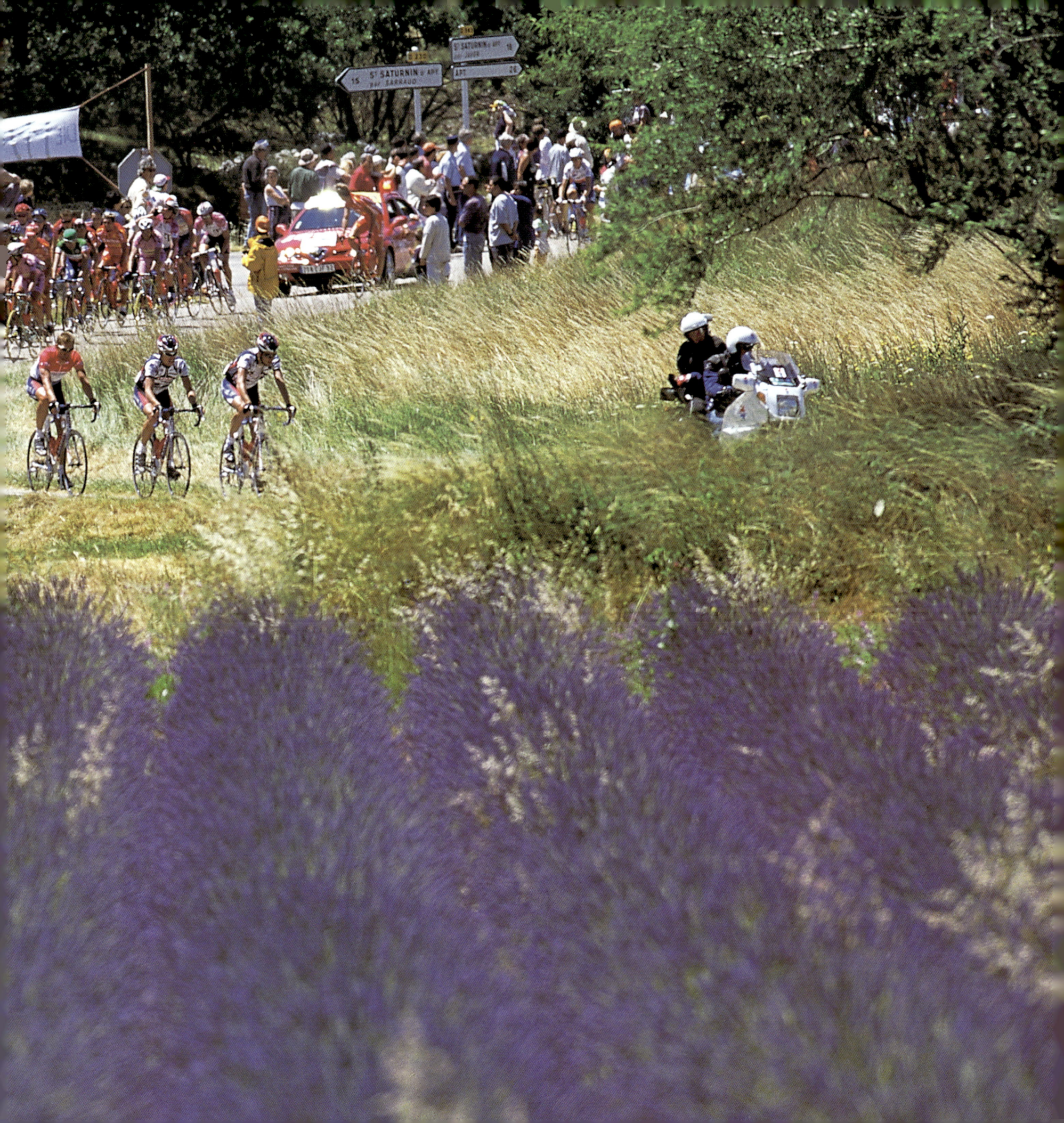

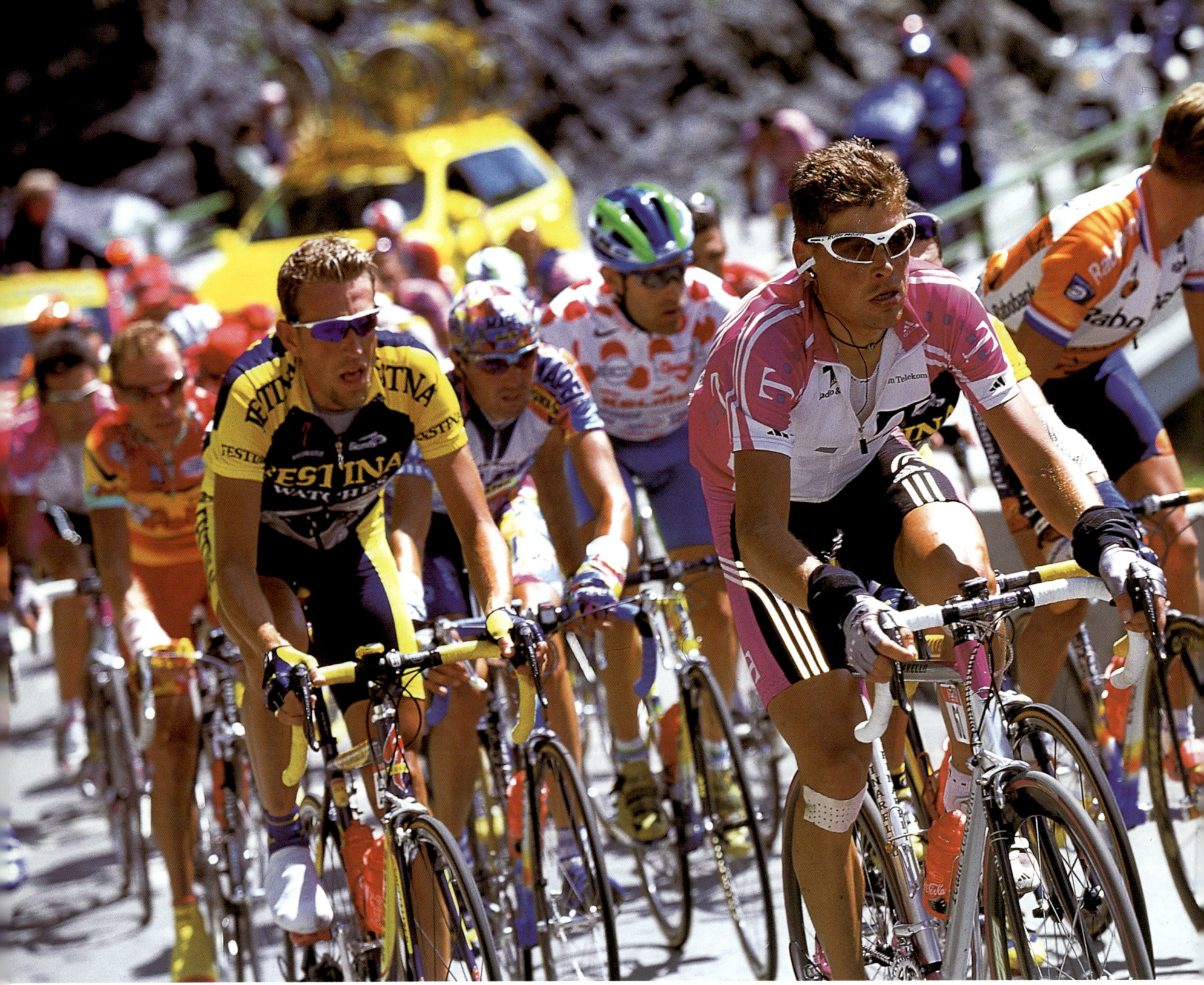

2000: TOUR DE FRANCE: FRENCH ALPS

Rabobank's Marc Wauters (right) turns to see who is the latest rider to be jettisoned by the tempo set by Lance Armstrong's Postal team on the Col de la Madeleine, while a grim-faced Jan Ullrich (center) follows the pace ahead of (right to left), Santiago Botero, Manuel Beltran, Christophe Moreau and Pascal Hervé.

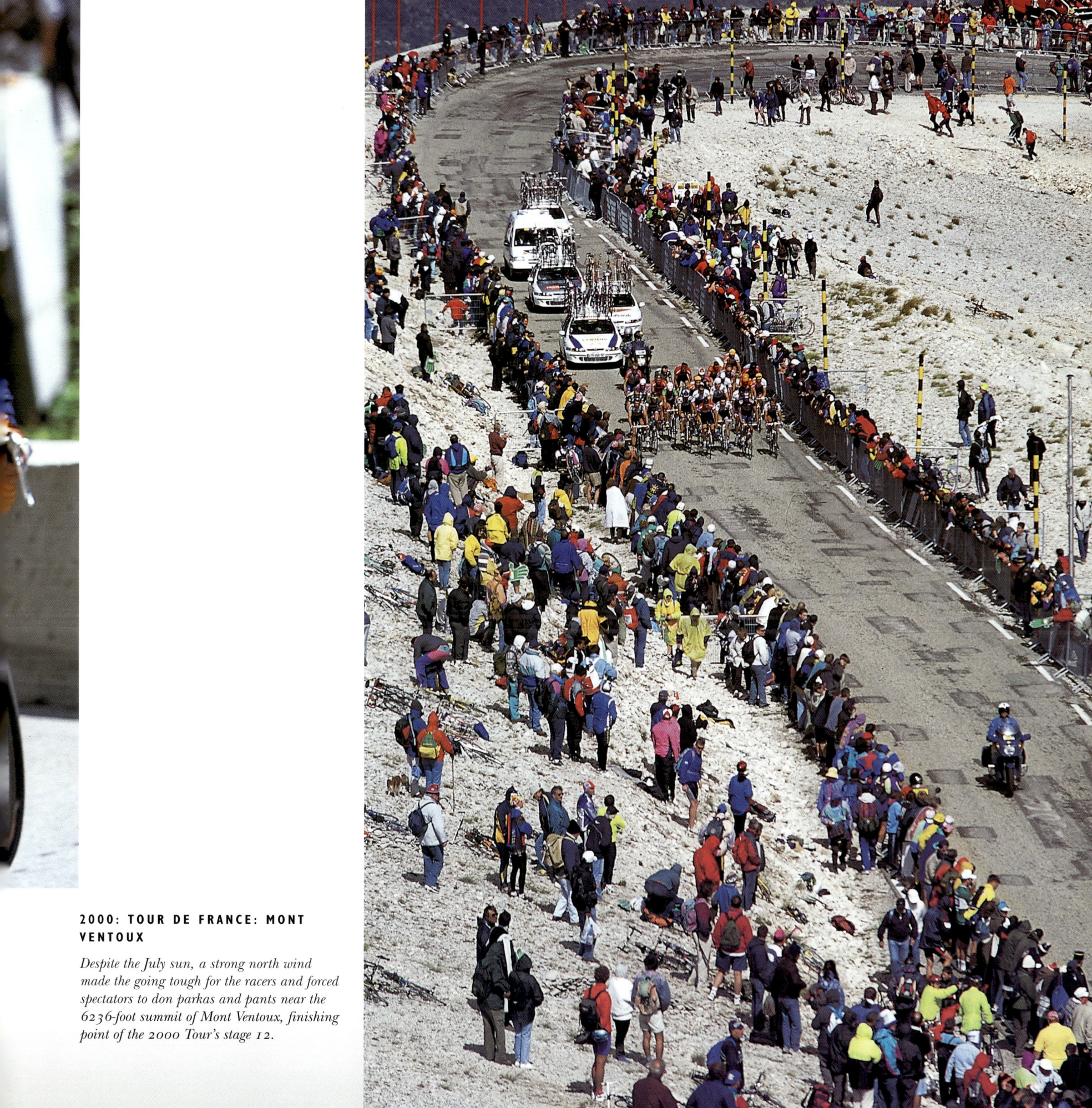

2000: TOUR DE FRANCE: MONT VENTOUX

Despite the July sun, a strong north wind made the going tough for the racers and forced spectators to don parkas and pants near the 6236-foot summit of Mont Ventoux, finishing point of the 2000 Tour's stage 12.

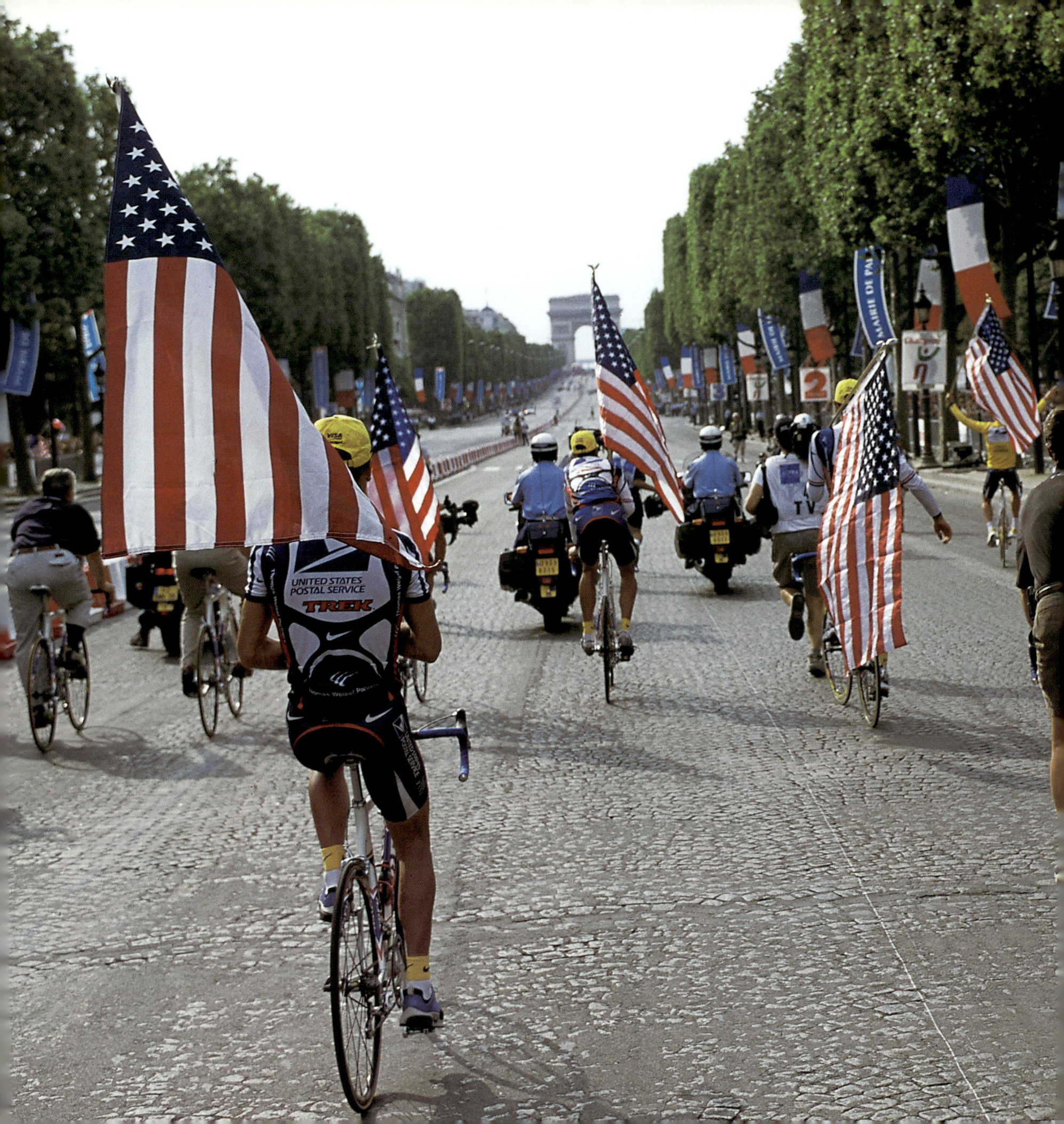

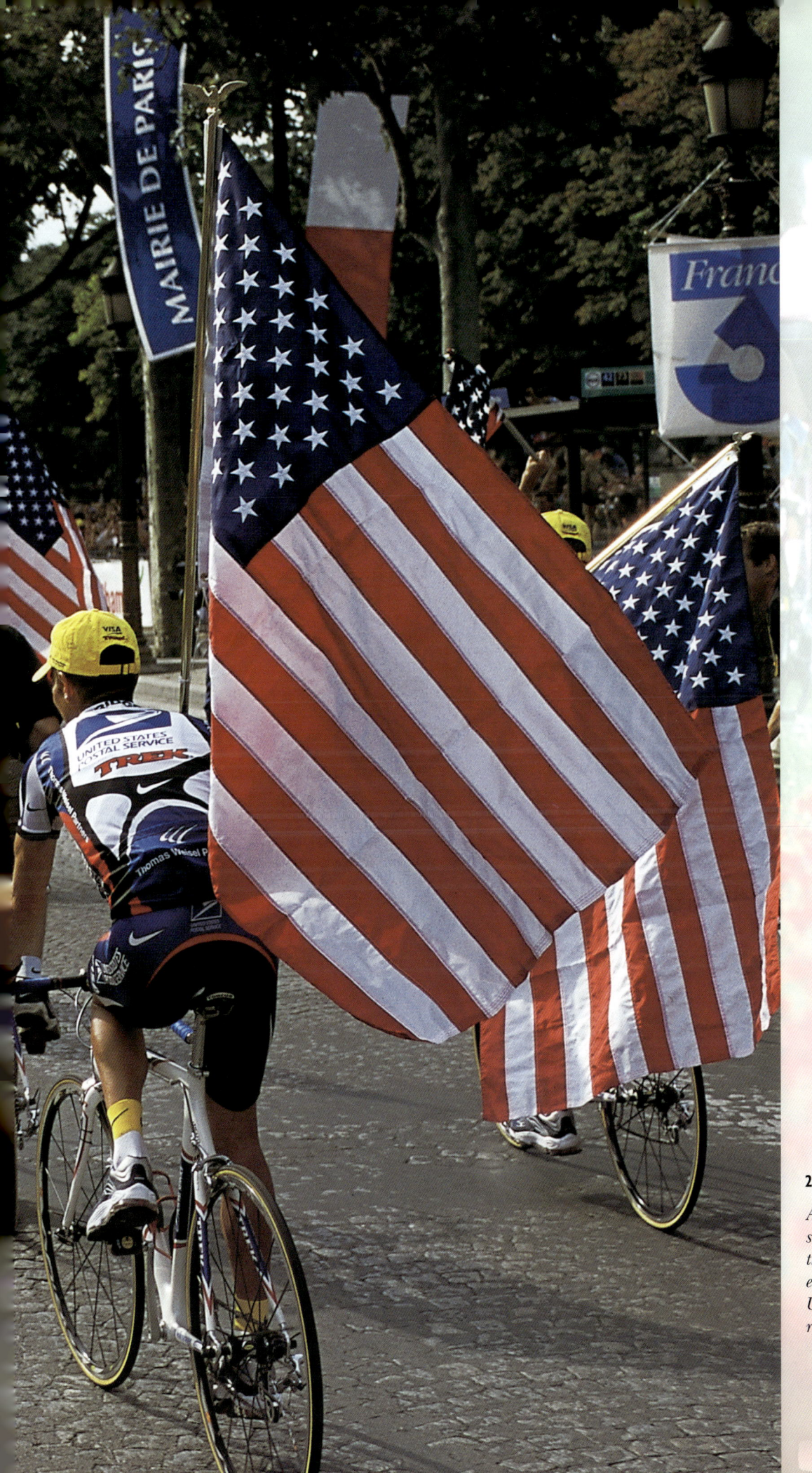

2000: TOUR DE FRANCE: PARIS

Avenue des Champs-Elysées, Paris, 6:25 p.m., July 23. The final stage of the 2000 Tour finished more than an hour ago, now it's the turn of the race winner's team to take its lap of honor in the evening sunlight. Headed by the man in yellow, Lance Armstrong, U.S. Postal Service is the only team that still has all nine of its riders (count the flags!) that started the Tour three weeks ago.

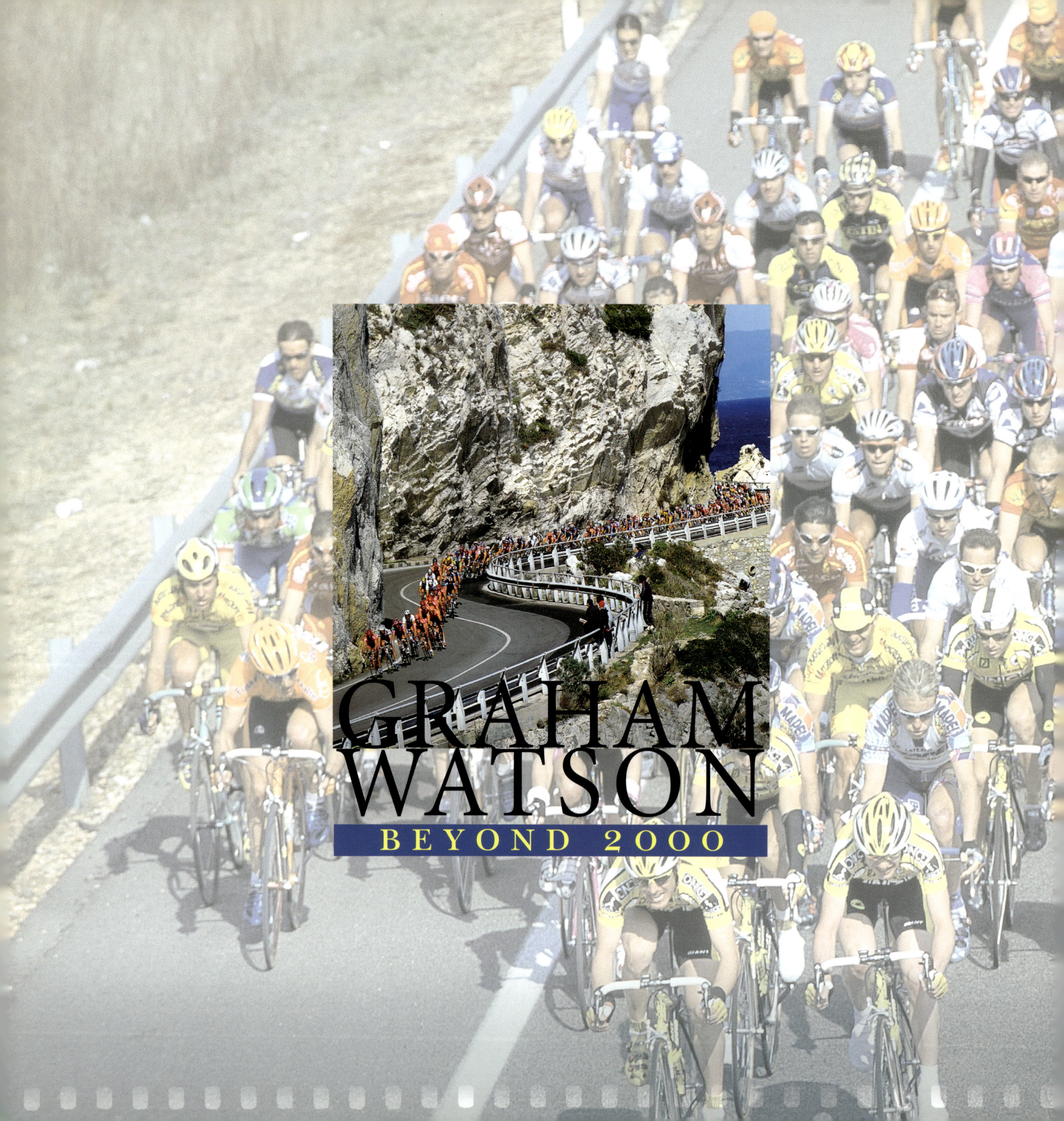

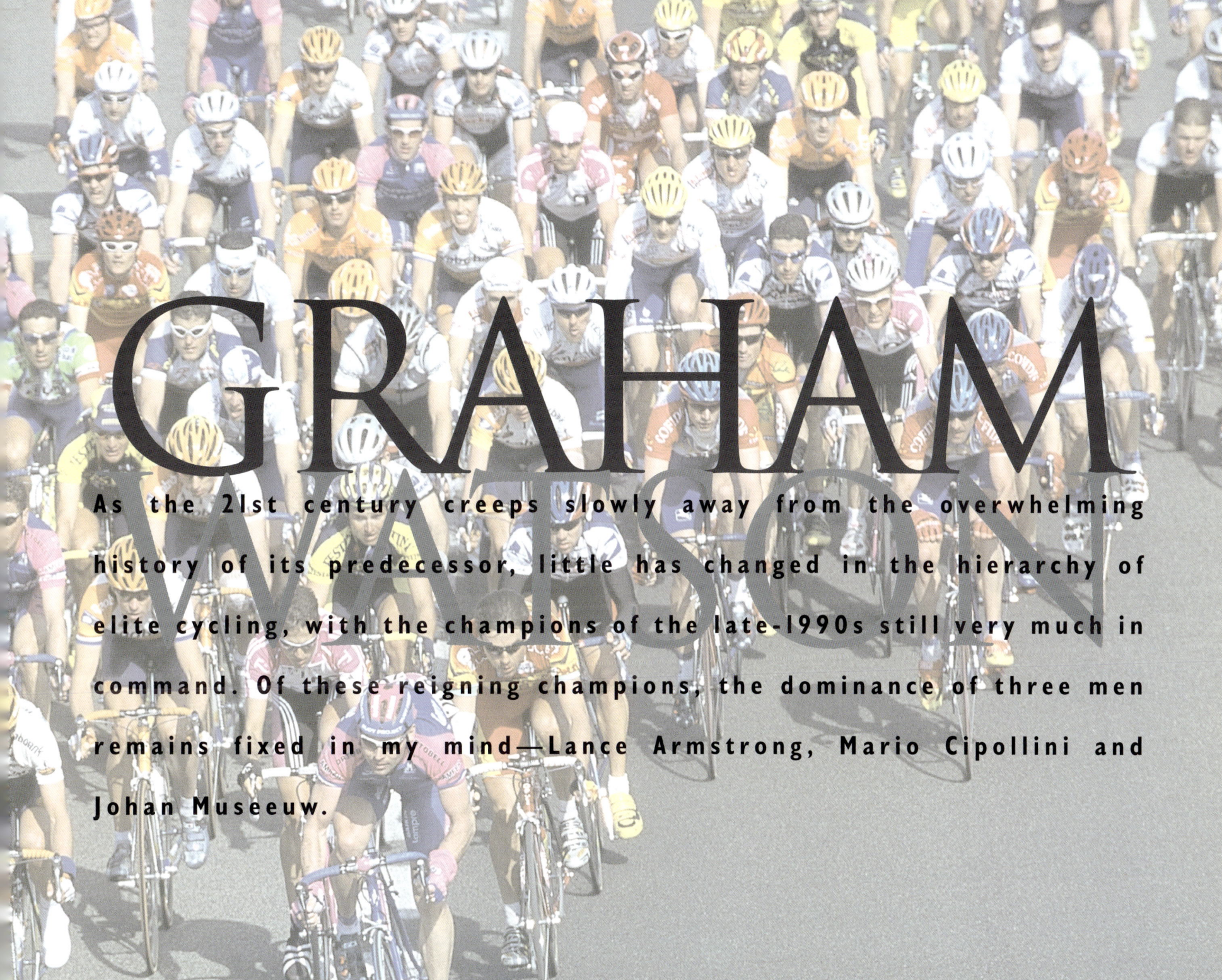

GRAHAM WATSON

As the 21st century creeps slowly away from the overwhelming history of its predecessor, little has changed in the hierarchy of elite cycling, with the champions of the late-1990s still very much in command. Of these reigning champions, the dominance of three men remains fixed in my mind—Lance Armstrong, Mario Cipollini and Johan Museeuw.

Armstrong, the youngest of the dominators, is heading for the history books as the first-ever American to win four Tours de France—and he may just go on to become the first-ever cyclist to win a sixth Tour, so potent is his cocktail of physical well-being, single-mindedness and obsessive approach to training. His only hindrance to ultimate greatness may lie in the fact that there seems to be no one strong enough to offer him his vitally needed competition. In dispensing with what could prove to be Jan Ullrich's final assault in 2001, Armstrong may actually have killed off the very trace of competition that fuels his hunger to win.

Mario Cipollini has started the new century as if it were the beginning of the 1990s, with legs, mind and body as good as when he first started winning professional races at age 22. In finally winning Milan-San Remo in 2002, Cipollini could have easily retired on the via Roma podium, yet this Italian's longevity shows no sign of failing him, and a new team seems set to have bolstered his hunger for at least another two years—when he will surely be looking retirement in the face. For now though, Cipollini is still indisputedly the fastest road sprinter in the world, ahead of his younger rivals like Erik Zabel, Tom Steels, Oscar Freire and Robbie McEwen.

Another of cycling's truly great characters is Johan Museeuw who, like Cipollini, has found life is even better post-35 years of age. Yet, in contrast to Cipollini's flourishing brand of showmanship, Museeuw's legend is carved out of a reclusive man's determination to overcome all odds. In recovering from an apparently life-threatening leg injury in 1998, Museeuw won a second Paris-Roubaix in 2000—then astounded the world (but not himself) by marching away to an incredible

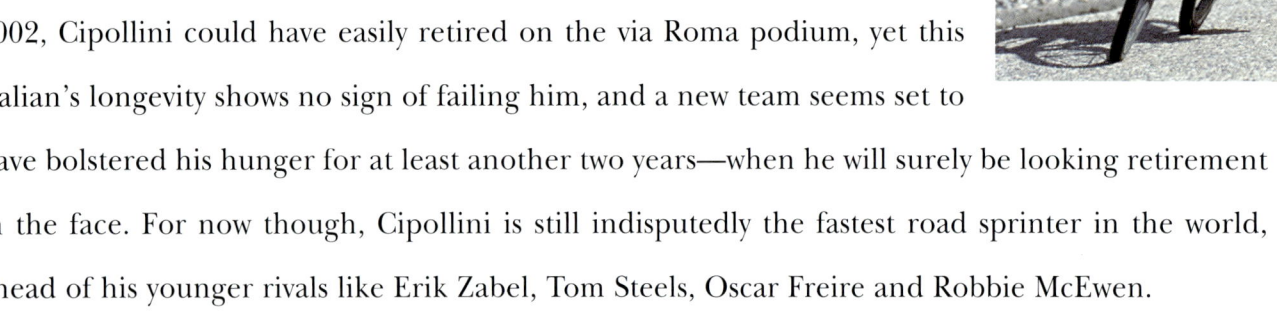

2001: AMSTEL GOLD RACE: THE NETHERLANDS
Lance Armstrong leads Erik Dekker in their two-man escape, with the Dutchman taking the win.

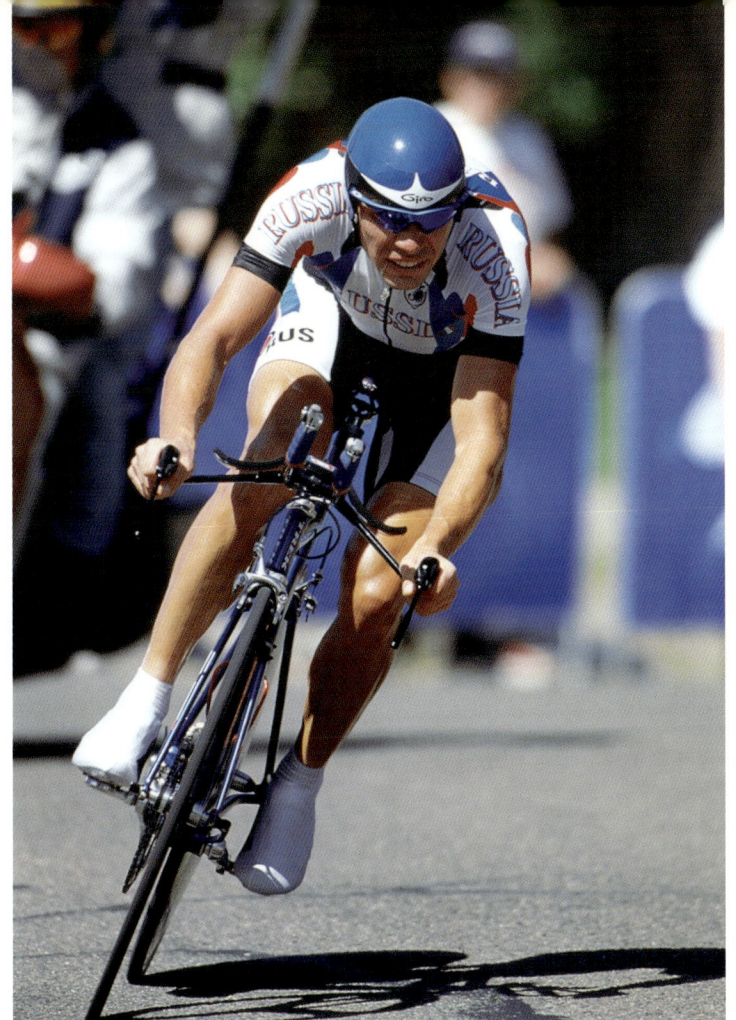
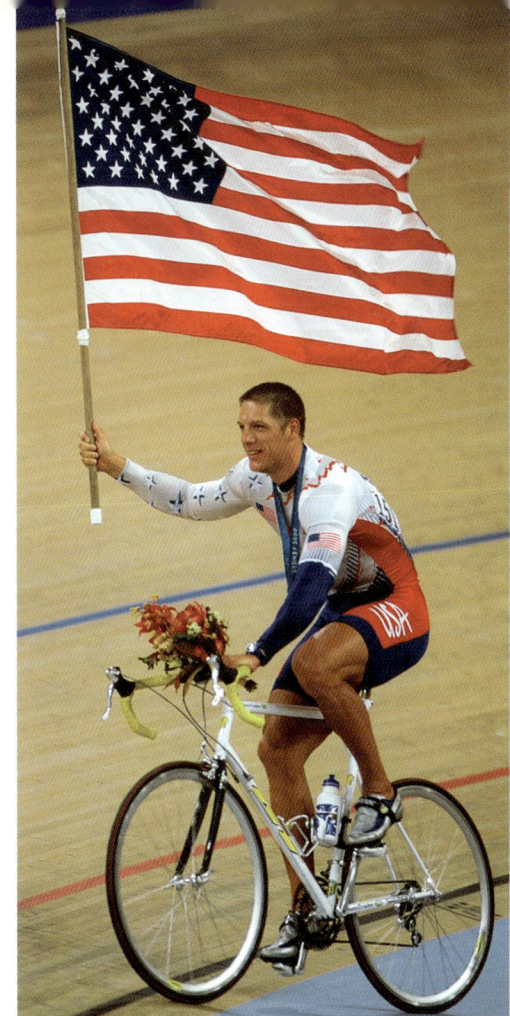

third victory in 2002 . . . a full three minutes clear of his nearest challenger. Perhaps revoking a promise to retire at the end of 2002, Museeuw may be tempted to go for a fourth "Hell of The North" in 2003.

If these three men solidify the fans' hopes that cycling has truly begun to resurrect its image after the woes of the drug-damaged Festina-Pantani years, the new century has dispensed lesser fortunes for men like Jan Ullrich and Marco Pantani—the respective winners of the 1997 and 1998 Tours de France. Being pitched together, ironically, against a reborn Armstrong has corralled both men into a somewhat sympathetic arena as worthy, but incapable, of much greater things. Pantani, still in the shadow of his Giro disgrace of 1999, has fallen deeper and deeper into a tide of anti-drug culture. Ullrich, utterly free of such accusations, has instead succumbed to the reality that he will never again regain the formidable strength that led him to win the 1997 Tour, the 1999 Vuelta a España, two world time trial championships and (perhaps the one-day highlight of his storied career) the 2000 Olympics road race.

2000: OLYMPIC GAMES: SYDNEY

Viatcheslv Ekimov heads for a gold medal in the individual time trial (left). Sprinter Marty Nothstein becomes the first American cyclist to win a gold medal since 1984 (right).

BEYOND 2000

The autumn of 2000 saw me puzzled by a mass-sprint finish of the world road championships in Plouay, France, where Latvia's Roman Vainsteins was the ultimate beneficiary of a somewhat easy circuit that failed to pitch an escape group into the final reckoning. The massive crowds at this popular circuit deserved more than this, I thought, but I was forced to appreciate how much the Olympic games—and the travel to Sydney and back—had decimated the true competitiveness of this world's, with absentees across the spectrum of world cycling.

That same autumn, in the north of England, Chris Boardman bid au revoir to a wonderful cycling career by establishing a "new" world hour record at Manchester's velodrome—to the hysterical applause of thousands of his loyal fans. Coming as it did during the world track championships, Boardman's feat was still the highlight of the week, hardly diluted by the Olympics. I felt more than a tinge of emotion witnessing this sincere gentleman's closing performance—his contribution to British and world cycling cannot be underestimated, and the controversially re-set hour record remains unbeaten a full three years from that epic night in Manchester.

The 2001 season began in the same spirit that closed out 2000, with sprint finishes at most of the opening spring classics—Erik Zabel in Milan-San Remo, Gianluca Bortolami in the Tour of Flanders, George Hincapie in Ghent-Wevelgem and Oskar Camenzind in Liège-Bastogne-Liège. Rik Verbrugghe was a brilliant solo winner of the Flèche Wallonne on a course that we must hope will never see a sprint finish, but for Anglo-Saxons it was Hincapie's win in Wevelgem that emerged as the highlight of the classics. Hincapie finally fulfilled the promise he had shown many years earlier and entered the realms of "to watch" men. But it was Hincapie's teammate, Lance Armstrong, who brought me back to reality with his annual assault on the Amstel Gold Race in the Netherlands—a race that jogs me out of classics mode and into stage racing.

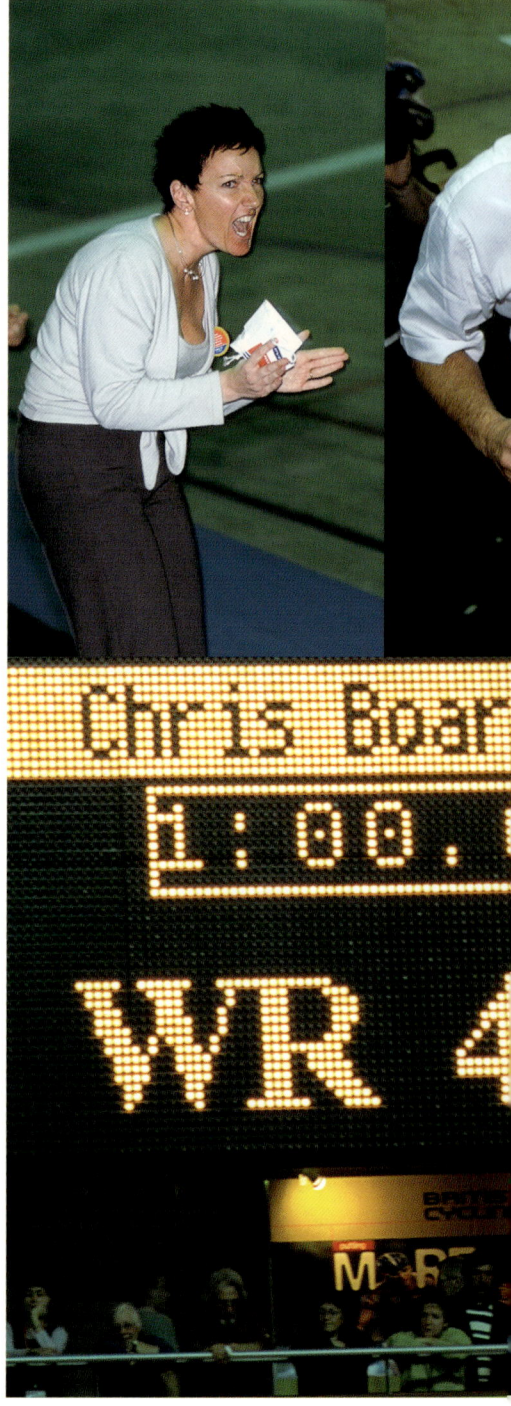

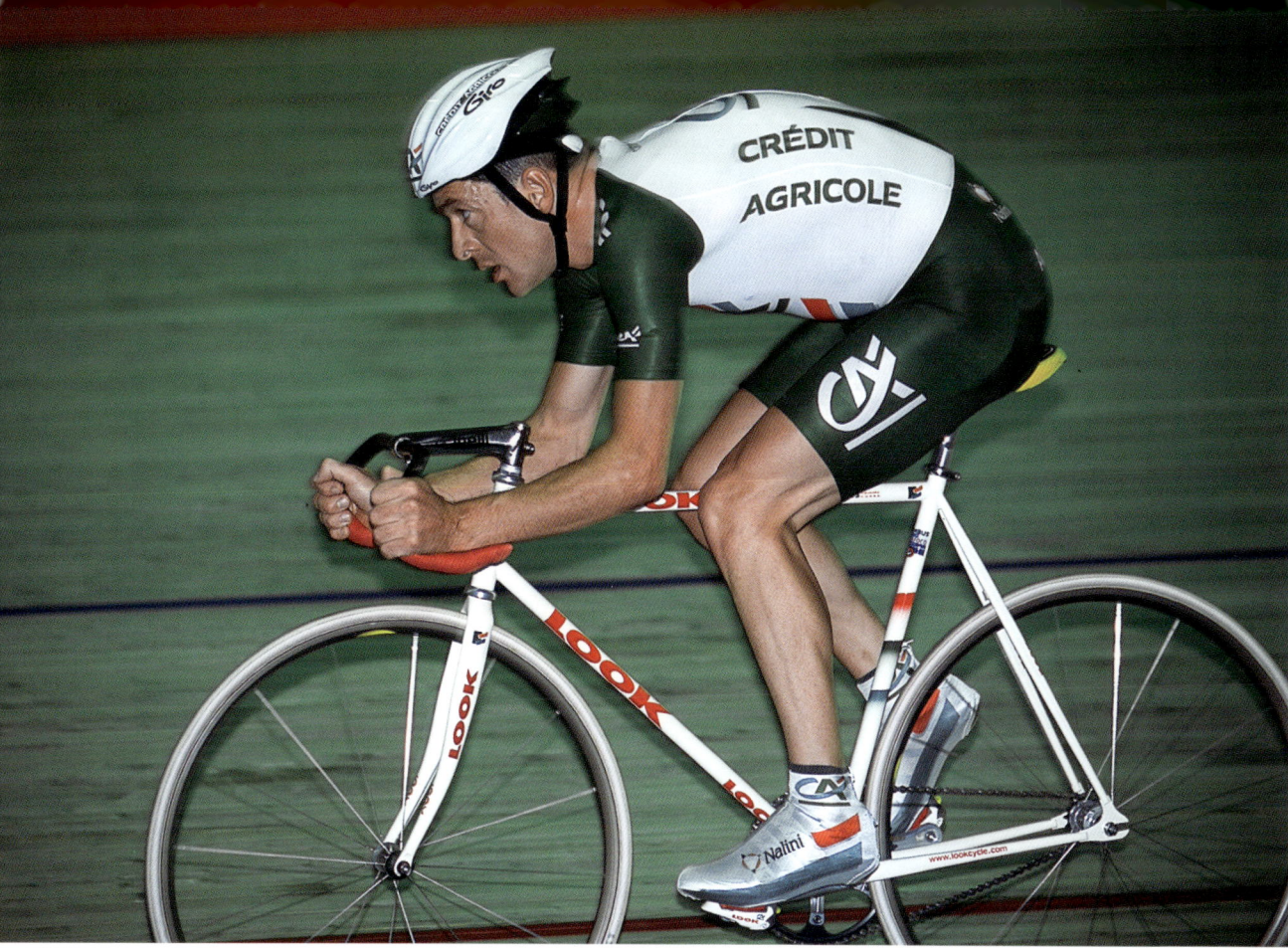
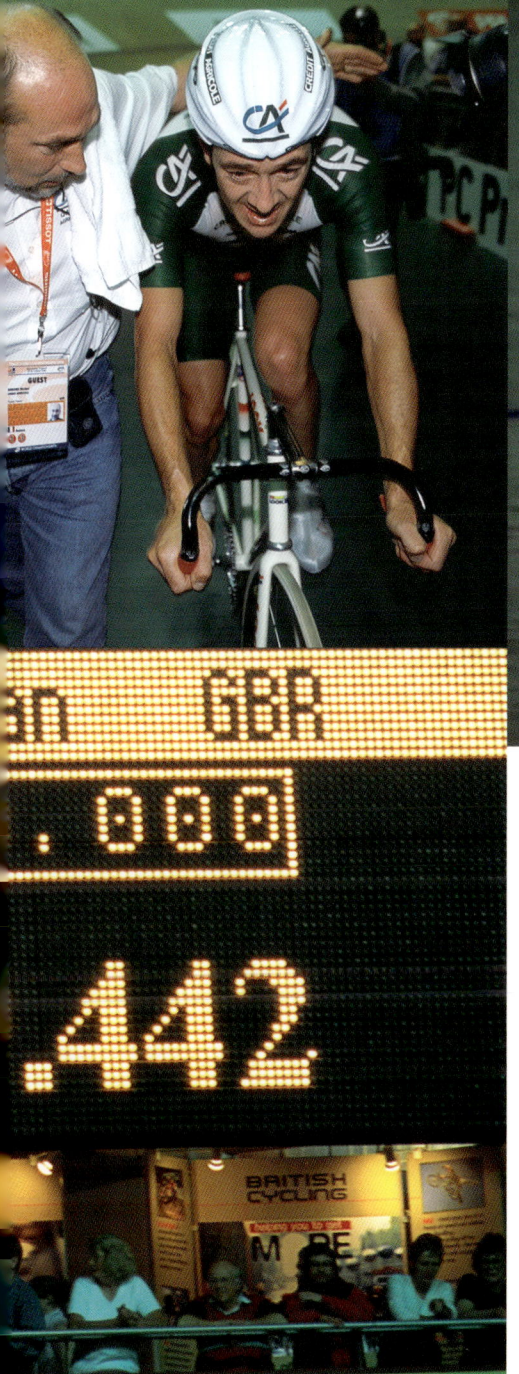

The 2001 Giro should have been one of the best, with some great racing terrain to be covered and the best stage reserved for the eighteenth day of the tour—from Imperia to Santa Anna di Vinadio, with the awesome climb of the Fauniera to test any champion's metal. Well, stage 18 never happened, following the infamous police raids during the previous night that netted a huge posse of cyclists found in possession of banned products. It was a stunning blow to the Giro, and to the sport as a whole, and it was painfully clear that this was a far more serious situation than the Festina affair in the 1998 Tour de France. Along with more than one hundred other media people, I spent a boring day at a hotel in San Remo, fervently optimistic that there might still be a stage to be raced if the riders emerged from a frantic meeting before midday. As it was, this spectacular stage was cancelled.

2000: WORLD HOUR RECORD: MANCHESTER

In the final event of his career, Chris Boardman adds 10 meters to the fabled "conventional bicycle" hour record of 49.432 kilometers set by Eddy Merckx in 1972. Boardman's wife voices her support during his epic ride, while his soigneur meets the exhausted Englishman at the finish.

All that was left of this sad race was the penultimate trek to Arona, with race-leader Gilberto Simoni's only challenger, Dario Frigo, now out of the race after confessing to having banned substances in his possession in San Remo. Simoni, who was not implicated in the police raids, illuminated the next stage with a display of panache on roads made lethally slippery by torrential rain. I left the Giro that evening and drove away from Arona with the promise of a decent Dauphiné Libéré to savor in the French Alps and the prospect of Britain's David Millar winning the prologue in Morzine the next day. Sadly, for me, Didier Rous won that time trial and memories of that Frenchman's implication in the Festina affair came back to haunt us all, just a few short days after Frigo's fall from grace in the Giro!

From the Dauphiné—won by another ex-Festina rider, Christophe Moreau—I trotted over to the Tour de Suisse, in serious need of an upbeat performance by Lance Armstrong after the recent weeks of controversy. He didn't disappoint, with a great win in the opening time trial in southern

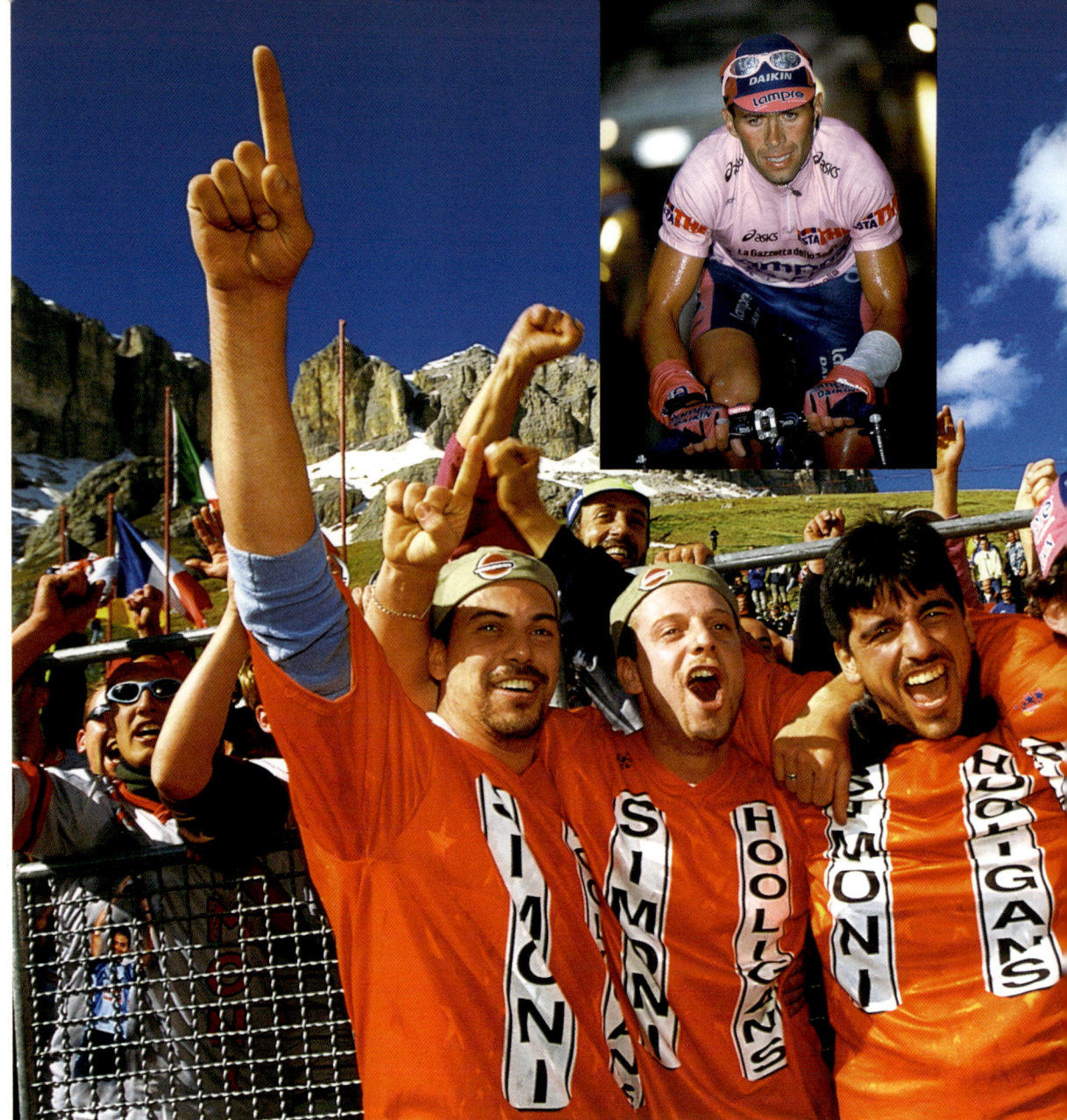

2001: GIRO D'ITALIA: ITALY

The self-proclaimed Simoni Hooligans come out en masse in the Dolomites (main photo), while their hero Gilberto Simoni goes on to win the final mountain stage (inset) in the leader's pink jersey.

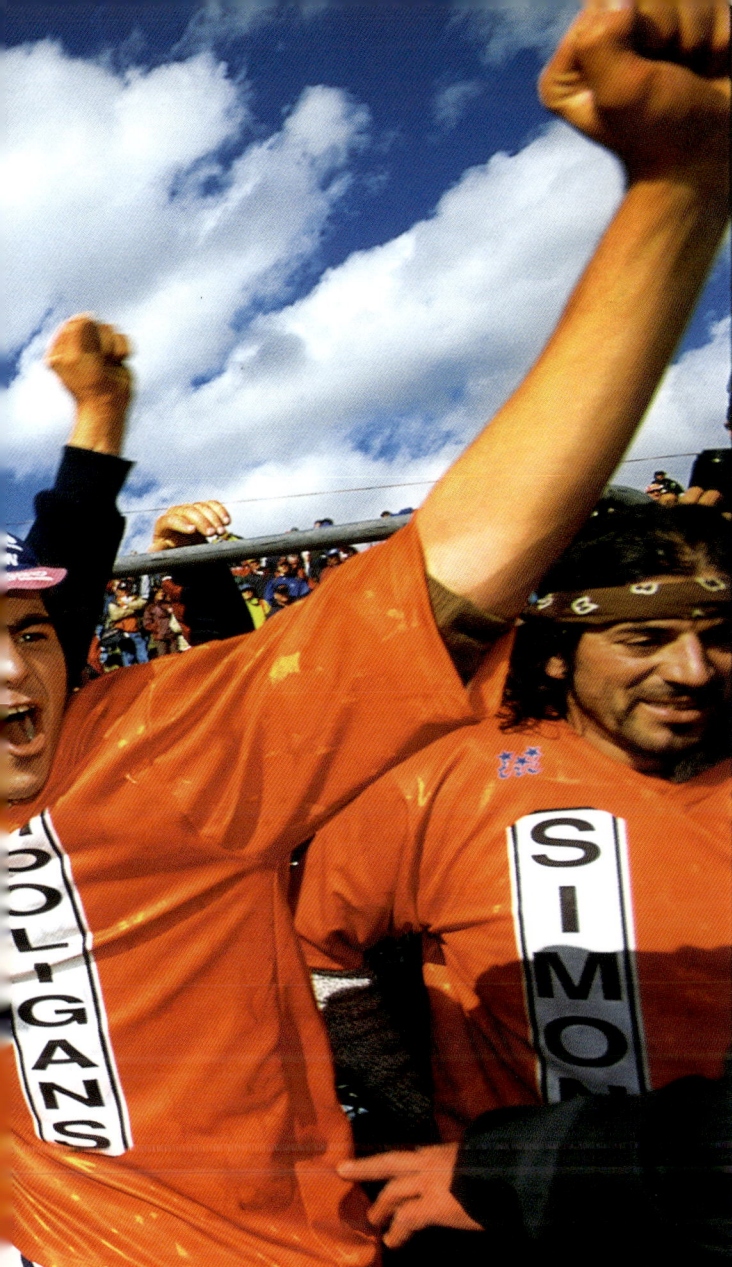

Germany, a superb ride in the vicious time trial up to Crans-Montana, and a masterful display in the mountains of the southern Swiss Alps. In winning the Tour de Suisse for the first time in his life, Armstrong was truly entering into the realm of the all-time greats.

The 2001 Tour started fairly normally, with Moreau winning the prologue a few precious seconds quicker than Armstrong, but became slightly farcical on stage 8 when an escape was allowed to gain a massive 35 minutes! My memory of that day was trying to stay within shooting distance of Armstrong, while still attempting to photograph this dangerous-looking breakaway that included people like Andrei Kivilev and François Simon. Even on a powerful motorbike, it takes a long time to cross a 35-minute gap—but it seemed like an eternity that day with the wet and slippery roads. . . . It came as no surprise that three or four of my colleagues crashed along the way. What transpired from that massive time-gain were blockbuster performances by Armstrong and Ullrich on each of the five mountain stages to come, the most potent one being to Alpe d'Huez two days later.

In just two short years, I have become accustomed to seeing Armstrong dance away from his rivals in the mountains, to the point that I think I know exactly what he is going to do, to whom, and exactly where . . . which is why stage 10 of the 2001 Tour was a strange one for me. I'd passed the main group on the Col de la Madeleine, somewhat surprised by the sight of so many Telekom riders at the front—shouldn't it be the Postal boys trying this intimidation trick? I saw

BEYOND 2000 *213*

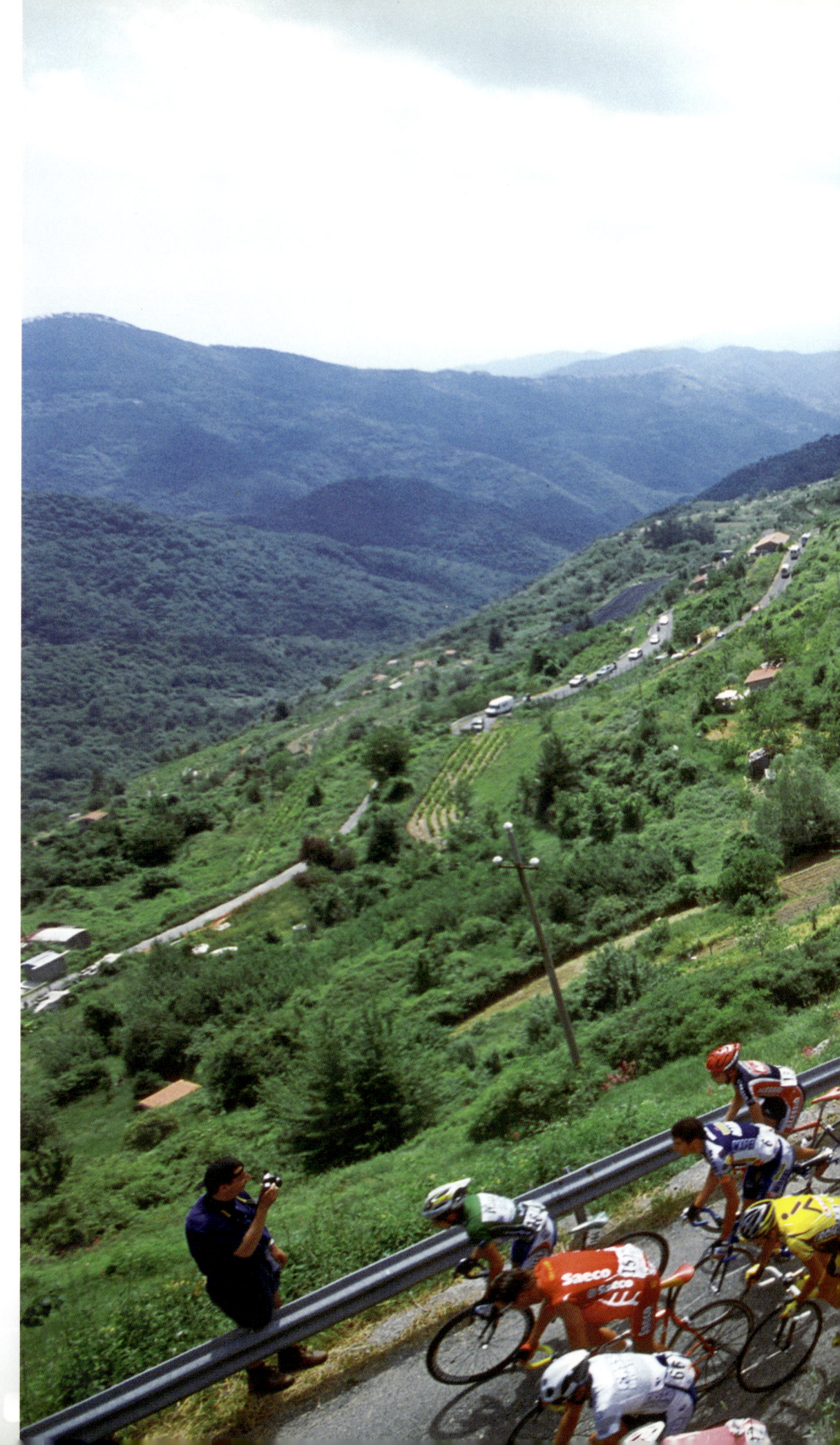

2001: GIRO D'ITALIA: MARITIME ALPS

The peloton climbs the Colle di Bajardo on the roundtrip stage 17 from San Remo. That night, all of the teams' hotel rooms were raided by police in a drug sweep.

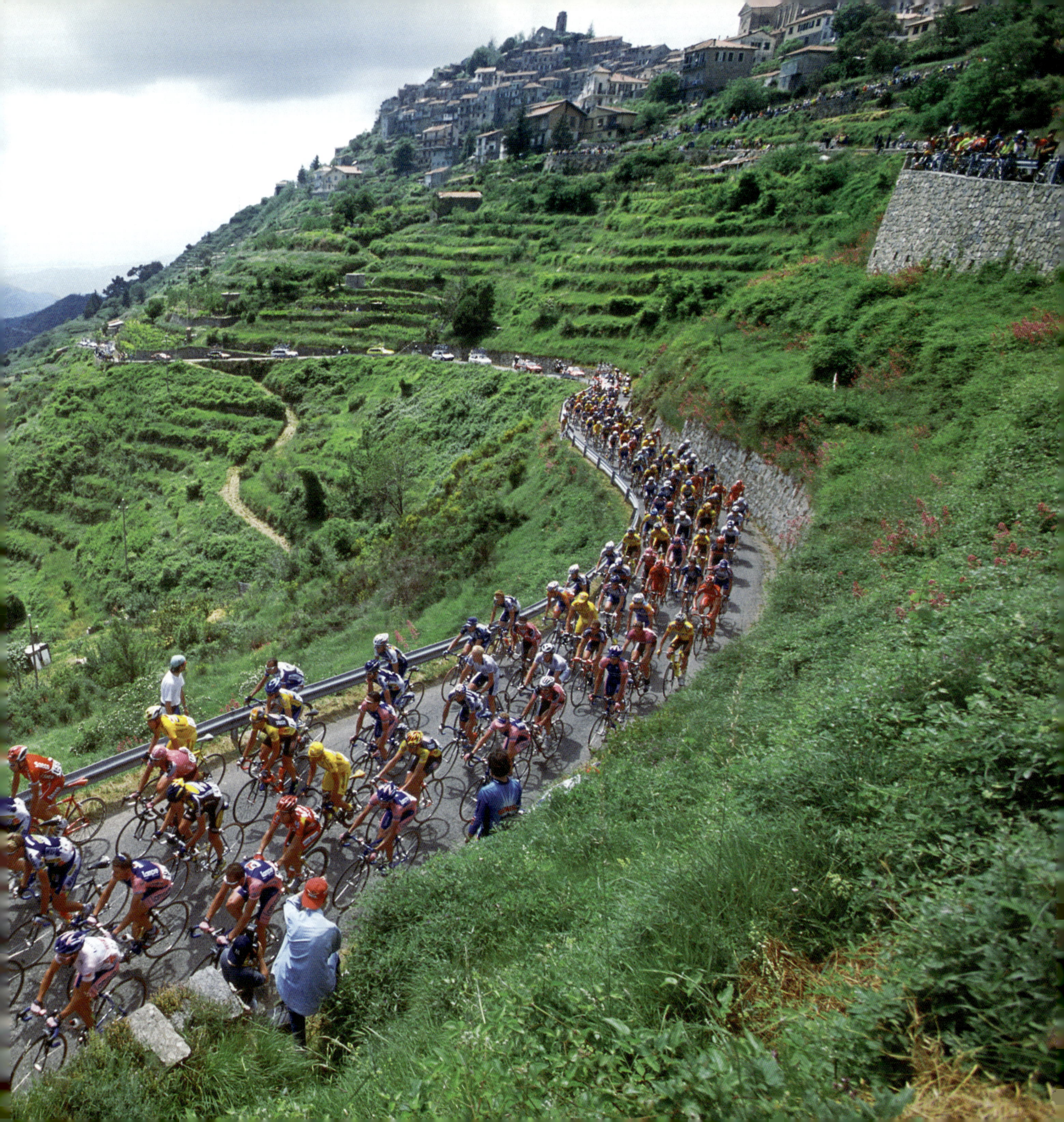

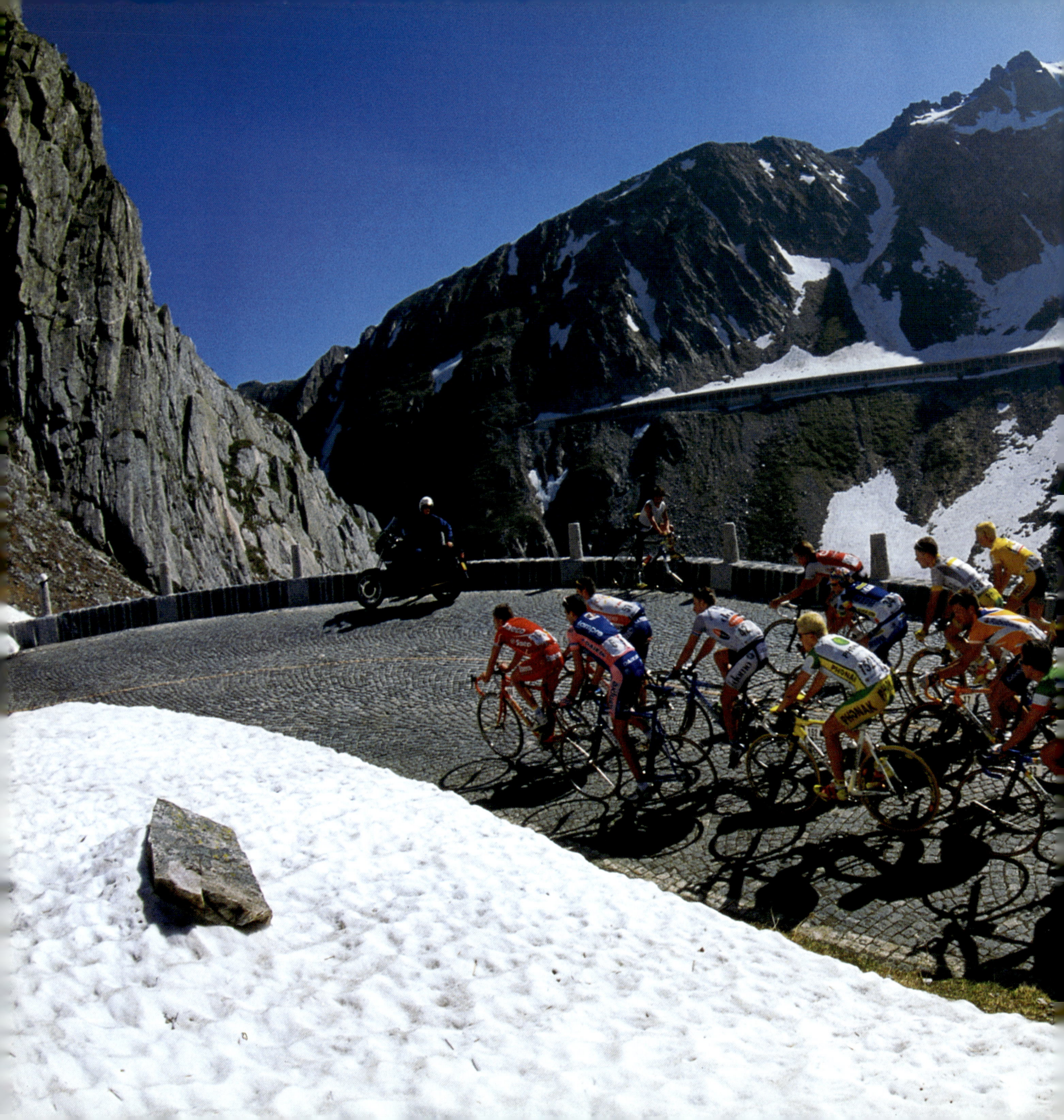

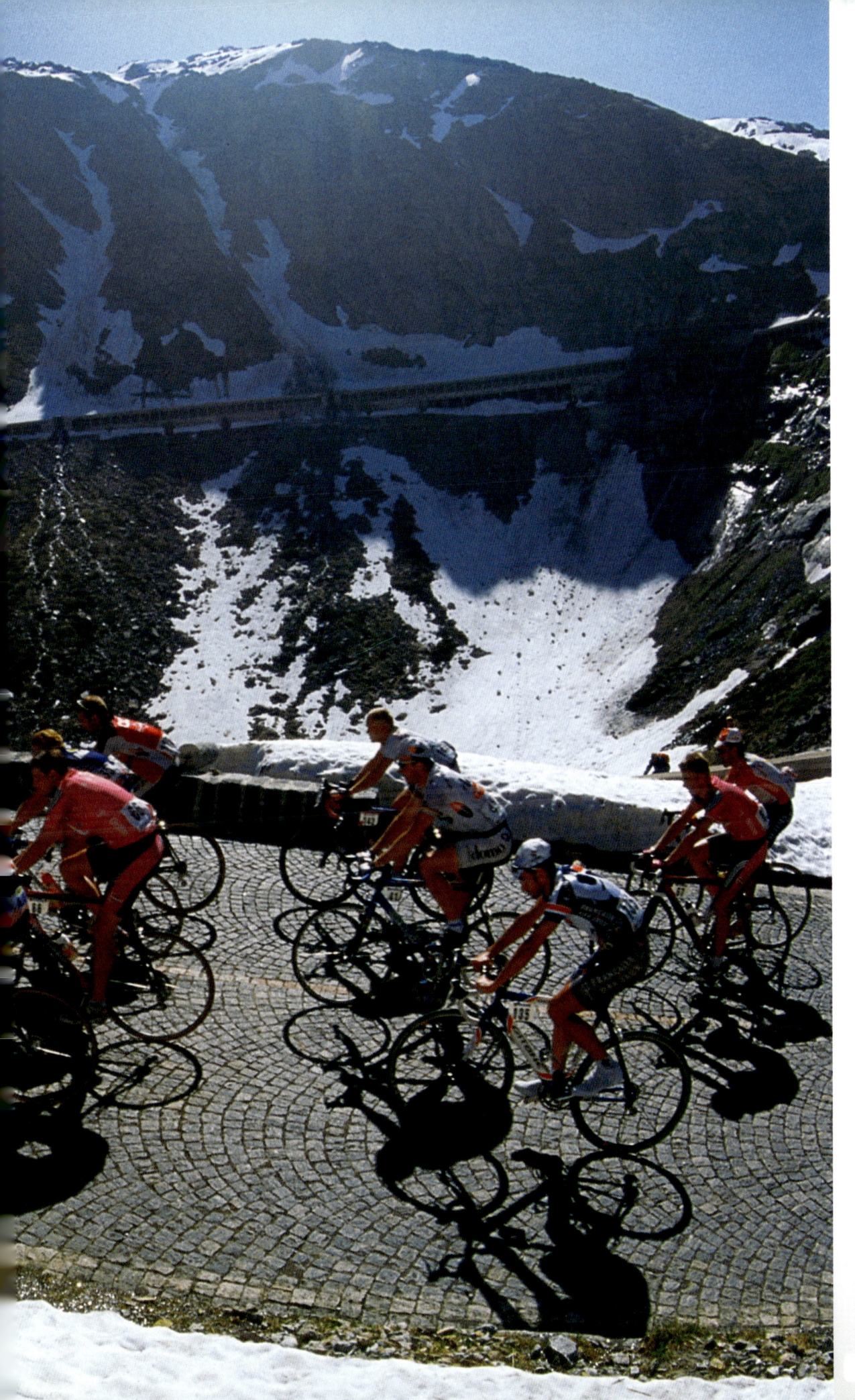

2001: TOUR DE SUISSE: SWITZERLAND

The backmarkers rumble up the cobblestone St. Gotthard Pass in the Swiss Alps.

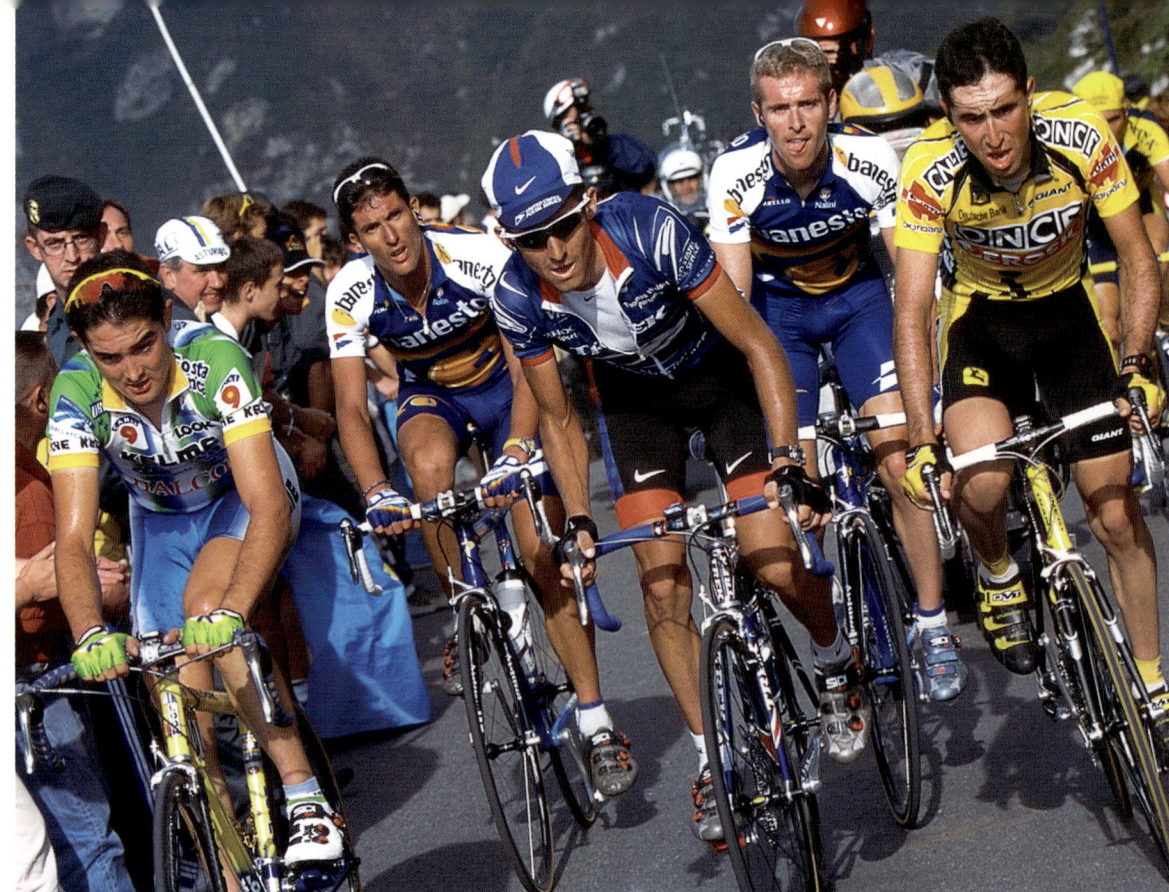

this group again near the Madeleine summit, and still Telekom was there, led by Italian Giuseppe Guerini—surely, something was wrong here! I stayed behind the now-dwindling group on the next climb, the narrow and nasty Col du Glandon, determined to see if Lance was okay, not having a bad day . . . but the signs were all there—he was repeatedly calling his team car up for more water, and consulting with manager Johan Bruyneel . . . oh, boy!

We drove past as slowly as we could under the stringent rules, and I saw that Lance's climbing was out of sync—his shoulders and backside looked distinctly uncomfortable, that much was clear. Yet his eyes and face didn't quite seem as stressed as they would typically be under this kind of pressure, so still I was unsure. At the front, his ex-teamate Kevin Livingston was applying the pressure on behalf of Telekom, and I started to dread what I might see on the Alpe d'Huez. It was because of this that I went on ahead to the Alpe, shooting some needless pictures of a two-man escape that would be gobbled up a few kilometers later. Then it happened: Radio Tour announced, "Acceleration by U.S. Postal, attack by Armstrong," and a moment later, "Ullrich unable to follow attack."

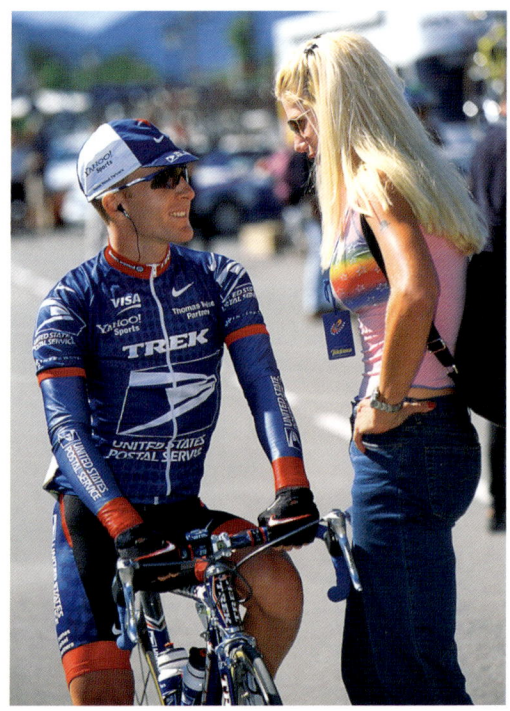

2001: VUELTA A ESPAÑA: LAGOS DE CORVODONGA
Defending champion Roberto Heras (center) struggles in stage five, eventually finishing fourth overall. Here, he climbs with (left to right) Oscar Sevilla, José Maria Jimenez, Aitor Osa and Joseba Beloki.

2001: VUELTA A ESPAÑA: SPAIN
A quiet moment for the new U.S. grand tour contender Levi Leipheimer and his wife Odessa Gunn.

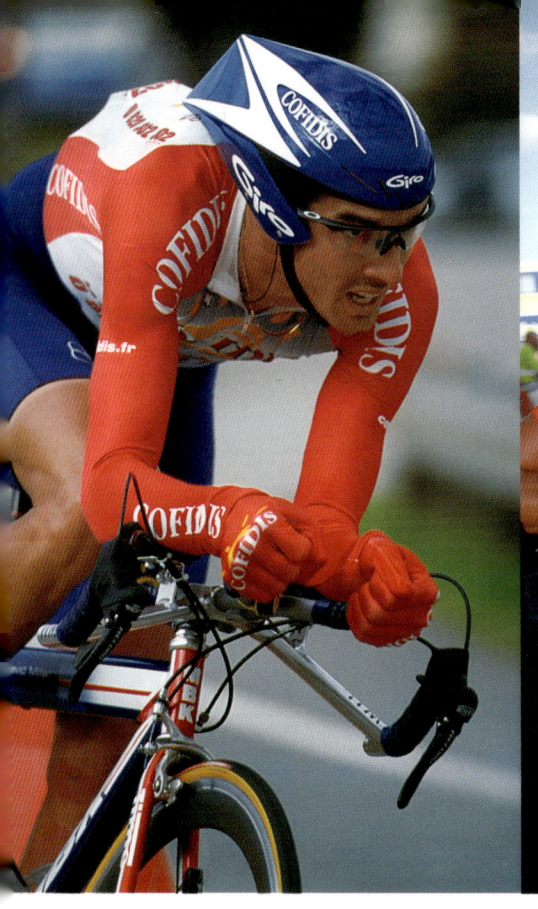
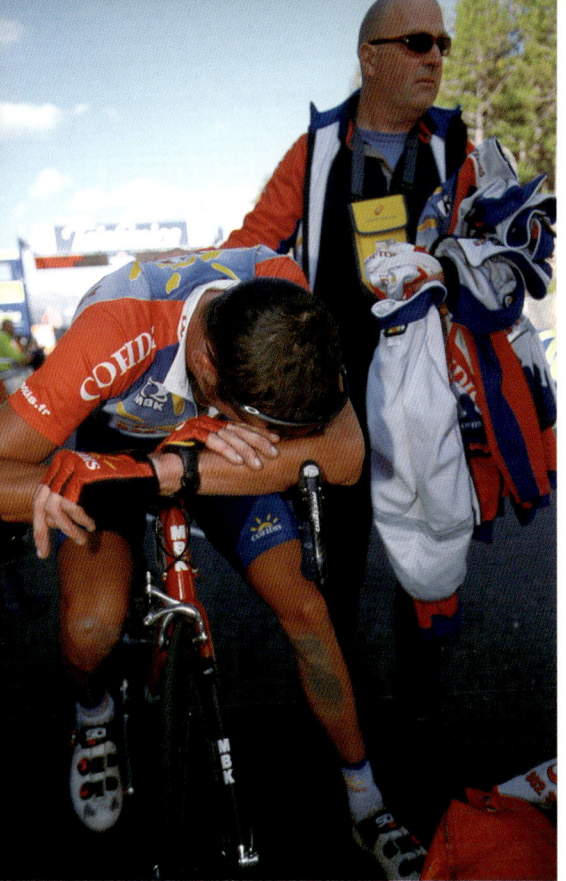

Cursing, yet more than slightly relieved by this news, I awaited Armstrong's arrival about 2 kilometers up the climb, banging off a handful of desperate shots as reality set in—he had been bluffing all along! What followed was a pursuit match between the two best cyclists in the world—though Alpe d'Huez is no flat velodrome, and neither Armstrong nor Ullrich were crouched low in aerodynamic tucks.

As the kilometers passed I began to settle down again, happy to be getting the vital shots of Lance in full cry while the radio confirmed what I myself could see each time I waited for Ullrich—the time gap was steadily increasing. Ullrich was now churning away in his big gear, at the front of a small group that contained Joseba Beloki, Oscar Sevilla, Roberto Laiseka and a determined Christophe Moreau. Farther back was Kivilev, riding steadily in hopes of the yellow jersey in the Pyrenees, while even farther back came Simon—the man most likely to take the yellow jersey at this stage finish, thanks to the huge time gap of two days ago.

Up front, I was at last beginning to enjoy myself, looking now for shots of crazy Americans running alongside Lance with their Stars 'n' Stripes flags, but sooner than I could anticipate, the climb ended among a wall of spectators, and Lance reached the finish with his arms spread wide, occasionally

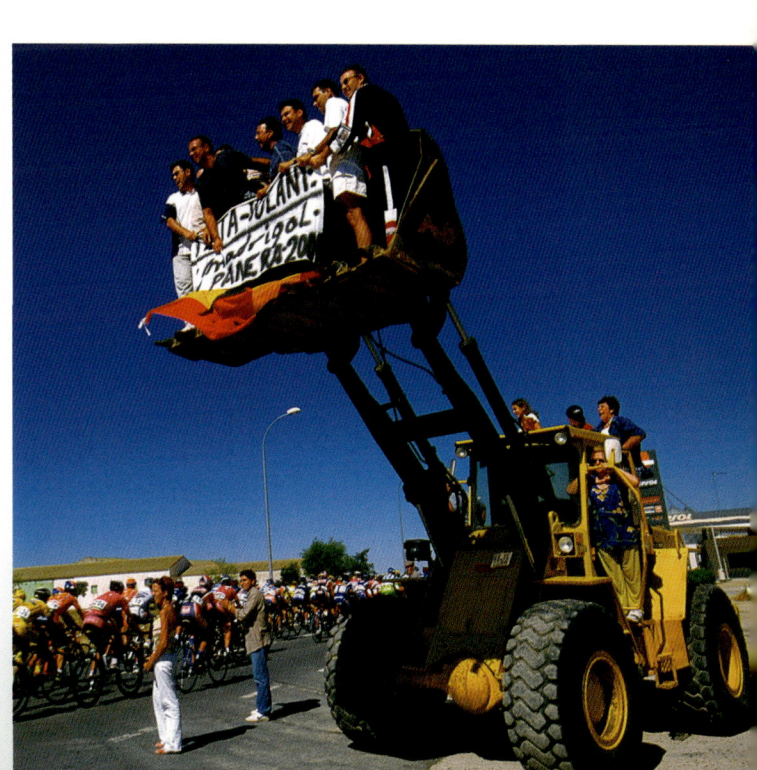

2001: VUELTA A ESPAÑA: SPAIN
Budding British star David Millar makes a breakthrough at the 2001 Vuelta, winning the stage one time trial (top left) and racing to his limit in the mountains (top right).

2001: VUELTA A ESPAÑA: SPAIN
Spanish spectators embody the enthusiasm for the race with their special viewing arrangement.

punching the air with delight, so happy was he with his performance. He had nearly matched the hill record set by Marco Pantani at the height of his powers in 1997. Yet as happy as I was that the Tour was finally turning around, I realized how important Armstrong's attack on Ullrich had been—I was bombarded with calls the next week from editors and sponsors wanting "that shot" when Lance had made Ullrich look utterly useless as the climb began. It became known around the world as "the look," so potent were the television images of Lance staring back at a distraught Ullrich. That exact moment had been taken by just two French photographers and I was ashamed to admit that I misread the signs on the Col du Glandon . . . so much for me knowing my job!

From there, Lance really went to work in the mountains until the final delight on stage 13 to Pla d'Adet, which finally saw Lance pull on the yellow jersey—and this time I did get the shot of him as he again left Ullrich for dead a few kilometers from the end.

One of the prominent riders on that epic stage 10 to Alpe d'Huez became the star performer of the Vuelta two months later—Oscar Sevilla. This youthful-looking rider had become the housewives' favorite even before he pulled on the "golden" race-leader's jersey at Lagos de Covadonga five days into the race and he was still Spain's favorite cyclist even after he'd lost the jersey to Angel Casero on the very last stage into Madrid—a morale-breaking time trial! Sevilla illuminated the Vuelta on all the mountain stages, and really left his mark on the race along with "foreigners" like Britain's David Millar, Colombia's Santiago Botero and Levi Leipheimer—the newest U.S. stage-race star. It was great to see Millar win the opening time trial in Salamanca, especially after seeing him crash in the Tour prologue in Dunkirk, and eventually lose his health and strength in France.

Millar had beaten Botero by just a few seconds, and the two sparred with each other throughout the Vuelta, with Millar outsprinting the Colombian on stage 6 into Oscar Freire's hometown,

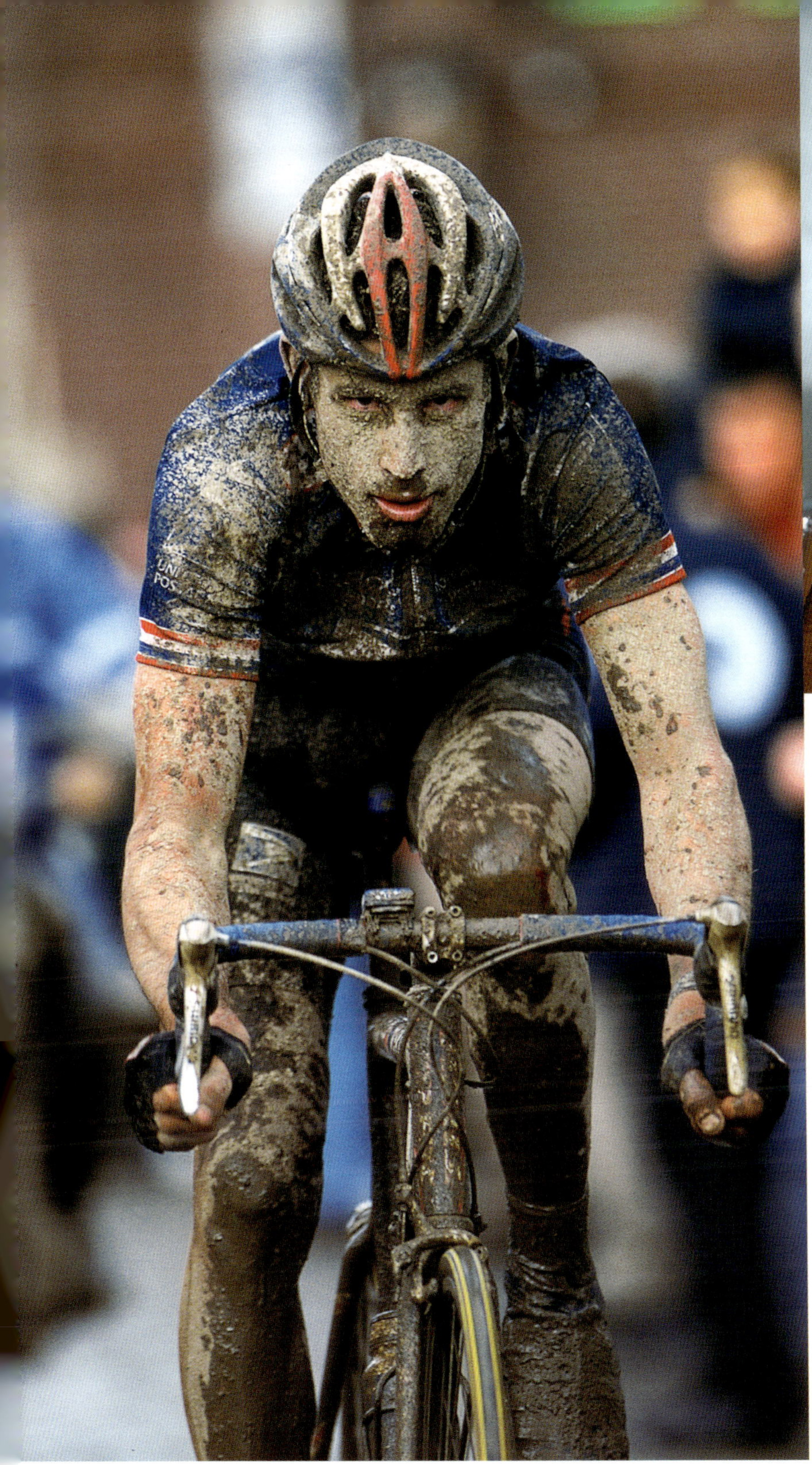

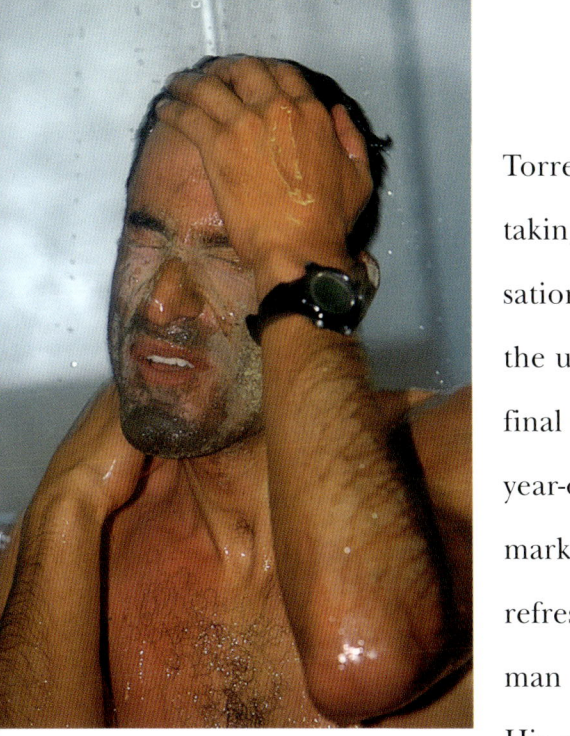

Torrelevega, but with Botero taking the race lead as compensation. Botero eventually got the upper hand by winning the final stage into Madrid, but 24-year-old-Millar had made his mark on the race, and it was refreshing to see this talented man make such great progress. His stage win into Torrelevega may well prove to be a turning point in Millar's career, for one could sense the elation of a time trialist turned roadman.

The 2001 world championships saw Millar again in contention, and I had a slightly difficult time consoling him after he was beaten to the gold medal by a stubbornly persistant Jan Ullrich in the time trial. Although he could not see it, Millar had scared the life out of experienced men like Ullrich and Botero (the bronze medal winner), and he made another remarkable step forward in his promising career. My emotions were confused as I felt sorry for Millar, yet admired the tenacity of Ullrich, who had finally managed to salvage something from an otherwise mediocre season. This highlight aside, the Portuguese world's will not go down in history as remotely great

2002: PARIS-ROUBAIX: FRANCE

George Hincapie was one of the heroes in the "Hell of the North" classic, but a post-race shower couldn't wash away the disappointment of defeat.

BEYOND 2000

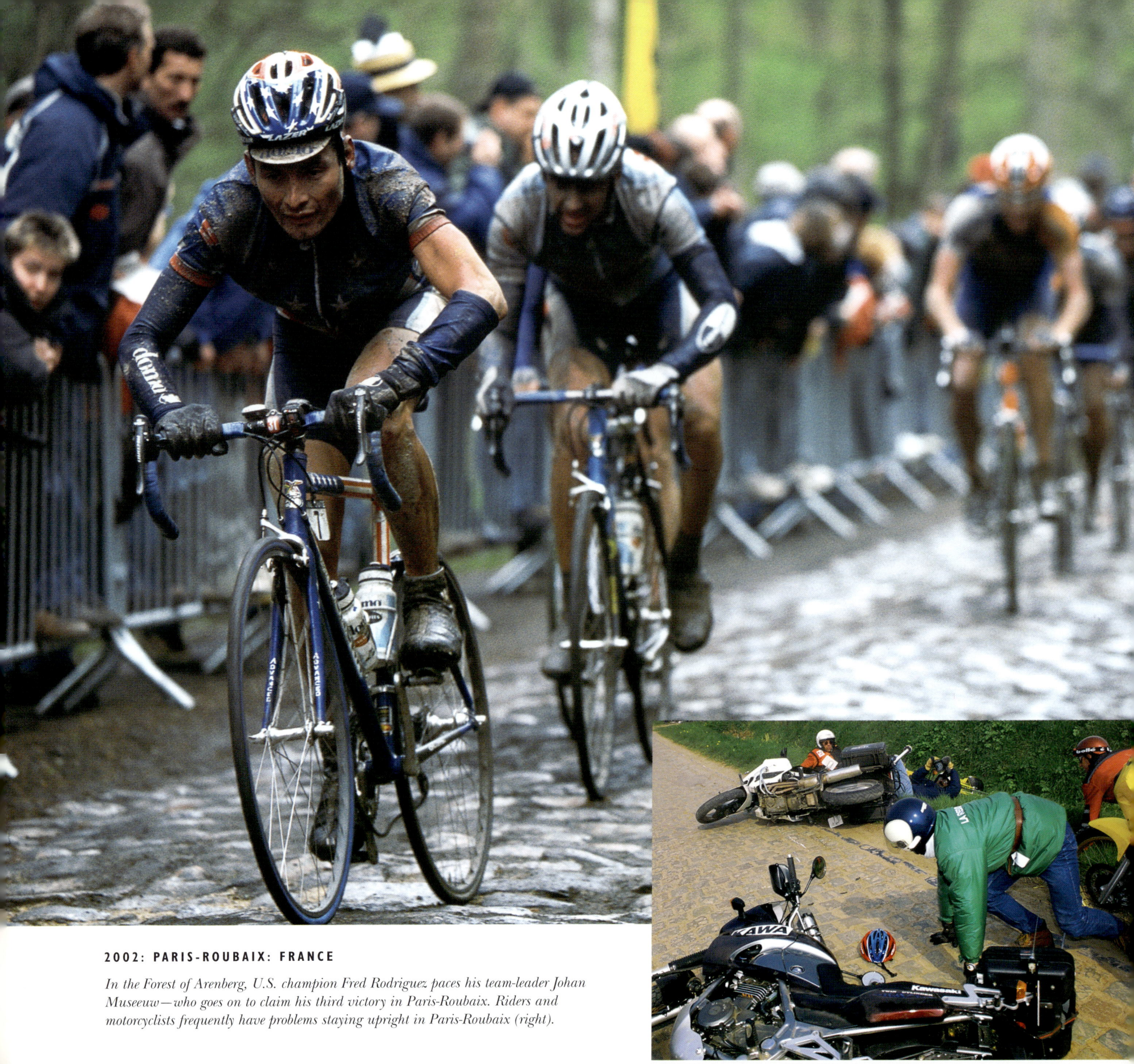

2002: PARIS-ROUBAIX: FRANCE

In the Forest of Arenberg, U.S. champion Fred Rodriguez paces his team-leader Johan Museeuw—who goes on to claim his third victory in Paris-Roubaix. Riders and motorcyclists frequently have problems staying upright in Paris-Roubaix (right).

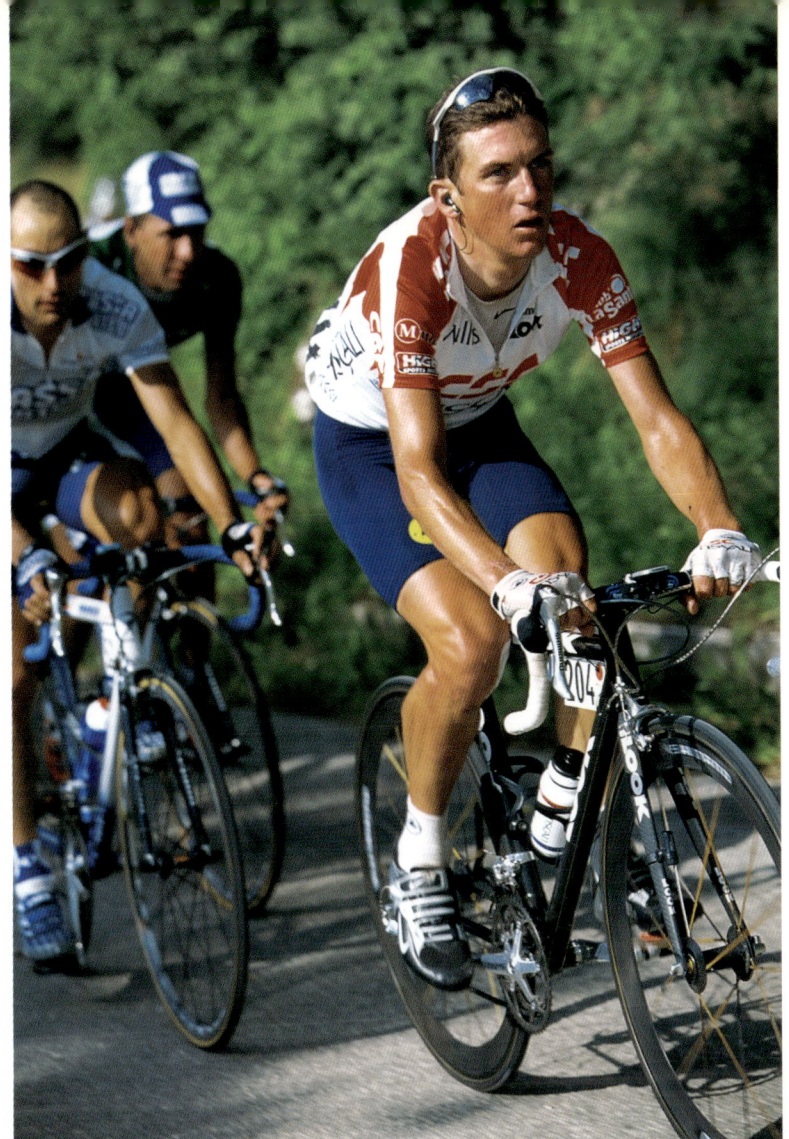

2002: GIRO D'ITALIA: ITALY

Tyler Hamilton (right) breaks through to win a time-trial stage and finish second overall.

given its almost nonexistent crowds, a totally ignorant local community, and a circuit that offered little in the way of great racing.

The 2002 season began on a better note with the wins at Milan-San Remo, the Tour of Flanders, and Paris-Roubaix going to three old greats—Mario Cipollini, Andrea Tafi and Johan Museeuw. Cipollini amazed himself with the manner in which he also won Ghent-Wevelgem, by chasing across to a useful-looking break containing Hincapie, Fred Rodriguez, and a pair of tough, wizened, Flemish roadmen, and then beating them at the finish.

The spring classics in 2002 were also notable for the atrocious conditions in Paris-Roubaix, far worse—if that was possible—than those of 2001, when days of rain made the cobbled paths almost impassable. After weeks without rain, inches of dried mud turned into a thick, slippery sludge on the cobblestones, sending cyclists, motorbikes and even team cars into all kinds of problems. But this Paris-Roubaix was a potential dream day for photographers—at least those of us who had had the foresight to be equipped with special bikes and tires. What transpired was an epic battle between the old master, Museeuw, and the combined might of younger hopefuls like Stefan Wesseman, Tom Boonen, Nico Mattan and Hincapie—but none of them were ever really a threat to a tough man like Museeuw, on as tough a day as this.

I often get to see the champions of tomorrow in the making, fresh into the professional ranks with their immaculate bikes and squeaky-clean new jerseys, their faces revealing a tender mixture of naiveté and hope. Sometimes that eagerness quickly turns to success as in the case of Australia's Cadel Evans at the 2002 Giro d'Italia. Or there are the late bloomers like American Tyler Hamilton at the same Giro. Cycling's champions of this era—Armstrong, Cipollini, Museeuw, Ullrich and Zabel—have comprised the great episodes in my life as well, and I thank them most sincerely for the pleasure I have drawn from their exploits.

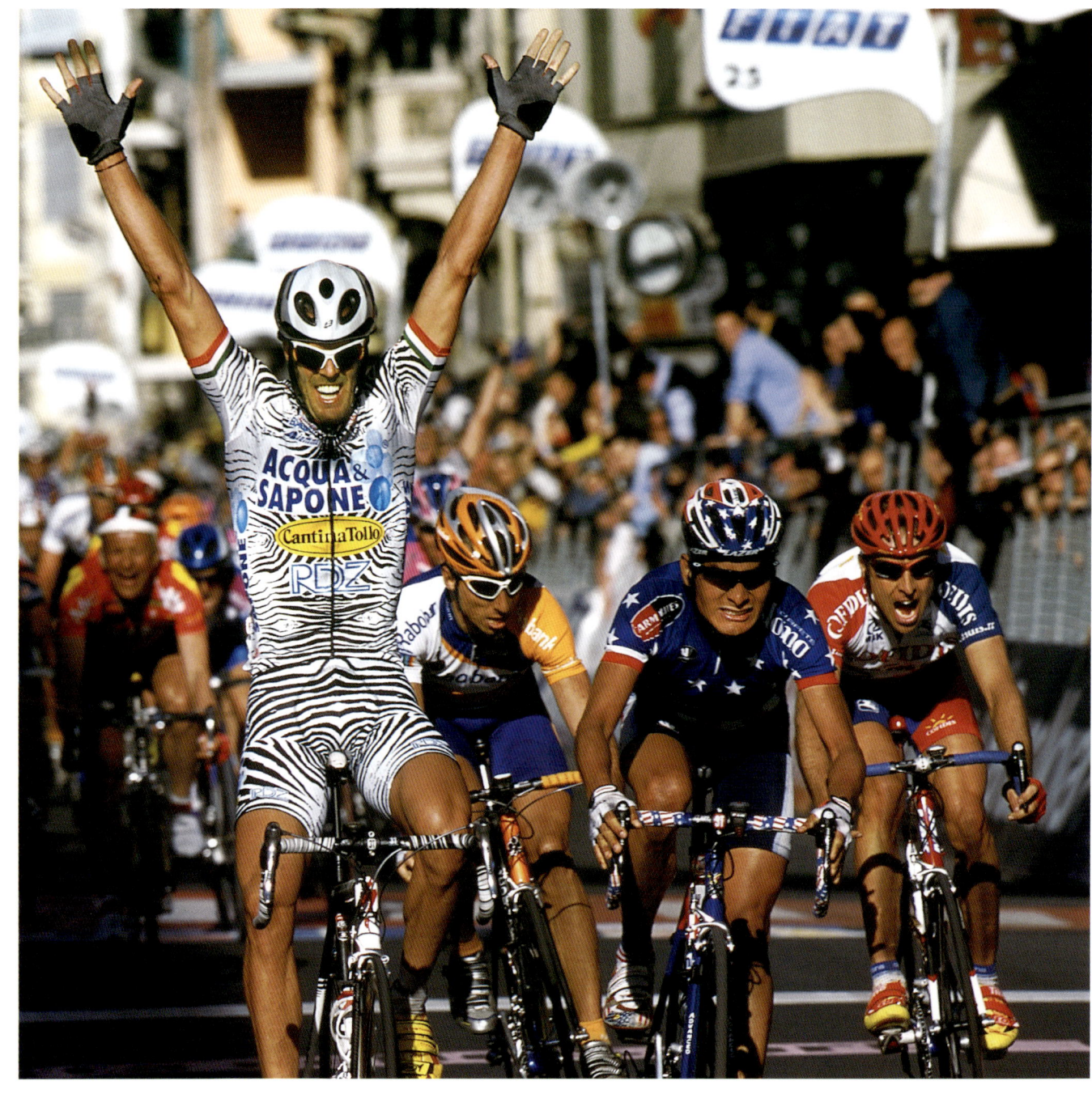

2002: MILAN-SAN REMO: ITALY

Mario Cipollini scores the biggest win of his career at age 35, defeating Fred Rodriguez (right) to win Milan-San Remo on the Via Roma.

PHOTOGRAPHIC INDEX

Agostinho, Joaquim:
   in Tour de France, (1978) 9
Alcála, Raúl:
   in Giro d'Italia, (1988) 62
   in Tour de France, (1988) 81
Anderson, Phil:
   in Het Volk, (1985) 53
   in Tour de France, (1985) 55, (1986) 65
   in Tour of Flanders, (1983) 21, 38
Andorra, 195
Andreu, Frankie:
   in Paris-Nice, (1995) 157
   in Tour de France, (1995) 159
Anquetil, Jacques:
   at Paris-Nice, (1986) 66
Argentin, Moreno:
   in Flèche Wallonne, (1994) 131
   in World Road Championships, (1983) 28, (1987) 64
Armstrong, Lance:
   in Amstel Gold, (2001) 208
   in Austin, 186
   in Paris-Nice, (1998) 181
   in Tour de France, (1993) 130, (1995) 159, (1999) 177, 194, 197, (2000) 198, 204-205
   in Tour of Flanders, (1994) 105
   in World Road Championships, (1990) 95-96, (1993) 130, 132, (1998) 5, 181
Australia:
   Sydney, 209
Austria:
   Villach, 64

Ballerini, Franco:
   in Paris-Roubaix, (1998) 193
Bartoli, Michele:
   In Rochester Classic, (1997) 166
Bauer, Steve:
   in Paris-Roubaix, (1998) 89, (1990) 84, (1992) 112
   in Tour de France, (1995) 159
   in World Road Championships, (1988) 80
Belgium, 12, 15, 21, 24, 53, 56-57, 71-72, 78, 104, 105, 109, 121, 131
   Houffalize, 179
   Liège, 162
   Renaix, 80
Bellutti, Antonella:
   in World Track Championships, (1990) 98-99
Beloki, Joseba:
   in Vuelta a España, (2001) 218
Beltran, Manuel:
   in Tour de France, (2000) 202
Berzin, Evgeni:
   in Flèche Wallonne, (1994) 131
Boardman, Chris:
   in Olympic Games, (1992) 123
   in World Hour Record Attempt, (1996) 140, (2000) 210-211
Botero, Santiago:
   in Tour de France, (2000) 202
Bondue, Alain:
   in Vuelta a España, (1986) 68
Boogerd, Michael:
   in Dauphiné Libéré, (1997) 149

Borges, Ismael, 63
Bourgignon, Thierry:
   in Paris-Nice, (1995) 157
Bouvet, Albert, 153, 197
Boyer, Jonathan:
   in Ghent-Wevelgem, (1986) 78
   in Tour de France, (1982) 48
Braun, Gregor:
   in Tour of Flanders, (1983) 24
Breu, Beat:
   in World Cyclo-cross Championships, (1988) 76
Bruyneel, Johan:
   in Tour de France, (1996) 143
Bungo, Gianni:
   in Giro d'Italia, (1990) 88
   in Tour de France, (1992) 116
   in World Road Championships, (1991) 110
Casagrande, Francesco:
   in Giro d'Italia, (2000) 173
Chiappucci, Claudio:
   in Giro d'Italia, (1991) 107
   in Milan-San Remo, (1991) 107
   in Tour de France, (1992) 116, (1990) 130
Cipollini, Mario:
   in Giro d'Italia, (1991) 111, (1995) 144
   in Milan-San Remo, (2002) 224
   in Tour de France, (1997) 145
   in Tuscany, 154
Clark, Danny:
   in Rotterdam Six Day, (1983) 32

Clasica San Sebastian, (1990) 85, 94-95
Copeland, Jim:
   in World Road Championships, (1990) 96
Criquielion, Claude:
   in World Road Championships, (1988) 80
Critérium International, (1996) 150
Czechoslovakia:
   Prague, 23

Dauphiné Libéré, (1997) 149, 165, (1999) 193
De Bosscher, Willy:
   in Skol Six, (1980) 16
Delgado, Pedro:
   in Giro d'Italia, (1991) 121
   in Tour de France, (1987) 74
De Meyer, Marc:
   in Paris Roubaix, (1981) 26
   in Tour of Flanders, (1980) 15
Dekker, Erik:
   in Amstel Gold, (2001) 208
Demol, Dirk:
   in Paris-Roubaix, (1988) 77
Denmark, 52
De Vlaeminck, Roger:
   in Paris-Roubaix, (1981) 26
   in Tour of Flanders, (1980) 12
Dew, Dave:
   in World Track Championships, (1992) 124
De Wolf, Fons:
   in Milan-San Remo, (1983) 32

Dhaenens, Rudy:
   in Tour of Flanders, (1991) 104
Diaz-Zabala, Herminio:
   in Vuelta a España, (1997) 141
Duclos-Lassalle, Gilbert:
   in Paris-Roubaix, (1994) 128
Duprel, Renée:
   in World Track Championships, (1990) 91
Durand, Jacky:
   in Paris-Tours, (1998) 197

Eaton, Matt:
   in Milk Race, (1983) 44
Ekimov, Viatcheslv:
   in Olympic Games, (2000) 209
England. *See* Great Britain
Escartin, Fernando:
   in Tour de France, (1999) 197

Fiedler, Jens:
   in Olympic Games, (1996) 139
Fignon, Laurent:
   in Paris-Nice, (1990) 86
   in Paris-Roubaix, (1989) 79
   in Tour de France, (1989) 74
Flèche Wallonne, (1994) 131
Fondriest, Maurizio:
   in World Road Championships, (1988) 80
Fontanelli, Fabio:
   in Giro d'Italia, (1999) 190
   in Tour de France, (1998) 184
France, ix, 14, 23, 26, 48, 70, 77, 79, 84, 89, 104, 108, 113-114, 128-129, 150, 187, 193, 197, 199
   L'Alpe d'Huez, 9, 82, 151
   Alps, 13, 17, 74, 78, 120, 147, 167
   Annecy Lake, 185
   Armentières, 115
   Avoriaz, 55
   Bourg d'Oisans, 177
   Brétigny, 97
   Brive-la-Gaillarde, 175
   Cannes, 30
   Col d'Eze, 66, 69
   Col d'Izoard, 149, 173, 198
   Col du Galibier, 183, 188
   Col du Glandon, 48
   Col de Madeleine, 167, 202
   Col de Porte, 165
   Col de la République, 192
   Cormet de Roseland, 143
   Disneyland Paris, 155
   Dordogne, 90
   Les Duex-Alpes, 189
   Forges-les-Eaux, 145
   Guzet-Neige, 81
   Hautacam, 142
   Lac de Vasivière, 54
   Limoges, 154
   Massif Central, 148, 157, 164-165
   Metz, 180
   Metz-Nancy, 10, 12
   Mont Faron, 86, 95
   Montreuil, viii
   Mont Ventoux, 86, 193, 203
   Paris, 50, 65, 68, 82, 85, 147, 153, 160, 167, 181, 184, 197, 204-205
   Pau, 159
   Provence, 200-201
   Puy-du-Fou, 194
   Pyrenees, 156
   Quimper, 115
   St. Emilion, 156
   St. Etienne, 83
   Tarascon-sur-Ariège, 185
   Verdun, 130
   Villard-de-Lans, 130
   Wallers, 180
   Wallers-Arenberg Forest, 112
Frank, Gert:
   in Ghent Six Day, (1984) 52
French Alps, 13, 17, 74, 78, 120, 147, 167
Furlan, Giorgio:
   in Flèche Wallonne, (1994) 131

Garzelli, Stefano:
   in Giro d'Italia, (2000) 173
Gavazzi, Pierino:
   in Tour of Lombardy, (1983) 40
Gentleman's Charity Race, 162
Germany, 58-59, 111
   Stuttgart, 110
Ghent Six Day, (1984) 52
Ghent-Wevelgem, (1985) 56-57, (1986) 78
Giro d'Italia, (1986) 62, (1988) 62, 69, (1990) 88, (1991) 107, 111, 120, (1994) 126, 133, (1995) 144, (1996) 167, (1997) 166, 168, (1998) 176, 182, (1999) 182, 190-191, (2000) 173, (2001) 212-215, (2002) 223
Goddet, Jacques, 86
Goubert, Stéphane:
   in Dauphiné Libéré, (1997) 165
Grand Prix des Nations, (1982) 30
Great Britain, 43-44, 46
   Dover Castle, 106
   Goodwood, 28, 46
   Leicester, 27, 30, 51
   London, 16
   Manchester, 140, 210-211
   Rochester, 166
   Royal Tunbridge Wells, 102-103

Gualdi, Mirko:
   in World Road Championships, (1990) 86
Guinness, Rupert, 115

Hage, Helen:
   in Tour de France Féminin, (1984) 50
Hall, Carey:
   in World Track Championships, (1991) 111
Hamilton, Tyler:
   in Giro d'Italia, (2002) 223
Hampsten, Andy:
   in Tour de France, (1986) 68
   in Giro d'Italia, (1988) 69, (1997) 166
Havik, Mieke:
   in Tour de France Féminin, (1984) 50
Henry, Jean-Jacques:
   in Paris-Tours, (1992) 113
Heras, Roberto:
   in Vuelta a España, (1999) 178, (2001) 218
Herety, John:
   in Nissan Classic, (1986) 71
Herrera, Lucho:
   in Tour de France, (1985) 55
Hervé, Pascal:
   in Tour de France, (2000) 202
Het Volk, (1985) 53
Hinault, Bernard:
   in Grand Prix des Nations, (1982) 30
   Milan-San Remo, (1983) 32
   in Paris-Roubaix, (1981) 26
   in Tour de France, (1978) 9-11, (1985) 54-55

Hincapie, George:
   in Paris-Roubaix, (2000) 187, 199, (2002) 221
   in Vuelta a España, (1995) 168
Hübner, Michael:
   in World Track Championships, (1994) 117

Induráin, Miguel:
   in Clasica San Sebastian, (1990) 85, 94-95
   in Giro d'Italia, (1994) 133
   at home in Villava, Spain, 132
   in Tour de France, (1992) 116, (1994) 120, (1995) 147, 164-165
   in Vuelta a España, (1985) 24
   in World Road Championships, (1991) 110
Ireland, 92-93
   Cliffs of Mohr, 71-72
   Cork, 66, 73
Italian Alps, 126
Italy, 24, 32, 36-37, 40, 42, 45, 47, 62, 121, 133, 168
   Alps, 88, 126
   Bassano Dell Grappa, 53
   Boario Terme, 182
   Casteggio, 107
   Colle di Bajardo, 214-215
   Dolomites, 212
   Marostica, 167
   Milan, 111, 127, 144
   Montecampione, 182
   Montello, 56
   Palermo, 117
   Passo Duran, 69
   Romagna, 190-191
   San Remo, 107, 196, 224
   Tuscany, 154, 166

Jalabert, Laurent:
   in Tour de France, (1994) 115, (1995) 148
   in Vuelta a España, (1995) 156
Japan, 96
   Maebashi, 91, 98-99
   Utsunomiya, 86, 95
Jiménez, José Maria:
   in Vuelta a España, (1999) 195, (2001) 218
Jones, Mandy:
   in World Road Championships, (1982) 46
Julich, Bobby:
   in Tour de France, (1998) 185, 188-189, 197, (1999) 180
   in Vuelta a España, (1996) 146

Kelly, Sean:
   in Nissan Classic, (1986) 66
   in Paris-Nice, (1986) 66
   in Paris-Roubaix, (1988) 89
   in Tour de France, (1978) 12, (1987) 90, (1991) 115
   in Tour of Flanders, (1991) 104, (1992) 121
   in Tour of Lombardy, (1983) 36-37
Kopylov, Sergei:
   in World Track Championships, (1983) 44
Kuiper, Hennie:
   in Tour de France, (1978) 9, (1980) 13, 17
   in Tour of Flanders, (1980) 12

Lacouline, Pierre:
   in World Track Championships, (1982) 27

Lancien, Frédéric:
   in World Track Championships, (1992) 124
Landa, Rafa, 63
Liège-Bastogne-Liège, (1988) 71, (1999) 179
Leblanc, Jean-Marie, 175
Leblanc, Luc:
   in Tour de France, (1991) 118-119
Leipheimer, Levi:
   in Vuelta a España, (2001) 218
LeMond, Greg:
   at home in Minnesota, 152-153
   in Paris-Nice, (1986) 69
   in Paris-Roubaix, (1985) 48
   in Tour de France, (1985) 54, (1986) 64, 68, 83, (1989) 82, (1990) 85, 97, (1992) 2
   in Tour of Flanders, (1991) 109
   in Tour of Lombardy, (1983) 36
   in World Road Championships, (1983) 34
Lemyre, Denis:
   in World Track Championships, (1992) 124
Lévitan, Félix, 68
Liboton, Roland:
   in Superprestige Cyclo-cross, (1983) 41
Liggett, Phil, ix

Madiot, Marc:
   in Paris-Roubaix, (1991) 114
Maertens, Freddy:
   in Paris-Roubaix, (1981) 26
   in Tour de France, (1978) 11

Martin, Marianne:
   in Tour de France, (1984) 50
Martin, Raymond:
   in Tour de France, (1980) 13
Masciarelli, Palmiro:
   in World Road Championships, (1983) 28
Massif Central, 148, 157, 164-165
McRae, Chann:
   in Vuelta a España, (1999) 195
Mejia, Alvaro:
   in Tour de France, (1995) 159
Merckx, Axel:
   in Vuelta a España, (1996) 162
Merckx, Eddy:
   in Gentleman's Charity Race, 162
   at Vuelta a España, (1996) 162
Milan-San Remo, (1983) 32, 42, 45, 47, (1985) 24, (1991) 107, 127, (1999) 196, (2002) 224
Milk Race, 49, (1983) 43-44, 46
Millar, David:
   in Vuelta a España, (2001) 219
Millar, Robert:
   in Paris-Nice, (1983) ix
   in Vuelta a España, (1985) 22
   in World Road Championships, (1984) 56
Molinari, Maurizio:
   in Giro d'Italia, (1995) 144
Moncassin, Frédéric:
   in Tour de France, (1997) 145
Moreau, Christophe:
   in Tour de France, (2000) 202
Morras, Miguel:
   in Critérium International, (1996) 150

Moser, Francesco:
  in Paris-Roubaix, (1980) 14, (1981) 26
  in Tour of Flanders, (1980) 15
  in World Track Championships, (1985) 52
Mottet, Charly:
  in Giro d'Italia, (1990) 88
Munich Six Day, (1985) 58-59
Museeuw, Johan:
  in Paris-Roubaix, (1998) 180, (2002) 222
  in Tour de France, (1994) 106

Nakano, Koichi:
  in World Track Championships, (1982) 27
Netherlands, The, 32, 39
  Valkenburg, 5, 181
  Valkenswaard, 75
Nissan Classic, (1986) 66, 71-73, (1990) 92-93
Norway:
  Hamar, 125
  Oslo, 105, 130, 132
Nothstein, Marty:
  in Olympic Games, (1996) 139, (2000) 209
  in World Track Championships, (1994) 117

Obree, Graeme:
  in World Track Championships, (1993) 125
Oersted, Hans-Henrik:
  in Herning Six Day, (1983) 52
Olano, Abraham:
  in Dauphiné Libéré, (1997) 149
Olympic Games, (1992) 123, (1996) 139, 161, (2000) 209

Osa, Aitor:
  in Vuelta a España, (2001) 218
Pantani, Marco:
  in Giro d'Italia, (1998) 176, 182
  in Tour de France, (1998) 183-185, 188, 197, (2000) 198
Paraskevin, Connie:
  in World Track Championships, (1982) 51, (1984) 51, (1990) 91
Paris-Nice, (1983) ix, 23, (1986) 66, 69, (1987) 86, (1990) 95, (1995) 157, (1998) 181, 192
Paris-Roubaix, (1980) 14, (1981) 26, (1985) 48, (1988) 77, 89, (1989) 70, 79, (1990) 84, (1991) 104, 108, 114, (1992) 112, (1994) 128-129, (1998) 180, 193, (2000) 187, 199, (2002) 221-222
Paris-Tours, (1992) 113, (1998) 197
Peden, Tony:
  in World Track Championships, (1992) 124
Peeters, Ludo:
  in Tour of Flanders, (1983) 24
Peiper, Allan:
  in Paris-Roubaix, (1991) 108
Peña, Miguel Angel:
  in Dauphiné Libéré, (1997) 149
Peron, Andrea:
  in Tour de France, (1995) 159
Phinney, Davis:
  in Liège-Bastogne-Liège, (1988) 71
Pijnen, René:
  in Rotterdam Six Day, (1983) 39

Planckaert, Eddy:
  in Paris-Roubaix, (1990) 84
Pollentier, Michel:
  in Tour de France, (1978) 9
  in Tour of Flanders, (1980) 15, (1983) 21
Post Tour de France Criterium, (1995) 163
Pyrénées, 63, 118-119, 136-137, 156, 158-159

Raas, Jan:
  in Tour of Flanders, (1980) 15, (1983) 38
Rasmaite, Rita:
  in World Track Championships, (1990) 91
Reiss, Nate:
  in World Road Championships, (1990) 96
Richard, Pascal:
  in World Cyclo-cross Championships, (1988) 79
Riis, Bjarne:
  in Tour de France, (1996) 142
Robin, Jean-Cyril:
  in Dauphiné Libéré, (1997) 149
Roche, Stephen:
  in World Road Championships, (1983) 34, (1987) 64
Rochester Classic, (1997) 166
Rodriguez, Fred:
  in Milan-San Remo, (2002) 224
  in Paris-Roubaix, (2002) 222
Roll, Bob:
  in Paris-Roubaix, (1989) 70
Rominger, Tony:
  in Vuelta a España, (1993) 122, (1996) 146

Rooks, Steven:
  in Tour de France, (1988) 78
  in World Road Championships, (1991) 110
Rotterdam Six Day, (1983) 32, 39
Russia:
  Moscow, 163

Saronni, Giuseppe:
  in Milan-San Remo, (1983) 45
  in World Road Championships, (1982) 28, (1983) 26
Senft, Didi, 154
Sercu, Patrick:
  in Rotterdam Six Day, (1983) 32, 39
Sevilla, Oscar:
  in Vuelta a España, (2001) 218
Sheafor, Nathan:
  in World Road Championships, (1990) 96
Simoni, Gilberto:
  in Giro d'Italia, (2001) 212-213
Singleton, Gordon:
  in World Track Championships, (1982) 27
Skibby, Jesper:
  in Tour of Flanders, (1987) 72
Skol Six, (1980) 16
Soukhoroutchenkov, Sergei:
  in Vuelta a España, (1986) 68
Spain, 22, 24, 68, 94-95, 122, 218-219
  Barcelona, 51, 56, 123
  Benasque, 162
  Calatayud, 168
  Castellar del Riu, 178
  Cordoba, 141
  Lanuza, 118-119
  Puerto de Serranillos, 146
  Pyrenees, 118-119

San Sebastian, 85
Segovia, 87
Valencia, 124
Villava, 132
Steels, Tom:
in Tour de France, (1997) 145
Superprestige Cyclo-cross, (1983) 41, (1990) 75
Swart, Stephen:
in Tour de France (1995) 159
Switzerland:
Alps, 216-217
Altenrhein, 28, 34-35
Hägendorf, 76, 79
Lausanne, 11
Lugano, 176
Mont Salève, 2, 116
Steinmaur, 41
Zürich, 44

Tafi, Andrea:
in Paris-Roubaix, (2000) 199
Tchmil, Andreï:
in Milan-San Remo, (1999) 196
Theunisse, Gert-Jan:
in Tour de France, (1988) 78, (1989) 82
Tomac, John:
in Paris-Roubaix, (1991) 104
Tonkov, Pavel:
in Giro d'Italia, (1996) 167, (1998) 182
in Vuelta a España, (1999) 195
Tonnoir, Aldo, 46
Tour de France, (1978) 9-12, (1980) 13, 17, (1982) 48, (1985) 54-55, (1986) 65, 68, 83, (1987) 74, 81, 86, 90, (1988) 78, 83, (1989) 74, 84, (1990) 63, 85, 97, 130, (1991) 115, 118-119, (1992) 2, 116, 122, (1993) 130, (1994) 102-103, 106, 115, 120, (1995) 136-137, 147-148, 153-154, 158-159, 164-165, (1996) 142, 143, 156, 160, (1997) 145, 155, 167, (1998) 175, 183-185, 188-189, (1999) 177, 180, 194, 197, (2000) 198, 200-205
Tour de France Féminin, (1984) 50
Tour of Flanders, (1980) 12, 15, (1983) 21, 24, 38, (1987) 72, (1991) 104, 109, (1992) 121, (1994) 105
Tour of Lombardy, (1983) 36-37, 40
Twigg, Rebecca:
in World Track Championships, (1982) 31

Ullrich, Jan:
in Tour de France, (1996) 156, (1997) 151, 167, (1998) 185, 188, 197, (2000) 202
in Vuelta a España, (1999) 178, 195
United States:
Atlanta, 139, 161
Austin, Texas, 186
Minnesota, 152-153

Valcke, Patrick, 65
Valkenburg, Rainer:
in World Track Championships, (1982) 27
Vandenbroucke, Frank:
in Paris-Nice, (1998) 192
Vanderaerden, Eric:
in Het Volk, (1985) 52

Van der Poel, Adri:
in Paris-Roubaix, (1988) 89, (1992) 112
in World Cyclo-cross Championships, (1988) 79
in World Road Championships, (1983) 34
Van der Velde, Johan:
in Tour de France, (1978) 11
Van Impe, Lucien:
in Tour de France, (1978) 9, (1980) 13, 17
Van Moorsel, Leontien:
World Road Championships, (1993) 105
Vaughters, Jonathan:
in Dauphiné-Libéré, (1999) 193
Verbruggen, Hein, 68
Virenque, Richard:
in Tour de France, (1997) 155, 167
Visentini, Roberto:
in Giro d'Italia, (1986) 62
Vos, Cor, 46
Vuelta a España, (1985) 22, 24, (1986) 68, (1989) 87, (1993) 122, (1995) 156, 168, (1996) 146, 162, (1997) 141, (1998) 184, (1999) 178, 195, (2001) 218-219

Walling, Linda, 132
Watson, Graham, viii, 24
Wauters, Marc:
in Tour de France, (2000) 202
Wegmüller, Thomas:
in Paris-Roubaix, (1988) 77
Wilcockson, John, 2, 115
Williams, Jeff:
in Milk Race, (1983) 43

World Cyclo-cross Championships, (1988) 76, 79, (1996) viii
World Hour Record Attempt, (1996) 140, (2000) 210-211
World Road Championships, (1982) 28, 46, (1983) 28, 34-35, (1984) 56, (1985) 56, (1987) 64, (1988) 80, (1990) 86, 95-96, (1991) 110, (1993) 105, 130, 132, (1998) 5, 181
World Team Time Trial Championships, (1981) 23
World Track Championships, (1982) 27, 30, 51, (1983) 44, (1984) 51, (1985) 52, (1990) 91, 98-99, (1991) 111, (1992) 124, (1993) 125, (1994) 117
Wüst, Marcel:
in Vuelta a España, (1995) 168

Yates, Sean:
in Milan-San Remo, (1983) 42
in Paris-Roubaix, (1994) 129
in Tour of Flanders, (1991) 107

Zabel, Erik:
in Tour de France, (1997) 145
Zimmermann, Urs:
in Giro d'Italia, (1988) 69
Zoetemelk, Joop:
in Tour de France, (1978) 9, 11, (1980) 13
in World Road Championships, (1985) 56
Zülle, Alex:
in Tour de France, (1999) 197
in Vuelta a España, (1993) 122, (1996) 146
Zweifel, Albert, 49

ABOUT THE AUTHOR

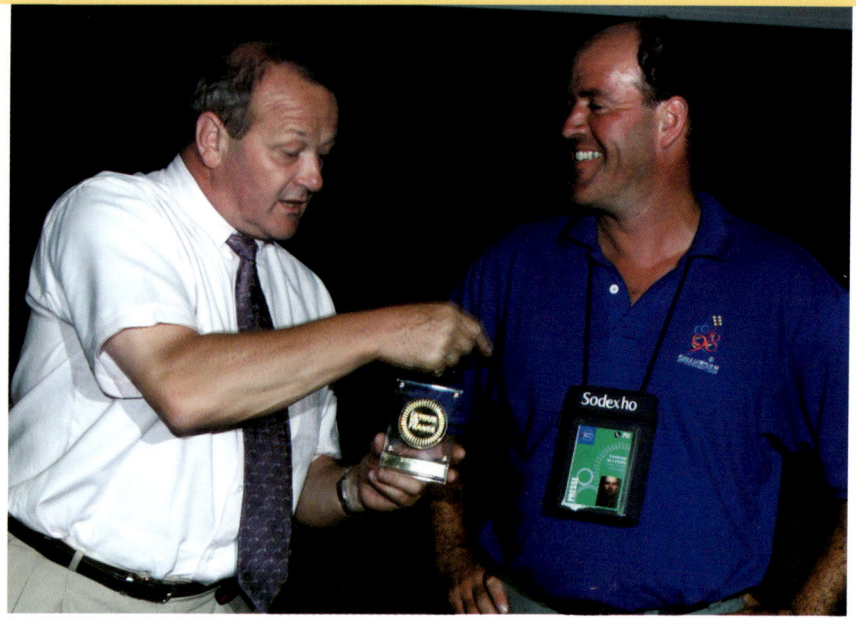

Graham Watson established himself as one of cycling's all-time great photographers after first photographing the sport in 1977 at the Tour de France, where he was merely a spectator watching the annual climax to the Tour on the Champs-Elysées. In the more than twenty years since that day, Watson has built an enviable reputation in a sport that is now global, but was once a very closeted European affair. He acknowledges how much his early career was helped by the successes of non-European cyclists like Greg LeMond, Phil Anderson, Sean Kelly, Andy Hampsten and Stephen Roche, and how much now, with equal successes by Chris Boardman, Stuart O'Grady and Lance Armstrong, his career is running at an all-time high.

Yet, Watson's reputation is also well established in Spain, Italy and France, where he regularly has his work published in books and magazines, and where he earns commercial assignments to cycling teams such as ONCE, Cofidis and U.S. Postal Service. He is the official photographer of the Union Cycliste Internationale, the sport's governing body, and celebrated his twentieth full year in cycling at the 2000 Tour de France.

This book features many of his more famous images of the sport's most renowned races, but devotes equal recognition to some of the less-established races, and to other disciplines of cycling not previously included in any of his other books—like cyclo-cross, world championship track racing and winter six-day racing. *Graham Watson: 20 Years of Cycling Photography* is the author's sixth book, having previously authored *Kings of The Road* (with Robin Magowan), *Visions of Cycling*, *The Tour de France and Its Heroes*, *The Road To Hell*, and *The Great Tours*.

2000: TOUR DE FRANCE: TOURS

Director-general of the Tour de France, Jean-Marie Leblanc, presents Graham with the coveted 20-year Tour medal.